CHIDUSHIM ON MOADIM

Rabbi Bernard Fox

Edited by
Rabbi Eliezer Barany

Table of Contents

Preface

It is with the help of *HaKadush Baruch Hu* and with tremendous joy that I can present the collected writings of Rabbi Bernie Fox on *Moadim*. Those familiar with his writings know how invaluable a *melamed* – teacher – he is. He disseminates *Torah* so clearly and helps others develop in learning and a love of *Hashem*. For those unacquainted, I can share with you a glimpse of what you're about to experience.

He articulates complex details in a way that is accessible to even casual students and helps guide them through the mazes of multifaceted issues. These books convey brilliant teachings that provide foundational lessons; allowing the reader to properly learn the *Torah*, delve into the *Talmud*, understand the *Rishonim*, and advance their own *Talmud Torah* abilities. The reader will gain broad knowledge on a myriad of topics while also diving deeply into specifics, thus enabling a substantial understanding of a verse and its surrounding topic. I write this with the idea that the reader will be prepared for how deep and comprehensive these writings are and also to instill the sense of excitement about what is in store, that I always feel when I read the Rabbi's thoughts and ponder his natural prose style. Studying these writings will allow one to truly approach *Kol HaTorah Kulo* – the entirety of Torah.

On a personal note, I am deeply grateful and honored to be able to share these lessons. Rabbi Fox's writings transfixed me from the very first analysis I read of his; a piece he wrote on *Megilat Ruth*. He established an appropriate approach to understanding the *Rishonim* on the text and allowed for a grasp of the text itself. Since then, I have learned answers to longstanding questions, have better understood passages in the *Torah*, have expanded my learning skills and have grown to love *Talmud Torah* even more! Compiling the Rabbi's writings has been a labor of love which has sustained me from start to finish.

It is my hope, in sharing his collected writings, to be able to be *Marbitz Torah* – disseminate *Torah* – and to help others experience the same enhanced love of learning that I did and which so many of Rabbi Fox's *Talmidim* –students, have.

With tremendous gratitude,

Eliezer Barany

Yom Tov

And Hashem spoke to Moshe saying: Speak to the Children of Israel and say to them: The appointed times of Hashem that you should declare them as sacred events; these are My appointed times. *(VaYikra 23:1-2)*

1. Yom Tov in One Simple Lesson

We have diverse attitudes toward Shabbat and our festivals. Some of us look forward to them and enjoy them. Some find meaning in Shabbat and festivals as opportunities to reconnect with family and friends. Others struggle to find meaning in their observance. Deprived of the opportunity to engage in professional activities or to pursue amusements, they are overcome with boredom.

In this discussion, we will explore the meaning of our festivals. In order to appreciate our Sages' understanding of their meaning we must be willing to make an honest acknowledgement and to give ourselves the opportunity to challenge our fundamental perspectives.

First, we must acknowledge that our lives are very much devoted to material accomplishments and material pleasures. Consequently, we assess activities or behaviors from the perspective of their material benefits. We define an activity as worthwhile if it contributes to our material wellbeing. An activity is pleasurable if it provides material pleasure.

Second, because of this orientation, we do not consider the possibility that activities that do not provide material benefit or pleasure may nonetheless be worthwhile. We are not open to the possibility that reward and pleasure can be found in activities that are spiritual.

Part of the reason that our minds are closed to this possibility is that achieving spiritual benefits and pleasures requires an investment of time and energy. Spiritual experiences are not like eating a cookie. One pops a cookie into one's mouth and pleasure follows. The capacity to appreciate and fully engage in a spiritual activity, benefit from it, and enjoy it must be developed. We respond to the challenge of developing this capacity like a child who refuses to learn how to swim because the challenge seems too great. But when that child gives him/herself permission to learn to swim, benefit, reward, and pleasure follow.

I speak of "we"and "us" in the above as a literary convenience. But I recognize that the challenge I describe does not apply to all of us and those facing this challenge are handicapped by various degrees of resistance. Read the comments of our Sages that follow with an open mind and hopefully they will provide direction in developing a greater appreciation for our festivals.

2. Sefer VaYikra describes the festivals

Shavuot is closely associated with Sefer VaYikra. In Parshat Emor the Torah describes Shabbat and the festivals. Shavuot is included in this section. Each festival has its own theme and message. Our festivals also have a shared meaning and significance. In the following discussion we will focus upon this shared character. The discussion is relevant to our observance of Shavuot and our observance of our other festivals.

The above passages introduce the section of Parshat Emor that discusses our festivals. Two terms are used to describe these festivals. They are described as *moed* and as *mikra kodesh*. The exact meaning of these terms is not self-evident. In the above translation *moed* is translated as an appointed time.[1] The term *mikra kodesh* is translated as a sacred event. These translations are based upon Unkelus' rendering of the terms as understood by Rashbam[2] and others.

In summary, the festivals are times that have a special designation (*moed*). They are designated as sacred events (*mikra kodesh*). In what way are these festivals sacred? In other words, what characteristic of the festivals endows them with their sanctity?

Withdrawal from material engagement

The simplest response is provided by Rambam – Maimonides. He explains that the sanctity of the festivals is derived from their prohibition against performing *melachah* – creative work. This restriction fundamentally distinguishes the festivals from typical days. On other days we are permitted and encouraged to fully engage with the material world. On festivals, we withdraw from this engagement. This withdrawal is intended to encourage us to focus upon our spiritual lives. According to Rambam, this withdrawal from material engagement – the prohibition against *melachah*– endows our festivals with their sanctity.[3]

Rambam's position is that sanctity is created by differentiating something or creating a separateness for some higher purpose. Our festivals are endowed with sanctity through the prohibition against *melechah*. How does this prohibition accomplish this? It creates the separateness that is fundamental to sanctity. Along with the higher purpose of this separateness – to focus upon our spiritual lives – it infuses our festivals with sanctity.

Three elements of festival sanctity

Ramban – Nachmanides – suggests an alternative description of the sanctity of the festivals. Let's consider his comments:

> The meaning of "sacred events" is that on this day we are collectively summoned and gather together to sanctify it. For it is a commandment upon Israel to gather together in the house of Hashem on the day of the festival and to sanctify the day publicly through prayer and praise to the L-rd and (through wearing) a clean garment.[4] And to make it a day of a festive meal....[5]

---

[1] The commentators disagree over whether the term *moed* can be applied to Shabbat or only to the festivals. According to Rashi, the term *moed* suggests a designation created by man. The term applies to festivals. We are charged with the responsibility of declaring each month and thereby, establishing the day on which each festival will occur. In contrast, Shabbat occurs on its appointed day and does not require our declaration. Rabbaynu Avraham ibn Ezra asserts that the term *moed* does apply to Shabbat. *Moed* means a time that has a designation. This designation need not be created by human beings. Rabbaynu Ovadia Sforno further develops this position.

[2] Rabbaynu Shemuel ben Meir (Rashbam) *Commentary on Sefer VaYikra* 23:2. This understanding of Unkelus is also suggested by Ramban. See also Rav Raphael Binyamin Pozen, *Parshegen, Sefer VaYikra* 23:2 and 23:4.

[3] Rabbaynu Moshe ben Maimon (Rambam) *Sefer HaMitzvot, Mitzvat Aseh* 159.

[4] The exact text on Ramban's comments is not certain. This text is based upon the source of his comments – *Torah Kohanim*. See Rav Pinchas Yehudah Liberman, *Pnai Yerushayalim – Notes and Clarifications on the Commentary of Ramban on the Torah*.

[5] Rabbaynu Moshe ben Nachman (Ramban), *Commentary on Sefer VaYikra* 23:2. According to Ramban, the term *mikra* suggests an assembly. Based on this interpretation, he concludes that the festival is observed through the assembly of the people in a public gathering.

According to Ramban, our festivals derive their sanctity from a number of sources. He acknowledges in a previous comment that the prohibition against *melachah* is a fundamental source of their sanctity. However, he adds that the sanctity of the festivals is also tied to their identity as a time of assembly in the house of Hashem and engagement in communal prayer and praise. Also, we sanctify our festivals though our treatment of them as celebrations. We wear special clothing and enjoy a festive meal. In other words, Ramban suggests the sanctity of our festivals is derived from three sources:

- The prohibition against *melachah* differentiates these days through designating them as times in which we withdraw from engagement in the material world.

- We assemble as a community in the house of Hashem to engage in prayer and praise of Hashem.

- We celebrate these occasions through our clothing and meals.

3. Communal prayer on festivals

Let's further consider these three elements. How are they related? How does each contribute to the character of our festivals? Let's begin by more carefully considering the second of these elements. Ramban explains that we assemble to pray to and praise Hashem. This element of our festivals requires further consideration. It seems that according to Ramban, on our festivals we are required to pray to Hashem as a congregation. Does this suggest that we are not required to come together as a congregation on typical days?

Rambam – Maimonides – discusses this issue and explains that the requirement that we pray within a congregation or *minyan* applies at all times.[6] He further explains that every community is required to create a *bait ha'hekeneset* – a synagogue – as a place designated for the community to assemble in prayer.[7] This requirement reflects the importance of praying as a member of an assembly. Rambam's rulings are based upon the discussion of the Talmud in Tractate Berachot.

Now, let us return to Ramban's comments. He asserts that assembling as a community in prayer and praise of Hashem is an activity associated with our festivals. It is difficult to understand this comment. Communal prayer is an ongoing obligation. It is not an obligation specific to our festivals!

Obviously, Ramban acknowledges that praying as part of a congregation is an ongoing obligation. This is not an obligation that is unique to festivals. However, Ramban's point is that on festivals communal prayer has an added meaning and dimension. On every other day praying with a congregation enhances the prayer experience. Rambam explains that the prayers of the congregation are superior to those of an individual.[8] However, on the festival communal prayer has an added significance. It is an important aspect of the observance of the festival.

In other words, one should always seek to pray with a congregation or *minyan*. This is because the prayers of the congregation are superior to those of the lone individual. On festivals there is another reason to pray with a congregation. Participation in communal prayer is a fundamental aspect of observance of our festivals.

---

[6] Rabbaynu Moshe ben Maimon (Rambam) *Mishne Torah*, Hilchot Tefilah 8:1.

[7] Rabbaynu Moshe ben Maimon (Rambam) *Mishne Torah*, Hilchot Tefilah 11:1.

[8] Rabbaynu Moshe ben Maimon (Rambam) *Mishne Torah*, Hilchot Tefilah 8:1.

4. Festivals are spiritual encounters

We can now understand the relationship between the first two elements of festival sanctity identified by Ramban. Rabbaynu Ovadia Sforno explains that our cessation from *melachah* is a withdrawal from engagement in the material world. This withdrawal alone does not endow the day with its spiritual character. A positive engagement is required to complement this withdrawal. Our engagement in communal prayer provides this positive element.[9]

In order to achieve a spiritual experience through prayer to and praise of Hashem an investment must be made in learning how to engage in these activities. Again, this is not like eating a cookie. How can we cultivate the capacity to experience prayer as a positive spiritual activity? First, we need to take the time to read the prayers and consider their content. Second, we need to develop the capacity to maintain our focus during prayer. Third, we need to discipline ourselves. This requires creating an environment that supports our focus on prayer. This may include avoiding friends who tend to distract us. However, if we can take these steps, we can discover meaning in our prayers and praises of Hashem and experience an authentic spiritual encounter.

5. Festivals and celebration

According to Ramban, The final element of our festivals is their celebratory aspect. We wear special garments and engage in festive meals. How does this element relate to the first two elements? This element seems out of place. The cessation of *melachah* and coming together as a community to approach and encounter Hashem are spiritual experiences. How do material expressions – special garments and lavish meals – contribute to this festival experience?

Sforno also addresses this issue. He explains that although the festival's focus is upon the spiritual encounter with Hashem, this experience must be celebrated. The special garments and the festive meal are our demonstration of joy in response to the spiritual encounter.[10]

Sforno is asserting that an authentic spiritual experience is a source of joy. We need to actually have a meaningful spiritual experience in order for this assertion to be credible. If we are willing to make the effort and to give ourselves the opportunity to have this encounter, then we can experience the joy Sforno describes.

6. A shared festival theme

Every festival has its own unique meaning and message. Shavuot celebrates receiving the Torah at Sinai. It is also a harvest festival – a thanksgiving festival for the abundance of the harvest. However, these differences between the festivals coexist with their common theme. All our festivals share the same essential character. They are a reorientation of our attention from the mundane to a search for spiritual meaning and fulfillment. We engage in this spiritual encounter as a community. We join together in prayer and praise of Hashem. Through this process we

---

[9] Rabbaynu Ovadia Sforno, *Commentary on Sefer VaYikra* , 23:2. Relevant to this discussion is the comment of the Talmud regarding the overall structure of the festival day. Rambam quotes this comment in his Hilchot Yom Tov, chapter 6. The Talmud explains that prayer is one of the elements of festival observance that provides its spiritual character. Another component is Torah study. According to the Talmud, our festivals are designated as a time for Torah study.

[10] Rabbaynu Ovadia Sforno, *Commentary on Sefer VaYikra* 23:2.

come closer to Him as a community and as individuals. The joy that we express during our festivals is a declaration of our values. We are proclaiming the importance of this spiritual experience and recognizing the richness that it brings into our lives.

And Hashem spoke to Moshe, saying: Speak to Bnai Yisrael and say unto them, "The appointed times of Hashem, which you shall proclaim to be sacred convocations, these are My appointed times:" (VaYikra 23:1-2)

And when you reap the harvest of your land, you shall not wholly reap the corner of your field. Neither shall you gather the gleanings of your harvest. You shall leave them for the poor, and for the stranger. I am Hashem your G-d. (VaYikra 23:22)

Two Aspects of Chesed

1. The Torah's review of Pe'ah and Leket

In Parshat Emor, the Torah repeats the commandments of Pe'ah and Leket. These commandments require the owner of a field of grain to share a portion of the harvest with the poor and needy. The mitzvah of Pe'ah directs the owner to leave standing the grain in one corner of the field. Those in need are permitted to enter the field and harvest this portion of its produce for themselves. Leket applies to the grain that inadvertently falls to the ground during the process of reaping. Individual ears or pairs of ears that drop to the ground are to be left to the poor and needy.

Both of these commandments were earlier introduced and described by the Torah. Why are these commandments delineated again? It is also interesting to note the context in which the Torah repeats these commandments. As is evident from the first set of passages cited above, this section of the Torah describes the annual festivals and holidays. It provides a complete list of all sacred days over the course of the calendar year. The text begins with a brief reference to Shabbat. It continues with a discussion of Pesach and concludes with a discussion of Sukkot. In the midst of this discussion of the festivals – immediately following the discussion of Shavuot – the Torah inserts the reference to Pe'ah and Leket. What relevance do these mitzvot have to the Torah's discussion of the festivals?

And HaShem spoke unto Moshe saying: Speak unto Bnai Yisrael, and say to them, "When you come into the land which I give to you and you shall reap its harvest, then you shall bring the Omer – the first-fruits of your harvest to the kohen. And he shall wave the Omer before Hashem, to be accepted for you; on the day after the shabbat the kohen shall wave it." (VaYikra 23:9-11)

You shall proclaim on the selfsame day; there shall be to you a sacred convocation. You shall do no manner of servile work. It is a statute forever in all your dwellings throughout your generations. (VaYikra 23:21)

2. Pesach, Shavuot, and Sukkot as harvest festivals

Some of the commentators respond to these questions based upon the specific context in which the mitzvot of Pe'ah and Leket are reiterated. As explained above, the section in which these mitzvot reappear discusses the annual festivals. However, more specifically, the review of these mitzvot is inserted immediately after the discussion of Shavuot.

8

The Torah's discussion of Shavuot is fascinating. The festival of Shavuot corresponds with the anniversary date of the Sinai Revelation. The liturgy for the festival consistently refers to Shavuot as the celebration of Revelation. However, the Torah never specifically describes Shavuot as a celebration of Revelation. In fact, the identification of Shavuot with Revelation and the characterization of Shavuot as a celebration of Revelation are found exclusively in the Oral Law or Tradition. How does the Torah – the Written Law – describe Shavuot?

The Torah describes Shavuot as a harvest festival. In the above text, the three annual harvest festivals are described. The first is Pesach. Pesach is observed at the beginning of the harvest season. The barley crop is the first grain harvested. On the second day of Pesach, the Omer sacrifice is offered. This is a grain offering composed of the first harvested ears of the barley crop. From the day of the offering of the Omer, seven weeks or forty-nine days are counted. On the fiftieth day, a second special grain offering is presented. This offering – the Two Loaves – is composed of two leavened loaves of bread baked from fine wheat flour. The final passage cited above explains that the day on which the Two Loaves – the Sh'tai HaLechem – are offered is a full festival replete with a prohibition against labor. Of course, the festival to which the passage refers is Shavuot – the Festival of the Weeks. The final festival described in the text is Sukkot. Sukkot is described as the third of the harvest festivals. It is observed at the time at which the grain has been gathered-in and stored. It celebrates the completion of the annual agricultural cycle.

In short, the Torah describes Shavuot as a harvest festival and the time of its observance corresponds with the harvest of the wheat crop. Fittingly, the description of Shavuot focuses upon the offering of the Sh'tai HaLechem – a grain offering composed of fine wheat loaves.

3. Observance of Pe'ah and Leket is equated to the rebuilding of the Temple

One of the interesting explanations for the insertion of a review of Pe'ah and Leket into this text is provided by Rashi. He asserts that the Torah inserts its review of Pe'ah and Leket at this point in order to communicate an essential lesson. One who fulfills the mitzvot of Pe'ah and Leket is regarded to be on par with a person who builds the Sacred Temple and offers his sacrifices therein.[11] Rashi at various points in his commentary echoes the message of the First Temple prophets. Hashem requires that we treat our fellow human beings with kindness, dignity, and justice. We cannot disregard this expectation and replace obedience of these standards with worship through sacrifices. Sacrifices are intended as a catalyst for personal growth and spiritual achievement. However, if instead devotion to worship through sacrifices replaces proper treatment of our fellow human beings or is employed as an excuse for disregarding the Torah's expectations of social conduct, then the sacrifices have been perverted and profaned.

4. The value and pitfalls of a personal sense of sanctity

Rashi's comment and the message that it communicates are important on two levels. First, Rashi is forewarning us against a very real and observable behavior. Ritual worship does provide the worshiper with a sense of sanctity. This sense of sanctity can have a positive or a negative effect. It can be a positive influence if it motivates a person to act to a higher standard in all aspects of his life. One's sense of heightened sanctity can motivate a person to relate to Hashem and to treat others in a manner that reflects the sanctity that the person feels. In this

---

[11] Rabbaynu Shlomo ben Yitzchak (Rashi), Commentary on Sefer VaYikra 23:22.

instance the person does not merely sense sanctity. He is aware of it. In other words, his actions reflect that he has truly sanctified himself and is acting out of an awareness of personal sanctity.

However, sometimes this sense of personal sanctity has a negative impact. This person feels that his sanctity is completely secured through meticulous attention to ritual law. Through the scrupulous attention to every detail of ritual law the person attains a sense – actually, a delusion – of personal sanctity. Secure in this delusion, the person neglects his obligations to his fellow human beings or may even act in a mean and abusive manner. Because of his delusion of sanctity, he feels entitled to disregard the needs and rights of others.

5. The Torah's revolutionary concept of G-d

Rashi's comment and message is significant on a second level. It is commonly acknowledged that through the Torah monotheism was established as a major theology. However, the Torah was revolutionary in another area. The pagan gods were perceived by their worshipers as powerful deities. These deities had many of the character flaws that were evident in humanity. In fact, the pagan worshipers based their understanding of their gods and their behaviors on a human model. The pagan gods were subject to greed, lust, jealousy, anger, and even capriciously careless behavior. Above all the heathen god was focused upon his own needs or desires. The worshiper's duty was to placate his deities and thereby earn their favor and protect himself from their wrath.

The Torah introduced a completely revolutionary concept. The G-d of the Torah demands that we serve Him through the manner in which we treat one another. He is perfect and selfless. We worship Him in order to elevate ourselves. Through growing closer to Him and more devoted to His will, we are inspired to act with kindness and justice toward others.

And when you reap the harvest of your land, you shall not wholly reap the corner of your field. Neither shall you gather the gleanings of your harvest. You shall not glean your vineyard. Neither shall you gather the fallen fruit of your vineyard. You shall leave them for the poor and for the stranger. I am Hashem your G-d. You shall not steal. Neither shall you deal falsely, nor lie to one another. You shall not swear by My name falsely, so that you profane the name of thy G-d. I am Hashem. You shall not oppress your neighbor, nor rob him. The wages of a hired servant shall not abide with you all night until the morning. (VaYikra 19:9-13)

6. Pe'ah and Leket are discussed in two contexts

Rabbaynu Avraham ibn Ezra offers an alternative explanation for the insertion of this review of the mitzvot of Pe'ah and Leket. He comments that because Shavuot is observed at the time of the harvest the Torah reviews other mitzvot – Pe'ah and Leket – that are performed at the time of the harvest.[12] Superficially, this comment seems simplistic and contrived. These commandments were described only a few chapters earlier. These commandments can only be understood as related to the harvest. Why does a discussion of the harvest festivals require a review of these commandments?

The above passages contain the previous discussion of Pe'ah and Leket. This discussion is somewhat different from the discussion in Parshat Emor. One of the most notable differences is the context of the discussion. In these passages, Pe'ah and Leket are described in the opening passages of a text that deals primarily with social responsibility. After describing Pe'ah, Leket,

---

[12] Rabbaynu Avraham ibn Ezra, Commentary on Sefer VaYikra 23:22.

and related mitzvot, the Torah outlines a number of commandments that direct us to deal honestly, fairly, and sensitively with one another. What message is communicated by the placement of Pe'ah and Leket in this context?

And it was in the days when the judges judged, that there was a famine in the land. A certain man of Bet-Lechem in Yehudah went to sojourn in the field of Moav – he, and his wife, and his two sons. The name of the man was Elimelech, and the name of his wife Na'ami, and the names of his two sons were Machlon and Chilyon – Ephrathites of Bet-Lechem in Yehudah. They came into the field of Moav, and continued there. And Elimelech, Na'ami's husband died. And she was left, and her two sons. (Megilat Ruth 1:1-3)

7. The practice of chesed as enlightened self-interest

Megilat Ruth opens with a description of the death of Elimelech. The passages do not provide an explicit explanation for his death. Later, Na'ami identifies his death as a punishment for a wrongdoing. However, she does not specifically identify the wrongdoing committed by her husband. The commentators explain that the opening passages provide an allusion to the wrongdoing committed by Elimelech and offer a number of suggestions as to the specific sin. Midrash Lekach Tov suggests that Elimelech fled the Land of Israel rather than share his wealth with those who were suffering from the famine. Lekach Tov continues and quotes an interesting comment of the Talmud. The Talmud explains that poverty is akin to a rotating wheel. It never vanishes. It may recede like a spot on a wheel that is rotating away from the observer. However, as the wheel continues to rotate, the spot will reappear before the observer. Poverty may seem distant to an individual. However, the misfortunes that produce poverty recur again and again. If a person avoids poverty in his own life, he cannot be assured that his children will have the same experience. Even if his children are not subjected to poverty, he should not expect that his grandchildren will also be safe from want.[13]

Lekach Tov is explaining that Elimelech's flight represented a lack of social responsibility. Society is a community of individuals interacting in a manner that benefits the members. Elimelech's failure to help others and promote chesed – kindness – represented a delusion or blindness. Everyone needs a helping hand at one time or another. If a person succeeds in avoiding poverty, he should not assume that his descendents will enjoy the same success. When we promote chesed, we are engaged in an activity of enlightened self-interest. At a future point, we may need the chesed and compassion of others. Certainly, our descendants will need the chesed of others.

This is the message of the Torah's earlier treatment of Pe'ah and Leket. In that discussion these mitzvot are presented as part of a system of social responsibility. Pe'ah and Leket are described in the context of measures commanded by the Torah that foster a mutually supportive and productive community.

8. Chesed as a reflection of Hashem

As noted above, the passages in Parshat Emor that discuss Pesach place emphasis on the Omer sacrifice. It is interesting to note that the discussion of the Omer begins with the statement, "When you come into the land which I give unto you, and shall reap its harvest, then you shall bring the Omer offering of the first-fruits of your harvest to the kohen". The phrase "which I give

---

[13] Rabbaynu Tuvia ben Eliezer, Midrash Lekach Tov, Introduction to Megilat Ruth.

to you" seems superfluous. However, this phrase communicates an important message that is introductory to the entire subsequent discussion. The Land of Israel is a gift from Hashem. Its harvest and its produce are an expression of His chesed. Sefer HaChinuch suggests that this message is the fundamental theme of the Omer sacrifice and the Sh'tai HaLechem of Shavuot. The harvest must be received with thanksgiving. We express our gratitude to Hashem and acknowledge His chesed through these sacrifices.[14]

Now, Ibn Ezra's comments can be more fully appreciated. Pesach and Shavuot are occasions on which we recognize Hashem's chesed toward us as expressed through the harvest. Our acknowledgement of this chesed gains expression not only through the offering of the Omer and Sh'tai HaLechem but also through our fulfillment of the mitzvot of Pe'ah and Leket. Our observance of these commandments is a personal reflection through our own behaviors of Hashem's chesed. Furthermore, by sharing with the less fortunate, we demonstrate that the produce of our fields is a gift of kindness from a benefactor who requires that we share with others.

In short, the Torah's two discussions of Pe'ah and Leket are designed to communicate two aspects of chesed. Chesed is behavior of enlightened self-interest. Only a fool believes that he or his descendants will not need the help of others. When we promote chesed, we help assure that others will respond to our needs when we are the less fortunate. Acts of chesed are also an acknowledgment of Hashem's chesed toward us. When we act with chesed toward others we emulate Hashem and acknowledge His kindness to ourselves.

And Hashem spoke to Moshe saying. Speak to Bnai Yisrael and say to them: The sacred occasions of Hashem that you should declare as occasions of sacred assembly – these are my sacred occasions. (VaYikra 23:1-2)

And when you harvest the produce of your field do not completely harvest the corner of your field in the course of your harvest. And the gleanings of your harvest you should not collect. Leave them to the poor and to the sojourner. I am Hashem your Lord. (VaYikra 23:22)

The Problem with Secular Humanism

1. Festivals are associated with care for the needy

The first quotation above introduces Parshat Emor's discussion of the annual festivals. The discussion begins by mentioning Shabbat and then enumerates each of the festivals observed during the cycle of the calendar. The description of the festivals opens with discussion of Pesach. In this context, the Torah describes the omer offering that is brought on Pesach. This offering is brought from the first grain of the annual barley harvest. The Torah also describes the grain sacrifice of the shetai ha'lechem – the two loaves – that are offered on Shavuot.

The second above quotation is inserted into the midst of the description of the festivals. It is placed immediately after the description of the shtai ha'lechem. It reviews two commandments regarding the harvest. The first of these commandments is pe'ah. This commandment requires that when a field is harvested a corner portion be left for the poor and needy. The field's owner leaves the grain in this corner standing. Those in need come to the field and harvest for

---

[14] Rav Aharon HaLeyve, Sefer HaChinuch, Mitzvah 302

themselves the standing grain. The second commandment is leket. This commandment requires that when the field is harvested, the gleanings – insignificant numbers of ears that fall to the ground – be left for the poor and needy.

After describing these two commandments, the Torah resumes its description of the annual festivals. This presentation raises an obvious question. Why are the mitzvot of pe'ah and leket inserted into the Torah's enumeration of the annual festivals?

Rashi offers a very interesting response. Quoting the midrash, he explains that one who observes the commandments of pe'ah and leket is comparable to one who builds the sacred temple and offers upon its alter his sacrifices. Rashi's response seems contrived. How is the observance of these two specific commandments comparable to building the temple and offering one's sacrifices?

2. Serving Hashem in our treatment of human beings

Possibly, it is not Rashi's intent to single out these commandments. Instead, he may intend to communicate a basic tenet of the Torah. Our treatment for our fellow human being is as important to Hashem as the sacrifices that we offer to Him. We serve Hashem through both our devotion to Him and through our observance of the commandments that regulate our interactions with our fellow human beings. We cannot fulfill our duty to Hashem by offering Him our sacrifices and prayers while ignoring the plight of our fellow human beings who need our compassion. According to this interpretation of Rashi's comments, the Torah inserts pe'ah and leket into its discussion of the festivals in order to demonstrate the unity of these commandments with our service to Hashem during the festivals. These commandments that regulate our treatment of other human beings are as fundamental to our relationship with Hashem as our observance of His festivals. However, perhaps Rashi is suggesting a more specific relationship between these two commandments and the festivals.

3. Recognizing that the harvest comes from Hashem

Before returning to Rashi, let us consider a comment of Gershonides. Gershonides suggests that there is a more specific relationship between these commandments and the festivals. Three of the festivals described in this portion are related to the harvest. Pesach and Shavuot coincide with the harvest. The omer sacrifice of Pesach and the shtai ha'lechem of Shavuot are thanksgiving offerings. Sukkot coincides with the completion of the collection of the grain from the field and its storage for the winter. All three thanksgiving festivals acknowledge Hashem for granting us the bounty that has been harvested and stored away. Through their observance, we thank Him for sustaining us.

Gershonides suggests that the process of thanksgiving is fundamentally an acknowledgment that everything that we have comes from Him. We recognize the very limited control we have over the factors that produce the harvest. Hashem provides the rain. He determines whether the grain will grow to maturity and be harvested or whether the grain will be destroyed by frost, attacked by disease, or consumed in some infestation. These and many other factors determine the success of the harvest. They are in His hands. We are virtually powerless.

According to Gershonides, this acknowledgment is communicated through our observance of the harvest festivals – Pesach, Shavuot, and Sukkot. It is also expressed through our observance of the mitzvot of pe'ah and leket. We recognize that Hashem has provided us with the bounty we have harvested and He commands that we share our blessings with those who are less fortunate than ourselves.

4. Similarities between Torah and secular humanism

In other words, Hashem is directing us to have compassion for those who are in need. He is commanding us to adopt humanitarian values and practices. This raises an interesting question. Virtually every enlightened society acknowledges the importance of humanitarian values. Humanitarianism is practiced by religious individuals and by devoted secularists. It seems clear that humanitarianism is a product of enlightenment and civilization and is not dependent upon acceptance of religious doctrine. Even an atheist will embrace the enlightened value of humanitarianism.

In view of this universal character of humanitarianism, why does the Torah find it necessary to tie its presentation of humanitarian values to our service of Hashem? The Torah admonishes us to care for the needy and poor in the context of our service to Hashem and in acknowledgment of His sovereignty. Does this connection between humanitarianism and devotion to Hashem shape or impact our implementation and application of humanitarian values?

One who curses Hashem shall surely die. The entire congregation shall stone him. Whether a sojourner or citizen, if he curses Hashem, he shall die. A person who strikes dead another human being shall surely die. (VaYikra 24:16-17)

5. The relationship between murder and cursing Hashem

The two passages above describe two capital crimes. The first crime is cursing Hashem. The Torah explains that one who does this is put to death. The second crime is violently taking the life of another. This crime is also punished with death. It is interesting that these two crimes are juxtaposed. What is the Torah's message in describing these two crimes and their punishments in adjacent passages?

One who spills the blood of a human being before witnesses, his blood should be spilled – for in the image of Hashem He made the human being. (Beresheit 9:6)

The above passage is part of the message that Hashem communicated to Noach when he left the ark and reentered the post-Deluge world. Hashem commanded Noach and his descendents that they may not take the life of another human being. One who violates this commandment is to be punished with death. Hashem explains to Noach that every human being reflects the Creator. This is because every human being, in some manner, is created in His image. Taking the life of human being is sacrilege.

Based on this passage, Rav Yosef Dov Soloveitchik zt'l explains the strange juxtaposition noted above. The crime of cursing Hashem is punished by death. The crime of murder is punished by death. These two sins and their punishments are described in adjacent passages. This is because the sins are actually similar. We must honor and revere Hashem. One who curses Him is severely punished. This same obligation to honor Hashem requires that we respect human life. Every human being reflects Hashem. Every human being is created in his Creator's image. The murder of a human being is a desecration of the sanctity of Hashem.

6. The sanctity of human life and Torah humanitarianism

Let us now return to Rashi's comments. Rashi explained that one who observes the commandments of pe'ah and leket is comparable to one who builds the sacred temple and offers on its alter his sacrifices. Rav Soloveitchik's insight suggests an alternative interpretation of Rashi's comments. Every human being is formed in the image of Hashem. When we reach out to the poor and needy we are not responding simply to our innate compassion. We are recognizing and acknowledging the divine in every single human being. We are recognizing that an individual blessed with wealth and his neighbor who is desperately struggling in the depths of poverty are created in the same sacred image. Both are sacred. The poor person needs our compassion. His divine image demands our respect and honor.

When we perform the commandments of pe'ah and leket we respond to the divine image that exists in every human being. We are honoring Hashem. In this sense, the performance of these commandments is comparable to the building of a temple to Hashem and offering our sacrifices upon its alter.

7. The limitations of secular humanism

This then is the ultimate foundation of the Torah's humanitarian values and practices. How does it impact our practices and how do the Torah's humanitarian practices differ from the practices of the secular humanist?

Secular humanism promotes compassion for those who are persecuted, or are in desperate need. It has not succeeded in establishing accepted standards for how we should treat every single human being. It does not compel us to visit a mourner. It does not demand that we treat others honestly and earnestly. It does demand that we show respect for every human being. Certainly, it does not suggest moderation in our treatment of our enemies.

The Torah's humanitarianism recognizes that every human being is endowed with sacred dignity. His sacredness demands our respect. Even one who is not a friend – even an enemy – retains his divine image. He must be respected and his sacred dignity must be honored.

"The first day shall be a sacred occasion for you. You should not perform any melechet avodah." (VaYikra 23:7)

Parshat Emor provides a list of the occasions on which it is prohibited to perform melachah. Loosely translated, the term melachah means work. The list begins with Shabbat. The Torah tells us that on Shabbat all melachah is prohibited. The Oral law teaches us that there are thirty-nine general categories of melachah. These thirty-nine forms of melachah are derived from the fabrication of the Tabernacle. All of the thirty-nine forms of melachah were essential processes in the construction of the Mishcan – the Tabernacle.

The list continues with an enumeration of the Yamim Tovim – the festivals and holidays. The pasuk above discusses the first day of Pesach. In this pasuk, the Torah tells us that the first day of Pesach is a sacred occasion and that it is prohibited to perform melechet avodah on that day. The Torah does not say that all melachah is prohibited on this occasion. Instead, the term melechet avodah is used to describe the labors that are prohibited. The Torah also tells us that melechet avodah is prohibited on the other Yamim Tovim. There is one exception. The Torah tells us that on Yom Kippur all melachah is prohibited.

In short, according to the passages in our parasha, on Shabbat and on Yom Kippur all melachah is prohibited but on the Yamim Tovim melechet avodah is prohibited. It seems clear that the Torah is contrasting Shabbat and Yom Kippur to these other Yamim Tovim. The term melechet avodah suggests that the prohibition against melachah on Yamim Tovim differs from the prohibition on Shabbat and Yom Kippur. But what is the precise difference?

In Parshat Bo the Torah describes in more detail the prohibition against melachah on Pesach. There, the Torah tells us that all melachah may not be performed on these days with the exception of melechet ochel nefesh – melachah needed for the preparation of food.[15] It is apparent that this is area in which the prohibition against labor on Shabbat and Yom Kippur differs from the prohibition on Yamim Tovim. On Shabbat and Yom Kippur all thirty-nine forms of melachah are prohibited. Even those types of melachah that are related to food preparation are prohibited. But on Yamim Tovim those types of melachah that are related to food preparation are permitted. For example, cooking and baking are prohibited on Shabbat. But on Yamim Tovim these types of melachah are permitted.

With this information we can understand the significance of the term melechet avodah. Nachmanides suggests that in Parshat Bo the Torah details the specific perimeters of the prohibition against melachah on Pesach. It tells us that melechet ochel nefesh is permitted. In our parasha, the Torah does not specifically reiterate that melechet ochel nefesh is permitted on Pesach. Instead, the Torah introduces the term melechet avodah. This term is intended to refer to those types of melachah that are not melechet ochel nefesh. The Torah tells us that – with the exception of Yom Kippur – all Yamim Tovim are subject to a prohibition of melechet avodah. This term is intended to communicate to us that on these occasions melechet ochel nefesh is permitted. In other words, the term melachah – when it is unqualified – includes all thirty-nine forms of melachah that are prohibited on Shabbat. The term melechet avodah includes only those forms of melachah that are not related to food preparation.

How does the term melechet avodah express this concept? Nachmanides discusses this issue in detail. He concludes that the term melachah includes two types of activities. It includes activities that one does in order to create or maintain possessions – for example: plowing, planting, harvesting. It also includes activities that one performs for rather immediate benefit – for example: cooking. In contrast, the term melechet avodah means only those types of melachah that are avodah – related to ones possessions. In other words, the term melechet avodah refers only to the forms of melachah are performed in order to create and maintain possessions. It does not include those forms of melachah that are designed for personal benefit – melechet ochel nefesh.[16]

Maimonides' understanding of the term melechet avodah is not as clear. In his Sefer HaMitzvot, Maimonides does not even use the term melechet avodah. In describing the prohibition against melachah on the festivals and the Yamim Tovim, he does not use the term melechet avodah. Instead, he explains that on these occasions melachah is prohibited. In his discussion of the positive command to refrain from melachah on the first day of Pesach does he mention that melechet ochel nefesh is permitted.[17] In his introduction to the laws of the Yamim Tovim, he lists the various mitzvot that will be discussed in this section of his code. These positive and negative commandments are all described as either prohibitions against melachah or positive commandments to refrain from melachah. In listing these commandments, he does not

---

[15] Sefer Shemot 12:16.

[16] Rabbaynu Moshe ben Nachman (Ramban), *Commentary on Sefer VaYikra* 23:7.

[17] Rabbaynu Moshe ben Maimon (Rambam) *Sefer HaMitzvot, Mitzvat Aseh* 159.

use the term melechet avodah. It seems that Maimonides has banished from his lexicon the term melechet avodah.

However, in the very first law of the section the term melechet avodah does appear. Maimonides explains that on Yamim Tovim all melechet avodah is prohibited, with the exception of melachah performed for the purpose of food preparation. If we consider this statement carefully, an ambiguity emerges. An example will illustrate this ambiguity. If I tell my students that they will all have a quiz with the exception of Reuven and Shimon, I am implying that Reuven and Shimon are students. However even though they are students, they will be exempted from the quiz. It is because Reuven and Shimon are students that I must specify that they are exempted. Maimonides tells us that all melechet avodah is prohibited on the Yamim Tovim with the exception of melechet ochel nefesh. This implies that the term melechet avodah includes melechet ochel nefesh. Because melechet avodah includes melechet ochel nefesh, Maimonides must tell us that there is an exception to the prohibition of melechet avodah. It does not include melachah performed for food preparation.

In short, Maimonides rarely uses the term melechet avodah. When he does use the term, he implies that it includes all thirty-nine forms of melachah – including those related to food preparation. So, the term melachah and melechet avodah seem to both include all forms of melachah. These two terms seem to be indistinguishable.

This raises two questions. First, Maimonides' position does not seem to be consistent with the message in our parasha. In our parasha, the Torah reserves the term melachah for Shabbat and Yom Kippur. The Torah consistently uses the term melechet avodah when referring to the prohibition on Yamim Tovim. It seems that Maimonides is suggesting that this distinction is meaningless. According to Maimonides, both terms – melachah and melechet avodah seem to be indistinguishable in their meanings. Second, it is odd that after completely neglecting to use the term melechet avodah in his description of the mitzvot that regulate melachah on Yamim Tovim, he suddenly makes reference to the term in the first law regarding the Yamim Tovim! Why suddenly introduce this term if it has no meaningful significance?

In order to understand Maimonides' position, it is useful to more carefully consider Nachmanides' understanding of the term melechet avodah. According to Nachmanides, this term refers to those types of melachah that are designed to create or develop our possessions. The term does not include those types of melachah that are performed for personal benefit. This means that according to Nachmanides, the set of activities that is prohibited on Yamim Tovim is a different set than the set prohibited on Shabbat. Nachmanides is telling us that there are no exceptions to the prohibition against melechet avodah on Yom Tov. Melechet ochel nefesh is not an exception to the prohibition against melechet avodah. Those forms of melachah that are melechet ochel nefesh are not part of the set of prohibited activities defined by the term melechet avodah.

It seems that Maimonides disagrees with this formulation. He states that melechet ochel nefesh is exempted from the general prohibition against melechet avodah. This raises a new question. Why are these forms of melachah exempted? Maimonides does not discuss this issue directly. However, he does allude to the solution. He explains that celebration of Yamim Tovim includes an obligation to partake in the festival meal. Celebration of the occasion through food and drink is a fundamental element of the observance of Yamim Tovim.[18]

Let us now return to Maimonides' understanding of the term melechet avodah. It seems that the term includes all forms of melachah. Yet, the term is somehow significant and unique to Yamim Tovim. In order to identify this unique meaning, it is helpful to dissect the term and then to compare it to the term melachah. Melechet avodah literally means melachah of avodah – or melachah that involves labor or toil. In contrast, the term melachah refers to creative activity. As noted, both terms refer to the same melachot. However, each term refers to a different aspect of the melachot. The term melachah refers to the creative element in these activities. The term melechet avodah stresses the toil and labor involved in these activities.

It seems that according to Maimonides, there is a fundamental difference between the prohibition against melachah on Shabbat and the prohibition against melechet avodah on Yamim Tovim. Both prohibitions include the same activities. However, the two prohibitions focus on different aspects of these activities. On Shabbat, melachah is prohibited. The prohibition against these activities stems from and focus upon the creative element in the melachot. On Yamim Tovim, melechet avodah is prohibited. The prohibition focuses upon the element of toil and labor involved in these activities. In other words, all forms of melachah are prohibited on Shabbat because we are commanded to refrain from creativity in the material world. But on Yamim Tovim we are not commanded to refrain from creativity. Instead, these are occasions of celebration and joy. On such occasions toil and labor are inappropriate.

Apparently, Maimonides introduces the term melechet avodah in the first law of Yom Tov because it is relevant to the exemption for melechet ochel nefesh. Maimonides maintains that melechet ochel nefesh is exempted from the prohibition of melechet avodah because food preparation is essential to the observance of the festivals and Yamim Tovim. However, he seems to also maintain that this exemption is reasonable because it is consistent with the aim and objective of the prohibition of melechet avodah. The prohibition is against toil and labor. It is designed to endow the Yamim Tovim with a character of celebration and joy. This very aim and objective suggest that melechet ochel nefesh – although involving toil and labor – deserve to be exempted from the prohibition. The exemption of these activities is consistent with the very theme and objective of the prohibition against melechet avodah. In other words, melechet ochel nefesh is permitted because it is not melechet avodah. Food preparation does involve toil and labor. However, the exemption of these activities from the prohibition against melechet avodah is thematically consistent with the very objective of the prohibition – to endow the occasion with a character of joy and celebration.

"When you reap your land's harvest, do not completely harvest the corner of your field. Do not collect the stalks that have fallen. Leave these to the poor and the stranger. I am Hashem your G-d." (VaYikra 23:22)

Priority of Tzedaka

1. Long arms

One Shabbat I was leaving the synagogue accompanied by my oldest son – Yosef. On our way home we passed an older gentleman and he and I entered into a brief conversation. Yosef asked me who this man was. I told Yosef that although this gentleman led a quiet, humble life,

---

[18] Rabbaynu Moshe ben Maimon (Rambam) *Mishne Torah*, Hilchot Yom Tov 6:17-19.

he was a very remarkable person. This man was not a wealthy person. Yet, many years before he had invested a significant portion of his savings into an endowment devoted to supporting Torah education. I explained that people think that endowments are created only by wealthy people. But this gentleman realized that he did not need to be wealthy to make a difference through creating an endowment. He only needed to make tzedaka, a priority.

I have been involved in raising funds for many years. It is a difficult responsibility. But the reason for the difficulty may not be because there is not enough funds out there. Perhaps, the reason it is so difficult is because – unlike this special gentleman – so many people are willing to fulfill their minimum obligation. I am convinced that if each Jew gave the required ten percent of their income to tzedaka, we would have no problem funding a community's needs. But instead of each person fulfilling this individual requirement, there is a tendency to dodge the responsibility of giving and insist that it someone else's job. Now, since everyone can think of someone else that should have the responsibility, it is very difficult to make progress. A friend of mine is fond of saying that to raise funds you don't need to find people with deep pockets. You need to find the ones with long arms!

Why do so many not fulfill their responsibility of giving tzedaka? How should we respond to these attitudes? These are questions addressed in this week's parasha.

2. *Peah* and *Leket* in the Bait Hamikdash

One of the subjects discussed at length in this week's parasha is the festivals. The Torah briefly describes each – beginning with Pesach and ending with Sukkot and Shemini Atzeret. However, there is an odd element in this discussion. In the middle of the narrative – directly after describing the festival of Shavuot – the Torah mentions the mitzvot of Peah and Leket. These mitzvot both involve the harvest. When a field is harvested, any stalks of grain that fall during collection must be left for the poor. This is the mitzvah of Leket. The mitzvah of Peah requires that the corner of the field not be harvested. Instead, this portion of the field is left for the needy. Why are these two mitzvot inserted into the middle of the discussion of the festivals?

Rashi offers an enigmatic answer. He explains that the Torah is intentionally juxtaposing the mitzvot of Peah and Leket with the description of the festivals in order to direct our attention to a common quality. In the discussion of the festivals, the Torah mentions that each requires its own sacrifices. The juxtaposition is intended to teach us that through observing the mitzvot of Peah and Leket, one is regarded as if he has rebuilt the Beit HaMikdash and offered sacrifices.[19] The difficulty with Rashi's explanation is that it is not clear how the observance of the mitzvot of Peah and Leket can be equated with building the Beit HaMikdash and offering sacrifices.

3. Your wealth

In order to understand Rashi's comments, we must begin by understanding some of the common, curious behaviors that people have regarding their wealth and the attitudes that underlie these behaviors. Let's begin with the behaviors. We sometimes find that individuals that are relatively scrupulous in their observance of halacha are not completely honest and ethical in business practices. Furthermore, even among those that are upright and ethical in business dealing, some do not fulfill their obligation in regards to tzedaka. What are the attitudes that underlie these behaviors? First, there is clearly a dichotomy that is being made between religious

---

[19] Rabbaynu Shlomo ben Yitzchak (Rashi), *Commentary on Sefer VaYikra* 23:22.

life and business dealings. One who is less than ethical in business but otherwise observant, apparently feels that Hashem has His domain within our personal lives. He has the right to require that we fulfill our religious rituals – Shabbat observance, davening, observing the laws of kashrut – but He has no right to manage our professional lives or business dealings. With this attitude this person dichotomizes and separates his life into two portions. In one portion he is faithful to Hashem. In the other, he is completely his own master.

Second, this person feels that his wealth is his own. He feels that although Hashem has a right to make demands upon us, He is not the master of our wealth. This attitude is closely related to a third attitude.

It seems that these behaviors reflect a world view regarding one's own mastery over one's personal fate. A person who excludes Hashem from his professional and business life, apparently believes that he does not need Hashem in this area. He is the master of his own fate. His own decisions control his fate. He is wise enough to secure his own success and does not need assistance from Hashem. It is not surprising that a person with this attitude will also feel that Hashem has no place in directing how one's wealth should be used. If a person has earned his wealth without Hashem, why should Hashem tell this person how to use it?

Now, let us return to Rashi's comments. Rashi equates the observance of the mitzvot of Peah and Leket with the building of the Beit HaMikdash and the offering of sacrifices. We all recognize that service in the Beit HaMikdash is a form of serving Hashem. But not everyone recognizes that the manner in which one conducts oneself with personal wealth is also a form of service to Hashem. A person who dichotomizes recognizes that we must serve Hashem. But through the dichotomizing the person eliminates Hashem from a part of his life – his relationship with his personal wealth. Rashi's comments attack this dichotomy. One cannot relegate service to Hashem to the Beit HaMikdash. Service to Hashem pervades all elements of our lives. We serve Hashem not only in the synagogue but also in the manner in which we manage and relate to our wealth.

4. You took out a loan

Gershonides offers another perspective on the juxtaposition in our parasha. He observes that the festivals of Pesach and Shavuot both involve elements relating to the harvest season. On Pesach, the Omer sacrifice is offered. This offering is brought from the first barley grain of the harvest. On Shavuot the Sh'tai HaLechem – the Two Loaves – are offered. This offering is the first grain offering of the harvest brought from fine wheat. Both offerings have a single theme. They are expressions of thanks to Hashem for the bounty of the harvest. They are intended to reinforce the recognition that we are dependant on Hashem for our wealth. Our wealth is not merely a result of our own wits and wisdom. We need the help of Hashem. Furthermore, Hashem does not bless us with this wealth so that we may do with it whatever we please. He requires that we use the wealth that He grants us as He directs. The mitzvot of Peah and Leket express the same theme. Hashem granted us this wealth. He granted it to us with the expectation that we will support the needy. It is not ours to use exclusively as we please.[20]

Gershonides' comments directly address the second and third attitudes outlined above. To the person that feels that he is completely in control of his fate, the Torah provides a reminder

---

[20] Rabbaynu Levi ben Gershon (Ralbag / Gershonides), *Commentary on Sefer VaYikra*, (Mosad HaRav Kook, 1997), pp. 340-341.

that this is not the case. Control is an illusion. Without the assistance of Hashem, we are helpless. We are also not the masters of our wealth. We have not earned it on our own. We only succeed through Hashem's benevolence. So, it follows that Hashem has every right to direct us in its use.

5. Investment advice

One of the most fascinating explanations of the juxtaposition in our parasha is offered by Sforno. Sforno begins by adopting Gershonides' approach. He explains that the grain offerings of Pesach and Shavuot are designed to remind us of Hashem's role in our material success. But Sforno adds that the Torah commands us in the mitzvot of Peah and Leket as a means to retain our wealth. Hashem tells us that if we wish to retain our wealth, we must share it with the less fortunate. Sforno continues by referencing an interesting set of statements of the Sages. The Sages comment, "What is the salt – the preservative – of wealth? Giving from one's wealth." Other Sages phrase the lesson somewhat differently. "What is the salt – the preservative – of wealth? Performing acts of kindness."[21,22]

The general message of Sforno's comments is easy to identify. Hashem gives us wealth. He rewards us and allows us to retain our wealth, if we fulfill our obligations towards the needy. If we ignore these obligations, we cannot expect Hashem to continue to act towards us with benevolence.

However, the comments from the Sages are more difficult to understand. More specifically, the Sages expressed their message in two slightly different comments. What is the precise difference between these two comments? Rashi provides some assistance. He explains that according to the first version of the Sages' comments, preservation of wealth requires that we reduce our wealth by giving to others. We can use Rashi's comments to understand more clearly the two perspectives contained in these two slightly different comments of the Sages.

The second version of the Sages' comments corresponds closely with Sforno's message. Hashem requires that we help the needy. He will only reward us with retention of our wealth, if we perform acts of kindness. But there is an additional subtle message in the first version. According to the first version, it is not enough that we perform acts of kindness. We must demonstrate a proper attitude towards our wealth. We cannot become so attached to our wealth that we cannot give from it. We must be willing to adopt an objective attitude towards our wealth and recognize that its accumulation is not an end in itself. We must be willing to step back and recognize that our wealth is a means to a greater end. If we cannot use our wealth appropriately, we cannot retain it.

6. Buying happiness

To this point, we have interpreted Sforno's comments as an insight into Hashem's providence. In other words, Sforno is telling us that there is message in the pasuk regarding Hashem's relationship to us. He rewards and punishes. We need to act according the prescribed commands of the Torah in order to receive the reward and avoid punishment. However, there is another possible way to understand Sforno's message.

The way we relate to wealth is fascinating. We feel that wealth brings us happiness. The more wealth we acquire, the happier we will be. But I have noticed that anecdotally this does not

---

[21] Rabbaynu Ovadia Sforno, *Commentary on Sefer VaYikra*, 23:22.
[22] Mesechet Ketubot 67b.

seem to be true. We all know people that are relatively wealthy but seem unhappy. And we know others that struggle financially but seem very content in life. If our attitude towards wealth is correct, we would expect that there would be a direct correlation between financial success and happiness. But there is not obvious evidence that this correlation exists.

In fact a USC economist – Richard Easterlin – recently conducted and published a study on this issue. And he discovered that there is no correlation between wealth and happiness. The study, released in August of 2003, surveyed 1,500 people and concluded that, "people are no happier when they acquire greater wealth." One explanation for this phenomenon is that the assumption that wealth is associated with happiness is founded on a faulty premise. This premise is that happiness can be purchased – or secured through purchasing objects. Every person discovers that, regardless of how desirable some object may be, once acquired it soon looses its attraction. Once this initial discovery is made, a person can come to two conclusions. One conclusion is that he simply has not purchased the right thing. And if he continues to make more and more purchases, eventually happiness will be secured. If a person adopts this conclusion, each purchase and disappointment is followed by an even more desperate attempt to buy happiness. This cycle can continue endlessly. But Easterlin's study suggests that the initial purchase and disappointment points to an alternative conclusion. Happiness cannot be purchased. As long as a person continues to pursue happiness through acquiring wealth and then purchasing more objects, the cycle of fantasy, purchase, and disappointment will continue – endlessly. Instead, happiness must be found elsewhere. Maybe, Sforno and our Sages are suggesting that happiness comes from spiritual development. One who wishes to maintain his wealth – for his wealth to be meaningful – must learn to relate to his wealth from a more spiritual perspective. As long as a person's attention remains focused on wealth and acquisition, happiness will evade the person. But once a person steps back and objectifies – once a person considers his wealth as a gift that can help others and advances to a more spiritual level of function – then happiness can be secured.

And it shall be, when you come into the land which Hashem your G-d gives you as an inheritance, and possess it, and dwell therein; that you shall take of the first of all the fruit of the ground, which you shall bring in from your land that Hashem your G-d gives you. And you shall put it in a basket and go unto the place which Hashem your G-d shall choose to cause His name to dwell there. (Devarim 26:1-2)

Say "Thank You"

1. Bikurim and cooking meat in milk

Parsaht Ki Tavo opens with a discussion of the mitzvah of Bikurim. This mitzvah requires that the first fruits of each year be brought to the Bait HaMikdash – the Holy Temple. The Bikurim are then given to the kohanim – the priests – for their consumption. The mitzvah of Bikurim does not apply to all crops. We are required to give Bikurim only from the seven species that are associated with the Land of Israel. The Land is considered blessed with these fruits and grains. The mitzvah of Bikurim is introduced in Sefer Shemot. The context in which the mitzvah is discussed is notable. In the passages preceding the discussion of Bikurim, the Torah outlines the three Pilgrimage Festivals – Pesach, Shavuot, and Sukkot. This is followed by the mitzvah of Bikurim. However, the very same passage that contains the mitzvah of Bikurim also outlines the prohibition against cooking together meat and milk. This implies a close relationship between

Bikurim and the prohibition against cooking meat with milk. What is this connection? A clearer understanding of the mitzvah of Bikurim is helpful in understanding this issue.

And you shall come unto the priest that shall be in those days, and say unto him: I profess this day unto Hashem your G-d, that I have come unto the land which Hashem swore unto our fathers to give us. And the priest shall take the basket out of your hand, and set it down before the altar of Hashem your G-d. And you shall speak and say before Hashem your G-d: A wandering Aramean was my father, and he went down to Egypt, and sojourned there, few in number. And he became there a nation, great, mighty, and populous. (Devarim 26:3-5)

2. The narrative for Bikurim reveals its nature

According to Maimonides, there are two mitzvot regarding the Bikurim. The first is to bring Bikurim to the Bait HaMikdash.[23] The second is Mikre Bikurim.[24] When the farmer brings the fruits, he is required to fulfill the mitzvah of Mikre Bikurim. He recites a specific portion of the Torah that is included in this week's parasha. In this recitation, he describes the tribulations experienced by our forefather Yaakov. He recounts his descent to Egypt. He describes the suffering and persecution our ancestors experienced in Egypt. Then, he briefly recounts our redemption by Hashem from bondage. He acknowledges that Hashem has given us the Land of Israel and that the produce that he is presenting is the product of that land. In short, the farmer describes the fruit he is presenting as a manifestation of Hashem's redemption of Bnai Yisrael and an expression of His providential relationship with the Jewish people.

The narrative of Mikre Bikurim reveals the nature of the mitzvah of Bikurim. The Bikurim are given to the kohanim for their consumption. However, the mitzvah is not merely a tax placed upon the farmers in order to support the kohanim. Bringing and offering Bikurim is an expression of thanksgiving. Through offering the first fruits in the Bait HaMikdash, the farmer acknowledges that the bounty of the harvest is an expression of Hashem's providence.

And you shall rejoice in all the good which Hashem your G-d has given to you, and to your house, you, and the Levite, and the stranger that is in your midst. (Devarim 26:11)

3. Bikurim and Regalim – a shared theme

Understanding the mitzvah of Bikurim explains the Torah's association of Bikurim with the Regalim – the Pilgrimage Festivals. This relationship can be understood on two levels. Rashi comments on the above passage that Mikre Bikurim is only recited when the Bikurim are brought during the season of rejoicing. He explains that the season of rejoicing is from Shavuot to Sukkot. After Sukkot the Bikurim may still be brought but Mikre Bikurim is not recited.[25]

Why is the period between Shavuot and Sukkot the season of rejoicing? Shavuot occurs at the opening of the wheat harvest. Sukkot coincides with the close of the harvest season. By Sukkot the harvest has been collected and placed in storage before the beginning of the rainy season. It is in the season between Shavuot and Sukkot that the farmer most rejoices over the bounty of the harvest.

Three times you shall observe a feast unto Me in the year. The feast of unleavened bread you shall keep. Seven days you shall eat unleavened bread, as I commanded you, at the time

---

[23] Rabbaynu Moshe ben Maimon, Sefer HaMitzvot, Mitzvat Aseh 125.
[24] Rabbaynu Moshe ben Maimon, Sefer HaMitzvot, Mitzvat Aseh 132.
[25] Rabbaynu Shlomo ben Yitzchak (Rashi), Commentary on Sefer Devarim 26:11.

appointed in the month Aviv – for in it you came out from Egypt. And none shall appear before Me empty; and the feast of harvest, the first-fruits of your labors, which you sowed in the field; and the feast of ingathering, at the end of the year, when you gather in your labors out of the field. Three times in the year all your males shall appear before the L-rd, G-D. (Shemot 23:14-17)

4. The Regalim as harvest festivals

The passages above from Sefer Shemot precede the Torah's commandment to offer Bikurim. These passages describe the three Regalim and the obligation to appear at the Bait HaMikdash during these festivals. In its treatment of Pesach, the Torah does note that the time of its celebration corresponds with the time of the redemption from Egypt. However, Shavuot and Sukkot are not associated, in these passages, with historical events. Instead, both are referred to as harvest festivals. Shavuot is described as the feast of the harvest of the first fruits and Sukkot is described as the festival of the in-gathering of the harvest. Even Pesach is associated with the harvest. It is observed in the month of Aviv. Rashi explains that the term aviv means that the grain is fully developed and approaching the time for harvest.[26]

In summary, although all of the Regalim are associated with important events in the history of Bnai Yisrael, they are also harvest festivals. They are occasions during which we are commanded to give thanks to Hashem for the bounty of the harvest. The association of Bikurim with the Regalim is not only because Mikre Bikurim can only be recited during the season from Shavuot to Sukkot. Bikurim and the Regalim are also associated through their shared objective. The Regalim and Bikurim are vehicles through which we offer thanksgiving to Hashem.

The choicest first-fruits of your land you shall bring into the house of Hashem your G-d. You shall not cook a kid in its mother's milk. (Shemot 23:19)

5. The prohibition against cooking meat in milk

The above passage follows the discussion of the Regalim and presents the commandment of Bikurim. The second half of the passage prohibits cooking a kid in its mother's milk. The Oral Tradition explains that this is a general prohibition against cooking meat in milk. The placement of this prohibition in the same passage that presents the mitzvah of Bikurim requires explanation. The commentators suggest a few alternative explanations. However, one of the most interesting is provided by Rabbaynu Ovadia Sforno. Sforno suggests that, in a restricted sense, the passage is to be understood literally. It refers to cooking specifically a kid in its mother's milk. He explains that in antiquity this was a ritual among the pagans. They believed that through cooking a kid in the milk of its mother, they would secure the benevolence of the spirits and secure a bountiful harvest.[27] From Sforno's perspective, the Torah does prohibit cooking any meat in milk. However the prohibition is aimed at discouraging a specific heathen practice – cooking a kid in its mother's milk.

According to Sforno, the message of the passage is that an abundant harvest is not secured through engaging in these primitive rituals. It is secured through the celebration of the Regalim and through offering Bikurim. These activities are means through which we offer

---

26   Rabbaynu Shlomo ben Yitzchak (Rashi), Commentary on Sefer Shemot 23:15.
27   Rabbaynu Ovadia Sforno, Commentary on Sefer Shemot, 23:19.

thanksgiving to Hashem. Through offering thanksgiving and acknowledging that our prosperity is a blessing bestowed by Hashem, we aspire to secure His continued blessings.[28]

6. To acknowledge Hashem we must learn to acknowledge one another

The fundamental message of the Regalim, Bikurim and Mikre Bikurim is that we can only expect to secure Hashem's blessings through realizing that our prosperity and happiness are a result of His blessings. How do we maintain this awareness of Hashem's role in our lives? How can we train or condition ourselves to be more cognizant of His blessings?

Rabbaynu Bachya ibn Paquda identifies three obstacles that one must overcome in order to feel a sense of appreciation for Hashem's blessings. First, the person must not disregard the blessings in one's life because of the needs or aspirations that have not been met. We commonly fail to appreciate our blessings because we are focused on the elements that we feel are lacking in our lives. Second, we tend to take our blessings for granted. We become accustomed to the comfort of our homes, the abundance of food on our tables, our safety and security. We take all of these wonderful blessings for granted – or worse – feel entitled to them. Third, we cannot appreciate our blessings because they are mixed with elements of sorrow and tragedy. No one lives a completely blessed life. We all are confronted with challenges and even tragedy. Sometimes, the negative elements of our lives become the focus of our attention and we have no effective cognizance of the blessings in our lives.[29]

Bachya extensively discusses the means by which we can overcome these obstacles. However, there is one simple, powerful step that we must take that will cultivate in us a greater appreciation of Hashem's blessings. We must be more mindful of the kindnesses done to us by other human beings and express gratitude to those who benefit us. Bachya treats the obligation to acknowledge Hashem's kindness as a self-evident ethical imperative.[30] If this is true, then it also extends to acknowledging kindnesses performed by human beings from which we benefit. Furthermore, if we are not able to acknowledge the concrete and perceivable benefits that are bestowed upon us through the efforts of others, then what chance do we have of appreciating Hashem? He is invisible to our senses. Awareness of His presence in our lives is not as easily cultivated and nurtured.

Specific commandments of the Torah express this message. The Torah directs us to honor our parents, and our teachers. The message in these commandments is not just that these individuals should be acknowledged for the lives that they have given to us. Rather, we must understand that these commandments are intimately linked to achieving an appreciation of Hashem, whose benevolence may not be as evident to us. We learn to be more appreciative of the blessings bestowed by Hashem, through acknowledging the benefits we receive from our fellow human beings.

---

[28] Rabbaynu Ovadia Sforno, Commentary on Sefer Shemot, 23:19.
[29] Rabbaynu Bachya ibn Paquda, Chovot HaLevavot (Feldheim, 1970), pp 125-128.
[30] Rabbaynu Bachya ibn Paquda, Chovot HaLevavot (Feldheim, 1970), pp 125-131.

Rosh Hashanah

It is customary to arise in the early morning to recite prayers of supplication from the beginning of the month of Elul until Yom HaKippurim. (Shulcah Aruch, Orech Chayim 581:1)

Differing Customs for the Reciting of Selichot

It is customary to recite *Selichot* – prayers of supplication – prior to *Rosh HaShanah*. Generally, these prayers are recited at night before daybreak. Both Ashkenazic and Sefardic communities recite *Selichot*. Each of the communities has its own version of the *Selichot* service. Many of the components of the service are different in the two versions. This can lead to the impression that two communities have developed very different versions of the service. However, this is incorrect. Both versions are constructed around a fixed set of essential components. Only the less essential components are different in the two versions.

Although their two versions of the *Selichot* service are structurally similar, there is one area in which the two communities' practices regarding *Selichot* do reflect a fundamental difference in their respective interpretations of the service. Accroding to Rav Yosef Karo, this service is initiated on the first day of Elul. This is the custom generally accepted by Sefardic communities. Rav Moshe Isserles comments that the Ashkenazic custom is to begin reciting the *Selichot* from the *Motzai Shabbat* prior to *Rosh HaShanah*.[1]

The source for these two customs is discussed by Rabbaynu Nissim. He explains that the custom of Barcelona was to begin *Selichot* on the twenty-fifth day of Elul.[2] The Gaon of Vilna explained that this is the source of the Ashkenazic custom.[3]

In order to appreciate the Gaon's conclusion, we need to better understand the practice of the Barcelona community. Rabbaynu Nissim explains the basis of this custom. This custom reflects the opinion that the sixth day of creation corresponds with *Rosh HaShanah*. Hashem chose this day for *Rosh HaShanah* because it is associated with forgiveness. On this day, Adam and Chavah, representing humanity, committed the first sin. They disobeyed Hashem. They ate the fruit that the Creator had forbidden. Hashem forgave this iniquity. On *Rosh HaShanah,* we too beseech Hashem for forgiveness. It is appropriate to appeal to Hashem on the anniversary of the date that forgiveness was introduced into the universe. If *Rosh HaShanah* corresponds with the sixth day of creation, what calendar date corresponds with the first day of creation? This date is the twenty-fifth of Elul (Elul having twenty-nine days).[4]

We can now understand the Gaon's comments. The conventional Ashkenazic practice simplifies the message of the Barcelona custom. The Barcelona custom is designed to remind us of the association between *Rosh HaShanah* and Adam and Chavah's experience of mercy and forgiveness. It accomplishes this through fixing the date for the initiation of *Selichot* with the calendar date corresponding with the first day of creation. In this manner, the days of the recitation of *Selichot* lead up to and climax with *Rosh HaShanah*. According to the Gaon, the

---

[1] Rav Moshe Isserles, *Comments on Shulchan Aruch, Orech Chayim* 581:1.
[2] R' Nissim, *Notes to Commentary of Rabbaynu Yitzchak Alfasi*, Mesechet Rosh HaShanah 3a.
[3] Rabbaynu Eliyahu of Vilna, *Biur HaGra, Shulchan Aruch, Orech Chayim* 581, note 8.
[4] R' Nissim, *Notes to Commentary of Rabbaynu Yitzchak Alfasi*, Mesechet Rosh HaShanah 3a.

conventional Ashkenazic custom fixes the day for the initiation of *Selichot* with the day to the week corresponding to the first day of creation. In place of associating the initiation of *Selichot* with the first day of creation by fixing it to a calendar date, it creates the association through fixing the initiation to a day of the week.

Rabbaynu Nissim explains the custom in Gerona was to begin the recitation of *Selichot* on the first day of Elul. This date was also chosen because of its association with forgiveness. After the sin of the *Egel HaZahav* – the Golden Calf, Moshe ascended Mount Sinai. He sought forgiveness for Bnai Yisrael. Moshe ascended the mountain of the first day of Elul. He secured Hashem's forgiveness forty days later. This day – the tenth of Tishrai – became *Yom Kippur*.

These two customs reflect two different aspects of Divine forgiveness. The forgiveness received by Adam and Chavah was not a result of repentance or prayer. In fact, both Adam and Chavah minimized their role in committing the sin. Why were they forgiven? Hashem created humanity and bestowed within us the unique ability to choose between good and evil. Every human enters life as an imperfect and instinctual creature. It is our responsibility to improve ourselves through the wise exercise of our freewill. It is inevitable that we will sin as we proceed along this path. Hashem forgives us for these failings just as He pardoned Adam and Chavah. In short, the very design of creation allows for an imperfect individual and implies Hashem's forbearance and forgiveness.

The forgiveness at Sinai was achieved through supplication and prayer. Moshe ascended the mountain and beseeched Hashem to forgive His people. As Moshe elevated Himself and rose to a higher spiritual level, he drew closer to Hashem. Through this process, his prayers were accepted and Bnai Yisrael was forgiven.

Each custom reflects one of these aspects of forgiveness. The Ashkenazic custom reminds us of the forgiveness received by Adam and Chavah. It recalls the forgiveness inherent in the design of creation. The Sefardic custom reminds us of the forgiveness achieved at Sinai. It recalls the forgiveness we can secure through personal spiritual effort and prayer.

However, there is no recitation of Hallel on Rosh HaShanah and Yom HaKippurim because these are days of repentance, awe, and fear. They are not days of excessive joy. (Maimonides, Hilchot Chanukah 3:6)

Rosh HaShanah Confusion

1. The Rosh HaShanah paradox

Rosh HaShanah is paradoxical. It seems that on this festival we are expected to experience both joy and dread. Maimonides explains that although *Hallel* is generally recited on festivals, it is not recited on Rosh HaShanah and Yom Kippur because these are days of repentance, awe and fear.[5] Yet, Maimonides teaches us that on *yamim tovim* we should be joyful. He lists the *yamim tovim* as the seven days of Pesach, the eight days of Sukkot, and the other festivals. Apparently, he includes Rosh HaShanah and even Yom Kippur![6]

---

[5] Rabbaynu Moshe ben Maimon (Rambam) *Mishne Torah*, Hilchot Chanukah 3:6.
[6] Rabbaynu Moshe ben Maimon (Rambam) *Mishne Torah*, Hilchot Yom Tov 6:17.

How can we reconcile the fear and anxiety that are natural reactions to judgment with the festive character of Rosh HaShanah?

You revealed Yourself in the cloud of Your glory to your sacred nation ... With thunder and lightning You revealed Yourself to them and with the sound of the shofar you appeared. (Musaf of Rosh HaShanah)

2. The dual message of the *shofar*

The answer lies in the *shofar*. Like Rosh HaShanah, the *shofar* expresses a paradox. The *musaf* of Rosh HaShanah includes three central blessings. The final of these discusses the message of the *shofar*. It describes the *shofar* blast as a pronouncement of Hashem revealing Himself as king. It declared His descent to Sinai and at the final redemption it will proclaim His revelation as king.

However, Maimonides explains that the *shofar* has another meaning. It is a call to repent. It awakens the slumbering person from his apathy and calls upon him to contemplate his actions and return to Hashem.[7]

In short, the *shofar* is a declaration of Hashem's glorious revelation. It is also the sound of an alarm and a call to repent. How can we reconcile or join together these two *shofar*-identities?

3. The challenge of being aware of Hashem

Let us set aside these questions for a moment and consider a different issue. During the *musaf* repetition, we will declare that "today the universe was born". For us, creation is not a historical event that occurred millennia in the past. It is an ongoing process. Every day in the blessings preceding the *Shema*, we declare that Hashem sustains or re-creates the universe every moment. His will is the ongoing source of the universe's existence. As Maimonides explains, if His will were to be removed from the universe for the briefest moment, creation would be voided.[8]

Every event in our lives, our triumphs and tragedies, our achievements and disappointments, are a consequence of His will. We plan; we labor; we strive. But the success of our efforts is not the product of our initiatives, wisdom, and dedication, as much they reflect His will and benevolence.

But this is not our everyday experience. I get up in the morning and I wash *netilat yadayim*. I do not doubt that water will emerge from the faucet as it has every morning. I get into my car, press the button to open the garage; it opens as it has every morning for many years. I arrive at the yeshiva. The building awaits me with its students, as it does every school day. Where is Hashem?

On an intellectual level, I recognize that health, prosperity, and security, are not to be taken for granted. I recognize that these are precarious blessings that can disappear in a moment. But I feel secure, smug and self-assured in my blessings. Hashem is creator. He is king. But He seems to be a very distant king. He is separated from me by the millennia since creation and by the perfect regularity of the very cosmos He designed, created, and sustains.

---

[7] Rabbaynu Moshe ben Maimon (Rambam) *Mishne Torah*, Hilchot Teshuvah 3:4.
[8] Rabbaynu Moshe ben Maimon (Rambam) *Mishne Torah*, Hilchot Yesodai HaTorah 1:2-3.

But what if tomorrow I were deprived of my health? What if I could not pay my mortgage? What if, G-d forbid, one of my students was seriously ill? Suddenly, the regularity of my world would be set asunder. My cocky, self-confidence would be replaced by fear and despair. I would be painfully aware of my limited control over my fate and the precariousness of my existence. G-d would quickly emerge as the true king and arbitrator. I would seek sanctuary and rescue in His shadow and call upon Him for salvation.

Can only tragedy or disaster awaken my awareness of Hashem's sovereignty?

4. Awakening in response to the *shofar* blast

Let us more carefully consider Maimonides's comments on the *shofar*. He tells us that the *shofar* calls to us: Arouse from your sleep. Those in a deep slumber awaken! Search your actions. Repent. Recall your creator!

What is this slumber that is suddenly disturbed by the *shofar*'s mighty blast? What is this sleep that the *shofar*'s call interrupts? That sleep and slumber are the very sense of security and smug self-assurance and are my everyday cognitive reality.

The *shofar* declares that judgment approaches. Our fate is not in our hands. The regularity and predictability of our lives are not assured and cannot be taken for granted. Today's health and prosperity are not precursors to tomorrow, and may suddenly vanish.

We hear the call of the *shofar* and we part the veil of regularity and predictability. Behind the veil we perceive the Almighty seated upon His throne. He is the creator, the king; and He is the judge. All of creation is before Him as He sits in judgment; He decides its fate and destiny.

Our awareness of judgment enthrones Hashem and establishes Him as our king.

5. Proclaiming and rejoicing in Hashem's sovereignty

The sound of the *shofar* is at once plaintive and glorious. It is a warning and an alarm. But by awakening us, it restores Hashem to His place as creator and ruler. It proclaims His sovereignty.

The dual characteristic of Rosh HaShanah is not paradoxical; it is a reflection of and a response to our own existential confusion. Intellectually, we recognize Hashem as creator and our king. Yet, we cannot feel His presence and His authority. He is hidden from us by the very regularity and predictability of the incredible universe He fashioned. We need help, some catalyst, to empower us to sweep away this deception so that we may gaze upon Hashem as our king.

Our awareness of judgment is this catalyst. With this awareness, we suddenly perceive Hashem as creator and sovereign of the universe.

Rosh HaShanah celebrates Hashem's kingship over the vastness of the universe and the minutiae of our individual lives. It establishes His sovereignty not as a distant, unreachable ruler but as a contemporary and personal G-d. We celebrate His sovereignty and rejoice in His presence. But we achieve this cognitive breakthrough through the awareness of judgment.

6. The Rosh HaShanah journey

On Rosh Hashanah we undertake a journey. The journey is not easy. It evokes our fears and anxieties. But at the end of this journey we arrive at a wonderful destination and we rejoice.

Our journey is along a path of self-evaluation and even criticism. It is a journey through an experience of judgment. As we proceed, we are anxious and fearful. But at the end of our journey we arrive at a wondrous destination. We observe – we encounter – Hashem enthroned in His glory. We rejoice in His presence. He is our king and we are His subjects. He is our father and we are His children.

And if you will not listen to the voice of Hashem your G-d to take care to perform all of His commandments and statutes that I command you today, then all of these curses will come upon you and overtake you. (Devarim 28:15).

Not Just another Warning

1. Moshe's warning is read before Rosh HaShanah

A large portion of Parshat Ki Tavo is devoted to Moshe's stern warning to the people. If they observe the commandments of the Torah, then they will be rewarded with wondrous blessings. If they are unfaithful, then they will bring upon themselves terrible suffering and exile. Moshe begins his description of the consequences of abandoning the commandments with a general description of the suffering that will befall the nation. He then provides a more detailed description of the terrible calamities that the nation will experience. In this description he foretells the most wretched and horrid ordeals that our nation has endured.

Our Sages refer to this section as Moshe's *tochachah* – his rebuke. Our Sages apportioned the sections of the Torah to their respective weeks so that this section is read two weeks prior to Rosh HaShanah. Rosh Hashanah initiates a period of judgment that is completed with Yom Kippur. The superficial connection between this Torah reading and the approaching period is easily identified. This is the period during which our people and all humanity are judged. The reading describes the blessings that will accrue to us if this judgment is favorable and the suffering that may befall us if the judgment is unfavorable. However, is there a deeper connection between this Torah reading and the period of judgment?

If you abhor My statutes and your souls reject My ordinances so as not to perform all of My commandments – so as to overturn My covenant, then I too will act thus toward you. I will punish you with consumption and fever that bring despair and sorrow. You will sow for naught your seeds. Your enemies will eat it. (VaYikra 26:15-16)

2. The rebuke of Parshat Bechukotai and its message of consolation

An additional section of the Torah is described, as a rebuke – a *tochachah*. This section is contained in Parshat Bechukotai. This rebuke describes with horrid detail the consequences of abandoning the Torah. However, there is a fundamental difference between this earlier version of rebuke and Moshe's warning.

Moshe's warning focuses exclusively upon the rewards for observance of the commandments and the consequences of abandoning the Torah. The rebuke in Parshat Bechukotai describes the consequences for abandonment of the Torah and then assures the nation of its ultimate redemption from its afflictions. The final passage assures the people that Hashem will recall His covenant with the Patriarchs. He will not forsake the nation He redeemed from Egypt.

This additional element seems to be intended to encourage and console the people. Even in the depth of suffering and when afflicted by the most intense persecution, the people should realize that they have not been abandoned. Hashem will remember His covenant with the Patriarchs and rescue His people.

Sefer Devarim is composed primarily of Moshe's final messages to the nation. Moshe includes in his address assurances similar to the consolatory material in Parshat Bechukotai's rebuke. Moshe understood that this message is essential to the nation's survival. It will provide hope at times of intense suffering and persecution. However, this message of consolation is expressed elsewhere in Sefer Devarim; it is not included in his rebuke. Why did he not include this message in his *tochachah*?

3. The eternity of the covenant

The conciliatory passages that conclude the Parshat Bechukotai rebuke provide a message of hope that will sustain the Jewish people in the darkest periods of its history. However, these passages also indicate that the Torah's presentation in Parshat Bechukotai is more than a rebuke. It is also an elaboration upon the covenant between Hashem and Bnai Yisrael. The covenant between the nation and Hashem demands that the nation observe the Torah. It is an agreement. Our fulfillment of our portion of the agreement secures Hashem's blessings. Our violation of the terms of the agreement will have severe consequences. However, because the presentation is an explanation of the covenant, it includes an additional element. The covenant will never be forgotten or abandoned. We will be chastised for wrongdoing but never forsaken. Redemption is an inevitable outcome of the covenant.

And observe the words of this covenant and perform them so that you will succeed in all that you do. (Devarim 28:8).

4. Moshe's rebuke, its message, and Rosh HaShanah

The above passage concludes a short section of our *parasha* that follows Moshe's rebuke. In this section Moshe reminds the people of the miracles of their redemption from Egypt. He recounts the wonders of their sojourn in the wilderness. He reminds the people of their triumph over the mighty kings Sichon and Og. He ends with the above passage – another admonition to observe the commandments. What is the connection between this admonition and the preceding passages?

Moshe's message is that the nation has witnessed Hashem's omnipotence. The people have seen His wonders and miracles. These provide testimony to His power over nature. Their own experience provides absolute proof that success and blessing are not products of nature and fate. They are an expression of divine will.

These passages directly follow Moshe's rebuke and reveal his intention. Moshe wishes to impress upon the people that their destiny will not be determined by their industry or wisdom. It will be determined by their commitment to observance. He understands that it is difficult to peer beyond the thick veil of the material world and recognize that it is but an expression of divine will. Our destiny is not decided by our efforts to manipulate and subdue nature to serve our purposes. Success is a product of Hashem's will and His blessings. These blessings are secured through our devotion to Him and to His Torah.

Moshe did not include in his message the conciliatory closing of Parshat Bechukotai's rebuke. These passages have no place in his message. His message is a charge to the nation to

31

recognize that their destiny will be guided by Hashem and it will reflect their choice – to serve Hashem or to abandon His Torah.

Why is the *tochachah* of Parshat KiTavo read before the approaching period of judgment? This period is not devoted only to judgment. Judgment is an expression of Hashem's majesty and glory. We realize that because He is creator and ruler, we are subject to His judgment. In other words, our realization that we are judged during the approaching days moves us to recognize Hashem's sovereignty. We read Moshe's *tochahah* not only because it speaks of judgment. We read it because it is a declaration of Hashem's kingship.

The relationship between judgment and recognition of Hashem's *malchut* – His kingship is reflected in the prayers of Rosh HaShanah. The focus of the liturgy is not upon judgment; its focus is upon His majesty over all creation. If our only response to these Days of Awe is limited to fear and trepidation evoked by the forthcoming judgment, then we have missed an important element of these days. We must recognize that judgment is an expression of Hashem's sovereignty over humanity and all of creation.

Our L-rd and the L-rd of our fathers, rule over the entire universe in Your glory, be exalted over the entire land in Your splendor, reveal Yourself in the majestic grandeur of Your strength over all who dwell in Your inhabited world. (Rosh HaShanah Amidah)

Living an Integrated Life

1. The festivals and their themes

Each of our holidays or festivals has a theme that is fundamental to the Torah. Pesach recalls our redemption from Egypt. The redemption is evidence of Hashem's omnipotence and through His redemption He established us as His nation. Shavuot recalls Revelation. Our observance of the Torah – its mitzvot and its lessons – is based upon Revelation. Sukkot recalls our travels in the wilderness. It reminds us of our dependence upon Hashem. It dispels the illusion that we have control over our destinies or that our efforts determine our successes or failures. Yom Kippur is devoted to repentance and atonement.

Even Chanukah and Purim emphasize fundamental themes. Rambam – Maimonides – explains that they reinforce the message that Hashem hears our prayers and "the Torah's assurance that 'What [other] great nation has a L-rd close to it like Hashem, our L-rd, in all instances that we call-out to Him.'"[9] In other words, when the Jewish people are in danger and we call-out to Hashem for salvation, He responds to our pleas.

2. The theme of Rosh HaShanah

The theme of Rosh HaShanah is easily overlooked. Rosh HaShanah initiates the Ten Days of Repentance. As Rambam explains, the blasts of the shofar are a signal that the time has arrived to devote ourselves to self-evaluation and repentance. "Awake! Awake, those who sleep, from your sleep. Bestir yourselves, those who slumber, from your slumber. Inspect your actions, repent and recall your Creator." [10] This emphasis on repentance and the approach of Yom Kippur – the day of which we will be judged – can obscure Rosh HaShanah's own unique theme.

---

9 Rabbaynu Moshe ben Maimon (Rambam) Mishne Torah, Introduction.
10 Rabbaynu Moshe ben Maimon (Rambam) Mishne Torah, Hilchot Teshuvah 3:4.

The theme of Rosh HaShanah is expressed in the above lines. They introduce the final paragraph of the Rosh HaShanah Amidah's central benediction. Rosh HaShanah celebrates Hashem's sovereignty. Rav Yosef Dov Soloveitchik Zt"l, quoting his childhood teacher, often described the day as Hashem's coronation.

Hashem's sovereignty is a fundamental message of the Torah. But, do we need Rosh HaShanah to remind us of this sovereignty? Every mitzvah we perform, our every prayer and petition attest to His sovereignty. Why is a festival devoted to a theme that is given ample emphasis every day?[11] An answer to this question is provided by an important insight developed by Rav Yosef Dov Soloveitchik in response to a baffling question.

I am Hashem your L-rd who took you out from the Land of Egypt, from the house of bondage.
(Shemot 20:2)

3. The commandment to believe in Hashem

Rambam understands the above passage to state a commandment. We are required to affirm the existence of Hashem.

"The first commandment is the commandment that He commanded us in the knowledge of the L-rd. [The commandment] is that it should be known that there exists a cause and He acts upon all that exists."[12]

Rambam elaborates upon this commandment in his Mishne Torah – his code of law. He explains that we are commanded to know that Hashem is the source of all that exists. The existence of the universe and all contained within it is sustained by the will of Hashem. If He would suspend His will for a moment the universe would immediately cease to exist.[13]

The difficulty with Rambam's position is blatantly evident in his phrasing of the commandment. "[It] is the commandment the He commanded us in the knowledge of the L-rd." In other words, Hashem commands us to affirm His existence. This seems completely circular. One's acceptance of the existence of such a command presupposes that Hashem exists and He issued the command. The command to affirm His existence is meaningless. Our affirmation is expressed in every commandment that we observe.

Furthermore, the very premise of the commandment is incomprehensible. To whom is the commandment directed? Does the commandment admonish the non-believer to believe? First, why would the non-believer accept the legitimacy of a commandment given by a L-rd in whom he does not believe. But if we imagine the non-believer to be moved by the commandment, what is he to do? Is he to try harder to believe? Beliefs are not like actions. Actions are volitional. Beliefs are involuntary. One cannot acquire a belief simply by closing one's eyes and imagining something is true.

Responding to this question Rav Soloveitchik suggests:

---

[11] This question does not apply to the other festivals. For example, it is true that we affirm Revelation with the performance of each commandment. However, the affirmation is implicit. In contrast, the performance of mitzvot is not an implicit acknowledgement of Hashem's authority or sovereignty; it is its explicit expression.

[12] Rabbaynu Moshe ben Maimon (Rambam) Sefer HaMitzvot, Mitzvat Aseh 1.

[13] Rabbaynu Moshe ben Maimon (Rambam) Mishne Torah, Hilchot Yesodai HaTorah 1:1-3.

"The first law in the Mishne Torah is the positive mitzvah to know that there exists a first cause [for all that exists]. By "know" the Rambam did not mean to know scientifically or philosophically. "Know" means to experience. The Rambam uses the word the way it's used sometimes in TaNaCh, in Chumash, "And Adam knew Chavah, his wife" or "And the L-rd knew." G-d knew? Of course, He knew, but "And the L-rd knew," the Ramban says it means He had mercy upon them, compassion. Or "And Hashem knew" means Hashem was involved in exile, His Divine presence was in exile. The Sacred One, Blessed be He, figuratively speaking, experienced exile."[14]

4. Experiencing Hashem

According to Rav Soloveitchik the commandment is addressed to one who believes in Hashem. This commandment does demand affirmation of Hashem's existence. It demands that we transform our belief into experience. We must experience His existence.

What does it mean to experience Hashem's existence? To answer this question, we must consider a phenomenon with which we are all familiar. One can know that something is true and not integrate that knowledge into one's decisions and life. Let's consider two examples.

First, consider a person who deeply loves his wife and children. He knows how important these people are to him and the meaning they bring into his life. This knowledge may or may not be integrated into the manner he behaves toward his family. Does he treat his wife with the respect and sensitivity that she deserves? Does he set aside time to spend with his children, take an interest in their daily lives, thoughtfully mentor and counsel them? Some of us struggle to give our love these forms of meaningful, concrete expression. This does not mean that we do not feel love and appreciation. Our failure is in integrating those feelings into our daily behaviors.

Second, a person knows that his cholesterol is high, his blood pressure should be lower. Despite his awareness and his recognition of the danger in which he is placing himself, he is not careful about his diet and does not exercise with regularity. He is not unaware of his peril. He has not succeeded in integrating the knowledge into his life-style.

Both examples illustrate the distinction between knowing a truth and experiencing it or integrating that truth into one's daily life. According to Rav Soloveitchik, this is the essence of the commandment to "know" Hashem. We are not commanded to affirm His existence. We are commanded to integrate our awareness of Hashem into our daily lives.

5. Integrating Hashem into our lives

An integrated life is one in which the awareness of Hashem is expressed in all its aspects. The awareness is not limited to the synagogue or to the moments at home when one is engaged in ritual. The awareness informs our interactions with the members of our family, our professional lives, even our personal habits and behaviors.

Rosh HaShanah celebrates Hashem's sovereignty. It is not intended to make us aware of His sovereignty. It is intended to move us to integrate that awareness into all aspects of our lives. Rosh HaShanah is observed the first two days of the year, but its impact is intended to extend to every moment of our lives.

---

[14] Rav David Holzer, The Rav Thinking Aloud on the Parasha, Sefer Shemot pp. 149-50. See Rav Holzer's footnote 291.

"Why do they sound the Shofar when they are sitting and again when they are standing? This is done in order to confound the accuser." (Tractate Rosh HaShanna 16a)

Adding to the Torah

1. When do we blow the shofar?

One of the mitzvot that is strongly associated with Rosh HaShanna is the sounding of the Shofar. According to the Torah, we are required to sound nine blasts – the combination of Tekiah, Teruah, Tekiah three times. We satisy this through thirty blasts.[15]

At what point in the service are we required to sound these thirty blasts? The Torah does not establish a specific point in the service during which the blasts should be sounded. However, the Sages did respond to this issue. The Sages established that the blasts should be sounded in the context of the blessings of the Musaf Amidah.[16] The prevalent Ashkenazic custom is to sound the blast during the repetition of the Amidah. The Sephardic custom is to sound the blasts during the silent Amidah and during the repetition.

However, the Sages also established a practice of sounding an additional series of thirty blasts following the Torah reading and before the Amidah. The Talmud asks, "Why do they sound the Shofar when they are sitting and again when they are standing?" In the time of the Talmud, during the blasts sounded before the Amidah it was customary for the congregation to remain sitting. During the blasts sounded during the Amidah, the congregation stood. So, the Talmud is asking, "Why do they we sound the required thirty blasts before the Amidah and again during the Amidah?" The Talmud responds that we sound the required thirty blasts twice in order to confound the Satan – the accuser. Rashi is concerned with the meaning of this response. He explains that the response is to be understood allegorically. Rashi explains the meaning of the Sages response is that we wish to demonstrate our love for the mitzvah of Shofar. We demonstrate this love by performing the mitzvah twice.[17] In other words, we are judged on Rosh HaShanna. We do not want to be accused of performing the mitzvah of Shofar in a mechanical, superficial manner. In order to respond to this possible accusation, we sound the required sounds twice. In doing so, we demonstrate our love for the commandment.

2. Adding Mitzvot

Tosefot asks an interesting question on the Talmud's response. The Torah commands us to not add or subtract from the commandments. The commandment against adding prohibits adding a new commandment or adding to an existing commandment. Tosefot ask, "How can the Sages add a practice to sound the required Shofar blasts both before the Amidah and during the Amidah? Why is this not a violation of the prohibition against adding to the commandments?" Tosefot respond that the prohibition against adding to the mitzvot is not violated by performing a mitzvah twice.[18] In other words, the Sages' requirement to sound the Shofar both before and during the Amidah might potentially involve a violation of the prohibition against adding to

---

[15] See next entry to understand this adjustment [ed.]

[16] Mesechet Rosh HaShanna 32a.

[17] R' Shlomo ben Yitzchak (Rashi), *Commentary on the Talmud,* Mesechet Rosh HaShanna 16b.

[18] Tosefot, Mesechet Rosh HaShanna 16b.

mitzvot. However, the prohibition is not violated because we are merely performing the mitzvah twice. Repeating the performance of a mitzvah is not prohibited.

Rashba asks an obvious question on Tosefot's comments. The premise of Tosefot's question is that an enactment of the Sages can be subject to the prohibition against adding to the mitzvot. Rashba objects to this premise. Rashba argues that the prohibition against adding to the commandments applies to individuals. As individuals, we do not have the authority to enhance mitzvot or modify them by adding or subtracting from them. However, this prohibition does not generally apply to the Sages. This can be easily proven. Outside of the land of Israel we observe Sukkot for eight days. The eighth day was established by the Sages. On this eighth day we are obligated to fulfill the mitzvah of living in the Succah. In other words, although the Torah obligation is to live in the Succah for seven days, the Sages require those outside of the land of Israel to live in the Succah for eight days. This requirement is not a violation of the prohibition against adding to the mitzvot. The reason this requirement does not violate the prohibition against adding to mitzvot is obviously because a requirement established by the Sages is not generally subject to this prohibition! So, why are Tosefot concerned with the Sages' requirement to sound two sets of Shofar blasts? [19]

3. Qualifying vs. adding

Rav Yitzchok Zev Soloveitchik suggests that in order to answer Rashba's question, it is necessary to more carefully analyze the two sets of Shofar blasts. Superficially, it would seem that a single set of thirty sounds is needed to satisfy our Torah level obligation and the Sages instituted a second set of thirty sounds in order to "confound the accuser." However, a more careful analysis indicates that this superficial interpretation of the two sets of Shofar blasts in not accurate.

As explained earlier, the Torah does not require that the Shofar be sounded at any particular moment in the services. However, the Sages require that the Shofar be sounded during the Amidah. How many sets of Shofar blasts are required to satisfy both of these obligations? A single set of thirty blasts sounded during the Amidah is adequate to satisfy both the Torah level obligation and the obligation established by the Sages. The Sages did not create a new set of Shofar blasts. They merely added a qualification to the Torah level obligation. So, by sounding thirty blasts during the Amidah, both the Torah level obligation and the obligation established by the Sages are satisfied. However, this is not our practice. First, we sound thirty blasts before the Amidah. These thirty blasts completely satisfy our Torah level obligation. But we then sound a second set of Shofar blasts which are required to satisfy the obligation established by the Sages to sound the Shofar during the Amidah. In other words, we could economize and satisfy both our Torah level and Rabbinic level obligation with a single set of thirty blasts sounded during the Amidah. But instead, we fulfill our Torah level obligation separately through the blasts sounded before the Amidah and then satisfy our Rabbinic level obligation with a second set of thirty blasts sounded during the Amidah. Why do we choose this more elaborate system of two sets of Shofar blasts over the more economic option of a single set of blasts during the Amidah? The Talmud is providing the answer to this question when it explains that we sound two sets of blasts in order to "confound the accuser." As interpreted by Rashi, the Talmud is explaining that in order to demonstrate our love for the mitzvah we do not try to economize. Instead, we intentionally fulfill our Torah level obligation separately from our Rabbinic level obligation.

---

[19] R' Shlomo ben Aderet (Rashba), *Commentary on the Talmud*, Mesechet Rosh HaShanna 16a.

4. The sages' authority

Now, we can restate the dispute between Tosafot and Rashba. Had the Sages established a requirement to sound a second set of Shofar blasts, there would be no dispute between Tosafot and Rashba. The Sages have the right to create new halachic entities. These new entities are not regarded as additions to the mitzvot. However, the Sages did not do this. Instead, they first required that the Shofar blasts be sounded during the Amidah. Second, they instructed us to fulfill this Rabbinic obligation separately from our Torah obligation. Tosefot argue that a single set of Shofar blasts would be adequate to fulfill both our Torah level and our Rabbinic level obligation, but we are required to sound an extra set of blasts. As a result, a unique situation evolves. The Sages did not create a new set of Shofar blasts but nonetheless, two set of blasts are required in order to fulfill our Torah level and Rabbinic level obligations. According to Tosefot, when the Sages create a new entity, this new entity is not subject to the prohibition against adding to mitzvot. But in our case, no new entity is created. An extra set of blasts is required. Tosefot argue that this extra set of blasts is subject to the prohibition against adding to the mitzvot. However, Tosefot explain that the prohibition is not violated because we are merely performing the mitzvah multiple times. Performing a mitzvah multiple times does not constitute adding to mitzvot.

Rashba argues that this extra set of Shofar blasts does not involve a potential violation of the prohibition against adding to mitzvot. The prohibition against adding to the mitzvot only applies to individuals. Any activity required in response to either a Torah level or a Rabbinic level obligation is not subject to the prohibition against adding to mitzvot. Therefore, since each set of Shofar blasts fulfills a specific obligation – either Torah level or Rabbinic level – the prohibition against adding to mitzvot does not apply.[20]

5. Innovation vs. permanence

It seems that according to Rashba, the primary objective of the prohibition against adding to or subtracting from mitzvot is to discourage innovations that in fact detract from the commandment. Therefore, the prohibition relates primarily to individuals. As individuals, we are not authorized to alter the commandments. However, the Sages are authorized to establish new laws and practices. They also have the wisdom to use this authority properly. Therefore, the laws and practices that they establish are not subject to the prohibition against adding to the mitzvot.

However, according to Tosefot, the objective of the prohibitions against adding to or subtracting from the mitzvot is not to discourage inappropriate innovations. These prohibitions even apply to the Sages. Therefore, it seems that according to Tosefot, these prohibitions are designed to permanently preserve the integrity of the Torah law. Even the Sages are subject to the prohibition against adding to a mitzvah in such a manner as to alter the Torah requirement. Instead, even the Sages are required to work within specific boundaries.

In summary, this dispute between Tosefot and Rashba reflects the unique structure of the Shofar blasts – specifically the interrelation between the set sounded before the Amidah and those sounded during the Amidah. The dispute also reflects two perspectives on the prohibition against adding to mitzvot.

---

[20] *Kuntres Moadim MeTorat Brisk*, p 12.

"It is a positive commandment of the Torah to hear the sounding of the Shofar on Rosh HaShanna as it states, "A day of Shofar blast it should be to you." (Maimonides, Mishe Torah, Laws of Shofar 1:1)

The sound of the Teruah

1. Sounding out the blasts

One of the mitzvot that is strongly associated with Rosh HaShanna is the sounding of the Shofar. According to the Torah, we are required to sound nine blasts – the combination of Tekiah, Teruah, Tekiah three times. This is represented by the following table:

Table 1. Requirement described by the Torah

Tekiah	Teruah	Tekiah
Tekiah	Teruah	Tekiah
Tekiah	Teruah	Tekiah

However, in order to fulfill this obligation, we are required to sound thirty blasts. How, does the Torah obligation to sound nine blasts translate into an obligation to sound thirty blasts?

There are two factors at play in this conversion of a requirement to sound nine blasts into the requirement to sound thirty. The Torah requires that we sound the series of Tekiah, Teruah, Tekiah three times. Part of this obligation is easily understood. The Tekiah is an uninterrupted blast. There is little or no room for uncertainty regarding its character. However, the Teruah is a sound characterized by interrupted notes. This is a much more complicated sound. Complication leaves room for doubts. What is the exact description of the "interrupted" blast? The Sages identified three possibilities. First, the Teruah may be a series of minimal sounds – the sound we refer to as Teruah. Second, the true Teruah may be a more substantial sound that is interrupted – the sound we refer to as Shevarim. Finally, the true Teruah may be a combination of these first two possibilities – the sound we refer to as Shevarim/Teruah. In short, the Torah requires that we sound the combination of a Teruah preceded and followed by a Tekiah three times – a total of nine blasts. However, this nature of the central Teruah is unknown. The three central blasts that we sound – Teruah, Shevarim and Shevarim/Teruah – are actually three possible identities of the true Teruah required by the Torah.[21] The following table represents the result of the doubt regarding the exact nature of the central Teruah sound:

Table 2. Minimum series of sounds required to satisfy the Torah obligation

Tekiah	Shevarim/Teruah	Tekiah
Tekiah	Shevarim/Teruah	Tekiah
Tekiah	Shevarim/Teruah	Tekiah
Tekiah	Shevarim	Tekiah
Tekiah	Shevarim	Tekiah

---

[21] Mesechet Rosh HaShanna 33b – 34a.

Tekiah	Shevarim	Tekiah
Tekiah	Teruah	Tekiah
Tekiah	Teruah	Tekiah
Tekiah	Teruah	Tekiah

How many sounds are there in the above table? One might reasonably conclude that the above table includes 27 sounds. However by convention, the Shevarim/Teruah sound is counted as two sounds. So, traditionally this table is described as including 30 sounds. This calculation is represented in the following table:

Table 3. Calculation of total number of sounds required to satisfy Torah obligation

Series	Number of sound in series
Tekiah, Shevarim/Teruah, Tekiah	4
Tekiah, Shevarim/Teruah, Tekiah	4
Tekiah, Shevarim/Teruah, Tekiah	4
Tekiah, Shevarim, Tekiah	3
Tekiah, Shevarim, Tekiah	3
Tekiah, Shevarim, Tekiah	3
Tekiah, Teruah, Tekiah	3
Tekiah, Teruah, Tekiah	3
Tekiah, Teruah, Tekiah	3
Total sounds	30

The dispute over the true nature of the Teruah is somewhat curious. It is clear that the Sages are certain that the character of the Teruah contrasts with the character of the Tekiah. Therefore, because the Tekiah is an uninterrupted blast, the Teruah must be an interrupted sound. However, how can we account for the development of these three alternative interpretations of the specific nature of the Teruah?

2. Crying interruption

Aruch HaShulchan offers an interesting explanation. He bases his explanation on a comment of the Sages. In the passage above from Mishne Torah, Maimonides quotes the pasuk in the Torah that is the source for the obligation to sound the Shofar on Rosh HaShanna. The literal translation of the pasuk is "a day of Teruah it should be for you." Unkelus translates the word Teruah in the passage as crying – "a day of crying it should be for you." The Talmud explains that the Sages' understand Unkelus's translation as providing a description of the Teruah. The Teruah imitates the sound of crying. However, crying can take three forms. Sometimes, one cries in long sobs. The Shevarim sound is an imitation of this form of crying. On other occasions, one cries in short shrieks. This form of crying is imitated by the sound that we refer to as Teruah. And sometimes crying combines these two forms of crying. This last possibility is imitated by the Shevarim/Teruah. In other words, the Sages know that the Teruah mentioned by the Torah is an imitation of crying.[22] However, they differ in precisely which of the various forms of crying the Teruah is intended to imitate.

3. The theme of crying

Aruch HaShulchan suggests that the Talmud's comparison of Teruah to crying is not merely intended to provide a description of the character of the sound. Instead, the Talmud is telling us that the Teruah is intended to express the activity of crying. In sounding the Teruah, we are engaging in an act of crying. We are expressing anguish. The dispute in the Talmud is over the nature of the anguish that we are required to express through the Teruah. According to Aruch HaShulchan's interpretation the Shevarim sound expresses groans of pain and the conventional Teruah sound expresses cries of lamentation.[23] Apparently, he maintains that pain and lamentation are each component themes of Rosh HaShanna. The dispute between the Sages is over which of these themes is to be reflected in the Shofar sound or if both themes are to be reflected.

Although this approach to explaining the debate of the true nature of the Teruah is interesting, it presents two problems. First, it is difficult to identify the actual alternative themes in Rosh HaShanna to which the various interpretations of the Teruah refer. In other words, we can easily understand that on Rosh HaShanna we should lament our condition and even anticipate with anxiety the coming judgment we will receive. But it is difficult to identify how this experience can be alternatively interpreted as an encounter with pain, an expression of lamentation, or both.

The second difficulty stems from a comment of Rav Hai mentioned by Aruch HaShulchan. Rav Hai maintains that all three of the interpretations of Teruah are valid and proper. There is no actual dispute regarding the character of the Teruah sound. Instead, all three interpretations essentially fulfill the requirement of sounding the Teruah sound. On a Torah level, any one of these three interpretations is acceptable.

However, in different communities different interpretations developed. The Sages wished to establish uniformity in the interpretation of Teruah. The Sages did not wish to choose one of these interpretations for universal implementation and suppress the alternatives. Instead, in order to establish a uniform, universal practice, they required that the Teruah should be sounded according to all of the various valid interpretations.[24]

Rav Hai's position is difficult to reconcile with Aruch HaShulchan's explanation of the three alternative interpretations of the Teruah. It is somewhat unlikely that each of these interpretations is a reference to an alternative theme in Rosh HaShanna – as Aruch HaShulchan suggests – and to maintain that each of these interpretations is valid according to the Torah! Certainly, the Torah is not unconcerned with the theme or themes of Rosh HaShanna that we are to express through the Shofar and leaves it to us to decide!

4. Broken as a description

These problems suggest an alternative interpretation of the discussion in the Talmud. As noted above, the Talmud interprets the term Teruah to mean "cry." Rabbaynu Yom Tov ben

---

[22] Mesechet Rosh HaShanna 33b.
[23] Rav Aharon HaLeyve Epstein, *Aruch HaShulchan*, Orech Chayim 590:2-3.
[24] Rav Aharon HaLeyve Epstein, *Aruch HaShulchan*, Orech Chayim 590:4.

Avraham Isbili – Ritva – suggests that the Talmud is not suggesting that the Teruah is intended to express crying. Instead, the Talmud is only providing a description of the Teruah sound. The intention of this description is to communicate that the Teruah is a broken sound. The discussion in the Talmud is over the specific nature of this broken sound.[25]

Ritva's approach suggests that the discussion in the Talmud should be interpreted as an analysis of the character of a "broken" Shofar blast. This broken character can be created by sounding a series of minimal notes that emerge as a Shofar blast through being sounded in a series. This is the conventional Teruah. Alternatively, the "broken" character can emerge through breaking the Tekiah into smaller components – at least three components. This interpretation is expressed in our Shevarim. In other words, the character of a "broken" blast can emerge from the inherent minimal nature of the component notes – the conventional Teruah. Alternatively, the broken character can emerge from the relative length of the component notes as compared to the Tekiah – our Shevarim. Finally, it is possible that the true Teruah must include both of these alternative interpretations – our Shevarim/Teruah.

This explanation of the Talmud allows for the discussion to be interpreted as a dispute between the Sages. It is also consistent with the position of Rav Hai. In other words, it is possible that the Sages are in agreement that the Teruah of the Torah is a broken sound but they dispute the exact character of this broken sound. It is also possible – as Rav Hai maintains – that the Torah merely requires the sounding of a broken sound but does not specify the precise manner in which we should create this sound. All of our interpretations of Teruah are valid and fulfill the Torah requirement.

"There are those who are accustomed to eat a sweet apple with honey. And they say, "It should be granted to us a sweet year". (Shulcah Aruch, Orech Chayim 583:1)

The Shulchan Aruch lists many foods eaten at the Rosh HaShanna meal. Each food alludes to a specific blessing. The eating is accompanied with a short prayer requesting from Hashem the blessing associated with the food. The eating of the apple is mentioned by Rav Moshe Isserles. In different communities customs vary as to which foods are consumed. However, the apple seems to have been widely incorporated into the Rosh HaShanna meal.

It is somewhat difficult to understand this custom. The Torah vigorously rejects all forms of superstition. It is very surprising that halacha should encourage a practice which seems to be based upon omen.

However, if carefully considered we can appreciate the meaning of this custom. It is not in any way an expression of superstition of primitive beliefs. For most of us the Rosh HaShanna experience is strongest while we are in the synagogue. There we pray for the fulfillment of our wishes in the coming year. We are actually aware of the process of heavenly judgment. Once we leave the synagogue we begin to become distracted. The Yom Tov meal and the opportunity to spend time with family and friends begin to compete for our attention. As the day passes we may forget the significance of the occasion.

---

[25] R' Yom Tov ben Avraham Isbili (Ritva), *Comm. on the Talmud*, Mes. Rosh HaShanna 34b.

Our Sages had a deep understanding of human behavior. They recognized this tendency towards distraction. Yet, the Rosh HaShanna experience should not be limited to the time spent in the synagogue. The atmosphere of judgment should extend throughout the day. In order to accomplish this end the Sages encouraged the custom of eating special foods during the Yom Tov meal. Through this process an element of prayer is incorporated into the experience. Rather than the meal becoming a distraction, it reinforces the special atmosphere of the occasion.

It is very praiseworthy for a repentant person to confess in public, make known his iniquities to them, and reveal to others the sins [he committed in his relationships] between himself and his friend. He should say to them, "In truth, I have sinned against so-and-so. I did to him such-and-such. Today, I am repentant and regretful." Anyone who is haughty and does not make known [his sins] but conceals his iniquities, his repentance is not complete as it says, *"One who conceals his sins will not succeed"* (Mishle 28:13). When does this apply? Concerning sins between a person and one's friend. But sins between one and the Omnipresent one need not publicize oneself, and it is brazen for one to reveal them. Rather, one should repent before the L-rd, Blessed be He, and confess them before the public in general terms. It is good for one to not reveal one's sin.... (Rambam, Hilchot Teshuva 2:5)

Human Rights

1. Public confession

Rosh Hashanah initiates the Ten Days of Repentance. These days are devoted to contemplating our lives, repenting from our sins, and returning to Hashem. Rambam – Maimonides – explains that repentance involves an internal and an external component. The internal component is the assessment of one's past sinful behavior, regret for the behavior, and the commitment to not return to it. The external component is viduy – verbal confession of the sin. This verbal confession includes specification of the sin and expression of the components of the internal process. The person states the sin and declares that he or she regrets the behavior and will not return to it.

In the above text, Rambam explains that sins should be confessed in public. This does not mean one is required to assemble the entire community. A group of people is adequate. This is an acknowledgment of one's shortcomings. One who does not confess publicly attempts to conceal these shortcomings. Repentance is incomplete without this public declaration.

Rambam adds a qualification. Only sins committed against another individual are confessed publicly. If a person sins against Hashem, one does not specify the sin in a public declaration. Instead, the person confesses one's specific sin privately, before Hashem. Then, one makes a general public declaration that one has sinned against Hashem without specifying the sin.

2. Not diminishing Hashem's honor

Why does one not specify in a public confession the sin committed against Hashem? Rambam explains that this is brazen. Rambam's position is based upon the Talmud's discussion of the issue. Commenting on this discussion, Rashi explains, "One does not reveal one's sin [against Hashem]. This is respect for Hashem. For any sin that a person commits in public is a diminution of the honor of [the One Who Rules the] Heavens."[26] In other words, making one's sin public through explicitly declaring it in public confession is an afront to Hashem's glory.[27] This ruling is difficult to understand. When one sins against another individual, one is also disobeying the Torah and Hashem. Why is it appropriate to confess a sin committed against another person? Is this not an affront to Hashem's honor?

Let's consider a simple example. If one slanders another, against whom has one sinned? One has sinned against the person slandered. One has also sinned against Hashem, Who commands us to not slander others. This is true for every sin one commits against another. Why is the public confession of this sin not considered an affront to Hashem's honor? Let us consider another issue that will provide an important insight.

And all positive mitzvot that are between a person and The Sacred One, Blessed Be He, whether [it is] a commandment that is obligatory or a mitzvah that is not obligatory, one recites a blessing before its performance. (Rambam, Mishne Torah, Hilchot Berachot 11:2.

3. Blessings for commandments

The Sages established blessings that are recited before the performance of a mitzvah. One recites a blessing before sounding the shofar. A blessing is recited before affixing a mezuzah on the doorpost. Rambam explains that, in general, we recite a blessing before performing a mitzvah between us and Hashem. Rambam's comment implies that one does not recite a blessing before a mitzvah between one individual and another. For example, we are required to return a lost object to its owner. Rambam implies that when one performs this commandment, one does not recite a blessing and that one does not recite a blessing before giving tzedakah – charity. Rav Yosef Karo confirms that Rambam intends this implication.[28]

The blessings recited before commandments share a uniform format. We state, "Blessed are You Hashem, our L-rd, King of the universe, Who sanctified us with His commandments and commanded us …." The blessing concludes with a description of the specific commandment one will immediately perform. This formula is suitable for any mitzvah. It is suitable for commandments between an individual and Hashem and commandments between one individual and another. Why is a blessing not recited before commandments between one individual and another?

4. The rights of the individual

Answering this question requires that we consider a fundamental issue concerning the commandments that regulate our interactions with one another. There are two ways one can understand these commandments. The first is that these commandments, like those between the individual and Hashem, are directives concerning personal behavior. Hashem commands us to not eat non-kosher foods, to observe Shabbat through abstaining from performing melachah – creative activity. He directs us to serve Him through prayer. Similarly, he commands us to love others, to respect and not steal their property, to not harm another through speech or action. All

---

[26] Mesechet Yoma 86b.

[27] Rashi is explaining the position in the Talmud that sins against Hashem that were committed publicly should be confessed publicly. Those committed in private are not to be confessed publicly. See Kesef Mishne on Rambam. He explains that Rambam agrees with this position. Rambam's ruling that sins against Hashem are not specified in public confession applies only to sins committed in private. Those committed in public should be specifically confessed in public.

[28] Rav Yosef Karo, Kesef Mishne, Hilchot Berachot 11:2.

these commandments regulate one's behaviors. The second possibility is that the commandments between one individual and another do more than regulate behavior. These commandments create rights and privileges.

An example will clarify this distinction. A person steals from another. This person violates the Torah commandment to not steal. Wherein lies the sin? One possibility is that the person sinned by engaging in prohibited behavior. The sin is akin to eating non-kosher food. Both are prohibited behaviors. The second possibility is that the commandment to not steal creates property rights. When one steals, one violates the property rights granted by the Torah. In short, when one steals, did one sin through acting unacceptably or shamefully, or is the sin the violation of another's rights?

5. Solving the blessing problem

What difference does it make whether one's sin is acting poorly or violating another's rights? One difference is whether one should make blessings over commandments that regulate our interpersonal interactions. If these commandments are regulating behaviors – as do other mitzvot, then they should require a blessing. However, if these commandments endow us with rights, then performing one of these commandments is responding to the rights of the individual.

Consider an example. We are required to pay workers promptly. When one makes payment to a worker, one is submitting to and respecting the right of the worker to prompt payment. A blessing is not appropriate. Why? The payment is not directly a response to the commandment. The commandment grants the worker the right to prompt payment. When one makes this payment, one is responding to and respecting this right. This does not mean that one is not fulfilling a commandment when making payment. One is performing a mitzvah. However, it is fulfilled through responding to the rights the commandment grants the worker. The commandment is fulfilled indirectly. Directly, the payment is a response to the rights of the worker.

6. Solving the confession problem

This explains Rambam's ruling that we do not recite a blessing before a commandment between one individual and another. This insight also explains why we publicly and specifically confess sins committed against another but not those sins committed against Hashem.

Reviewing the question will reveal the answer. When we act improperly to another, have we not violated a commandment of the Torah? If specific sins against Hashem are not publicly confessed, why should a sin that is also against another individual be specifically, publicly confessed?

When one acts improperly toward another one has sinned only indirectly against Hashem. The Torah's mitzvot create rights and privileges. Directly, the sin was the violation of these rights and privileges. Rambam's ruling emphasizes this issue. When one sins against another, one is required to confess specifically and publicly. The confession is an explicit acknowledgment that another's rights and privileges were violated. One declares, "I have sinned against so-and-so. I did such-and-such to him."

7. Individual sanctity

This is an important message about the sanctity of the individual. If the commandments regulating our behavior toward one another were akin to other commandments, they would not communicate to us a message about the sanctity of the individual. If stealing were prohibited because it is inappropriate and demeaning behavior, then the commandment says nothing about the importance and significance of the individual.

As explained above, the commandments governing interpersonal interactions grant individual rights and privileges. This communicates an important message. Every person has sanctity. Every person is significant. This sanctity and individual significance are reflected in one's Divinely granted rights.

Even though repentance and petition are always appropriate, during the ten days between Rosh HaShanah and Yom HaKipurim it is even more appropriate and it is accepted immediately, as it is stated: Seek Hashem when He is to be found…. Yom HaKipurim is the time for repentance for the individual and for the congregation. It is the time of forbearance and forgiveness for Israel. Therefore, everyone is required to repent and to confess on Yom HaKipurim … (Maimonides, Laws of Repentance 2:6-7)

Just as the merits and iniquities of a person are weighted at the time of his death, so each and every year each and every person's sins are weighed against his merits on the festival of Rosh HaShanah. One who is found to be righteous is sealed for life and one who is found to be wicked is sealed for death. Those of an intermediate status are placed in suspension until Yom HaKipurim. If he repents, he is sealed for life and if not, he is sealed for death. (Maimonides Laws of Repentance 3:3)

Seek Hashem When He is to be Found

1. **Maimonides' understanding of the significance of the ten days between Rosh HaShanah and Yom Kippur**

Maimonides' Mishne Torah is one of the earliest codifications of Torah law. The work covers the breadth of halachah, providing the basic laws relevant to each of the Torah's 613 mitzvot. However, the work is not only notable for its thoroughness. It is also very carefully organized. In his organizational theme, Maimonides often opts for an order that expresses the conceptual relationship between components over an order that would facilitate ease of use as a reference work. For example, each of the festivals is discussed. Purim and Chanukah are grouped together with Purim placed first and Chanukah following. This is the opposite of the order in which these celebrations occur on the calendar. Rav Yosef Dov Soloveitchik Zt'l explains that Maimonides groups these two celebrations together because both were established by the Sages. He places Purim before Chanukah because Purim was first established and served as the precedent for the creation of Chanukah.

Both of the excerpts above are from Maimonides' Laws of Repentance. The first excerpt explains that the period beginning with Rosh HaShanah and continuing through Yom Kippur is designated by the Torah as a time for repentance. Hashem is "near" and easily reached during these days. Maimonides does not – at this point – provide any indication why these days have been selected and singled-out for this designation. However, in the second excerpt – from the next chapter, Maimonides returns to his discussion of these special days and explains that we each stand in judgment before Hashem during this period. Maimonides' order is counter-intuitive. One would have expected him to first explain that we are each evaluated and judged during the ten days between Rosh HaShanah and Yom Kippur and then to explain that because we are each being judged, it behooves us to repent during this period. What is Maimonides' message in choosing his enigmatic order over the more straight-forward presentation?

Maimonides does not provide a response to this question. However, one conclusion can be drawn. The selection of these days for designation as a time devoted to repentance is not a function merely of their status as a time of judgment. In other words, these days are selected as a time for repentance for some reason other than their role as the period of judgment. What is this reason?

The intent of the Divine law is to lead people towards achieving the true success which is spiritual success and eternity. It makes known to them the paths they should tread upon to achieve it. It makes known to them the true good so that they will endeavor to achieve it and it makes known to them the true evil so that they will guard themselves from it. It accustoms them to abandon the imaginary forms of success so that they should not long for them and should not feel sorrow over their abandonment. It also sets forth the ways of justice so that society will be organized in an appropriate and effective manner and so that poor social organization will not detract them from achieving the true success and will not divert them from striving to achieve this success and the ultimate goal of humanity which is the objective of the Divine law. In this manner the Divine law is superior to the secular law. (Rabbaynu Yosef Albo, Sefer HaIkkarim, 1:7)

2. The difference between secular law and the Torah

In his Sefer HaIkkarim, Rabbaynu Yosef Albo discusses at length the differences between the Torah and a secular system of law. A system of secular law is designed primarily to ensure peace and cooperation among the members of the society it governs. The laws of the Torah are also designed to fulfill this objective. The Torah includes an extensive system of law that regulates commerce and interpersonal relationships and conduct. However, the Torah system has a second objective not included in a secular system of law. The Torah is designed to instill within those it governs basic, truths, virtues, and values.

This second objective is expressed in the Torah in two manners. First, the Torah reveals these truths, virtues, and values. For example, it teaches us that there is one G-d and that Hashem is a unity. It teaches us the value of charity and the virtue of humility. Second, "it makes known to them the paths they should tread upon to achieve" or secure commitment to these truths, virtues, and values. In other words, the Torah does not merely reveal and teach these truths, virtues, and values. It instills them within its followers. This second element is a significant addition to the first. Every parent and teacher appreciates the importance of this second element and the difficulty in devising a strategy for its accomplishment. It is far easier to merely communicate a truth than to inspire a student or child to embrace that truth. Albo is observing that the Torah includes not only a description of fundamental truths, virtues, and values. In includes also a strategy for instilling them within the hearts of its followers. Many of the mitzvot of the Torah are devoted to this process of cultivation and nurturing. These mitzvot create a path designed to lead to our embrace of the Torah's truths. However, in order to understand the Torah's strategy for instilling these truths, it is necessary to understand the Torah's unique perspective on the human cognitive process.

And the nation saw that Moshe was delayed in descending from the mountain. And the nations gathered around Aharon and said to him: Make for us a god that will go before us. Because this man Moshe that brought us up from the Land of Egypt – we do not know what has become of him. (Shemot 32:1)

3. The strange account of the incident of the Egel

One of the strangest portions of the Torah is its description of the sin of the Egel – the Golden Calf. The nation came to Sinai and heard the commandments of the Decalogue. Moshe left the people and ascended the mountain to receive the Tablets and the Torah. He remained on the mountain for forty days and nights. The people became alarmed that Moshe had not returned and concluded that he had not survived his sojourn on the mountain. They appealed to Aharon to make for them an idol to replace Moshe. Ultimately, their request was fulfilled; the idol was fashioned, and the people adopted its worship. Two aspects of the narrative are remarkable. First, this nation, a short time before, had heard the voice of Hashem declare that they should have no other gods. How is it possible that it abandoned this commandment and adopted the worship of a primitive idol? Second, why does the Torah not offer any explanation for the nation's rapid and startling demise? Perhaps, this second question is more disquieting than the first. By not offering any explanation for the people's sudden abandonment of the very commandment that had just been delivered to them through a phenomenal act of revelation, the Torah implies that this behavior requires no explanation or that it is self-explanatory! Yet to us, the behavior of the people seems bizarre and beyond any explanation.

And Moshe went forth with the nation from the camp towards G-d. And they stood at the foot of the mountain. (Devarim 19:17)

The passage teaches that the Holy One Blessed be He uprooted the mountain from its place and He held it over them like a huge vessel. He said to them: if you accept the Torah, good. If not, there will be your burial place. (Tractate Shabbat 88a)

4. Acceptance of the Torah was the culmination of the nation's mission

The above passage describes the nation approaching Mount Sinai. The passage states that the nation stood at the foot of the mountain. However, a more literal rendering of the passage is that the nation stood at the underside of the mountain. Based upon this more literal interpretation, the Talmud explains that Hashem uprooted the mountain, suspended it above the nation, and compelled them to accept the Torah. This interpretation is difficult to understand because it contradicts an important detail of the narrative in the Torah. The Torah tells us that the nation freely accepted upon themselves the Torah with the statement: *All that Hashem says we will do and observe.*[29]

The apparent message of the Talmud is two-fold. One element of the message is that the nation had experienced Hashem's providence because of its role in a Divine plan. Hashem had selected the nation to receive His Torah. He had redeemed them from Egypt and brought them to Sinai for this purpose. The nation's very existence was conceived and preserved in anticipation of this moment. If the nation will accept the Torah, then its existence will have meaning. However, if the nation will decline to accept the Torah, then its existence will no longer have meaning or significance.[30]

5. The Torah's perspective on the limits of human cognition

---

[29] Shemot 24:7

[30] This message emerges whether the Talmud's comments are interpreted literally or figuratively

There is a second element in the Talmud's message. The nation was compelled to accept the Torah. This does not mean that the people were deprived of their freewill. However, they had experienced redemption from Egypt, the parting of the Reed Sea, and traveled through the wilderness. Now, they stood in the presence of Hashem before Sinai. The combined impact and influence of this series of astounding events was so powerful, their acceptance of the Torah was inevitable. In other words, the evidence of Hashem's omnipotence and presence was overwhelming and the proper path was completely clear.

However, it was the overwhelming impression created by this unique series of experiences that compelled the nation to accept the idea of a single omnipotent and ever-present Creator. Although this generation had been reared in a pagan culture and was steeped in idolatrous practices, the people were able to reject their pagan beliefs and practices because of the combined overwhelming impact of all they had recently experienced. These experiences opened their minds and at the moment they stood before Sinai, the people were able to perceive and embrace a truth that was the antithesis of their former beliefs.

However, this intellectual and emotional breakthrough did not represent a thorough reworking of the people's personalities and behaviors. Instead, it was a momentary parting of the clouds of ignorance and primitivism that allowed a profound truth to shine through. But these clouds had not yet been banished from the sky. They yet threatened to return and to obscure the truth. With Moshe's ascent to the mountain and his failure to return, these clouds returned. No longer, could the people see the truth that was clear forty days earlier. In their panic and anxiety, old learned behaviors and attitudes reasserted themselves. The nation responded according to patterns that were familiar and reassuring. They sought an idol to replace the unreliable Moshe.

The narrative of the Egel teaches us a fundamental lesson. Often our ability to perceive and embrace the truth is a consequence of the context in which we find ourselves. We often perceive a truth only because at the moment it is revealed we are open to it. At another time, in a different situation, or in a different mood, we might completely misinterpret the very same evidence. The Torah does not explain the nation's re-descent into idolatry because no explanation is required. It is their profound – but transient – grasp of truth that requires an explanation. It is explained by the experiences that preceded it. However, the obscuring of this truth requires no explanation other than an understanding of the limits of human cognition.

You grant knowledge to humanity. Grant us from you knowledge, insight, and understanding.
(Weekday Amidah)

6. Praying for knowledge

Every weekday in the Amidah prayer, we petition Hashem to provide us with knowledge. On the surface, this is a very strange petition. Most of the other petitions in the Amidah relate to needs that we clearly cannot satisfy without the help of Hashem. We ask Hashem to heal us, to redeem us, to forgive our failings. These are not ends we can secure without Him. However, the acquisition of knowledge, insight, and understanding seem to be within the human purview. If we wish to acquire knowledge, then let us study. If it is insight or understanding we seek, then we must reflect, consider, and analyze. In what manner do we expect Hashem to assist us in this quest? For what are we petitioning?

This petition is another expression of the Torah's perspective on the limits of the human cognitive process. We believe that we are empowered with the ability to secure knowledge and understanding. We need merely to apply our powerful intellects and the secrets of the Torah, life, or nature will reveal themselves to our probing scrutiny. The Torah's perspective is that our intellectual prowess is only one aspect of the cognitive process. Our ability to discover and grasp the truth – regardless of our intelligence – is determined by the context in which we find ourselves. If we are in the proper situation, we have been exposed to the appropriate hints, have encountered the facts in the proper sequence, are in the requisite frame of mind, and we are free of any blinding bias, then we may discover the truth. However, without all of these factors properly aligned, the truth may just as easily elude us. Our petition to Hashem represents an acknowledgment of the limits of human cognitive ability and recognition of our dependence on Him for even our grasp of basic reality.

Do not think, my son, to criticize my words and say: Why did Hashem the Blessed One command us to perform all of these (commandments) that are commemorative of that miracle? Would not the matter be implanted upon our consciousness and not forgotten by our descendants with a single commemorative (commandment)? Know that it is not from wisdom that you criticize me on this matter. Immature thinking influences you to speak thus…. (Sefer HaChinuch, Mitzvah 16)

7. Mitzvot as a cognitive aid

Sefer HaChinuch was composed by a Sage as an educational text for his son. In the above excerpt, the author confronts a question that he anticipates his son will pose. According to Sefer HaChinuch, multiple mitzvot share the same objective. These commandments are designed to remind us of our redemption from Egypt. One can easily identify some of the commandments that share this objective. We are required to read a paragraph of the Torah twice every day that reminds us of our redemption. We mention our redemption in the Kiddush for Shabbat and festivals. We celebrate Pesach with its many mitzvot devoted to this same theme. Sefer HaChinuch anticipates that its reader will wonder why so many commandments are required to communicate a single idea.

Sefer HaChinuch responds that this question reflects a naive perspective on human nature. As explained by Albo, the Torah's objective is not to merely communicate truths. Its objective is to encourage our embrace and assimilation of these truths. These multiple mitzvot are not required to communicate the message that we were redeemed. However, they are essential to the process of assimilation of this idea into our worldview and perspective.

Sefer HaChinuch continues and explains that we prefer to believe that our actions are a product of our thoughts – that we act in response to our thoughts. However, the opposite is also true. Our thoughts are formed by our actions. Our actions influence our thoughts and perceptions. If we develop a habit of giving charity – tzedakah – in a proper manner, then we acquire compassion for the less fortunate. If we pray daily, then we become more aware of Hashem's presence. If we constantly remind ourselves of our redemption, then this redemption becomes more than an episode in the history of our ancestors. It becomes part of our personal reality and worldview.

Seek Hashem when He is to be found. Call unto Him when He is close. Let the wicked person abandon his path and every person the iniquity of his thoughts. And let him return to Hashem and He will have mercy upon him and to our G-d for He is abundant in his forgiveness.
(Yishayahu 55:6-7)

8. The ten days as an expression of Hashem's compassion

The prophet urges that we seek Hashem when He is to be found. Of course, Hashem is omniscient. His knowledge of our thoughts and actions is constant. Nonetheless, our Sages understand this passage as a reference to the ten days from Rosh HaShanah through Yom Kippur. Maimonides quotes this passage as supporting his assertion that these days have special designation as a time for repentance. In what sense is Hashem closer to us during these days?

Repentance is a fundamental process in human development. We error, sin, stray, but we have the capacity to repent and to restore our relationship with Hashem. However, the desire to return to Hashem is an expression of an awareness of His presence. Repentance is an imperative that emerges from a clear cognition of Hashem's closeness. This cognition should be as constant as Hashem's relationship with us. This relationship never falters neither should our awareness of Hashem. However, the Torah recognizes that this is not the nature of human cognition. Human cognition is fickle and fragile. Our awareness of Hashem must be complete, powerful, and intense if it is to compel us to repent. Potent, repetitive messages are required to part the clouds of our mundane perspective and allow the truth of Hashem's presence to penetrate. These ten days provide those messages. The blast of the shofar, the moving liturgy, the solemnity of the Yom Kippur fast are a strong wind that – at least for a time – clear one's consciousness of clouds and allow the truth to penetrate in its full dazzling brilliance. And although Hashem has not changed, to us, He indeed does seem closer and more accessible.

Perhaps this is Maimonides' message. The special status of these days as a time for repentance is not a consequence merely of judgment taking place. This status is an expression of Hashem's compassion and kindness. For these ten days, He creates the special context that we need in order to recognize, feel, and embrace His presence. It is through this cognitive breakthrough that we experience the urge to draw closer to Him and to repent.

"One who does not observe the restriction concerning bread baked by a non-Jew should observe the restriction during the *Asseret Yemai Teshuva*." (Shulchan Aruch, Orech Chayim 603:1)

Respect

1. Social interaction

The ten days beginning with Rosh HaShanna and ending with Yom Kippur are the *Asseret Yemai Teshuva* – the Ten Days of Repentance. This a period devoted to introspection and repentance. Shulchan Aruch comments that during this period it is appropriate to observe the restriction against bread baked by a non-Jew. In order to understand this comment, some background is required.

Our Sages established a prohibition against eating food cooked by a non-Jew. This law is often misunderstood. The law is not a precaution against eating non-Kosher food. Supervising the preparation of the food does not alleviate the prohibition. In other words, food cooked by a non-Jew is prohibited even if the entire process is supervised by a trustworthy Jew.

What is the reason for this restriction? Maimonides provides the reason for this enactment in his Mishne Torah. He explains that the prohibition is designed to prevent intermarriage! The Sages were very sensitive to the forces encouraging assimilation and eventual intermarriage. They concluded that these forces can only be overcome by creating barriers against intimate social relations. Familiarity is fostered through sharing a meal. Conversely, the inability to share a meal is a barrier to social intercourse. As a result of these considerations, the Sages prohibited the consumption of foods cooked by a non-Jew.[31]

It should be noted that this prohibition is not merely directed against the food prepared by an idolater. The restriction extends to the food cooked by any non-Jew. This is consistent with Maimonides' basic reasoning. The decree does not involve any judgement regarding the morality or integrity of the non-Jew. Instead, it is designed to discourage assimilation and preserve Torah values. Accordingly, it extends to food prepared by any non-Jew.

It must be noted that this prohibition does not extend to all cooked foods. The restriction only includes foods that "are worthy to be served on the table of a king." In more modern terms, only foods that would be served at a banquet are prohibited. For example, pop-corn prepared by a non-Jew is permitted. A steak is prohibited.

2. Chumrot in *halacha*

There is a dispute among the Sages regarding bread baked by a non-Jew. According to some authorities, this bread is prohibited. Other authorities argue. They maintain that the prohibition only extends to bread that is produced in the home of a non-Jew. Commercially produced bread, baked by a non-Jew is permitted. The reasoning underlying this position is obvious. The entire enactment is designed to discourage intermarriage. The restriction is a barrier against intimate social gatherings. Consumption of commercially baked bread does not result in sharing a meal with the baker! Therefore, there is no reason to apply the restriction to this product.[32]

We are now prepared to understand the above law. Shulchan Aruch begins by acknowledging that there is a basis in *halacha* for permitting bread baked commercially by a non-Jew. However, he explains that this leniency should not be practiced during the *Asseret Yemai Teshuva*. During this period, the more strict interpretation of the law should be observed. Even commercially baked bread should not be consumed.

The basic message of Shulchan Aruch is that during the *Asseret Yemai Teshuva* we should be more scrupulous in our observance of *halacha*. We should adopt practices that we do not observe during the remainder of the year.

It is very important to note the specific practice that Shulchan Aruch cites as an example. Shulchan Aruch provides the example of refraining from eating bread commercially baked by a non-Jew. What are the implications of this example? Clearly, Shulchan Aruch is not suggesting that we adopt stringencies that lack a firm basis in *halacha*. Instead, Shulchan Aruch cites an instance in which there are two equally reasonable positions. During most of the year, it is acceptable for a person to adopt the more lenient position and eat bread commercially baked by a non-Jew. During the *Asseret Yemai Teshuva* we should conduct ourselves according to the more stringent position. However, it is important to recognize that this more stringent position is consistent with normative *halacha*. In short, a person who adopts arbitrary stringencies that do not have a basis in *halacha* is not following the directions of Shulchan Aruch.

3. Deception

---

[31] Rabbaynu Moshe ben Maimon (Rambam) *Mishne Torah*, Hilchot Maachalot Assurot 17:9.
[32] Rav Yosef Karo, *Shulchan Aruch, Yoreh Dayah* 112:1-2 and notes of Rav Moshe Isserles.

We have now explained the basic message of Shulchan Aruch. Let us now analyze Shulchan Aruch's law at a deeper level. On a superficial level, the law presents a problem. Shulchan Aruch is suggesting that we adopt practices during the *Asseret Yemai Teshuva* that we do not observe during the rest of year. It seems that we are attempting to deceive Hashem. We are portraying ourselves in a manner that is not reflective of our behavior during the rest of the year!

This question is based upon a misunderstanding of Shulchan Aruch's law. The question assumes that our scrupulous observance of *halacha* during the *Asseret Yemai Teshuva* is an attempt to demonstrate our righteousness. If this is the intent of Shulchan Aruch, our self-portrayal is indeed dishonest and inappropriate.

4. Demonstrating awe

Rav Yitzchak Mirsky offers an alternative explanation of Shulchan Aruch's law. He begins with an analogy. Imagine you are invited to the White House for a meeting with the President. For this meeting, you would probably dress very carefully. Perhaps, during the week you rarely wear a suit. But for this important meeting you wear your finest outfit. You meet with the President attired in your carefully selected clothing. The President realizes that the clothing you are wearing is not your usual garb. He knows that you have adapted your dress for the occasion. There is no deception involved in your decision. You are demonstrating your respect for the office of the presidency.

Rav Mirsky explains that during the *Asseret Yemai Teshuva* the Almighty's presence should be acutely felt. We should feel the awe of Hashem's closeness. This is analogous to meeting with the President. This sense of awe should inspire us to conduct ourselves in an exemplary manner. This is not a deception. Instead, it is an expression of respect for Hashem.[33]

After the Torah is read and returned to its place, the congregation is seated. One person stands and recites the blessing: Blessed are You, Hashem, L-rd of the universe, who has sanctified us with His commandments and commanded us to hear the sound of the shofar. (Maimonides, Mishne Torah, Hilchot Shofar, Lulav, v'Sucah 3:10)

Rosh HaShanah and Yom Kippur

1. The *shofar* communicates a message we are called upon to obey

The sounding of the *shofar* is the central practice of Rosh HaShanah. Hearing its sounds is one of the Torah's 613 commandments. The performance of many positive commandments is preceded by a blessing. There are a number of opinions regarding the proper blessing for the *mitzvah* of *shofar*. The accepted opinion is presented above. Maimonides rules that the blessing ends with the words *lishmoa kol shofar* – to hear the sound of the *shofar*. In this blessing we acknowledge that Hashem commanded us to hear the sounds of the *shofar*.

Rabbaynu Asher accepts the opinion above but notes variants of the benediction suggested by other authorities. One alternative is to end the blessing with the words *lishmoa ba'kol shofar*. This variant adds the *ba* prefix to the word *kol* – sound. Although this addition

---

[33] Rav Yitzchak Mirsky, *Higyonai Halacha* (Jerusalem 1997), volume 3, p. 23.

seems minor, it changes the meaning of the blessing. With this addition, the blessing means to *obey* the sound of the *shofar*.

We do not accept this opinion. However, its premise is important. This opinion points out that the fulfillment of the *mitzvah* of *shofar* requires that we not only hear its sounds but that we obey their command. What is the command communicated by the *shofar*? The first step toward answering this question is to identify the theme of Rosh HaShanah.

You were revealed in Your cloud of glory to Your sacred people to speak with them. From the heavens You made them hear Your voice and revealed Yourself to them in thick clouds of purity. Moreover, the entire universe shuddered before You and the creatures of creation trembled before You during Your revelation, Our King, on Mount Sinai to teach Your people Torah and commandments. ..... You were revealed to them and with the sound of the shofar You appeared to them. (Musaf Amidah of Rosh HaShanah)

2. The theme of Rosh HaShanah is Hashem's kingship

The *musaf amidah* of Rosh HaShanah includes three unique central blessings. The first of these blessings – *malchiyot* – deals with Hashem's sovereignty. The second – *zichrinot* – discusses His providence over humankind and the Jewish people. The final blessing – *shofrot* – is devoted to exploring the meaning of the *shofar*. The opening paragraph of this blessing is quoted above. It associates the *shofar* with the Sinai revelation. The blessing suggests that the *shofar* blast announces the revealed presence of Hashem as sovereign of the universe. In other words, the *shofar* is akin to the trumpet blast proclaiming the entrance of a king.

The *shofar's* proclamation of Hashem's presence is an expression of the day's overall theme. Rosh HaShanah is the celebration of Hashem's sovereignty over the universe. This theme is fully developed in the first of the central blessings of the *musaf amidah*. This is the blessing of *malchiyot* which discusses the sovereignty of Hashem. The blessing has a second theme. It is also the blessing of *kedushat ha'yom*. It is devoted to describing the unique sanctity of Rosh HaShanah. The combination of these two themes suggests that they are closely related or even synonymous. The day's sanctity is derived from its designation as our celebration of Hashem's sovereignty.

We now have a response to our question. What is the message of the *shofar* that we are called upon to obey? Rosh HaShanah celebrates Hashem's sovereignty. The *shofar* announces the entrance of the king. The *shofar* declares that Hashem is our king and that He is the ruler of the entire universe. We obey the voice of the *shofar* by acknowledging Hashem's kingship and serving Him as our ruler.

Even though the sounding of the shofar on Rosh HaShanah is a decree, it contains an allusion. It is as if [the shofar's call] is saying: Wake up, sleepy ones from your sleep and you who slumber, arise. Inspect your deeds, repent, remember your Creator. Those who forget the truth in the vanities of time and throughout the entire year, devote their energies to vanity and emptiness which will not benefit or save: Look to your souls. Improve your ways and your deeds and let every one of you abandon his evil path and thoughts. (Maimonides, Mishne Torah, Hilchot Teshuvah 3:4)

3. The sounds of the *shofar* call upon us to repent

In the above quotation, Maimonides discusses the meaning of the *shofar*. He explains that the *shofar* serves as a wake-up call. It urges us to reconsider our lives, renew our devotion to

Hashem, abandon our sins, and repent. This message seems to be different from the *amidah*'s commentary of the meaning of the *shofar*. According to Maimonindes, the *shofar* beckons us to repent. According to the commentary of the *amidah,* the *shofar* proclaims Hashem's sovereignty. In order to respond to this issue, let us consider other comments of Maimonides.

Even though repentance and calling out [to Hashem] are desirable at all times, during the ten days between Rosh HaShanah and Yom Kippur, they are even more desirable and will be accepted immediately as [Isaiah 55:6] states: "Seek Hashem when He is to be found." (Maimonides, Mishne Torah, Hilchot Teshuvah 2:6)

For these reasons, it is customary for all of Israel to give profusely to charity, perform many good deeds, and be occupied with mitzvot from Rosh HaShanah until Yom Kippur to a greater extent than during the remainder of the year. During these ten days, the custom is for everyone to rise [while it is still] night and pray in the synagogues with heart-rending words of supplication until daybreak. (Maimonides, Mishne Torah, Hilchot Teshuvah 3:4)

4. The Ten Days of Repentance

Maimonides explains that during the period beginning with Rosh HaShannah and continuing through Yom Kippur emphasis should be given to repentance. Conventionally, this period is referred to as the *Aseret Yemai Teshuvah* – the Ten Days of Repentance. The special character of this period is reflected in the practices that Maimonides associates with it. These include giving more intense and consistent attention to the performance of *mitzvot* and rising in the morning to recite *selichot* – prayers of supplication and penitence. In practice, the liturgy of Rosh HaShanah does not include such prayers. We do not recite *vedoi* – the confession of our sins. We do not engage in expression of contrition. This is because Rosh HaShanah celebrates Hashem's sovereignty. Its mood is festive and joyous. It is not appropriate in this context to dwell upon our sins and engage in expressions of contrition. But how do we reconcile our observance of Rosh HaShanah with Maimonides' assertion that it initiates a period of repentance? Where in our observance of Rosh HaShanah is there any element of repentance or contrition?

If a person transgresses any of the mitzvot of the Torah, whether a positive command or a negative command – whether willingly or inadvertently – when he repents, and returns from his sin, he must confess before the L-rd, blessed be He, as [Numbers 5:6-7] states: "If a man or a woman commit any of the sins of man... they must confess the sin that they committed." (Maimonides, Mishne Torah, Hilchot Teshuvah 1:1)

Teshuvah is great for it draws a man close to the Shechinah as [Hoshea 14:2] states: "Return, O Israel, to Hashem, your L-rd;" [Amos 4:6] states: "'You have not returned to Me,' declares Hashem;" and [Jeremiah 4:1] states: "'If you will return, Oh Israel,' declares Hashem, `You will return to Me.'" Implied is that if you will return in teshuvah, you will cling to Me. Teshuvah brings near those who were far removed. Previously, this person was hated by the Omnipresent, disgusting, far removed, and abominable. Now, he is beloved and desirable, close, and dear. (Maimonides, Mishne Torah, Hilchot Teshuvah 7:6)

5. Two aspects of repentance

The answer lies in appreciating that there are two aspects to *teshuvah* – to repentance. First, the commitment of a sin requires that we repent. This aspect is explained by Maimonides in the first quotation above. In the second quotation, Maimonides focuses upon the second aspect of *teshuvah*. When we sin we move away from Hashem. Our sins create a partition between us and Hashem. *Teshuvah* is the means of restoring our relationship with Him. It rips down the barrier that separates between us and Hashem. In short, *teshuvah* is a response to sin and it is a restoration of our relationship with Hashem.

The *Aseret Yemai Teshuvah* are devoted to both aspects of *teshuvah*. They are a time to repent our sins and atone for the specific sins we have committed. They are also a time to return to Hashem and restore our relationship with Him. Appropriately, Rosh HaShanah initiates this period. We begin our return to Hashem by acknowledging and personally accepting His sovereignty. Rosh HaShanah does not feature *vedoi* or expression of contrition. But its clear resounding declaration of Hashem's majesty is the beginning of the process of returning to Him and restoring our relationship with Him.

Let us consider an analogy. Many of us have entered into a conflict with a friend and after time wished to bring the conflict to a close. We apologized and perhaps, we exchanged apologies with the other person. But even after apologies were exchanged, tension remained. The relationship that we enjoyed before the conflict was not restored.

How could we have secured a better outcome? What measure would have restored the relationship that we miss? Well, what would have happened if instead of offering a simple apology, we had first spoken to our friend about the meaningfulness of the relationship that we shared, then described how much we miss this relationship, and finally apologized for specific wrongs? I suspect that this apology would have been more effective. This is because our friend would understand that it is not merely an apology for a specific wrongdoing; it is an apology for discounting the importance of our relationship and allowing this conflict to undermine it.

The point of this analogy is that like two friends in conflict, we too must take responsibility for our wrongdoings and apologize; we must repent for our sins. But this repentance is more meaningful when it is founded upon a desire to restore our relationship with Hashem. Rosh HaShanah expresses that desire to restore our relationship with Hashem. Through our declaration of His sovereignty, we declare that we wish to return to Him. Upon this foundation, we move forward during the remaining days of the *Aseret Yemai Teshuvah* and offer our *vedoi* and supplications.

6. Acknowledgment of Hashem's kingship is the foundation of our repentance

We can now return to our original question. What is the message of the *shofar*? Is it a proclamation of Hashem's presence as our king or is it a wake-up call to perform *teshuvah*?

It is fundamentally a declaration of Hashem's kingship. But in the context of Rosh HaShanah, this declaration wakes us up to the imperative to perform *teshuvah*. We declare that Hashem is our king and proclaim our desire to renew our relationship with Him. This is our wake-up call. Once we acknowledge His sovereignty and embrace the challenge of returning to Him, we feel compelled to consider our lives, repent from our sins and seek His forgiveness.

Tshuva

1. *Sukkot* celebrating the Exodus

We are now in the midst of the Yom Tov season. This season begins with Rosh HaShannah and ends with the celebration of Sukkot, and specifically, Shemini Atzeret. What is the relationship between these three festivals or sacred days?

The connection between Rosh HaShannah and Yom Kippur is well known. The process of judgment begins with Rosh HaShannah and is completed with Yom Kippur. But is there a relationship between the observance of Sukkot and the two prior holidays – Rosh HaShannah and Yom Kippur? I believe that the answer to this question is not only significant to our appreciation of the message of Sukkot, but also provides an important insight into our observance of Rosh HaShannah and Yom Kippur.

This issue is discussed by our Sages in the context of a different question. Our Sages were troubled by the observance of Sukkot in the fall. Sukkot recalls the sojourn of our ancestors in the wilderness. The *sukkot* we build, and in which we live, during Sukkot recalls the Divine protection our ancestors enjoyed during their travels in the *midbar* – the wilderness. The wilderness was a hostile environment. It was barren and dry. The environment was bereft of the elements necessary for survival and the climate was life threatening. As the nation traveled through the wilderness, it lived in flimsy huts similar to our *sukkot*. These insubstantial shelters were inadequate to protect the people from the assault of the elements. Hashem covered the nation with His clouds and these clouds protected the nation for the forty years of travel through the *midbar*.

Bnai Yisrael left Egypt and entered the wilderness in the spring and we would expect the festival of Sukkot to be celebrated in that season. Why is the observance of Sukkot postponed to the fall?

2. Observing *Mitzvah* observance

Our Sages offer a number of responses to this question. The most well-known explanation is offered by the Tur. He begins with a premise. The commandment to dwell in the *succah* is formulated in a manner that demonstrates this activity is performed as a mitzvah. In other words, in formulating this mitzvah, the Torah wishes to demonstrate that we are dwelling in the *succah* in response to a commandment.

Based upon this premise, Tur explains the celebration of Sukkot in the fall. If Sukkot were celebrated in the spring, it would not be clear that we are dwelling in the *succah* in response to a mitzvah. Spring weather is pleasant. We enjoy spending time outdoors in the spring. However, in the fall the outdoors is less inviting. The rainy season is beginning. It is damp and the air is crisp and cooler. The summer has ended and we now wish to return to the indoors. Dwelling in the *succah* in the fall cannot be mistaken for an act of leisure. It is clearly the response to a commandment.[34]

Tur's explanation does not suggest any relationship between Sukkot and the preceding holidays. According to his explanation, Sukkot is not observed in the fall because of any relationship with the preceding observances. It is observed in the fall in order to demonstrate that our dwelling in the *succah* is a response to a commandment.

However, it is possible to propose an alternative explanation for the observance of Sukkot in the fall. This explanation requires that we further consider the significance of Sukkot.

---

[34] Rabbaynu Yaakov ben HaRash, *Tur Shulchan Aruch, Orech Chayim* 625.

3. Serve *Hashem* in joy

Maimonides explains that although we are required to rejoice on all festivals, Sukkot is *especially* associated with rejoicing. What is the nature of this rejoicing? Over what are we rejoicing? Maimonides explains that we should not perceive our service to Hashem as a burden. Instead, we should serve Hashem and perform His commandments with joy. The rejoicing we express on Sukkot is intended to convey this attitude of joy in the service of Hashem and performance of His *mitzvot*.[35]

Let us compare this Sukkot "theme" with the dominant theme of Rosh HaShannah and Yom Kippur. These two holidays are associated with judgment. The emphasis is on Hashem's majesty and kingship. On Rosh HaShannah and Yom Kippur we experience a sense of awe. Yet, we are obligated to rejoice on Rosh HaShannah – even Yom Kippur has an element of rejoicing. However, this is not the dominant theme of these holidays. Our rejoicing is inevitably overwhelmed by the recognition that we stand before Hashem in judgment. Our sense of awe dominates.

However, the awe we experience on Rosh HaShannah and Yom Kippur is only one element of our relationship with Hashem. We are also obligated to rejoice in our relationship with Hashem. If the holidays ended with Yom Kippur, our expression of our relationship with Hashem would be incomplete. It would lack the second element of our relationship – our joy in serving Hashem and performing His commandments. The celebration of Sukkot complements our observance of Rosh HaShannah and Yom Kippur by focusing on the second element of our relationship with Hashem – the element of rejoicing and joy.

According to this interpretation, the celebration of Sukkot in the fall is linked to our observance of Rosh HaShannah and Yom Kippur. It completes the process of renewing our full relationship with Hashem.

4. The mercy of *Hashem*

Aruch HaShulchan offers a third explanation for the observance of Sukkot in the fall. Before considering his comments, it will be helpful do reflect on another issue.

In Sefer Devarim, Moshe delivers his final message to Bnai Yisrael. He is addressing the generation that will enter and conquer the Land of Israel. His message begins with an enumeration of the various incidents in which Bnai Yisrael sinned against Hashem during its travels in the wilderness. Why does Moshe feel compelled to remind this generation of the various failings and sins of its parents?

The most obvious explanation is that Moshe is providing a warning. He is recounting the sins of the parents in order to admonish their children. He is warning this next generation against repeating the mistakes of its parents. Nachmanides accepts this explanation but he makes an important addition. He explains that Moshe was not only reminding the nation of the sins of its parents and warning it against repeating these behaviors, but he was also reminding this new generation that despite these sins and shortcomings, Hashem did not abandon its parents.

Nachmanides continues and explains the importance of this message. This new generation was charged with the role of conquering and possessing the Land of Israel. This was a

---

[35] Rabbaynu Moshe ben Maimon (Rambam) *Mishne Torah*, Hilchot Lulav 8:12-15.

role that they knew they could only fulfill with Hashem's assistance. Yet, sin is part of the human condition. This new generation would realize that regardless of its efforts, it would be inevitable that its conduct would not be perfect. When it predictably sins, will Hashem abandon it?

5. Effective *Teshuvah*

Moshe's address is designed to respond to this doubt. He reminds this new generation that their parents also sinned against Hashem. But Hashem's mercy is abundant. He never abandoned their parents. Instead, He helped them repent and return to His service. Moshe assured this new generation that it too would enjoy the same relationship with Hashem. They will make mistakes and sin. But Hashem – in His mercy – will not abandon them.[36]

Nachmanides' message is that we are not created as perfect human beings. We are each faced with a lifelong mission of gradual and steady self-improvement and self-realization. *Teshuvah* – repentance – is a lifelong process. In order to devote ourselves to this process and mission, we must feel confident that Hashem will indulge us by treating us with patience. If Hashem judges us according to the strict standard of *din* – justice – we cannot survive and fulfill our mission. In other words, we will only engage in the process of personal growth and *teshuvah* if we feel confident that Hashem will forgive our failings and provide us with the opportunity to grow and support our efforts. If we lack this confidence, it is likely we will dismiss the process of repentance as a wasted effort.

Aruch HaShulchan derives from Nachmanides' comments a further explanation of the celebration of Sukkot in the fall. He explains that on Rosh HaShannah and Yom Kippur we confront our failings. We devote ourselves to *teshuvah* and to the objective of securing atonement. But as we confront our shortcomings and failings, we may question – or even doubt – the efficacy of our efforts to restore our relationship with Hashem. We may question whether we deserve and can secure Hashem's forgiveness. These doubts can easily undermine our efforts to repent and change. We may even question whether the effort required to change is justified.

Sukkot responds to these doubts. Sukkot recalls Hashem's mercy and providence over our ancestors in the wilderness. It reminds us that our ancestors sinned gravely in creating and worshipping the *egel* – the golden calf. But their repentance and Moshe's intercession secured their forgiveness. Despite their sin, Hashem spread His clouds and protection over our ancestors and protected them during their sojourn in the *midbar*. In short, Sukkot reminds us of Hashem's forbearance, mercy, and the efficacy of repentance. As we observe Rosh HaShannah and Yom Kippur, we remember that Sukkot is approaching. We are struggling with the imperative to change and repent. But our knowledge that Sukkot is approaching encourages us and reminds us of the efficacy of our efforts. It communicates to us that Hashem is eager to forgive us. If we restore our relationship with Him, He will forgive us and redeem us.[37]

---

[36] Rabbaynu Moshe ben Nachman (Ramban), *Commentary on Sefer Devarim*, Introduction.
[37] Rav Aharon HaLeyve Epstein, *Aruch HaShulchan*, Orech Chayim 625:5.

Yom Kippur

Honoring Human Beings – With all Our Flaws

1. Repentance communicates personal responsibility

No one is perfect. Each of us has faults and every person commits sins. One of the amazing aspects of the Torah is its response to this aspect of the human condition. Our sins and wrongdoings are not overlooked because of their inevitability. We are held responsible for our wrongdoings. But neither are our sins beyond forgiveness. We are encouraged to confront our flaws, make the commitment to address them, and strive to correct them. With this commitment we can secure Hashem's forgiveness.

In other words the Torah communicates a message of personal responsibility. Our flaws and sins are not overlooked as the inevitable outcome of human imperfection. Neither are we rendered beyond redemption by virtue of our sins. We are responsible for embarking upon the path that will secure Hashem's forgiveness. We must take the initiative and demonstrate commitment.

How do we take responsibility for our wrongdoings? We accomplish this through the process of repentance. This is not a simple process. Repentance is not easily accomplished. Authentic repentance requires harsh, sincere introspection, tenacity, and determination.

The process begins with recognizing and fully accepting that one has acted wrongly – that one has sinned. This is the aspect of the process that requires introspection. Repentance is not a mere superficial acknowledgment of wrongdoing. It is a sincere recognition of one's flaws. This recognition is only achieved when a person actually feels a sense of deep regret or embarrassment regarding the behavior.[1] This intense regret expresses recognition of the full dimensions of one's sins. It reflects the sinner's realization that he has violated Hashem's Torah and defiled one's personal sanctity.

Recognition is followed by commitment. Once a person has recognized that he has sinned and he feels the associated regret or disappointment, he must commit to change.[2] This aspect of the repentance process requires tenacity and determination. Change is never easy. Yet, repentance requires firm commitment to never return to one's abandoned behavior.

In short, we can secure forgiveness for our sins through repentance but this process requires a meaningful commitment to introspection and change.

2. Repentance requires concrete verbalization

There is another aspect to repentance. In addition to the internal aspects described above, repentance includes a verbal declaration. The person engaging in repentance must give expression in words to his commitment. This process is often referred to as confession but involves more than merely verbally acknowledging the sin. The declaration must verbally express all aspects of the repentance process.[3] In other words, the person must verbally acknowledge his sin. He must express his remorse or shame. He must declare his determination to not return to the abandoned behavior.

---

[1] Rabbaynu Moshe ben Maimon (Rambam) *Mishne Torah*, Hilchot Teshuvah 2:2.

[2] Rabbaynu Moshe ben Maimon (Rambam) *Mishne Torah*, Hilchot Teshuvah 2:2.

[3] Rabbaynu Moshe ben Maimon (Rambam) *Mishne Torah*, Hilchot Teshuvah 2:2.

3. The public element

Maimonides adds that this declaration should ideally be made in public. In other words, one should – essentially – declare his faults, regret, and intention to change in front of an audience of peers and neighbors. However, Maimonides qualifies this statement. He explains that public declaration is required only in regard to sins we have committed against others. Sins that we have committed against Hashem should not be publicly declared. The verbal declaration of sins committed against Hashem is required but it should be made privately rather than publicly.[4]

Maimonides' ruling is difficult to understand. The sins that we commit against our peers or against strangers are also prohibited by the Torah. When we commit such sins, we violate the Torah's laws and disobey Hashem. So, even though these sins are against our fellow human beings, we have also rebelled against Hashem and His Torah.

Let us consider an example. Sometimes, we become angry at a friend or peer. Maybe, in our rage we say terrible things about this person to others. We have sinned against this person. When we are prepared to repent, we must seek the forgiveness of the person against whom we sinned. We must also publicly declare the elements of repentance – regret, shame, and commitment to change. This is because we sinned against another human being. Therefore, our declaration must be public. But have we not also sinned against Hashem? Does He not command us in His Torah to not speak against others behind their backs? Are we not enjoined by His Torah against defamation of others? We have sinned against this person but also against Hashem. Why should our declaration be made in public? Our wrongdoing includes a sin against Hashem. Sins against Hashem are not to be publicly declared!

And if a man committed a sin worthy of death, and he be put to death, and you hang him on a tree; his body shall not remain all night upon the tree, but you shall surely bury him the same day; for he that is hanged is a reproach unto G-d; that you shall not defile your land which Hashem your G-d gives you as an inheritance. (Devarim 21:22-23)

4. The public hanging of the body of the sinner

Before considering the above passages, some background information is required. When the most serious prohibitions of the Torah are violated the consequences are severe. In the most serious cases, the courts are authorized and required to apply capital punishment. There are four forms of execution available to the courts. The specific form of execution employed corresponds with the severity of the prohibition violated. Stoning is reserved for the most serious violations.

The above passages communicate two laws that are somewhat paradoxical. The first law is that after a person is executed through stoning his body is hung on display. However, the second law in these passages is that the body must be removed from display and buried by evening. In other words, although the body of the person committing the most severe sin must be hung and displayed, this display must be very brief. By the evening the body must be interred.

5. The hanging body of the sinner is an affront against Hashem

Rabbaynu Yosef Bechor Shur comments on the requirement to bury the body of the sinner after a brief display. He explains that this display is reserved for the bodies of only those who have been stoned — those who have committed the worst sins. Among the sins punished by

---

[4] Rabbaynu Moshe ben Maimon (Rambam) *Mishne Torah*, Hilchot Teshuvah 2:5.

stoning is blaspheming Hashem. The observer of the displayed body may reasonably speculate that this sinner had blasphemed Hashem. This speculation is described in the above passages as a "reproach unto G-d". Entertaining the thought of blasphemy is in itself an affront to the glory and honor of Hashem.

Rabbaynu Yosef Bechor Shur suggests that we envision a person who slapped his king. The king punished the person publicly for the affront. There are two consequences of the king's public punishment of this criminal – one intended consequence and one not intended. The king's intention is to demonstrate that one who dishonors his monarch deserves severe punishment and public humiliation. The unintended consequence is that those who view the spectacle of the punishment come to realize that the king can be struck and dishonored. They realize that, in fact, some people actually do so. Spectators who previously would never have imagined it possible to dishonor their monarch now know that behaviors unimaginable to them are performed by others. The king's honor has been diminished and the awe in which his subjects held him has been compromised.

Similarly, the display of the body of a person is presumed to be a blasphemer does communicate the severity of his sin. But the display also communicates that some people do blaspheme Hashem and that this unimaginable affront is actually committed by some people. Hashem is dishonored and the spectators' awe of Hashem is, to some degree, diminished.[5]

6. Promoting Hashem's honor

We can apply Rabbaynu Yosef Bechor Shur's reasoning to our question. When we sin against another human being, we also sin against Hashem and His Torah. When we hear the confession of one who has sinned against another person, we recognize that the sin was provoked by disregard for a fellow human being. We know that the sin includes an implicit sin against Hashem and his Torah but we recognize that the action was not directed against Hashem. Hashem's honor and glory are "collateral damage" – unintended casualties of the behavior. In contrast, when we sin against Hashem, the only element or aspect of the sin is the violation of His Torah. In this instance, the public declaration of the sin has an affect akin to displaying the body of one who was stoned. Yes, the declaration expresses recognition of the severity of the sin and it bemoans the defilement it engendered. But the declaration also compromises the honor of Hashem. Those who hear the confession learn that the sinner violated Hashem's will and His Torah. Hashem's glory is compromised and our awe of Hashem is diminished.

7. Hashem compromises His honor for the sake of human sanctity

It is possible that Rabbaynu Yosef Bechur Shur's comments suggest an alternative response to our problem. Perhaps, even when a person declares his repentance from a sin against his fellow human being, this declaration diminishes Hashem's honor. After all, the sinner has also violated His will and Torah. Yet, Hashem allows – even requires – that His honor be compromised for the sake of reinforcing a message. We defile ourselves when we sin against others. In other words, Hashem compromises His own honor in order to encourage us to honor and respect one another.

---

[5] Rabbaynu Yosef Bechor Shur, *Commentary on Sefer Devarim* 21:23.

How does one confess? He says, "I beseech you Hashem. I have erred. I have willfully acted wrongly. I have acted rebelliously before you. I have (specify wrongdoing). I have regret. I am embarrassed with my actions. I will never return to this behavior. (Maimonides, Mishne Torah, Laws of Repentance 1:1)

The Formula for Confessing One's Sins

The process of repentance must be accompanied by a verbal confession. This confession has a specific format. Maimonides' formulation of the confession is based upon a discussion found in Tractate Yoma. The majority of Sages suggest the formulation adopted by Maimonides. In this version, first errors or unintentional sins are confessed. Then, reference is made to intentional wrong doings. Last, acts of rebellion are included. The reasoning underlying this order is that a person should first seek forgiveness for lesser sins and then the more serious wrong doings.

However, the Talmud explains that Rebbe Meir suggests an alternative form for the confession. He suggests that first the confession should mention the willful sins. This is followed by mentioning acts of rebellion. The confession ends with reference to unintentional errors. Rebbe Meir derives his order from the prayers of Moshe. In seeking forgiveness for Bnai Yisrael, Moshe describes Hashem's attributes of mercy and kindness. He declares that because of these attributes, Hashem forgives willful sins, acts of rebellion, and unintentional errors. Rebbe Meir adopted this order for his formulation of the confession.[6]

What is the basis of the dispute between the Sages and Rebbe Meir. The Sages order the sins referred to in the confession from the least serious to the most severe. This order is dictated by a clear logic. The confession is a request for forgiveness. It is appropriate to begin with the lesser offenses. Rebbe Meir maintains that the confession includes an additional element. It makes reference to Moshe's intercession on behalf of Bnai Yisrael. Moshe began by enumerating the attributes of Hashem responsible for forgiveness. In order to incorporate the reference to Moshe's appeal for forgiveness based upon the attributes of mercy and forbearance, Rebbe Meir's confession adopts the order Moshe used in describing the sins of the nation. In other words, Rebbe Meir maintains that as we ask for forgiveness, we must acknowledge and appeal to the benevolence of Hashem implicit in this forbearance.

Although the opinion of the Sages is accepted, the issue raised by Rebbe Meir finds expression is *halachah*. The confession contained in the liturgy is often accompanied by a recitation of the Divine attributes of Hashem described by Moshe. This is in accord with Rebbe Meir's opinion that confession is associated with recognition of Hashem's kindness as expressed in the attributes. Although this recognition is not incorporated into the confession itself, it is associated with the confession through the liturgy.

"If a person violates any commandment of the Torah – a positive or a negative command – whether this violation is intentional or unintentional, when one performs repentance and repents from the sin, he is obligated to confess before G-d, Blessed Be He ... This confession is a positive command." (Maimonides, Mishne Torah, laws of Repentance 1:1)

---

6   Mesechet Yoma 36b.

Life of *Teshuva*

1. *Teshuva* or *vedoi?*

The period from Rosh HaShannah through Yom Kippur is devoted to the process of repentance. Each of us must attempt to engage in this fundamental process. What are we attempting to accomplish? What do we hope to achieve through this process?

Maimonides, in his Mishne Torah devotes ten chapters to the Laws of Repentance. The quote above is a portion of the first law in this section. Maimonides explains that the violation of any commandment engenders a requirement to perform *teshuva* – repentance. Whether we sin through commission or omission, whether the sin is intentional or unintentional, we are required to repent. This repentance must be followed by *vedoi* – a verbal confession of the sin and a commitment to change our behavior. Maimonides emphasizes the importance of this verbal declaration. He explains that this declaration is a positive commandment of the Torah.

In short, Maimonides teaches us that wrongdoing requires a twofold response. We must perform *teshuva* and *vedoi*. *Vedoi* is a verbalization of the process of *teshuva*. We put into words our regret for past behavior and our commitment to change.

Which of these two responses is more fundamental – *teshuva* or *vedoi?* We would imagine that *teshuva* is the more essential element. However, Maimonides seems to indicate that *vedoi* is the more fundamental component. He explains that the *vedoi* is a positive command.

Apparently, Maimonides maintains that repentance requires that a person address the Almighty and declare one's contrition. Without the declaration, the process of repentance is incomplete. An unstated, internal sense of regret is inadequate. The repentant person must address Hashem and accept responsibility for his or her misdeeds.

This suggests that the process of *teshuva* is a prerequisite to *vedoi*. A person cannot make a meaningful declaration without an internal commitment. Therefore in order to perform *vedoi*, *teshuva* must occur. Maimonides confirms this interpretation of his comments in the next chapter of his discussion of repentance. There, he explains that one who performs *vedoi* without an internal commitment to change accomplishes little or nothing.[7]

2. Two different descriptions of v*edoi*

"What is repentance? It requires that the sinner abandon the sin. And one must discontinue any contemplation of it. One must commit to not return to the behavior ... In addition, one must regret the past ... One should call upon Hashem as a witness that he will never return to the sin ... And one must declare these matters to which one has made an internal commitment."
(Maimonides, Mishne Torah, Laws of Repentance 2:2)

Here, Maimonides describes in detail the process of repentance. He identifies five elements within the process. First, one must discontinue the sinful behavior. Second, one must refrain from even contemplating or fantasizing about the behavior. Third, the person must review past behaviors and feel sincere regret. Fourth, one must make a firm commitment to not return to the behavior. Maimonides then adds the person must verbalize these matters. This is the process of *vedoi*.

---

[7] Rabbaynu Moshe ben Maimon (Rambam) *Mishne Torah*, Hilchot Teshuva 2:3.

What is Maimonides telling us about *teshuva* and *vedoi*? Maimonides begins with a question. He asks, "What is *teshuva*?" He then responds. He explains that the verbal *vedoi* must follow the internal process. This is part of his description of *teshuva*. This strongly suggests that *vedoi* is part of the process of *teshuva*. It completes the process. How does *vedoi* complete the process? It seems that *vedoi* provides substance and finality to one's commitment. Through expressing one's thoughts in word, the person becomes more firmly committed to change.

It seems that Maimonides provides two different views on the role and significance of *vedoi*. In this chapter *vedoi* is characterized as a part of the *teshuva* process. It is the element that lends finality to the process. This is a very different characterization than that provided in the first chapter. That characterization is described above. In the first chapter, Maimonides explains that *vedoi* is the fundamental response to sin. *Teshuva* is a prerequisite to a meaningful *vedoi*. How can these two views be reconciled?

3. Much to repent

"One should not imagine that teshuva is limited to sins that involve some action – for example promiscuity, theft or larceny. Rather, just as one must repent from these, so one must seek out one's improper attitudes and repent from them – for example from anger, hatred, jealousy ..."
(Maimonides, Mishne Torah, Laws of Repentance 7:3)

In order to answer our question, we must consider another apparent contradiction in Maimonides' treatment of repentance. We have discussed Maimonides' description of the process of repentance. Let us now consider his position regarding the types of behavior that require repentance.

In the law quoted above Maimonides explains that the requirement to repent is not engendered solely by the violation of a commandment. We are also required to repent from improper attitudes or character traits. For example, we must attempt to abandon our hatreds and to temper and control our anger. We must evaluate all of our attitudes, identify our character flaws and address them. In other words, even if a person has not violated a specific commandment, *teshuva* is required.

This conclusion does not seem to agree with Maimonides' statement in the opening law of this section. In that law, Maimonides explains that *teshuva* and *vedoi* are required when a person violates a law of the Torah. This means that the violation of a commandment engenders the requirement to perform *teshuva* and *vedoi*. Some commission or omission must occur. This implies that poor attitude alone does not create an obligation to repent! How can these two positions be reconciled?

Let us return to our opening question. What are we attempting to accomplish through *teshuva*? What do we hope to achieve through this process? First, we must recognize that in sinning we violate the Torah. We disregarded the will of the Almighty. We rebel against the ultimate King. The *vedoi* that accompanies *teshuva* begins with the acknowledgment that we have sinned against the Torah. Through repentance, we attempt to earn atonement for this sin. We wish to avoid retribution or unpleasant consequences. In short, one objective of *teshuva* is atonement – *kapparah*. But does *teshuva* have any other objective?

"Since one is granted volition ... one should endeavor to perform teshuva and vedoi in response to sin ..." (Maimonides, Mishne Torah, Laws of Repentance 7:1)

Maimonides does outline another objective in the process of *teshuva*. In order to identify this objective, we must consider the above quote. Maimonides explains that human beings are unique. We are endowed with freewill. We have the ability to choose between right and wrong. He explains that as a result of this faculty we are required to engage in *teshuva*.

Why does the element of human volition engender an obligation to perform *Teshuva*? Freewill means that we are in charge of our self-improvement. To a great extent, we determine the degree to which we fulfill our individual potential. We decide whether we will squander our talents and lives or whether we will strive to fulfill our potential.

We can only achieve personal fulfillment through an ongoing process of *teshuva*. In this process we constantly reevaluate our lives and attitudes. We reconsider our personal mission and constantly seek self-improvement. The objective is not to atone but to purify – *tahara*.

4. *Teshuva* and *kapparah*

In short, *teshuva* has two objectives. One objective is *kapparah* – atonement for our sins. The second objective is *tahara* – personal improvement.[8]

This explains Maimonides' position regarding which sins engender the obligation to perform *teshuva*. In the first chapter, Maimonides indicates that *teshuva* is a response to violation of the law. Maimonides is discussing the *teshuva* of *kapparah*. Atonement is required when the law is violated. If the law has not been violated, the obligation to seek *kapparah* is not engendered.

However, Maimonides teaches us that we should repent from improper attitudes and character traits. This is because in addition to *kapparah*, *teshuva* has a second objective. This objective is *tahara* – self-improvement. In order to achieve this objective, we must engage in an ongoing process of introspection. This process requires that we consider and evaluate our attitudes and character traits.

We can now explain Maimonides' treatment of *vedoi*. In the first chapter of the Law of Repentance, Maimonides is explaining the process of atonement. In this process the *vedoi* is the fundamental element. We have sinned against Hashem's Torah. It is appropriate to verbally appeal to Hashem for forgiveness and atonement. Accordingly, *vedoi* is fundamental to achieving atonement. In this context, the *vedoi* is not merely the final step in *teshuva*. It is the essential element in the process of *kapparah*.

However, *teshuva* is not merely a prerequisite in the process of achieving atonement. It is also a process that purifies and improves a person. In this process, the internal element is essential. Self-improvement requires thorough introspection. In the second chapter of the Laws of Repentance, Maimonides is explaining the process of *teshuva*. He describes it as a process of self-improvement. Its objective is internal change. In this context, *vedoi* completes the *teshuva*. It finalizes the internal commitments that result from the process of introspection. Therefore, in this context Maimonides describes *vedoi* as the final element in the process of *teshuva*.

---

[8] See Rav Yosef Dov Soloveitchik, *Al HaTeshuva* (Jerusalem, 5739), Part 1.

What exactly is repentance? It is that a person should abandon the sin and remove it from his thought. He should resolve not to again commit it as it says, "The wicked should abandon his path..." Also, he should regret his past behavior as it says, "For after I repented I had remorse..." And He who knows the inner thoughts of man should testify on his behalf that he will not ever return to this sin as it says, "Nor shall we say any more to the work of our hands 'our god'...". And he is required to verbally confess and pronounce these ideas that he has resolved. (Maimonides Mishne Torah, Hilchot Teshuvah 2:2)

The Dialectic of Teshuvah

1. Objective outcomes of repentance

Maimonides devotes ten chapters of his code of Torah law to a discussion of the laws of *teshuvah* – repentance. In the second chapter he describes *teshuvah*. His definition includes three fundamental components. First, the repentant individual must commit to abandon the sinful behavior. This abandonment must be both in action and in thought. His commitment must be to not repeat the sin and also to no longer contemplate it. Second, he must view his past sinful behavior with remorse. Third, he must commit to words the resolve that he has developed in his heart. This requires that he verbally acknowledge his sin and state his remorse and commitment to abandon the behavior.

The impression that emerges from this description of *teshuvah* is that it is achieved through attainment of specific outcomes. In other words, *teshuvah* is achieved when a person is prepared to acknowledge the fault of the past with remorse and is willing to commit to abandon the sinful behavior.

It also seems from this description that the path by which a person comes to these outcomes is not relevant to *teshuvah*. In other words, the causes of a person's remorse and his motives for abandoning the sinful behavior do not seem to be relevant.

2. Is all *teshuvah* equal?

This raises an interesting and important question. Consider a person who has been engaged in sinful behavior. Perhaps, he has only sporadically and minimally contributed to charity. However, this person regularly takes inventory of his personal behaviors and eventually considers his attitudes toward *tzedakah* – charity. After carefully evaluating his values and his treatment of the *mitzvah* of *tzedakah*, he feels embarrassed over his past behavior. He recognizes that he was acting out of greed. He decides that he must change. Henceforth, he will contribute regularly and he will give according to his blessings and means.

Let us compare this person to another individual who has struggled with the *mitzvah* of *tzedakah*. He experienced a transformation similar to the first individual. He was reluctant to participate in the *mitzvah* of *tzedakah* but he eventually felt remorse and committed to being more generous. However, his transformation involved traveling a very different path than the first individual. The second individual became aware of the reputation that he had earned in the community. His peers regarded him as selfish and unempathic. They observed him with wonder and were astounded by his capacity to turn a blind eye to the suffering of others. Eventually, he recognized that his peers shunned him. Their harsh treatment gave him cause to consider the reason for the rejection he was receiving. Suddenly he realized that he could only earn the approval of his peers by changing his behavior. He was seized with remorse over his past stinginess and he committed to be more generous in the future.

Both of these individuals ultimately achieved the outcomes that Maimonides identifies as essential to *teshuvah*. Are they therefore to be regarded as equals or is one individual's *teshuvah* superior to the other's?

What is complete teshuvah? This is one who encounters an opportunity to repeat a transgression, he has the capacity to do it and he does not because of repentance and not in response to fear, or lack of strength. For example, he transgressed through intimacy with a woman. After a period of time he is alone with her, he still loves her, he is still physically capable, he is in the physical environment in which he transgressed, and he abstains and does not transgress, this is regarded as fully repentant. This is what Shlomo said, "And remember your Creator in your youth…" If one only repents in his old age and when it is not possible for him to do that which he did in the past, then even though it is not perfect repentance, it is effective for him and he is regarded as repentant. Even if he transgressed his entire life and repented on the day of his death and dies in his repentance, all of his sins are forgiven, as it says"…before the sun, or the light, or the moon, or the stars are darkened, and the clouds return after the rain", which refers to the day of one's death. It is implied that if one remembers his Creator and repents before he dies, he is forgiven. (Maimonides Mishne Torah, Hilchot Teshuvah 2:1)

3. Three levels of repentance

Maimonides describes the perfect repentance. He explains that perfect repentance is achieved when one commits a transgression. He repents and is then confronted with circumstances that are essentially equivalent to those in which he formerly sinned. In Maimonides' example, a person sinned through prohibited intimacy with a woman. After repenting, he is confronted with a new opportunity to repeat the transgression. The circumstances of the opportunity are fundamentally the same as those in which he previously committed the transgression. However, this time he resists because of his repentance. Maimonides declares that this is the perfect repentance!

Maimonides continues to explain that if the person who initially succumbed to his passions is confronted with a new opportunity to transgress but the circumstances are fundamentally altered from the initial episode, and as a consequence of his repentance the person resists, then the repentance is regarded as effective. However, it is not as perfect as the repentance of the person who resisted under circumstances that are equivalent to those of the transgression.

Finally, Maimonides explains that even if a person repeatedly sins throughout his life and only repents in his last moments, his repentance is accepted and his sins are forgiven. However, it seems that Maimonides regards this last instance of repentance as far inferior to the two versions that he previously described.

If repentance is achieved solely through securing outcomes – remorse and an effective commitment to not repeat the sin – then Maimonides' description of three levels of repentance is difficult to explain. All three of the individuals have experienced remorse and all have effectively avoided repeating their sin. Yet, Maimonides does assert that these three individuals are not equal and that their repentance should be assessed on a declining scale. Perfect repentance is achieved when the repentant individual demonstrates his resolve in fundamentally the same circumstances that formerly were his downfall. The penultimate level of repentance is achieved when a person resists repeating the sin, albeit, he is not confronted with the circumstances that led to his prior failure. The lowest level of repentance is that of the person confronted with his impending death and only at this moment achieves the resolve required to repent his past sins.

4. *Teshuvah*: Conquest of perception over desire

Rabbaynu Menachem Me'eri describes nine levels of *teshuvah*. In his delineation, the highest level is identical to the highest level described by Maimonides. Me'eri idenitifies two characteristics that distinguish this highest level of repentance. First, the *teshuvah* occurs in response to the sinner's internal initiative. He is not compelled to repent because of any external factor – for example, fear of punishment or the distain of his peers. Second, the *teshuvah* expresses the triumph of objective perception over desire or lust. The individual who earlier was overpowered by desire and unable to resist its pressure now recognizes that desire is an illusion. He appreciates the value of virtue and its superiority over pursuit of short-lived immediate pleasure. He may achieve this understanding through reforming his self-perception and appreciating that we are essentially spiritual creations sojourning in the material world. He may come to his understanding of virtue and sin through appreciating the wisdom of the Torah and its mitzvot and recognizing that they are the truest and most effective path to contentment in this world. Regardless of the specific realization, the person's perception of truth is so effective that it penetrates the haze generated by desire and lust. It pushes aside the cloud of confusion and, now, the reformed, repentant sinner sees truth.[9]

Now, the distinction between Maimonides' three levels of repentance can be more clearly understood. The highest level is achieved when a penetrating perception subdues and overpowers desire. The reformed sinner finds himself in the same situation that before led to his downfall. Now, he is not overpowered or misled by desire. Instead, perception penetrates the confusion generated by desire and he recognizes that the better choice is to reject sin or to restrain himself from acting on his desires.

The second level of repentance does not confront the reformed sinner with the same challenge. He is not confronted with the circumstances that previously ensnared him. True, even in this new challenge he must resist desire and see truth through the cloud of passion. However, the cloud is not as thick as in the past and the longings of his instincts are not as intense as in the past.

In the final level, the former sinner finds himself confronted with his own mortality. He recognizes that the lusts and desires that he longed to fulfill throughout his life have no meaning any longer. He cannot take with him the passing pleasures of the material world and neither will his material accomplishments save him from the gaping abyss that now awaits him. He cannot avoid the conclusion that he has acted foolishly and squandered the gift of life. His remorse is unbearable and his perception completely penetrating. However, he has not actually triumphed in the struggle with instinct and desire. Instead, these opponents have been vanquished by the reality of impending death. His encounter with his mortality has destroyed all illusions.

5. The *teshuvah* dialectic

This analysis suggests that Maimonides ascribes two components to *teshuvah*. One component of *teshuvah* is objective. It is characterized by outcomes – remorse over the past sin

---

[9] Rabbaynu Menachem Me'eri, *Chibur HaTeshuvah, Mayshiv Nefesh*, chapter 2.

and commitment to not repeat the behavior. Were this the only component of *teshuvah*, then all repentant individuals would be equals. The motives or circumstances of a person's repentance would be irrelevant.

However, repentance has a second component. This component is an internal dialectic. It is characterized by the conquest of perception over desire. The presence of this component in the *teshuvah* of the individual is subject to variation. This component achieves its greatest expression in the repentant individual whose perception is so absolute that even the circumstances of his earlier downfall can now be resisted. Those whose perception is less absolute or who achieve clarity of perception only when confronted with the reality of mortality are repentant. However, the dialectic component exists to a lesser or minimal extent in their *teshuvah*.

"Among the repentant behaviors are for the repentant individual to constantly call-out to Hashem with cries and supplications. And one should give charity according to one's ability. One should distance oneself from one's sin. One should change one's name. One is stating that I am a different person. I am not the person who did those inappropriate actions. One should alter all of one's actions so that they are positive and just..." (Maimonides, Mishne Torah, Hilchot Teshuva 2:4)

Maimonides describes the behaviors of the repentant individual. One of these behaviors is somewhat confusing. Maimonides suggests that the repentant individual should alter all of his or her actions. One must be positive and just in all of their actions.

In order to understand the difficulty regarding this suggestion, a short introduction is required. What is repentance? Repentance is not accomplished through a temporary cessation of the sinful behavior. *Teshuva* is much more demanding. *Teshuva* requires that a person make a complete break with the sinful behavior. This complete break is only achieved through a commitment to never again commit the sin. Maimonides' position on this issue is emphatic. He explains that a person who confesses a sin and does not resolve to completely discontinue the sinful behavior has not fulfilled the *mitzvah* of *teshuva*. He compares this person to one who immerses in a *mikveh* – a body of water – while holding an impure object. The immersion cannot affect a state of purity until the person releases the impure object. Similarly, the purification and process of *teshuva* cannot proceed without a complete break from the sin. This complete break is expressed in a firm commitment to abandon the sinful behavior.[10]

Maimonides suggests that the repentant individual must alter all of his or her behaviors. Does this mean that repentance must be all-encompassing and include all aspects of a person's life? Is Maimonides suggesting that the repentance from a specific sin requires a person to repent from all other inappropriate behaviors? This is not a reasonable interpretation of Maimonides' words. As we have explained, *teshuva* requires a complete and permanent cessation of the sinful behavior. Maimonides cannot intend to suggest that repentance from a single sin requires that we permanently abandon all other wrongdoing. Such a requirement would render *teshuva* virtually unattainable!

---

[10] Rabbaynu Moshe ben Maimon (Rambam) *Mishne Torah*, Hilchot Teshuva 2:3.

We must conclude that Maimonides is not suggesting that the repentant individual must permanently discontinue all other inappropriate behaviors. Instead, Maimonides is acknowledging the value of change that is not accompanied by complete commitment. The repentant person should endeavor to discontinue all inappropriate behavior. It is true that such a drastic undertaking will not result in a permanent cessation of all wrongdoing. That is an unrealistic expectation. Nonetheless, temporary change has a value. The sincerely repentant person should appreciate that value and seek change – even temporary change.

This interpretation of Maimonides' suggestion is implied by his carefully chosen wording. He does not suggest that the repentant individual should repent from all other wrongdoing. He suggests that repentant person alter his or her behavior. There is a tremendous difference between altering a behavior and repenting from the behavior. An alteration is achieved even through a temporary suspension of wrongdoing. Repentance requires a complete commitment to permanently discontinue the behavior. This analysis confirms our interpretation of Maimonides' suggestion. He is acknowledging the value of positive change – even temporary change.

"Among the ways of repentance is for the repentant individual to constantly bemoan his sin before Hashem with crying and supplications. And he should give charity according to his ability. And he should distance himself, to an extreme, from the area concerning which he sinned. And he should change his name. In this he states, "I am someone else and not that person who performed those actions." (Maimonides, Mishne Torah, Laws of Repentance 2:4)

Maimonides describes, in this halacha, some of the behaviors which accompany repentance. He includes the establishment of a new identity. The sinner sees him/herself as a different person from the individual who committed the wrongdoing.

A person's behavior is strongly affected by self image. Once we establish a behavior or attitude it is difficult to imagine ourselves without this element. This psychological barrier must be overcome if the process of Teshuva is to be successful. The person must become accustomed to a different self-image.

The Talmud discusses the life of Elisha ben Avuyah. This great scholar was the teacher of Rav Meir. In his studies, Elisha ben Avuyah delved into the most difficult areas of the Torah. He eventually discovered truths for which he was not prepared. He could not accept these concepts and rejected the Torah. Elisha ben Avuyah went so far, in rejecting his former life, that he changed his name. Interestingly, he chose the name Acher. Literally translated, this name means "other". Through adopting this name, he explained that he intended to indicate that he was no longer Elisha ben Avuyah. He was a different person with new attitudes.

The Talmud comments that the Almighty declared that although all humanity has the opportunity to repent, Acher is an exception. He cannot repent his sins.

Rav Yosef Dov Soloveitchik ZTL explained that it is not the intention of the Talmud to indicate the Almighty will not accept Acher's repentance. Instead, the message of the Talmud is that Acher simply cannot repent. He does not have the ability.

Based on the teaching of Maimonides, this message can be easily understood. Elisha ben Avuyah established a new identity of Acher. Acher was an individual who lived a life antithetical to the Torah. As long as Elisha ben Avuyah viewed himself as Acher it would be impossible for him to repent. His self-image would prevent him from establishing a Torah outlook and life. Only once he removed this identity could he hope to repent.

Among the characteristics of repentance is for the repentant individual to constantly call out before Hashem tearfully and with petitions. One should give charity according to one's capacity. One should distance oneself from one's sinful behavior... (Maimonides, Laws of Repentance 2:4)

How Much Tzedakah Should We Give?

1. Behaviors associated with teshuvah

Maimonides explains that the process of teshuvah – repentance – should be accompanied by other activities. Among the behaviors that he enumerates are petitional prayer and tzedakah – giving charity. Maimonides' position is reflected in the comments of the Talmud. The Talmud explains that three activities have the capacity to cancel a negative decree. These activities are prayer, teshuvah and tzedakah.[11] According to the Talmud, these activities do not only impact Hashem's judgment of us. They also have the power to reverse a negative verdict. In other words, even if as a consequence of our misdeeds we are judged as deserving punishment, these activities have the capacity to reverse the decree of punishment.

My people, upon whom My name is called, humble themselves and pray and seek My presence and repent of their evil ways, I shall hear from heaven and forgive their sin and heal their land.
(Devrai HaYamim II 7:14)

2. The Talmud's textual source for tzedakah's role in the teshuvah process

The Talmud cites the above passage as the source for its comments. This passage is part of a prophecy received by King Shlomo upon his completion of the construction of the Bait HaMikdash. Hashem tells Shlomo that when the people sin and are punished, they should call out to Him from the Bait HaMikdash and He will listen to their prayers. However, the pasuk identifies three activities that can rescue the nation – prayer, repentance, and seeking Hashem's presence. The Talmud explains that "seeking Hashem's presence" is a reference to tzedakah.[12]

And Hashem spoke to Moshe saying: Speak to Bnai Yisrael and they should take for Me an offering. From every person, that which his heart moves him to give, you should take as My offering. (Shemot 25:1-2)

3. Teshuvah and Tzedakah in the Torah

Rav Yosef Dov Soloveitchik Zt"l suggests that the Torah itself provides a source for the role of tzedakah in the teshuvah process and in moderating negative decrees. In order to understand his comments, a brief introduction is necessary. In Sefer Shemot, the incident of the Egel – the Golden Calf – interrupts the Torah's discussion of the building of the Mishcan – the Tabernacle. The discussion of the Mishcan begins with the above passages. In these passages, Hashem commands Moshe to initiate the process of collecting the materials from which the Mishcan and its contents will be fabricated. These materials are to be collected through freely

---

[11] Talmud Yerushalmi, Mesechet Ta'anit 2:1.
[12] Based upon Tehilim 17:16 the Talmud associates tzedakah with being in Hashem's presence.

71

contributed donations. The Torah's account continues with a description of the design of the Mishcan and its contents, and related issues. Then, suddenly the incident of the Egel and its aftermath are described. Upon completion of its discussion of the Egel, the Torah resumes its narrative regarding the Mishcan. This order suggests that the incident of the Egel occurred at some point after Hashem commanded the nation to create the Mishcan and before the completion of the project. However, the Sages' analysis of the texts led them to a different conclusion. The Sages explained that the commandment to create the Mishcan was revealed to Moshe after the incident of the Egel. Moshe ascended Mount Sinai and petitioned Hashem to forgive Bnai Yisrael. On Yom Kippur he descended having secured Hashem's pardon and immediately received the command to create the Mishcan.[13]

Rabbaynu Ovadia Sforno and others suggest that the commandment to create the Mishcan was a response to the incident of the Egel.[14] Sforno seems to maintain that the sin of the Egel demonstrated that the people remained vulnerable to the familiar attractions of idolatry. In order to assure that service to Hashem would not become tainted with idolatrous practices, this service was relegated to the tightly supervised environment of the Mishcan.

Rav Soloveitchik suggests that there is another element of the command to create the Mishcan that responded to the sin of the Egel. The Mishcan was created primarily through voluntary offerings. In other words, in response to the sin of the Egel the people were commanded to give tzedakah.[15]

In summary: Maimonides identifies tzedakah as an element of the teshuvah process. The Talmud asserts that tzedakah can even nullify a negative decree. Rav Soloveitchik explains that the relevance of tzedakah to teshuvah and forgiveness is demonstrated by the incident of the Egel. Hashem responded to this horrible sin by commanding the nation to engage in tzedakah.

Why is specifically the mitzvah of tzedakah associated with the teshuvah process? The Torah has many other commandments that seem to have the potential to restore the repentant sinner's relationship with Hashem. Observance of Shabbat and Torah study are powerful experiences of encounter with Hashem. Why are not these mitzvot associated with the teshuvah process? Furthermore, according to the Talmud, tzedakah has even the power to moderate a decree of punishment. From where does tzedakah derive its powerful efficacy?

4. Giving tzedakah to the extent of one's capacity

Maimonides makes an interesting comment that provides an important insight. He explains that the repentant individual should give tzedakah according to his capacity. The implication of this comment is that it is not the mere giving of charity that is associated with

---

[13] Rabbaynu Shlomo ben Yitzchak (Rashi), Commentary on Sefer Shemot 31:18.

[14] Rabbaynu Ovadia Sforno, Commentary on Sefer Shemot 31:18.

[15] Rav Soloveitchik explained that in the wilderness the implementation of a command to give tzedakah presented a unique challenge. Generally, tzedakah is given in order to provide for a less fortunate person's needs. In the wilderness, tzedakah could not be given for this purpose. Hashem provided miraculously for all of the needs of the people. He provided manna, water, and all other necessities. In order to implement a commandment to give tzedakah, some project was required to which the people would contribute. The Mishcan was the project that Hashem selected for this purpose. (Recorded lecture. See also Harerai Kedem, vol 1, p 76)

teshuvah. The repentant individual should give tzedakah to an extent that is personally substantial.

In order to understand the significance of this distinction, some explanation is necessary. All of us give tzedakah. How much do most of us give? The amount differs widely. So, does the proportion of income that one gives. Some give the requisite ten percent. Some give more and others less. In short, from a quantitative perspective, there is enormous diversity in giving habits. However, from a qualitative perspective, there is overwhelming consistency. Most people will give up to the point that requires personal sacrifice. When we reach the point at which further giving will require giving up something of significance, we stop giving. For example, if a person realizes by making a further or larger contribution to charity, he will have to postpone the anticipated purchase of a new car, he will not make the additional or larger donation. We each have our limit. However, the limit is generally determined by the same factor. Development professionals refer to it as the "ouch factor". Giving ends at the "ouch".

Maimonides' position is that the tzedakah is associated with teshuvah only when it evokes the "ouch". The contributor can afford it but he feels it. He is making a sacrifice. Why is this important?

What is repentance? It is the sinner abandoning his sinful behavior. He removes it from his thoughts. He commits in his heart to not repeat it (the behavior)... Also, he regrets the past (behavior)... (Maimonides, Mishne Torah, Laws of Repentance, 2:2)

5. Teshuvah is a behavioral and internal change

Maimonides describes the elements of teshuvah. Repentance is not only a commitment to reform one's behavior. It is also an analysis of one's past behavior. In fact, according to Maimonides, this honest reflection, assessment, and understanding of one's past behavior is an essential element of repentance. This seems odd. If a person reforms his behavior – for whatever reason – is he not repentant? He has embarked upon a new, more appropriate path. He is committed to turn his life around. Why must he return to his past, painfully recall his wrongdoings, dwell upon his errors and declare his regrets? The past cannot be changed! Why not focus on the future before us?

Apparently, teshuvah requires more than behavioral change. It demands that we reform our attitudes and refine our values. Introspection, value clarification, and reshaping of our attitudes and beliefs are as essential as the behavioral change. The process of teshuvah only achieves its full meaning when it is predicated upon purification of one inner-self.

When this process takes place in its entirety, the repentant individual changes his behavior because he understands that they were misguided. He sees his previous behavior as predicated upon false values, flawed beliefs, and erroneous notions. He is moved to change by a sincere sense of regret. He has emerged from darkness and confusion into the light of true understanding. He is a transformed individual.

6. Tzedakah and value clarification

Now, the association between tzedakah – as described by Maimonides – as teshuvah is obvious. A person who gives up to the "ouch" but no further has weighed the spiritual value of supporting a cause or need that he understands as compelling against his relatively trivial material desires. After weighing one against the other, he has decided his material desires are more important. This person is struggling to embrace the reality of spiritual values. However, he cannot fully incorporate into his decision making process a cognizance of the spiritual as imperative. His material desires and experiences remain more real and more compelling than spiritual values. He can give tzedakah up to the "ouch" but no further.

In overcoming the "ouch", a transformation takes place. A threshold is passed over. The spiritual asserts itself as more real and compelling than the fleeting gratification of material experiences and the meaningless pursuit of material desires.

This is the special significance and power of the tzedakah associated with teshuvah. It is predicated upon a process of value clarification. It is an extension and expression of the internal transformation that is essential to teshuvah. Through his tzedakah, the repentant individual reaffirms, demonstrates and implements his sincere transformation. The person who was condemned to be punished no longer exists. He has departed and been replaced by a new enlightened individual. The decree is nullified because the emergent individual is innocent of his predecessor's sins.

Realizing our Humanity

The repentant person should not imagine that he is far from the level of the righteous because of the iniquities and sins he has committed. This is not so. Rather, he is beloved and cherished before the Creator – as if he had never sinned. Furthermore, his reward is great, for he tasted the taste of the prohibited and he separated himself from it. He conquered his desires. Our Sages said:

> In the place that repentant individuals stand, the perfectly righteous cannot, there, stand. This means that their excellence is greater than the excellence of those who have never sinned because they (repentant individuals) conquer their desires more than they (who have never sinned).[16]

1. The greatness of the repentant individual

In the above comments, Maimonides – Rambam – addresses the ba'al teshuvah – the repentant person. He makes two related points. First, he assures this person that he is not tarnished by the sins from which he has repented. His relationship with Hashem is not compromised because of the wrongdoings from which he has repented.

Second, Rambam makes an important and amazing assertion. He explains that the ba'al teshuvah has achieved a higher degree of personal excellence through the process of sinning and then repenting. This is because he has experienced the pleasure of the sin and then rejected and disavowed the behavior. He has conquered his desires.

Rambam describes a person who has never sinned in his life. Who has achieved a higher level of personal excellence – this person, who has never sinned, or the repentant person? Rambam asserts it is the ba'al teshuvah. This is because the person who has never sinned is apparently endowed with a very unusual disposition. He does not struggle with containing his desires and controlling his passions. Acting properly comes naturally. In contrast, the ba'al teshuvah struggles to overcome his passions and to triumph over his desires. He has waged this

---

[16] Maimonides, Mishne Torah, Hilchot Teshuvah 7:4

battle and emerged victorious. Therefore, he has achieved the higher degree of personal excellence.

These comments are difficult to understand. Is not the goal to act properly and to not sin? If this is a goal, then the person who easily achieves it and endures no struggle is equally excellent. Consider an analogy. Imagine two sprinters. One is a natural and has won every competition in which he has entered. The other is not as naturally endowed and must work very hard to compete. He sometimes wins races and sometimes loses. These two sprinters face each other in a race and tie at the finish. Should the judges award the victory to the less naturally endowed contestant because he had to try harder? Of course not! Victory is defined by reaching the finish-line first. They both reached it at the same exact moment. Neither deserves to be awarded the victory more than the other. Yet, when it comes to observance of the Torah's commandments, Rambam asserts that the ba'al teshuvah is greater than the one who has never sinned. Why is this?

I bring to bear witness against you today the heavens and the earth. Life and death I have given before you – blessing and curse. Choose life so that you will live and your descendants.
(Devarim 30:19)

2. Freewill is a fundamental Torah principle

Moshe has described to the people the blessings that will be bestowed upon them if they observe the Torah and the consequences that will befall them if they abandon it. Now, he tells them that they must choose between these destinies. They can observe the commandments and secure the blessings or they can reject them and endure the consequences. It is their responsibility to make this choice.

What is Moshe's point? What is he telling the people that they do not know? Already, he has described their possible destinies in detail. Of course, it is up to them to choose the path they will tread!

Rambam explains that Moshe is making a very important point. We have freewill. Rambam asserts regarding freewill that "It is an important fundamental principle and it is a pillar of the Torah and the mitzvot."[17] We have the capacity to accept the Torah or disregard it. It is this capacity that obligates us to observe its commandments. Freewill makes us responsible for a decision to abandon the Torah. Freewill endows us with the capacity to repent and is the foundation of our obligation to engage in teshuvah – repentance.[18]

And the L-rd said: Let us make Adam in our form, in our likeness, and they will rule over the fish of the sea, the birds of the heavens, the animals, all the land, and all that swarms upon the land.
(Beresheit 1:26)

3. Freewill is a unique characteristic of human beings

The above pasuk introduces the creation of Adam – the first human being. Hashem describes Adam as a creature who will have the form and likeness of Hashem and His angels. Rabbaynu Ovadia Sforno comments that in some ways Adam will have the likeness of Hashem and in some respects, he will have the likeness of the angels. How is Adam ''like'' Hashem?

---

[17] Hilchot Teshuvah 5:3
[18] ibid 5:4, 7:1

Sforno explains that human beings are unique among all creations – including the angels. We have freewill. In this sense, we are like Hashem. Like Hashem we are the cause of our own actions.[19] In other words, the angels can only act as commanded by Hashem. They cannot initiate their own actions or programs. The elements and creatures of the universe formed by Hashem also lack volition. They respond to the unyielding commands of nature and its laws or to instinct. Only human beings are like Hashem; we have the capacity to choose, to initiate. We are the cause of our actions.

Other commentators differ with Sforno on his interpretation of this passage. However, they do not contest his observation that the human being is unique among all creations. The human being has the capacity to be like Hashem.

4. Emulating Hashem

This is an observation of fundamental importance. When one's life is ruled by instinct and passions, one has exchanged humanity for the existence of an animal or a rock. This person by wholly following the urges of instinct has sacrificed that unique gift that defines the human being – the capacity to choose to overcome instinct. When a person chooses to defy instinct and passion, to rise above one's material urges, this person is embracing one's humanity and emulating Hashem.

5. Repentance expresses the uniqueness of humanity

We can now return to Rambam's comparison of the ba'al teshuvah to one who has never sinned. Rambam championed the superiority of the ba'al teshuvah. Why is he greater than the person who never sinned? The highest expression of one's humanity is to choose the proper path. Both of these individuals have acted properly. However, the person who has never sinned is endowed with an unusual character. This person is not accosted by typical passions and urges. Therefore, he acts properly in every situation but not through making choices. He simply acts according to his character. The ba'al teshuvah intensely feels urges and passions. He has faltered and followed their counsel. But he has arisen, striven with desire, and made choices. He has used his freewill to wage a valiant battle and ultimately has triumphed. He has realized the highest expression of his humanity through choosing to observe the Torah – through demonstrating freewill.

"Do not think… that the Holy One, Blessed be He, decrees upon a person from the moment of creation that the individual will be a *tzadik* or *rasha*. It is not so! Rather every individual is capable of being a *tzadik* like Moshe or a *rasha* like Yiravam…." (Mishne Torah, Hilchot Teshuva 5:2)

Maimonides explains that we are endowed with freewill. We are the product of our choices. The Almighty does not decree upon any individual that this person will be wicked or righteous. Instead, the Creator empowers us. We choose, and through our choices, fashion ourselves.

Maimonides explains that we are not limited by predetermined constraints. Each of us can be as righteous as Moshe. This comment seems to contradict other statements by Maimonides. In Hilchot Yesodai HaTorah, Maimonides discusses prophesy. He explains the

---

[19] Beresheit 1:26

differences between the prophesy of Moshe and of other prophets. Maimonides comments that Moshe is the master of all prophets. His prophesy is distinguished from all prophets that preceded him and that follow him.[20] It seems clear that Maimonides maintains that no other individual will achieve the level of Moshe! Yet, in our text, Maimonides tells us that each of us can be a Moshe!

This question can be answered on different levels. On the simplest level, we can resolve this apparent contradiction through better understanding the phenomenon of prophecy. Maimonides explains that prophecy is not acquired through the unilateral efforts of the individual. Spiritual perfection is a prerequisite for prophecy. However, one's personal perfection does not assure that prophecy will be achieved.[21] Hashem may grant the person a vision. It is also possible that the Almighty will not respond with a prophetic communication.

This understanding of prophecy provides an obvious answer to our question. We can each achieve the righteousness of Moshe. It does not follow that this righteousness will secure the prophetic vision of Moshe. Prophecy, at its various levels, cannot be claimed through individual effort alone. The Almighty bestows prophetic vision. He has indicated that He will not elevate another individual to the prophetic level of Moshe.

We can also resolve our question in a different manner. Maimonides comments that any individual can be a *tzadik* like Moshe. What does the term *tzadik* mean? The term is derived from the word *tzedek*. *Tzedek* means justice. This indicates that the *tzadik* is a person associated with justice. Justice is a difficult concept to define. However, we can make the following observation. The concept of justice assumes the existence of an order within the universe and society. Justice requires that a person live within this order. Let us consider an example. Assume two individuals come to court. One claims to be owed money by the other. How does the court resolve the issue? The court assumes that an order exists. This order dictates specific rights between individuals. The court attempts to resolve the issue through applying these rights to this case. In short, justice is achieved through applying a system of order to the case.

What does this tell us about the *tzadik*? The *tzadik* wishes to fulfill his or her role in the universe created by the Creator. What is this role? It certainly differs for various individuals. However, we know the outline. We must observe the Torah and serve the Almighty. We are each created with unique talents and abilities. These traits dictate different specific roles for various individuals. No individual can be a prophet on par with Moshe. This is not part of our individual missions. However, personal righteousness is an expression of faithfulness to the highest role each individual can achieve.

Now we can understand Maimonides' comments. In order to be a *tzadik*, a person does not need to be as wise as Moshe or a prophet. Yet, every person can work towards fully actualizing his or her potential and fulfilling one's individual role.

"It is a *mitzvah* to eat and drink on the eve of *Yom HaKippurim* and to partake of an extensive meal." (Shulchan Aruch, Orech Chayim 604:1)

---

[20] Rabbaynu Moshe ben Maimon (Rambam) *Mishne Torah*, Hilchot Yesodai HaTorah 7:6.
[21] Rabbaynu Moshe ben Maimon (Rambam) *Mishne Torah*, Hilchot Yesodai HaTorah 7:5.

Shulchan Aruch explains that we are commanded to partake of an extensive meal on the eve of *Yom Kippur*. This *halacha* is discussed in the Talmud. The Talmud explains that one who eats and drinks extensively on the eve of *Yom Kippur* is regarded as having fasted for two days.[22]

The commentaries offer various explanations for this requirement. Rashi explains that the Torah requires us to partake of a substantial meal on the eve of the fast in order to prepare ourselves for the ordeal of fasting.[23]

Rashi essentially maintains that meal on the eve of *Yom Kippur* is a preparation for the fast. This is a difficult concept to understand. Every *mitzvah* requires preparation. On *Sukkot*, we live in the *Succah*. In order to fulfill this *mitzvah*, we must build a *Succah*. This is a necessary preparation for the fulfillment of the commandment. Yet, the building of the *Succah* is not regarded as a part of the *mitzvah* of living in the *Succah*. It is a preparation. In contrast, Rashi seems to indicate that preparation for *Yom Kippur*, through eating and drinking, is part of the actual performance of the command!

Rabbaynu Asher deals with this issue. He too, explains the requirement to eat and drink prior to the fast. He offers the same explanation as Rashi. However he adds important comments. He explains that this law is designed to demonstrate the Almighty's love for Bnai Yisrael. He offers a parable, which illustrates the concept. A king decrees that his son should fast on a predetermined date. He then commands his servants to feed his son on the day prior to the fast. The king wishes to assure that the son will be well prepared to endure the challenge of the fast. Similarly, the Almighty assigns us a day of the year to fast. This is an opportunity to atone for our transgressions. He than commands us to eat and drink the previous day. He wishes to help us through the ordeal.[24]

The comments of Rabbaynu Asher provide an answer to our question. The preparation for *Yom Kippur* is different from the preparations for *Sukkot*. We build a *Succah* because of strictly practical considerations. These preparations are not part of the actual *mitzvah* of living in the *Succah*. The preparations for *Yom Kippur* are not motivated by practical considerations. Instead, these preparations are designed to place *Yom Kippur* in the proper context. The day must be viewed as an expression of the Almighty's compassion for His people. This is accomplished through fulfilling the obligation of eating and drinking on the eve of the fast. This helps present *Yom Kippur* as an expression of the Almighty's compassion for His people. Therefore, the meal on the eve of *Yom Kippur* is a fundamental component of the actual *mitzvah*.

"For the commandment that I have commanded you today is not too difficult for you. Neither is it too distant from you." (Devarim 30:11)

"And you will return to Hashem your G-d and you will listen to His voice according to all that I have commanded you today – you and your children with all your heart and all your soul." (Devarim 30:2)

Communal and Individual Repentance

1. **Two *pesukim* one *Mitzvah***

---

22 Mesechet Yoma 81b.
23 Rabbaynu Shlomo ben Yitzchak (Rashi), *Commentary on the Talmud,* Mesechet Yoma 81b.
24 Rabbaynu Asher, *Commentary on the Talmud,* Mesechet Yoma, Chapter 8, note 22.

One of the 613 commandments is the *mitzvah* of repentance – *teshuva*. *Teshuva* requires an evaluation of one's behaviors and attitudes. This evaluation is followed by a decision to change. *Teshuva* is a very personal experience and an individual effort. The *Yamim Noraim* – the High Holidays – center upon the theme of *Teshuva*. Therefore, it interesting that so much of the activity of the *Yamim Noraim* takes place in a community or congregation. We spend long hours in synagogue. Many of the prayers we recite can only be recited in this public forum. Even our confessions, supplications and prayers for forgiveness take place in this communal setting. These are days that require personal introspection. Why is so much of our time spent in a public setting?

The two passages quoted above provide an important insight into the *mitzvah* of *Teshuva*. This insight will provide one response to our question.

In the first passage, Moshe admonishes the people regarding observance of a commandment. Moshe assures the people that they can perform this commandment. It is not too difficult or too complicated. They have the ability. To which commandment does Moshe refer?

The commentaries offer various responses to this question. Nachmanides suggests an answer based upon the surrounding context of the *pasuk*. He explains that Moshe is referring to the *mitzvah* of *teshuva*. He is assuring us that we have the ability to renew ourselves. We can change. Nachmanides contends that this passage is the source in the Torah for the *mitzvah* to *teshuva*.[25]

The second *pasuk* quoted above is from the same chapter of the Torah. In this passage also, Moshe discusses *teshuva*. In the passages preceding this *pasuk* Moshe predicts that the people will sin. They will be expelled from the land of Israel and forced into exile. In our *pasuk*, he assures Bnai Yisrael that they will ultimately repent. Once the nation repents, Hashem will redeem His nation from exile. Nachmanides contends that this second passage is also the source of the *mitzvah* of *teshuva*.[26]

This raises a question. Every *mitzvah* is derived from a single passage in the Torah. Other passages may amplify and add detail. However, the basic command is derived from a single *pasuk*. In Nachmanides' comments he seems to ignore this principle. He identifies two separate passages as the source for the *mitzvah* of *teshuva*.

2. Two types of *teshuvah*

Rav Ahron Soloveitchik suggests an answer to this question. This answer involves two simple steps. First, Rav Soloveitchik suggests that the citing of two sources suggests that there are two different commandments dealing with *teshuva*. In other words, each passage is the source for one of the two *mitzvot* of *teshuva*.

Second, Rav Soloveitchik defines these two separate *mitzvot*. He explains that the first passage is directed to the individual. This *mitzvah* of *teshuva* instructs the individual to repent. The second passage addresses the nation. It communicates another *mitzvah* of *teshuva*. This second *mitzvah* is placed upon the community. We are required to repent as a congregation.

---

[25] Rabbaynu Moshe ben Nachman (Ramban), *Commentary on Sefer Devarim* 30:11.
[26] Rabbaynu Moshe ben Nachman (Ramban), *Commentary on Sefer Devarim* 30:2.

In short, according to Nachmanides, there are two *mitzvot* of *teshuva*. One is a commandment upon the individual to repent. The second command admonishes the community to perform *teshuva*.[27]

This raises a new question. How are these two *mitzvot* different? Why are both needed? Why are the community and the individual commanded to perform *teshuva* by two separate *mitzvot*?

Perhaps, the answer lies in again considering the context of these passages. This second passage appears in the context of a prophecy. The people will sin. They will be exiled. They will repent – as a community – and they will be redeemed. The *mitzvah* of communal repentance is presented in the context of national redemption. *Teshuva* is described as the method for restoring Bnai Yisrael. This context reflects on the nature of the *mitzvah*. The context explains the basis for the communal imperative to repent. We must repent in order to restore Bnai Yisrael. We cannot be redeemed from exile without returning to Hashem.

The Torah is telling us that we have a mission and destiny as Bnai Yisrael. We are responsible for the fulfillment of this mission and destiny. We must be redeemed. We are responsible for our own redemption through the performance of *teshuva*.

Individual repentance is required for a very different set of reasons. This second form of repentance is a response to our individual sins and imperfections. The purpose of individual repentance is not national redemption. Its objective is personal and individual renewal and development. We must seek to perfect ourselves. We can only achieve this objective through ongoing, individual *teshuva*.

We can now answer our original question. Rosh HaShannah and Yom Kippur are devoted to *teshuva*. However, there are two *mitzvot* of *teshuva*. We are required to repent as individuals. We are also commanded to repent as a community. Therefore, the emphasis on community is appropriate. We should be concerned with our personal repentance. We must also be involved in the community's repentance.

When September 11 Precedes Yom Kippur

1. From where are personal values derived?

How do we develop values? Are our personal values a consequence of our education and our culture? Are there other factors that influence the emergence of an individual's personal ethical standards and moral priorities?

And He said to Avram: Know that your descendants will be strangers in a land that is not theirs. They will subjugate them and afflict them for four hundred years. And I will also judge the nation that they will serve. Afterwards, they will go forth with abundant possessions. (Beresheit 15:13-14)

2. The mystery of Bnai Yisrael's suffering in Egypt

In order to respond to this question, let us consider a difficult set of passages in the Torah. The above passages are a portion of a prophecy of Avraham. In this prophecy Hashem

---

[27] Rav Ahron Soloveitchik, *Sefer Perach Mateh Ahron*, (1997), volume 1, p 175.

reveals to Avraham that his descendants will develop into a great nation. He also reveals to Avraham that the journey of his descendants will include travails, terrible suffering, and persecution. They will experience four hundred years of exile. During their exile, they will be subjected to servitude. They will become the slaves of the citizens of their host country. Their masters will persecute and afflict them. Only after this period of intense suffering will they emerge as a nation with its own land and home.

Later in the Torah this prophecy is fulfilled. Avraham's descendants become residents of Egypt. There they are subjugated and made slaves. They are persecuted and even murdered. Only after enduring centuries of suffering are Avraham's descendants redeemed from Egypt and transformed into the nation of Bnai Yisrael.

The Torah does not provide an explanation for this persecution. Why was it deserved? If it was not the result of some terrible sin but the result of necessity, then what was that necessity?

Rav Yosef Dov Soloveitcvhik *Zt'l* suggests that the context of this prophecy of persecution suggests at least a partial explanation for it. Hashem is revealing to Avraham that his descendants will develop into a great nation. It is in this context that He tells Avraham about the suffering that is the destiny of his progeny. This context suggests that this terrible suffering was somehow fundamental to the nation-building process of Bnai Yisrael. Why was it essential?

3. The impact of a personal encounter with evil

Although we can develop an understanding of good and evil through an intellectual process, this process will not necessarily result in our own personal commitment to the good. The absolute commitment to a life of virtue often requires personal exposure to the opposite – exposure to intense evil. Exposure to evil transforms our intellectual concept of virtue into a meaningful personal ethic. Through this exposure one more vividly appreciates the immense destructive power of evil and hatred.

Rav Soloveitchik explains that the destiny that Hashem revealed to Avraham was not merely that his descendents would form a nation. Their destiny was to become a nation that would embody their forefather's values and ethics. They would teach to humanity Avraham's message of compassion and kindness. They would reject the mindless life of pagan hedonism and adopt a lifestyle committed to ethical treatment of others, pursuit of knowledge, and service to Hashem.

Certainly, Avraham would transmit his values and outlook to his descendants. They would be educated in the religion of Avraham. But would they share Avraham's commitment to these values and this outlook? How could a nation be formed that would fully commit itself to Avraham's revolutionary values? The Egypt experience helped assure this outcome.

Egypt was a laboratory of evil. However, Avraham's descendants were not passive observers of these demonstrations of humanity's capacity for evil. They were the subjects and victims of the demonstrations. In Egypt, Avraham's descendants came to understand the ethical degeneracy that is the product of the hedonist's decadence. They fully grasped the capacity of humankind to inflict terrible suffering upon one another. They comprehended the sinister power of hatred. They came to completely recognize the impact of the dehumanization of others and the malevolent behavior that this dehumanization evokes and promotes.

These lessons were designed to inspire Bnai Yisrael to be a different type of nation. They would be a people who would embrace and promote compassion for others. They would protect those who are poor or alone. They would welcome and sustain strangers. They would reject the decadence of pagan hedonism and replace it with a life devoted to the highest values. They would adopt and embrace as a national identity the values Avraham would transmit.[28]

4. 9/11 and the lessons learned from horror

Rav Soloveitchik's analysis suggests that we can learn from even the most dreadful personal experiences. Lessons of fundamental importance were powerfully communicated by the horror of the Egypt experiences. The encounter with intense evil can be the most effective means of communicating the value of virtue. From this perspective, the tragedy of human suffering can be moderated if we learn from the suffering. The tragedy of suffering is compounded if its lessons are unheard or unheeded.

The terrorist attacks of September 11, 2001 are one of the worst horrors that most of us have experienced. But there is a lesson that is communicated by the immensity of that tragedy. In order to identify that message, we will turn to Yom Kippur.

And Yona arose and he fled to Tarshish from before Hashem. He went to Yaffo and he found a ship that had arrived from Tarshish. He paid its fare and boarded the ship to travel with them to Tarshish from before Hashem. (Sefer Yona 1:3)

5. The story of Yona and his perspective

On the afternoon of Yom Kippur we read the Book of Yona. The book tells the story of the prophet Yona. Yona was commanded to travel to Ninveh, to rebuke its citizens, and warn them of their approaching doom. He was instructed to inform them that their repentance would save them. Doom and disaster would be avoided.

In the above passage, Yona rejects this mission and attempts to flee from before Hashem. He fails to escape. He reluctantly undertakes the mission that he abhorred. He preaches to the citizens of Ninveh and pleads with them to repent. They respond to Yona's message. They change their lives and reshape their destiny.

The text does not provide an explanation for Yona's resistance to Hashem's directive. The commentators offer a number of possibilities. Malbim explains that Ninveh was a great metropolis in the country of Ashur. Ashur was Israel's enemy. Yona feared that some time soon Ashur would march its armies against Israel. He concluded that saving Ninveh and Ashur would contribute to the destruction of his own people. Israel could be saved or at least preserved longer if Ashur would be destroyed. Yona made the decision to allow Ninveh to be destroyed for its sins rather than facilitate the misery and suffering of his own people.[29]

Yona was successful in saving Ninveh. However, he did not celebrate his success. Instead, he intensely mourned the approaching tragedy that he had facilitated.

Should I not have compassion for Ninveh – the great city? In it are more than one hundred twelve thousand people who do not know their right from left and much livestock. (Sefer Yona 4:11)

6. Hashem's response to Yona: the sacredness of human life

---

[28] Rav Yosef Dov Soloveitchik, *Yemai Zikaron* (Jerusalem, 1986), pp. 92-97.
[29] Rabbaynu Meir Libush (Malbim), *Commentary on Sefer Yona* 1:1.

Hashem again spoke to Yona. The above passage is the final words of Hashem's message. Hashem taught Yona the importance of every human being. Jew and non-Jew are created in the divine image. Hashem's love extends to all of His creations. Yona does not have the right to place the interests of Bnai Yisrael above the mission of saving the people of Ninveh.

What is the relevance of this reading on Yom Kippur? Rav Soloveitchik explains that throughout Yom Kippur we pray for personal salvation. We petition Hashem to spare our families, our communities, and our nation. However, on Yom Kippur all of humanity is judged. The fate of every human being – Jew and non-Jew – is decided. The reading admonishes us to not make Yona's mistake. We should not become so absorbed in our prayers for ourselves that we forget to have compassion for others. We review the lesson that Hashem taught to Yona, and through him, to us. Every human soul is precious. Every human being is fashioned in the Divine image.[30]

The horror of 9/11 is a powerful illustration of the impact of forgetting this lesson. How were intelligent, educated individuals capable of destroying so many innocent lives? Where was their compassion for the small children sitting in the seats of airliners that they transformed into lethal missiles? How could they not feel compassion for the families that would be deprived of father or mothers, the children that they would orphan that day?

The answer is that these terrorists were products of hatred and their vicious, merciless behavior is the expression of a jaundiced world-view shaped by this hatred. In this world-view those who are different in their religion, opponents in their political views, or members of another ethnicity are not human – or not as human. Their death and suffering is justified and even deserved. Attacker and victim do not share a common humanity. In this world-view there is no room for compassion or mercy on behalf of one's opponent.

The horror of 9/11 attests to the relevance and significance of the Book of Yona's message. It provides incontrovertible and compelling testimony to the importance of remembering that all human beings are Hashem's creations and that every life is sacred. We are all members of the community of humanity. The story of Yona compels us to include all of humanity in our prayers or to risk demeaning our own humanity.

The word of Hashem came to Yonah the son of Amittai, saying: Arise, go to Nineveh, that great city, and proclaim against it; for their wickedness is come up before Me. Yonah rose up to flee to Tarshish from the presence of Hashem; and he went down to Yaffo, and found a ship coming to Tarshish. He paid the fare for it. He went down into it, to go with them to Tarshish, from the presence of Hashem. (Sefer Yonah 1:1-3)

The Prophet who Defied G-d

1. Yonah's flight from before Hashem

Sefer Yona delivers an account of Yonah's mission to the people of Ninveh. He is directed by Hashem to warn the people of this non-Jewish nation, that Hashem is prepared to destroy them because of their wickedness. Yonah initially resists this mission but eventually relents. He delivers Hashem's message to the citizens of Nineveh. They respond to Yonah's message by repenting. The destruction of Nineveh is averted. However, Yonah is not pleased

---

[30] Rav Yosef Dov Soloveitchik, *Mesorat HaRav Yom Kippur Machzor* (N.Y., 2006), p. 692-693.

with this outcome. He is disappointed that Nineveh is spared. In the closing chapter of the book, Hashem provides Yonah with a revelation that addresses Yonah's anguish.

One of the most troublesome elements of the narrative is Yonah's initial refusal to carry out the mission to which Hashem appoints him. There are two questions that arise from Yonah's response. The first question to be considered is why was Yonah opposed to warning the people of Nineveh? One of the functions of a prophet is to rebuke the people and to urge them to be faithful to Hashem. Yonah was a prophet. He must have rebuked Bnai Yisrael many times during his tenure as a prophet of the nation. Yet, initially, he refused to warn the people of Nineveh of their forthcoming demise. Why did Yonah object to this assignment?

There are a number of responses suggested to this question. Malbim and others suggest that Yonah understood that Nineveh was the capital of an emerging political and military power. He also foresaw that this state would be an adversary of the Jewish people. He concluded that the destruction of Nineveh would benefit Bnai Yisrael. Therefore, he was reluctant to rescue a likely enemy of his own people.[31]

A similar answer is suggested by the Talmud and quoted widely among the commentators. Yonah strongly suspected that the people of Nineveh would indeed repent in response to his forecast of doom. This would starkly contrast with the response of the Jewish people to the many prophets that Hashem had sent to them. Despite the urgings of its prophets, the Jewish people had not repented. Yonah feared that the contrast between Bnai Yisrael's stubborn adherence to its wickedness and the immediate repentance of the people of Nineveh would render his people even more liable for their behavior. He did not want to bring further shame upon his people and magnify their failings.[32]

And he prayed to Hashem, and said: Please, Hashem, was not this my saying, when I was yet in my own country? Therefore I fled beforehand to Tarshish; for I knew that You are a gracious G-d, and compassionate, long-suffering, and abundant in mercy, and You repent from the evil.
(Sefer Yonah 4:2)

2. Yonah believes Hashem is too merciful

Neither of these explanations for Yonah's resistance is clearly stated in the text. In fact, the narrative describes Yonah's initial refusal to accept his mission without providing any explanation for Yonah's behavior. However, in the final chapter of the sefer, Yonah himself provides a very disturbing explanation for his attitude. He has delivered his warning to the people of Nineveh; they have repented. Hashem has spared them. Yonah says to Hashem that this is the outcome that he had feared from the moment he was assigned his mission. He understood that Hashem is merciful and forgiving. He anticipated that the people would repent and Hashem would spare them.

This is a remarkable complaint. Do we not benefit from Hashem's mercy and forbearance? We all sin and at times we act wickedly. Because Hashem is merciful and forgives us, we are spared from destruction and from the consequences we deserve. How can Yonah criticize Hashem's mercy?

---

[31] Rav Meir Leibush ben Yechiel Michel (Malbim), *Nachalat Yehoshua – Comm. on Yonah* 1:2.
[32] Michilta, Parshat Bo, Introduction.

Yonah was not objecting to Hashem's mercy. However, he believed that there is a point at which a wicked person has forfeited the right to be forgiven. He argued that at some point a person has been afforded adequate opportunity to repent his sins and to abandon his evil ways. If this point is passed and the person has not been moved to repent, then the person should be punished. Yonah was convinced that the people of Nineveh had passed this point. Their opportunity to repent and to be forgiven had passed. They did not deserve this last opportunity. They deserved to be punished.[33]

And he came there to a cave, and lodged there; and, behold, the word of the L-rd came to him, and He said to him, "What are you doing here, Elijah?" And he said, "I have been very zealous for Hashem the L-rd of hosts: for the children of Israel have forsaken your covenant, thrown down your altars, and slain your prophets with the sword; and I, even I only, am left; and they seek my life, to take it away." (Melachim 1 19:8-9)

3. Yonah refused to obey Hashem

Yonah's response to Hashem's instructions raises a second issue. Yonah had reason for questioning and resisting the mission Hashem assigned to him. However, we expect a prophet to surrender to the will of Hashem. Every person is required to observe the commandments of the Torah. Some of these commandments we do not understand. Some are beyond the realm of human comprehension. Despite our inability to comprehend the rationale of some of the commandments of the Torah, we observe them. Yonah received a personal commandment from Hashem. He was instructed to travel to Nineveh and warn the people of their impending doom. He did not understand and objected to the commandment. He should have suspended his own judgment, and submitted himself to the will of Hashem.

Furthermore, this is not the only instance in which a prophet declined a mission assigned to him by Hashem. The prophet Elijah – Eliyahu – declined to fulfill the mission assigned to him by Hashem. In the above passages, Eliyahu tells Hashem that he has acted zealously on behalf of

---

[33] Rav Ari Ginsberg
(http://www.yutorah.org/lectures/lecture.cfm/797608/Rabbi_Ari_Ginsberg/Yonah_-_Escaping_from_Hashem) develops more thoroughly Yonah's outlook. He notes that Maimonides explains in chapter 5 of his Laws of Repentance that repentance is not a right guaranteed to a person. Instead, it is a privilege. In some instances, Hashem does deprive a person of this privilege. The Torah describes Hashem hardening the heart of Paroh. This phrase means that Hashem deprived Paroh of the capacity to exercise his free will and chose to repent his sins. Hashem hardened Paroh's heart in response to his prolonged and stubborn wickedness. According to Maimonides, Hashem suspended Paroh's capacity to repent in order that he should receive the punishment he deserved. Maimonides provides other examples, from the Torah, in which Hashem suspended free will in order that a wicked person should receive the punishment deserved. Rav Ginsberg explains that Yonah understood the phenomenon described by Maimonides. Yonah believed that the people of Nineveh deserved the same fate as Paroh and the Egyptians. They should not be given further opportunity to repent. Instead, they should be destroyed for their sins. An interesting aspect of Maimonides' position is that Hashem never ignores a person's repentance. Regardless of the degree and extent of one's wickedness, if that person repents, he is saved from punishment. Therefore, when a person has exhausted Hashem's mercy and must be punished, his capacity to repent is suspended. He cannot repent and he receives the punishment that he deserves.

Hashem. The people have rejected the messages of the prophets that Hashem has sent to them. Rather than heeding their rebukes and warnings they have pursued, persecuted, and even murdered their prophets. Eliyahu does not want to continue to serve as prophet to the nation. They do not deserve continued warnings and opportunities to repent.

Eliyahu's objection is similar to Yonah's. He cannot understand Hashem's mercy. Is there not a point at which evil must be punished? Where is Hashem's justice? However, Eliyahu's behavior raises the same problem as Yonah's. Why did Eliyahu not submit to Hashem's will? We should not expect to fully understand Hashem's will. We must be obedient and serve Hashem even when we do not understand his commandments.

In summary, both Eliyahu and Yonah resisted the missions assigned to them by Hashem. Both were prophets. They were individuals of remarkable wisdom, humility, and virtue. Yet, somehow these exceptional individuals could not surrender to the will of Hashem and perform His commandments to them. How can we understand their behavior?

4. A prophet must be more than obedient

Perhaps, the answer lies in reconsidering the analogy between the commandments of the Torah and the personal assignment given to the prophet. The commandments of the Torah demand our obedience. Because observance of these commandments is an expression of obedience to Hashem, our performance is not compromised by our inability to understand the rationale underlying a commandment. In fact, obedience is an act of submission and surrender. In order to surrender to the authority of the Torah, we need not understand the rationale of its commandments.

Apparently, the prophet cannot discharge his mission simply through obedience. He must embrace and integrate into his outlook the mission that is assigned to him. Each personal commandment that is assigned to him is both a directive and a revelation. He cannot be obedient to the directive, yet untouched by the revelation. The revelation aspect must shape his outlook and his understanding of Hashem. In a sense, the prophet is required to partner with Hashem. He must embrace his mission and feel personally compelled by it. Hashem demands more from the prophet than obedience. He demands that he conform his thinking and outlook to the revealed truth of his mission.[34]

Now, Yonah's and Eliyahu's behaviors can be reinterpreted. They were not refusing to perform their missions. They were responding to their inability to integrate them into their outlook and thinking. Without this integration, they could not discharge their missions. In other words, neither refused to perform his mission. Each expressed his lack of capacity, his inability to understand his mission. Without this understanding the prophet cannot proceed.

5. Sefer Yonah's theme and Yom Kippur

Various explanations are offered for reading the story of Yonah on Yom Kippur. The variety and number of plausible explanations is understandable. Sefer Yonah deals extensively with the themes of *teshuvah* and *mechilah* – repentance and forgiveness. These themes are central to our observance of Yom Kippur. The lessons communicated by the story of Yonah provide us a deeper appreciation and understanding of these themes and the day.

---

[34] This explanation of Yona's and Eliyahu's behavior is similar to Rav Yisrael Chait's comments on this issue. (TTL catalogue # Sefer Yona N-042 and 043)

On Yom Kippur we appeal to Hashem for His mercy. We ask that he accept our repentance and forgive us for our sins and wrongdoings. We might feel that we are entitled to repent from our sins and to be forgiven by Hashem. The story of Yonah reveals that there is no simple explanation for Hashem's mercy and His acceptance of our repentance. Yonah could not understand the secret of Hashem's mercy and we should not assume that we have penetrated this mystery. Certainly, we should recognize that the opportunity to repent and to secure atonement is not an entitlement.

Sukkot

"You should dwell in *Sukkot* for seven days. Every member of the nation of Israel must dwell in *Sukkot*. This is so that your future generations will know that I caused Bnai Yisrael to dwell in *Sukkot* when I brought them forth from the land of Egypt. I am Hashem your G-d." (VaYikra 23:42-43)

Finding Purpose

1. Within your vision

Our passages describe a fundamental *mitzvah* of the festival of *Sukkot*. We are required to live in thatched huts – *Sukkot* – for seven days. The Torah explains the reason for this commandment. The *mitzvah* reminds us of the *Sukkot* of the wilderness. During the sojourn in the wilderness, the nation dwelled in these insignificant structures. These huts provided minimal protection from the harsh elements of the wilderness. Nonetheless, the nation survived the sojourn and even thrived. This experience provides testimony to the providence of the Almighty over His people. During the festival of *Sukkot,* we reenact the experience of the wilderness. Through this process we are reminded of the Almighty's providence.

In Tractate Succah, the Talmud suggests that an important law can be derived from these passages. The first mishne of the Tractate records various laws regarding the structure of the *succah*. One of these requirements is that the structure may not be higher than twenty cubits – the equivalent of thirty to forty feet. The mishne does not state the reason for this restriction. However, the Gemara poses the question. What is the reason for the limit on the *succah*'s height? The Talmud offers various explanations. One is derived from our passages.

The Sage Rabba suggests that our passages provide a reason for restricting the height of the *succah*. According to Rabba's interpretation, the passage requires the height of the *succah* to be consistent with the purpose or character of the structure. The essential component of the *succah* is its roof or covering. This covering must be composed of *sechach* – branches or vegetation. The character of the roof must be evident to its occupant. A person's immediate range of vision extends to a height of only twenty cubits. If the *succah* is within twenty cubits, the occupant is aware of the *sechach*. If the height exceeds twenty cubits, the *sechach* is above the person's range of vision. The occupant will not be cognizant of the *sechach*.[1]

2. Why is *Succah* different?

Rabba's position raises a number of questions. First, how does Rabba derive his principle from our passages? Our passages state that we are required to dwell in the *succah* during the festival. The passages also explain the reason for this *mitzvah*. It is intended to remind us of the huts in the wilderness. The passage does not seem to state any structural restriction.

The second difficulty with Rabba's position requires a brief introduction. The Torah contains 613 commandments. Each commandment has a reason or purpose. In some instances, the purpose of a commandment is not revealed. In other cases, the reason is revealed. What intentions or thoughts must a person have in performing a commandment? Certainly, a full understanding of a commandment enhances its performance. But what is the minimum cognizance required in performing a *mitzvah*?

---

[1] Mesechet Succah 2a.

There is a dispute among the Sages regarding this issue. Some maintain that a person must be aware that the activity is a commandment. Others take a different position. They assert that the person must consciously perform the activity required by the *mitzvah*. However, the person is not required to recognize that the performance is a commandment.

An example will illustrate the dispute. Assume a person picks us the Four Species. The person is not thinking about the activity and is barely aware of the action. Both authorities agree that the commandment has not been performed. Now, assume a person picks up the species. The action is done with intention and forethought. However, the person is not aware of the *mitzvah* of the Four Species. Has the commandment been performed? The more lenient view is that the *mitzvah* has been fulfilled. The more stringent view is that the commandment has not been performed. The person was not aware of performing a commandment.

It must be noted that neither position maintains that the person must be aware of the purpose of the *mitzvah*! This higher level of understanding and thought is not required for the minimal performance of a *mitzvah*.

We can now understand the second question on Rabba's position. Rabba maintains that the occupant of the *succah* must be aware of the *sechach*. Why is this necessary? The most obvious explanation is that the *sechach* reminds us of the purpose of the commandment. The occupant's awareness of the *sechach* assures recognition of the purpose of the *mitzvah*. In other words, performance of the *mitzvah* of *succah* requires cognizance of its purpose!

This requirement is an anomaly in *halacha*. At most, we are required to be aware that we are performing a commandment. Generally, a *mitzvah* is achieved without awareness of its purpose. In other words, Rabba posits that it is insufficient for the *succah* to merely reflect the purpose of the *mitzvah*. The height must assure that the occupant is actually aware of the purpose in performing the commandment. This level of awareness is not generally required.

3. A word or two

The commentaries offer a number of responses to our first question. One of the simple explanations is provided by Rabbaynu Nissim. He begins by acknowledging that the passages have a clear simple interpretation. The passages state a commandment and its purpose. He then explains that these objectives could be accomplished in a more concise manner. The passages could have merely stated that we are required to live in the *succah* during the festival because Hashem caused us to live in huts during the sojourn in the wilderness. Instead, the passages contain a seemingly superfluous phrase. This phrase is, "This is so that your future generations will know". This entire phrase could have been replaced by the single word "because". Every word and phrase in the Torah has a message. Rabba is providing an interpretation of the seeming verbose wording of the passages. The additional phrase has a message. The message is that the *succah* must be constructed in a manner that makes known to its occupants the purpose of the commandment. This is accomplished by restricting the height of the *succah*. Through this regulation, the *sechach* is within the visual range of the occupants. The *sechach* reminds these occupants of the purpose of the *mitzvah*.[2]

BaCh extends Rabbaynu Nissim's reasoning in order to answer our second question. He begins by noting an oddity in the Tur's discussion of the *mitzvah* of *succah*. The Tur is a code of

---

[2] R' Nissim ben Reuven, (Ran) *Notes to Com. of R' Yitzchak Alfasi*, Mesechet Succah 1a.

halacha. Generally, the Tur does not expound upon the theological purpose of commandments. However, in a few instances the Tur deviates from this policy. One of these instances is the *mitzvah* of *succah*. The Tur's discussion begins with an elaboration on the purpose of the *mitzvah*. The Tur then explain various laws and requirements of the *mitzvah* in light of its purpose.[3] BaCh asks the obvious question. Why does the Tur deviate from its usual method of presentation and digress into this theological discussion?

4. The proof is in the *halacha*

BaCh responds that the answer lies in our passages. Rabbaynu Nissim observes that the passages are apparently verbose. He explains that the seemingly extra phrase is establishing a structural requirement. BaCh asks a simple question. How do the passages communicate this message? He responds that the passages tell us that it is not sufficient for the *succah* to reflect its purpose. The *succah* must effectively communicate its message to the occupants. This communication is accomplished through fostering an awareness of the *sechach*. In other words, the passages establish a unique requirement for this *mitzvah*. The reason for the *mitzvah* must be communicated. Cognizance of purpose is fundamental to the performance of the commandment.

BaCh explains that now we can understand the Tur's digression into the purpose of the *mitzvah* of *succah*. In the case of most *mitzvot* this discussion is irrelevant. Performance of the commandment does not require appreciation of its purpose. The Tur's mission is to define the elements required for proper performance of the *mitzvah*. A discussion of the *mitzvah*'s purpose is not relevant to this objective.

The *mitzvah* of *succah* is different. Our passages establish a unique requirement for the fulfillment of the *mitzvah* of *succah*. In this instance, cognizance of purpose is fundamental to the proper performance of the *mitzvah*. Therefore, it is appropriate for the Tur to discuss this purpose.[4]

We can now answer our second question on Rabba. Our interpretation of Rabba is correct. He does acknowledge the role of a special cognizance in the performance of the *mitzvah* of *succah*. The structure must foster an awareness of purpose. Generally, this level of awareness is not needed. However, our passages establish a special requirement for the *mitzvah* of *succah*. In the performance of this *mitzvah,* cognizance of purpose is fundamental to the performance.

In sukkot you should dwell for seven days. Every citizen of Yisrael should dwell in sukkot. (This is) so that your generation will know that I caused Bnai Yisrael to dwell in sukkot when I brought them forth from the Land of Egypt. I am Hashem your G-d. (VaYikra 23:42-43)

Sukkot, Fantasy, and Delusion

1. The succah commemorates the wilderness experience

In Sefer VaYikra, the Torah describes the commandment to dwell in sukkot during the celebration of Sukkot. The Torah explains that we are required to perform this commandment as a commemoration of the sojourn of our ancestors in the wilderness following their rescue from

---

3   Rabbaynu Yaakov ben HaRash, *Tur Shulchan Aruch, Orech Chayim* 625.
4   Rav Yoel Sircus, (BaCh), *Bayit Chadash Commentary on Tur*, *Orech Chayim* 625.

Egypt. The sukkot in which we live during the celebration of Sukkot recall the sukkot in which our ancestors dwelled during their travels.

The Sages dispute the meaning of the Torah's reference to the sukkot of our ancestors. According to Ribbi Eliezer, the sukkot of our ancestors were the cloud that accompanied and protected our ancestors in the wilderness. According to Ribbi Akiva, our ancestors fashioned for themselves shelters similar to our sukkot and these flimsy shelters provided them with protection from the harsh elements of the wilderness' environment. However, regardless of the specific nature of our ancestors' sukkot, the meaning and significance of our observance is clear. Sefer HaChinuch explains that we live in sukkot to recall the wilderness experience of our ancestors. Our ancestors traveled through and survived the hostile environment of the wilderness. Hashem protected and sustained them and brought them to the Land of Israel. We celebrate the festival and live in our sukkot in order to recall our ancestors' miraculous experience in the wilderness and, through recollection, we acknowledge Hashem and thank Him for His mercy and kindness.[5]

However, on the fifteenth of the seventh month when you gather the produce of the land you should observe a celebration for Hashem for seven days. The first day should be observed as a Sabbath and the eighth day should be observed as a Sabbath. (VaYikra 23:39)

2. Sukkot is a harvest festival

Rashbam suggests an alternative understanding of the mitzvah of dwelling in the succah. His analysis addresses two issues in the above passage. First, the passage indicates that the Sukkot festival is to be observed in the fall. The events that the festival recalls were initiated with our redemption from Egypt in the springtime. At that time, Bnai Yisrael were redeemed from Egypt and entered the wilderness. Why is the commemoration of wilderness experience postponed to the fall? Second, the above passage relates the Sukkot festival to the conclusion of the harvest season with the in-gathering of the grain from the fields. What is the connection between Sukkot and the conclusion of the harvest season?

Rashbam's response begins with a discussion of the feelings and attitudes evoked by the successful harvest. As the harvest season is concluded and the grain is gathered from the fields and stored away, a sense of accomplishment can be expected to emerge. However, this sense of accomplishment can evolve into a feeling of pride, exaggerated self-assurance, and unwarranted security. The harvest has been gathered and stored away for the season. We feel secure in the conviction that our material needs will be met. We will have food for our tables and grain for trade. We are proud that through our efforts, we have secured prosperity. We feel assured that we have the power to manipulate the forces of nature to fulfill our will and conform to our needs. The abundance of the harvest testifies to our conquest over our environment.

Lest you eat and be satiated and you will build good houses and dwell (therein). You will become haughty and forget Hashem your G-d that brought you out from the Land of Egypt, from the house of bondage... And you will say in your heart my strength and the power of my hand made for me this wealth. You should remember that Hashem your G-d, He gives you the power to create this wealth in order to fulfill the covenant that He vowed to your forefather as He (fulfills) today. (Devarim 8:12-18)

3. Unwarranted security leads to abandonment of Hashem and His Torah

---

[5] Rav Aharon HaLeyve, Sefer HaChinuch, Mitzvah 325.

Rashbam notes that Moshe warned that this very attitude leads to abandonment of Hashem. Moshe explained that if we adopt this inflated sense of self-reliance and mastery over our destiny, we will quickly forget that Hashem is the source of our success and accomplishments.

Rashbam suggests that it is at this moment of unrestrained self-satisfaction that we must remind ourselves of the wilderness experience. We recall that Hashem miraculously sustained our ancestors in the wilderness, and through this recollection, we will understand that the success of our harvest is not a consequence of our power to manipulate nature. It is an expression of Hashem's omnipotence. This explains the observance of the festival at the end of the harvest season, in the fall. It is at this time of the year that the message of the festival is most relevant – even imperative.[6]

Rashbam's comments require some interpretation. He identifies an issue that the festival of Sukkot addresses – the unfounded sense of self-sufficiency and power that may be evoked by a successful harvest. He identifies the Torah's means of addressing this issue – through recalling the miracles of the wilderness experience. However, he does not explicitly explain how this recollection corrects our misconceptions and faulty self-perception. Furthermore, Rashbam notes that this attitude of false self-sufficiency will lead to abandonment of Hashem and His Torah. Indeed, this concern was expressed by Moshe. But Rashbam does not explain how this overestimation of our own control over our fates affects a denial of Hashem.

And He afflicted you and He caused you hunger and He fed you the manna that you had not known and your ancestors had not known in order to make known to you that it is not on bread alone that man lives but on all brought forth by the word of Hashem man lives. (Devarim 8:3)

4. The desire for security and the delusions it induces

The above passage is from Moshe's final address to the people. He discusses with them the meaning and significance of the wilderness experience. He explains that Hashem led the nation into the wilderness. He allowed them to experience suffering and hunger and then rescued them from starvation with the mun – manna. Moshe provides an enigmatic explanation for this process of suffering and salvation. Hashem did this in order to demonstrate to the people that humankind does not require bread to be sustained. Hashem can sustain humankind with anything brought forth by His word. What does Moshe mean? What is this lesson of the wilderness experience that he is attributing to Hashem?

Moshe seems to suggest that Hashem led Bnai Yisrael into the wilderness in order to place the nation in a completely helpless situation. He allowed the people to experience affliction and even severe hunger. He then rescued the nation from agony and starvation through providing all of the nation's needs. Why did Hashem first afflict the nation and then rescue the people from the very suffering He had brought upon them? He did this in order to reduce the nation to a state of complete helplessness and despair. Then, through rescuing the people, He demonstrated their complete dependence on Hashem. In other words, Moshe seems to say that Hashem wished to strip from the people any sense of self-reliance and control over their own destiny. He wished to place the people in a situation in which they would be clearly and completely dependent on Hashem. Only when the nation fully recognized its absolute dependency on Hashem did He rescue the nation and provide for its needs.

---

[6] Rabbaynu Shemuel ben Meir (Rashbam) Commentary on Sefer VaYikra 23:43.

This seems to be Moshe's message. However, the message is completely amazing! Moshe is suggesting that Hashem deemed it necessary to demonstrate to the nation He rescued from Egypt that it is completely dependent upon Hashem. Moshe's interpretation of the wilderness experience implies that the redeemed nation harbored a false sense of security and power. This seems absurd! These people were newly freed slaves. Certainly, slaves are well aware of their vulnerability and helplessness!

The conclusion that must be drawn from Moshe's interpretation of Hashem's actions is that even an oppressed and subjugated slave can easily overestimate his influence over his destiny and may not fully understand his actual vulnerability and dependence on Hashem. How can this be?

Apparently, human nature compels us to seek a sense of security. We need to feel that we have some safety and stability in our lives. We are incapable of living in constant fear and anxiety. Therefore, we strive to insulate ourselves from the forces that we feel threaten our safety and security. We attempt to assert control over any and every aspect of our environment and surroundings that we regard as significant to our safety and well-being. Even a slave is subject to this aspect of human nature. He knows that he is subject to the will of his master. Yet, he attempts to assert control wherever possible and to sustain whatever stability and security possible. More significantly, our need to feel safe and secure – to alleviate our fears and anxieties over the uncertainty of our destinies – seduces us into retreating into a fantasy in which we exaggerate our influence over our destinies.

5. The wilderness experience as an antidote to delusion

This conception of human nature resolves two of the questions posed above. First, Moshe's interpretation of Hashem's strategy can be understood. Even the slaves, rescued from a horrid life of persecution, did not fully appreciate their complete dependence upon Hashem. In the wilderness, Hashem stripped these freed slaves from every false and fantastic delusion of control and influence over their own fate. In the wilderness, they entered into a state in which it was impossible to maintain any vestige of such fantasies. Day-to-day survival was completely a consequence of Hashem's miracles and kindness.

The pathway from personal accomplishment and success to rejection of Hashem can also be understood. If a lowly slave is susceptible to delusions of personal power and influence, then a successful, accomplished person is even more vulnerable to such fantasies. Success and personal accomplishment provide "evidence" of our power and influence over our destinies and environment. Our successes resonate with our need to perceive our lives as safe and secure. We imagine that these successes "prove" that we are indeed in-control of our fates and that we need not fear the future. We can care and provide for ourselves and meet any challenges that we may face. In our flight into a fantasy of control and security, we obscure our fundamental helplessness, vulnerability, and dependence upon Hashem.

6. The contrast between human perceptions and the reality described by the Torah

This discussion can be viewed from another perspective. The message of Moshe in his interpretation of the wilderness experience and in his warning to the people is that there is a fundamental conflict between our innate perceptions and the reality described by the Torah. We seek security and safety. We strive to create stability in our lives and delude ourselves into exaggerating the degree to which we control of our destinies. To the extent that we imagine that we control our destinies, we do not need Hashem. The Torah's reality is quite different from our fantasies. In the Torah's reality, humanity is frail and helpless. We are expected to act on our own behalf and to seek to better ourselves and our world. However, ultimately the success of our efforts and strivings depend upon Hashem. A person who is scrupulously conscientious in regards to his health may fall victim to cancer. A city that carefully plans its neighborhoods, transportation system, and infrastructure can, in a moment, be devastated by an earthquake. Plagues and diseases can threaten thriving cities, states, and even nations. We certainly cannot prevent a meteor from striking the earth and destroying all life! Ultimately, we are dependent on Hashem. We are relatively minor players in the drama of human advancement. One of the fundamental objectives of the Torah is to help us abandon our delusion and see reality as described by the Torah. Rashbam is suggesting that the festival of Sukkot is one of the measures in the Torah designed to instill within us an accurate appraisal of reality and the limits of our influence over our fates.

How does Sukkot accomplish this? Possibly, Sukkot reminds us that even our ancestors – newly freed slaves – were victims of delusions of security. They required the experience of the wilderness – an experience of total reliance on Hashem – to correct their false perceptions. If these freed slaves were capable of nurturing fantasies of control over their destinies, then we certainly need to examine our attitudes and free ourselves of fantasy and delusion.

The foundation of foundations and the pillar of all wisdom is to know that there exists a primary existence that gives existence to all existence and all that exists from the heavens to the earth and all between them only exists consequential to His absolute existence. (Maimonides, Moshe Torah, Hilchot Yesodai HaTorah 1:1)

7. Even our limited control over our destinies is only apparent

However, there is another possible explanation of the role of Sukkot in addressing our delusions of control. As explained above, human nature seeks security and this drive can encourage fantasies of control. However, to what extent do we ever have control or power over our destiny or environment? Is our control ever real or is it always merely imagined?

In order to consider this issue, it is helpful to begin with an analogy. Each weekday morning, I get into my car and I drive to school. I imagine that I arrive at school as a consequence of personal endeavor and effort. But let us consider the issue more carefully. I drive a car I neither designed nor constructed. It is fueled by gasoline I did not refine or bring to market. I travel on roads I did not build and which I do not maintain. Actually, my role in bringing myself to school is remarkably minor. I merely take advantage of the wisdom, work, and planning of so many others whom I do not even know! Without them, I would be walking to school. No, I would walk to the shore of Lake Washington and swim to Mercer Island!

The universe in which we live is Hashem's creation. He fashioned it, brought it into existence, and sustains it every moment. My every accomplishment, every act, merely utilizes the resources, properties, and natural laws which are expressions of Hashem's will. I only take advantage of the wonders He created and sustains. It is not accurate for me to describe my arrival at school as a consequence of my efforts and endeavors. Similarly, it is foolish for me to imagine that I am the source of any accomplishments; I am merely availing myself of the resources with which Hashem provides me.

In other words, although we are most aware of Hashem's omnipotence when confronted with a miracle or a breach of the natural order, it is the created universe that is the most wondrous and consistent manifestation of His omnipotence. The miracle demonstrates that Hashem is the creator and sustainer of the universe and can therefore, suspend or abrogate its laws. However, once His omnipotence is demonstrated through miracles, then His universe provides constant testimony that He is its creator and sustainer.

The miracles of the wilderness demonstrated to the nation His omnipotence. Through this demonstration, they came to understand He is Creator and He sustains all existence. We are not the cause of our accomplishments. We merely avail ourselves of the resources He places before us. The celebration of Sukkot reminds us of the miracles of the wilderness and the lesson of Hashem's omnipotence that they communicate.

"A lulav that is stolen or dried out is disqualified." (Tractate Succah 3:1)

Praising Hashem

1. Glorifying Hashem

One of the unique commandments of the festival of Sukkot is the requirement to take the four species. The four species are the palm branch, citron, two willow branches, and three myrtle branches. The mishne above explains that a lulav – a palm branch – that is dried-out is unacceptable. The mishne does not provide a reason for this law. However, Rashi explains that we are required to use a lulav that is beautiful, and one that is dried-out does not meet this requirement. What is the source for the requirement that the lulav be beautiful? Rashi suggests that the requirement is derived from the passage, "This is my G-d and I will glorify Him."[7]

Some background information is required to understand Rashi's suggested derivation for this requirement. In Tractate Shabbat, the Talmud explains that there is a general requirement to beautify mitzvot. The Talmud derives this requirement from the passage quoted by Rashi – "This is my G-d and I will glorify Him."[8] The Talmud explains that we should beautify ourselves before Hashem with mitzvot. The Talmud provides specific examples. Our succah should be beautiful; our lulav should be beautiful; our tzitzit – the fringes we are required to place upon the corners of four-cornered garments – should be beautiful; a Sefer Torah should be beautiful.[9] The Talmud is teaching us that we should not merely create a succah that meets the minimum requirements. We should build a beautiful succah. Similarly, when securing other objects that will be used in the performance of a commandment, we should not be satisfied with an object that meets the minimum specifications. We should try to secure an object whose beauty surpasses these minimum requirements.

Rashi's comments seem to indicate that the dried-out lulav is disqualified because it does not meet the general requirement to beautify mitzvot. Tosefot identify a number of difficulties with Rashi's explanation. We will focus on one of these objections. Tosefot notes that the general requirement to beautify mitzvot – derived from "This is my G-d and I will glorify Him" – is not fundamental to fulfilling the commandment. For example, if one builds a succah that

---

[7] Rabbaynu Shlomo ben Yitzchak (Rashi), *Commentary on the Talmud,* Mesechet Succah 29a.
[8] Sefer Shemot 15:2.
[9] Mesechet Shabbat 133b.

meets the essential requirements, but does not fulfill the requirement of beautification of the commandment, one can still fulfill the mitzvah with this succah. Tosefot offer an even more compelling example in order to prove their point. The Talmud explains that the lulav, the willow branches, and the myrtle branches should be bound together. The Talmud explains that this is an expression of the general requirement derived from the passage, "This is my G-d and I will glorify Him."[10] Nonetheless, if one does not bind these species together, one fulfills the commandment. Clearly, even in the case of the four species, meeting the requirement of beautification is not essential to fulfilling the basic commandment. Based on these two questions, Tosefot reject Rashi's explanation for the disqualification of the dried-out lulav.[11]

How can Rashi's position be explained? It is clear that Rashi must acknowledge that meeting the general requirement to beautify mitzvot is usually not essential to the fulfillment of the commandment. But, Rashi seems to contend that in this case – the four species – this requirement is raised to a higher level and therefore, it becomes essential. According to Rashi, why is the mitzvah of the four species special?

2. Beautification of a Mitzvah

Are there any other instances in which meeting the requirement for beautification is essential? There is one other instance in which fulfilling this requirement is essential. The Talmud explains that in writing a Sefer Torah, the name of Hashem must be written with intention. In other words, each time the scribe writes Hashem's name, he must do so with the specific intention to write this name. If this requirement is not fulfilled, the Sefer Torah is rendered invalid. The Talmud asks whether there is a corrective measure that can be taken if the name of Hashem is written without the required intentions. Can the scribe rewrite the name – with the required intention – over the existing letters that were inscribed without the required intention? The Talmud rejects this solution. So, even if the scribe rewrites the name over the unintended original letters, the Sefer Torah is not acceptable. The Talmud continues to explain the basis for its position. It comments that the Sefer Torah must meet the requirement of beautification expressed in the passage "This is my G-d and I will glorify Him." The rewriting of Hashem's name will result in an inconsistent appearance. The rewritten name of Hashem will be darker than the surrounding text. This detracts from the appearance of the text and renders it invalid.[12]

It emerges that in some cases, beautification is essential, and in other cases, the basic mitzvah can be fulfilled without beautification. How can this distinction be explained? What determines whether the requirement of beautification is essential to the performance of the mitzvah?

3. Associate with G-d

Rav Yosef Dov Soloveitchik Zt"l suggests an explanation for the law of the Sefer Torah. He explains that the issue of whether beautification is essential is determined by the level of association between the object of the mitzvah and Hashem. Most objects used in the performance of a mitzvah are only associated with Hashem, himself, in the sense that they are used to serve Him. A succah is associated with Hashem because we use it to fulfill a mitzvah commanded by

---

[10] Mesechet Succah 11b.

[11] Tosefot, Mesechet Succah 29b.

[12] Mesechet Gitten 20a.

Him. Let us compare this to the name of Hashem in a Sefer Torah. The name of Hashem is not associated with Hashem merely because the Sefer Torah is used to serve Hashem. The name is more directly associated with Hashem. It is the word that we use to refer to Hashem. Rav Soloveitchik suggests that the closeness of this association demands a higher degree of requirement for beautification. The requirement of beautification is absolute. It must be met in order for the commandment to be fulfilled.[13]

It should be noted that Rav Soloveitchik's conclusion is very consistent with the passage. The passage tells us that we must glorify Hashem. Although this is accomplished through the beautification of mitzvot, the objective is to glorify Hashem. The degree of association of the object with Hashem determines the level of the requirement of glorification. The name of Hashem is directly associated with Him. It follows that the requirement to glorify Him will express itself most fully – as an absolute requirement – in writing His name in a Sefer Torah. The beautification of other objects used in mitzvot also glorifies Hashem. However, the glorification is less direct. This is because the object is only associated with Hashem because it is used in the performance of a mitzvah. It is not a direct reference to Hashem.

Rav Soloveitchik's comments explain the reason for an absolute requirement of beautification of the name of Hashem in a Sefer Torah. How can this reasoning be applied to the lulav? Rav Soloveitchik suggests that in order to answer this question, we must have a clearer understanding of the nature of the mitzvah of the four species.

4. The four species

Maimonides explains that the mitzvah of the four species is fulfilled with their lifting. In other words, when a person lifts up the species, he has fulfilled the commandment. However, the mitzvah is only fulfilled in its entirety when the species are waved during the recitation of the Hallel.[14] Maimonides' comments indicate that there is a fundamental relationship between the Hallel and the four species. What is this relationship? Hallel is composed of praise to Hashem. The association of the four species with Hallel seems to indicate that the waving of the four species is an act of praise to Hashem.

This insight solves another problem. We fulfill the mitzvah of the four species all seven days of the festival. However, the Torah level obligation is limited to the first day. The Sages established the obligation to perform the mitzvah of the other six days of the festival. However, in the Bait HaMikdash – the Sacred Temple – the Torah level obligation extends to all seven days of the festival. The seven-day obligation in the Bait HaMikdash is expressed in the passage, "And you should rejoice before Hashem your G-d seven days."[15] Our Sages explained that the term "before Hashem" refers to the Bait HaMikdash. The phrase "you should rejoice" refers to the performance of the mitzvah of the four species. This raises an important question. Why does the passage not make specific reference to the mitzvah of the four species? Why does the passage replace a direct reference with the somewhat vague instruction to rejoice?

Rav Soloveitchik explains that this problem can be resolved based on a comment of Maimonides. Maimonides explains that although we are required to rejoice on all festivals, this requirement is more extensive on Sukkot. Maimonides explains that this obligation is fulfilled

---

[13] Rav Yosef Dov Soloveitchik, *Harerai Kedem*, volume 1, p 222.
[14] Rabbaynu Moshe ben Maimon (Rambam) *Mishne Torah*, Hilchot *Lulav* 7:9-10.
[15] Sefer VaYikra 23:40.

through the special services performed in the Bait HaMikdash all seven days of the festival. In Maimonides' description of these services, the main component is the singing of praises of Hashem.[16] It is clear from Maimonides' comments that rejoicing is primarily expressed through giving praise to Hashem.

Based on Maimonides' comments, we can reinterpret the passage above. It is not merely telling us to rejoice in the Bait HaMikdash for the seven days of the festival. It is instructing us to rejoice through offering praise to Hashem.

As explained above, our Sages understood this requirement - to rejoice through praise - as the source for the mitzvah to perform the mitzvah of the seven species all seven days of the festival in the Bait HaMikdash. This indicates that the mitzvah of the seven species is clearly an expression of praise to Hashem. The Torah refers to the obligation to perform the mitzvah of the four species as an act of rejoicing in order to communicate the basic nature of the mitzvah. The Torah is teaching us that this mitzvah is an act of rejoicing – through offering praise to Hashem.

5. Absolutely beautiful

Rav Soloveitchik explains that the nature of the mitzvah of the four species accounts for the absolute requirement of beautification. The mitzvah is essentially to praise Hashem through the four species. It is only reasonable that an object used for the praise of Hashem should fulfill the requirement of, "This is my G-d and I will glorify Him." It is incomprehensible that an object lacking beauty should be acceptable as a vehicle of praise.[17] This is consistent with the general principle of beautification. The closer an object is associated with Hashem, the more stringent is the requirement. Rav Soloveitchik notes that an object used to praise Hashem is more closely associated with Hashem than an object used in the performance of another mitzvah. Therefore, objects used in praise are treated more stringently.

It should be noted that not all requirements of beautification of the four species are absolute. It is required to bind the lulav with the myrtle and willow branches. However, if they are not bound together, the commandment is still fulfilled. Even in the instance of the four species, some beautification requirements are absolute and others are not. Rav Soloveitchik's analysis suggests a basis for this distinction. It follows from his analysis that those beautification requirements that relate to the object used in praise are absolute. The object is not acceptable if it does not meet these requirements. Therefore, the dried out lulav is disqualified. However, it seems that the binding is not a beautification of the objects. Instead, the binding is a beautification because it facilitates the performance of the mitzvah. In other words, the mitzvah can be performed less awkwardly through the binding. Rashi seems to maintain that those beautifications that pertain to the object used in praise are essential. Those that facilitate the activity of taking the lulav – the binding – enhance the performance of the mitzvah; but they are not absolute requirements.

Rav Soloveitchik's analysis provides two important insights into the festival of Sukkot. First, he provides a basic understanding of the mitzvah of the four species. Rav Soloveitchik demonstrates that this mitzvah is essentially a process of offering praise to Hashem.

---

[16] Rabbaynu Moshe ben Maimon (Rambam) *Mishne Torah*, Hilchot *Lulav* 8:12-13.
[17] Rav Yosef Dov Soloveitchik, *Harerai Kedem* , volume 1, p 222.

Second, Rav Soloveitchik explains the nature of our rejoicing on festivals, and especially on Sukkot. Our rejoicing is an expression of our appreciation of our relationship with Hashem. For this reason, it is expressed through the offering of praise.

Forgive us our father for we have sinned…. (Weekday Amidah)

Where Did Hashem Go? He's Waiting for Sukkot!

1. The close of Yom Kippur and the sense of Hashem's departure

Immediately after the completion of Yom Kippur we recite the weekday Maariv/Aravit service – the evening service. The service includes the Amidah which is composed of nineteen berachot – benedictions. The sixth benediction is a petition to Hashem for forgiveness. This blessing is the basis of an amusing witticism. How is it possible that a few moments after the completion of Yom Kippur, which hopefully secured Hashem's forgiveness, we are again asking for His forbearance? What sin could we have committed in these few moments? The answer is that in our eagerness to rush home and break our fast, we barely pay attention to the prayers we are reciting. The very manner in which we are praying is the sin that requires forgiveness.

Of course, the question is only asked for the purpose of introducing the answer. The true answer to the question is very simple. The Amidah has a specific design and the weekday version is composed of its nineteen benedictions. Whenever the weekday version is recited all of the blessings are included. However, although the question is not serious, the answer does capture a disturbing paradox. Yom Kippur is a day of solemn majesty. We stand before Hashem and we are being judged. Our actions are being reviewed and our destiny decided. We are overcome with awe. We sense the presence of the Divine influence. Rav Yosef Dov Soloveitchik Zt"l compared the Shofar blast sounded at the end of the Yom Kippur service to the blast heard by Bnai Yisrael after the Sinai Revelation. That blast communicated that Revelation had ended and that Divine influence had "ascended" back to the heavens. The Shofar blast at the close of the Yom Kippur service communicates that our encounter with Hashem has ended. Our sense of intimacy with Him is lost.[18]

How do we translate the Yom Kippur experience into an ongoing awareness of Hashem's presence or influence? How do we extend the intimacy of Yom Kippur into the whole year?

You are sacred and Your name inspires awe. There is no other G-d like unto you, as it is written, "And Hashem the Lord of Hosts will be exalted in judgment and the sacred G-d will be sanctified in justice." (Amidah of High Holidays)

2. The High Holidays and Hashem's reign over the universe

The first step in answering this question is to more carefully consider the capacity of the Yamim Noraim – the High Holidays to inspire us. There are two inter-related elements of the Yamim Noraim that endow these days with their inspirational power. The first is that these days celebrate Hashem's kingship over the entire universe. Repeatedly we describe Him as master of all. We recognize that every event that occurs and every process that takes place is an expression of His will. He is revealed in the blowing of the wind and the shining sun. The spider inexorably spinning its web is responding to the nature that the Creator implanted within it. The branch

---

[18] Rav Herschel Schachter, Recorded lecture, YUTorah.org.

reaching up to the rays of the sun is acting according to a set of commandments decreed by the ruler of all natural phenomena.

We come to understand that during the Yamim Noraim we are participating in an inexplicable drama. This omnipotent ruler of all that exists eagerly beckons us – mortal, powerless, flawed creations – to return to Him and renew our relationship with Him.

Blessed are You, Hashem, the King Who pardons and forgives our iniquities and the iniquities of His people, the Family of Israel and removes our sins every year, King over all the world, Who sanctifies Israel and the Day of Atonement (Yom Kippur Amidah)

3. The High Holidays and judgement

Second, we recognize that the King has ascended His throne and is judging His subjects. No one can escape His judgment and His decree cannot be ameliorated. We recognize that our destiny is being decided by Hashem – who knows all and whose judgment is absolute.

These perceptions overcome the illusions we foster regarding our destiny. Generally, we consistently assure ourselves that we control our fates. We believe in the power of our own wisdom, the efficacy of our efforts, and our capacity to overcome all obstacles by dint of our determination. The Yamim Noraim strip away this self-indulgent illusion. They break through the barriers of conceit that we have erected around us and impose upon us the realization that we are actually puny, impotent creatures. We lack the capacity to protect ourselves from a virus carried by a tiny insect – one the most insignificant creatures in our environment. How can we delude ourselves into believing that we are the masters of our destiny? Within us emerges the realization that we are completely dependent upon Hashem. Our destiny is determined by His decree and we are powerless to defy His will.

And You gave us, Hashem our G-d, with love, this day of Yom Kippur for pardon and forgiveness, and to pardon on it all of our sins, a sacred occasion, a memorial to the exodus from Egypt. (Yom Kippur Amidah)

I am for my beloved and my beloved is for me… (Shir HaShirim 6:3)

4. The High Holidays as a rendezvous with Hashem

This overwhelming sense of awe is accompanied by a sense of intimacy. Hashem beckons unto us to return to Him. He invites us to come before Him. He calls unto us to restore the relationship that we have weakened through our trespasses, our willfulness, and even our rebellion. Awe and intimacy combine to create an overpowering force that inspires us. We feel the presence of the Creator and we renew our commitment to serve Him and to be faithful to His commandments.

In short, the intensity of the Yamim Noraim experience derives from the replacement of our self-imposed delusions of strength and independence with the reality of our frailty, our absolute dependence upon Hashem, and His ever-present invitation to approach Him – His beckoning call that we return to Him.

If we can resist our innate tendency to delude ourselves with fantasies of our own omnipotence and retain our perception of both our dependence upon Hashem and His accessibility, then we can extend the inspiration of the Yamim Noraim beyond its boundaries and endow our entire year with the inspiration of these special days. But how can we overcome our natural tendency to succumb to our illusions?

Let the heavens be glad, and let the earth rejoice; let the sea roar, and the fullness thereof; Let the field exult; and all that is therein; then shall all the trees of the wood sing for joy; (Psalms 96:11-12)

5. The four species of Sukkot and their message

The festival of Sukkot centers around two mitzvot. One is the mitzvah of the four species. These are the palm branch, the citron, the myrtle, and the willow. The four species are elements of the natural world that is Hashem's obedient servant. The species and the universe they represent perfectly obey the master Who commands the laws that govern all natural phenomena. Every element of the universe from the angels in the heavens to the sub-atomic particle in unison extols Him. Their unflagging obedience to His irresistible will expresses the most beautiful and sublime praise.

However, He challenges humanity to choose to reflect His will. This exalted state is not imposed upon humankind. Instead, humankind must come to this state through election. Humanity can elect to reflect His will. This election completes the tapestry of the universe and a work of breathtaking beauty and wonder emerges. Alternatively, humanity can reject Hashem and deny His will. This election mars the tapestry with discord and confusion.

On Sukkot we grasp these species. We hold them and wave them as we praise our Creator. We express our earnest desire to join the universe in its exalted praise of Hashem. We acknowledge that the natural world is but a reflection of the wisdom and omnipotence of Hashem. It is His servant and messenger responding obediently to His irresistible will. In the quiet passing of the breeze and the soft flutter of the wings of a tiny bird, we hear the thunder of nature's praise for its Creator. As we grasp these species we express our deep desire to join this chorus and to blend our praise into the song of the universe.[19]

You shall dwell in booths for seven days. All that are home-born in Israel shall dwell in booths, so that your generations may know that I caused the children of Israel to dwell in booths, when I brought them out of the land of Egypt. I am Hashem your G-d. (VaYikra 23:42-43)

6. The message of the succah

The second commandment that is unique to the celebration of Sukkot is dwelling in the succah – a booth. The Torah directs us to leave our homes and to live in these temporary booths for the duration of the festival. According to the Torah, the mitzvah recalls the booths or the coverings of clouds that protected Bnai Yisrael during its sojourn in the wilderness. The commentators note that the sole intent of the mitzvah is not to recall this historical event. Instead, the mitzvah directs us to leave the security of our homes and to establish these flimsy booths as

---

[19] This explanation of the message of the four species is suggested by various sources that associate the mitzvah with Tehilim 96:12. In this chapter King David asserts that the heavens, earth and their component parts give praise unto Hashem. Among the texts that associate the mitzvah with this chapter are Yalkut Shimoni, VaYikra, 23:651; Midrash Tanchumah, Emor, chapter 18; Shaarei Teshuvah, 660:1. The association of the mitzvah with this chapter indicates that the mitzvah makes reference of the praise to Hashem that is reflected in the universe of natural phenomena. This association does not explain the selection of these four specific species for the purpose of communicating this idea. The selection of specifically these species is discussed extensively in the midrash and among the commentaries.

our residencies. Through this experience we are reminded of our dependence upon Hashem and we recall that in the hostile environment of the wilderness, He provided us with complete protection and security.[20]

However, the mitzvah has an even greater significance in the context of its season. The Yamim Noraim emphasized our dependence upon Hashem. With the passing of the Yamim Noraim, we are challenged to cling to this cognizance of our helplessness and our dependence upon Hashem. In order to succeed, we must confront the elaborate measures we take to convince ourselves that we are the masters of our destinies and that we have the power to secure favorable futures and to ward-off disaster.

Our homes are one of the most powerful components of our delusion. Within our home we feel a sense of security. We feel that we are protected from those who would harm us. The elements are held at bay. For many of us, our homes project our sense of authority, our pride, and our feelings of accomplishment and triumph. Of course, this is an illusion. Our homes provide little protection against an adversary who truly wishes to harm us. In our homes we are sheltered from mild variations in the elements. We are protected from common winds and rain. However, our homes provide no protection against a true onslaught of the terrible forces of nature – a hurricane or earthquake. We may delude ourselves into believing that the grandeur of our homes reflects our own greatness. However, how many great fortunes have been lost overnight? How many vibrant, healthy lives have been taken by a sudden inexplicable illness or tragic accident?

Hark! My beloved! Behold, he cometh, leaping upon the mountains, skipping upon the hills. (Shir HaShirim 2:8)

7. Rediscovering Hashem in the succah and synagogue

Forced to abandon our homes for the duration of the festival we feel exposed, vulnerable, and almost helpless. Suddenly, we reencounter Hashem! Stripped of the delusion of power and control, we rediscover the Creator of the Yamim Noraim. Again, as we listen intently, we hear Him beckon unto us. He awaits us in the succah. He anticipates us at the synagogue. He is eager to hear our voices added to the chorus of creation that extols His praises.

Through Sukkot, we renew and extend our encounter with Hashem. We confront the complex delusions that we construct around us to ward away our insecurities. With the deconstruction of these delusions, we rediscover that the only true security is provided by Hashem. Again, we realize that He awaits us.

"If rain begins to fall, one enters the house. At what point can one leave? Once enough drops are falling so that were they to fall into the food, they would ruin it... Rama: This applies even if there is no food present. If one is not competent in making this measurement, one can evaluate the rain as follows: If this much rain leaked into one's house, would one leave the house? If so, one leaves the *succah*." (Shulchan Aruch, Orech Chayim 639:5)

"Anyone who is exempt from the *succah* and does not leave it, does not receive a reward for this behavior. Rather he is considered simple-minded...." (Rama, Shulchan Aruch, Orech Chayim 639:7)

---

[20] See for example, Rashbam VaYikra 23:43.

Raining on your parade

1. Exempt from a *Mitzvah*

During the festival of *Sukkot* we are commanded to live in the *succah*. We must make the *succah* our dwelling or residence. This *mitzvah* is fulfilled through transferring basic daily activities to the *succah*. At a minimum, we should eat and sleep in the *succah*. Performing additional activities in the *succah* increases the fulfillment of the *mitzvah*.

Generally, we are exempt from the *mitzvah* of living in the *succah* if rain renders it unfit for use. At what point is the *succah* unfit? Rama provides a simple rule. The *succah* should be treated as one's house. If the rain would cause a person to leave one's house and seek better shelter, one can leave the *succah*.

This raises an important question. Assume it is raining. The downpour is heavy enough to exempt me from dwelling in my *succah*. Is there any reason to stay in the *succah*? In the case of most commandments we would respond in the affirmative. Even if one is exempt from a commandment, one is still rewarded for its fulfillment. Women are exempt from the commandment of *Shofar*. Yet, common practice is for women to hear the *shofar* blasts. We would expect the same principle to apply here. Based on this reasoning, there would be a reward for eating in a dripping *succah*.

Rama explains that this is not the case. In the instance of a *succah* that is dripping rain, there is no benefit in remaining in the *succah*. He supports his view by quoting the Talmud Yerushalmi. The Talmud explains that anyone who is exempt from a command and nonetheless performs it, is considered a simpleton.[21]

As we have shown above, the rule of the Yerushalmi cannot be universally applied. In many cases, we recognize the validity of an exempt person performing a *mitzvah*. When does the Yerushalmi's principle apply? Why does it apply to the rain sodden *succah*?

2. Impossible vs. independent

It seems that there are two circumstances under which a person is exempt from a *mitzvah*. First, a person can be exempt because the obligation to perform the command does not extend to this individual. Our case of a woman and the *mitzvah* of *shofar* is an example of this situation. Women are not obligated in the *mitzvah*. Similarly, women are not obligated in the *mitzvah* of shaking the four species. However, if a woman executes these commandments, the performance is valid. Therefore, a woman is rewarded for listening to the *shofar* blasts and shaking the four species. Despite their exemption, they have executed a valid performance of the *mitzvah*.

Second, a person can be exempt from a *mitzvah* because this individual cannot perform the commandment. Imagine a person who, unfortunately, has lost both arms. This person cannot perform the *mitzvah* of placing one of the *teffilin* on his arm. This person is not merely exempted from the *mitzvah*. Performance is impossible. In such a case, any attempt to perform the commandment is obviously foolish. Apparently, the Yerushalmi refers to this situation.

Based on this distinction, Rav Chaim Soloveitchik *Zt"l* explains the position of Rama. We are required to dwell in the *succah*. If a person cannot be comfortable in the *succah* because of rain, extreme cold or some other condition, the person is exempt. Rav Chaim explained that

---

[21] Talmud Yerushalmi, Mesechet Berachot 2:9.

this exemption is not because the obligation does not extend to this person. The exemption results from a more basic issue. Dwelling in the *succah*, under such circumstances, is not recognized as the type of dwelling required by the *mitzvah*. As Rama explains, we must evaluate whether a person would dwell in one's house under such circumstances. If the answer is negative, then this is not the type of dwelling required by the *mitzvah*. The rain makes it impossible to perform the commandment. Therefore, remaining in the *succah* serves no purpose.[22]

"The Holy One Blessed Be He wished to benefit Israel. Therefore He provided them with many laws and commandments." (Tractate Makkot 23b)

On *Simchat Torah* we celebrate the annual completion of the reading of the Torah and the initiation of a new cycle. This celebration is an acknowledgement of the importance of the Torah. Implicitly, we affirm the Almighty's kindness in providing us with the Torah.

The quotation above discusses the benefit we derive from the Torah. In order to understand this insight, we must begin with the simple meaning of the quotation. The Torah is composed of six hundred thirteen commandments. Each of these commandments includes a multitude of laws. The laws define the manner in which the commandment is fulfilled. For example, the Torah directs us to dwell in a *succah* during the celebration of *Sukkot*. This is a *mitzvah*. Various laws are needed to define the means of fulfilling this obligation. The laws describe the structure of the *succah*. The laws also define the meaning of "dwelling". In other words, the laws delineate the specific acts required to establish a state of dwelling in the *succah*.

Many of these *mitzvot* seem to serve similar purposes. We are required to dwell in the *succah* in order to remember our exodus from Egypt and our sojourn in the wilderness. The celebration of *Pesach* also recalls our exodus from Egypt. *Shabbat* is associated with the redemption form Egypt. The requirement to recite the last paragraph of the *Shema* is designed to remind us of our rescue from bondage. Why are so many *mitzvot* required? Why is a single theme reinforced by a multiplicity of commandments?

This is the issue addressed by our Sages in the above quotation. The Sages respond that this very redundancy somehow enriches us. The Sages do not clearly explain the nature of this benefit. We must solve this mystery. We must identify the exact benefit to which they allude.

Sefer HaChinuch provides a solution to this problem. He explains that the Torah is both a system of laws and a personal philosophy and outlook. Clearly, an objective of the Torah is to teach us this outlook and encourage our assimilation of this philosophy.

How is this objective met? Commonly, a teacher or scholar wishing to teach a novel philosophy communicates its tenets. The student must master these tenets and incorporate them into a person world-view. This is a formidable task. If the philosophy is truly unique, it will be difficult to assimilate. The student may clearly understand its principles. Yet, it is difficult to revise one's perspective and world-view. These attitudes are ingrained. They are part of the personality. Therefore, this new philosophy fails to effect a real change in the student.

The Torah solved this problem through combining its philosophy with *mitzvot*. The commandments provide the means for assimilating the Torah outlook. These *mitzvot* train us to see reality though the perspective of the Torah. Let us return to our example. There are many

---

[22] Rav Yosef Dov Soloveitchik, *Reshimat Shuirim, Succah*, pp. 92-93.

mitzvot that share the goal of reminding us of our redemption from Egypt. These *mitzvot* are redundant. But there is a reason for the redundancy. Through repeated actions that reinforce the message of redemption, we assimilate this concept into our personal outlook. The *mitzvot* translate the Torah's philosophy into a personal outlook.

We can now understand the insight of our Sages. The Almighty wanted us to actually benefit from the wisdom of the Torah. This requires that we absorb this wisdom and incorporate it into our personal world-view. Therefore, He gave us a multitude of laws and *mitzvot*. These laws and *mitzvot* enable us to mold our personal perspective.[23]

---

[23] Rav Ahron HaLeyve, *Sefer HaChinuch*, Mitzvah 16.

Chanukah

Reflections on Chanukah

1. The obvious question

One of the most well-known discussions regarding Chanukah is found in Bait Yosef's comments on the very first chapter of the laws of Chanukah. He asks why we celebrate Chaunkah for eight days rather than seven days. The small cruse of undefiled oil discovered by the Hashmonaim miraculously sufficed for the eight days required to produce a new supply of suitable oil. On seven of these days, the lights of the Menorah were the result of a miracle. One day was not the result of a miracle; the cruse contained one day's oil!

Bait Yosef offers a number of responses. Let's just note two of these. One is that the oil was divided into eight portions; and one portion was placed into the Menorah each night. On each of the eight nights, this one eighth of the cruse fueled the Menorah the entire night. Another response is that the entire contents of the cruse were placed in the Menorah the first night but the cruse remained full.

Bait Yosef's question and his responses can be traced back to Tosefot HaRosh. However, as Minchat Asher points out, no other Rishonim raise this issue. In other words, for some reason, virtually all our greatest Talmudic scholars are completely untroubled by what seems to be a rather compelling and obvious question. This nearly universal dismissal of the issue suggests that there is an obvious solution to the problem posed by Bait Yosef and that this solution was embraced by almost all of Rosh's contemporaries. What is this response?

2. Objective vs. method

There are two paradigms through which one can view the miracle of the oil. One can view it mechanically or in terms of its objective. To view it mechanically is to ask how exactly the miracle unfolded. To view it in terms of its objective is to focus not on the details of how the miracle occurred but upon the objective it achieved.

Bait Yosef and Rosh assume that Chanukah commemorates the miracle viewed from a mechanical framework. It recalls the specific miracle taking place each day. It follows that they are perplexed by why the celebration is observed for eight days when oil for one day was on-hand.

Apparently, the other Rishonim are unconcerned with the mechanics of the miracle. In their view, Chanukah commemorates the miracle of the oil through viewing it from the perspective of its objective. What was the objective of the miracle? It was that somehow this one cruse of oil should prove adequate to fuel the Menorah for eight days. Chanukah commemorates the miracle by viewing it from the perspective of its objective – that the cruse sufficed for eight days. Viewed from this perspective, of course the celebration is observed for eight days. The objective of the miracle was to produce the light of the Menorah for eight nights!

3. Looking to our lives

The blessings we enjoy in life can also be viewed from these two perspectives. We can focus on outcomes or we can scrutinize the details of our lives seeking hints of the presence of providence in specific events. This second approach is very popular. Many of us imagine that we can detect Hashem's presence in or influence upon individual events in our lives – securing a job, being fired from a position and moving on to a better opportunity, avoiding a serious auto accident, or quickly recuperating from an illness. The challenge with these speculations is reflected in the responses Bait Yosef provides to his question. It is impossible to choose one over the other. We can know that there was a miracle but we can only speculate regarding its specific mechanics. Similarly, when we attempt to identify specific instances in which Hashem's influence guided events in our lives, we speculate about that which is actually unknowable to us. In contrast, when we step back from scrutinizing the details and look upon the broader picture of the blessings we enjoy, then we can feel true, authentic gratitude. We are not merely indulging in imaginative speculation; we are feeling appreciation and expressing thanks for actual blessings that we are experiencing.

Chanukah is a time of giving thanks. We recall our triumph over an ancient oppressor and we commemorate the miracle of the Menorah. However, we enjoy countless personal blessings every day. Hopefully, the spirit of appreciation that infuses Chanukah will carry-over to the rest of the year and inspire within us a sense of gratitude for the blessings Hashem bestows upon us.

"For this reason the Sages of that generation established that these eight days.... should be days of rejoicing and *Hallel*. And we light on them candles, at night, at the doors of the homes each night ... to demonstrate and reveal the miracle." (Mishne Torah, Laws of Megilah and Chanukah, 3:3)

Maimonides explains that the celebration of Chanukah is observed through rejoicing, the recitation of the *Hallel* prayer and the lighting of candles. There is no requirement of indulging in elaborate meals. In this respect Chanukah differs from Purim. On Purim, the holiday meal is central to the celebration. In fact, many of the Purim obligations including sending gifts to friends and to the poor are related to the holiday meal! Why is Chanukah different?

Mishne Berurah quotes the response of Levush to this question. He comments that the distinction between Chanukah and Purim can be explained through understanding the circumstances of each celebration. Purim commemorates the deliverance of the Jewish people from Haman. Haman attempted to annihilate Bnei Yisrael. The salvation of Purim was from this physical destruction.

Chanukah recalls a different form of deliverance. The villains of the Chanukah episode were Assyrians, committed to Hellenistic culture. Their primary aim was not to cause physical harm to the Jewish people. Instead, their intention was to wipe out observance of the Torah. This would encourage assimilation into the Hellenistic culture. The salvation of Chanukah was essentially of a spiritual nature. Therefore, it is fitting that the Chanukah celebration emphasizes the spiritual character of the redemption. To create this emphasis the celebration is overwhelmingly spiritual in character. There is no requirement of an elaborate holiday meal. Instead, the *Hallel* prayer is recited. A section of praise – *Al HaNissim* – is added to the *Amidah* and *Birkat HaMazon*. Candles are lit to recall the miracle of the re-establishment of service in the Temple.[1]

---

[1] Rav Yisrael Meir Kagan, *Mishne Berurah*, 670:6.

On the miracles, on the redemption, on the mighty acts, on the salvations, and on the wars that You performed for our fathers in those days, in this time. (Al HaNisim prayer)

Chanukah: The Solace in Being Hated

1. The Chanukah and Purim versions of the *Al HaNisim* prayer

Chanukah and Purim both recall dramatic episodes in Jewish history. In both of these episodes we were confronted by threats of annihilation and in each we were rescued by Hashem. There are also similarities in the observance of these two celebrations. On both, we insert into the *Amidah* and into *Birkat HaMazon* a version of the *Al HaNisim* thanksgiving prayer.

Let us compare and contrast these two versions of the prayer. Both versions share a fundamental theme – salvation from our enemies. This theme is presented through the three basic components of the prayer. The *Al HaNisim* prayer opens with the above statement of thanksgiving. We acknowledge the salvation of our people by Hashem. Second, the prayer describes a conflict that threatened to destroy us. In regards to Purim, this is the plan of Haman to annihilate the Jewish people in the kingdom of Achashverosh. Chanukah recalls our conflict with the Hellenist Assyrian kingdom. The third element describes our triumph over our wicked adversary or our salvation from catastrophe.

The Purim version of the *Al HaNisim* prayer is briefer than the Chanukah version. The reason for its brevity is that it does not include as elaborate a description of our rescue. The Purim version merely states that Hashem undermined Haman's plans. Rather than annihilating the Jews, Haman and his sons were destroyed.

You adopted their grievance. You enforced their judgement. You avenged them. You delivered the mighty into the hand of the weak, the many into the hand of the few, the defiled into the hand of the pure, the wicked into the hand of the righteous, the willfully evil into the hand of those who study Your Torah. And for Yourself, You made Your name great and sanctified in Your world. (Al HaNisim prayer for Chanukah)

2. The unique elements of the Chanukah version of *Al HaNisim*

In the Chanukah version the third element is much more elaborate and descriptive. It includes the following material:

A. Hashem is described as working through the Jewish people. He empowers them to overcome their adversaries.

B. Two paradigms are used to describe the Jewish people's triumph over their enemies. One paradigm is military. The might and superior numbers of the enemy were overcome by a smaller and weaker force. The second paradigm is a moral one. The righteous and pure defeated the wicked and defiled.

C. The triumph of the Jews over their enemies is described as a sanctification of Hashem's name.

Let us consider these last two components.

In the days of Matityahu the son of Yochanan, the Kohen Gadol of the Hashmonaim family and his sons. When the evil Hellenist kingdom arose against Your nation to force them to forget Your Torah and to violate the statutes of Your will. (Al HaNisim prayer for Chanukah)

108

3. The character of the Chanukah conflict

In order to appreciate the significance of this added material, we must consider more carefully the fundamental nature of each of these conflicts. The Purim miracle was that Hashem saved His people from Haman's plan to destroy the Jewish nation. It is true that he was motivated by issues stemming from our commitment to Torah. Specifically, he understood that Judaism opposes the exaltation and worship of any human being. He resented the Jewish people because they were an obstacle to his promulgation of the self-myth of greatness. However, despite this religious underpinning, the conflict did not manifest itself as a religious struggle. Haman was not interested in altering the religious doctrines of the Jewish people. He wished to annihilate us. In short, the religious conflicts were in the background and latent. The manifest expression was a campaign to destroy our people.

In contrast, Chanukah focuses upon an historical religious conflict. The Hellenists were not bent upon destroying the Jewish people. They sought to convert us to their world view. This was a conflict between perspectives and cultures. The Hellenists directed their aggression against our Torah. They suppressed Torah study and observance and they defiled the *Bait HaMikdash* – the Sacred Temple. This battle was over religious issues.

This difference between the two conflicts is reflected in the way they are respectively described in the *Al HaNisim* prayer. The Chanukah victory is not described merely in military terms – the few and weak overcame the strong and the many. It is described in religious and moral terms. The righteous overcame the wicked and the sacred vanquished the defiled. Why is this religious/moral paradigm employed? It provides a description of the conflict – it was religious in nature.

4. The Chanukah victory sanctified Hashem's name

Understanding this difference between the two conflicts explains another aspect of their respective treatments in the *Al HaNisim* prayer. The defeat of Haman and the preservation of the Jewish people is not characterized in the *Al HaNisim* prayer as a sanctification of Hashem's name. This is because the overt conflict was not focused upon good versus evil. It was a conflict between two peoples. The defeat of the Hellenists is described as a sanctification of Hashem's name because this conflict was focused upon issues of right and wrong, good and evil. It is the triumph of righteousness over wickedness that sanctifies Hashem's name.

5. The foundation of our enemies' hatred

As noted above, both conflicts were motivated by religious antipathies. They differ in the manner in which the religious resentments were expressed. Haman's strategy was to destroy our nation. The Assyrian Hellenists sought to uproot our commitment to our Torah. In both instances we survived and our enemies were defeated. These are two of many instances in which our enemies have tried to destroy us. We have survived these countless persecutions only through the intervention of Hashem. However, despite the incessant nature of the antipathy directed against our people, we have reason to actually derive solace from our historical plight. If our enemies truly believed in the superiority of their own world-view, they would have no reason to wish to destroy us. They would merely dismiss us as a clan of primitives. Why did Haman and the Hellenists not merely ignore us? Implicitly expressed in our enemies' consistent hatred and aggression is their acknowledgment of their insecurities. Haman, the Assyrians, and so many other subsequent adversaries could not dismiss us because they knew deep in their hearts that we represent a truth that they could not ignore and that threatened their own world-view. So, although we continue to be the target of hatred and aggression, we receive some comfort. We know that their regard for the truth of our Torah underlies their behavior.

"What is Chanukah? Our Sages taught: On the twenty-fifth of Kislev Chanukah is observed. This is for eight days on which it is prohibited to eulogize or fast. For when the Hellenists entered the Temple they defiled all of the oil. And when the Hashmonaim rose to power and overcame them, they only found one container of oil sealed with the seal of the Kohen Gadol. It only contained sufficient oil for one day. But a miracle was performed with this oil and they lit from it for eight nights. In a different year they established and made these days a festival with Hallel and giving thanks." (Tractate Shabbat 21b)

Miracle from Hashem

1. Which miracle?

The Talmud explains that the celebration of Chanukah recalls the miracle of the oil. The Hashmonaim defeated the Assyrians and reoccupied the Bait HaMikdash. They wished to rekindle the Menorah – the candelabra – of the Temple. They required ritually pure oil. The Assyrians had defiled the oil in the Temple. The Hashmonaim found only a small container of oil that remained fit. It held sufficient oil to fuel the Menorah for a single night. They would require eight days to procure additional oil. A miracle occurred and the small container of oil provided sufficient fuel for all eight nights. The Talmud explains that the days on which this miracle occurred were established as a holiday. The festival is celebrated through reciting Hallel and offering thanks to Hashem. How do we offer thanks? We add the prayer of Al HaNissim to the Birkat HaMazon and the Amidah. It is clear, from the discussion in the Talmud that, the miracle of the Menorah is the central event commemorated by Chanukah. We would expect that Al HaNissim would thank the Almighty for this miracle. However, a review of Al HaNissim reveals that the miracle of the Menorah is not even mentioned. Instead, the prayer deals exclusively with the salvation of the Jewish people from their enemies. The Talmud indicates that this prayer is a fundamental aspect of the celebration of Chanukah. Why does this prayer not mention the central miracle? Furthermore, the comments of the Talmud are difficult to understand. It is true that the burning of the oil for eight nights was a miracle. However, far greater miracles are recorded in TaNaCH. These more impressive wonders are not commemorated through any celebration. For example, Yehoshua split the Jordan, he stopped the sun in its passage through the sky, and he brought down the walls of Yericho with a shofar blast. None of these awesome wonders are commemorated through their own celebration. The miracle of the oil is quite modest compared to these other events. Why is this miracle commemorated with its own holiday and not these other wonders?

Chanukah is one of two holidays established by the Sages of the Talmud. Prior to creating the celebration of Chanukah, the Sages instituted Purim. Maimonides discusses the reason the Sages established Purim. He explains that the Torah assures us that the Almighty will never forsake His people. In times of suffering Hashem will redeem us. The events of Purim provide testimony to the truth of this promise. In discussing Chanukah, Maimonides mentions the miracle of the oil. However, he also stresses our salvation, through Hashem, from our enemies. It seems that Maimonides is explaining an important concept. The celebrations of Purim and Chanukah share a common theme. The Almighty will never allow the Jewish people

110

to be destroyed. Both celebrations reinforce this covenant. Both recall episodes from our history. In each incident Bnai Yisrael's existence was in peril. The Almighty intervened to save us. Both reinforce the reality of the Torah's promise. We can now begin to answer our questions.

Not every miracle is the occasion for the establishment of a holiday. The celebrations of Purim and Chanukah do not commemorate miracles. They testify to the truth of the Almighty's promise that He will never abandon His people. Other miracles, of greater magnitude are not commemorated by holidays. This is because these miracles did not involve the salvation of the Jewish people. We can now understand the Al HaNissim prayer. This prayer captures the essential theme of Chanukah. It discusses the rescue of the Jewish people from their oppressors. This prayer is also recited on Purim. This is appropriate. Purim also communicates the same theme of salvation. We must still explain the comments of the Talmud. The Talmud relates the celebration of Chanukah to the miracle of the Menorah. Maimonides also acknowledges the fundamental role of this miracle. This miracle would not seem to be an appropriate reason for creating a holiday!

2. Hashem reveals Himself

Let us return to Purim. How do we know that the Almighty was the cause of our salvation? Perhaps events just unfolded, by chance, in a manner that saved the Jews from Haman! The answer is found in Megilat Esther. The Megilah reveals Hashem's manipulation of events. It provides us with insight into the events. Based on the Megilah, we know that our salvation was through the Almighty. This revelation was fundamental to the creation of Purim. Only a rescue clearly engineered by Hashem confirms the promise of the Torah. Two criteria must be met to establish a holiday. There must be redemption from certain destruction. This rescue must clearly be through the Almighty's intervention. The events of Purim meet these criteria.

We can now appreciate the fundamental role of the miracle of the oil. Victory in battle is not a sufficient foundation for the creation of Chanukah. The Almighty must reveal Himself as the cause of the triumph and salvation. This revelation took place through the miracle of the oil. With this miracle, Hashem indicated His influence and role in the events of Chanukah. Just as the Almighty had performed the miracle of the oil, so too He had been the force behind the salvation. We can now understand the comments of the Talmud. True, Chanukah celebrates our salvation. However, the celebration could not have been established without the miracle of the Menorah. This miracle indicated that the salvation was through the intervention of the Almighty. Only on the basis of this revelation could the celebration of Chanukah be created.

"During the Second Temple period, the Hellenist kings made decrees against the Jewish people, suppressed their religion, did not allow them to learn Torah or to perform *mitzvot*, seized their money and daughters, entered the Temple and broke down its walls, and defiled the objects of purity. And, they greatly afflicted the Jewish people and oppressed them tremendously until the G-d of their fathers had mercy upon them, provided salvation and saved them from their hands. And the house of the Hashmonaim – High Priests – triumphed over them, killed them and provided the Jewish people with salvation from their hands. And they established a king from among the Priests. Kingship returned to the Jewish people for more than two hundred years – until the destruction of the Second Temple." (Maimonides, Mishne Torah, Hilchot Chanukah 3:1)

111

Praise the Lord

1. The ruling class

Maimonides describes the events that are recalled through the celebration of Chanukah. He explains that the Hellenist kings ruled the land of Israel and the Jewish people. Their reign was characterized by comprehensive religious oppression and material persecution. Eventually, the Hashmonaim – a family of *Kohanim* – led a rebellion and overthrew the oppressors. They reestablished the Jewish kingship. They appointed a king from their own family. The kingdom that they established lasted for over two hundred years and only ended with the destruction of the Second Temple.

It is clear from Maimonides' comments that he views the two hundred year rule by the kings of the Hashmonaim positively. There are a number of problems with Maimonides' position. One of these problems is his indication that the longevity of the rule of the Hashmonaim kings is relevant to the celebration of Chanukah. It is not immediately obvious why this factor should be worthy of note. The Jewish people were oppressed by the Hellenists – both spiritually and materially. Hashem had mercy upon His people and through the Hashmonaim, he rescued them from oppression. This seems to be an adequate reason to give thanks to Hashem through the observance of a celebration. Why is the length of rule of the Hashmonaim relevant?

2. A foreign affair

Rav Yosef Dov Soloveitchik *Zt"l* offers an interesting explanation of Maimonides' position. He bases his explanation upon a teaching from the Talmud. Like Chanukah, Purim recalls the salvation of the Jewish people from an enemy determined to destroy them. Haman carefully planned the destruction of the Jewish people. Through Hashem's intervention, Mordechai and Esther succeeded in defeating his designs and destroyed the enemies of the Jewish people. It would seem appropriate to commemorate the salvation of the Jewish people with the recitation of the Hallel. Why is the Hallel not recited on Purim? The Talmud offers three possible explanations. First, the events of Purim occurred in the exile. The Hallel is not recited on miracles that occur in the exile. Second, the Hallel is not needed on Purim. The reading of the Meggilah replaces the Hallel. Third, the salvation commemorated by Purim was not complete. The Jewish people were rescued from Haman. However, they remained in exile – subjects of the heathen king.[2]

Rav Soloveitchik suggests that Maimonides, apparently, adopts the Talmud's final explanation. Hallel is not recited on Purim because the Jewish people remained the subjects of a foreign king. Rav Soloveitchik contends that Maimonides extrapolated from this ruling a general principle. The Hallel cannot be recited to commemorate any miracle that does not result in complete salvation – leaving the Jewish people under the rule of a foreign king. Based on this interpretation of Maimonides' position, Rav Soloveitchik suggests that we can understand Maimonides' reference to the two hundred years of rule of the Hashmonaim kings.

According to Rav Soloveitchik, Maimonides is applying his understanding of the Talmud to the practice of reciting the Hallel on Chanukah. The Hallel is recited on each day of Chanukah. This is only consistent with Maimonides' understanding of the Talmud's ruling if Chanukah commemorates a complete salvation. A complete salvation must restore the Jewish

---

[2] Mesechet Meggilah 14a.

leadership. Had the Hashmonaim not succeeded in reestablishing Jewish rule, it would not be appropriate to recite the Hallel on Chanukah. But, because the Hashmonaim did reign over the Jewish people for over two hundred years, the requirements for the recitation of the Hallel are met and the Hallel is recited on Chanukah.[3]

3. The house of David

Rav Soloveitchik's interpretation of Maimonides' comments resolves another problem. Nachmanides comments that the Hashmonaim did not have the right to elevate themselves to the position of kings. He explains that once Hashem chose David as king, the institution of kingship was awarded to David and his descendants in perpetuity. In assuming the kingship, the Hashmonaim were usurpers. Nachmanides argues that they were severely punished for this trespass.[4] Of course, it is possible that Maimonides does not agree with Nachmanides' position regarding the prohibition against the appointment of a king from outside of the family of David. Maimonides seems to indicate that although kingship will ultimately return to the family of David, it is not inappropriate to appoint a king from another family or *shevet*, if necessary. The Torah instructs us only that the kingship cannot be permanently transferred to another family.[5]

However, according to Rav Soloveitchik's interpretation of Maimonindes' comments, there is no reason to assume that Maimonindes disagrees with Nachmanides' position. It is possible that Maimonides would agree that the Hashmonaim were not entitled to assume the mantle of kingship. Maimonides is not endorsing their behavior. Instead, he is dealing with a different issue – was the salvation commemorated by Chanukah complete. The complete salvation required for the recitation of the Hallel requires the reestablishment of Jewish rule. This was done by the Hashmonaim. Whether they were correct in their behavior or were usurpers is not relevant to this issue. Irregardless of the advisability of their behavior, kingship was restored.

4. But it's against the Rambam

Rav Soloveitchik points out that there is a serious problem with his interpretation of Maimonides' comments. Maimonides discusses the omission of the Hallel from the observances of Purim. According to Rav Soloveitchik's interpretation of Maimonides' position, we would expect Maimonides to explain that the Hallel is not recited on Purim because the salvation commemorated by Purim was not complete. However, Maimonides does not offer this explanation. Instead, he explains that the Hallel is not recited on Purim because the reading of the Meggilah takes its place.[6]

In order to attempt to resolve this problem, it is important to define the question more clearly. Maimonides' comments in regard to Purim seem to indicate that the deficiency of the salvation commemorated by Purim does not prevent the recitation of the Hallel. In fact, there is an obligation to recite the Hallel on Purim. However, this obligation is fulfilled through the reading of the Meggilah. In contrast, his comments in regard to Chanukah seem to indicate that an incomplete salvation would not have sufficed for the recitation of the Hallel. How can this contradiction be resolved?

---

[3] Rav Yosef Dov Soloveitchik, *Harerai Kedem* , volume 1, p 272.
[4] Rabbaynu Moshe ben Nachman (Ramban), *Commentary on Sefer Beresheit* 49:10.
[5] Rabbaynu Moshe ben Maimon (Rambam) *Mishne Torah*, Hilchot Melachim 1:7-9.
[6] Rabbaynu Moshe ben Maimon (Rambam) *Mishne Torah*, Hilchot Meggilah 3:6.

5. Proportional results

The Talmud explains that, in general, when the Jewish people are rescued from an affliction, we are required to recite the Hallel.[7] In other words, the Talmud is identifying two elements that together create an obligation to recite the Hallel. First, there must be an affliction. Second, the Jewish people must be rescued from the affliction. It follows that in order to determine whether the redemption is complete, it is necessary to determine the nature of the affliction that the redemption addresses. For example, if the Jewish people are faced with religious persecution, then redemption would be defined as the rescue from this religious persecution. Alternatively, if the Jewish people were confronted with annihilation, then redemption would be defined as the rescue of the nation from this destruction.

Let us apply the same analysis to the events commemorated by Purim and Chanukah respectively. Haman's design was to totally destroy the Jewish people. Redemption from this affliction would be defined as the rescue of the nation from Haman's elaborate plans to destroy the nation. In contrast, the Hellenists did not wish to destroy the Jewish people. They practiced religious persecution and they attempted to subjugate the Jewish people. Rescue from this affliction would be defined as the cessation of religious persecution and the freeing of the nation from foreign domination.

As Rav Soloveitchik explains, Maimonides maintains that the Hallel is not recited for a salvation that is not complete. But, the completeness of the salvation must be evaluated relative to the affliction. The events commemorated by Purim represent a complete salvation. The Jewish people were in exile. Exile is a tragedy. But, Purim is not designed to recall our return to the land of Israel. Instead, it recalls that Haman wished to destroy the nation. Hashem intervened and defeated Haman. Was this rescue complete? When evaluated relative to the affliction, it is clear that it was. It is not relevant that the Jewish people remained in exile, ruled by a foreign king. The tragedy of exile is not the affliction that is recalled on Purim. However, the events commemorated by Chanukah occurred in the land of Israel. The affliction consisted of religious persecution and an attempt to subjugate the people in their own land. In this instance, the definition of salvation includes not only the cessation of religious persecution, but, also, the restoration of the independence of the nation and its regaining of freedom from foreign domination. In such an instance, the reestablishment of Jewish kingship is an essential element of the salvation. If the Hashmonaim had succeeded in bringing an end to religious prosecution, but had failed to rescue the nation from foreign domination, the salvation could not have been regarded as complete.

This explains Maimonides' position. Maimonides maintains that only a complete salvation obligates us in the recitation of the Hallel. On Purim, the salvation was complete. The Jewish people were saved from destruction at the hands of Haman. That they remained in exile does not negate the completeness of their salvation from Haman. Therefore, Maimonides rules that Purim requires the recitation of the Hallel, and this obligation is fulfilled through the reading of the Meggilah. However, the salvation of Chanukah was only completed through the reestablishment of Jewish rule in the land of Israel. Therefore, the restoration of the kingship is cited by Maimonides as an essential element of the salvation.

---

[7] Mesechet Pesachim 111a.

"What is Chanukah? Our Sages taught: On the twenty-fifth of Kislev Chanukah is observed. This is for eight days on which it is prohibited to eulogize or fast. For when the Hellenists entered the Temple they defiled all of the oil. And when the Hashmonaim rose to power and overcame them, they only found one container of oil sealed with the seal of the *Kohen Gadol*. It only contained sufficient oil for one day. But a miracle was performed with this oil and they lit from it for eight nights. In a different year they established and made these days a festival with *Hallel* and giving thanks." (Tractate Shabbat 21b)

This is the Talmud's discussion of the source of the Chanukah celebration. The Talmud explains the miracle of the oil. The Sages also describe the festival of Chanukah. However, the comments of the Sages are not easily understood. The Talmud tells us that the celebration was established as a result of the miracle of the oil. However, in its description of the celebration the Talmud does not mention the lighting of the Chanukah lights! We generally regard the lighting of the *Chanukiyah* – the *menorah* – as the most fundamental observance of the festival. Yet, in the above description of Chanukah, the Talmud does not mention this observance. Furthermore, if we consider the context of the above text, this omission is even more bizarre. The section of Talmud, in which the above quote is found, is discussing the various laws governing the lighting of the Chanukah lights!

Maimonides, in his Mishne Torah, provides an important hint towards answering these questions. Maimonides begins his discussion of Chanukah with a review of the historical events underlying the celebration. He discusses the oppression of the Jewish people by the Hellenist Assyrians. He then describes the triumph of Bnai Yisrael. Finally, he discusses the miracle of the oil. Then Maimonides writes, "And for this reason the Sages of that generation established that these days, beginning with the 25th of Kislev, should be days of happiness and *Hallel*. We light candles on these days, at night, at the doors of the homes, on each night of the eight nights, in order to show and reveal the miracle."[8]

Maimonides always chooses his words very carefully. Therefore, it is appropriate to consider every nuance of his wording. The Rav – Rav Yosef Dov Soloveitchik *Zt"l* - makes an important observation based upon this wording. Maimonides did not write that the Sages established Chanukah as days of happiness, *Hallel* and lighting candles. Instead, he wrote that these days were established as days of happiness and *Hallel* – and that we light candles on these days. The implication of this wording is that the lighting of the Chanukah lights was not part of the original enactment of the Sages. Originally, the Sages established Chanukah as a time of happiness and *Hallel*. At some latter point the practice of lighting candles was established.

This provides a partial answer to our questions. The Talmud is explaining the original enactment of Chanukah. The initial response of the Sages to the miracles of the victory and oil was to establish a celebration of *Hallel* and thanks. It did not include a requirement to light the Chanukah lights. This was a latter development. However, we are left with a new question. Why was the lighting of the *Chanukiyah* not included in the original enactment. Furthermore, why was this practice latter added?

The Rav suggests that the lighting of the Chanukah lights was established after the destruction of the *Bait HaMikdash*. Prior to this time, the *Menorah* of the *Mikdash* existed and the practice of lighting the Chanukah lights did not exist.

---

[8]   Rabbaynu Moshe ben Maimon (Rambam) *Mishne Torah*, Hilchot Chanukah 1:3.

Why was this practice established only after the destruction of the Temple? Nachmanides explains, in his commentary on the Chumash, that the Chanukah lights recall the *Menorah* of the Temple.[9] The Rav explains that any practice designed to recall the Temple cannot coexist with the *Bait HaMikdash*. Such practices only become meaningful after the destruction of the Temple.[10]

Bait Shammai say that on the first night, one kindles eight. From then onward, one decreases the number. And Bait Hillel says that on the first night, one kindles one. From then onward, one adds to the number. (Tractate Shabbat 21b)

So Many Candles!

1. Bait Shammai and Bait Hillel

One of the most well-known disputes concerning the mitzvah of the Chanukah lights concerns the number of lights that are kindled each night. We follow the practice of Bait Hillel. On the first night, we kindle a single light. Each following night, we add a candle. This process culminates with kindling eight candles on the eighth night. However, Bait Shammai suggests an alternative and opposite procedure. According to Bait Shammai, eight lights are kindled on the first night and one light is subtracted on each subsequent night. On the eighth night, a single candle is kindled.

2. The Talmud's first explanation

The Talmud offers two explanations of this dispute. The first is rather simple. According to Bait Shammai, the number of lights kindled represents the number of days of Chanukah that remain. On the first night, all eight days remain; eight lights are kindled. On the last night, only a single day remains; a single light is kindled. Bait Hillel maintains that the number of lights kindled represents the number of days that have passed – including the current night. On the first night, no days have yet passed. However, we kindle one light – corresponding to the current night. On the second night, we kindle two lights – corresponding with the day that has passed and the current night.

Although this is a reasonable explanation of the dispute between Bait Shammai and Bait Hillel, it presents a problem. Both agree that the number of lights kindled corresponds with the night of Chanukah. In other words, we are counting the nights of Chanukah through the number of lights that we kindle. However, it seems that Bait Hillel's method of counting is more reasonable. It is straightforward and simple. Bait Shammai's method is somewhat convoluted. Why does Bait Shammai require that we indicate the night of Chanukah through demonstrating how many nights remain?

3. Numbers and messages

Rav Yisroel Chait offers an insightful explanation of Bait Shammai's opinion. He begins by asking a simple question. How does one determine how many lights one will kindle on any night? One considers which night it is and then subtracts from eight. So, on the third night, two days of Chanukah have passed. These two days are subtracted from eight and six lights are

---

[9] Rabbaynu Moshe ben Nachman (Ramban), *Commentary on Sefer BeMidbar* 8:2.

[10] Rav Yosef Dov Soloveitchik, "Notes on Rambam's Hilchot Chanukah," *Mesora,* Adar 5757, pp. 17-18.

kindled. Each night, the number of lights kindled reflects two quantities – the number of days that have passed and the total number of days of Chanukah.

This analysis demonstrates that according to Bait Shammai, the number of lights kindled must reflect both of these quantities. The opinion of Bait Shammai is that it is not adequate for the number of lights to merely reflect the number of days that have passed. The lights must also reflect that Chanukah is an eight-day celebration.

Now, we understand the dispute between Bait Shammai and Bait Hillel. According to Bait Hillel, the number of lights kindled reflects only a single quantity – the number of days that have passed. But according to Bait Shammai, the number of lights kindled reflects the number of days that have passed and the total number of days of the celebration. For example, on the third night, Bait Hillel's lights communicate only one message; it is the third night of the celebration. Bait Shammai's lights communicate that it is the third night of an eight-day celebration.

4. Priorities on communication

This raises a new question. According to Bait Shammai, why is it necessary to communicate through the lights kindled, that Chanukah is an eight-day celebration? Why is it not adequate to simply indicate – through the lights – the number of days of the celebration that have passed?

Rav Chait suggests a simple answer to this question. He explains that the Chanukah lights are more than a method for counting the nights of Chanukah. The lights are designed to communicate and recall the miracle of the Menorah; a container holding enough oil for a single day sufficed for eight days. In this context, we can understand Bait Shammai's position. According to Bait Shammai, we must communicate that Chanukah is an eight-day celebration commemorating a miracle that extended over eight days. Each night, we declare which day we are celebrating of an eight-day celebration that commemorates an eight-day miracle.

Now, we can better understand the dispute between Bait Hillel and Bait Shammai. Both agree each night the candles communicate the number of the day of Chanukah and the corresponding number of days the miracle had extended. As noted, Bait Hillel's method of lighting is clear and straightforward. It communicates to the observer the current night of the miracle and the Chanukah celebration. Bait Shammai's method is not as straightforward. But it communicates more information. It communicates the current night of Chanukah and the corresponding miracle. It also communicates the total length of the miracle and celebration.

Both methods communicate the miracle of the Menorah, but they prioritize different aspects of the communication. Bait Hillel's method emphasizes the clarity of the communication. Bait Shammai's emphasizes the quantity or completeness of the information communicated. Therefore, Bait Shammai sacrifices some clarity to communicate a more complete message.[11]

5. The Talmud's second explanation

The Talmud offers a second explanation of the dispute between Bait Shammai and Bait Hillel. According to this explanation, Bait Shammai maintains that the number of lights kindled each night is patterned after the sacrifices offered on Succot. These are described in Parshat Pinchas. Thirteen bulls are offered on the first day, and on each subsequent day, one less bull is offered. On the final day – the seventh day of Succot – seven bulls are offered.[12]

[11] See P'nai Yehosua, Commentary on Mesechet Shabbat 21b.
[12] Sefer BeMidbar 29:12-34.

117

In other words, just as the number of bulls offered decreases with the passing of each day of Succot, so too, the number of lights kindled decreases with the passing of each day of Chanukah. Bait Hillel maintains that the number of lights increases each night. This position is based upon a general principle in halacha – we are required to bring about ascension in sanctity and not descent. This principle is expressed in various laws. For example, if we sell an object that has sanctity, then we are required to use the funds to purchase an object of greater sanctity. We cannot use the funds for the purchase of an object of lesser sanctity.[13] Based on this principle, Bait Hillel reasons that we are required to increase the number of lights and we cannot decrease them. Therefore, we add a light each night.

This answer presents an obvious problem. What is the connection between Succot and Chanukah? Why should the pattern of sacrifices on Succot be the model for the number of lights kindled on Chanukah?

6. Hallel of Succot and Pesach

To answer this question, it is useful to begin with a related issue. As we have explained, there is a general principle in halacha of ma'alin ba'kodesh ve'ayn moredin – we are required to cause ascension in sanctity and not descent. However, the number of bulls offered on Succot does decrease. Why does the principle of ma'alin ba'kodesh not apply to these sacrifices?

There is an interesting discussion in the Talmud that seems to answer this question. The Talmud explains that we are required to recite the entire Hallel on each day of Succot. However, on Pesach, we are only required to recite the entire Hallel on the first day.

The Talmud explains that we recite the full Hallel in each day of Succot because the number of bulls offered differs on each day. Their different sacrifices distinguish the days of Succot from one another. Because the days are differentiated through their sacrifices, the complete Hallel is recited each day. In contrast, on Pesach the same daily sacrifices are offered on each of the seven days.[14] Because its days are not differentiated through their sacrifices, the complete Hallel is recited only the first day.[15]

What is the connection between the differentiation of the days of Succot through their various sacrifices and the recitation of a complete Hallel? The different sacrifices offered on each day endow each day of Succot with a unique sanctity. Because each day of Succot has a unique sanctity, it requires a complete Hallel. In contrast, the days of Pesach are not differentiated by their sacrifices. Therefore, they all partake of a single extended sanctity. This single sanctity extends through the entire seven days of Pesach. The single sanctity of Pesach requires a single recitation of the complete Hallel.

This discussion suggests that there is a fundamental difference between Succot and Pesach. The festival of Succot is composed of a sequence of seven unique, but separate days. Each day has its special sanctity. Pesach is a single sanctity that extends over seven days.

7. The days of Chanukah

Now, we understand why the principle of ma'alin ba'kodesh does not apply to Succot. The principle of ma'alin ba'kodesh only applies when there is a relationship between a prior and later sanctity – generally, through both relating to a single object. In our above example, the

---

[13] Rabbaynu Moshe ben Maimon (Rambam) Mishne Torah, Hilchot Tefilah 11:14.
[14] Sefer BeMidbar 28:18-24.
[15] Mesechet Erechin 10b.

funds received for the sale of an object of sanctity cannot be used to purchase an object of lesser sanctity. This is because the funds would descent from their association with a higher level of sanctity to association with a lesser level. This principle cannot be applied to Succot. The various sacrifices endow each day with a unique and separate sanctity. The sacrifices of one day are not associated with the sacrifices of the next. Therefore, the principle of ma'alin ba'kodesh is not applicable.

This helps us understand the Talmud's second explanation of the dispute between Bait Hillel and Bait Shammai. According to Bait Hillel, the eight days of Chanukah are patterned after the seven days of Pesach. The eight days share a single designation as Chanukah. Because all eight days partake of a single designation, the principle of ma'alin ba'kodesh applies. Bait Shammai contends that eight days of Chanukah are patterned after the seven days of Succot. Each day of Chanukah has its own separate identity. To create and communicate each day's uniqueness, the lights are kindled in the pattern of the Succot sacrifices. The lights of Chanukah differentiate the days of the celebration – much as the sacrifices of Succot differentiate the days of the festival. The pattern in which the lights are kindled communicates that, like the days of Succot, the various days of Chanukah are separate from one another.

"How many candles should one light? On the first night one should light one flame. From that point onward, he should add one flame each night until the last night on which there will be eight flames." (Shulchan Aruch, Orech Chayim 671:2)

Eight lights eight nights

1. Three levels

Shulchan Aruch describes the procedure for lighting the Chanukah candles. The first night one candle is lit. An additional candle is added each night. Finally, on the eighth night eight candles are lit.

This law is derived directly from the Talmud in Tractate Shabbat. The Talmud explains that the obligation of lighting the Chanukah lights can be fulfilled on three levels. On the basic level, it is sufficient to light a single candle for the entire household, regardless of the night. In other words, one candle is lit the first night. A single candle is lit the last night. At the next level, the *mitzvah* is enhanced. The number of candles lit each night corresponds with the number of members in the household. A household of four would light four Chanukah candles each night. The optimum performance of the *mitzvah* requires that the number of candles correspond with the night. This is the level described by Shulchan Aruch. The first night one candle is lit. By the eighth night, eight candles are kindled.[16]

A comparison of Shulchan Aruch to the Talmud suggests an obvious question. According to the Talmud, there are three levels of performance for the *mitzvah* of the Chanukah lights. Shulchan Aruch does not mention the two lower levels. Only the optimum method is described in Shulchan Aruch. Why are the two lower levels deleted?

2. Hiddur Mitzvah

---

[16] Mesechet Shabbat 21b.

The discussion in the Talmud also presents a difficult problem. The Talmud is describing a basic performance of the *mitzvah* and enhancements of the performance. The Talmud in Tractate Baba Kamma discusses the issue of enhancements of *mitzvot*. It discusses the amount one should spend in order to enhance a *mitzvah*. The conclusion is that one should only spend up to one third of the value of the basic *mitzvah*.[17] An example will illustrate this rule. Assume a person wishes to buy a *mezuzah*. A *kasher* – fit – *mezuzah* can be purchased for twenty dollars. However, the purchaser wishes to buy a better *mezuzah*. How much should the buyer spend for a finer *mezuzah*? According to the rule in the Talmud, the maximum the person should spend is $26.60.

This rule obviously contradicts the discussion in Tractate Shabbat. The basic *mitzvah* of Chanukah only requires the lighting of a single candle each night. The enhanced and optimum levels require far more than a one third increase in expenditure. For example, by the last night the optimum method of lighting requires kindling eight lights. The basic level would only require a single light.

These two questions seem to indicate that there is a basic difference between the enhancements of the Chanukah lights and the enhancement of other *mitzvot*. Let us consider the general concept of enhancement. In most cases a *mitzvah* is performed in its entirety without the enhancement. In our example of the *mezuzah*, the *mitzvah* is performed perfectly with the twenty-dollar *mezuzah*. However, there is a separate obligation to enhance one's performance of all *mitzvot*. This is the obligation one fulfills through purchasing the better *mezuzah*. In regard to this obligation to enhance all *mitzvot*, the Talmud establishes a spending ceiling.

3. Lacking enhancement, lacking the Mitzvah

Shulchan Aruch does not mention the subsidiary levels of performance of the *mitzvah* of Chanukah. This indicates that, according to Shulchan Aruch, we are obligated in the optimum method. The implication of this statement is clear. Enhancement of the *mitzvah* is not merely required because of the general obligation to enhance all *mitzvot*. Instead, enhancement is an essential component of the *mitzvah* of the Chanukah lights. This *mitzvah* is only performed properly when the optimum method is used. In other words, one who lights a single candle, rather than eight, on the last night has not merely failed to fulfill a general obligation to enhance all *mitzvot*. The performance of the *mitzvah* of the Chanukah lights is incomplete.

It follows that the spending ceiling for enhancements does not apply to the Chanukah lights. That limit is applied to the general obligation to enhance all *mitzvot*. Here, enhancement is not an extraneous obligation. Enhancement is fundamental and required for the proper performance of the *mitzvah* of the Chanukah lights.

We can also understand the Shulchan Aruch's reason for deleting any mention of the subsidiary levels of the *mitzvah*. The Shulchan Aruch posits that the Talmud is not suggesting that we use the most basic method or even the enhanced method of lighting. We are obligated to use the optimum method. However, the Talmud is required to define the subsidiary methods of performing the *mitzvah*. Optimum is a relative concept. For a performance to be defined as optimum, other lower levels of performance must exist. The creation of an optimum performance requires, by definition, the creation of lower levels of performance. The Talmud establishes these

---

[17] Mesechet Baba Kamma 9a.

120

lower levels of performance in order to provide a basis and meaning for the optimum level. The Talmud does not intend for these levels to be used.

"How many candles does one light? On the first night, one lights one candle. Thenceforth, one adds one candle each night so that on the last night there will be eight candles. And if there are many household members, they should not light more than this number. Some say each household member should light." (Shulchan Aruch Orech Chayim 671:2)

The Talmud explains that the commandment to light the Chanukah lights can be fulfilled on three levels.[18] The basic level requires that each night a single candle is lit for the entire household. The preferred method is to light a number of candles corresponding to the number of members of the household. This number of candles is lit every night. The optimal method is to light a number of candles corresponding to the night of the festival. The first night one candle is lit. The second night two candles are lit. One candle is added each night until, on the last night, eight are lit.[19] An illustration will demonstrate these various levels. Consider a household composed of a father, mother and two children. The basic level of performance requires that this household light a single candle each night of Chanukah. This number never increases. The preferred method requires four candles to be lit each night. This number corresponds to the size of the household. The number remains constant throughout the festival.[20] Applying our illustrative case to the optimal level presents a difficulty. The Shulchan Aruch maintains that our family will light a single candle the first night. An additional candle is added each night, until a total of eight is reached. Rav Moshe Isserlis, in his glosses on the Shulchan Aruch, disagrees.[21] He maintains that the household must still light a number of candles corresponding with the number of its members. Therefore, the first night four candles are lit. This number represents the four members of the family. On subsequent nights one candle is added to each of the four. Following this plan, on the second night eight candles are lit two candles for each family member. On the third night twelve candles are lit. On the eighth night thirty-two candles are lit. Superficially, the position of Ramah Rav Moshe Isserlis is more logical. The preferred method of lighting requires a candle be lit for each member of the household. The optimal level requires that the number of candles correspond with the night of the festival. Ramah assumes that these two methods should be combined. Performance of the commandment at the optimal level should not preclude the inclusion of the preferred method. Therefore, each night, the number of candles corresponds with both the number of members of the household and the night of the festival. This makes sense!

Shulchan Aruch insists that once the optimal level is selected the preferred method must be abandoned. At the optimal level, the number of candles can only correspond to the number of nights. Any reference to the number of household members must be abandoned. What is Shulchan Aruch's reasoning? The source of the dispute between Shulchan Aruch and Ramah is found in the early commentators on the Talmud. Shulchan Aruch's position is expressed by the Tosefot.[22] They explain that when performing the mitzvah at the optimal level, the preferred

---

[18] Rabbaynu Shlomo ben Yitzchak (Rashi), Commentary on the Talmud, Mesechet Shabbat 21b.
[19] Rabbaynu Moshe ben Maimon (Rambam) Mishne Torah, Introduction.
[20] Rabbaynu Moshe ben Maimon (Rambam) Mishne Torah, Hilchot Chanukah 3:1-3.
[21] Rav Moshe Isserles, Comments on Shulchan Aruch, Orech Chayim 671:2
[22] Mesechet Shabbat 21b. Tosefot, Mesechet Shabbat 21b.

method must be abandoned. Their conclusion is based on a practical consideration. The candles can only represent a single numerical value. It is simply not possible to simultaneously represent the number of family members and the day of the festival. Therefore, when performing the mitzvah on the optimal level any reference to the number of family members must be abandoned. If reference to the number of household members remains included at the optimal level, complete confusion results. Consider a simple example. The second night a household lights two candles. This could represent a single individual lighting on the second night. This could also represent a family of two and one candle is lit for each member. In order to avoid this confusion, all reference to the number of household members is omitted. Now, there is no longer any confusion. The number only represents the night of the festival.

Ramah adopts the opinion of Maimonides.[23] He does not seem concerned with the issues raised by Tosefot. According to Ramah, how can a single number of candles represent two numbers? How can it represent both the number of household members and the night of the festival? Ramah suggests a simple solution to this problem. He requires each household member be represented by a separate set of candles. The separation between the sets removes any confusion. On the second night a family of four does not merely light eight candles. It lights four separate sets of two candles. The number of sets represents the number of family members. The number of candles in each set, corresponds with the night of the festival. This discussion suggests an interesting insight. Shulchan Aruch and Ramah dispute the requirements of the optimal method of performance. However, the basis of their disagreement is their interpretation of the preferred method. Shulchan Aruch understands the preferred method to require lighting a single set of candles. This set corresponds to the number of household members. The optimal method cannot be superimposed on the preferred method. Only one set of candles is lit. It cannot represent two numbers the members of the family and the night of the festival. Ramah maintains that the preferred method requires lighting multiple sets of candles. Each family member is represented by a separate set. This allows fulfillment of the optimal requirement without abandoning this preferred method. Each separate set can be expanded to represent the night of the festival. There is no cause for confusion. The number of sets represents the number of family members. The number of candles in each set represents the night.[24]

---

[23] Rabbaynu Moshe ben Maimon (Rambam) Mishne Torah, Hilchot Chanukah 4:1-2.
[24] Rav Israel Chait, Chanukah Shiurim 1974.

Purim

And it will be that when Hashem, your L-rd, grants you rest from all your enemies that surround you, in the land that Hashem, your L-rd, gives to you as a portion to possess, you should destroy the memory of Amalek from under the heavens. Do not forget. (Devarim 25:29)

Know your Enemies

1. The relevance of the commandment to destroy Amalek

The above passage is the source for the commandment to destroy Amalek. Who is Amalek? This nation attacked the Jewish people as they traveled from Egypt to the Land of Israel. We can no longer identify the descendants of this nation. Does this mean that this commandment is no longer relevant?

Rambam seems to indicate that this commandment retains its relevance even though the nation of Amalek has ceased to exist.[1] How can we be obligated to discharge this obligation if we cannot identify the nation of Amalek? Rav Yosef Dov Soloveitchik Zt"l suggested a response to this question that was shared with him by his father – Rav Moshe Zt"l. Rav Moshe suggested that the term Amalek refers to both a specific nation and to all others who adopt the outlook of this nation. The Torah deems a nation and individual who adopt the Amalek philosophy to be members of the Amalek nation.

And Amalek came and waged war with Israel at Refidim. (Shemot 17:8)

2. Identifying Amalek

What is the Amalek philosophy? Rav Soloveitchik quotes his father as explaining that Amalek sought to eradicate the Jewish people. A person or nation seeking our destruction is regarded as Amalek.[2]

A study of the comments of our Sages suggests a more precise definition of the Amalek philosophy. What motivated Amalek to attack Bnai Yisrael? Rashi explains that Amalek was not motivated by fear of conquest. It did not anticipate that Bnai Yisrael would attempt to conquer its land. It was not acting to forestall such an attempt. Amalek's motivations were more perverse. Amalek was driven by hatred for the Jewish people.[3]

Our Sages suggest different sources for this hatred. However, for the purpose of defining the Amalek philosophy, one need not know the source of the hatred. The essential characteristic of Amalek is that its aggression against the Jewish people is not a response to a real danger; it is an expression of base hatred.[4] This suggests that mere aggression toward the Jewish people does not identify a person or nation as Amalek. Aggression may be motivated by a legitimate fear or

---

[1] Rabbaynu Moshe ben Maimon (Rambam) Mishne Torah, Hilchot Melachim 5:4-5. Rambam explains that we cannot identify the nations of Cana'an. He does not extend this comment to Amalek. This implies Amalek can be identified.

[2] Rav Yosef Dov Soloveitchik, Harerai Kedem vol 1, chapter 186.

[3] Rabbaynu Shlomo ben Yitzchak (Rashi), Commentary on Sefer Devarim 25:18.

[4] R' Meir Leibush B' Yechiel Michel (Malbim), HaTorah VeHaMitzvah, Com. on Shemot, 17:8.

intended to protect a true self-interest. This is not Amalek's aggression. Amalek's aggression is an expression of baseless hatred.[5]

A consequence of this discussion is that it is difficult to identify the contemporary Amalek. Aggression toward the Jewish people does not, itself, render a person or nation Amalek. The motivation must be base hatred. Is it ever possible to determine who is Amalek? This question provides an insight into Megilat Esther.

As on the days that the Jews rested from their enemies and the month that was reversed from anguish to rejoicing and from a time of grieving to a festival – to make them days of feasting and rejoicing, sending portions of food to one another and gifts to the poor. (Megilat Esther 9:22)

3. The Megillah's overt plot

The above passage describes the creation of the Purim festival. Mordechai directed the Jewish people to observe Purim and established practices to be observed on the occasion. These include the Purim feast, friends sending gifts to one another, and giving gifts to the poor. The passage also describes the theme of Purim. It recalls the rescue of the Jewish people from annihilation.

This theme is developed in the Megillah. It tells the story of the rise of Haman to eminence in the court of King Achashverosh. Haman hates the Jewish people and persuades Achashverosh to allow him to issue a decree against the Jews. On the thirteenth day of Adar the people of Achashverosh's kingdom are invited and urged to rise-up against their Jewish neighbors and destroy them.

Achashverosh comes to suspect Haman's loyalty and to appreciate the integrity of Mordechai, the Jew. Esther succeeds in exposing Haman to the King. Achashverosh orders the execution of Haman. He empowers Mordechai and Esther to issue a decree allowing and encouraging the Jewish people to defend themselves from their enemies. This the Megillah's overt plot. The Sages suggest that the Megillah includes another less obvious sub-plot.

After these events, Achashverosh gave prominence to Haman, the son of Hamdatah, the Aggagi, and he elevated him. He placed his seat above all the ministers that were with him. (Megilat Esther 3:1)

4. The Megillah's sub-plot

The above passage describes Haman's rise to eminence. Achashverosh appoints him as his senior minister. Commenting on this passage, the Sages explain that Hashem allowed Haman to be granted this position as a prelude to and foundation for his destruction.[6] The appointment of Haman provided him the opportunity to plan the destruction of the Jews. Haman's campaign to annihilate the Jewish people eventually led to his own destruction. This is a difficult idea to

---

[5] This distinction has a contemporary application. Are the Palestinians a modern-day expression of Amalek? This depends upon the source of their aggression toward the State of Israel. If it is motivated by a sincere desire to regain a homeland that they believe is their own, then they are not Amalek. If this is not the underlying motivation, but instead, they are motivated by a hatred of the Jewish people, then they are Amalek. As we shall discover, determining whether an individual or nation is Amalek is challenging.

[6] Midrash Rabba, Megilat Esther 7:1.

understand. If Hashem's objective was to destroy Haman, could this not have been accomplished without jeopardizing the survival of the Jewish people?

As noted above, it is difficult to identify Amalek. The solution to this problem is the Megillah's sub-plot. It explains how the Jewish people were able to identify the Amalek of their time.

The Megillah's narrative describes the coincidence of two circumstances that exposed those who were Amalek.

- The Jewish people were citizens of Achashverosh's kingdom. They did not have sovereignty and were not a threat to any nation or people. Aggression directed against the Jewish people could only derive from base hatred and not in response to a real threat.
- Expression of this hatred was allowed and even sanctioned. This encouraged the haters to reveal themselves and become known to their Jewish neighbors.

Imagine the experience of the Jews at that time. Haman's decree was issued. The day was selected for the massacre of the Jewish people. Haman would not send forth the king's armies to carry out this mission. He invited the citizens of the kingdom to be his henchmen. The Jews observed the reactions of their neighbors. Some regarded Haman's decree as an abomination. They would never consider turning upon their neighbors. Others responded with indifference. But some eagerly awaited and planned for the coming massacre. They gathered weapons and designed the operations they would carry out. They eagerly and openly awaited the day on which they would give full expression to their vile hatred.

Like Haman, they exposed themselves as Amalek. When Achashverosh turned against Haman and empowered Mordechai and Esther, the Jews knew which of their neighbors were Amalek. They used this knowledge to confront and destroy the Amalek of their time.

5. Watch our Amalek!

Haman's decree caused the Jews enormous anxiety and anguish. Their lives were in jeopardy. They faced annihilation. However, this suffering was the means through which their enemies were fully exposed. Amalek was identified.

It is painful to observe the resurgence of anti-Semitism throughout the world. However, it is also true that the prerequisite for its destruction is the exposure of those who are Amalek.

"There are those that maintain that the reading of Parshat Zachor and Parshat Parah is a Torah obligation. Therefore, people living in an area in which there is not a congregation are obligated to come to a place that has a minyan for these Shabbatot. This is in order to hear these Torah readings that are Torah commandments." (Shulchan Aruch, Orech Chaim 685:7)

Waging War

The Shabbat prior to Purim, we read Parshat Zachor. This special reading is found at the end of Parshat Ki Tetzei. It discusses two mitzvot. The first is the obligation to remember the evil of Amalek. The second is the obligation to destroy the very memory of this corrupt nation. Shulchan Aruch notes that, according to many authorities, the reading of Parshat Zachor is required in order to fulfill the mitzvah of remembering Amalek. Therefore, it is important for every person to hear this reading.

Parshat Zachor is one of two sections in the Torah that discusses the wickedness of Amalek. The second section is at the end of Parshat Beshalach. These passages describe the unprovoked war that Amalek waged against Bnai Yisrael. This section also records Hashem's pledge to destroy Amalek. These passages are the Torah reading for Purim. Magen Avraham raises an interesting question. Can one fulfill the obligation to recall the wickedness of Amalek through the Purim Torah reading? This reading also discusses the wickedness of Amalek.

Magen Avraham suggests that one can fulfill the obligation to remember Amalek with the Purim reading. He argues that there is no reason for specifically requiring one to read the passages at the end of Parshat Ki Tetzei. Neither is there any obvious reason for requiring that one fulfill the mitzvah the week before Purim.

Rav Yosef Dov Soloveitchik Ztl disagrees. He points out that there is a basic difference between these two sections. Parshat Zachor discusses the mitzvot regarding Amalek. These are the mitzvot to remember Amalek and to destroy the nation. The reading of Purim does not describe these commandments.

Rav Soloveitchik continues his analysis with a very simple question. What is the nature of this mitzvah to remember Amalek?

In his Mishne Torah, Maimonides implies that this commandment to remember Amalek is closely linked to the mitzvah to destroy the nation. Maimonides explains that we are required to destroy Amalek. Then, he adds that we are required to regularly recall the evil of Amalek in order to evoke an abhorrence of this nation. Maimonides seems to imply that remembering Amalek is a precursor to waging war against the nation. We remember Amalek in order to motivate us to fulfill the commandment to destroy Amalek.[7]

This implication is confirmed by Maimonides' formulation of the mitzvah to destroy Amalek in his Sefer HaMitzvot. There, Maimonides writes that we are obligated to recall the evil of Amalek in order to motivate the Bnai Yisrael to wage war with this wicked nation.[8]

Rav Soloveitchik suggests that Maimonides' formulation of the mitzvah to remember Amalek suggests that Parshat Zachor may be specifically required. It is possible that the Purim reading is not adequate. The mitzvah to remember Amalek is designed to provide motivation for waging war. It is reasonable to assume that the mitzvah can only be fulfilled through a Torah reading that specifies the obligation to destroy Amalek. Through this reading, the recollection of Amalek's wickedness is linked to the commandment to destroy the nation. The Purim reading does not discuss the requirement to wage war against Amalek. This commandment is only mentioned in Parshat Zachor.[9]

"One is obligated to read the Megilah at night and to repeat it during the day." (Shulcah Aruch, Orech Chayyim 687:1)

---

[7] Rabbaynu Moshe ben Maimon (Rambam) Mishne Torah, Hilchot Melachim 5:5.
[8] Rabbaynu Moshe ben Maimon (Rambam) Sefer HaMitzvot, Mitzvat Aseh 189.
[9] Rav Michel Sherkin, Harrai Kedem, Chapter 195.

Repetition is the Key

1. More important

Shulchan Aruch explains that the Megilah is read twice on Purim. It is read at night and during the day. This law is derived from the Talmud in Tractate Megilah.[10] Tosefot and many other commentaries explain that the two readings of the Megilah are not of equal importance. The more fundamental reading is during the day. There are numerous proofs for this assertion. One simple proof is that the fundamental mitzvot of Purim are observed during the day. For example, the Purim feast can only be held during the day. The Talmud equates these observances to the reading of the Megilah. The equation seems to imply that, just as other mitzvot of Purim must be performed during the day, so too the reading of the Megilah is related to the day of Purim and not the night.[11]

This raises an interesting question. Why, then is the Megilah read at night? Secondly, the wording of Shulchan Aruch and the Talmud seems to imply that the nighttime reading is the more fundamental. Both refer to the daytime reading as a repetition of the nighttime reading. Referring to the second reading as a repetition indicates that it is secondary!

2. The need to study

Rav Naftali Tzvi Yehudah Berlin (Netziv) Ztl answers this question through a brilliant explanation of the relationship between the two readings. In order to understand his explanation, we must more carefully study the text of the Talmud.

The discussion in the Talmud begins by quoting Rebbe Yehoshua ben Levi. He explains that a person is required to read the Megilah at night and "le'shnotah" by day. The term leshnotah can be interpreted in two ways. It can mean "to learn" or it can be understood as "to repeat". At first, the Talmud understands the term to mean "to learn". According to this interpretation, we are required to read the Megilah at night and to study the laws during the day. The Talmud rejects this interpretation and concludes that le'shnotah means "to repeat". Therefore, the requirement is to read the Megilah at night and repeat the reading during the day.

Netziv asks, "How could the Talmud initially assume that the Megilah is not read during the day?" Yet, this seems to be the Talmud's original understanding of Rebbe Yehoshua ben Levi's lesson. The Talmud interprets his statement to mean that the Megilah is read at night and the laws of Purim are studied during the day!

Netziv responds that the Talmud never assumed that the laws of Purim should be learned to the exclusion of reading the Megilah. The Talmud always understood that the fundamental reading of the Megilah takes place during the daytime. Instead, the Talmud originally assumed that Rebbe Yehoshua ben Levi was establishing an additional requirement. Beyond the mere reading of the Megilah, one must study the laws. This enriches the reading of the Megilah.

3. An enhanced understanding

Through the study of the laws, the student acquires a more advanced comprehension of the Megilah's contents. Netziv further points out that this initial interpretation of Rebbe Yehoshua ben Levi's dictum reveals an essential premise of the Talmud.

---

[10] Mesechet Megilah 4a.

[11] Tosefot, Mesechet Megilah 4a.

The Talmud assumes that Rebbe Yehoshua ben Levi is not describing the fundamental mitzvah of reading the Megilah. The fundamental mitzvah is to merely read the Megilah during the day! Rebbe Yehoshua ben Levi is establishing a requirement to enhance this performance.

Through identifying the Talmud's premise, Netziv answers our questions. The Talmud rejects its initial interpretation of Rebbe Yehoshua ben Levi's lesson. His intention is to require the reading of the Megilah at night and its repetition during the day. However, the Talmud never abandons its essential premise! Rebbe Yehoshua ben Levi is establishing a requirement to enhance the performance of the mitzvah. In order to enhance the reading during the day, it must be preceded by a reading during the night. The daytime reading will be a repetition of the nighttime reading. Like any material, the Megilah is understood more clearly with review! Because the daytime reading is a second review, it will be better understood and appreciated.

Netziv explains that the nighttime reading is required to prepare us for the daytime reading. The daytime reading must be a repetition of the nighttime reading. True, the Talmud and Shulchan Aruch refer to the daytime reading as a repetition. However, this is not intended to diminish the importance of this second reading. The intention is to stress its fundamental nature. Through rendering this daytime reading into a repetition, it is enhanced with greater understanding and appreciation.[12]

And it was in the days of Achashverosh – the Achashverosh who ruled from Hodu to Kush – one hundred and twenty provinces. (Megilat Esther 1:1)

Lessons from Achashverosh

1. The messages of the Megilah story

The story related in Megilat Esther is constructed around the interplay between four personalities. Mordechai and Esther are the hero and heroin of the narrative. Haman is villain. Achashverosh is somewhat of an enigma. He is initially deftly manipulated by Haman, but later he emerges as the protector of the Jewish people. In other words, Achashverosh seems to be a passive figure in the narrative. Rather than initiating action, he is acted upon by others. Given this role, it would be expected for the Megilah to give him scant attention. Yet, the Megilah lavishes its attention upon Achashverosh and devotes the entire first chapter to developing a portrait of his personality.

According to the Talmud, the events described in the Megilah had a significant impact upon the attitudes of the Jewish people. Their experiences during the events, portrayed in the Megilah, provided compelling evidence of Hashem's ongoing providential relationship with the Jewish people. In addition, the events provided a moving lesson regarding human behavior and its consequences.

They observed two powerful figures – Achashverosh and Haman – trapped by the failings of their own personalities. Their observations of these two personalities provided an object-lesson in the consequences of blind pursuit of honor and power or self-indulgent pleasure. Therefore, the Megilah does not only include a description of events unfolding according to the irresistible plan of providence, it also explores the behaviors, attitudes, and personalities of the

---

[12] Rav Naftali Tzvi Yehuda Berlin (Netziv), Meromai Sadeh, Commentary on Mes. Megilah 4a.

main characters. This biographical component is designed to communicate the rewards of virtue and the consequences of evil and corruption.[13]

The first character sketch in the Megilah is of the king – Achashverosh. In the following discussion, a few aspects of that sketch will be explored.

In the third year of his reign, he made a party for all of his ministers and servants, the army of Paras and Madai, the nobility and the ministers of the provinces, before him. (Megilat Esther 1:3)

2. Achashverosh's celebration

Megilat Esther begins with a description of the celebration convened by Achashverosh in the third year of his ascent to the throne. This celebration ultimately led to a confrontation between Achashverosh and his queen, Vashti. Her defiance of the king resulted in her removal from the throne. This created the opportunity for Esther to replace Vashti as queen.

In other words, Achashverosh's celebration played an important role in the events that are described in the Megilah. Nonetheless, the reason that the Megilah devotes so much attention to the celebration is not evident from the text. It would seem adequate for the Megilah to explain that Vashti was deposed as a consequence of a dispute with the king and that Achashverosh, in response to his loneliness, sought out a new consort. Why does the Megilah devote so much attention to Achashverosh's celebration? Apparently, the details of the celebration and the events that occurred there provide a revealing portrait of Achashverosh's personality and his failings.

There, he displayed the riches of his glorious kingdom and the honor of his excellent majesty, many days – one hundred and eighty days. When these days were completed, the king made a feast for all of the people that were present in Shushan the castle, both great and minor people, seven days, in the court of the garden of the king's palace. (Megilat Esther 1:4-5)

3. The strange design of Achashverosh's celebration

The Megilah explains that Achashverosh's celebration was composed of two separate feasts. The first was conducted for a period of 180 days. All of the dignitaries, ministers, and nobility were invited to this fete. The second feast was held for seven days. At this party, Achashverosh hosted the entire population of Shushan. Even the most common citizens were invited to attend. What was the purpose of Achashverosh's celebration and why did he create two events?

In discussing the first celebration, the Megilah explains that Achashverosh wished to display his wealth and glory. This objective becomes very meaningful when considered in the context of a comment by Rashi. Rashi explains that the celebration was occasioned by Achashverosh's consolidation of power and authority.[14] Apparently, Achashverosh felt it necessary to impress upon the leaders, ministers, nobility, and the bureaucracy of his extended kingdom that he was now firmly in control and that he was the absolute monarch of the realm.

This explains Achashverosh's motives for convening the first feast. Why did he follow this 180-day fete with a second feast on behalf of the citizens of Shushan?

---

[13] Mesechet Megilah 19a.

[14] Rabbaynu Shlomo ben Yitzchak (Rashi), *Commentary on Megilat Esther* 1:2.

And they gave them drink in vessels of gold – vessels of diverse types – and the royal wine was abundant, according to the bounty of the king. The drinking was according to the instruction; no one was compelled. For so the king had directed to all the administrators of his household, that they should do according to every man's desire. (Megilat Esther 1:7-8)

4. The relationship of Achashverosh's dual objectives

In describing the second party, the Megilah explains that the participants were served wine in vessels of gold of diverse styles. An unlimited quantity of drink was made available to the guests. Then, the Megilah adds that Achashverosh instructed his household servants to carefully respect the preferences of his guests. Every guest was to be given as much wine as he wished. No one was to be denied the opportunity to fully indulge his appetite for drink and no one was to be forced to drink more than he wished. Rashi explains the importance of this instruction and its intention. At many parties, guests are required to drink cup after cup of wine as a courtesy to the host.[15] Achashverosh specifically instructed his staff to not create such an expectation. Achashverosh wanted his guests to truly enjoy themselves. He did not want their enjoyment to be marred by the necessities of protocol or social custom. Each guest was free to conduct himself – in regard to drink – as he pleased, free from the imposition of protocol or custom.

This suggests that Achashverosh had a second objective in creating his celebration. He wished to create a party in which the participants would be encouraged to fully indulge their desires free of social protocol or restrictive custom. This objective was achieved in the second feast. This party was a hedonistic experience.

In short, each of the two component feasts of the celebration had its own purpose. The first fete was designed to impress upon the political and social leadership of the kingdom that Achashverosh was their supreme and absolute ruler. The second component focused on pure pleasure, unfettered by social protocol. However, the identification of the objectives of each component feast does not completely explain Achashverosh's plan. Why could the two objectives not be combined in a single feast? Why did each feast with its unique objective also have its unique guest list?

4. Achashverosh's story

In order to understand the odd structure of Achashverosh's celebration, it is necessary to know more about his background. The Sages explain that Achashverosh was not the scion of noble lineage. He was a commoner who rose to power and deposed the royal family. This insight adds a dimension to the purpose of the first party. For 180 days Achashverosh hosted the leadership, royalty, and bureaucracy of his vast kingdom. He asserted his authority. The common people of Shushan were not included among the invited guests to this affair. Achashverosh did not need to impress the commoners. He did not need to assert his power over or demonstrate his authority to the plebeian class of Shushan. However, after the first feast ended, he immediately convened a party for the common people of Shushan. What does this reveal about Achashverosh?

Apparently, the second party was Achashverosh's response to the first affair. For 180 days he had been required to appear before and to impress the notables and nobility of his

---

[15] Rabbaynu Shlomo ben Yitzchak (Rashi), *Commentary on Megilat Esther* 1:8.

kingdom. Furthermore, his objective was to impress upon his guests his authority and grandeur. In order to accomplish his objective, he was required to conduct himself with dignity and restraint. He succeeded and he completed the 180-day celebration without mishap. However, the lengthy, dignified, and restrained affair was an ordeal for Achashverosh. Therefore, he immediately convened a second celebration.

The second party was designed to correct the defect of the first party and provide Achashverosh with a release that he needed desperately and felt he had earned. The second party paid no attention to protocol or social convention. Demonstrations of authority were replaced by abandonment to pleasure. This was not a feast for royalty and dignitaries. Achashverosh realized the elite of society would scoff at such an undignified adventure in hedonism. Instead, Achashverosh chose as his companions the common people – the members of the plebeian class who were his brothers. For Achashverosh, this second feast was the true party and the reward for his previous ordeal. However, at this second feast, Achashverosh faltered, and thereby, he placed his reign in jeopardy.

On the seventh day, when the heart of the king was merry with wine, he commanded Mehuman, Bizta, Harbona, Bigta, Abagta, Zetar, and Carcas, the seven chamberlains that ministered before the king Achashverosh to bring Vashti the queen before the king with the crown royal, to show the people and the princes her beauty; for she was fair in appearance. (Megilat Esther 1:10-11)

5. Achashverosh's confrontation with Vashti

On the final day of the second feast, Achashverosh precipitated a fateful confrontation with his queen, Vashti. After 186 days of celebration, Achashverosh became mindlessly drunk. In his intoxicated state, he commanded that Vashti appear before his guests so that he might display her astounding beauty. How was Achashverosh able to contain his appetites and remain sober until this point and why did he now permit himself to become intoxicated? Furthermore, why did his loss of control express itself in his precipitation of a confrontation with his queen? Even drunk, Achashverosh must have realized that he was inviting a confrontation with Vashti!

Our Sages provide an additional bit of information that is essential to understanding the confrontation that unfolded between Achashverosh and Vashti. They explain that Achashverosh and Vashti came to the throne from very different backgrounds. In contrast to Achashverosh's humble origins, Vashti boasted royal lineage. Achashverosh was a commoner and usurper who seized the throne and took Vashti as his queen.[16] It is very likely that his marriage to Vashti was designed to consolidate and legitimize his position as sovereign.

In this context, Achashverosh's treatment of Vashti provides another insight into his personality. His treatment of Vashti expresses a need to demean her and to deprive her of dignity. This suggests that Achashverosh felt intimidated by Vashti's royal lineage and somewhat inadequate in comparison to his queen. In other words, despite his power and authority, Achashverosh remained insecure. He could not dispel his own sense, that ultimately, he was a commoner who had usurped the throne from the royal family. Vashti evoked a deep sense of inadequacy. Under normal circumstances, Achashverosh was in control of his feelings and did not give public expression to his attitude toward Vashti. Now, in his drunken state, his

---

[16] Mesechet Megilah 12b and 11a.

resentments and his sense of inferiority overpowered his good sense and he engineered a showdown with his royal queen.

It is not surprising that only now – well into his second feast – did Achashverosh become drunk and lose his self-control. As explained, Achashverosh was intimidated by Vashti's noble heritage. If this was Vashti's affect upon him, one can imagine the strain he experienced during the first 180-day feast.

For 180 days, Achashverosh was surrounded by nobility and notables. He was required to impress his guests and demonstrate authority. However, these very people, whom he labored to impress, reminded him of his own plebeian origins and evoked a deep sense of inferiority. Now, at his second feast, his ego was buoyed by the company of the common people of Shushan – the people among whom he felt secure and confident. In this environment, he felt comfortable fully indulging his hedonistic desires.

He also became engrossed in his resentment of those who made him feel inferior and unworthy. To Achashverosh, no person represented the class of privilege more than his own queen – Vashti. Eventually, his state of mind and judgment were compromised by his drunkenness. His anger and resentment gained control over him and he precipitated the confrontation with Vashti.

And the queen Vashti refused to come at the instructions of the king through the chamberlains. And the king became very angry and his wrath burned within him. (Megilat Esther 1:12)

6. Vashti's refusal and Achashverosh's reaction

Achashverosh's reaction of Vashti's refusal to attend to his wishes was immediate and extreme. He was overcome with anger. The remarkable intensity of Achashverosh's reaction can be appreciated in the context of another comment of our Sages. They explain that in response to Achashverosh's ill-mannered invitation, Vashti delivered a sharp rebuke. She reminded Achashverosh of his humble origins. She attributed his drunkenness and boorish behavior to these origins and contrasted Achashverosh to her own regal father who never demeaned himself publicly.[17] In other words, rather than achieving his goal of humbling Vashti, Achashverosh was reminded by her of his own inadequacy. The very insecurities that motivated his confrontation with Vashti were intensified and transformed into indignant anger.

In summary, the first chapter of Megilat Esther provides two important insights into Achashverosh's personality. First, despite his ascent to the throne, in his heart he remained a member of the plebeian class. He was capable of acting with restraint and dignity – for a period of time. However, he was drawn toward the hedonistic lifestyle and could not resist its allure. Second, Achashverosh was a powerful king. Yet, he was plagued by a sense of inferiority and inadequacy. He had risen to the highest rank within society. Yet, he viewed himself as a usurper and interloper. These character traits fatefully combined and led Achashverosh into a confrontation with Vashti and ultimately caused him to depose and kill his queen.

Now it came to pass in the days of Achashverosh – he was the Achashverosh who reigned from Hodu to Cush, one hundred twenty-seven provinces. (Megilat Esther 1:1)

---

[17] Mesechet Megilah 12b.

An Important Message from Achashverosh

1. Megilat Esther tells two stories

Megilat Esther tells two stories. One is the narrative of the salvation of the Jewish people from an evil adversary who would have destroyed them. In this narrative, a set of unlikely events leads to placing the heroine, Esther, in a position from which she is uniquely suited and situated to intervene to save her people. At the same time, a series of equally unlikely events, leads the king, Achashverosh, to suspect the loyalty of his most trusted advisor – the evil Haman.

As the story unfolds, one unlikely event establishes the foundation for the next unlikely event. The message of the narrative is that an invisible hand is at work behind the scenes. This hand – Hashem's providence – is preparing the means for Bnai Yisrael's salvation even before, and while, Haman executes his plan for their destruction.

The second story told by the Megilah concerns the interactions of disparate personalities. The characters in this narrative are Achashverosh, Haman, Mordechai, and Esther. Each is unique and different from the others. The account of their interactions with one another and the influence that each has on the others is an exploration of human personality, our strengths and our challenges. If we study these characters, we discover that a little of each of us can be discerned in each of these disparate characters.

And when these days were over, the king made for all the people present in Shushan the capital, for [everyone] both great and small, a banquet for seven days, in the court of the garden of the king's orchard. (Megilat Esther 1:5)

In the evening she would go, and in the morning she would return to the second house of the women, to the custody of Shaashgaz, the king's chamberlain, the guard of the concubines; she would no longer come to the king unless the king wanted her, and she was called by name. (Megilat Esther 2:14)

2. Achashverosh the hedonist

Let us begin with Achashverosh. What type of person was this mighty king? What does the Megilah reveal about his personality? He was a powerful ruler. He demanded and received the loyalty and obedience of princes and ministers from throughout the far-flung territories of his vast kingdom. Yet, the formality of the Persian court and its standards of decorum made the mighty King Achashverosh uneasy.

After celebrating the consolidation of his rule for 180 days with the princes, ministers, and officers of his kingdom, Achashverosh convened a second seven-day feast. Unlike the first celebration, this feast was not intended primarily for the dignitaries of the kingdom. It was held for the common citizens of Shushan – his capital.

Apparently, Achashverosh needed a release. The demands of the court were oppressive. The prolonged celebration and the responsibility of entertaining the royalty and dignitaries of his kingdom placed enormous strain upon Achashverosh. He rewarded himself with a celebration with the common people, in which wine flowed freely, and each person drank as he desired. At this party, Achashverosh finally felt at ease. He allowed himself the indulgent pleasure of drunkenness, with an outcome that he later regretted.

Achashverosh was also a person of enormous appetites. In his loneliness, he sought the companionship of women. He created a harem populated by the most beautiful women of his

133

kingdom. Women were recruited from every province, and presumably the king would select one to be queen in place of the deposed Vashti. But Achashverosh spent only one night with each young woman. His quest for a queen was replaced by an adventure in lust. Appetite ruled his actions. Achashverosh was a hedonist. Yet, this uncouth hedonist fell completely in love with Esther. Who was Esther and how did she secure the devotion of such an unlikely suitor?

And the maiden pleased him, and she won his favor, and he hastened her ointments and her portions to give [them] to her, and the seven maidens fitting to give her from the king's house, and he changed her and her maidens to the best [portions in] the house of the women. (Megilat Esther 2:9)

3. Esther: Beauty and virtue

The Megilah reveals two qualities of Esther. She was beautiful. She was also a woman of charm and virtue. In the above passage, we are told that while held in the harem, she earned the respect and devotion of its master. This man – who was essentially a purveyor of women to the king – lavished upon Esther his care and attention. Something about her won the admiration of even this base creature.

The Talmud in Tractate Ketubot describes a practice of Rav Shmuel the son of Rav Yitzchak. This sage would dance before the bride while grasping three myrtle branches. The Talmud applauds his practice of celebrating before the bride and groom, and specifically his enthusiasm in the practice of this mitzvah. But the Talmud does not comment on the significance of the three myrtle branches that Rav Shmuel grasped while dancing.

There is a hint to the significance of these branches in the Megilah. The Hebrew word for myrtle is *hadasah*. The Megilah tells us that Esther had a Hebrew name. That name was Hadasah. Perhaps, the significance of the branches that Rav Shmuel grasped when dancing before the bride is that they represent the Hadasah of the Megilah – Esther. In grasping these branches, Rav Shmuel compared the bride to Esther.

The declaration of Rav Shmuel is consistent with an earlier discussion in the Talmud. There, the school of Hillel rules that one should declare before every bride that she is pleasant in both appearance and character. The school of Shamai disagrees. This school rules that although it is appropriate to praise a bride, one's praise should be truthful. Therefore, the praise should be adapted to the actual qualities of the particular bride. If she is, in fact, pleasant in appearance and character, then that praise should be used. But if such praise would be untruthful, then a more accurate praise should be substituted.

Rav Shmuel grasped his myrtle branches at every wedding celebration and danced with them before the bride. He compared every bride to Esther – pleasant in appearance and in character. Through this practice, he adopted the position of the school of Hillel.

4. Beauty and virtue in marriage

The discussion in the Talmud stresses the importance of virtue in a bride in addition to beauty. It is the combination of both traits that secures the love of the husband. Beauty may secure the groom's fascination, and even infatuation. But it is the combination of beauty and virtue that secures his devotion.

Now, let us return to Esther and her relationship with Achashverosh. Esther was beautiful. But so were the other members of the extensive harem created for Achashverosh. It is not likely that she was the most beautiful woman with whom the king had a liaison. What won his devotion? Esther was unique in her character. Apparently, this character earned Esther the dedication of the master of the harem and also secured the absolute devotion of Achashverosh.

In short, the hedonistic Achashverosh, who was seeking only orgiastic pleasure, was completely taken by Esther. But his complete devotion was not because of some unique physical beauty that Esther possessed. It was a result of a spiritual character that somehow radiated from her. How strange that the hedonist was smitten by virtuous Esther! How can this be explained?

But it seemed contemptible to him to lay hands on Mordechai alone, for they had told him Mordechai's nationality, and Haman sought to destroy all the Jews who were throughout Achashverosh's entire kingdom, Mordechai's people. (Megilat Esther 3:6)

5. Haman's hatred of Mordechai

We will return to this issue. But first, let us consider another of the relationships described in the Megilah – the relationship between Haman and Mordechai. What do we know about these characters? The Megilah describes Haman as driven by the desire to secure power and influence. At first, this drive propelled him to the highest levels of influence in the court. Eventually, this same drive led to his downfall when Achashverosh recognized Haman's true character and motives.

Mordecahi was above all guided by his religion and ethics. He protected his sovereign from conspirators who sought to depose and murder him. He guarded Esther and cared for her. He fought for the welfare of his people. He absolutely refused to bow to Haman and worship him. And Haman intensely hated Mordechai.

How strange! Mordechai and Haman, Achashverosh and Esther. Two pairs of opposites. In one pair the opposites repel one other. Haman hates Mordechai and is consumed by a hatred that he can only conceive of satisfying through the murder of his adversary and the total annihilation of his people. In the other pair, opposites are attracted. The hedonistic Achashverosh is completely smitten by the virtuous Esther. He must have her as his queen. How are such different reactions to be explained?

6. Responding to those who have virtues we lack

The answer is very simple and basic. Despite his many shortcomings, Achashverosh had the capacity to appreciate virtue. He did not have the capacity to achieve it and he struggled to just contain his passions and impulses. But he recognized virtue and he appreciated it. He was drawn to Esther and eventually he placed his trust in Mordechai.

In contrast, Haman was threatened by virtue. He could not tolerate it and sought to destroy it. Mordechai's refusal to bow to him was intolerable. It evoked in Haman a self-awareness of his own inescapable humanity and mortality. Haman was attempting to kill not just Mordechai and the Jewish people, but a fundamental truth. We are all finite, mortal human beings. Our power is illusionary and even the illusion can last no longer than the fleeting passage of a lifetime.

Haman and Achashverosh had much in common. Both were confronted by individuals who represented to them a set of virtues very alien to their own values and lifestyles. Both were challenged by their respective partners to consider an alternative to their own path in life. Haman was confronted by Mordechai. Achashverosh was challenged by Esther. Haman responded by attempting to uproot and destroy the truth he could not endure. Achashverosh had the capacity to recognize and value that truth even though he could not personally live his life according to its demands.

Some years ago I had an interesting conversation with a former student. This young man had given up many aspects of his Torah observance. I told him that I understood that many Torah practices were difficult for him. But certainly, many other aspects were not so challenging. Why not continue those practices that resonated with him? He responded that were he to resume those practices, he would be reminded of his failure to observe other practices. If he observed kashrut, he would be reminded of his failure to observe Shabbat. Rather than be haunted by this reminder of failure, he preferred to abandon virtually all observance.

Years passed and he slowly began to increase his level of observance. What changed and allowed this person to reverse course and reengage in Judaism? He came to see life as a journey. We travel toward a distant goal. That goal is to make the most of ourselves. At every moment, we are more than the person we might have been and less than the person we may yet become. If we understand that we are on a journey, then we can be like Achashverosh. We can recognize virtue, value and even treasure it, even though at the moment it escapes our grasp. But if see ourselves only as we are at the moment, without the vision of a great journey that lay before us, then every virtue we lack is an insult hurled at us. We become Haman – intolerant of the virtues that remind us of our failings.

I believe that this young man, as he matured, came to see his life as a journey. The realization that he could be more than he was at the moment, gave him the capacity to travel the path toward self-realization and fulfillment.

Now in Shushan the palace there was a certain Jew, whose name was Mordechai, the son of Yair, the son of Shimei, the son of Kish, a Benjamite; who had been carried away from Jerusalem with the captivity which had been carried away with Yechoniah king of Judah, whom Nevuchadnezzar the king of Babylon had carried away. And he brought up Hadassah, that is, Esther, his uncle's daughter: for she had neither father nor mother, and the young girl was fair and beautiful; whom Mordechai, when her father and mother were dead, took for his own daughter. (Megilat Esther 2:5-7)

The Megilah's Account of Multiple Intelligences[18]

1. The heroes of the Megilah

The above passages introduce the two heroes of the Purim story – Mordechai and Esther. Mordechai is described as a refugee who came to Persia with the exile of the Jewish people from their homeland. Esther is his orphaned cousin. The passages explain that Mordechai adopted Esther and raised her as his own daughter. Together, these two individuals saved the Jewish people. What was the role of each of these heroes in the salvation of their people? In order to answer this question, we must better understand each of these individuals. This process begins through considering three incidents described in Megilat Esther.

---

[18] Although lectures of Rav Yosef Dov Soloveitchik are not directly citde, many aspects of this presentation are inspired by, influenced by, and even identical to his analysis of the Megilah.

When Mordechai perceived all that was done, Mordechai rent his clothes, and put on sackcloth with ashes, and went out into the midst of the city, and cried with a loud and a bitter cry; and came even before the king's gate: for none might enter into the king's gate clothed with sackcloth. (Megilat Esther 4:1-2)

2. Mordechai's response to Haman's plan to destroy the Jews

The first of these incidents is described in the above passages. The Megilah tells the story of Haman's attempt to destroy the Jewish people and the defeat of his evil plan. Haman rises to the position of grand vizier to the king of Persia – Achashverosh. Haman resents Mordechai's refusal to bow to him and develops a plan to destroy Mordechai and his people. He persuades Achashverosh to allow a pogrom to be carried out against the Jews throughout the vast Persian Empire. Mordechai becomes aware of the king's pact with Haman and reacts. The above passages describe his response. He rends his clothing and dons garments of sackcloth. He goes forth into the city and cries out in mourning. He proceeds as far as the gate to the king's compound and there he remains.

What did Mordechai hope to accomplish through this very public display? Perhaps, he wished only to attract Queen Esther's attention in order to secure her help in saving their people. Malbim suggests that Mordechai had another objective.

The posts went out, being hastened by the king's commandment, and the decree was given in Shushan the palace. And the king and Haman sat down to drink; but the city Shushan was perplexed. (Megilat Esther 3:15)

3. Mordechai acting while others were paralyzed

The above passage describes the reaction in the capital to the announcement of the planned annihilation of the Jews of Persia. The news was received with astonishment. It is not clear exactly who was astonished. Rashi suggests that the Jews of the capital – Shushan – were astonished.[19] Why were the Jews who were refugees in a foreign land shocked that they should be persecuted?

The opening passages to the Megilah describe the celebration that Achashverosh sponsored to celebrate the consolidation of his rule over his extensive kingdom. The Megilah explains that Achashverosh included his Jewish subjects in this elaborate celebration. The inclusion of the capital's Jewish citizens among the king's guests indicates that they were not regarded as aliens. They had integrated themselves into their host community and they did not regard themselves as exiles and foreigners. This view of their position within their adopted home brought with it a sense of security. Jews regarded themselves as accepted and respected.

Suddenly, the Jews learned that they were to be butchered. Their king had endorsed the plan to eradicate them. They received this news with shock and dismay. Their security was shattered and their understanding of their place within the Persian Empire was instantly destroyed.

Gershonides suggests that there is another possible interpretation of the above passage. All of the citizens of the capital were stunned.[20] The Jews were not mistaken in their appraisal of their status. They were accepted by the enlightened community in which they lived. Their

---

[19] Rabbaynu Shlomo ben Yitzchak (Rashi), *Commentary on Megilat Esther* 3:15.

[20] Rabbaynu Levi ben Gershon (Ralbag / Gershonides), *Commentary on Megilat Esther* 3:15.

neighbors joined them in responding with complete astonishment and dismay to the news that an integral part of the Persian community would be eradicated by decree of the king.

In short, the passage is explaining that the Jews of Shushan, and perhaps, even their neighbors were stunned by the king's decree and his behavior. However, Rabbaynu Avraham ibn Ezra adds another element to the message of the passage. He explains that the passage is revealing not only the people's sense of confusion but also that the people did not know how to respond. They were overwhelmed by their astonishment. They understood that they were confronted by disaster but they took no action.[21] They were confused, but silent.

Now, Mordechai's objective can be identified. Malbim explains that Mordechai was demonstrating against the king's decree. He intentionally traveled through the streets of the capital and up to the gates of the king's palace in the garb of a mourner, boldly crying out his distress. His objective was to shake observers out of their lethargy. His demonstration was directed to the Jews and to the larger community. He was marching, protesting, and challenging all those who observed or heard of his actions to step forward and take action. And among those to whom he appealed was the queen – Esther.[22]

> Then Mordecai commanded to answer Esther: Think not with yourself that you shall escape in the king's house, more than all the Jews. For if you altogether hold your peace at this time, then relief and deliverance shall arise to the Jews from another place; but you and your father's house shall be destroyed. And who knows whether you have come to the royal court for such a time as this? (Megilat Esther 4:13-14)

4. Mordechai's confronting of Esther

The second revealing episode of the Megilah now occurs. Esther learns of Mordechai's actions and the planned annihilation of her people. Mordechai directs Esther to appeal to the king on behalf of her people. Esther criticizes Mordechai's plans. She explains to her cousin that protocol of the court requires that she await a summons before approaching the king. Those who approach the king without an invitation do so at the risk of their lives. Malbim explains that Esther was not refusing to act on behalf of her people. She was arguing that rather than appearing uninvited at the king's court, she should await Achashverosh's inevitable invitation. The invitation would express the king's desire to see her and be with her. Certainly, that would be the best time to appeal to the king on behalf of the Jewish people.[23]

In the above passages, Mordechai rejects Esther's reasoning. He tells her that she should not assume that she is protected by her position in the royal court. She must step forward on behalf of her people. If she refuses to act, Hashem will preserve His people through some other agent or means and she and her family will be destroyed. Mordechai ends his response by suggesting to Esther that maybe it was for this very task that she had become queen.

Clearly, Mordechai suspects that Esther is responding with fear when courage is required. He argues that Esther's personal safety is not assured because of her position in the court. Instead, she can only hope to save herself through acting courageously on behalf of her people.

---

[21] Rabbaynu Avraham ibn Ezra, *Commentary on Megilat Esther* 3:15.
[22] Rabbaynu Meir Libush (Malbim), *Commentary on Megilat Esther* 4:1.
[23] Rabbaynu Meir Libush (Malbim), *Commentary on Megilat Esther* 4:11.

However, there are three elements of Mordechai's response to Esther that are difficult to understand. First, he suggests that if she does not act, she and her family will be destroyed. How does Mordechai know this? Second, he tells Esther that if she does not act, then salvation will come from some other source. This seems to contradict his message of urgency. If the Jews will be saved even without Esther risking her life, why should she place herself in danger? Third, Mordechai suggests that, perhaps, Esther became queen in order that she take action at this moment. This is an amazing claim. Why did Mordechai offer this speculation and how did it strengthen his argument?

Ibn Ezra explains that Mordechai was making two points to Esther. The first is that Hashem will not allow His people to be destroyed. Esther's actions will not decide the destiny of her people. However, Esther does need to decide whether she will be the instrument for the salvation of the Jews or whether she will allow that responsibility to pass to another. Second, in making her decision, she should consider that, perhaps, providence had made her queen so, at this moment, she would be Hashem's instrument in the salvation of His people. If this is her appointed mission, then she must pursue it. If she refuses, then she will be acting against the plan of providence and her ascension to the throne will be meaningless and worthless. And Mordechai reminds Esther that her security is not derived from her royal status. Like her predecessor, she can be stripped of that status in a moment. Her security lies in Hashem. She must act according to His providential plan if she wishes to enjoy His protection.[24]

At this point in the narrative an impression of the personalities of Mordechai and Esther begins to emerge. Mordechai has demonstrated two qualities. First, he is a person of action. While others are stunned and incapacitated by their shock, he is moving forward with a plan of action. Second, he has the remarkable capacity to step outside of the events into which he is entwined and analyze them from the perspective of an unattached observer. He quickly senses the fear that underlies his cousin's response. He looks at the events that have unfolded from the ascension of Esther to her throne up to the present moment. He sees the hand of Hashem, and understands what must be done. In contrast, Esther seems to be dominated by her fear and, like the Jews of Shushan, unable to take action.

If I have found favor in the sight of the king, and if it please the king to grant my petition, and to perform my request, let the king and Haman come to the banquet that I shall prepare for them, and I will do tomorrow as the king has said. (Megilat Esther 5:8)

5. Esther only partially adopts Mordechai's plan

The above passage describes the third incident we must consider. Esther does not completely adopt Mordechai's plan. She does appear before the king without a summons but she does not bare her soul to him. Instead, she invites the king to come to her home accompanied by Haman for an intimate party. The king accepts the invitation and with Haman he comes to Esther's party. He recognizes that Esther has some request that she wishes to place before him and he encourages her to present her petition. Esther responds that she seeks most the king's and Haman's company at a second intimate party the following day.

Why did Esther not follow Mordechai's directions, immediately approach the king, and beg for the deliverance of her people? When the king and Haman came to her party and the king urged Esther to state her request, why did she again not take advantage of the king's invitation

---

[24] Rabbaynu Avraham ibn Ezra, *Commentary on Megilat Esther* 4:14.

and seek the salvation of her people? Why instead did she merely invite the king and Haman to a second party?

Go, gather together all the Jews that are present in Shushan, and fast for me, and neither eat nor drink three days, night or day. I also and my maidens will fast likewise; and so will I go in unto the king, which is not according to the law: and if I perish, I perish. (Megilat Esther 4:16)

6. Esther's elaborate strategy

Let us consider an earlier episode in the narrative. Esther prepared before appearing before Achashverosh. She asked Mordechai to declare a three-day fast. She and her household would also join in this fast. This would be a period of repentance and prayer. On the third day Esther appeared before the king without invitation.

Ibn Ezra raises an important question. Esther appeared before the king at the end of a three day fast. The long fast would have impacted her appearance. She would not have looked her best. She had come to court hoping to appeal to the king's love and desire for her. She should have done everything possible to enhance her beauty. Instead, she came at the end of a long fast. She could not have looked her best.

Ibn Ezra responds that Esther understood that the fast would compromise her appearance. But she was relying more upon the prayers and repentance of the people and less upon her appearance.[25]

Gershonides adds an important insight. Esther was coming to Achashverosh to beg him to spare her people. She was not appealing to his sense of justice or his love for the Jewish people. She hoped that he would grant her request because of his love for her. She needed to impress upon Achashverosh that the issue that she wished to place before him was of the greatest importance to her. She accomplished this through two measures. First, she came to the court without invitation. Immediately, the king recognized that she had come to appeal to him about an issue of immense personal importance. She was willing to risk her life. Second, she communicated to Achashverosh that the issue was of such enormous concern that it fundamentally impacted her wellbeing, happiness, and even her health. She wanted him to conclude that she was laboring under a burden of terrible worry and that her concern over the unrevealed issue was so intense as to physically impact her.[26]

It emerges from this insight that Esther had developed and was implementing a strategy. She had accepted Mordechai's charge to act. However, she concluded that the straightforward approach advocated by Mordechai was not the best strategy. Mordechai's urgings moved Esther to act. But the strategy that she employed was completely hers.

Let us now consider Esther's behavior at the first party. Ibn Ezra suggests that Esther was waiting for the best moment to appeal to the king. At the first party, she did not feel that the circumstances were optimal. She decided to postpone her appeal to the king, hoping that some development might improve these circumstances.[27] This did take place. That night, the king was reminded of Mordechai's discovery of and intervention into a plot to assassinate the king. He also discovered that Haman was not only greedy, but also ambitious and, perhaps, even coveted

---

[25] Rabbaynu Avraham ibn Ezra, *Commentary on Megilat Esther* 4:16.

[26] Rabbaynu Levi ben Gershon (Ralbag), *Commentary on Megilat Esther, Toelet* 35.

[27] Rabbaynu Avraham ibn Ezra, *Commentary on Megilat Esther* 5:8.

his throne. The next day Esther realized that the time was right to ask the king to save the people of Mordechai from the evil machinations of the power-hungry Haman.

GRA sees another motive in Esther's behavior. Achashverosh would wonder at Esther's reluctance to reveal her request. He would interpret this reluctance as indicative of her overwhelming distress. He would conclude that Esther's issue was consuming her. That she was in such pain, that heroic effort was required for her to present it to the king.[28] According to GRA, Esther was systematically moving the king toward a state of deep anxiety, and even panic over her wellbeing.

Gershonides adds another dimension to Esther's behavior. He explains that in each invitation, Esther included Haman. The impression this communicated to Achashverosh was that Esther believed she could not present her weighty issue to the king alone. Haman's acquiescence would be required to resolve the matter.[29] For a tyrant like Achashverosh, the recognition that his own beloved queen was uncertain of his power and authority was unsettling. It aroused his suspicion of Haman and prepared him for the accusation of disloyalty that Esther planned to present.

7. The complementary roles of Esther and Mordechai

Hashem saved his people from Haman through Esther and Mordechai. Each had a distinct role in the salvation of the Jewish people. Only through the combination of their traits was the rescue affected. Mordechai contributed clarity of vision, the ability to quickly understand and assess a situation, and act while others remain confused and paralyzed. However, Mordechai approached challenges with direct, transparent methods.

Esther contributed a keen understanding of human motivations and emotions. She possessed the uncanny ability to foresee how another person – in this case Achashverosh – sees his surroundings and circumstances. She also had a remarkable capacity for developing and implementing creative strategies. She combined these gifts in her response to Mordechai's prompting. She designed and implemented the strategy that saved the Jewish people.

8. How to create partnerships

No person possesses all of the gifts and talents required to address every challenge. We are strongest when we join our gifts and talents with those of others. For these powerful combinations to be formed, the participants must recognize that each individual is blessed with unique gifts. Each of us must appreciate the blessings of our own gifts and have the humility to recognize one's own limits and the gifts and talents that Hashem has bestowed upon others. With this recognition we can come together to achieve outcomes we cannot individually attain.

And when Haman saw that Mordechai bowed not down, nor prostrated himself before him, then Haman was full of wrath. But it seemed contemptible in his eyes to lay hands on Mordechai alone; for they had made known to him the people of Mordechai. And Haman sought to destroy all the Jews that were throughout the whole kingdom of Achashverosh, even the people of Mordechai. (Megilat Esther 3:5-6)

---

[28] Rav Eliyahu of Vilna (GRA), *Commentary on Megilat Esther* 5:8.
[29] Rabbaynu Levi ben Gershon (Ralbag), *Commentary on Megilat Esther, Toelet* 35.

It's not Easy being Haman

1. The confrontation between Haman and Mordechai

Megilat Esther focuses on two aspects of Haman's character. It explains the strategy he employed in order to manipulate Achashverosh. The Megilah also explores the nature of Haman's wickedness. It delves into the source of his pathological fixation upon Mordechai and the Jewish people. However, the Megilah's treatment of this issue is not manifestly expressed in its passages. Instead, careful consideration of two incidents is required for the Megilah's message to emerge.

Haman seems to acquire his hatred for the Jewish people soon after his appointment as Achashverosh's vizier. The Megilah explains that with this appointment came a directive that all members of the court and subjects of the king pay homage to Haman by kneeling and prostrating themselves before him. This directive was obeyed by the king's servants and subjects. Mordechai, alone, refused to obey the royal directive and pay homage to the king's vizier.

Apparently, Mordechai's behavior did not immediately disturb Haman. It seems that initially he was not even aware of Mordechai's refusal to follow the king's edict. However, among those who observed Mordechai's behavior, his refusal to kneel and prostrate himself before Haman was sensational. These observers understood from Mordechai that his actions expressed his convictions as a Jew. They made Haman aware of Mordechai's behavior. They wanted to precipitate a conflict between Haman and Mordechai and see who would triumph. The Megilah explains that at this point Haman first took notice of Mordechai and discovered that the report brought to him was accurate. Indeed, Mordechai would not kneel or prostrate himself before him.

Haman was consumed with anger. His anger was provoked by Mordechai, but it extended to all Jews. Haman decided that he would seek the destruction of all Jews in the kingdom.

Two aspects of Haman's reaction to Mordechai require further consideration. First, the Megilah explains that when Haman became aware of Mordechai's resistance, he was filled with anger. Haman enjoyed virtually universal recognition. One single individual – Mordechai – refused to efface himself. Mordechai's lonely protest was so insignificant that Haman did not even notice it until instigators brought it to his attention. Why was Haman so infuriated by Mordechai's actions? Second, the Megilah describes Mordechai as an outlier, even among Jews. Apparently, other Jews obeyed the king's directive. Why did Haman decide to destroy all of the Jews because of Mordechai's behavior?

And Haman recounted unto them the glory of his riches, and the multitude of his children, and everything as to how the king had promoted him, and how he had advanced him above the princes and servants of the king. Haman said moreover: Yea, Esther the queen did let any man come in with the king to the banquet that she had prepared but myself; and tomorrow also am I invited by her together with the king. Yet, all this avails me nothing, so long as I see Mordechai the Jew sitting at the king's gate. (Megilat Esther 5:11-13)

2. Mordechai's profound effect on Haman

In order to answer these questions, another incident should be considered. As the story of the Megilah progresses, Haman persuades Achashverosh to allow him to issue a decree promoting the annihilation of the kingdom's Jews. Mordechai appeals to Esther the queen to intercede with Achashverosh and ask that he revoke the decree. Esther decides against directly appealing to Achashverosh. Instead, she invites the king and Haman to a party she has prepared exclusively for them. This party does not provide Esther with an opportunity to appeal to Achashverosh. Esther invites Haman and Achashverosh to second exclusive party the following night.

Upon leaving the queen's residence, Haman encounters Mordechai. Again, Haman's nemesis refuses to pay him homage. Haman in enraged. He returns to his home and gathers his closest confidants and his wife. He delivers an address. He begins by describing his fame and wealth. He boasts of his many sons. He proudly notes that even the queen acknowledges his singular position in the kingdom. She has twice included him alone in intimate parties she has made for the king. Then, Haman makes an amazing statement. He declares that all his accomplishments, his wealth, and his glory are rendered meaningless by Mordechai's defiance.

How can this be explained? Why did Mordechai's behavior have such a powerful effect on Haman? How is it possible that all of Haman's accomplishments were rendered meaningless by the defiance of this one lonely Jew?

3. A foreign deity

The answer to all of these questions is provided by a comment of our Sages. The Sages are discussing Mordechai's reason for not obeying the king's directive to pay homage to Haman. They explain that Mordechai refused to obey the directive because Haman had made himself into a deity.[30]

The actual narrative of the Megilah does not seem to support the conclusion that Haman ascribed supernatural powers or omnipotence to himself. The Sages are not necessarily suggesting that the Megilah omitted this important element of the narrative. Instead, perhaps the Sages are suggesting that Haman was enamored with his perception of his own greatness. He believed himself to be singular, powerful, and brilliant. He perceived himself as the master of fate and destiny and as the potentate who either ruled or manipulated all others. He deserved the acknowledgement of lesser human beings and their adulation.[31]

Of course, this outlook is an absurd presumption for any human being. We are all frail creatures. We cannot control nature or protect ourselves from its extremes. A single sick cell within our complex bodies can multiply unchecked and bring us to an untimely end. Our power and our influence over our destiny are illusionary. At times we may entertain an illusion of greatness, but a sudden change in our finances, the illness of a friend or family member brings reality home to us.

Because the discordance between reality and Haman's fantasy was so extreme, he was required to resort to extreme measures to maintain his illusion. His energy was devoted to supporting his fantasy and suppressing any evidence that contradicted his illusion of greatness. We can imagine Haman's thinking. If others experienced sudden financial ruin, it was because they were not as wise as he. If others were confronted by children or wives who rebelled against their authority, it was because they did not wield their authority as effectively as he. If others were struck by illness, or even death, it was because they lacked his physical vigor.

---

[30] Midrash Rabba, Esther 7:8.
[31] See Rav Yosef Dov Soloveitchik, *Days of Deliverance*, pp. 35-37.

Now, Haman's reaction to Mordechai has a context and is understandable. Mordechai was a lone, humble, exiled Jew. He was not a notable significant personage. In fact, before it was brought to his attention, Haman had no reason to monitor or even notice Mordechai's behavior. However, once brought to his attention, Mordechai's insignificance made his resistance an even greater affront and threat to Haman. That a simple, powerless, single, exiled Jew could resist his power and authority, was a complete contradiction to Haman's illusion of greatness. It was impossible for Haman to reconcile Mordechai's brave resistance with his all-consuming fantasy of power and grandeur.

4. Torah basis

The Megilah beautifully captures all this in its description of Haman's conversation with his wife and closest confidants. He enumerates his accomplishments. He presents the impressive evidence of his greatness. Then, he declares that all of this is rendered meaningless and worthless by Mordechai's resistance. How did Mordechai acquire such powerful sway over Haman? Ironically, Mordechai's humble status and his insignificance gave him this power. His resistance undermined all of Haman's efforts to create and maintain his fantasy of human greatness. If this insignificant Jew could not be controlled and subdued, Haman's claims to greatness would be proven to be nothing more than an illusionary pretense.

However, Haman recognized that Mordechai was the product of a worldview. Although the other Jews of Shushan may not have shared Mordechai's bravery, Haman realized that the Torah was the source of Mordechai's worldview and resistance. According to this worldview, no human being is all-powerful. The success of every human endeavor depends on the benevolence of a Creator who is truly omnipotent. Man is actually a weak and fragile creature dependent upon the kindness bestowed upon him by his true heavenly master. This day Mordechai stood alone in his courageous disobedience. However, as long as the people of the Torah existed, new "Mordechais" would emerge. Haman knew that the threat to his fantasy was not only Mordechai. The true danger was presented by the Torah and those who studied and adhered to its lessons. This meant that the Jewish people must be destroyed with Mordechai.

And Haman said unto King Achashverosh: There is a certain people scattered abroad and dispersed among the peoples in all the provinces of your kingdom; and their laws are diverse from those of every people; neither do they keep the king's laws. Therefore, it profits not the king to suffer them. (Megilat Esther 3:8)

5. Ignoring Achashverosh's authority

Haman's fantasy of greatness was not contradicted by his subservience to the king. Haman realized that the king had ultimate authority. However, he was confident in his ability to manipulate Achashverosh to achieve his own ends. His success in convincing Achashverosh to kill his own loyal subjects confirmed to Haman that he was the true power in the kingdom. How was Haman able to so effectively control his king? What was his strategy?

The Megilah provides an indication of his methods in its introduction of Haman. It explains that Haman's appointment as vizier followed the events described in the prior chapter. The final episode in the prior chapter was the plot by two of the king's entourage to assassinate him. The Megilah explains that their plot was uncovered by Mordechai, reported to the king, and they were executed. Apparently, this episode led to the appointment of Haman.

The opening passages of the Megilah describe two elaborate celebrations that Achashverosh convened to commemorate his consolidation of control over his kingdom. Our Sages explain that Achashverosh did not inherit his throne. He seized it.[32] The plot against him by members of his own entourage suggested some members of the court continued to oppose him. Haman's appointment followed Achashverosh's narrow escape from assassination. This indicates that Achashverosh's appointment of Haman was at least partially motivated by concern over his personal security and the stability of his control over his kingdom.

6. Haman's manipulation of Achashverosh

Haman recognized Achashverosh's preoccupation with his personal security and his fear that rebellion might erupt at any moment. He used these fears to manipulate his king. He described the Jews as an ethnically discrete people that held itself apart from the rest of the population. He also noted that the Jews lived throughout the kingdom. Haman understood that Achashverosh would perceive the Jews – described in this way – as a perfect fifth column. Their separateness would suggest to a paranoid Achashverosh that their loyalty should not be assumed. Their dispersion throughout the kingdom would suggest to him that they were potentially the basis for a widespread network of resistance to his authority. Achashverosh would conclude that the Jews posed an ongoing threat to his security. He would eagerly hand them over to Haman for extermination.[33]

In short, Haman was a perceptive interpreter of Achashverosh's needs, desires, and fears. He understood how to utilize his insight into Achashverosh to pursue his own personal agenda. He combined this understanding with a capacity to package his own objectives in a form that would appeal to his king's fears and insecurities. Perhaps, these characteristics of Haman are the basis of the contention of the Sages that Haman and Memuchan were a single character.[34]

> And Memuchan answered before the king and the princes: Vashti the queen has not done wrong to the king only, but also to all the princes, and to all the peoples, who are in all the provinces of the king Achashverosh. For this deed of the queen will come abroad unto all women, to make their husbands contemptible in their eyes, when it will be said: The king Achashverosh commanded Vashti the queen to be brought in before him, but she came not. And this day will the princesses of Persia and Media who have heard of the deed of the queen say the like unto all the king's princes. So will there arise enough contempt and wrath. (Megilat Esther 1:16-18)

7. Memuchan is Haman

Memuchan appears earlier in the Megilah than Haman. In this earlier episode, Queen Vashti was summoned by a drunken Achashverosh to display herself before the commoners of Shushan. Our Sages explain that Vashti was the scion of the royal family and refused to be made into a spectacle for the entertainment of the boorish king and his commoner companions. Achashverosh understood Vashti's response as a rebuke, a reminder of his humble origins, and as an expression of the queen's pretensions of superiority. He responded with intense anger.[35]

---

[32] Rabbaynu Shlomo ben Yitzchak (Rashi), *Commentary on Megilat Esther* 1:1.

[33] Rav Yosef Dov Soloveitchik, *Days of Deliverance*, pp. 81-85.

[34] Mesechet Megilah 12b.

[35] Mesechet Megilah 12b.

Yet, he saw no means by which he could punish the queen. Apparently, he did not feel he could enter into a confrontation with a member of the royal family.

Memuchan provided Achashverosh with a solution. He suggested that Achashverosh recast his conflict with Vashti. He should portray Vashti as a social radical promoting a dangerous attack on conventional family values – as a subversive social revolutionary determined to undermine the authority of husbands in their own homes. Thus recast, the conflict could be addressed. The king would play the role of champion of traditional values. He would be free to act against Vashti and punish her as he pleased.

Memuchan understood his master's true desires. He recognized that Achashverosh was not interested in his counselors' advice regarding how to best respond to Vashti's challenge to his authority. Achashverosh knew how he wanted to respond. He wished to severely punish his queen. Memuchan perceived that Achashverosh was seeking a means by which to exact his vengeance. Also, Memuchan demonstrated a remarkable capacity to package Achashverosh's destruction of Vashti as a moral imperative. He transformed an act of personal vengeance into a courageous defense of fundamental social values. Both of these traits are identical to the talents demonstrated by Haman. Perhaps, these similarities suggested to the Sages that Haman and Memuchan were a single character.

"And Mordechai told him all that had befallen him, and the full account of the silver that Haman had proposed to weigh out into the king's treasuries on the Jews' account, to cause them to perish. And the copy of the writ of the decree that was given in Shushan he gave him, to show Esther and to tell her, and to order her to come before the king to beseech him and to beg him for her people." (**Megilat** Esther 4:7-8)

Disguising Achashverosh's movitves

1. Responding to Haman

Megilat Esther narrates the efforts of Haman to destroy the Jewish people and the response of Mordechai and Esther to this threat. Haman slanders the Jewish people to the king, Achashverosh. He tells the king that the Jewish people adhere to their own standards and laws. They are not faithful to the king and do not obey his directives. He urges the king to decree the destruction of the Jewish people. He offers to deliver to the king's treasury ten-thousand silver talents in exchange for the king's acquiescence to his advice. Achashverosh accepts Haman's offer and advice. He authorizes Haman to write and promulgate an appropriate decree in his name regarding the Jews. Haman selects the thirteenth day of Adar as the day for the destruction of the Jewish people throughout the kingdom. He writes the decree announcing this plan and distributes it throughout the kingdom.

Mordecahai appeals to Esther to intercede with the king. He communicates with a messenger sent by Esther. Our pesukim record Mordechai's message to Esther. Mordechai's description of the events leading to Haman's decree is interesting. Mordechai tells Esther that Haman has placed a sum of silver into the king's treasury in order to procure the right to destroy the Jews. But he makes no mention of Haman's slander of the Jews to Achashverosh. This is an odd omission. Mordechai is appealing to Esther to intercede with the king. In order to be successful, she will require the best possible intelligence regarding the king's motives for handing over to Haman the fate of the Jewish people. Haman's accusation of disloyalty was a

146

fundamental element of the argument he made to Achashverosh. Why does Mordechai omit this information?

"Then Memuchan declared before the king and the princes, "Not against the king alone has Vashti the queen done wrong, but against all the princes and all the peoples that are in all King Achashverosh's provinces. For the word of the queen will spread to all the women, to make them despise their husbands in their eyes, when they say, 'King Achashverosh ordered to bring Vashti the queen before him, but she did not come.' And this day, the princesses of Persia and Media who heard the word of the queen will say [the like] to all the princes of the king, and [there will be] much contempt and wrath. If it please the king, let a royal edict go forth from before him, and let it be inscribed in the laws of Persia and Media, and let it not be revoked, that Vashti did not come before King Achashverosh, and let the king give her royal position to her peer who is better than she. And let the verdict of the king be heard throughout his entire kingdom, although it is great, and all the women shall give honor to their husbands, both great and small." (Meggilat Esther 1:16-20)

2. Understanding Achashverosh

Achashverosh is the most mysterious character in the Meggilah. We can easily grasp and appreciate the righteous motivations of Mordechai and Esther. Haman is the villain. He is motivated by a deep personal hatred of the Jewish people and their Torah. But what are Achashverosh's motivations? Is he a fool – easily influenced by devious advisors? Does he share Haman's hatred for the Jews? In order to understand Mordechai's message to Esther, we must develop a firmer grasp of Achashverosh's personality and behaviors.

There are two enigmatic episodes in the Meggilah that must be explored in order to better understand Achashverosh. Achashverosh made an elaborate celebration for his ministers and subjects. During the celebration, he directed his queen, Vashti, to appear before this audience. His intention was to demonstrate her remarkable beauty. Vashti refused to appear. Our Sages offer various explanations for Vashti's refusal. But the simple explanation is that Vashti recognized the king's motivations. She regarded his request as demeaning. She was not willing to compromise her dignity as queen by being paraded in front of an assembly of drunken ministers and subjects.

Achashverosh responded to this refusal with intense anger. But he could not identify the proper course of action to take against Vashti. He consulted with his advisors. One of his counselors – Memuchan – suggested a response. He told Achashverosh that he should not treat Vashti's refusal as a personal issue. Instead, he should deal with it as an affair of state. Vashti's rebuff should be regarded as the beginning of a social movement. Vashti's behavior will suggest to all women that they need not obey the wishes of their husbands. Vashti's expression of independence will be the catalyst for a liberation movement that will undermine structure of the family and the authority of all husbands. Vashti must be removed as queen and replaced by a more suitable role model. This action will send a message to all women that they must honor and obey their husbands. Achashverosh accepted this suggestion, designed and distributed the decree, and removed Vashti.

3. Seeking a pretext

It seems that Memuchan's essential advice to Achashverosh was that Vashti should be deposed as queen. Obviously, this was an option that Achashverosh would have contemplated without Memuchan's help. But Memuchan added an innovation. He suggested that Achashverosh explain his decision to oust Vashti as a response to a subversive social movement. Why was this necessary? How did this suggestion suddenly resolve Achashverosh's quandary regarding the appropriate course of action?

Apparently, Achashverosh was reluctant to depose Vashti simply because she refused to comply with a command of questionable propriety. Achashverosh was eager to punish Vashti and depose her. But he was reluctant to add another display of unseemly behavior to his previous licentiousness. He needed some pretext behind which he could hide his true motive. Memuchan recognized the nature of Achashverosh's dilemma and provided the requisite pretext. In other words, Achashverosh's true motive for deposing Vashti was personal, juvenile anger. Achasheverosh recognized the shabby nature of these motives but did not abandon them. Instead, the sought some pretext behind which he could hide his true motivations.

> "After these events, when King Achashverosh's fury subsided, he remembered Vashti and what she had done, and what had been decreed upon her. And the king's young men, his servants, said, "Let them seek for the king young maidens of comely appearance. And let the king appoint commissioners to all the provinces of his kingdom, and let them gather every young maiden of comely appearance to Shushan the capital, to the house of the women, to the custody of Heyge, the king's chamberlain, the keeper of the women, and let their ointments be given them. And let the maiden who pleases the king reign instead of Vashti." And the matter pleased the king, and he did so." (Megilat Esther 2:1-4)

There is a second incident – described in the above pesukim – that seems to confirm this interpretation of Achashverosh's behavior. Achashverosh's anger abates. He misses Vashti and regrets deposing her. The king's young servants suggest a solution to his problem. The king should collect all of the beautiful young women of the kingdom into a compound in Shushan, the capital. Each will be brought, in turn, to the king. He will select the most worthy of these candidates as his new queen.

This seems like a remarkably absurd suggestion. Achasheverosh was a powerful king. An appropriate queen for such a ruler would be a woman of royal lineage and prominence. Achasheverosh's servants suggested that he select a replacement for Vashti through a process that was essentially a beauty pageant! However, despite the absurdity of this suggestion, Achashverosh readily and immediately accepted the proposal.

The apparent conclusion is that Achashverosh accepted this suggestion because he was not seeking an appropriate woman to replace Vashti. Neither was he seeking a single woman to serve as his queen. He wanted a female companion with whom he could enjoy intimacy, not another queen. However, a king cannot compromise his dignity by inviting a series of women into brief intimate encounters. Again, Achashverosh needed a pretext under which he could pursue his licentious desires. His servants provided the required pretext. Achashverosh would announce an elaborate plan for finding a new queen. This pretext would provide him with the opportunity to enter into intimate relationships with a virtually endless series of beautiful women.

In other words, Achashverosh understood that, if revealed, his true motive would be easily recognized as simple lust. But he was unwilling to reconsider this motive. Instead, he sought, found, and implemented a strategy for concealing his true motive. He would disguise it as an elaborate process by which he would select a new queen.

"And the king took his ring off his hand and gave it to Haman the son of Hammedata the Agagite, the adversary of the Jews. And the king said to Haman, "The silver is given to you, and the people to do to them as it pleases you." (Megilat Esther 3:10-11)

4. Not buying it

Before explaining Mordechai's message to Esther, one further observation will be helpful. The above pesukim describes Achashverosh's response to Haman's proposal to destroy the Jewish people. It is interesting that Achashverosh does not instruct Haman to carry out his plan. He accepts Haman's proposal to deposit a large sum of silver into the king's treasury. In exchange, he gives Haman the authority to deal with the Jews as he pleases.

This is a strange response. Haman had argued that the Jews were unfaithful. They deserved to be destroyed as dangerous subversives. Yet, Achashverosh showed no enthusiasm for the destruction of his supposed enemies. He made no comment regarding his wishes for the treatment of these seditious traitors. He left their fate in Haman's hands.

It seems that Achashverosh was not convinced that the Jews were traitors. He was not concerned with their supposed sedition. He did not feel compelled to address this presumed threat. He recognized that Haman's accusation was not credible. But if Achashverosh recognized Haman's duplicity, why did he turn the Jews over to their enemy? The inescapable conclusion is that Achashverosh coveted the money Haman offered to pay into his treasury.

If this is the case, why did Haman feel it necessary to slander the Jews? Why did he not just offer the king the silver he craved and demand that in exchange he receive control over the fate of the Jews?

Haman understood Achashverosh's personality. He knew that Achashverosh could be motivated by his intense desire for even greater wealth. But also he knew that Achashverosh would not demean himself by responding to this offer of wealth. He would need some pretext in order to acquiesce to his offer. Haman provided the pretext. Haman recognized that in order to secure Achashverosh's support, he did not need to convince him of the justice of his accusations. He merely needed to provide some pretext.

We can now understand Mordechai's message to Esther. Mordechai understood Achashverosh's personality and behavior. He knew that Haman had accused the Jews of disloyalty. But he realized that this accusation had not motivated the king to hand over the Jews to Haman. He knew that this accusation was intended, and served, as a pretext. He did not tell Esther about Haman's slander against the Jews because this accusation was not the true reason for Achasheverosh's agreement to Haman's proposal.

Esther need not develop a defense of the Jews. She did not need to prove their loyalty. Any effort to defend her people would be misguided and ineffectual. He revealed to Esther Achashverosh's true motivation – Haman's silver. His message to Esther was that she needed to counter Achashverosh's desire for silver with an even stronger desire.

Mordechai hoped that Achashverosh's devotion to Esther and his need for her would serve as this opposing desire. Achashverosh would not risk losing Esther's love. Mordechai hoped that Achashverosh's deep need for Esther would motivate him to abandon Haman and rescind his decree.

And Mordechai said to respond to Esther: Do not imagine about yourself that you can escape in the house of the king from (the destiny) of the Jews. For if you are silent at this time, relief and rescue will arise for the Jews from some other place and you and your father's household will be destroyed. Who knows if for a moment such as this you arrived to your royal position. (Megilat Esther 4:13-14)

Lives in Balance

1. Esther and Mordechai debate

One of the most moving portions of the Megilah is a dialogue between Mordechai and Esther. Haman has persuaded King Achashverosh to allow him to issue a decree authorizing the wholesale slaughter of the Jews within the kingdom. Mordechai appeals to Esther to approach the king and plead for the lives of her people. Esther initially objects that this is not the proper time for her to act. She shares with Mordechai that she has not been summoned by the king for thirty days. In order to speak with the king, she must appear at his palace and seek an audience. This is a dangerous venture. Appearing at the palace without a summons is regarded as an affront to the king's dignity. Anyone who approaches the king in this manner is subject to death. Only if the king specifically directs, is the person spared.

Esther does not suggest a specific alternative to Mordechai's plan, but she apparently believes it best to wait for a more opportune time. When that time comes, she will plead with Achashverosh to spare her people.[36]

Mordechai responds to Esther. His response has four components. First, he tells her that she cannot save herself from the fate of her people. She should not imagine that her position as queen will shield her. Second, he explains to Esther that whether she acts or surrenders to her fears, the Jews will be saved. Hashem will not allow His people to be destroyed. Third, if the Jews are saved through some means other than her intervention, then she and her father's household will be destroyed. Fourth, he suggests to Esther that perhaps, providence placed her in the role of queen specifically for this moment.[37]

---

[36] Esther told Mordechai that she had not been summoned by the king for thirty days. What message was she communicating to Mordechai with this information? According to Malbim, she was explaining to Mordechai that she expected Achashverosh to soon ask for her. She was suggesting that when this occurs, she will plead with him to spare the Jewish people. Gersonides – Ralbag – proposes a different interpretation of Esther's comments. She was explaining to Mordechai that she would be placing herself in danger. The king did not summon her often. She had not been invited to his palace in thirty days. She could not know when he would next extend an invitation. Therefore, she could petition the king on behalf of the Jews only by approaching him without an invitation. This would be dangerous.
These two interpretations represent very different views on the intent of Esther's reply.
According to Malbim, Esther was suggesting to Mordechai an alternative plan. Let's just wait for a better moment to appeal to Achashverosh. This opportunity is likely to occur soon. According to Ralbag, Esther did not present Mordechai with an alternative plan. She was expressing her fear.
[37] How certain was Mordechai of his interpretation of providence's intent? He said to Esther,

150

Do not bear tales among your nation. Do not stand upon the blood of your neighbor. I am Hashem. (VaYikra 19:16)

2. The obligation to rescue another Jew from danger

The above passage commands us to not be idle when a fellow Jew's life is in danger. Maimonides explains that this commandment requires that we use our resources to save our fellow Jew from danger. For example, if I observe someone drowning and I can swim, then I must swim out to the person and save him.

It is clear from this example that one is not obligated to sacrifice oneself in order to rescue another. Maimonides is not suggesting that one who cannot swim rush into a river to save his friend. However, Bait Yosef raises a question. Is one required to place one's life *at risk*[38] to save another whose death is otherwise virtually certain?[39] For example, I observe someone drowning in the river and I know how to swim. However, I must swim a challenging distance to affect the rescue and the current is swift. I assess that I will *endanger* myself through the attempt. In other words, my friend's life will certainly be lost if I do not act. However, by acting I endanger my own life. Am I required to risk death in order to save my fellow Jew from certain death?

Bait Yosef concludes that one is obligated to affect the rescue despite the personal risk. Others question this conclusion and suggest that one is not obligated to incur even the risk of death in order to recue another.[40]

3. Mordechai told Esther to endanger her life

This discussion presents two related problems. First, it seems that Bait Yosef should have availed himself of an obvious and compelling proof for his position. Was not the dialogue

---

"Who knows". He seems to acknowledge some degree of doubt regarding his conclusion. Among the commentators there are two opinions on the nature of his uncertainty. According to Rabbaynu Avraham ibn Ezra, Mordechai was not prepared to declare with certainty that providence had placed Esther in this position so that she could now save her people. Malbim and Rashi suggest that Mordechai was not expressing doubt regarding the mission assigned by providence. He was addressing Esther's suggestion that she delay taking action until a more favorable moment. Mordechai responded that perhaps, providence placed her in this situation in order to act at this point in time. His uncertainty was not in regards to the mission assigned by providence; it related to how that mission should best be executed.

[38] To *risk* or *endanger* one's life means to incur the *possibility* of death

[39] Of course, "certain" in this context does not mean 100% certainty. A more detailed analysis is required to precisely define the point of demarcation between "risk" and "certain" death. See, for example, Rav Aharon Soloveitchik, *Perech Mateh Aharon,* volume 2, pp 139-140. For the purposes of this discussion this analysis is not essential.

[40] Shulchan Aruch does not include a ruling. S'MA suggests that the ruling is omitted because the issue is not discussed by any of the authorities upon whom Shulchan Aruch generally relies. Seemingly, according to S'MA, Shulchan Aruch is declining to rule on the issue. Pitchai Teshuvah suggests that the issue is not discussed by these authorities because they do not distinguish between placing oneself in certain or possible danger. In other words, even if one will subject oneself to possible danger in the rescue of his fellow from certain death, one is not obligated to affect the rescue.

between Mordechai and Esther a discussion of this issue? Mordechai told Esther that her fellow Jews were destined to be slaughtered and that she needed to intervene and save them. She responded that taking action would place her own life at risk. Mordechai told her that despite the risk to her life, she must act to rescue her people. Mordechai ruled that one must risk one's life in order to intervene on behalf of another who will otherwise die. Yet, although Bait Yosef's ruling is supported by this explicit narrative in the Megilah, he makes no mention of it.

Second, as noted above, Bait Yosef's conclusion is disputed by others. These authorities maintain that one is not required to place one's life in danger to save another from certain death. How can these authorities reconcile their position with Mordechai's ruling? According to their view, Esther was actually completely justified in her response and Mordechai's position was incorrect.[41]

4. Passivity would place Esther's life in forfeit

Rav Yisrael Chait suggests a solution to this problem. He bases his suggestion upon a closer analysis of Mordechai's comments to Esther. As noted above, Mordechai's response has four components. However, his main focus is upon a single issue.

Mordechai is telling Esther that she is in certain danger. She should not delude herself. She cannot save herself through passivity. If Haman succeeds in his ruthless campaign to destroy the Jewish people, she will not be saved by hiding herself in her palace. Her royal status will not protect her. In fact, by not acting she places her life in even greater jeopardy. Hashem will save His people through some other means. But perhaps, providence has preserved her specifically to now take action.[42] If she does not accept this responsibility upon herself, then providence will abandon her. Hashem will preserve His people but she will perish.[43]

---

[41] Mordechai could not have been certain that Esther's intervention would be successful. Is one obligated to place one's own life at risk when it is uncertain that this will save another? BaCh suggests that the answer is unclear and the authorities dispute whether one must risk one's own life under such circumstances. He suggests that Tur records both positions without clearly ruling. BaCh's view suggests a further question. Mordechai was not certain that Esther's efforts to rescue the Jewish people would be successful. Mordechai asked that she place her life in danger to possibly recue her people. This seems to conclusively prove that one is obligated to risk one's own life to possibly rescue another's life. Yet, according to BaCh, despite Mordechai's clear ruling, the authorities dispute the issue.

[42] It is generally agreed among the commentators that Mordechai was certain that Esther would perish if she declined to act. However, they have different views on his specific reasoning. According to Ibn Ezra (note above), Mordechai made two separate points. One was that Esther and her father's household would perish if she did not act. He did not share with Esther how he came to that conclusion. His second point was that perhaps providence gave her this mission. According to Rashi and Malbim, Mordechai had no doubt regrading Esther's mission. His only doubt related to the specifics of providence's plan. Malbim explains that because Mordechai was certain that the existential meaning of Esther's life was tied to this mission, her failure to act would place her life and her father's household in forfeit.

[43] This understanding to Mordechai's comments seems to be supported by GRA. See his comments on 4:13.

In short, Mordechai told Esther she must act now to save her people and to save herself. According to this analysis, Mordechai's instructions to Esther are not relevant to the discussion of the circumstances under which one must risk oneself for another. Mordechai was not instructing Esther to risk her life only to save another. He was telling her to save herself by saving her people. Bait Yosef and his opponents are dealing with placing one's life at risk to save another. Mordechai was telling Esther that she should risk her life to save her people and herself!

5. Living a meaningful life

Mordechai told Esther that he suspected providence had brought about her ascent to the throne for this moment. Malbim comments that his suspicion was based on the unlikelihood of such an occurrence. Mordechai felt justified in warning her that her failure to act would undermine the plan of providence and place her life in jeopardy.

There is a message in Mordechai's comments that can be extended beyond Esther. Our lives must have meaning and purpose. In Esther's case, Mordechai felt that this meaning and purpose could be identified. She was placed in her position as queen to save her people.

In assessing our own lives, it more difficult to identify a specific mission that has been assigned to each individual. Yet, Mordechai's message has relevance for us. His message urges us to make our lives meaningful and to seek purpose. If we live only to exist, then we deprive our lives of significance. If we accept the challenge of identifying and pursuing a purposeful life, then we endow our lives with meaning and consequence.

And Esther said: If it pleases the king, let the king and Haman come today to the banquet that I have prepared for him. (Megilat Esther 5:4)

And the king arose in his fury from the wine feast to the orchard garden, and Haman stood to beg for his life of Queen Esther, for he saw that evil was determined against him by the king. (Megilat Esther 7:7)

Hidden Messages

1. Hashem's hidden presence in the Megillah

These above passages capture contrasting moments in Haman's life. In the first passage, Esther summons him to accompany the king to a banquet she plans for them. Haman believed that this reflected his ascension to the highest level of influence in the Persian empire. The queen invited him to accompany the king!

The second passage describes Haman's downfall. The king turned against Haman. He recognized his duplicity. He was convinced that Haman was his mortal enemy.

Rabbaynu Eliezer Eskenazi notes that Hashem's name is hidden in the key phrase of each passage. The first Hebrew letters in the words "Let the king and Haman come today" are yud, hey, vav, and hey. These are the letters of the Tetragrammaton – Hashem's most sacred four-letter name. The final Hebrew letters in the words "that evil was determined against him" also spell the Tetragrammaton.[44] The name of Hashem does not appear in the Megillah. Instead, Hashem's role in the narrative is implied. Perhaps, as Rabbaynu Eliezer suggests, it is "coded"

---

[44] Rabbaynu Eliezer Eskenazi, Yosef Lekach, Commentary of Megilat Esther 1:1.

into these passages. Why does the Megillah not explicitly describe and acknowledge Hashem's role in our salvation?

2. The dilemma confronting Mordechai and Esther

Rabbaynu Avraham ibn Ezra comments:

It is the case, that in this megillah there is no mention of Hashem's name. [Yet,] it is one of the books of the Canon.... In my opinion, the proper [explanation] is that this megillah was authored by Mordechai. This is the meaning of 'And he sent forth books.[45]' All [these books] were copies of a single text – that is the Megillah...The Persians copied it and wrote it into the history of their kings. They were idolaters. They [would have] written the name of their abominations in the place of the Exalted and Awe-inspiring Name...[Therefore,] it was an honor for the name of Hashem for Mordechai to not mention it in the Megillah.[46]

Let us consider these comments closely. Ibn Ezra begins with a question. How can Megilat Esther be part of TaNaCh – the Canon – but not include mention of Hashem? The narrative portions of TaNaCh focus upon Hashem's interaction with humanity. The Torah describes His creation of the universe and His providential relationship with the Avot – the Patriarchs – and the Jewish people. The Prophets continue this discussion. None of the works included in TaNaCh are histories composed from a secular viewpoint. Megilat Esther is different from these other books of TaNaCh. It does not mention Hashem or explicitly attribute to Him a role in the salvation of the Jewish people.

Ibn Ezra responds that this deviation from the style common to TaNaCh is in response to a practical consideration. Esther was Achashverosh's wife and Mordechai was his minister. Their record of the events recalled by Purim was regarded as authoritative. It was adopted by the Persians and incorporated into the court's official history.

Mordechai and Esther composed the Megilah aware that this would occur. They faced a dilemma. If they composed their narrative in the style common to TaNaCh, they would provoke the Persians to modify it. A typical TaNaCh-style account would describe Hashem intervening in human affairs to rescue His people. The Persians were idol worshippers and would not adopt such a document as their official account of the events. Instead, they would edit it to replace Hashem with their own deities. A work composed to give thanks to Hashem would be perverted into an instrument of idolatry.

Mordechai and Esther address their dilemma by leaving out of the Megilah any overt mention of Hashem. The work describes an unlikely series of events that lead to the rescue of the Jewish people from destruction. The astute reader understands that these events reflect Hashem's providence. However, the Persian or secular reader can conclude that the Jews benefited from good fortune. The overt religious neutrality of the text was not offensive to the Persians and did not conflict with their idolatrous beliefs.

A similar explanation is suggested by Rabbaynu Eliezer Eskenazi. Based on this explanation, he develops an interesting insight into a strange passage in the Megilah.

And all the acts of his power and his might and the full account of Mordechai's greatness, how the king advanced him – are they not written in the book of the chronicles of the kings of Media and Persia? (Megilat Esther 10:2)

---

[45] Megilat Esther 9:20.

[46] Rabbaynu Avraham ibn Ezra, Commentary on Megilat Esther, introduction

3. An imperfect work

The above passage notes that the events recalled by Purim were recorded in the official court history of Media and Persia. Why is this mentioned? Perhaps, these chronicles are cited as corroboration for the Megillah. Rabbaynu Eliezer suggests another explanation:

"The passage states that [the Megilah] was recorded in the chronicles of Media and Persia. This accords with that which our Sages of blessed memory said there [in the Talmud]. When she asked that [the Megilah] be incorporated into the Hagiographa, Esther said, 'It is already recorded in the chronicles of Persia.' The benefit of this – making known that it was recorded in the chronicles of Persia and Media – was to explain why the name of the Blessed One is not mentioned and why many aspects are stated in [the account] through hints and in a hidden manner. These are elements that were appropriate to mention explicitly! For this reason, they are [mentioned] through allusion and recorded in a hidden manner – because of fear of the sovereign. He might be angered and say, 'They praise their god for that which I did out of my love for Esther. [Instead of acknowledging my role] they say our strength and might through our faith did this for us'"[47]

Rabbaynu Eliezer Eskenazi suggests an alternative description of the dilemma that confronted Mordechai and Esther. The chronicles of the king record his activities and achievements. Achashverosh – the king – viewed himself as the hero of this story. He saved the Jewish people as an expression of his love for his queen, Esther. An accurate account that acknowledged Hashem's role would reduce Achashverosh to a minor character in the story. He would resent this portrayal of his role. Also, he would resent the Jewish people for their failure to express their gratitude to him and for instead, directing their gratitude toward their god.

According to Rabbaynu Eliezer Eskenazi, the above passage is included in the Megilah to explain the absence of Hashem's name from the text. The text was incorporated into the chronicles of the Persian kings. This prevented Mordechai and Esther from explicitly acknowledging Hashem in its text. The above passage is essential to the Megilah. It explains its strange style.

Both of these explanations characterize the Megilah as an imperfect work. Ideally, the Megilah would explicitly describe Hashem as saving His people. Circumstances prevented Mordechai and Esther from composing this ideal work. Instead, they resorted to hint, allusion, and suggestion.

4. Hashem hides His face

Another comment of Rabbaynu Eliezer Eskenazi suggests an alternative explanation for the Megilah's atypical style.

"When our iniquities multiplied and our merits became fewer, and our Sacred Temple was destroyed, we were not worthy of the performance of an overt miracle for us when He fought [on our behalf] on the day of battle. Then, He saved us [acting] in a hidden manner... Thus, Hashem, the Blessed One, since He is with us in exile [but] hides His face, He brings about causes through which we are saved from the hand of those who arise against us. However, it is not overtly evident that this salvation is from Him, the Blessed One. We are the sheep of his flock. He makes known to Bnai Yisrael His actions

---

[47] Rabbaynu Eliezer Eskenazi, Yosef Lekach, Commentary of Megilat Esther 5:4

and makes them explicit to us through the many, immediate, events [that are] unnatural [and] uncommon. This is even more the case, when we see the overturning of the counsels [of our enemies] and the nullification and reversal of their plots. This affirms to us even more [that these events] are the result of the One in Whose hand is every life and Who searches the innermost thoughts [of every person]."[48]

Rabbaynu Eliezer Eskenazi explains that the Jewish people of the Purim story did not deserve to be save through overt miracles. However, they were not abandoned by Hashem. He saved His people through manipulating events and engineering a rescue. This rescue might seem natural and unextraordinary. The objective of the Megilah is to identify the many key events that occurred at precise times and in a critical order designed to bring about our salvation. Through its description of this timing and order, the Megilah reveals to the sensitive and astute reader the hand of Hashem.

5. Portrayal of a hidden miracle

These comments suggest an explanation for the Megilah's unusual style. The Megilah is the story of a hidden miracle. In bringing about our rescue, Hashem did not overtly reveal Himself. Instead, His providence was hidden and evident only through careful study of the events that combined to save the Jewish people. The Megillah's style is perfect for describing this type of salvation.

The Jews saved by Hashem did not experience an overt miracle. Hashem did not manifestly reveal Himself. The Megilah describes this experience. Hashem is evident only through the unusual and remarkable combination of events it describes. His name does not appear because His influence is not manifest in the events.

This explanation of the Megilah's style differs from the explanation offered by Ibn Ezra and initial one by Rabbaynu Eliezer Eskenazi. They concluded that the Megilah is an imperfect work. Ideally, it would clearly describe Hashem's role. Perhaps, the Megilah is not an imperfect work. Its style is ideal for describing the experience of the Jews of the Purim story.

"That was on the thirteenth day of the month of Adar; and they gained relief on the fourteenth day, making it a day of feasting and gladness. But the Jews that were in Shushan assembled on the thirteenth and the fourteenth, and rested on the fifteenth, making it a day of feasting and gladness." (Megilat Esther 9:17-18)

1. Two days

The events of Purim culminated in the Jews defeating their enemies. In general, this battle took place on the thirteenth of Adar. However, in Shushan the battle continued an additional day. In Shushan the conflict ended on the fourteenth. This salvation is celebrated through the festival of Purim.

Purim is celebrated on two days. Most cities observe Purim on the fourteenth of Adar. This was the date on which most Jews rested from their conflict with their enemies. However, some cities observe Purim on the fifteenth of Adar. These cities recall, through their celebration, the events in Shushan. In Shushan, the Jews fought on the fourteenth and did not rest until the fifteenth.

---

[48] Rabbaynu Eliezer Eskenazi, Yosef Lekach, Commentary on Megilat Esther 1:1

Which cities observe Purim on the fourteenth and which celebrate the fifteenth? Shushan was a walled city. Therefore, those cities defined as walled celebrate on the fifteenth of Adar. Accordingly, the fifteenth of Adar is referred to as Shushan Purim. Cities that are defined as open or cities without walls celebrate on the fourteenth of Adar.

How does halacha determine the status of a city as walled or open? The Talmud explains that any city that was walled at the time Yehoshua conquered the Land of Israel is regarded as walled.[49] This criterion applies even to cities whose walls were destroyed by the time of the events commemorated by Purim. Cities that were not walled in Yehoshua's days are regarded as open cities. If the city was subsequently walled, its status remains unchanged. It is regarded as an open city. The only exception to this rule is Shushan, itself. Shushan was walled after the time of Yehoshua. Nonetheless, it is defined as a walled city.

2. Respecting Israel

The question regarding these criteria is obvious. Why is the determination based on the city's status at the time of Yehoshua? The purpose of distinguishing between walled and open cities is to recall the different days of celebration in Shushan and other cities. It seems that a city's designation should be established by its status at the time of the Purim miracle!

Maimonides responds to this question.[50] He explains that at the time of the miracle of Purim the land of Israel was desolate. The walls of its cities had been destroyed. If the criteria were determined by a city's condition at that time, an unacceptable outcome would result. The cities of Israel would be reminded of their fall and destitution. This would disgrace the Land of Israel. In order to preserve the honor of the Land of Israel, the determination of a city's status was based upon its condition prior to the desolation of the land.

This raises two interesting questions. First, there seems to be a simpler solution to the problem of respecting the honor of the land of Israel. The creation of Shushan Purim is designed to commemorate the unique experience in Shushan. Why not limit observation of Shushan Purim to Shushan? This would avoid any slight to the land of Israel. Second, we can well appreciate the importance of honoring the land of Israel. However, we expect halacha to be governed by logical principles. Basing a city's status on its condition at the time of Yehoshua seems arbitrary and inappropriate. The fact that a city was walled centuries before the miracle of Purim is not a basis for comparing the city to Shushan!

3. Reliving Purim

These two questions lead to an important insight into the celebration of Purim. Purim is not merely a celebration of a past miracle and salvation. It is not solely an experience of thanking the Almighty for our salvation. Instead, it is a process of duplicating and reliving the events. For example, we fast on Ta'anit Esther and then enter the celebration of Purim in order to relive the transition from peril to salvation. The enactment of Shushan Purim serves this purpose of reenactment. It is designed to recall the various dates of salvation. Therefore, it is crucial that Shushan Purim receive prominent attention.

---

[49] Mesechet Megilah 2a.
[50] Rabbaynu Moshe ben Maimon (Rambam) Mishne Torah, Megilah and Chanukah 1:5.

Observing Shushan Purim in Shushan alone would be completely inadequate. This would not provide adequate recognition of the events. Instead, a set of cities was selected that assured that the two alternate days of salvation would be fully relived and recalled.

We can now understand the criterion chosen by the Sages. Our Sages did not establish Shushan Purim because a city's similarity to Shushan required this alternative date of celebration. Instead, they created the celebration in order to establish a vehicle for more fully recreating the events of Purim. This necessitated selecting some group of cities to preserve and demonstrate the events of Purim. Some similarity to Shushan was necessary to communicate the message. However, a strict resemblance to Shushan was not required. Therefore, the Sages had latitude in defining the criteria for walled cities. They had the option of respecting the honor of the land of Israel. This respect did not detract from fulfilling their purpose.

To accept upon themselves to observe the fourteenth day of the month of Adar and fifteenth in it in every year. (Megilat Esther 9:21)

False Security

1. Purim's two dates

Most communities observe Purim on the fourteenth of Adar. In cities that were walled in ancient times, Purim is observed on the fifteenth of Adar. It is not relevant whether the walls of the city are currently standing. If the city was walled at the time of Yehoshua's conquest of the Land of Israel, it is treated as a walled city. What is the significance of these two dates?

Haman decreed that the enemies of the Jewish people should destroy them on the thirteenth of Adar. Mordechai and Esther were successful in overcoming Haman but could not rescind his royal decree. The Jews' enemies arose against them. Throughout the kingdom of Achashverosh, the conflict raged on the thirteenth of Adar and in Shushan, the capital, it continued through the fourteenth of Adar. The Jews triumphed and vanquished their enemies. They celebrated their salvation on the following day. Throughout the kingdom, the celebration took place on the fourteenth of Adar. In Shushan, the conflict continued through the fourteenth. The Jews of Shushan celebrated their salvation on the fifteenth.

These two days of celebration are recalled though our observance of Purim on the fourteenth and fifteenth of Adar. In Shushan and cities walled in ancient times, Purim is observed on the fifteenth of Adar. In all other communities, it is observed on the fourteenth of Adar.

2. Uniform observance

Ramban – Nachmanides – explains that the celebration of Purim on two separate dates is inconsistent with an important principle of Torah law. Torah law requires uniformity of practice. Basic laws are observed in the same manner by everyone.

Of course, communities have their own unique customs and practices. But this diversity is restricted to the details of observance and does not extend to fundamental practices. For example, communities have different practices regarding the point in the service at which the Sefer Torah is returned to its ark. However, they do not differ on whether the Torah is read on Shabbat. Communities have different practices regarding the permissibility of legumes and near-grains on Pesach. However, there is no debate regarding actual chametz – leavened grain. It is universally prohibited.

Purim is an exception to the requirement of uniformity. Communities celebrate Purim on different days. Shushan and cities that were walled in ancient times celebrate Purim on the fifteenth of Adar, and all other communities observe it on the fourteenth of Adar. What compelled the Sages to create this exception to the otherwise universal requirement of uniformity of practice? In order to respond to this question, Ramban traces the development of the festival of Purim.

3. Reactions to Haman's decree

Ramban's response is based upon his understanding of Jewish history. He explains that although the scene of the Megilah's narrative is Shushan in Persia, the Persian empire was no longer the center of Jewish life. The return to the Land of Israel was underway. The greater part of the return from exile had taken place.[51] The process of rebuilding the land had begun.

Haman's decree threatened the fragile Jewish community in the Land of Israel. The danger was greatest for those living in unwalled communities. These communities were completely exposed to the aggression of their surrounding neighbors. Communities within walled cities had reason to feel more secure. The walls of their cities provided them with some protection, and the Jewish population dominated many of these cities. The Jewish inhabitants were less threatened from within and more protected from threats from outside the city. The respective attitudes of these two types of communities directly impacted the development of Purim.

Therefore, the Jews of unwalled cities, who lived in unwalled cities, observed the fourteenth day of the month of Adar with celebration and festive drinking, as a festival, and through sending portions of food to one another. (Megilat Esther 9:19)

4. The early history of Purim

Purim was established in stages. In its early stage, Purim was a "grassroots" celebration. This is described in the above passage. The people, acting on their own initiative, created the celebration. As indicated by the passage, this early adoption was not universal. Communities in unwalled cities were the early adopters. Communities in walled cities did not participate in this initial stage. Why did they not adopt the observance?

Ramban deduces from their behavior, that the communities in walled cities did not feel that they were in as great danger as those living in unwalled cities. Therefore, the communities in walled cities did not continue to celebrate their victory in the years following it.

Because Haman the son of Hamdata, the Aggagi, afflicter of the Jews, contemplated the Jews to destroy them. He conducted a "pur" – that is the lottery – to terrify them and to destroy them. (Megilat Esther 9:24)

5. The establishment of Purim

---

[51] Ramban's assertions regarding the timeline of resettlement of the Land of Israel are not generally accepted. RaN (Comments on Alfasi, Mesechet Megilah 1a) rejects Ramban's position. He contends that the greater part of the return to and resettlement of the Land of Israel took place after the events recalled by Purim.

In the second and final stage of the development of Purim, the Sages established it as a permanent festival. They were persuaded to take this step by Esther and Mordechai. Mordechai recorded the decision of the Sages in the Megilah and distributed the Megilah throughout the Persian kingdom. In the above passage, he explains that all communities will celebrate the festival. Haman's intention was to destroy all Jews. According to Ramban, this passage addressed the attitude of the Jews living in walled cities. He told the Jews of these communities that every Jew had been in danger, even those who believed that they would be afforded protection by the walls surrounding their city.

Based on this understanding of the development of Purim, Ramban explains its two dates of celebration. Communities in unwalled cities were assigned the fourteenth of Adar as their day of celebration. This is the date on which these communities celebrated in the year of their salvation. The assignment of this date to these communities reflected two considerations. First, these communities adopted the annual celebration on their own initiative. Second, these communities were in the greatest danger and experienced the greatest miracle. Communities in walled cities were assigned the fifteenth of Adar as their day of celebration – the day celebrated in Shushan.[52]

In other words, the observance of Purim on the fourteenth of Adar by communities in unwalled cities preserves the record of their initiative to create the festival and it recognizes their clear perception of the danger from which they were rescued. Because communities in walled cities did not participate in this initiative, they are assigned the fifteenth of Adar as their Purim.

Ramban is answering his question. Why is Purim an exception to the Torah's emphasis on uniformity? Ramban responds that if the Sages had initiated Purim, they would have created a single date for its uniform observance. But they did not create Purim. Its observance preceded the Sages' formal establishment of the annual festival. The Sages, in their formalization of Purim, did not discard the initiative of the communities of unwalled cities. They preserved the record of their initiative in their formalization of Purim observance. They achieved this by assigning the fourteenth of Adar to unwalled cities alone.

Ramban's explanation raises a question. He explains that communities in walled cities did not participate in the early initiative. They did not recognize the extent of the danger facing them. Therefore, they are required to delay their observance of Purim to the fifteenth. This is an interesting response to the disappointing behavior of these communities. They observe Purim on the same day as the Jews of Shushan. This seems more a prestigious distinction than an expression of criticism. As RaN observes, Shushan was the site of the events described in the Megilah. It is the place in which the miracle unfolded.[53] Is there a further message in partnering communities in walled cities with Shushan for their celebration of Purim? Let's consider another issue that will help answer this question.

Therefore, they called these days Purim – because of the lottery, because of all the words of this letter, and what they saw concerning this matter, and what happened to them. (Megilat Esther 9:26)

6. The meaning of Purim

---

[52] Rabbaynu Moshe ben Nachman (Ramban), Commentary on Mesechet Megilah 2a.
[53] R' Nissim ben Reuven, (RaN) Notes to Commentary of R" Yitzchak Alfasi, Mes. Megilah 1a

The Megilah explains that the celebration of Purim derives its name from the pur – the lottery – used by Haman to select the day on which battle would be waged against the Jews of the empire. Why was this lottery so significant that it is commemorated in the name of the festival?

Rav Yosef Dov Soloveitchik Zt"l responds that the lottery represents the role of the accidental and the unpredictable in human affairs. What is a lottery? One outcome is arbitrarily selected from among other possible outcomes. In his lottery, by chance and accident, Haman selected the thirteenth of Adar as the day for the Jews' destruction. Purim reminds us that we are vulnerable. We can and must take action in response to problems and challenges that confront us. However, we cannot prepare for the unforeseeable. Unforeseeable and unlikely events can suddenly place our wellbeing and our lives in jeopardy. These events are like the outcome of a lottery. They are unpredictable. The lottery represents human vulnerability and our helplessness to prepare for the unforeseeable.[54]

And Mordechai said to respond to Esther: Do not imagine to yourself to escape in the house of the king from among all the Jews. (Megilat 4:13)

7. Mordechai's message to Esther

The theme of our vulnerability is expressed in the above passage. Mordechai directs Esther to intervene with Achashverosh on behalf of the Jews. Esther responds with hesitation. She argues that the time is not best for her to act. She should wait for a more favorable moment to intercede with the king. Mordechai responds in the above passage. He cautions Esther to not deceive herself. She should not imagine that she is safe in her palace. Her destiny is tied to that of her people. In other words, Mordechai questioned the motivation behind her hesitancy. Perhaps, she believed that her position would save her from the destruction planned for her people. Mordechai explained that human beings are vulnerable. At any moment chance and unforeseen events can destroy our lives. Did Vashti imagine she would be deposed? What is Esther's guarantee that she will be saved?

We can look only to Hashem for our protection. We have very limited control over our destiny. Events and circumstances that we cannot foresee and over which we have no control can instantaneously alter the course of our lives. Only Hashem has true control over the affairs of humanity and over human destiny.

The couriers went forth in haste by the king's order, and the edict was given in Shushan the capital, and the king and Haman sat down to drink, and the city of Shushan was perturbed. (Megilat Esther 3:15)

8. The message of Purim's two dates

Let us now return to our question. Why were communities in walled cities paired with Shushan to celebrate Purim on the fifteenth of Adar? The communities in walled cities did not fully understand Mordechai's lesson. They were guilty of the perspective that Mordechai suspected motivated Esther. They believed they would be protected by the walls surrounding their communities. Mordechai explained to them that their sense of security was delusionary. He directed them to observe Purim with those who were most aware of human vulnerability and our dependence upon Hashem. This was the community of Shushan.

---

[54] Rav Yosef Dov Soloveitchik, Days of Deliverance, (KTAV 2007), p 12.

The Jews of Shushan were at the center of the events that unfolded. They were welcome guests of the king's feast and soon after scheduled for annihilation. Mordechai assigned to the communities in walled cities the fifteenth of Adar as a message. Let the community of Shushan be your role-model. Replace your delusion of control and safety with their recognition of human frailty and vulnerability. Turn to Hashem and recognize your dependence upon Him.

9. An insight into prayer

Rav Soloveithchik explains that this is one of the basic messages of prayer. In prayer we turn to Hashem. We ask for health, safety, salvation, sustenance, and the fulfillment of our other needs and desires. The process of petitioning Hashem has a twofold purpose. We hope that our prayers will be answered. Also, we are acknowledging our frailty and dependence upon Hashem.[55]

And these days will be remembered and observed in every generation, by every family, in every country, and every city. These days of Purim will not pass away from among the Jews and its memory will not cease from their descendants. (Megilat Esther 9:28)

Who Cares about Purim? Let's Have a Good Time!

1. The fate of temporary minor festivals

The above passage explains that the celebration of Purim will be observed in all generations. From our contemporary perspective, this is a difficult statement to understand. After all, we are observing the celebration of Purim and more than two thousand years have passed since the events took place that it commemorates. We regard Purim as one of our festivals and as on par with Pesach and Sukkot. Of course, it will be observed in all generations. Why does the Megilah need to make this assertion?

In order to understand the intent of the Megilah's statement, some background is required. Purim is unique and different from our other festivals. Before the establishment of Purim, all major festivals were established by the Torah.

Other minor festivals not recorded in the Torah were observed. These festivals recalled significant events or occasions of salvation. We have a record of these minor festivals. They are recorded in Megilat Ta'anit. These minor festivals were observed through refraining from fasting or refraining from fasting and eulogizing. These minor festivals were not permanent enactments of the Sages and their observance has been abandoned by the Sages.

Purim was enacted by the Sages as a permanent festival. Unlike the minor festivals enumerated in Megilat Ta'anit, it is not subject to repeal. Its observance will continue for all generations.

And Esther the queen, the daughter of Avichayil, wrote with Mordechai, the Jew, an account of the potent miracle in order that the words of this second Purim epistle should be established. (Megilat Esther 9:29)

2. Two Purim epistles and their impact.

The Talmud explains that the establishment of Purim as a permanent enactment was not easily accomplished. Esther proposed this enactment. The Sages resisted. They questioned their

---

55 Rav Yosef Dov Soloveitchik, Days of Deliverance, (KTAV 2007), p 6.

authority to add a permanent festival to the Torah's calendar. Ultimately, Esther prevailed and the festival of Purim was established. The resolution of this controversy also established the basis for later creating the festival of Chanukah.

The above passage explains that Esther and Mordechai sent to all of the Jews this epistle – Megilat Esther – and directed the people to observe the Purim festival. The passage notes that this was the second epistle sent to the people. Earlier in the chapter, the Megilah explains that Mordechai composed a prior epistle and sent it to the Jews. In his epistle, he directed the Jews to observe the Purim festival. The Megilah explains that the Jews accepted this directive upon themselves. Why did Esther and Mordechai compose the second epistle and send it to the people? Why was Mordechai's first epistle not adequate?

The Talmud explains that this second epistle represents Esther's triumph over the Sages' resistance. Mordechai's original epistle established the observance of Purim as an accepted practice among the people. However, his epistle did not establish the observance as a festival enacted by the Sages, applicable to all generations of Jews wherever they live and for all eras. The second epistle announced this enactment.[56]

3. The messianic era, Purim observance, and the Megilah.

Maimonides ends his presentation of the laws of Purim with a passage that opens the above discussion. He explains that in the messianic era we will no longer contemplate past persecutions and suffering. Celebrations commemorating our deliverance from such persecutions will be abandoned. However, Purim will be observed. Its observance will not be abandoned.

Preceding these comments, Maimonides records an amazing ruling. He explains that in the messianic era, all of the books of the Prophets and Hagiographa – NaCh – will be annulled. However, Megilat Esther will retain its place as part of the canon. In other words, in the messianic era the canon will be composed of the five books of the Torah and Megilat Esther.[57]

Maimonides' comments are drawn from the Jerusalem Talmud.[58] The ruling poses two problems. First, why will the books of the Prophets and the Hagiographa lose its canon status? Second, why is Megilah Esther an exception? Why will it remain included in the canon?

4. The purpose of the Prophets and the Hagiographa.

Karban HaEydah addresses the first issue. His explanation is based upon a vision of the messianic era. This vision is described by Maimonides in the final sentences of his code. He explains that in the messianic era, humanity will achieve wisdom and understanding. We will understand secrets that are now hidden from us and we will understand the Creator to the extent that such wisdom is attainable by a human being.[59]

Karban HaEydah explains that the books of the Prophets and the Hagiagrapha are designed to elucidate and expound upon the message of the Torah. Through the works of the Prophets and the Hagiagrapha, we are able to identify and better understand messages in the Torah that might be hidden from us without these works. Because in the messianic era humanity will achieve a much higher level of understanding, these lessons of the Torah will be obvious to

---

[56] Mesechet Megilah 7a.

[57] Rabbaynu Moshe ben Maimon (Rambam) *Mishne Torah*, Hilchot Megilah 2:18.

[58] Mesechet Megilah 1:5.

[59] Rabbaynu Moshe ben Maimon (Rambam) *Mishne Torah*, Hilchot Melachim 12:5.

us without the aid of the books of NaCh. These works will no longer be needed. Therefore, they will be dropped from the canon.[60]

5. The unique content of Megilat Esther.

Why will Megilat Esther retain its status? Maimonides does not directly answer this question. However, perhaps there is an allusion to an explanation in his phrasing which is a paraphrase of the Talmud's comments. Maimonides writes that Megilat Esther will remain intact in the messianic era "just as the five books of the Torah and the Oral Law." This is an odd statement. Maimonides' comparison of the stature of the Megilah to the books of the Torah makes sense. He is explaining that, unlike the other elements of NaCh, the Megilah will remain part of the canon. However, Maimonides also compares the Megilah to the Oral Law. Why did he add this comparison?

This comparison seems to reflect a unique aspect of the Megilah's content. Other books of NaCh include references to Torah law, and occasionally laws are derived or supported from passages in NaCh. However, these works are not works of Torah law. They deal with the Torah's spiritual and ethical message. Megilat Esther does include an extensive presentation of the laws of Purim.

Similarly, Purim differs from other enactments of the Sages. Other enactments are presented in the Talmud or other works of the Oral Law. Purim is presented in one of the works included in the canon.

In short, Purim and Megilat Esther are both unique. The Megilah includes a presentation of the law. Purim is a rare and perhaps completely unparalleled instance, in which an enactment of the Sages is presented though a work of the canon.

6. The Megilah is a work of law.

Now, let us reconsider Maimonides' comments. He explains that Megilat Esther will remain a permanent part of the canon. It is like the Torah and comparable to the Oral Law. It is like the Torah because it is a permanent part of the canon. Its status will not be nullified like the other books of NaCh, because it is different from them. These other works are an amplification of laws in the Torah. They add nothing that is not accessible in the Torah to the astute student. This cannot be said of Megilat Esther. It contains laws that are not recorded in the Torah. It includes laws that were enacted by the Sages and included in the Megilah.

7. Appreciating Purim.

Purim can mistakenly be regarded as a minor festival. After all, it is not accompanied by the prohibition against work – *melachah*. It is arguably the most festive of our celebrations. It includes a feast. It is a time for jovial conduct and mirth. However, the conclusion that Purim is a minor celebration, or that it lacks the grandeur or spiritual content of our other festivals is incorrect.

Purim and its Megilah are beautiful and unique. The preceding discussion only touches open their special character. The Sages created a festival and they incorporated its laws into TaNaCh – the canon. Through this they gave Purim and its Megilah eternal life within the Jewish

---

[60] Rav David Frankel, *Karban HaEydah on the Jerusalem Talmud*, Mesechet Megilah 1:5 (7a).

people. Purim and the Megilah represent the merger of human initiative and the Divine will. The Sages augmented the Torah's festivals and created a permanent addition to TaNaCh.

Pesach

The Shabbat before Pesach is called Shabbat HaGadol – the Great Shabbat – because of the miracle that was performed on it. (Shulchan Aruch, Orach Chayim)

Questions without Answers

1. The commemoration of *Shabbat HaGadol*

The Shabbat prior to Pesach is referred to as *Shabbat HaGadol*. Its name is derived from the miracle that occurred on that Shabbat at the time of the exodus from Egypt. In the year of the redemption, the date of this Shabbat was the 10th of Nisan. Moshe told the people that they would soon be redeemed. The process of redemption required their abandonment of the idolatry of Egypt. Each household was to slaughter a lamb and place its blood on the doorposts and lintel of its home. The Egyptians regarded lambs as sacred. Obedience to this command was their renouncement of the idolatry of Egypt. Moshe also told them that each household must secure on the 10th of the month the lamb for slaughter. On that day, the Jews gathered their lambs and the Egyptians questioned them. They told the Egyptian that in a few days they would slaughter their sacred animals. The Egyptians dared not oppose the Jews. Instead, they stood by as these former slaves defied their religion and culture.[1]

The 10th of Nisan does not always correspond with the Shabbat preceding Pesach. Nonetheless, the events of the 10th of Nisan are recalled on that Shabbat every year.

2. Reading the *Haggadah* on *Shabbat HaGadol*

Shabbat HaGadol is observed in a number of ways. One of these is that the *rav* – the rabbi – of the community delivers a discourse on the laws of Pesach. Many communities have another observance. A major section of the *Haggadah* is read. The portion begins with *Avadim Hayinu* and concludes with the paragraph following *Dayeinu*. The simplest and most obvious reason for this practice is that the Shabbat recalls the events of the 10th of Nisan. On that date, the Jews took their first pro-active step toward denouncing idolatry and achieving liberation. The reading of the *Haggadah* is a fitting means of honoring the day and recalling its significance.[2]

---

[1] Shulchan Aruch does not identify the miracle that *Shabbat HaGadol* recalls. The explanation cited above is provided by a number of commentaries. According to this explanation, the events of the 10th of Nisan did not include a miracle. However, the Egyptians' behavior reflected the enormous impact of the miracles that had occurred up to this point. They did not oppose the Jews because they recognized that they could not defy the will of the god of the Jews.

[2] Rav Eliyahu of Vilna – the GRA – opposed reading the *Haggadah* on *Shabbat HaGadol*. His reasoning is based upon a law cited in the *Haggadah*. The *Haggadah* explains that the commandment to retell the events of our redemption applies only to the night of Pesach. The *mitzvah* cannot be performed and fulfilled before its time.

A number of authorities question the ruling of the GRA. They point out the above noted excerpt from the *Haggadah* does not prohibit reading the *Haggadah* or retelling the story of our redemption at times other than the night of Pesach. The ruling in the *Haggadah* deals only with the fulfillment of the commandment to retell the story. One does not read the *Haggadah* on *Shabbat HaGadol* in order to fulfill the commandment of retelling the story of redemption. It is read as a means of commemorating the events of 10th of Nisan. Therefore, there is no reason to prohibit the activity.

One of the most ancient explanations for the practice of reading the *Haggadah* on *Shabbat HaGadol* is provided by Rabbaynu Amram Gaon. He begins by reinterpreting the actual practice. He suggests that the practice is for only the children to read the *Haggadah* on *Shabbat HaGadol*. The children preview the *Haggadah* before Pesach night to prepare for their participation in the *Seder*.

This participation is central to the *Seder*. The children are encouraged to ask questions and the discussion at the *Seder* should take place in response their inquiries. Without this preview, the children can be easily overwhelmed by the *Seder*'s activities and by the unfamiliar *Haggadah* text. Their preview and understanding of the *Haggadah*'s contents enables them to ask far better questions.[3]

According to Rabbeinu Amram Gaon, the *Shabbat HaGadol* practice is related to one of the most fundamental aspects of the *Seder*. On Pesach night, we do not read the *Haggadah*; we teach and learn it. This is also an aspect of the *Seder* that is confusing and difficult to understand. Let us consider the problem that it presents.

3. The role of the children at the *Seder*

The *Haggadah* includes the *Ma Nishtanah*. This portion of the *Haggadah* is a set of sample questions that the children at the *Seder* might pose. However, the *Ma Nishtanah* does not represent the ideal extent of the children's participation. The ideal is for the children to ask numerous questions encompassing every aspect of the *Seder* and its redemption narrative. Their specific questions are the product of their understanding, intelligence, and imagination. We cannot anticipate in advance every question that our children may ask. Similarly, the *Haggadah* presents responses to the questions included in the *Haggadah*. However, the *Haggadah* does not and cannot include responses to the many and varied questions that our children are encouraged to pose.

In other words, if we succeed in inspiring our children to participate fully in the *Seder* and to apply their inquisitive minds, we will surely find that the material included in the *Haggadah* is inadequate to answer their questions. How are we to respond to questions we did not anticipate and whose answers are not in the *Haggadah*?

We can better understand this problem by comparing this aspect of the *Seder* to its other performances. The other *mitzvot* performed at the *Seder* have precise parameters. By conducting ourselves within these parameters, we fulfill these *mitzvot*. For example, *Kiddush* has a specific text. If we recite its text and meet the other simple specifications, then we fulfill the *mitzvah* of making *Kiddush*. The *mitzvah* of eating *matzah* is another example. We are required to eat a specific amount of *matzah* in a designated length of time. By meeting these requirements, we fulfill the *mitzvah*.

Of course, the GRA understood that the law cited in the *Haggadah* is stated in regards to the *mitzvah* of retelling the story of redemption. However, he maintains that the inclusion of this law in the *Haggadah* is intended to communicate that the text of the *Haggadah* is designed and designated for the fulfillment of the *mitzvah* of Pesach night. Reading the *Haggadah* on *Shabbat HaGadol* suggests that the text does not have this specific design and designation.

[3] Rav Yisroel Yosef Bronstein, *Haggadah shel Pesach, Including Teachings of Rav Moshe Feinstein*, p 21.

Now let's contrast these examples to our obligation to retell the story of our redemption. We perform this *mitzvah* by engaging our children. They may pose questions we do not expect and that we cannot answer by referring to the text of the *Haggadah*. We may not know the answers to these questions. How do we respond to these questions and create a meaningful learning experience?

"And our toil" these are the sons. As it says: every son who is born should be thrown into the river and every daughter should be preserved. (Haggadah of Pesach)

4. The toil of bondage

A hint to the answer to our question is found in an unexpected place. Let's consider the above excerpt from the *Haggadah*. In the section of the *Haggadah* from which the excerpt is taken we retell the story of our bondage and redemption in detail. The story is communicated through a process of Biblical study and interpretation – a process of Torah study. The *Haggadah* focuses upon a short set of *pesukim* in Sefer Devarim. These passages provide an abbreviated account of the story. The passages are carefully analyzed and compared to the more detailed account in Sefer Shemot. Through this process, the more complete story emerges.

In the above excerpt, the *Haggadah* expounds upon a specific portion of the Sefer Devarim section. In that portion, Hashem is described as observing our suffering and our toil. The *Haggadah* explains that the term "toil" refers to the Egyptian program of genocide. Paroh decreed that every male child should be thrown into the river and drowned.

Malbim asks: How did the Sages know that the term "toil" refers to the Egyptian program of extermination? He responds that the Hebrew term *amal* – toil – means to exert effort without a meaningful outcome. Malbim explains that a person who endures grueling labor is not necessarily engaged in *amal*. If the tribulations are endured in order to achieve a positive outcome, then the experience is a hardship but it is not meaningless toil. However, if this misery is endured and no positive outcome can be envisioned, then the person's affliction is transformed into *amal* – pointless toil.

Based on this interpretation of the term *amal*, Malbim explains the Sages' reasoning. Before Paroh's genocidal decree the people believed that they would endure their suffering and that the Jewish people would survive. Their affliction was harrowing but it was not pointless. They were preserving the Jewish people. When Paroh decreed that every male should be killed, their endurance no longer served a purpose. Paroh's program was designed to destroy the Jewish people. No longer was there any point to enduring. The grueling routine was transformed into pointless toil.[4]

We give thanks before You, Hashem – our L-rd and the L-rd of our fathers – that You placed our portion among those who dwell in the bait ha'midrash and You did not place our portion among those who dwell at street corners. We rise early and they rise early. We arise to the words of

---

[4] Rav Meir Leibush ben Yechiel Michel (Malbim), *Midrah Haggadah – Commentary on Pesach Haggadah*, p 31. Malbim's phrasing is not completely clear. The following is the text of his comments: *"Our toil". The term* amal *refers to a person who toils without benefiting oneself. Instead, his toil is pointless and does not achieve its objective… "This is the decree of the sons". Insofar as they toiled on their behalf and it was pointless because Paroh decreed that they should be destroyed.*

Torah and they arise to meaningless affairs. We toil and they toil. We toil and receive reward.
They toil and do not receive reward. (Hadran prayer)

5. The *amal* of Torah study

This interesting insight into the *Haggadah* has an important implication in regards to Torah study. This is because the term *amal* is used to describe Torah study. The above quote is taken from the *Hadran* prayer. This prayer is customarily recited upon the completion of a tractate of the Talmud.[5] In this prayer we describe the study of Torah as toil – *amal*. This presents three problems.

First, how can the study of Torah be characterized as a pointless activity. Second, we declare in this prayer that our toil in the study of Torah is rewarded. If it is rewarded, then it is not *amal*! There is a meaningful outcome! Third, the *Hadran* prayer compares the study of Torah to other endeavors. These other activities are described as meaningless activities that are not rewarded. This seems to be an unfair assertion. The recompense for other activities may not be a reward from Hashem, but certainly they are rewarded. For example, a person who makes a wise investment in securities or in some other asset is rewarded. The asset appreciates and his wealth grows. Why does the *Hadran* treat this endeavor as meaningless and without reward?

6. Activity without product

We must begin by understanding how the term *amal* is being used in this prayer. In order to understand this usage, we must more carefully consider how we view or describe endeavors. An endeavor has two aspects. It involves an activity and it includes an outcome. Let's return to the example of our investor. His endeavor includes a set of activities in which he engages. He identifies potential investments. He evaluates their potential for producing profit. He evaluates risk. He deploys his capital among his various investment options. His endeavor also produces an outcome. He earns a profit from his investments.

The same analysis applies to the endeavors of a student of Torah. He engages in an activity of study and discovery. He produces an outcome. The outcome is his correct understanding of the material he studies.

The term *amal* in the *Hadran* prayer, refers to the activity of an endeavor – divorced from and viewed irrespective of its outcome. This usage is slightly different than the usage in the *Haggadah*. However, both usages share a common root. In both instances, *amal* describes activity divorced of product. However, in the *Haggadah*, the activity is divorced of a meaningful product because that product – the survival of the people – has been eliminated by Paroh's decree. In the *Hadran* prayer, the term *amal* describes activity divorced of its product. However, in this instance, the product is achievable; we are choosing to consider the activity alone and without its product.[6]

---

[5] The current text has been in use for a few hundred years (Rav Aden Steinsaltz). The practice of celebrating the completion of a tractate is derived from Mesechet Shabbat 118b. See: Rav Shlomo Luria, *Yam shel Shlomo*, Masechet Bava Kamma, Chapter 7, afterword.

[6] It seems that the more fundamental usage is that of the *Hadran* prayer. *Amal* is the activity involved in an endeavor, considered separately from its product. The use of the term to describe the misery of bondage is intended to communicate that they engaged in activity alone. In other words, their activity – their intense labor – was not associated with the achievement of a

7. The unique character of Torah study

This clearer understanding of the use of the term *amal* in the *Hadran* prayer answers our first two questions. The term is used to describe an activity that is viewed separately from its outcome. The prayer does not suggest that learning does not produce an outcome or that the outcome is meaningless.

Now, we are ready to understand the strange declarations of the *Hadran* prayer. The investor's *amal*– his activities when considered irrespective of their outcomes – have no reward. They are meaningless. It is only the hoped-for outcome that inspires the investor. He engages in the elaborate and tedious process of investment evaluation and analysis in order to make money. If he did not believe that his activities would lead to that outcome, he would engage in other endeavors. In short, his *amal* – his activities, alone – has no inherent value or reward.

The *Hadran* prayer is explaining that the activity of Torah study does have inherent value – regardless of the success of the student. It makes no difference whether the student develops a deeper understanding of the material or ends his study session more confused than when he started. The value of and reward for the endeavor is to be found in the activity and not only in its outcome.

All of our questions on the prayer are answered by this insight. The point made by the *Hadran* prayer is not that Torah study produces reward and other activities do not. The point is that we receive reward for the *amal* of Torah study. This means that the activity of Torah study has value and reward regardless of its success. In this sense, Torah study is unique. All other endeavors are worthwhile by virtue of their product. The *amal* alone is meaningless. The activity's meaningfulness is derived from the success of its outcome. Only in the case of Torah study does the *amal* – the activity itself – have inherent value.[7]

8. Questions without answers

Now, we can return to and answer our original question. We have discovered that our question is founded upon a flawed understanding of the nature and objective of Torah study. We assumed that unanswered questions detract from the quality of one's Torah study. We assumed that if our children pose questions that we cannot answer, then we have failed to fulfill the obligation to study with them the story of our exodus. This is not true. The study of Torah is not dependent upon coming to definite conclusions and discovering the answers to our questions. We are required to engage in study, to connect to the Torah. Whether our engagement leads to answers or to even greater questions, we have fulfilled the *mitzvah* of Torah study.

As parents and as teachers, we must understand that our primary responsibility is not to provide our children and students with answers. Instead, we must inspire our children and students to engage in Torah study and in the pursuit of understanding. Sometimes, study leads to answers and greater understanding. Sometimes, authentic study uncovers mistaken assumptions and flaws in presumed answers. Recognizing these mistakes and flaws is also an increase in our understanding – even though the encounter does not provide conclusive results.

---

meaningful outcome.

[7] This is not an original interpretation. I regret that I cannot recall its source.

Before one begins to search one recites the blessing, "that sanctified us with His commandments and commanded us on the removal of chametz"... (Shulchan Aruch, Orech Chayim 432:1)

And there are those who observe the custom of placing pieces of *chametz* in a place that they will be found. This is in order that the blessing will not be recited needlessly. However, if these pieces are not distributed, it does not prevent the recital of the blessing. This is because a person's intention in reciting the blessing is to remove *chametz* if it is found. (Ibid, Rema 432:2)

Chametz-free

1. Needless blessing

On *Pesach*, leavened substances – *chametz* – are forbidden. A number of commandments regulate our interaction with these substances. These *mitzvot* prohibit consumption and possession of *chametz*. It is prohibited to even benefit from this forbidden substance. In addition to these prohibitions, there is a positive command regarding *chametz*. One must remove all *chametz* from one's possession prior to Pesach. Two processes are employed to fulfill this positive command. First, a thorough search is conducted on the night of the fourteenth of Nissan – the night prior to *Pesach*. Any *chametz* found during this search is subsequently destroyed. Second, we nullify our ownership of all *chametz*. This is accomplished through the pronouncement of a specific legal formula. This formula is recited after the search for the *chametz* and repeated after the destruction of the *chametz*.

The search for the *chametz* fulfills a positive command to remove the *chametz* from our possession. Therefore, it is preceded by a blessing. This blessing is described in the above quotation from Shulchan Aruch. Rema – Rav Moshe Isserles – deals with an interesting problem.

It is prohibited to recite a blessing needlessly. This blessing is recited prior to fulfilling the commandment to remove *chametz* from one's possession. It is possible that the person reciting the blessing will not find *chametz*. No *chametz* will be removed. If this should occur, the *mitzvah* of removing *chametz* has not been fulfilled. The blessing was recited needlessly.

Rema, suggests that this consideration led to the development of a popular custom. Pieces of *chametz* are placed in a specific place in the house. The search is conducted. At least these pre-placed pieces of *chametz* are found. This assures that some *chametz* is removed. The *mitzvah* is fulfilled. The blessing is not recited needlessly.

2. Intention doesn't matter

It easy to appreciate the logic of this custom. It seems to respond to a valid consideration. However, Shulchan Aruch does not require the placement of these pieces of bread. Furthermore, Rema explains that there is a basis for Shulchan Aruch's dismissal of this issue. He points out that it is not absolutely necessary to find *chametz* in order for the blessing to be recited. He argues that the meaning of the blessing is determined by the intention of the person by whom it is recited. This person does refer to the commandment of the destruction of *chametz*. However, one's real intention is that we are commanded to destroy any *chametz* one may find. Therefore, this objective is fulfilled regardless of finding actual *chametz*. This explains the position of Shulchan Aruch. There is simply no need to validate the blessing though distributing pieces of bread.

171

Rema's argument is somewhat difficult to understand. The terms in the blessing are not an expression of personal thoughts. Our personal interpretation of the blessing is irrelevant. The blessing refers to a specific commandment. In order to determine the meaning of the blessing, we cannot consider a subjective interpretation of one reciting the blessing. We must analyze the actual commandment. This blessing acknowledges the *mitzvah* to remove *chametz* from one's possession. Rema seems to concede that the commandment requires the actual removal of *chametz*. If so, the personal interpretation of the individual reciting the blessing is unimportant! If the *mitzvah* is fulfilled, the blessing is valid. This requires the actual removal of *chametz*.

3. Chametz free home

An alternative explanation of Shulchan Aruch's position can be derived from a discussion in the mishne. The mishne raises an interesting question. The search for *chametz* seems to ignore a practical problem. How can the search actually assure that one's domain is free of *chametz*? Assume a person checks one room of his or her home. This individual then moves on to another room. In the interim, prior to completing the inspection of the second room it cannot be regarded as free of *chametz*. Any *chametz* in that room could be dragged by a mouse to the already inspected room. As a result, it seems impossible to determine that the house is completely free of *chametz*. The mishne responds to this issue. It explains that we do not concern ourselves with this consideration![8] This is a rather odd response. How can a valid consideration be dismissed?

4. Legal state

This mishne is conveying a basic concept underlying the process of searching for *chametz*. The search is not merely a practical means of determining that the domain is free of *chametz*. In an absolute sense, this is impossible. One cannot inspect the entire domain simultaneously. Even were this possible, the inspected domain could become contaminated by *chametz*. This *chametz* could be bought into the inspected domain from another home not yet inspected.[9] What then is the value of the search?

The mishne is telling us that the search is effective because it confers upon the domain a legal status. Once a room is inspected this legal status is created. The room is legally regarded as *chametz*-free. This legal status exists despite the possibility of contamination. *Halacha* can and does chose to disregard the possibility of contamination. *Halacha* has the right to determine the requirement for creating a legal state. In short, the search is effective because it creates a legal status of *chametz*-free. It is not effective because it creates an actual practical assurance.

We can now understand Shulchan Aruch's position regarding the blessing over the search. The search is not merely a means for finding and removing *chametz*. The search creates a *chametz*-free status in the domain. This suggests an alternative understanding of the *mitzvah* to remove *chametz*. We are not actually required to remove all *chametz* from our domain. The mishne explains that this is virtually impossible. Instead, we are required to create a legally *chametz*-free domain. The blessing prior to the search acknowledges that we are fulfilling this commandment. Therefore, it is valid whether or not *chametz* is found. It is valid because the *mitzvah* is not to remove *chametz*. The *mitzvah* is to render one's domain *chametz*-free.

---

[8] Mesechet Pesachim 9a.
[9] Mesechet Pesachim 9a.

It is a positive command of the Torah to discuss the miracles and wonders that were done for our ancestors in Egypt on the night of the fifteenth of Nisan.[10] **[This is] as it says, "Remember this day that you went forth from Egypt."** (Rambam, Mishne Torah, Hilchot Chametz U'Matzah 7:1)

Personal Redemption

1. Searching for the meaning of the *seder*

Rambam – Maimonides – explains that we are obligated to recount the events of our redemption. This commandment is fulfilled at the Pesach *seder*. Arguably, it is the *seder*'s central *mitzvah*. Why is recalling this historical event so critical? What is the message or meaning that we are to take from the *seder* and the narrative to which it is devoted? Perhaps, the answer to this question lies in understanding the meaning of our redemption. Afterall, the *seder* recalls our redemption. If we wish to understand the importance of recalling an event, it is reasonable to begin by understanding the meaning of the event, itself!

And I will take you to Me as a nation, and I will be to you the L-rd, and you will know that I am Hashem, your L-rd, Who brought you forth from under the burdens of Egypt. (Shemot 6:7)

2. Redemption's educational objective

Hashem instructs Moshe to describe to the Jewish people their impending redemption. In the above passage, Hashem explains the final objective of the redemption. The Jewish people will know Hashem and be His nation.[11]

Commenting on this passage, Ramban – Nachmanides – explains that the events of the redemption will demonstrate to the world Hashem's omnipotence and that the Jewish people are His chosen nation. In other words, Ramban contends that the objective of redemption is educational. It will reveal or demonstrate important truths to the Jewish people and to humanity.

In this passage and Ramban's comment, an important idea is communicated. The objective of the redemption was not our freedom, ending the injustice of our suffering, or punishment of the wicked. The objective was the education of the Jewish people and humanity.

3. Redemption demonstrated fundamental truths

Ramban elaborates on the educational objectives of the redemption. He explains that among the basic truths demonstrated by the redemption are the following:

---

[10] The phrase, "on the fifteenth night of Nisan" is a dangling participle. It is not clear whether it describes the events to be recalled – those that occurred on the fifteenth of the month, or whether it refers to the date on which the *mitzvah* is performed. However, the passage cited by Rambam suggests that the first interpretation is correct. The *mitzvah* is to recall the events that took place on the fifteenth. If this is correct, the inclusion in the *seder* discussion of events leading up and subsequent to the fifteenth of Nisan provides context, but is not the fundamental element of the *mitzvah*.

[11] In the following passage, Hashem explains that the Jewish people will be brought to the Land of Israel and given the land. This can take place only after the nation knows and accepts Hashem. The Land of Israel is given to the descendants of the Patriarchs because they are their spiritual heirs.

•Hashem is omnipotent. He is not restricted by the laws of nature, because He IS the Creator.

•His knowledge encompasses the actions and affairs on humanity.

•He interacts with humanity.

•Hashem communicates with humanity through His prophets.

Ramban further explains that Hashem endowed humanity with intelligence. We have the capacity to discover and know truths. These truths are the foundation of our relationship with Hashem. It is through this relationship that creation's objective is achieved. Because these fundamental principles are confirmed through the events of the redemption, multiple *mitzvot* are designed to focus our attention upon it.

These include the commandment to retell the story of our bondage and redemption on the *seder* night.[12]

It seems we have answered our initial question. What is the message of the *seder*? We retell the story of our redemption to reaffirm the fundamental tenets that these events established.

And it is us that He brought forth from there to bring us, to give us, this land that He promised to our forefathers. (Devarim 6:23)

4. Reliving redemption

The Torah describes an encounter between a parent and an inquisitive child. The child asks the parent to explain the significance and meaning of the Torah's commandments. The parent responds by relating our history to the child. The parent recounts our slavery in Egypt and our deliverance. The parent tells the child that after redeeming us, Hashem brought us to the Land of Israel and gave it to us as He promised our forefathers. Hashem commanded us to observe His commandments and to fear Him. Our obedience to His commandments will benefit us and enrich our lives.[13]

This passage is incorporated into the Hagadah:

"In every generation one is obligated to see oneself as if he went forth from Egypt. [This is] as is stated: And you shall tell your son on that day, "Because of this Hashem did [these wonders] for me when I went forth from Egypt." (Shemot 13:9)

It is not only our ancestors that the Holy One, Blessed be He, redeemed. Rather, also, we were redeemed with them. [This is] as it is stated: And it is us that He brought forth from there to bring us, to give us, this land that He promised to our forefathers. (Devarim 6:23)"

The Haggadah is explaining the meaning of our passage. We are required to recall and to recount the story of our bondage in Egypt and our redemption. However, we do not fulfill this obligation through simply reviewing or retelling the events. We must perceive the events as a personal experience. We fulfill our obligation only when we regard the bondage in Egypt and our redemption as more than historical events. We must relate to these experiences as our personal story.

---

[12] Rabbaynu Moshe ben Nachman (Ramban), *Commentary on Sefer Shemot* 13:16.

[13] This inquisitive child's question is posed by the Hagadah's wise son.

Rambam – Maimonides – codifies this requirement. In his discussion of the *mitzvah* of retelling the story of our redemption, he explains:

"In every generation one is obligated to conduct oneself as if he, himself, went forth – at this moment – from Egypt... (Mishne Torah, Hilchot Chametz U'Matzah 7:6)"[14]

Through relating to these events as personal experiences, we intensify their meaning. We are moved to express our gratitude to Hashem with *Hallel* and praise. We are motivated to observe His commandments.

We discovered above that through retelling the story of our redemption, we reaffirm fundamental principles of Judaism. We have discovered also that we are obligated to recount this event as a personal experience. Are these two elements of the *mitzvah* related? Does this personalization of redemption play a role in the educational objective of the *seder*? Is this personalization a necessary prerequisite to the affirmation of the truths outlined by Ramban?

5. Appreciating one's blessings

Rabbaynu Bachya ibn Paquda, in his *Chovot HaLevavot*, explains that we can know and appreciate Hashem's infinite wisdom and kindness through the study of the universe He created. In its greatest elements – the sun and the stars – and in its most minute – a tiny insect– we discover immense wisdom. In the ways in which the components of the universe interact with one another and sustain humanity, Hashem's immeasurable kindness is demonstrated. However, it is difficult for us to recognize the evidence of His wisdom and kindness. Three factors interfere with our assessment:

- We are distracted. Our involvement in the mundane affairs of life and our pursuit of our desires deflects our attention from consideration of the world from which we benefit.

- From the moment that our intelligence asserts itself we are accustomed to the wonders that surround us. Because we cannot imagine an alternative to our world, we do not recognize its wonders. We are like children who have been reared in opulence. Such children struggle and generally fail to recognize their good fortune. They cannot imagine another life; so, they take for granted their blessings.

- Inevitably, we experience sorrows and disappointments. These events have a tenacious hold upon our attention and obscure from us the infinite blessings that surround us. We assess the world from the perspective of our suffering and not with objectivity and balance. We see an imperfect and even wicked world rather than Hashem's wisdom and kindness.

What is the effect of these obstacles? They prevent us from contemplating the meaning and message of the world. To appreciate the wisdom and kindness of Hashem, we must overcome these obstacles.[15]

---

[14] Rambam replaces the obligation to "see oneself as if one went forth from Egypt" with an obligation to conduct oneself in this manner. This is not a contradiction. Apparently, he agrees that the goal is for one to view the events of bondage and redemption as personal experiences. However, this objective is achieved through acts of demonstration that take place at the *seder*. These include reclining when eating and drinking, and drinking the four cups of wine.

[15] Rabbaynu Bachya ibn Paquda, *Chovot HaLevavot*, Introduction to *Sha'ar HaBechinah*.

Let us apply Rabbaynu Bachya's insight to the *seder*. The objective of the redemption was to

6. Appreciation precedes contemplation

There is an important lesson in Rabbaynu Bachya's comments. The prerequisite to contemplating the wonderous phenomena that surround us is appreciation. We will contemplate natural phenomena and discover the wisdom expressed in the design of the universe only after we take notice of and appreciate these wonders. If we are too distracted to notice them, discount these wonders, or take them for granted, we will not contemplate them or recognize the wisdom they embody.

7. The *mitzvah* of recalling redemption – two elements

In conclusion, the *mitzvah* of recalling and retelling the story of redemption incorporates two related and complementary components. First, we must retell the story. Second, we must experience it as our personal history. We are moved to contemplate the meaning of the events and discover and reaffirm the truths demonstrated by redemption through our personal relationship with the redemption.

"It is a positive command to tell of the miracles and wonders that were done for our fathers in Egypt on the night of the fifteenth of Nisan, as it says: "Remember this day that you went out from Egypt" just as it says: "Remember the day of the Shabbat." (Mishne Torah, Hilchot Chametz U'Matzah 7:1)

Explaining the Mitzvah

1. Tzipur

One of the most fundamental commandments that we perform on Pesach is *tzipur yetziat mitzrayim* – the recounting of our redemption from Egypt. The *mitzvah* of *tzipur* seems rather easy to understand. Pesach is the first of the three annual festivals. It is followed by Shavuot, which recalls the revelation at Sinai, and by Sukkot, which recalls our sojourn in the wilderness. It seems reasonable that on Pesach when we renew this annual cycle of festivals, we should discuss the redemption from Egypt. This discussion provides us with an understanding and appreciation of Pesach and also provides us with the fundamental knowledge needed to understand and appreciate the festivals that will follow Pesach in this annual cycle.

The Torah also presents us with a rather clear description of the manner in which the *mitzvah* of *tzipur* is to be performed. The Torah tells us that we are to retell the events to our children.[16] In other words, we are required to provide our children with an oral account of the events of our redemption.

---

establish fundamental truths. At the *seder* we recount the story of our redemption to reaffirm these truths. However, if we are to fully contemplate the events surrounding our redemption and to uncover their meaning and the tenets that these events demonstrate, we must take redemption seriously. If we regard it as a chapter in the history of long-forgotten ancestors, then we will not contemplate the meaning of redemption or appreciate the principles it establishes. We must connect with it on a personal level. The personal experience of redemption is the catalyst for our serious contemplation of redemption and our discovery and affirmation of the truths it reveals.
[16] Sefer Shemot 13:8.

However, Maimonides' explanation of the *mitzvah* of *tzipur* does present some troubling difficulties. Maimonides begins his explanation of the *mitzvah* of *tzipur* by indicating the source in the Torah for the *mitzvah*. He explains that the *mitzvah* is derived from a passage in Sefer Shemot. The passage tells us to recall the day that we left the bondage of Egypt.[17] Maimonides then compares this passage to the passage that commands us to recall the Shabbat. This passage is also in Sefer Shemot.[18] It is part of the Decalogue. Maimonides understands this passage to be the source for the *mitzvah* to recite *Kiddush* at the advent of Shabbat.[19] In other words, Maimonides is telling us that the *mitzvah* of *tzipur* is similar or comparable to the requirement to recite *Kiddush* at the beginning of Shabbat. However, Maimonides' comments do not indicate the manner in which the *mitzvah* of *tzipur* is comparable to the *mitzvah* of *Kiddush*.

2. Source for the *mitzvah*

It is clear from Maimonides' comments that he regards as ambiguous the statement in the Torah that we are to recall the day that we left Egypt. He refers us to the enigmatic comparison to *Kiddush* to provide an explanation for this statement. Given that the meaning of this statement – that we are to recall the day of our redemption – is unclear, it seems odd that Maimonides should select this passage as the source in Torah for the commandment of *tzipur*. After all, as noted above, there is a perfectly clear passage that also discusses the commandment of *tzipur*. We are commanded to retell the events to our children. Why did Maimonides not use this passage as the source for the commandment and instead insist that the source is the more ambiguous directive to remember the day of our redemption?

"And you should tell your son on that day saying, "Because of this Hashem did (this) for me when I went out from Egypt." (Shemot 13:8)

"One might think that the mitzvah of tzipur can be fulfilled from the first of the month. But the Torah tells us "on that day." If the Torah only said, "on that day", one might conclude that the mitzvah can be fulfilled before nightfall. Therefore the Torah tells us, "because of this." "Because of this" only refers to the time at which matzah and marror are before you."
(Haggadah of Pesach)

3. On that day

The passage above is the *pasuk* that tells us that the *mitzvah* of *tzipur* requires that we retell the events of our redemption to our children. The Haggadah quotes *Mechilta's* explanation of this *pasuk*. *Mechilta* learns from this passage that the *mitzvah* of *tzipur* can only be fulfilled on the night of Pesach – at the time that *matzah* and *marror* are before us.

This discussion in *Mechilta* deserves careful analysis. *Mechilta* proposes that one might reasonably assume that the *mitzvah* of *tzipur* can be fulfilled from the beginning of the month of Nisan. This is a remarkable statement! Why would one make such an assumption? Either it is self-evident that the *mitzvah* of *tzipur* is related to Pesach or it is not self-evident! If we assume that it is self-evident that the *mitzvah* is one of the *mitzvot* of Pesach, then obviously it cannot be fulfilled from the beginning of the month. Alternatively, if it is not self-evident that the *mitzvah* is related to Pesach, why would one conclude that the *mitzvah* can be fulfilled only from the

---

[17] Sefer Shemot 13:3.
[18] Sefer Shemot 20:8.
[19] Rabbaynu Moshe ben Maimon (Rambam) *Mishne Torah*, Hilchot Shabbat 29:1.

beginning of the month of Nisan? If one does not assume that the *mitzvah* of *tzipur* is related to Pesach, then why could it not be fulfilled any time during the year?

"This month should be for you the first of the months. It should be for you the first of the months of the year." (Shemot 12:2)

4. The month of redemption

This passage instructs us to designate the month of Nisan as the first of the months of the year. Nachmanides, in his comments on this passage, explains that Nisan is selected as the first month of the year because it is the month of our redemption. All other months are identified in their relationship to Nisan. For example, Iyar is identified as the second month of the year and Tishrei is the seventh month of the year. Nachmanides further explains that this system is designed to assure that we constantly recall and make reference to the redemption. Each time we identify the date and mention the month, we will identify the month in relationship to Nisan – the month of our redemption.[20]

It seems from Nachmanides' comments that the month of Nisan has a unique identity. It is the month of our redemption. In other words, the events that took place in Nisan actually endow the month with an identity. It is the month associated with redemption.

Based on these comments, we can begin to understand the reasoning of *Mechilta*. *Mechilta* assumes that the *mitzvah* of *tzipur* can only be fulfilled at a time that is relevant to the redemption that *tzipur* recalls. However, *Mechilta* proposes that this requirement can be fulfilled from the beginning of Nisan. Nisan has a unique identity. It is the month of our redemption. Therefore, one would reasonably assume that the *mitzvah* of *tzipur* can be fulfilled from the beginning of the month.

However, *Mechilta* explains that we cannot fulfill the *mitzvah* of *tzipur* from the beginning of the month. The *mitzvah* can only be fulfilled at the time that we have *matzah* and *marror* before us. In other words, *Mechilta* posits that the *mitzvah* of *tzipur* is somehow tied to the other *mitzvot* performed on the night of Pesach. What is this connection between *tzipur* and the other *mitzvot* of Pesach?

5. Providing an explanation

Let us now return to our original question. What is the connection between *tzipur* and *Kiddush*? Maimoindes provides a succinct definition of the *mitzvah* of *Kiddush*. He tells us that the *mitzvah* of *Kiddush* is to describe the greatness of Shabbat, its exalted and distinctive nature that differentiates it from the other days of the week.[21] In short, the *mitzvah* of *Kiddush* is to express in words the significance of Shabbat – the day we are prepared to observe.

Apparently, we cannot adequately observe the Shabbat by simply abstaining from the activities that are prohibited on the day. We must first express in words the significance of this observance. Mere abstention from creative labor is not an adequate observance of Shabbat. We must first explain the significance of this conduct.

Perhaps, this is the basis of Maimonides' comparison between *tzipur* and *Kiddush*. *Tzipur*'s objective is similar to the objective of *Kiddush*. We are required to provide – through

---

[20] Rabbaynu Moshe ben Nachman (Ramban), *Commentary on Sefer Shemot* 12:2.
[21] Rabbaynu Moshe ben Maimon (Rambam) *Sefer HaMitzvot, Mitzvat Aseh* 155.

tzipur – an explanation of the *mitzvot* we are to perform on the night of Pesach. Just as *Kiddush* provides an explanation of the observance of Shabbat, *tzipur* provides an explanation and framework for the *mitzvot* performed the night of Pesach.

We can now appreciate the reasoning of *Mechilta*. In order to relate *Kiddush* to Shabbat, we recite the *Kiddush* at the advent of Shabbat. However, the entire month of Nisan has the identity of the month of our redemption. The entire month is related to and is an extension of the observances performed the night of Pesach. Therefore, one might reasonably assume that the *mitzvah* of *tzipur* can be performed from the beginning of the month. However, the Torah tells us that the performance of *tzipur* must be more closely related to the *mitzvot* of the night of Pesach. It must be performed at the time at which these *mitzvot* of Pesach are performed.

6. Mitzvah formulation

Let us now consider our second question on Maimonides. Why did Maimonides not cite as the source for the *mitzvah* of *tzipur* the more explicit *pasuk* requiring us to retell the events of our redemption to our children? The passage that instructs us to retell these events to our children provides us with clear instructions for the manner in which the *mitzvah* of *tzipur* is to be performed. However, the passage tells us nothing about the nature of the *mitzvah*. In contrast, the passage telling us to recall the day of our redemption provides us with an insight into the meaning and significance of the *mitzvah*. The passage employs language similar and reminiscent of the language the Torah uses to describe the *mitzvah* of *Kiddush*. Through alluding to this comparison, the passage reveals to us that the *mitzvah* of *tzipur* is fundamentally similar to the *mitzvah* of *Kiddush*. Both are designed to provide a framework for the observances that will follow.

It is a positive commandment of the Torah to recount the miracles and wonders that occurred to our fathers on the night of the fifteenth of Nisan as it says: Remember this day that I took you forth from Egypt. (This should be understood in a manner) similar to that which it says: Remember the Shabbat day... (Maimonides, Mishne Torah, Hilchot Chametz u'Matzah 7:1)

Retelling our Redemption

1. The story of our redemption

With the above comments Maimonides introduces his discussion of the commandment to recount, on the Seder night, the story of our redemption from Egypt. Maimonides suggests that a passage in Sefer Shemot is the source for this mitzvah. In this passage, Moshe instructs the nation to remember the day that they were redeemed from slavery in Egypt and that on the days that commemorate this event – the festival of Pesach – they should not each chametz – leavened products. Maimonides explains that the first portion of this passage, in which Moshe instructs the nation to recall the day of its redemption, is the biblical source for the commandment to retell the events of the redemption at the annual Pesach Seder.

Maimonides adds that the meaning of the passage's admonition to "remember" the day we were taken out of Egypt can be understood by comparing this passage to another in which we are instructed to "remember." We are commanded to "remember" Shabbat.

Maimonides' intention in these comments is not clear. He seems to acknowledge that the specific obligation engendered by a commandment to "remember" our redemption is unclear. What do we do in order to remember? What is required of us? He responds to this problem by directing us to the term "remember" in reference to Shabbat. By understanding the meaning of the commandment to "remember" Shabbat, presumably, we can understand the meaning of the commandment to "remember" our redemption. But Maimonides does not explain the meaning of the term when used in reference to Shabbat. So, he seems to be explaining one enigma by referring us to another enigma.

2. Shabbat and our redemption

Actually, Maimonides elsewhere does explain the meaning of the commandment to "remember" Shabbat. He explains that this passage requires that we verbally sanctify Shabbat upon its arrival and departure. This is accomplished through recitation of Kiddush at Shabbat's onset and Havdalah at its ending – short paragraphs that describe the sanctity of Shabbat.

Now, Maimonides' intention is somewhat clearer. Our understanding of the admonition to "remember" our redemption should be informed by our knowledge that this term, when used in reference to Shabbat, engenders the obligation to recite Kiddush and Havdalah. So, Maimonides is telling us that there is a similarity between the commandments to "remember" our redemption and the obligation of Kiddush and Havdalah. However, he does not seem to provide any indication of the nature of this similarity.

Rav Aharon Soloveitchik Zt"l suggests that Maimonides is dealing with a very specific problem. The Torah obligates us to remember various events. Maimonides maintains that in some of these instances, no specific obligation is engendered by the admonition. For example, we are admonished to remember – or more specifically to not forget – the events of Sinai. According to Maimonides, this does not generate a commandment to regularly engage in a specific activity of recalling Revelation. In other instances, the admonition does generate a specific obligation.

For example, we are commanded to remember the evil of Amalek. This nation attacked us without cause in the early stages of our journey from Egypt to the Land of Israel. In this instance, the instruction to remember Amalek is interpreted as a commandment. It requires that the episode be recalled through verbalization. However, according to Maimonides, this mitzvah does not include specific ideas or themes that must be recalled and reviewed. We are merely required to recall the incident and to feel an appropriate degree of anger and animosity towards these enemies of Hashem and His nation.

The instruction to remember Shabbat is also a commandment. However, it requires a far more specific performance. Maimonides explains that this mitzvah requires that we describe the exalted nature of the day and its distinction from the other days of the week. A vague utterance acknowledging that Shabbat has arrived or departed is not adequate.

In short, the Torah includes various admonitions to remember. Some do not generate a specific commandment. In the instance of the commandment to remember Amalek, a loosely formulated obligation is generated by the passage. In the case of Shabbat, a more specific obligation to recite Kiddush and Havdalah is engendered.

Now, Maimonides' comments are more easily understood. The Torah tells us we must remember the events of our redemption. Maimonides' intention is to explore the meaning, in this instance, of the admonition to remember. He explains that in this case, our Sages understood the term "remember" to communicate a commandment. Furthermore, as in the case of the commandment to remember Shabbat, the commandment requires we remember through verbalization and that we recall with this verbalization specific events, themes, and ideas.

And you should tell to your son on that day saying: For this reason Hashem acted on my behalf when I went forth from Egypt. (Shemot 13:8)

3. Sipur or Haggadah

Maimonides describes the commandment to retell the events of our redemption with the term sipur. However, the Torah uses a different term in describing the commandment. The above passage is discussing the commandment to recount the events of our redemption and it uses the term ve'hegadeta. This is a form of the same Hebrew root from which Haggadah is derived. In other words, in describing this mitzvah, Maimonides and virtually all other authorities use the Hebrew verb sipur. However, the Torah itself uses the verb ve'hegadeta. Both of these verbs communicate the process of recounting the events. However, the two verbs are not synonyms. The difference between these two verbs is evident in the Torah's account of Yosef's two dreams of dominance.

Yosef had two dreams. In the first dream he and his brothers were in a field. They were binding grain into sheaves. Yosef's sheaf arose and stood. The brothers' sheaves surrounded Yosef's sheaf and bowed to it. Yosef told his brothers of his dream. The Torah tells us that the brothers' hatred for Yosef was heightened by this dream.

Yosef's second dream involved the sun, moon and eleven stars. Yosef envisioned these bodies bowing to him. Again, he related the dream to his brothers. He also retold the dream to his father. The Torah tells us that after hearing this second dream, the brothers were jealous of Yosef.

Apparently, the brothers had different reactions to the two dreams. They hated Yosef after the first dream. After hearing the second dream, they were also jealous. Why did the dreams evoke these different reactions?

One reason may be that Yosef himself had a different response to the two dreams. Yosef retold both dreams. However, the Torah uses different verbs for the two instances. In Yosef's retelling of the first dream, the Torah uses the verb vayaged – a conjugation of the same verb from which ve'hegadeta and Haggadah are derived. In the second instance, the Torah uses the verb va'yesaper – a conjugation of the same verb from which sipur is derived. Both of these verbs communicate that Yosef retold his dreams to his brothers. But these verbs indicate different forms of retelling. A few examples will illustrate the difference between these verbs.

4. Recounting with enthusiasm

Eliezer returns with Rivka. He tells Yitzchak of the wondrous events that led to the selection of Rivka. He wants to communicate that he has experienced an encounter with providence. We can expect that he spoke to his master with enthusiasm and shared with him the details of his adventure. The Torah uses the verb va'yesaper to describe Eliezer's retelling of the events.

Yitro, Moshe's father-in-law, joins Bnai Yisrael in the wilderness. Moshe tells Yitro of all the miracles experienced by Bnai Yisrael. He wants to impress Yitro with these events and their implication. He must have spoken with enthusiasm and provided colorful detail. Again, the verb va'yesaper is used.

5. Brief report

Va'yaged communicates a different meaning. This verb describes a person delivering a brief, to-the-point account or report. Avraham's nephew Lote was captured in war. A refugee from the conflict reported the capture to Avraham. The Torah uses the term va'yaged to describe the refugee's delivery of the report. Avraham did not require a detailed account of the battle or of the experiences of the refugee. He required a brief, even concise, account of his nephew's capture.

Bnai Yisrael are at Sinai awaiting Revelation. They declare their commitment to do all that Hashem commands. Moshe reports their commitment to Hashem. Again, Moshe's report is described with the verb va'yaged. Moshe did not provide a detailed account of his communications with the nation or attempt to communicate the process through which the nation determined that it would enter into a commitment to obey Hashem's Torah. A precise report of their decision was required. The verb va'yaged is appropriately used.

In describing Yosef's relating of his first dream, the verb va'yaged is used. Yosef retold the first dream in a brief and concise manner. The term va'yaged does not imply the speaker has any particular attitude or attachment to the information. In describing his retelling of the second dream, the verb va'yesaper is used. This term also means to tell. However, it is used in the Torah to indicate that the speaker is recounting the events in detail and with enthusiasm.

Apparently, Yosef did not attach tremendous importance to the first dream. He viewed it as an interesting curiosity. The brothers perceived the dream as an expression of a latent desire to dominate and they resented Yosef's egotism. However, the second dream made a much greater impression upon Yosef. He felt this dream had meaning. He carefully, eagerly, and in detail described it to his listeners. Yosef's enchantment with this second dream – as expressed in his impassioned recounting of its contents – suggested to the brothers that Yosef took seriously this second dream of dominance. This evoked the brothers concern and their jealousy.

The Torah uses the term ve'hegadeta in describing the requirement to recount the events of our redemption. This term communicates an obligation to recount events in a concise and precise manner. However, when Maimonides and others describe the commandment, they use the term sipur. This term has a different meaning. It communicates an obligation to recount the events with vigor and in detail. Why did these authorities adopt a term that seems to communicate a description of the commandment that differs from the Torah's description?

Anyone who does not recite these three things on the night of the 15th does not fulfill his obligation. These are the things: Pesach, Matzah, and Maror... These things in their entirety are referred to as Haggadah. (Maimonides, Mishne Torah, Hilchot Chametz u'Matzah 7:5)

Even great scholars are required to recount the exodus from Egypt. Anyone who discusses at length the events that occurred and that which happened is praiseworthy. (Maimonides, Mishne Torah, Hilchot Chametz u'Matzah 7:1)

5. The meaning of the term Haggadah

Maimonides explains that the mitzvah of sipur is only fulfilled by a discussion of the redemption that includes specific components. Maimonides carefully lists all of the elements that must be included in the discussion in order for the commandment to be fulfilled. For example, the discussion must include a description of the obligations to eat the Pesach sacrifice, matzah, and marror. These mitzvot must be discussed and their meaning and message communicated. He concludes his delineation of the required elements of sipur with the comment that these elements – taken together – are referred to as Haggadah. Why is the term Haggadah used to describe this body of information?

Before responding to this question, it will be helpful to consider another law regarding sipur. Maimonides explains that although the mitzvah of sipur requires a discussion that includes certain fundamental elements, these elements represent a minimum standard for the discussion. The discussion has no upper limit. In other words, there is no point at which the discussion of our redemption has been exhausted and further consideration of the events is irrelevant to the mitzvah. The more one discusses the redemption, the greater the magnitude of the fulfillment of the mitzvah of sipur.

In short, the mitzvah of sipur requires that we discuss our redemption. The Torah establishes a minimum content for this discussion but there is no maximum. The more content added to the discussion, the greater the fulfillment of the commandment.

Now, Maimonides' use of the term Haggadah can be understood. Rav Yosef Dov Soloveitchik Zt"l explains that the term Haggadah aptly describes this minimum content requirement. The elements that compose Haggadah form the basic framework for the discussion. Because these elements are the essential components and the framework for the discussion, it is appropriate to describe them as Haggadah. Haggadah communicates a recounting of events in a minimal presentation that is limited to the fundamentals.

6. The messages of the terms ve'hegadeta and sipur

The Torah uses the term ve'hegadeta to describe the mitzvah of recounting the events of our redemption. This term communicates that specific fundamental information must be imparted. We do not fulfill the commandment by simply relating any detail or aspect of the events that comes to mind. A specific body of information must be communicated. The term sipur communicates an additional message regarding the mitzvah. What is this message?

Maimonides and others consistently describe the mitzvah of retelling the events of our redemption as lesaper (sipur) be'yetziat mitzrayim. This is a very unusual grammatical construction and somewhat enigmatic. The use of the prefix 'be' following a form of the verb sipur is uncommon. The term sipur – in its various conjugations – appears frequently in the Torah. It is usually followed by some form of the word 'et.' What is the significance of the replacement of the more common 'et' with 'be?'

The term 'et' identifies the material that is the subject and content of the sipur. Yosef recounted – et – his dreams. The dreams are the content of his account. Moshe described to Yitro – et – the events that had befallen Bnai Yisrael. These events were the substance and content of his account to Yitro. The term 'be' literally means "in". The phrase lesaper (sipur) be'yetziat mitzrayim means to engage in a discussion "in" or regarding the topic of our redemption. In other words the phrase used by our Sages to describe the mitzvah communicates an important idea.

According to Rav Soloveitchik, the mitzvah is not to merely recount specific events – albeit in detail. The mitzvah is to engage in a discussion regarding the topic of our redemption.

These finite events are not the content and substance of our discussion. They are the topic of a discussion that can be virtually endless.

An illustration will help clarify this distinction. A contract contains an account of an agreement. The agreement is the content and substance of the document. It provides a complete description of all aspects of the agreement. The contract can be said to recount et the agreement. In contrast a biology text – even a very thick one – can only be said to discuss the topic of biology. It is an account 'be' biology. Biology is the subject discussed, but the text makes no attempt to exhaust this immense topic.

The conventional description of the mitzvah as lesaper (sipur) be'yetziat mitzrayim conveys the message that the mitzvah is not to merely recount a specific set of events. The commandment requires that we engage in an unbounded discussion on the topic of our redemption.

Now, the Sages' use of the verb sipur – rather than Haggadah – in describing the mitzvah is understood. As explained above, the term Haggadah communicates that the discussion is not completely open-ended. It must include fundamental elements that form its framework. However, the mitzvah is not to merely identify and review these elements. The commandment is lesaper (sipur) be'yetziat mitzrayim. We are commanded to engage in a discussion that is about these elements. However, these elements only form the topic for the discussion. The exploration and analysis of these elements has no limit. Every additional observation, comment, and insight on the topic contributes to the fulfillment of the mitzvah and increases the degree to which the mitzvah is fulfilled.

Therefore, when one conducts a meal on this night, he is required to eat and to drink while reclining in the manner of a free person. Every person – man and woman – is obligated to drink on this night four cups of wine. One should not diminish from them. Even a poor person who provides for himself through charity should not be given less than four cups ... (Maimonides, Laws of Chametz and Matzah 7:7)

Redemption

1. Reclining at the *seder* and drinking wine

One of the features of the Pesach night *seder* is that during the course of its execution we each drink four cups of wine. Maimonides discusses this requirement in the above quote from his code. It is important to note the context in which he introduces this obligation. He begins his discussion by explaining that on Pesach night we are required to conduct ourselves in a manner that is demonstrative of the attainment of freedom. Pesach, and specifically the *seder,* recall our redemption from Egypt and from bondage. We retell the narrative of our rescue from Egypt though reading and discussing the material in the Haggadah and also through demonstration.

Maimonides specifies the requirement to recline during the meal. This is one of the demonstrative elements of the *seder.* Our reclining is an expression of our freedom. The practice is based upon the ancient practice to recline on couches or pillows when eating a meal. This practice was reserved for those who were their own masters. Slaves did not recline. They lived austere lives. We recline to demonstrate that we have been redeemed from our bondage and we are free.

After introducing the requirement of reclining, Maimonides discusses the obligation to drink four cups of wine. There are two interesting aspects of Maimonides' comments regarding the four cups of wine. First, he does not provide an explanation for the specific number of cups required. In other words, he does not explain why we drink four cups of wine and not five or three. Second, in this statement of the basic requirement to consume four cups of wine, he does not explain how they are integrated into the *seder*. Later in his discussion he does elaborate on this issue and he explains that each cup is consumed at a specific point in the *seder*. However, the above quote suggests that although the cups are consumed at specific points of the *seder*, the consumption of four cups of wine is significant in itself and is not merely an embellishment of the benedictions in the Haggadah that they accompany.

2. The unique role of the *seder's* four cups of wine

In this sense, these four cups of wine are unique. We are required to drink wine on other occasions. For example, we recite the Friday night *kiddush* over a cup of wine and then drink the cup. This cup of wine accompanies the recitation of the *kiddush* as an embellishment. In other words, the *kiddush* attains a higher status through its recital over a cup of wine. In contrast, the wine of the *seder* is significant in its own right. It is not merely an embellishment for the benediction recited over it. What is the wine's special significance on the *seder* night?

Maimonides is succinctly responding to this issue in his treatment of the four cups. He introduces them in the context of the obligation to demonstrate our freedom. In other words, according to Maimonides, drinking four cups of wine is one of the means through which we demonstrate that we are free men and women. We indulge ourselves and we even pamper ourselves with wine. He adds that even one who is impoverished and lacks the resources to purchase four cups of wine should resort to appealing for charity in order to fulfill this requirement. On the following day this poor person may feel the full weight of his poverty, but this night he must endeavor to celebrate his freedom and perceive himself as a prince and not as a pauper.

Therefore, speak unto Bnai Yisrael: I am Hashem. I will take you forth from under the burdens of Egypt. I will save you from their servitude. I will redeem you with an outstretched arm and with great wonders. I will take you to Me as a nation and I will be to you a G-d. You will know that I am Hashem your G-d Who has taken you forth from under the burdens of Egypt. (Shemot 6:5-7)

3. The four expressions of redemption

As noted, Maimonides does not feel compelled to provide a reason for the requirement of four cups of wine instead of some other number of cups. However, our Sages were concerned with this issue and they concluded that the number is not arbitrary. The above passages are most often cited as the source for the number of cups.

In these passages, Hashem tells Moshe that he should speak to Bnai Yisrael and assure them of their approaching redemption. Moshe is instructed to employ in his message four terms that describe the redemption:

1) I will take you forth.

2) I will save you.

3) I will redeem you.

4) I will take you to Me.

These terms describe four distinct aspects of the forthcoming redemption. The people will be rescued from the oppression of slavery. They will no longer be the subjects of Paroh. They will be enlightened through witnessing the wonders that Hashem will perform. They will enter into a covenantal relationship with Hashem. These four aspects are recalled at the *seder* through the four cups of wine.

4. Alternative explanations for the four cups of the *seder*

Although these passages are the most often cited as the source for the number of cups at the *seder*, this is not the only explanation our Sages provided. In fact, this explanation is one of four possibilities suggested by the Sages of the Talmud.

And the wine-butler told to Yosef his dream. He said to him: In my dream there were three grape vines before me. (Beresheit 40:9)

Another explanation for the number of cups at the *seder* is based upon the conversation introduced in the above passage. Some background information is needed to appreciate this conversation.

Yosef was sold by his brothers into slavery. Initially, Yosef became the servant of a powerful Egyptian minister. However, eventually, he was thrown into prison suspected of a crime he had not committed. While in prison, he was assigned the responsibility of caring for a fellow inmate – Paroh's former wine-butler. One night this prisoner had a disturbing dream. Yosef persuaded him to share with him the dream so that he might attempt to interpret it. Yosef interpreted the dream as a harbinger of the wine-butler's rehabilitation and restoration to his position in court.

Yosef's interpretation proved prescient. The wine-butler was restored to his position in court. Later, when Paroh was disturbed by a troubling dream, the wine-butler told Paroh about the young Hebrew with the remarkable capacity to interpret dreams. Paroh summoned Yosef and told him his dream. Yosef interpreted the dream and expounded upon its meaning and significance. Paroh was so impressed by Yosef that he appointed him as his vizier.

The Talmud notes that in the conversation between Yosef and the wine-butler, they four times use the word cup. The Talmud suggests that possibly the four cups of wine at the *seder* correspond with these mentions of a cup in this conversation.

And Edom rebelled from the authority of Yehudah to this day. At that time Livnah rebelled. (Sefer Melachim II 8:22)

From the time that Bnai Yisrael emerged into nationhood, it has been subject to persecutions. Our Sages enumerated four nations – including Edom – who have been our persecutors. The Sages suggest that the four cups of wine at the *seder* may correspond with these four nations who have been our adversaries.

For so says Hashem the G-d of Israel to me: Take this cup of wine – of anger – from My hand. Give to drink from it to all of the nations to which I send you. (Sefer Yermiyahu 25:15)

In the above passage, Hashem tells the prophet Yermiyahu that He will punish the nations that have persecuted and oppressed His nation. Hashem describes their punishment employing a figure. They will be forced to drink four cups of retribution. The Sages suggest that the *seder's* four cups may correspond with these four cups of retribution.

In summary, the Sages suggest four possible explanations for the four cups of the *seder*:

- The cups correspond with the four expressions of redemption that Moshe was to employ in describing to the people their impending rescue.

- The cups correspond to the four times the term cup occurred in the conversation between Yosef and Paroh's wine-butler.

- The four cups correspond to the four nations that are Bnai Yisrael's historic oppressors.

- The four cups correspond with the four cups of retribution that these nations will experience in the future.

We can easily appreciate the first possibility. It is a reasonable explanation for the four cups. The *seder* celebrates our redemption and these terms describe the aspects or dimensions of that redemption. The other suggestions are much more difficult to understand. Why would the *seder* include a reference to the nations that have persecuted us? What is the connection between the *seder* and Yosef's conversation with Paroh's wine-butler? The *seder* recalls our redemption from Egypt. Why insert a reference to the foretold retribution that will be visited upon our enemies?

5. Contemporary lessons from ancient history

A careful study of the Haggadah reveals that it is not merely an historical narrative of our redemption from an ancient oppression. Instead, it is an analysis of the experience. Its goal is not to merely recall the past. Its goal is to study that past and learn from it. We review this ancient episode of oppression and redemption in order to enlighten ourselves and to inform our understanding of our contemporary experience.

Each of these interpretations of the four cups relates these cups to a prominent theme of the Haggadah. Of course, the first interpretation understands the cups to be an expression of the overall drama of the Haggadah. The cups urge us to consider all the dimensions of this ancient redemption. They direct our attention to its various aspects. They point out to us that our redemption did not only free us from servitude; it enlightened us and it initiated us into a unique relationship with Hashem.

6. The inexorable progression of providence

The second interpretation relates the *seder's* cups to Yosef's conversation with Paroh's wine-butler. Like Bnai Yisrael, Yosef was condemned to bondage. As a youth, he had dreamt of achieving greatness, and even sovereignty. However, rather than being a leader or ruler, he was a lowly servant in a prison. He could not see or imagine how he might be redeemed from his miserable state. He could not imagine how his youthful dreams might be fulfilled. But even in his destitution, providence moved forward according to its irresistible design.

The wine-butler's dream proved to the be catalyst that would lead to Yosef's liberation and his ascent to power. The reference, through the *seder's* four cups, to this catalyst, draws our attention to the Haggadah's discussion of our nation's providential journey.

Blessed is the One Who keeps His promise to Israel. Blessed is He. The Holy One, Blessed is He, considered the destined end, so as to do as He had told to Avraham our forefather at the Covenant of the Halves. (Pesach Haggadah)

This theme is expressed in the above quotation from the Haggadah. In it, the Haggadah expounds upon the inexorable progression of providence. It presents the redemption from Egypt as the fulfillment of an ancient promise and covenant that Hashem made with Avraham. Like Yosef, the Jews enslaved in Egypt could not foretell how they would be redeemed. Certainly, the covenant made to their forefather must have seemed to them a failed promise. Although invisible to them, providence was proceeding along its path and toward its appointed end. The destiny of our people was set and the sojourn in Egypt was a stage along the journey to fulfillment of the sacred covenant.

And this has stood by our ancestors and by us. Not only one has stood opposed to us and sought to destroy us. Rather in every generation they have stood against us to destroy us. And the Holy one Blessed is He has saved us from their hand. (Pesach Haggadah)

7. The constancy of Hashem's relationship with the Jewish people

The destiny of our people and the irresistible design of providence combined to bring about our redemption from Egypt. But the Haggadah is not interested in the Egyptian episode alone. In the above quote, the Haggadah explores this moment in our history to mine from it meaning and lessons for every generation.

We were persecuted throughout our history. Much of humanity continues to regard our people as a pariah. Our journey is not along a straight path. It has many painful detours and horrible interruptions. Four nations will oppress us over the course of our long journey. But Hashem and His covenant will stand by our side. They will protect us and save us from every enemy.

The reference through the *seder's* cups to our four historic persecutors corresponds with this theme. It reminds us that although in every generation we will be confronted with enemies who seek our destruction, Hashem will preserve us as He has throughout our long journey.

So Hashem our G-d will bring us to other appointed times and festivals that approach us in peace.

We will rejoice in the building of Your city and we will delight in Your service. There we will eat from the sacrifices and the Pesach offerings whose blood will reach the wall of your altar as an appeasement. We will give You thanks with a new song for our redemption and for the redemption of our souls. (Pesach Haggadah)

8. Our faith in the final redemption

The Haggadah also focuses on the eschatological age. Perhaps, reinforcement of our faith in the inevitability of the Messianic vision is the ultimate "take-away" from the *seder*. This theme is referenced by four *seder* cups corresponding with the four cups of retribution that our enemies will be forced to ultimately endure. The above blessing closes the Haggadah's narrative section. It reflects our faith in our inevitable redemption. Its message is that our redemption from Egypt provides us with the model and guarantee of our future redemption.

This is the bread of affliction that our fathers ate in the land of Egypt. Let all that are hungry come and eat. Let all that so require come and join in the Pesach offering. Now, we are here. Next year, may we be in the land of Israel. Now, we are servants. Next year, may we be free people. (Haggadah of Pesach)

Haggadah Themes

1. The themes

This short paragraph is recited prior to breaking the *matzah* at the opening of the *Seder*. The paragraph contains a number of elements. It describes the *matzah* as the bread eaten by our ancestors during the bondage. It includes an invitation to others to join in our meal. Finally, it closes with a confirmation of our conviction in the coming of the Messiah. The Messiah will come and we will be a free people in the land of Israel.

Rabbaynu Saadia does not include this paragraph in his Haggadah. He replaces it with a similar paragraph. Rabbaynu Saadia's version contains two of the three elements. It begins with an invitation to join in the *Seder*. It concludes with the confirmation of our conviction in the coming of the Messiah.

In both versions we affirm our conviction in the Messianic era. This conviction is one of the fundamental principles of Judaism. However, why do we begin the *Seder* with this affirmation?

The Haggadah indicates that there is a close connection between the redemption from Egypt and the Messianic era. The end of the *Magid* – the portion of the Haggadah that retells the story of the exodus – we recite the blessing of *Ga'al Yisrael*. In this *beracha* we thank Hashem for redeeming us from Egypt. We acknowledge that we now celebrate the *Seder* as a result of this redemption. We then express our wish to soon be able to celebrate the festivals in the rebuilt holy Temple.

This blessing indicates that the celebration of Pesach is related to the Messianic era? What is the relationship?

2. Redeem and redeem

There are two basic possibilities. The first is that the redemption from Egypt is incomplete. We are in exile. Our affirmation of the Messianic era is a request to the Almighty to hasten the Messiah's coming. This explanation is consistent with the formulation of the blessing of *Ga'al Yisrael*. We begin the blessing thanking Hashem for our redemption. We then acknowledge that this redemption is incomplete. We cannot serve the Almighty in the *Bait HaMikdash*. We pray that Hashem will rebuild the Temple so we can serve Him more fully.

However, this interpretation does not explain the affirmation of the Messianic era at the opening of the *Seder*. According to this first explanation, we mention the Messianic era only after recalling our redemption. We are asking Hashem to complete the redemption. It would not make sense to affirm our conviction in the Messianic era before we discuss the redemption from Egypt.

Therefore, an alternative explanation is needed. It seems that through introducing the *Seder* with an acknowledgement of the Messianic era, we are identifying one of the objectives of the *Seder*. The purpose of the *Seder* is not solely to recall our exodus from Egypt. Retelling the story of our redemption serves another purpose.

189

We are obligated to fully accept that the Messiah will ultimately arrive. How do we know that there is a basis for this conviction? The redemption from Egypt provides the proof. The Almighty rescued our ancestors from slavery. He created a free nation from an oppressed people. If we accept the truth of these events, we have a firm basis for our conviction in a second redemption through the Messiah.

The order of the *Seder* expresses this theme. We begin with an affirmation of the Messianic era. We then discuss the basis for our conviction – the redemption from Egypt. We close by articulating the connection. Hashem redeemed us from Egypt. Therefore, we can be sure that He will redeem us again.

This matzah that we eat – what does it represent? It recalls that the dough of our fathers did not have sufficient time to rise before the King of all Kings – the Holy One Blessed be He – appeared to them and redeemed them; as it is stated, "And they baked the dough that they brought out of Egypt into cakes of matzah. Because it did not rise for the Egyptians chased them out. And they could not delay. And they also did not prepare provisions". (Pesach Haggadah)

3. Sun-baked *matzah*

The Haggadah explains the symbolism of *matzah*. The *matzah* recalls the haste of the exodus from Egypt. The Egyptians were eager for Bnai Yisrael to leave Egypt. They begged the Jews to leave as soon as possible. The Jews did not have time to allow their dough to rise properly. Therefore, the dough baked into unleavened cakes.

The Haggadah quotes a *pasuk* from the Torah that describes the haste of the departure from Egypt and the preparation of the *matzah*. The passage does not refer to the *matzah* brought out from Egypt as loaves – *lechem*. Instead, it calls the *matzah* "cakes" – *ugot*. Rashbam explains that the term *lechem* is not applicable to these *matzot*. The term *lechem* is only used to describe bread baked in an oven. These *matzot* were not placed in an oven. Instead, the dough was carried by Bnai Yisrael and baked by the heat of the sun. In order to indicate that these *matzot* were not baked in an oven, the term *ugot* is used.[22]

This raises an interesting question. On Pesach, we are commanded to eat *matzah*. Can one fulfill the commandment of eating *matzah* with sun-baked dough? The Aruch HaShulchan maintains that this product is unfit for use as *matzah*. He explains that it is difficult to sun-bake the dough before it leavens. He adds that even were leavening avoided, the product would not be suitable for the *mitzvah* of *matzah*. This is because *matzah* is a type of *lechem*. *Lechem* is dough processed through the heat of an oven.[23]

4. Round cakes

Other authorities offer an alternative explanation of the term *ugot*. Their explanation is based on a comment of Rashi in Tractate Taanit. Rashi explains that the term *ugah* – the singular of *ugot* – means round.[24] These authorities conclude that it is appropriate to use round *matzot* for the *mitzvah* of *matzah*.[25]

---

[22] Rabbaynu Shemuel ben Meir (Rashbam) *Commentary on Sefer Shemot* 12:39.
[23] Rav Yechiel Michal HaLeyve Epstein, *Aruch HaShulchan, Orech Chayim* 461:5.
[24] Rabbaynu Shlomo ben Yitzchak (Rashi), *Commentary on the Talmud,* Mesechet Taanit 23a.
[25] Rav Yitzchak Mirsky, *Haggadat Hegyonai Halacha* (Jerusalem, 5755), p 19, note 32.

This interpretation is difficult to understand. Why would the Chumash stress the shape of the *matzot* Bnai Yisrael baked when leaving Egypt? Furthermore, why should we be required to imitate this characteristic of Bnai Yisrael's *matzah*?

A solution to these questions is provided by the *pasuk* quoted in the Haggadah. The passage explains that the *matzah* symbolize the haste of the departure from Egypt. Bnai Yisrael did not have the time to allow the dough to rise. Therefore, it baked as unleavened cakes. This haste also explains the round shape.

The dough was mixed, kneaded and flattened. The resultant cake was round. Any other form would have required shaping. There was no time to form shaped loaves. We can now understand the requirement to use round *matzot* for the *mitzvah* of *matzah*. Our *matzah* must reflect the haste of the departure from Egypt. The *matzah* is unleavened. This captures the image of haste. However, the round shape adds another reminder of the haste of the departure.

This is the bread of affliction that our fathers ate in the land of Egypt. Let all who are hungry come and eat. Let all who so require come and join in the Pesach meal. Now, we are here. Next year, may we be in the Land of Israel. Now, we are servants. Next year, may we be free people. (Hagadah of Pesach)

Two Themes of the Seder

1. *Ha Lachma Anya* – Its components and context

The *Seder* begins with the recitation of *Kiddush*. The *Kiddush* is not unique to the *Seder* night. Every Shabbat and Yom Tov is introduced with *Kiddush*. We continue the *Seder* by washing our hands and then dipping a vegetable into saltwater and eating it. This process is unique to the *Seder* night and is specifically designed to stand out, draw attention, and evoke questions.

The *Seder* focuses upon the children and its objective is to involve them in learning about our redemption from Egypt. We can only succeed in teaching our children once we evoke their curiosity and engage their minds. We intentionally adopt this unusual activity of dipping and eating a vegetable to initiate the learning process by seizing our children's attention.

The *Seder* continues with *Yachatz* – the breaking of the middle of three *matzot* that are on the table.[26] *Ha Lachma Anya* – the short paragraph above – is recited immediately after breaking the *matzah*.[27] The paragraph contains three elements[28]:

---

[26] This practice is in accordance with the ruling of Shulchan Aruch (O.C. 473:6) and reflects general practice. However, according to Maimonides (M.T. *Hilchot Chametz u'Matzah* 8:6) *Yachatz* is performed immediately before eating the *matzah*.

[27] The recitation of *Ha Lachma Anya* immediately after *Yachatz* is in accordance with the ruling of Shulchan Aruch (Ibid.) However, According to Rabbaynu Amram Gaon, *Ha Lachma Anya* is recited after the *Seder* Plate when the *matzot* are removed from the table and the second cup of wine has been poured. It immediately precedes *Ma Nishtanah*. Maimonides' position is unclear on this issue. In his discussion of the laws of the *Seder* (M.T. *Hilchot Chametz u'Matzah* Chapter 8) he excludes any mention of *Ha Lachma Anya*. However, in the versions of the *Hagadah* attributed to him it is included without indication of whether it is recited before the *Seder* Plate with the *matzot* is removed or after pouring the second cup.

A. It begins by describing the *matzah* as the bread eaten by our ancestors during their bondage.

B. It includes an invitation to others to join in our meal.

C. It closes with an affirmation of our conviction in the coming of the Messiah. The Messiah will come and we will be a free people in the Land of Israel.

The relevance of the first of these three elements is easily grasped. In *Yachatz* we divided the middle *matzah* into two parts. The first component of *Ha Lachma Anya* provides an explanation for this step of the *Seder*. Why do we perform *Yachatz*? Rav Yosef Dov Solovaitchik *Z"l* offers a simple explanation for this practice. The Torah refers to *matzah* as *"lechem oni."* [29] The Talmud offers various interpretations of this phrase. One interpretation is based upon the traditional pronunciation of the phrase. Translated on this basis, the term means bread over which we recite. We are required to recite the *Hagadah* over the *matzah*.

An alternative interpretation is based upon the spelling of the phrase. If the phrased is pronounced exactly as spelled, it would be read *"lechem ani"* which means bread of affliction or impoverished bread. The *matzah* is a form of bread that reflects poverty and suffering. It is hastily baked and composed of simple ingredients. However, the Talmud adds that our ancestors rarely had the opportunity to eat a full *matzah*. Instead, they sufficed with a portion of a *matzah*.[30] *Yachatz* reflects both of these interpretations. As we prepare to recite the *Hagadah* over the *matzot* – the *lechem oni*, we break the *matzah* so that it will more accurately reflect *lechem ani* – bread of affliction and poverty that our ancestors ate in Egypt. In other words, we initiate the *matzot* into their role as bread used in our recital of the *Hagadah* by rendering the *matzot* into a perfect simulation of the fractured bread of poverty and affliction that our ancestors ate in Egypt.[31]

The first element of *Ha Lachma Anya* explains the significance of *Yachatz*. We state that with the breaking of the *matzah*, it now perfectly represents the bread of affliction and poverty that our ancestors ate in their bondage.

2. Pesach and our longing for the redemption

The final element of the *Ha Lachma Anya* is an expression of our confident expectation of redemption and our return to the Land of Israel. Why is this sentiment expressed at this point in the *Seder*?

Some have suggested that this sentence is added as an expression of a *halachah* that was established by the Sages after the destruction of the first Temple. Maimonides discusses this law in the final chapter of his Laws of Fasts. He explains that after the *Churban* – the destruction of

---

The origins of *Ha Lachma Anya* are not clear. It is not mentioned in the Mishnah, Talmud, or Midrash. The earliest references to this portion of the *Hagadah* appear in the writings of the Geonim. Both Rabbaynu Amram Goan and Rabbaynu Saadia Gaon include a variant of *Ha Lachma Anya* in their *Hagadot*. The versions currently in use closely model Rabbaynu Amram's version.

[28] R' Saadia Gaon's version contains two of the three elements. It begins with an invitation to join in the *Seder* and concludes with affirming our conviction in the coming of the Messiah.

[29] Sefer Devarim 16:3.

[30] Mesechet Pesachim 115b.

[31] Rav Yosef Dov Soloveitchik, *Harerai Kedem* vol 2 p 161.

the First Temple – the Sages established a number of observances designed to draw our attention to our loss. Many of the observances share a common design. They moderate or in some way qualify our happiness on joyous occasions. In this manner, we are reminded at times of happiness that our joy cannot be complete as long as we remain in Exile and the Temple is in ruins.

One of the practices established by the Sages is placing ashes on the head of the *chatan* – the groom – at his wedding. Another of these practices is that when entertaining guests at a meal, we are required to introduce an element that qualifies and diminishes the celebration. We leave out some component from the meal or we leave one place at the table unset.[32] Some have suggested that our reference in *Ha Lachma Anya* to our longing for and anticipation of our return to the Land of Israel is an expression of this *halachah*. According to this interpretation, this sentence is not uniquely relevant to the *Seder*; it is a sentiment that should be expressed at every festive or festival meal. However, these other festive meals do not have a text associated with them. Only the *Seder* has a text. Therefore, at other festive meals, we must express our inconsolable disappointment with our continued exile through another method – those discussed by Maimonides.[33]

This explanation is not unreasonable. However, it ignores the context of the sentence. Were this sentence in *Ha Lachma Anya* the sole mention of our longing for redemption, this explanation would be more plausible. However, even a cursory examination of the *Hagadah* indicates that this is a basic and recurrent theme of the *Seder*. In fact, the *Seder* shifts its focus between two redemptions – our redemption from Egypt and our awaited redemption from our current exile.

3. The two redemptions in the Blessing of *Ga'al Yisrael*

At the end of *Magid* – the portion of the *Hagadah* that retells the story of the exodus – we recite the blessing of *Ga'al Yisrael* – Redemption. In this *berachah* we begin by thanking Hashem for redeeming us from Egypt. We acknowledge that we now celebrate the *Seder* as a result of this redemption. We, then, express our wish to soon be able to celebrate the festivals in the rebuilt Holy Temple.

This reference to two redemptions – our historic redemption from Egypt and our anticipated redemption from our current exile – is reflected in our recital of *Hallel* at the *Seder*. We recite the first two paragraphs of the *Hallel* before the meal and recite the balance of the *Hallel* after the meal. The interruption of the *Hallel* between the first two paragraphs and the remaining paragraphs is not arbitrary, but instead, reflects the different themes of these two parts of the *Hallel*.

The first two paragraphs of the *Hallel* are composed entirely of praise and thanksgiving. These paragraphs relate to our redemption from Egypt. The second portion of the *Hallel* that is recited after the meal also contains praise and thanksgiving. However, an element of petition is also present. This portion of the *Hallel* deals with our anticipated, final redemption and return to the Land of Israel. We petition Hashem to deliver us from our exile and restore our people.[34]

---

[32] Rabbaynu Moshe ben Maimon (Rambam) *Mishne Torah*, Hilchot Ta'aniyot 5:13.

[33] Rav Yosef Dov Soloveitchik discusses this position in his lecture of *Ha Lachma Anya*. He rejects this position as not having a basis in *halachah*.
(http://download.bcbm.org/Media/RavSoloveitchik/Moadim/)

Like the blessing of *Ga'al Yisrael*, the *Hallel* deals with two redemptions – our redemption from Egypt and our coming redemption.

So, it is not surprising that the *Ha Lachma Anya* introduces the *Seder* by expressing our prayers for our ultimate redemption. But how is the celebration of Pesach related to the Messianic era? What is the exact relationship?

4. The Pesach redemption is completed by the Messianic Era

There are two basic approaches to understanding the relationship between Pesach and the final redemption. The first is that the redemption from Egypt was incomplete; it lacked finality. We are again in exile. Our affirmation of the approach of the Messianic Era and our petition to Hashem to hasten the Messiah's coming express our longing for the completion of the drama that began with our redemption from Egypt. This explanation is consistent with the formulation of the blessing of *Ga'al Yisrael*. We begin the blessing thanking Hashem for our redemption. Then, we implicitly acknowledge that this redemption is incomplete. We cannot serve Hashem in the *Bait HaMikdash* – the Holy Temple. We pray that Hashem rebuild the Temple so we can serve Him more perfectly and completely.

The Talmud asserts that just as we were redeemed from Egypt in the month of Nisan, our current exile will end in Nisan.[35] What is the message communicated to us through both redemptions occurring in the same month? The apparent message is that the final redemption is the completion of the first. Their shared month communicates to us that the awaited redemption is the continuation of a process that began in the month of Nisan long ago.

At the *Seder* we drink four cups of wine. These four cups correspond with the four expressions of redemption that Hashem employed in describing to Moshe the approaching deliverance of Bnai Yisrael from Egypt. Hashem told Moshe that He would "take out" the people, "save" them, "redeem" them, and "take" them to Himself as His nation.[36,37] However, it is customary among Ashkenazim to pour a fifth cup of wine which we do not drink. This custom seems difficult to understand. The fifth cup is clearly different from the others; we do not drink it.[38] What is the meaning of this cup and how can its ambiguous nature be explained?

This fifth cup is commonly referred to as the "Cup of Eliyahu."[39] It corresponds with a fifth expression of redemption which Hashem used to describe our rescue from Egypt. He told Moshe that He would "bring" us to the Land of Israel.[40] The incorporation of this fifth cup alerts us that there is an expression of redemption in addition to the four represented by the four cups we drink. However, this final expression of redemption is different than the first four.[41] It awaits Eliyahu, whom the Prophet Malachi tells us will be the harbinger of the approach of the Messiah.[42]

---

[34] Rav Yitzchak Mirsky attributes this explanation to Levush. (*Hagadah Higyonai Halachah*, p 133, Rav Yosef Dov Soloveitchik discusses the explanation in his lecture on *Ha Lachma Anya* (Ibid.) and adopts this explanation.

[35] Mesechet Rosh HaShanah 11a.

[36] Sefer Shemot 6:6-7

[37] Talmud Yerushalmi, Mesechet Pesachim 10:1.

[38] Rav Yisrael Meir Kagan, *Mishne Berurah*, 480:10.

[39] Ibid. See Yosef Lewey, *Minhag Yisrael Torah*, vol 3, pp. 158-60 for an extensive discussion.

[40] Sefer Shemot 6:8.

[41] Rav Yosef Dov Soloveitchik, *Harerai Kedem* vol 2 p 208-9.

This cup is poured but we do not drink it. It refers to a final step of the redemption that we confidently await but which we cannot yet celebrate through drinking its cup.

In conclusion, there are many indications that the *Seder* calls upon us to recognize that our redemption is not complete and we still await its conclusion with the coming of the Messiah. However, this insight does not seem to explain the affirmation of the Messianic Era at the opening of the Seder in the *Ha Lachma Anya*. This interpretation only explains our mentioning of the Messianic Era after recalling our redemption from Egypt. We are asking Hashem to complete the redemption. But in *Ha Lachma Anya* we express our longing for the Messiah's arrival before we even mention our redemption from Egypt. It does not seem sensible to petition Hashem to complete our redemption from Egypt before we discuss our historic rescue from bondage.

5. The Messianic Era is a Fundamental Element of the Torah

Maimonides identifies thirteen convictions that are essential to Torah observance. He contends that only through accepting these convictions can a person be regarded as a member of our religious community and attain the afterlife – *Olam HaBah*.[43] Many of these thirteen convictions are obviously elemental to our religion. They include belief in a cause Who is the source of all that exits, belief in Revelation and the immutability of the Torah. However, Maimonides' characterization of some of his principles as elemental to the Torah has been criticized. One of these thirteen fundamentals is the belief in the coming of the Messiah. Abravanel formulated the question well. What is lacking in my observance if I do not believe that the advent of the Messianic Era is predestined? How is my observance or commitment to Hashem and His Torah compromised?[44]

In order to answer this question, it is necessary to understand the nature of Maimonides' thirteen principles.[45] The answer is that Maimonides maintains that the Torah is more than a set

---

[42] Malachi 3:23.

[43] Rabbaynu Moshe ben Maimon (Rambam) *Commentary on the Mishne*, Mes. Sanhedrin 10:1.

[44] Don Yitzchak Abravanel, *Rosh Amanah*, Chapter 3.

[45] Various scholars have provided differing interpretations of Maimonides' intention in describing these principles as fundamental. It is difficult to describe these principles as postulates. Postulates are independent principles that cannot be derived from one another. This is clearly not true of Maimonindes' principles. For example, his second principle is that Hashem is an absolute unity. This means the He has no parts, divisions, or aspects; it is not appropriate to describe attributes to Him in their literal sense or characteristics. From this principle one can easily derive the conclusion that Hashem cannot be material. Any material entity cannot be described as an absolute unity. Nonetheless, Maimonides lists as his third principle that Hashem is not material.

Others have suggested that these thirteen principles are not a set of postulates but instead are fundamental beliefs. We are required to be aware of and to accept each explicitly. Implicit acceptance of any of these principles does not suffice. Therefore, it is necessary for Maimonides to specifically describe the principle of Hashem's non-material nature even though this can be deduced from the principle of His unity.

However, even if we assume that these are fundamental convictions which require explicit acceptance, it remains unclear why Maimonides selected these beliefs and no other or fewer. Some are clearly within the class of beliefs we would ascribe as appropriate to a religious system

of religious beliefs and practices; it is a perspective upon and interpretation of our world. Our belief in Hashem is not merely a religious affirmation; it is an understanding of how our universe operates and is constructed. For this reason, he does not describe the first of these thirteen principles as belief in Hashem as the G-d of the Revelation or the G-d described in the Torah. Instead, the first of his principles is to accept that there is a cause of all that exists. All that exists depends upon this prime cause for its continued existence and this first cause does not require any prior cause to sustain its existence. This first principle is not merely a religious affirmation; it is an outlook or interpretation of the universe that surrounds us. Similarly, our belief in the divine origins of the Torah is not just an expression of devotion and commitment to its observance; it is a perspective on Hashem's relationship with humanity in general and the Jewish People specifically.

Our conviction in the advent of the Messianic Era must be understood in a similar manner. It is not merely a religious or national aspiration; it is an interpretation of the history of humankind. It is an assertion that there is meaning in history. It has a direction and end. History is not the sum total of human endeavors and achievements; it is the inexorable progression to an inevitable outcome.[46]

6. The Redemption from Egypt confirms our ultimate redemption

Through introducing the *Seder* with an acknowledgement of the Messianic Era we are identifying one of the objectives of the *Seder*. The purpose of the *Seder* is not solely to recall our exodus from Egypt. Retelling the story of our redemption serves another purpose. We are obligated to fully accept that the Messiah will ultimately arrive. How do we know that there is a basis for this conviction? During periods of suffering throughout our history our ancestors' confidence in our ultimate redemption must have been severely tested. The redemption from Egypt provided them and continues to provide us with proof of our destiny. Hashem rescued our ancestors from slavery. He created a free nation from an oppressed people. If we accept the truth of these events, we have a firm basis for our conviction in a second redemption through the Messiah.

– belief in the existence of an ultimate cause for all that exists, that He is a unity, Revelation, that He interacts with humanity. Others of the thirteen beliefs outlined by Maimonides seem less essential. Abravanel identifies two beliefs in Maimonides' list that he regards as subject to this criticism: belief in the Messianic Era and in the resurrection of the dead.

Abravanel points out that it is difficult to imagine that one's religious experience, outlook or practice would be significantly impacted if one did not ascribe to these beliefs. Of course, it is not Abravanel's intention to imply that these beliefs are not part of the Torah and or not absolutely correct and even required. However, he questions why they should be identified as fundamental.

[46] Implicit in Maimonindes' perspective is rejection of the division commonly suggested between religious and scientific knowledge. According to Maimonides, both combine into a comprehensive understanding of the universe. The scientist who arbitrarily interrupts his study of the universe and his search for causes and will not consider the source of the natural laws has only a partial understanding of the universe that he studies. Similarly, the student of religion who regards G-d as the Creator but is ignorant of and uninterested in the means by which Hashem governs His universe has artificially truncated his study of Hashem and His ways.

The order of the *Seder* expresses this theme. We begin with an affirmation of the Messianic Era. We then discuss the basis for our conviction – the redemption from Egypt. We close the *Magid* section of the *Hagadah* with the blessing of *Ga'al Yisrael* in which we articulate the connection. Hashem redeemed us from Egypt. Therefore, we can be sure that He will redeem us again.

7. Inviting the needy – Rav Huna's practice

The middle element of the *Ha Lachma Anya* is an invitation to the needy and less fortunate to share with us our *matzah* and join us in the Pesach meal. This invitation seems out of place. Why at this point do we invite the hungry and the less fortunate to join with us in our celebration? Of course, this is a commendable sentiment and we cannot be surprised that the *Seder* should include an invitation to the less fortunate to share in our meal. But it seems odd that this invitation should be inserted into the *Hagadah* at this specific point.

Ha Lachma Anya begins by explaining *Yachatz* and ends by introducing a basic theme of the *Seder* – our anticipation of our coming redemption. Why are we interrupting our discussion of issues specifically relevant to the *Seder* with this invitation?

Rabbaynu Matityahu Gaon suggests that the source of the phrasing of this invitation can be traced to the Talmud. The Talmud explains that Rav Huna's practice before every meal was to announce that any person who is hungry is welcome to participate in the meal.[47,48] We do not generally engage is this practice and Torah law does not require of us this remarkable level of kindness and hospitality. Why, then, are we required to adopt Rav Huna's practice on Pesach night?

8. Including the needy in the Yom Tov meal

One possibility is suggested by a comment of Maimonides. Maimonides explains that we are required to experience joy and happiness on our festivals. One of the means through which we experience and express our happiness is the festival meal. Maimonides continues and explains that we are required to include among the participants in the Yom Tov – the Festival – meal the poor, destitute, bitter and the less fortunate. He explains that a person who bars his doors against the intrusion of these less fortunate, needy people and shares his meal with only his family has distorted the joyous celebration of the Festival transforming it into a hedonistic pleasure. [49,50]

If this is the source for our invitation to the hungry and needy, then we are engaging in a practice that is appropriate to every Yom Tov meal. The proffering of this invitation is not a requirement specific to the *Seder* or even Pesach. According to Maimonides, we should pronounce this same invitation before all Pesach meals and our Shavuot and Sukkot meals. Of course, there is no text that is recited at these other meals; there is no *Hagadah* to provide a formula for the invitation. Nonetheless, the *Ha Lachma Anya* is only providing an appropriate formula for the pronouncement of an invitation that is required before every Yom Tov meal.

9. Special considerations related to Pesach

---

[47] Mesechet Ta'anit 20b.

[48] See Yekutiel Cohen, Hagadat HaGeonim ve'HaRambam p 39.

[49] Rabbaynu Moshe ben Maimon (Rambam) *Mishne Torah*, Hilchot Yom Tov 6:17-18.

[50] See Yekutiel Cohen, Hagadat HaGeonim ve'HaRambam p 40.

Rav Matityahu Gaon seems to suggest that the *Seder* engenders an additional obligation to invite the needy. He explains that the invitation extended in the *Ha Lachma Anya* is the completion of a process that begins earlier in the day, perhaps even days and weeks before Pesach. Before the night of Pesach, the members of the community would search for all those who were in need of assistance or companionship and invite them to their various homes for the celebration of the *Seder*. The pronouncement of the *Ha Lachma Anya* invitation was the completion of this process.[51]

Rav Matityahu Goan seems to suggest that this practice was specific to Pesach. In other words, in addition to the general obligation to include the poor and needy in every Yom Tov meal, Pesach engenders its own unique obligation to reach out to those who are less fortunate.

There is other evidence that Pesach prompts its own unique obligation to include the poor and less fortunate in our celebration. Rama comments that it is customary in the weeks leading up to Pesach to purchase wheat or the *matzot* themselves on behalf of the poor and to distribute these provisions to them.[52] The Gra points out that this custom is very ancient; it is mentioned in the Talmud Yerushalmi.[53,54]

In summary, there are three sources for the *Ha Lachma Anya's* invitation to the needy. The wording seems to be derived from the practice of Rav Huna who would extend this invitation to the poor any time he engaged in a substantial meal. We do not engage in Rav Huna's remarkable degree of charity and compassion. However, we do borrow the wording of his invitation for the *Ha Lachma Anya*.

Why are we more demanding of ourselves on the night of Pesach? There are two reasons. First, every Yom Tov meal is only properly celebrated when we include among our guests the less fortunate. Second, the celebration of Pesach engenders its own unique obligation to offer support and encouragement to the needy and less fortunate.

What is it about Pesach that engenders this additional requirement that we reach out our hands to the needy? In order to answer this question we must consider another aspect of the *Seder* and its *Hagadah*.

10. The Pesach narrative style – Ascension from humble origins

The process of recounting the events of our redemption is performed according to a specific formula. Of course, we are encouraged to explore the themes found in the *Hagadah* to the extent of our ability. The *mitzvah* of recounting the events of our redemption is not fulfilled in its most complete form through merely recounting a specific narrative. Instead, the material in

---

[51] See Yekutiel Cohen, Hagadat HaGeonim ve'HaRambam p 39. It is not completely clear from the earliest sources of Rabbaynu Matityahu's comments that he regarded this procedure as unique to Pesach. However, Avudraham seems to interpret Rabbaynu Matityahu's comments as referring only to Pesach. Rav Yosef Dov Soloveitchik discusses Rabbaynu Matityahu's comments in his lecture on *Ha Lachma Anya* and assumes the comments are specific to Pesach. The above interpretation of Rabbaynu Matityahu's comments is based on Rav Soloveitchik's understanding of his position.

[52] Rav Moshe Isserles (Rama), *Comments on Shulchan Aruch, Orech Chayim* 429:1.

[53] Rav Eliyahu of Vilna (Gra), Biur HaGra, Orech Chayim 429:1.

[54] Talmud Yerushalmi, Mesechet Baba Batra, 1:4.

the *Hagadah* provides a minimum standard. But we are charged to expand upon and to enrich this material to the extent of our ability. Nonetheless, we cannot abandon the format and formulation of the *Hagadah*. We must embellish, but we must not revise or ignore the framework contained in the *Hagadah*.

One aspect of the formula we follow is discussed by the Talmud in Tractate Pesachim. The Mishne explains that we begin our account by describing the humble beginnings of our people and we then proceed to describe its ascent to greatness. What is the specific historic process that we describe?

The Talmud explains that Rav and Shemuel dispute this issue. Rav suggests that we are required to acknowledge that our ancestors – Avraham's own father and later our more immediate ancestors in Egypt – were idolators. But Hashem chose us as His people and He gave us His Torah. Shemuel suggests that we begin the process of recounting our redemption by describing the bondage of our forefathers in Egypt. We then describe our redemption through the miracles and wonders that Hashem performed.[55]

We can easily understand Shemuel's interpretation of the formula. We must recount our redemption by first describing our humiliating servitude and then we describe the process of our redemption. This is exactly as we would expect the narrative of our redemption to be developed. But how do we explain Rav's alternative interpretation? Why begin our Pesach narrative by recalling our primitive ancestors from before the time of Avraham? It is difficult to even characterize these pagans as our antecedents. With the emergence of our forefather Avraham we rejected the culture, values and religious fallacies of his predecessors. We refer to Avraham as our first forefather; this is because he is our beginning and not his ancestors.

Rav and Shemuel agree on the basic theme of the Pesach narrative. They both agree that the formulation of the narrative is designed to communicate that we did not ascend to greatness through our own might, wisdom, or tenacity. We climbed out of the depths of despair or spiritual corruption through the mercy and intervention of Hashem. This message of our dependence on Hashem forms the underlying motif of the Haggadah.

Rav and Shemuel only differ on a relatively minor issue: Do we demonstrate our helplessness and our dependence upon Hashem through acknowledging His redemption of our ancestors from inevitable material destruction or do we provide this demonstration through acknowledging His rescue or our ancestors from moral and religious debasement?

Shemuel suggests that we acknowledge our helplessness and dependence through the experience that is most relevant to the *Seder* – our rescue from Egypt. Rav suggests that our recalling of our redemption from Egypt should occasion our recognition of our general helplessness and dependency. We expand upon the lesson of our redemption from Egypt and extend that lesson to the earliest history of our nation.

11. Helplessness and dependence upon Hashem

---

[55] Mesechet Pesachim 116:a. In the standard text of the discussion in the Talmud, Rav does not mention the idolatry of our ancestors in Egypt, only the practices of Avraham's predecessors. Rashbatz, in his commentary on the *Hagadah*, includes in Rav's position the idolatry of our ancestors in Egypt.

This dispute provides a basic insight into the celebration of Pesach. Pesach recalls and celebrates the emergence of the Jewish nation – *Um Yisrael*. Our redemption from Egypt is a central event in the drama of our ascent to the position of *Um Hashem* – Hashem's chosen nation. But the central motif of the Festival is not the celebration of our accomplishments and our pride in earning Hashem's covenant. The central motif is acknowledgement of Hashem's role in this process. He redeemed us. He rescued us. We did not shape and engineer our fate; we are the beneficiaries of Hashem's benevolence.

We can now appreciate our focus on Pesach upon charity and our sensitivity for others less fortunate than ourselves. A person who does not feel the misery of others and cannot empathize with those who are suffering, has lost touch with his own essential helplessness and dependence. When we identify with the less fortunate, when we empathize with them, we recognize that we are the same.

Had Hashem not redeemed us, we would be more desperate than those to whom we are extending a helping hand. If He had not rescued us, we would be far more lost than those we are including at our *Seder* meal. Any person who recognizes that his own good fortune is the result of the kindness that Hashem has bestowed upon Him will naturally reach out to others.

12. Dependence and Redemption

The second and final components of the *Ha Lachma Anya* reflect two basic themes of the *Seder*. The middle component reminds us of our kinship with the less fortunate and needy. We reach out to them in recognition of our own helplessness and our reliance upon Hashem. The final component expresses our anticipation of redemption from our current exile. These two themes are closely connected.

The Torah informs us that before Bnai Yisrael were redeemed from Egypt, they called out in prayer to Hashem.[56] Hashem tells Moshe that He will redeem the people in response to their prayers.[57] Turning to Hashem, recognizing that He alone could provide salvation was a prerequisite to Bnai Yisrael's redemption. Maimonides generalizes this lesson. He explains that any affliction visited upon the Jewish People requires that we respond with prayer and acknowledgement of our dependence upon Hashem. Only through this response can we illicit His intervention.[58]

We precede our longing for our redemption with an invitation to our brethren who are in need. In this way, we affirm our own dependence upon Hashem. From the depths of our acceptance of our own helplessness and our dependence upon Hashem, we reach out to Him with our prayers and yearnings for redemption.

We were servants to Paroh in Egypt and Hashem, our G-d, took us forth from there with a mighty hand and an outstretched arm. If the Holy One Blessed Be He had not taken our fathers out of Egypt, then we, our children, and our grandchildren would be enslaved to Paroh in Egypt. Even if we are all scholars, we are all understanding people, we are all wise elders, we all know the Torah, it is incumbent upon us to engage in discussion of the exodus

---

[56] Sefer Shemot 2:23-25
[57] Sefer Shemot 3:7-8
[58] Rabbaynu Moshe ben Maimon (Rambam) *Mishne Torah*, Hilchot Taaniyot 1:2-3.

from Egypt. The more extensive the discussion of the exodus from Egypt the more praiseworthy. (Pesach Haggadah)

The Daily Acknowledgement of Redemption

1. The father's initial response to the son's questions

The Pesach *Seder* is constructed in the form of a dialogue between father and son. The son poses questions to his father regarding the *Seder* night and its mysterious practices. The father responds, speaking to his son, the others present, and even to himself. The father begins his response with the above lines. He explains that our ancestors were enslaved by Paroh and the Egyptians and that Hashem rescued His people from bondage. We assert that our own freedom today is a direct consequence of Hashem's rescue of our ancestors. We are obligated to retell and relive the events of our liberations.

This obligation applies to every Jew – the simple lay person and the erudite scholar. The obligation is not limited to recounting specific elements of a redemption narrative. Instead, the more one delves into the events of the redemption and explores their meaning and significance, the greater the fulfillment of the *mitzvah*.

After this brief, direct response to the son's inquiry, the focus of the Haggadah moves away from describing and exploring our redemption. Understanding this section of the Haggadah requires a brief introduction.

It is a positive commandment of the Torah to retell – on the night of the fifteenth of Nisan – the miracles and wonders performed for our fathers in Egypt .... (Maimonides, Mishne Torah, Hilchot Chametz U'Matzah 7:1)

2. The commandment of *sippur* and its laws

Maimonindes explains that we are commanded to retell and discuss the events of our redemption on the *Seder* night. This *mitzvah* is referred to as *sippur* – retelling. After stating that the discussion at the *Seder* is the subject of a Torah commandment, Maimonides explains the various requirements established by the Torah and the Sages for the fulfillment of this *mitzvah*.

In other words, like all *mitzvot* of the Torah, the *mitzvah* of *sippur* is provided by Jewish law – *halachah* – with specific form. *Halachah* dictates the elements that must be included in the discussion, the time when the commandment can be performed, the method of presentation, and other aspects of the *mitzvah*.

The Haggadah includes a discussion of the *halachot* (plural of *halachah*) of *sippur*. This section begins immediately after the father's initial response to his son's inquiry. In fact, the father's initial response is actually the beginning of the Haggadah's discourse in *halachah*.

The father explains the basis of our obligation to engage in *sippur* – because our ancestors and indeed we, ourselves, attained freedom through the redemption. He explains that every Jew is required to participate in this *mitzvah*. Then, he explains that the more extensive our discussion and exploration of redemption, the greater the fulfillment of the *mitzvah*.

Ribbi Elazar ben Azariah said: I am as one of seventy years of age and I had not merited to account for the recitation of (the story of) the exodus from Egypt at night until Ben Zoma explained it. It states in the passage "in order that you remember the day of your going forth from the Land of Egypt all the days of your life". "The days of your life" refers to the daytime.

"All the days of your life" refers to the nighttime. The Sages say: "The days of your life" refers to this world. "All the days of your life" refers to the Messianic era. (Pesach Haggadah)

3. *Sippur* and *Zechirah*

The above excerpt is found in the Haggadah's discourse on *halachah*. The quote describes a dispute between Ribbi Elazar ben Azariah and the Sages regarding the commandment to recall our redemption every day – the obligation of *zechirah*. In order to understand the dispute an introduction is necessary.

In addition to the *mitzvah* of *sippur*, which is fulfilled at the *Seder*, we are obligated to recall our redemption from Egypt daily – *zechirah*. *Zechirah* is executed through recitation of the third paragraph of the *Shema,* which includes a reference to our redemption. Ribbi Elazar ben Azariah assumed that this third paragraph was included in the recitation of the *Shema* in the morning and also at nighttime. However, he could not, himself, prove from a Torah passage that the nighttime recital of *Shema* should include reference to our redemption from Egypt.

Ribbi Elazar ben Azariah then explains that Ben Zoma provided a Torah reference from the very passage that stipulates the requirement of *zechirah*. The portion of the passage that establishes the obligation states, "in order that you remember the day of your going forth from the Land of Egypt all the days of your life". The word "all" seems superfluous. Ben Zoma explained that the word "all" is included in the passage in order to include the nighttimes – not just the daytimes of our lives – in the *mitzvah*.

The Sages rejected Ben Zoma's interpretation of the word "all". They argued that the word is included in the passage in order to extend the obligation of *zechirah* into the Messianic era. In other words, without the insertion of the word "all" into the text of the passage, the passage would be understood to direct us to recall our redemption from Egypt until the advent of the Messianic era. However, with the arrival of the Messiah, the obligation of *zechirah* would lapse. The insertion of the word "all" extends the obligation into the Messianic era. In other words, even when the Messiah arrives and redeems Bnai Yisrael from its final exile, the obligation of *zechirah* will persist.

4. All of "all"'s meanings

The dispute between Ben Zoma and the Sages can be understood on various levels. One aspect of their dispute is in regard to the meaning of the word "all" in the passage that obligates us in *zechirah* "all of the days of your life". The term "all" can mean "in its entirety". For example, the mouse-pad on the desk is all black; it is entirely black. Alternatively, the word "all" can mean every member of a group. For example, I hope that all – every member of the group – of readers of this article will enjoy it.

According to Ben Zoma, the directive to recall our redemption "all of the days" means that we are required to recall the exodus the whole day. Of course, this does not mean that we are to constantly dwell upon the redemption. It means that both components of the day – the daytime and the nighttime must include an acknowledgement of our redemption. The Sages understand the directive to mean that every day – even those of the Messianic era, must include an acknowledgement of our redemption from Egypt.

5. *Zechirah* during the Messianic era

Another aspect of the dispute is in regard to Ben Zoma's and the Sages' different understandings to the obligation of *zechirah*. The Talmud explains that Ben Zoma disputes the Sages' contention that the obligation extends into the Messianic era. He argues that the obligation to recall the redemption from Egypt will lapse with the advent of the Messianic era.[59]

It is noteworthy that the Sages disagree with Ben Zoma but tacitly acknowledge the fundamental virtue of his position. The Sages maintain that the obligation of *zechirah* is only extended into the Messianic era because the Torah specifically directs its application to that era. Other commandments, as a matter of course and without any special stipulation, extend into the Messianic era. This obligation is accompanied by a specific directive which extends it into the Messianic era. Even the Sages agree that there is some basis for assuming that *zechirah* should lapse with the Messiah's arrival. However, they contend that the Torah responds to this potential erroneous assumption by specifically extending the obligation into the Messianic era.

6. Greater revelation

Hashem's presence is evidenced in two ways. The miracles and wonders that He performed in redeeming Bnai Yisrael from Egypt testified to His omnipotence. This omnipotence can only be attributed to the Creator.[60] Our patriarch Avraham concluded that the universe has a Creator without witnessing miracles and wonders. He based his conclusion upon the wonders that he observed in the design of the natural world. He did not require a miracle to arrive at his conviction.[61]

The advent of the Messianic era will provide a revelation akin to but exceeding the revelation discovered by Avraham. With the coming of the Messiah, Hashem's plan for humanity will become evident. Finally, humanity will arrive at the destination of its wandering journey through the ages. Humankind will recognize that there is a design for humanity and that all of history has unfolded consistent with this design. The emergence of this revelation will constitute profound evidence of Hashem, the Creator and Sovereign. No longer will humankind need to look for miracles and wonders to evidence Hashem.

Ben Zoma and the Sages recognize that in the Messianic era we will no longer recall the wonders and miracles of our redemption from Egypt in order to find Hashem. We will be surrounded by a more profound testimony to His sovereignty. Therefore, Ben Zoma argues that with the Messianic era, the obligation of *zechirah* – to each and every day recall our exodus from Egypt – will lapse.

The Sages do not accept Ben Zoma's conclusion. However, the Talmud explains that they do acknowledge his basic premise. They agree that the revelation of the Messianic era will exceed the revelation provided by the miracles of the redemption.[62]

The Haggadah's discussion of the *zechirah* is inserted into the midst of its discussion of the *halachot* of *sippur*. Why does the Haggadah digresses from its discussion of *sippur*?

---

[59] Mesechet Berachot 12b.
[60] Rabbaynu Moshe ben Nachman (Ramban), *Commentary on Sefer Shemot* 13:16.
[61] Rabbaynu Moshe ben Maimon (Rambam) *Mishne Torah*, Hilchot Avotad Kochavim 1:3.
[62] Mesechet Berachot 13a.

Do not eat with it leavened bread. For seven days eat with it matzot – the bread of affliction – because you went out of the Land of Egypt in haste. (This is) in order that you remember the day of your going forth from the Land of Egypt all of the days of your life. (Sefer Devarim 16:3)

6. The relationship between *sippur* and *zechirah*

The above passage contains the directive cited by Ben Zoma and the Sages as the source for the obligation of *zechirah*. This passage is actually discussing the prohibition against eating *chametz* – leavened bread – on Pesach and the eating of *matzah*. Ben Zoma and the Sages are taking the final phrase out of its context and citing it as the textual source for the obligation of *zechirah*.

This interpretation of the passage's final phrase can be understood based upon a comment of Rav Naftali Tzvi Yehudah Berlin – Netziv. Netziv explains that the *mitzvah* of *sippur* and the obligation of *zechirah* are operationally related; they are intended to operate in tandem. *Sippur* is performed on an annual basis. It creates an elaborate and inspiring experience. We not only recall our redemption; *sippur* asks for and facilitates our reliving of the redemption from Egypt. *Zechirah* extends the message and experience of the *Seder* night to the remainder of the year.

Netziv explains an evening devoted to the recounting and contemplation of our redemption is required each year in order to inspire us. After this evening, we recapture that inspiration throughout the year through *zechirah* – a daily reminder.[63]

The Torah inserts its directive regarding *zechirah* into a passage discussing Pesach in order to communicate this idea. The daily recollection is intended to refresh within us the inspiration drawn from the observance of Pesach and the experience of the *Seder*.

Now, the inclusion of a discussion of the obligation of *zechirah* within the Haggadah's discussion of *sippur* is understood. The Haggadah is communicating that the messages and inspiration developed at the *Seder* through the *mitzvah* of *sippur* must remain with us every day throughout the year. *Sippur* is not to be performed and forgotten the next day. It is the foundation of an ongoing cognizance that extends throughout the year. Each day it is renewed through *zechirah* in the recitation of the *Shema*.

What does the wise one say? What are these testimonies, laws and rules that Hashem our G-d commanded you? And you tell him of the laws of the Pesach. One may not eat a dessert after the Pesach sacrifice." (Haggadah of Pesach)

Study of the law

One of the *mitzvot* fulfilled at the *Seder* is recounting the exodus from Egypt. This *mitzvah* is ideally fulfilled through a discussion between father and son. The Torah requires the father to employ a pedagogic style that matches the needs of the specific child. The above passage describes the question of the wise son and the appropriate response.

The wise son asks the father to explain the meaning of the various commandments of *Pesach*. The Haggadah instructs the father to answer the son through teaching the laws of *Pesach*.

---

[63] Rav Naftali Tzvi Yehudah Berlin (Netziv), *Commentary Hamek Davar on Sefer Devarim* 16:3.

This response is difficult to understand. The father must retell the story of our redemption. Although the method of teaching must match the child, the goal is to discuss these events. Yet, the answer suggested by the Haggadah does not mention the redemption.

The first step in answering this question is to understand that the Haggadah is not dictating the complete answer to be given to the son. The Haggadah is indicating the appropriate approach. The answer is far more comprehensive than the short response included in the above passage. The response must include a complete recounting of the events of the redemption. However, the discussion must begin with a lesson concerning the laws of *Pesach*.

Why begin with a discussion of the laws? What would be missing if the father immediately retold the story of the exodus and bypassed this discussion of the laws?

The wise son recognizes that the Torah can only be fully understood through study of its law. The father is required to reinforce this conclusion. He encourages this study. He shows the son that the profound lessons of the Torah emerge from the study of the law. Through this approach, the wise son discovers that the exodus is not just an event, but also the basis for the laws of the Torah.

"The following are the ten plagues that the Holy One Blessed Be He brought upon the Egyptians in Egypt: Dam (Blood), Tzfardeah (Frogs), Kinim (Lice), Arov (Wild Beasts), Dever (Pestilence), Sh'chin (Boils), Barad (Hail), Arbeh (Locusts), Choshech (Darkness), Macat Bechorot (The Plague of the Firstborn). Rabi Yehuda expressed them through their initials – D'TzACh, ADaSh, BeAChaB." (Hagaddah of Pesach)

Hashem's Omnipotence

1. Ordering the plagues

The redemption from Egypt was preceded by ten plagues. The *Pesach* Hagaddah lists these plagues. The Hagaddah then tells us that the Sage Rabi Yehuda created a mnemonic from the initials of the ten plagues. This mnemonic cannot be accurately transliterated from Hebrew to English. This is because some Hebrew letters have alternate pronunciations. Therefore, in some instances a letter is pronounced in one manner in the Hebrew word for the plague and in another manner in the mnemonic.

The commentaries discuss the purpose of this mnemonic. We usually employ such devices in order to commit complicated or intricate material to memory. This is not the likely explanation of Rabi Yehuda's device. Ten plagues are not terribly difficult to memorize. What was Rabi Yehuda's objective in creating this mnemonic?

There are various approaches to answering this question. Many of these Sages note that the plagues are recorded in Sefer Tehillim. There, the order is somewhat altered.[64] This might create some confusion as to the actual order. Rabi Yehuda wished to indicate that the actual order is found in the Torah. He created a mnemonic that represents the plagues in the order in the Torah.[65]

---

[64] Sefer Tehillim, Chapters 78 and 105.

[65] Rabbaynu Shlomo ben Yitzchak (Rashi), *Commentary on the Hagaddah of Pesach*.

This explanation assumes that the order in which the plagues occurred was significant. In other words, there was a specific reason for this order and no other. The Midrash seems to confirm this assumption. The Midrash comments that the names of the plagues were carved onto Moshe's staff. These names were arranged in the order of their occurrence. This seems to confirm the importance of the order.[66]

This raises a question. Why was the order important? Why did the plagues occur in a specific sequence? Again, the commentaries offer a variety of responses. One well-known explanation is offered by the Midrash. The Midrash explains that the order is similar to the strategy followed by a king putting down a rebellion. First, the king places a siege around the rebellious city. He cuts off the water supply. Similarly, the Almighty turned the water in Egypt to blood. Then the king commands his troops to sound their trumpets. This is an attempt to confuse and discourage the rebels. The frogs fulfilled this function. Their constant croaking unnerved the Egyptians. The Midrash continues to delineate the similarities between the order of the plagues and the strategy of the king.[67]

2. Separating the plagues

Other commentaries offer a completely different explanation of Rabi Yehuda's mnemonic. They explain that Rabi Yehuda was not merely attempting to indicate the sequence of the plagues. Instead, he was dividing the plagues into three distinct groups. What are these three groups? The first three plagues were plagues of the earth or water. The water was turned to blood. Then, an infestation of frogs was generated from the water. Next, the dust of the earth turned to lice.

The next group is harder to characterize. These seem to be plagues that emerge from the general surroundings. The first of these was an infestation of wild beast. These animals emerged from the surrounding wilderness. Pestilence and boils followed this.

The final group of plagues descended from the heavens. These were the plagues of hail, locusts and darkness. Tacked on to this last group is the plague of the firstborn. This plague is not truly a member of this group. However, it is attached to the last group in order to create an effective mnemonic.[68]

There is a basic difference between these two approaches to explaining Rabi Yehuda's mnemonic. In order to better understand this dispute, it will help to consider a *pasuk* in the Torah.

Hashem sends Moshe to Paroh to warn him of the coming plague of Hail. Moshe makes an interesting statement. He tells Paroh that Hashem could immediately end the bondage of Bnai Yisrael in Egypt. He could bring a plague of pestilence upon Egypt that would obliterate the Egyptians. However, the Almighty does not choose to do this. Instead, it is His will to extend His conflict with Paroh. Why does Hashem wish to continue the struggle? Moshe explains that Hashem wishes to demonstrate and publicize His omnipotence.[69]

---

[66] Rabbaynu Shlomo ben Yitzchak (Rashi), *Commentary on the Hagaddah of Pesach.*
[67] Midrash Tanchuma, Parsaht Bo, Chapter 4.
[68] Rabbaynu Shemuel ben Meir (Rashbam), *Commentary on the Hagaddah.*
[69] Sefer Shemot, 9:15-16.

What is Moshe's message to Paroh? Moshe is explaining that Hashem could destroy Paroh and his nation immediately. Why is Hashem not acting more forcibly? Moshe explains that this part of the Almighty's will to demonstrate His omnipotence.

3. Design vs. control

How did the plagues illustrate Hashem's omnipotence? This demonstration required two elements. First, the plagues could not be mistaken for a natural set of catastrophes. Second, they demonstrated the extent of the Almighty's control over all elements of the environment. The plagues included both of these elements. They followed a plan. This is the message of the Midrash.

The plagues followed the strategy of a king suppressing a rebellion. The expression of this strategy in the sequence of plagues demonstrated the element of design. Clearly, these plagues were not a series of natural catastrophes.

The plagues also affected every element of the environment. The first three plagues originated in the earth and water. The second set of three was produced by the general surroundings. The lash three descended from the heavens. This demonstrated the Almighty's control over every element of the environments.

We can now understand the dispute between the commentaries. Which of these elements is represented by Rabi Yehuda's mnemonic? According to the first interpretation, the mnemonic represents the element of design in the plagues. According to the second interpretation, the mnemonic communicates the Almighty's control over the various elements of the environment that was illustrated by the plagues.

"Raban Gamliel said, "Anyone that does not discuss these three things does not fulfill one's obligation. And these are the things: the Pesach sacrifice, Matzah, and Marror." (Hagaddah of Pesach)

The Seder

1. The mitzvah of sippur

This selection from the Hagaddah is derived from the Talmud in Tractate Pesachim. Raban Gamliel explains that in order for a person to fulfill his obligation on the night of Pesach, he must discuss the mitzvot of the Pesach sacrifice, Matzah and Marror.

There are two difficulties with Raban Gamliel's law. Raban Gamliel does not specify the obligation that is fulfilled through this discussion. In other words, if a person does not discuss the mitzvot of Pesach, Matzah and Marror, what is the obligation that the person has failed to fulfill? Second, Raban Gamliel does not indicate the source for his law.

First, let us focus on the first question. What obligation has not been fulfilled if the Pesach, Matzah and Marror have not been discussed? Maimonides provides a simple answer to this question. Maimonides places Raban Gamliel's law in the chapter of his code that discusses the laws regarding the mitzvah to discuss the redemption from Egypt on the first night of Pesach. It is clear from the placement of Raban Gamliel's law in this chapter that Maimonides maintains that the discussion of Pesach, Matzah and Marror is essential to the mitzvah of retelling the events of our redemption from Egypt. Furthermore, Maimonides explains that the discussion of these three topics – Pesach, Matzah and Marror – is referred to as Haggadah.[70] This seems to confirm that the discussion is part of the mitzvah to retell the events of the redemption.

"And you shall say, 'This is the Pesach sacrifice to Hashem who passed over the homes of Bnai Yisrael when He struck Egypt and our homes He saved.' And the nation bowed and prostrated itself." (Shemot 12:27)

2. Through the Pesach

Tosefot do not directly deal with our first question. Instead, they discuss our second question. What is the source for Raban Gamliel's law? Tosefot explain that the source is the above passage. The passage indicates that there is an obligation to explain the significance of the Pesach sacrifice.

However, Tosefot realize that this answer creates a problem. The passage only specifies that the Pesach sacrifice must be discussed. Raban Gamliel extends this obligation to the Matzah and Marror. The pasuk makes no mention of Matzah and Marror. What is the source for the obligation to discuss these mitzvot? Tosefot offer a rather strange answer to this question.

"And you shall eat the flesh (of the Pesach) on this night roasted by fire and with Matzah and Marror you should eat it." (Shemot 12:8)

3. Discussion, not sippur

Tosefot suggest that the obligation to discuss Matzah and Marror is derived from the above passage. According to Tosefot, the pasuk equates or associates the Matzah and Marror with the Pesach. Tosefot explain that based on this association, the requirement to discuss the Pesach is extended to the Matzah and Marror.

Tosefot's reasoning is not immediately obvious. The above passage tells us the Pesach must be eaten with Matzah and Marror. In other words, the obligation to eat the Pesach is not fulfilled in its entirety by eating the Pesach alone. Instead, in order to completely fulfill the mitzvah of eating the Pesach, it must be eaten with Matzah and Marror.

Tosefot's contention that the pasuk associates the Pesach with Matzah and Marror is certainly accurate. However, this association is insofar as the obligation to eat the Pesach. The passage does not discuss the obligation to speak about the Pesach. In no sense does the pasuk associate the Matzah and Marror with the Pesach in regards to the obligation to discuss the Pesach.

Rav Yitzchak Mirsky suggests that according to Tosefot, the obligation to discuss the Pesach sacrifice is part of the mitzvah to eat the Pesach. In other words, the eating of the Pesach must be preceded by a discussion of the significance of the mitzvah. Based on this insight, he explains Tosefot's reasoning.

Since the eating of the Matzah and Marror is part of the mitzvah of eating the Pesach – as indicated by our pasuk – the obligation to discuss the Pesach extends to the Matzah and Marror which is eaten with the Pesach.[71]

---

[70] Rabbaynu Moshe ben Maimon (Rambam) *Mishne Torah*, Hilchot Chametz U'*Matzah* 7:5.
[71] Rav Yitzchak Mirsky, *Haggadat Hegyonai Halacha* (Jerusalem, 5762), p 111.

So, although Tosefot do not directly discuss the mitzvah that is not fulfilled if Pesach, Matzah and Marror are not discussed, their position has emerged. This discussion is needed in order to completely fulfill the mitzvah of eating the Pesach with its Matzah and Marror.

Tosefot's position presents an interesting problem. Generally, in performing a mitzvah we are not required to understand the purpose and full significance of the commandment. At most, we are obligated to be cognizant of the obligatory nature of the performance. But according to Tosefot, the mitzvah of eating the Pesach with its Matzah and Marror must be discussed and understood in order to be completely fulfilled. Why is the mitzvah of the Pesach different from other mitzvot?

"And you should tell to your son" One might think that the mitzvah can be fulfilled from the beginning of the month. The Torah tells us, "On that day." If one was only told that the mitzvah must be fulfilled on that day, one might think that it can be fulfilled before nightfall. The Torah tells us "For the sake of this." "For the sake of this" only applies at the time the Matzah and Marror are placed before you." (Hagaddah of Pesach)

4. Co-mingled mitzvot

This section of the Hagaddah is derived from and paraphrases the Michilta. The section deals with the derivation for the proper time for the fulfillment of the mitzvah of recounting our redemption from Egypt. The Mechilta explains that the mitzvah can only be fulfilled on the night of the fifteenth of Nisan. This requirement is not explicitly stated in the Torah. Instead, it is derived from a passage that indicates the mitzvah can only be fulfilled at the time of the mitzvot of Matzah and Marror. The mitzvot of Matzah and Marror are fulfilled on the fifteenth of Nisan after nightfall. Therefore, according to the Mechilta, the mitzvah of Sippur – the retelling of the redemption – is also relegated to the night of the fifteenth of Nisan.

The implications of this lesson from the Mechilta are very important. According to the Mechilta, the mitzvot of Matzah, Marror and Sippur are inextricably interrelated – to the extent that the mitzvah of Sippur can only be fulfilled at the time of the mitzvot of Matzah and Marror. What is the basis of this interrelationship?

It seems clear from the Mechilta that the Torah designed the mitzvot of Matzah and Marror to be fulfilled in the context of Sippur. These mitzvot do not merely coexist on the night of the fifteenth. Together, they merge into a single entity.

5. One unit

This relationship is reflected in Maimonides' treatment of these mitzvot. In his code, he discusses the mitzvah of Matzah, then the mitzvah of sippur. He then describes how these mitzvot are performed on the night of the fifteenth of Nisan. In other words, after discussing the various mitzvot performed on the night of the fifteenth, Maimonides provides a detailed description of the Seder.

From Maimonides' treatment of these mitzvot and the Seder, it seems that the Seder is more than a set of instructions for the fulfillment of a set of unrelated mitzvot that happen to occur at the same time. Instead, the various mitzvot of the night merge into a single unified and coordinated entity – the Seder. In other words, the Seder is the halachic entity in which the various mitzvot of the night merge and become unified.

We can now more fully understand Tosefot's reasoning. Why do the mitzvot of Pesach, Matzah and Marror require discussion, explanation and understanding? This is because the mitzvot are designed to occur in the context of the mitzvah of Sippur. Because of this context the mitzvot cannot be properly fulfilled without explanation and understanding.

"You shall not eat leaven with it; for seven days you shall eat with it matzot, the bread of affliction, for in haste you went out of the land of Egypt, so that you shall remember the day when you went out of the land of Egypt all the days of your life." (Devarim 16:3)

Matzah

1. Eaten during bondage

One of the mitzvot of Pesach is the prohibition against eating leavened bread. In place of leavened bread, we eat matzah. The first night of Pesach we are obligated to eat matzah. The remaining days of the festival, we are not obligated to eat matzah, but we are prohibited from eating chametz – leavened products.

In the above passage, the Torah explains that the matzah recalls the bread eaten during bondage. How does the matzah recall the bread eaten during bondage? Rabbaynu Ovadia Sforno explains that the while in bondage, the Jews were forced to constantly labor for their Egyptian masters. The Egyptians would not provide their Jewish slaves with the time required to mix the dough for their bread and then allow it to rise. Instead, once the dough was mixed, the Jews were forced to immediately bake the bread. The dough did not have the opportunity to rise. The resulting loaves had the unleavened form of matzah.[72]

"And one takes the middle matzah and breaks into two parts ... and he lifts the Seder plate and recites, "This is the bread of affliction," until "How is this night different." (Shulchan Aruch 473:6)

Another fundamental commandment performed on Pesach is sipur yetziat mitzrayim – the recounting of our redemption from Egypt. This mitzvah is fulfilled through the Pesach Seder. One of the early steps in the Seder is YaChatz – breaking the middle matzah. Shulchan Aruch explains this process. The middle matzah is broken and half is retuned to the Seder plate. The plate is then lifted and the reader recites: "This is the bread of affliction which our fathers ate in Egypt."

In other words, the reader explains that the broken matzah recalls the bread that the Jews ate during their bondage in Egypt. The identification of matzah with the affliction in Egypt is based upon our passage in which the Torah refers to the matzah as "bread of affliction."

"They baked the dough that they had taken out of Egypt as unleavened cakes, for it had not leavened, for they were driven out of Egypt, and they could not tarry, and also, they had not made provisions for themselves." (Shemot 12:39)

2. Bondage and redemption

---

[72] Rabbaynu Ovadia Sforno, *Commentary on Sefer Devarim*, 16:3.

210

In the above passage, the Torah explains that Bnai Yisrael left Egypt in tremendous haste. They did not have the opportunity to prepare adequately for their journey. They could not allow their dough to mix. Instead, they mixed the dough and immediately baked it. The product was unleavened cakes.

Based on this passage, the Talmud explains the significance of the *matzah*. Raban Gamliel explains that the *matzah* recalls our redemption. He explains that at the *Seder* we are required to explain that the *matzah* we will eat is intended to remind us of the haste with which our ancestors left Egypt.[73] His comments are based u16pon our passage in the Torah. The comments of Raban Gamliel are incorporated into the *Seder* and read prior to fulfilling the commandment to eat *matzah*.

In short, the Torah suggests two alternative explanations for *matzah*. In Sefer Devarim, the Torah explains that *matzah* recalls our affliction in Egypt. In Sefer Shemot, the Torah suggests that *matzah* recalls that haste of our redemption from Egypt.

Paradoxically, both of these messages are associated with *matzah* during the course of the *Seder*. At the opening of the *Seder*, we declare that the *matzah* recalls our bondage. But before eating the *matzah*, we read Raban Gamliel's interpretation of *matzah*. In this interpretation, the *matzah* is associated with the redemption from bondage. In other words, the process of *sipur* requires that we recall both our bondage and our redemption. Both of these phenomena are symbolized by the *matzah*.

We can easily understand the importance of recalling our bondage and our redemption. The full meaning and significance of our redemption can be fully appreciated when we remember the bondage from which we were redeemed. However, it is odd and paradoxical that the same object – *matzah* – is used to symbolize both of these elements of our experience in Egypt. Why did the Torah not create two separate objects – each designed to recall one of the two elements?

3. Urgency

Sforno's comments also address this issue. He explains that the Torah intends to communicate a message. During their bondage in Egypt, the Jews were oppressed by their masters. The oppression of Bnai Yisrael was epitomized by the bread they were forced to eat. The Egyptians would not even afford their Jewish slaves the time to bake their bread properly. They pressured the Jews to hurriedly prepare and bake their bread. The result was unleavened *matzah*.

At the moment of redemption, the demoralized Egyptians urged the Jews to hurry. Again, the bread that the Jews baked epitomized the urgency of the Egyptians. But this urgency was not motivated by their desire to oppress the Jews. Instead, their urgency was motivated by panic. They could not endure another moment of suffering![74]

Sforno is explaining that the Egyptians demonstrated urgency in two situations. In both instances, their urgency was expressed in a similar behavior. They hastened Bnai Yisrael to

---

[73] Mesechet Pesachim 116a.
[74] Rabbaynu Ovadia Sforno, *Commentary on Sefer Devarim*, 16:3.

prepare their bread without allowing their dough to rise. But in the first instance – during their oppression of the Jews – this urgency was an expression of oppression. In the second instance – at the moment of redemption – this urgency expressed the complete humiliation and defeat of the Egyptians. Sforno's comments indicate that the urgency of the Egyptians in these two different situations in some manner communicates a fundamental message regarding the redemption. What is this message?

4. Sudden reversal

Apparently, the miracle of the redemption from Egypt is not merely that a nation of slaves was liberated from the oppression of the most powerful nation in the civilized world. But the miracle can only be fully appreciated if we recognize the total and sudden reversal that Bnai Yisrael and the Egyptians experienced. Bnai Yisrael did not gradually achieve liberation from oppression and freedom as the power and authority of their masters slowly declined. Instead, in a few months, the Jewish people emerged from a condition of abject subjugation and tyranny into a state of total freedom. Their masters – who once would not allow them a few moments to properly prepare their bread – were reduced to trembling petitioners. They begged their former slaves to spare them and to leave posthaste and end their suffering! It is this total and abrupt reversal that captures the gravity and magnitude of the miracle of the redemption.

Still, why is *matzah* used to symbolize both the severity of the oppression and the totality of the Egyptians' demise? Sforno is answering this question. An illustration will help explain this point. It is difficult to appreciate the speed of a fastball thrown by an accomplished pitcher. We lack a basis for comparison. But if we want to truly appreciate the talent and skills of this pitcher, we must create a contrast. We can do this by placing on a single-viewing screen two pitches. One is the fastball of the professional and the other is the best effort of an accomplished amateur. On the split screen, we can see both pitches progress through time and over distance towards the batter. Now, we can more fully comprehend the remarkable speed of the professional's pitch.

According to Sforno, the full miracle of the redemption can only be appreciated by recognizing the totality and abruptness of the reversal experienced by Bnai Yisrael and the Egyptians. The reversal only becomes clear when the severity of the oppression is contrasted with the panic of the Egyptians at the moment of redemption. But, like the two pitches in our illustration, the contrast between the oppression and the redemption can only be fully appreciated when they are viewed side-by-side – on a split screen.

The *matzah* provides this "split screen." A single object – the *matzah* – captures and communicates the degree of oppression and the total demise of the Egyptians. In *matzah*, the two experiences are communicated side-by-side. This dual symbolism within a single object eloquently communicates to us the totality and suddenness of the redemption and thereby, the extent of the miracle of the redemption.

And Moshe said to the nation: Remember this day that you went forth from Egypt, from the house of bondage – for with a mighty hand Hashem took you forth from this. Leaven products should not be eaten. (Shemot 13:3)

Retelling the Redemption from Egypt

1. A biblical source for the commandment of *Sipur*

In this passage, Moshe instructs the nation that they must remember the day that they were redeemed from slavery in Egypt and that on the days that commemorate this event – the festival of Pesach – they should not each *chametz* – leavened products. In his code of law – Mishne Torah – Maimonides explains that the first portion of this passage in which Moshe instructs the nation to recall the day of its redemption is the biblical source for the commandment to retell the events of the redemption at the annual Pesach *Seder*.[75],[76]

2. An alternative biblical source for the commandment of *Sipur*

In his *Sefer HaMitzvot*, Maimonides suggests an alternative source for the commandment to retell the events of our redemption. There he cites the passage: *And you should tell to your son on that day saying, "For this purpose Hashem did this for me when I went out of Egypt."*[77] Why does Maimonides present different passages as the biblical source for the *mitzvah* in these two works?

3. The two aspects of the commandment of *Sipur* represented by its two sources

Every commandment has a purpose and objective. However, in most instances the halachic – the legal obligation – associated with the commandment is limited to its performance. Achievement of the *mitzvah*'s objective is laudable. However, the commandment is fulfilled at its basic requisite level without achievement of its objects. For example, we are required to pick up and wave the four species on Sukkot. Certainly, this commandment has some meaning and purpose. However, a person who performs the physical action of the commandment fulfills its requirements even if the person has no understanding of the meaning and significance of the performance.

However, there are some commandments in which the performance of the physical activity associated with the *mitzvah* is meaningless without achievement of the commandment's objective. The best known example is repentance. Rav Yosef Dov Soloveitchik *Zt"l* explains that this commandment consists of two components or aspects:

---

[75] Rabbaynu Moshe ben Maimon (Rambam) *Mishne Torah*, Hilchot *Chametz* U'Matzah 7:1.
[76] Rav Yosef Dov Soloveichik notes that the commandment as expressed in the passage is to recall the events of the date of the redemption – the 15th of Nisan. Maimonides' formulation of the commandment in his code reflects this formulation. He states: It is a positive commandment to retell the miracles and wonders that were preformed for our ancestors in Egypt on the night of the 15th of Nisan. (*Mishne Torah*, Hilchot *Chametz* U'Matzah 7:1). Maimonides' wording is unclear. One possibility is that the reference to the 15th of Nisan is intended to identify the date that the commandment is performed. In other words, Maimonides is saying that the commandment is to be performed on this date. Alternatively, he could mean that the commandment is to focus on the events that occurred on the 15th of Nisan. If this is the correct explanation, then the *mitzvah* of *Sipur* performed at the *Seder* would be limited to the discussion of those events leading up to the redemption and the redemption itself. Subsequent events – including the parting of the Reed Sea – would not belong in this discussion. Rav Soloveitchik suspected that this second interpretation was in fact Maimonides' position. He cited peculiar omissions from the *Hagadah* attributed to Maimonides to support this position.
[77] Shemot 13:8

A. The activity of verbal confession of one's sin.

B. The internal commitment to repent from the sin and evil behavior.

The *mitzvah* is fulfilled only through the merger of its two aspects. A person who makes the commitment to change but does not verbalize his confession has not fulfilled the requirements of the commandment. Neither has the person who utters the required confession without the commitment to alter his behavior.[78]

Any commandment that consists of these multiple aspects – an activity and an objective – can be defined in terms of its activity or in terms of its objective. In the example of repentance it is equally correct to define the commandment as an obligation to confess one's sin or as an obligation to repent or reform one's behavior. Both definitions are correct. The first defines the commandment in terms of its required physical activity. The other definition focuses on the commandment's purpose or objective.

Maimonides seems to suggest that the commandment of *Sipur* – retelling the events of our rescue from Egypt is a member of this class of commandments. The commandment consists of an outward activity designed to achieve an internal objective. We are required to engage in retelling the events of our exodus. Through this activity we must recall and internalize the significance of these events.

4. Understanding the *Haggadah*

This insight provides a basis for Ramah's ruling that the Pesach *Haggadah* cannot be merely recited in Hebrew without understanding its meaning. Instead, it must be read in a language understood by the participants or read in Hebrew and then explained.[79] The process of *Sipur* must impact the participants. Therefore, the process must be carried out in a manner that communicates the events.

5. The aspects of redemption that must be recalled

A careful analysis of the above passage suggests that there are three issues or aspects of the redemption that must be recalled in the process of *Sipur*. The passage states: Remember this day…

A. that you went forth from Egypt,

B. from the house of bondage –

C. for with a mighty hand Hashem took you forth from this.

---

[78] Rav Yosef Dov Soloveitchik, *Al HaTeshuva* (Jerusalem, 5739), Part 1.

[79] Rav Yosef Karo, *Shulchan Aruch, Orech Chayim* 473:6. See Mishne Berurah ibid, note 63. Mishne Berurah suggests that the passage "And you should tell to your son… (Shemot 13:8) is the basis for this requirement. "Telling" means to communicate information. This cannot be accomplished unless the communicator and recipient of the information understand the message communicated. However, the term "tell" in the Torah does not always imply that the communication must be understood. When presenting the first fruit – the *Bikurim* – in Yerushalayim, the presenter is required to recite a set of Torah passages. These are recited in Hebrew and the presenter reciting the passages need not understand their meaning. In its formulation of this requirement, the Torah describes the presenter as "telling" the contents of the passages.

In other words, our recollection of the events must encompass three aspects. First, we were brought forth from Egypt. Second, we were in bondage in Egypt. Third, the process through which we were redeemed demonstrated Hashem's omnipotence – His mighty hand.

Raban Gamliel said: Anyone who does not discuss these three things on Pesach does not fulfill his obligation. These are the things: Pesach, Matzah, and Maror.

For what reason did our ancestors eat the Pesach when the Temple was in existence? Because the Holy One Blessed be He passed over the houses of our ancestors in Egypt...

What is the reason that we eat this Matzah? Because there was not adequate time for the dough of our ancestors to leaven before the King of All Kings, The Holy One Blessed be He was revealed to them and redeemed them...

What is the reason that we eat this Maror? Because the Egyptians made the lives of our ancestors bitter in Egypt.... (Pesach Hagadah)

6. Retelling the events of our redemption through *Pesach*, *Matzah*, and *Maror*

The above section of the Pesach *Haggadah* is derived directly from the Mishne of Tractate Pesachim. Raban Gamliel explains that we are required to retell the events of our redemption from Egypt through explaining the significance of the Pesach sacrifice, the *Matzah*, and the *Maror*.

We explain that the *Pesach* reminds us that Hashem passed over the households of Bnai Yisrael when He struck the Egyptians with the most destructive and terrible of His plagues – the Plague of the Firstborn. *Matzah* reminds us of the suddenness of our redemption. Our ancestors were hastily released from bondage and quickly and eagerly ushered from the land by the very masters who only days before had refused to grant them their freedom. *Maror* reminds us of the suffering and torment that our ancestors experienced in Egypt.

7.　The essential elements of *Sipur*

Apparently, these three messages comprise the essential elements of the *mitzvah* of *Sipur*. Each of the objects central to the *Seder* – the *Pesach*, *Matzah*, and *Maror* – communicate one of these elements and these elements must be presented in the context of explaining the meaning of these objects.

Let us more carefully consider these messages. Pesach reminds us that Hashem spared the household of Bnai Yisrael when He struck the Egyptians with the Plague of the Firstborn. It communicates the miraculous nature of the redemption and the revelation in the redemption of Hashem's omnipotence. *Matzah* reminds us of the sudden transformation to freedom; the redemption occurred so swiftly the people could not adequately prepare their provisions for their unexpected journey into the wilderness. *Maror* reminds us of the cruelty of our bondage in Egypt.

Why are these messages – communicated by the central objects of the *Seder* – so central to the *mitzvah* of *Sipur*? They are the essential elements because they exactly correspond with the elements identified in the first of the passages cited by Maimonides as the biblical source for the commandment. These are the three elements that we are required by the passage to remember!

And Moshe said to the nation: Remember this day that you went forth from Egypt from the house of bondage. For with a mighty hand Hashem took you forth from this. And do not eat leavened bread. (Shemot 13:3)

Enough for What?

1. The elements of the *mitzvah* of *sipur*

Maimonides cites the above passage as the Torah source for the commandment to retell the story of our redemption from Egypt on the night of Pesach.[80] This commandment – *sipur* – is the focus of Pesach *seder*. In his Sefer HaMitzvot, Maimonides enumerates the components of this *mitzvah*. We must include the following elements in our discussion:

- The works of Hashem that He performed on our behalf in order to rescue us.

- Our oppression at the hands of the Egyptians with focus on their cruelty and wickedness.

- Hashem's punishment of the Egyptians for their evil treatment of us.

- Offering thanksgiving to Hashem.

He adds that the more one discusses our redemption, the greater the fulfillment of the *mitzvah*.[81]

It is clear from Maimonides' comments that fulfillment of the commandment is not completed by simply providing an historical account of the events of our exodus from Egypt. The recounting must focus on the role of Hashem in the events, His administration of judgment and justice, and of thanksgiving. In other words, the *mitzvah* does not focus on our emergence as a nation as much as upon Hashem's role and our debt to Him.

How many elevating acts of goodness did the Omnipresent do for us! (Pesach Hagadah)

2. The *dayanu* mystery

Maimonides' comments provide an explanation for one of the more enigmatic components of the *Hagadah*. This is a recitation of fifteen verses introduced by the above phrase. Each verse describes a kindness that Hashem performed on our behalf. The verses are sequential describing these kindnesses in the order in which they occurred. Each verse ends with the declaration *dayanu* – it would be enough for us!

This composition presents a number of difficulties. Seemingly, the phrase *dayanu* means that we would have been satisfied with any one of the kindnesses mentioned in the fifteen verses, even were it not followed by the subsequent kindnesses. This interpretation makes sense in regard to some of the verses. For example, the first verse states that if Hashem had taken us forth from Egypt but not punished the Egyptians it would have sufficed for us. However, other verses are more difficult to understand.

A subsequent verse states that if Hashem had parted the waters of the Reed Sea but had not brought us through it upon dry land, it would have been sufficient for us. How would the parting of the sea sufficed for us, had we not passed through it and escaped the pursuing Egyptians? Similarly, another verse states that if Hashem had brought us to Sinai but not given

---

[80] Rabbaynu Moshe ben Maimon (Rambam) *Mishne Torah*, Hilchot Hametz u'Matzah 7:1.
[81] Rabbaynu Moshe ben Maimon (Rambam) *Sefer HaMitzvot, Mitzvat Aseh* 157.

us the Torah it would have sufficed for us. It is certainly true that at Sinai the people observed the presence of Hashem expressed upon the mountain. But this was a prelude to Revelation and the presenting of the Torah to the Jewish people. How would the Sinai experience have sufficed for us without receiving the Torah?

Rav Yosef Dov Soloveitcvhik *Zt"l* suggests an interpretation of the *dayanu* verses that responds to these questions. He reinterprets the *dayanu* refrain in a manner that corresponds with Maimonides' descriptions of the components of *sipur*. He explains that the *dayanu* refrain does not mean that any one of these kindnesses would have sufficed for us without the subsequent kindnesses. Instead, it means that each and every element of our deliverance requires our recognition of the kindness of Hashem and deserves or suffices to require our thanksgiving.

In other words, we do not satisfy our obligation to thank Hashem for our redemption by simply thanking Him for our deliverance and our return to the Land of Israel. Instead, we are required to recognize each kindness of Hashem that we experienced along our journey from oppression to freedom and independence. We must respond with recognition of each of these kindnesses by offering our thanks to Hashem.[82]

Rav Soloveitchik's interpretation of the *dayanu* verses is consistent with Maimonides' description of the elements of *sipur*. Maimonides explains that this *mitzvah* combines the recounting of our redemption with thanksgiving. The *dayanu* verses emphasize the thanksgiving element of *sipur* and acknowledge each step in the process of our redemption and ensuing journey as deserving its own thanksgiving.

Therefore, we are obligated to give thanks, to extol, to praise, to glorify, to exult ... the One Who did for our fathers and for us all these miracles. He brought us forth from bondage to freedom, from sorrow to happiness ... and let us say before Him a new song of prasie. Hallelu-h!
(Hagadah)

3. The strange formulation of *Hallel HaGadol*

Typically, thanksgiving is combined with praise. The *Hagadah* provides an example of this principle. After completing the narrative portion of the *Hagadah,* we recite the paragraph beginning with the above phrase. Also, this paragraph reflects Maimonides' comments. We have completed our retelling the story of our redemption and we then acknowledge that the events we have just discussed obligate us to offer thanksgiving and praise to Hashem. In other words, we do not fulfill our obligation of *sipur* though a dry recounting of the events. We must be inspired by the account and recognize the presence of Hashem in the shaping of our nation and in the freedom that we each enjoy today. This inspiration must move us to offer praise and thanksgiving to Hashem.

This paragraph is immediately followed by the recitation of the first two paragraphs of *Hallel*. The balance of the *Hallel* is recited after completing the Pesach meal. After completion of *Hallel* we recite *Hallel HaGadol*. This composition from Psalms consists of twenty six short verses. Each verse acknowledges a kindness of Hashem and ends with the phrase "for His kindness is eternal". Most of the verses describe kindnesses that were performed by Hashem in redeeming us from Egypt and in giving us possession of the Land of Israel. However, these verses are preceded and seceded by verses that are not related to this theme.

---

[82] Rav Yosef Dov Soloveitchik, Quoted by Rav Yisrael Chait, Author's personal notes.

We begin *Hallel HaGadol* by giving praise to Hashem as Creator. We acknowledge His creation of the heavens with His understanding, His creation of the sun, the moon, and the stars. *Hallel HaGadol* closes with recognizing that Hashem provides sustenance to all flesh and that He is the L-rd of the heavens.

This is an odd combination of verses. Most of the verses are related to the journey of our people from bondage to independence in the Land of Israel. Why are these passages preceded and seceded by the acknowledgment of Hashem as Creator?

There are a number of possible explanations. One is that the combination of verses communicates the message that Hashem is the L-rd of the entire universe. He is its creator and He rules the entire expanse of the vast universe that He created. Yet, despite His infinity and His exulted sovereignty over the vast expanse of the entire universe, He guides the destiny of our people. Hashem, Who created the universe, is also our redeemer from Egypt. In other words, *Hallel HaGadol* juxtaposes the omnipotence of Hashem to His kindness to the Jewish people. Apparently, this juxtaposition adds an element to our thanksgiving. What is this element?

What can we say before You Hashem, our G-d and the G-d of our fathers! Are not all the mighty as naught before You and men of repute as if they never were! And the wise are as without understanding and those with understanding are without intelligence. For their abundant actions are meaningless and their lives are empty before You. And the superiority of the human over the beast is naught for all of their actions are emptiness.

But we are Your nation, the children of Your covenant, the children of Avraham, Your beloved. That You swore unto him at Mount Moriah. The descendants of Yitzchak his only son who was bound upon the altar. The congregation of Yaakov, Your firstborn son. That from Your love for him and Your rejoicing in him You called his name Yisrael and Yeshurun. (Daily morning prayer)

4. Two elements of thanksgiving

This same juxtaposition is even more evident in the above prayer. It is its focus. We begin by comparing ourselves to Hashem. We acknowledge that all of our wisdom and accomplishments are insignificant, and even meaningless, when we compare ourselves to Hashem. But we then recognize that despite our relative insignificance, Hashem has chosen us as His nation.

In the context of this prayer, the message of the juxtaposition emerges. When we offer thanksgiving to Hashem, our objective is to acknowledge two truths. First, we recognize a kindness that He has performed for us. Second, we recognize that we have no claim to this kindness. Our descriptions of Hashem's greatness add this second element. We describe His greatness. Our own relative insignificance is either implicit or actually overtly noted – as in the above prayer. We follow with our thanksgiving. The juxtaposition communicates that we have no claim upon Hashem and we cannot explain or comprehend the mystery of His kindness to us.

Hallel HaGadol communicates this same message. Verses thanking Hashem for His kindness to us are preceded and seceded by verses that extoll His greatness as Creator. These introductory and concluding verses give context to our thanksgiving. We give thanks for kindnesses that we cannot begin to explain and understand.

5. Hashem's presence at the *seder*

Pesach is the most widely observed of our festivals. Its themes of liberation and freedom from oppression resonate with Jews, and even with non-Jews. It reminds us of the potential of human beings and the right of the individual to pursue one's dreams and strive to achieve one's aspirations. These themes are important, and deserve our confirmation. However, for us, Pesach is much more than an endorsement of these universal values. These values are a celebration of the greatness of humanity as expressed in the potential of the individual.

Our observance of Pesach is not a celebration of humanity. Instead, it is designed to bring us closer to Hashem. It directs us to consider the role that Hashem has played in the emergence of the Jewish people. It implores us to consider the wonder of our relationship with Hashem. He is the creator and sovereign of the universe. Yet, He has guided our history and shaped our destiny. It inspires us to draw closer to Hashem and to welcome him into our lives.

And you shall tell your son on that day, saying: It is because of that which Hashem did for me when I came forth out of Egypt. (Shemot 13:3)

It's Not Just a lot of Talk

1. Recounting our redemption

The central *mitzvah* of the *seder* is recounting the story of our redemption from Egypt. Other commandments are fulfilled at the *seder*. We eat *matzah* and *marror*. We recite *kiddush*. However, all of the performances are wrapped into our retelling the story of our redemption.

Our discussion of our redemption fulfills the obligation expressed in the above passage. We are required to relate the story to our children. Although, the passage is not very specific regarding the manner in which the account must be communicated, the Torah does establish specific requirements for the manner in which the *mitzvah* is to be fulfilled. These requirements are the foundation of the *Haggadah* and the *seder*.

And you shall speak and say before Hashem your G-d: A wandering Aramean was my father, and he went down into Egypt, and sojourned there, few in number; and he became there a nation, great, mighty, and populous. (Devarim 25:5)

2. Guidelines for retelling the story

One of these requirements is that the story must be communicated through the study of relevant Torah passages. One would expect the Sages to select the Torah's account of the exodus that is contained in Sefer Shemot as the text for the *seder*. They did not. Instead, they selected an abbreviated account of the events that is recited by the pilgrim who brings his first fruits to the *Bait HaMikdash* – the Sacred Temple. This selection opens with the above passage. The *Haggadah* contains a passage by passage analysis of this brief section of the Torah. Each passage is read and then analyzed based upon midrashic interpretation.

During the early post-Talmudic era a practice developed to replace this portion of the *Haggadah* with the relevant narrative from Sefer Shemot. This seems to be a reasonable innovation. The Sages of the era – the Geonim – condemned the practice. There are a number of reasons for the reaction of the Geonim. One was that they suspected that the practice was rooted in the Karaite tradition. The established text of the *Haggadah* is composed of a short text from the Written Torah which is explored and developed through a midrashic analysis from the Oral Torah. The Karaite tradition accepted the Written Torah but denied the authenticity of Oral

219

Tradition. Replacement of the established text with a text completely from the Written Torah suggested to the Geonim a rejection of the Oral Torah.

Another reason for rejection of this innovation is that the Torah requires that we retell the story of redemption through Torah study. Torah study is not achieved through mere reading of passages. Instead, the passages must be studied and analyzed. This requires consideration of the passages from the perspective of the Oral Torah. Therefore, the reading of a set of passages from Sefer Shemot does not fulfill the obligation of retelling the events of our redemption.[83]

We were slaves to Paroh in Egypt, and the L-rd, our G-d, took us out from there with a strong hand and with an outstretched arm. (Pesach Haggadah)

In the beginning our fathers served idols; but now the Omnipresent One has brought us close to His service. (Pesach Haggadah)

3. Humble beginnings leading to great achievements

Another requirement for fulfillment of the *mitzvah* of retelling the events of our redemption is that we begin our account by describing the humble origins of our nation and complete it by describing our achievements.[84] This requirement addresses the style or the manner in which we retell the story. However, this requirement does not address the issue of the material that must be included in the account.

This issue is disputed by the Sages. According to Rav, we are to begin by acknowledging that our ancestors – Avraham's father and those who preceded him – were idolaters. He requires that we use the second of the above texts. According to Shmuel, we begin by describing our servitude to Paroh. His text is the first of those above.[85] Our *Haggadah* accommodates both of these opinions. First, we fulfill our obligation as required by Shmuel. We explain that we were slaves to Paroh and Hashem rescued us. Later in the *Haggadah* we accommodate Rav's position. We explain that our ancestors were idolaters and now Hashem has drawn us into His service.

Shmuel's position seems more reasonable than Rav's. Pesach recalls our redemption from Egypt. Shmuel's text focuses exclusively on this theme. Rav's text begins with Terach – Avraham's father. What relevance does Terach's idolatry have to Pesach?

The first step in understanding this dispute is to better understand Rav and Shmuel's common ground. As explained above, Rav and Shmuel agree on the style of the narrative. It must begin with a description of our humble beginnings and conclude with an account of our achievements. They disagree on the starting point to the narrative. Why are we required to begin by recounting our humble origins?

4. Recognizing the role of Hashem

The objective of the *mitzvah* to retell the story of our redemption is not to merely preserve our historical memory of the event. Instead, our objective is to renew our awareness of the providential role in our development into a nation. We tell the unlikely story of a nation's emergence from obscurity into greatness. We describe this process as an expression of Hashem's providence and not as an accomplishment for which we can take credit. We recognize that what

---

[83] Rav Yosef Dov Soloveitchik as retold by Rav Yisroel Chait, Taped lecture.
[84] Mesechet Pesachim 116a.
[85] Mesechet Pesachim 116a.

we have achieved is not through our own might, wisdom, or endeavors, but a result of His kindness and providence.

5. Nationhood: Political autonomy and national destiny

Now, the dispute between Rav and Shmuel can be better understood. According to Rav, we emphasize the providential element of our emergence into nationhood. We demonstrate the presence of the hand of Hashem by directing our focus upon our redemption from Egypt which provides the clearest evidence of Hashem's role in our development.

Rav requires that we begin our story from before the emergence of our Patriarchs. His account differs from Shmuel's in two ways. First, Shmuel's account deals with our development into a nation in the political sense – our liberation from the oppression and domination of Egypt. Rav's narrative deals with the broader issue of our development into a nation with a unique spiritual destiny and mission. It describes our journey from idolatry to the Sinai Revelation and its covenant.

Our rescue from Egypt is included in Rav's narrative. It is an essential element. Only through our redemption was our spiritual mission realized. The miracles of our rescue demonstrated to the emerging nation that Hashem is the omnipotent Creator. This experience, and the realization it engendered, prepared the nation to achieve its spiritual destiny at Sinai. In short, the story of our redemption is told from a teleological perspective. In this context, the meaning and reason for our redemption become part of the narrative.

Second, Shmuel's account emphasizes the miraculous element of our rescue from Egypt. Rav's narrative, because of its breadth, places less emphasis on the overtly miraculous. The miracles of our redemption from Egypt are contained within the broader narrative of our spiritual journey.

6. Focus on which aspect of redemption?

Now, the dispute between Rav and Shmuel can be better understood. Both agree that our objective on the *seder* night is to retell the story of our redemption and to recognize that our freedom was given to us by Hashem. However, Rav and Shmuel differ over the emphasis. Rav's focus is on meaning and context. Our redemption can only be appreciated and understood when placed within the context of our national destiny and mission. Therefore, although our objective on the *seder* night is to relate the story of our rescue from Egypt, we can only accomplish our task fully by describing our rescue as an essential step toward achievement of our spiritual mission.

Shmuel responds that our emphasis must be on recognizing the miraculous. We tighten the scope of the narrative in order to sharpen the focus. The teleological element is important but it is not emphasized. It cannot be permitted to distract the *seder* participants from the role of Hashem in our emergence as a nation. We begin with our bondage in Egypt. We describe the miracles of the plagues, the destruction of our oppressors and emphasize Hashem's mighty hand and outstretched arm.

In other words, Rav and Shmuel agree that the *seder* discussion is about our redemption from bondage. They disagree over how we prioritize two conflicting objectives. In order to fully understand the significance and meaning of our redemption, the scope of the discussion must be expanded to incorporate its teleological aspect. However, this broader discussion can distract the participants from recognizing the miraculous element of our redemption. Rav prioritizes achieving a deeper understanding of the redemption from Egypt. Shmuel prioritizes recognition of the miraculous nature of the redemption.

"It came to pass when Paroh sent forth the people, that G-d did not lead them [by] way of the land of the Philistines for it was near, because G-d said, "Lest the people reconsider when they see war and return to Egypt." (Shemot 13:17)

Looking Forward or Behind?

1. Ease, lest retreat

Hashem leads Bnai Yisrael from Egypt. He will now guide the people to the Land of Israel. Our passage explains that Hashem did not lead the people to the land of Israel by the shortest, most direct route. The most direct route would have brought the people to the Land of the Pelishtim – the Philistines. In our passage, the Torah explains Hashem's reasoning for foregoing this more direct route and selecting a circuitous path. However, the exact meaning of this passage is disputed among the commentaries.

The above translation of the passage is based upon Rashi's commentary. He explains that the passage indicates two considerations that influenced Hashem's decision to select the more circuitous route. First, the route leading through the territory of the Pelishtim was more direct. Second, Hashem reasoned that when faced with war, the people might panic and attempt to return to Egypt. This second element is easily understood. However, the first factor – the directness of the route leading through the territory of the Pelishtim – does not seem to be a liability. On the contrary, the directness of the route would seem to favor its selection. Rashi explains that a direct route is more easily retraced. In contrast, a more circuitous route cannot be easily retraced. According to Rashi, these two elements are related. If Bnai Yisrael panicked when confronted with battle, the people would consider retreat back to Egypt. A direct route could easily be retraced. This option would encourage the people to surrender to their panic and return to Egypt. A more circuitous route cannot be easily retraced. Faced with war, the option to return to Egypt would be closed. Bnai Yisrael would be forced to confront their fears and go to battle; they simply would not have the option of retreat.[86]

2. Disjointed

Nachmanides rejects Rashi's interpretation of the passage. He raises an obvious objection: According to Rashi's interpretation, the passage is disjointed. Hashem's decision was based upon two related factors – the ease of retreat along the more direct route and the possibility of panic.

If this is the intention of the passage, then it should group these two factors together and present both as Hashem's considerations. The passage should read: G-d did not lead them [by] way of the land of the Philistines because G-d said, "It was near. Lest the people reconsider when they see war and return to Egypt." Instead, the passage tells us that the route through the territory of the Pelishtim was more direct, and then the passage introduces Hashem's reasoning with the phrase "because G-d said."

3. Time to prepare

---

[86] Rabbaynu Shlomo ben Yitzchak (Rashi), *Commentary on Sefer Shemot* 13:17.

Nachmanides offers an alternative translation for the passage: According to Nachmanides, the proper translation is: G-d did not lead them [by] way of the land of the Philistines, although it was near, because G-d said, "Lest the people reconsider when they see war and return to Egypt." The passage provides a single reason for forsaking the direct route: The people might panic when confronted by war and attempt to return to Egypt.

According to Nachmanides' interpretation, the more direct route was not abandoned because it would facilitate retreat. The route was forsaken because it would more quickly bring the nation into conflict with the inhabitants of the Land of Canaan – the land Bnai Yisrael must conquer. Hashem wished to delay this inevitable battle. Bnai Yisrael were not prepared to face the terror of an armed conflict. Therefore, a circuitous route that would delay this inevitable conflict was preferable.

Nachmanides recognizes that his interpretation of the passage presents a problem: Bnai Yisrael did enter into battle soon after leaving Egypt. The nation was attacked by Amalek. According to Nachmanides' interpretation of the passage, it seems that Hashem's plan was not completely successful! Although the route selected by Hashem delayed the inevitable battle with the inhabitants of Canaan, the Land of Israel, Bnai Yisrael was not shielded from an immediate confrontation with Amalek.

4. Defensive, not offensive

Nachmanides offers an interesting response to this problem: He explains that Hashem was not concerned with the response of Bnai Yisrael to this confrontation with Amalek. Nachmanides notes a fundamental difference between Amalek and the nations of Canaan: The nations of Canaan fought Bnai Yisrael in order to protect themselves from conquest and to retain possession of their land. They responded to a threat posed by Bnai Yisrael. Their war was defensive. Amalek was not motivated by these considerations -- it waged a war of aggression. Although Bnai Yisrael did not pose a threat to its security, Amalek attacked Bnai Yisrael out of hatred.

Based on this distinction, Nachmanides resolves the difficulty in his position. Hashem knew that Bnai Yisrael would fight Amalek. But, in this battle, retreat would not be a reasonable option. Bnai Yisrael would recognize the character of Amalek's attack. They would understand that Amalek was waging a war of aggression. Retreat would not save Bnai Yisrael. Amalek would continue to pursue the nation even as it retreated.

In contrast, Bnai Yisrael might be tempted to consider retreat when confronted with the battle over the Land of Israel. In this instance, retreat would be an option. The nations of Canaan would be fighting a defensive battle. They would be unlikely to pursue Bnai Yisrael once they felt they were no longer threatened.[87]

Of course, Rashi disagrees with this distinction. He explains that the circuitous route selected by Hashem was designed to discourage retreat when attacked by Amalek. According to Rashi, Hashem was concerned that Bnai Yisrael might panic when attacked by Amalek. In their panic, they might make the foolish decision to attempt a retreat. The circuitous route discouraged this choice.[88]

---

[87] Rabbaynu Moshe ben Nachman (Ramban), *Commentary on Sefer Shemot* 13:17.
[88] Rabbaynu Shlomo ben Yitzchak (Rashi), *Commentary on Sefer Shemot* 13:17.

5. Allusion

How might Rashi respond to Nachmanides' objection to his interpretation of the passage? According to Rashi's interpretation, the wording of the passage is somewhat disjointed. One of the most interesting responses to this objection is offered by Gur Aryeh. He suggests that Rashi was aware of the objection posed by Nachmanides and provided a response. Gur Aryeh notes that Rashi adds to his interpretation of the passage an enigmatic statement. Rashi comments that there are numerous interpretations of the phrase "for it was near" in the midrash.[89] Rashi does not quote any of the interpretations. Why does Rashi alert us to the existence of these interpretations?

Gur Aryeh suggests that Rashi's reference to the midrash is a response to Nachmanides' objection. Rashi is acknowledging that the passage's wording is not completely consistent with his interpretation. However, Rashi is explaining that the wording is designed to accommodate an allusion to the various insights provided by the midrash.

Gur Aryeh offers an illustration that clarifies his comments. Avraham made a covenant of peace with the Pelishtim. This covenant was to extend a number of generations. According to the midrash, the phrase "for it was near" refers to this covenant. Bnai Yisrael could not enter into battle with the Pelishtim because of Avraham's covenant. It was "too near" – too recent. The period of the covenant had not yet passed.[90,91] The passage's odd construction provides an allusion to this and similar interpretations.

The passage describes Hashem attributing his decision to two factors: One is clearly related to the insecurities of Bnai Yisrael – they may retreat when confronted by battle. According to Rashi, the other factor, "for it was near," is an amplification of this concern. A direct route would facilitate retreat.

Rashi maintains that this is the simple meaning of the passage. However, the disjointed phrasing in the passage alludes to an additional interpretation. The wording implies that an additional factor – separate and independent of Bnai Yisrael's insecurities – influenced the selection of this route. In short, the passage is constructed so as to communicate an overt message and to allude to the additional messages suggested by the midrash.

6. Back or forth

It is important to note that there are two fundamental differences between Rashi and Nachmanides' interpretations. First, according to Rashi, Hashem was concerned with Bnai Yisrael's response to an attack by Amalek. He was concerned that Bnai Yisrael would panic and attempt a foolish retreat. This would be a foolish response. Amalek would not break off its attack. Even as Bnai Yisrael fled, Amalek would press the attack. Hashem selected a circuitous route in order to discourage this panicked reaction.

According to Nachmanides, Hashem's decision was not directed towards addressing the challenge posed by Amalek. It was designed to prepare the nation for its inevitable confrontation with the nations of Canaan. In this confrontation, retreat would be a practical option. Bnai Yisrael could avoid war through retreat. Hashem's plan was designed to create an interlude

---

[89] Rabbaynu Shlomo ben Yitzchak (Rashi), *Commentary on Sefer Shemot* 13:17.

[90] Rav Yehuda Loew of Prague (Maharal), *Gur Aryeh Commentary on Sefer Shemot* 13:17.

[91] Mechilta, Parshat BeShalach, Chapter 1.

between the escape from Egypt and the conquest of the land. During the interlude, the nation would mature and develop the confidence to face battle. Rashi and Nachmanides do not necessarily differ on Bnai Yisrael's likely response to Amalek's attack. But, they do differ on whether Hashem's plan was designed to address this issue.

Second, according to Rashi, Hashem's decision was an extension of the redemption from Egypt. It was designed to assure that the redemption would not falter. Hashem wished to prevent a negation of the redemption. He had redeemed Bnai Yisrael from Egypt. They were not to return.

However, according to Nachmanides, Hashem's decision was designed to prepare the nation for the conquest of the Land of Israel. In other words, the travels in the wilderness provided an interlude between the redemption from Egypt and the conquest of the Land of Israel. This interlude had a purpose. It was designed to prepare the nation for the conquest of the land. Also, it was essential that during this interlude the redemption remain intact. It was essential that the redemption not be negated by the return to Egypt.

Rashi and Nachmanides differ on which aspect of this interlude dictated the selection of a circuitous route. According to Rashi, the selection of this route was designed to assure the preservation of the redemption. According to Nachmanides, the route was selected in order to facilitate the conquest of the Land of Israel.

And it was when Paroh had sent forth the people that G-d did not lead them by the way of the Land of the Philistines, because it was near; for G-d said: Lest the people reassess when they see war, and they return to Egypt. And G-d led the people about, by the way of the wilderness, by the Reed Sea. And Bnai Yisrael went up armed out of the Land of Egypt. (Shemot 13:17-18)

Time for a Road Trip

1. Hashem led Bnai Yisrael on a detour

The passages above describe the initial travel plan of Bnai Yisrael in its exodus from the Land of Egypt. The Torah explains that the most direct route to the promised Land of Cana'an was the northern route. This route would have brought the Jewish people to the western border of the land in less than ten days.[92] However, Hashem did not lead them along this route. Instead, He led the Jewish people along a southerly route. This route would bring the people to the Reed Sea that separated Egypt from most of the Sinai Peninsula and its harsh desert. After crossing the Reed Sea, Bnai Yisrael would be able to approach the Land of Israel from the south or even enter the land from the east.

Why did Hashem lead the people along this detour? The passages seem to say that the Pelishtim blocked the western approach to the Land of Israel. They would oppose Bnai Yisrael's passage. Within a few days from escaping the Land of Egypt, the Jewish people would be confronted by a very capable and intimidating adversary. Rather than confront the Pelishtim, Bnai Yisrael would panic and seek to return to Egypt. Therefore, Hashem led the nation along a more southerly course. Immediate confrontation with an imposing enemy was avoided.

---

[92] Rabbaynu Avraham ibn Ezra, *Extended Commentary on Sefer Shemot*, 13:17.

And Hashem spoke unto Moshe, saying: Speak to Bnai Yisrael, that they should turn back and encamp before Pi-Hachirot, between Migdol and the sea, before Baal-Tz'fon, over against it shall you encamp by the sea. And Paroh will say of Bnai Yisrael, "They are entangled in the land, the wilderness has shut them in." And I will harden Paroh's heart, and he shall follow after them. And I will glorify Myself through Paroh, and through all his host. And the Egyptians shall know that I am Hashem. And they did so. (Shemot 14:1-4)

2. The objective of the miracle of the Reed Sea

There are a number of difficulties with the Torah's explanation of this detour. This first difficulty is found in an interesting comment of Maimonides. Maimonides discusses the various wonders Moshe performed. He explains that each of these was done in order to address a need of the moment. He then details these wonders and their purposes. Among these is the splitting of the Reed Sea. He explains that this wonder was performed by Moshe in order to destroy the Egyptians.

Avodat HaMelech notes that this is an odd characterization of this wonder's purpose. We would expect Maimonides to describe its purpose as the salvation of the Jewish people from their pursuers. In other words, why does Maimonides focus upon the death and destruction of the Egyptians and not upon the rescue and salvation of Bnai Yisrael?

Avodat HaMelech responds that a careful reading of the relevant passages confirms Maimonides's characterization of the splitting of the Reed Sea. In the above passages, Hashem tells Moshe that he should lead the nation back toward Egypt and encamp the people opposite Ba'al Tz'fon. Paroh will believe that the people are lost and wandering. This will induce him to reconsider his decision to free Bnai Yisrael. He will quickly assemble a force to recapture his escaped slaves. In other words, Hashem describes to Moshe a plan to entrap Paroh.

Of course, this elaborate scheme leads to Paroh chasing Bnai Yisrsael into the Reed Sea. Paroh and his mighty army are crushed by the collapsing waters of the Reed sea and destroyed. Avodat HaMelech explains that these passages clearly state that the purpose of the splitting of the Reed Sea was not to save the Jewish people. The purpose was to destroy Paroh and his legions.[93]

This analysis presents the first problem with the opening passages to the *parasha*. Those passages seem to explain that Bnai Yisrael was led along the more southerly route in order to avoid confrontation with the Pelishtim. However, the above analysis demonstrates that there was another more immediate reason for selecting the more southerly route. This route would lead to the shore of the Reed Sea and to the destruction of the Egyptians.

And Moshe said to G-d: Who am I, that I should go to Paroh, and that I should bring forth Bnai Yisrael out of Egypt? And He said: Certainly I will be with you. And this shall be the sign for you that I have sent you: when you have brought forth the people out of Egypt, you shall serve G-d upon this mountain. (Shemot 3:11-12)

3. Before entering Israel the nation must receive the Torah

The second problem with these opening passages is more obvious. The Torah describes Moshe's first prophecy. He experienced a vision while shepherding flocks. He took the flocks to

---

[93] Rav Menachem Krakavski, *Avodat HaMelech, Commentary of Mishne Torah*, Hilchot Yesodai HaTorah 8:1.

the Sinai wilderness and at Mount Sinai he experienced a vision. In that prophecy, Hashem told Moshe that he will lead Bnai Yisrael out of Egypt. He will bring them to this mountain and there they will experience the Revelation.

In order for this prophecy to be fulfilled, Moshe would need to lead the nation out of Egypt and deep into the Sinai wilderness. A southerly route was required to arrive at the mountain of the Revelation. In other words, the most fundamental reason for not taking the northern route is that the nation's first destination was not the Land of Israel. Their first destination was a lonely mountain deep in the Sinai wilderness.

4. The less traveled road

Rabbaynu Ovadia Sforno answers these questions through reinterpreting the opening passages of the *parasha*. He understands these opening passages as communicating an enormous amount of information in a very abridged form.

According to Sforno, the most-traveled and developed route from Egypt to the Land of Cana'an was the "Land of the Pelishtim Road". Hashem's plan was to lead the nation to Sinai and to Revelation. Along the way, he would bring Bnai Yisrael to the Reed Sea. He would induce Paroh and his army to chase after the Jewish nation and He would destroy these enemies. Only after Revelation would the nation turn north and proceed to the Land of Can'an. In other words, the Pelishtim Road could not bring the people to their initial destinations – the Sinai wilderness and to the site of Revelation. However, it would have been efficient to use this well maintained route for the initial stages of the journey and then to divert from the road and turn south. Instead, Hashem immediately led the nation into the wilderness.

The initial passages provide the reason for avoiding the well-traveled route. This is because it was the most efficient route between Egypt and the Land of Cana'an. The Torah continues to explain why this made the route unacceptable. Hashem will induce the Paroh to launch a campaign to recapture his escaped slaves. If Bnai Yisrael travels along the Pelishtim Road, they will quickly learn of Paroh's plans from the many travelers leaving Egypt. Bnai Yisrael will be overcome with fear and surrender their freedom.[94]

In other words, according to Sforno, the passage is not suggesting that Hashem's plan was to immediately take Bnai Yisrael to the Land of Cana'an. The plan was for the nation to proceed to the Reed Sea. There, their enemies will be destroyed. From the sea, they will travel into the Sinai wilderness and to Revelation. The passage is explaining why Hashem did not lead the nation along the most developed route for even the shortest portion of their journey. It is communicating the fragile state of the nation. Because of the nation's timidity, Hashem did not allow them to become aware of Paroh's pursuit until the very last moment.

Speak to Bnai Yisrael, and say to them: When you pass over the Jordan into the Land of Cana'an, then you shall drive out all the inhabitants of the land from before you, and destroy all their figured stones, and destroy all their molten images, and demolish all their high places.
(BeMidbar 33:51-52)

5. Bnai Yisrael's delayed entry

Rav Naftali Tzvi Berlin – Netziv – provides a simpler but more remarkable explanation of the *parasha's* opening passages. He explains that Hashem did not lead the people along the

---

[94] Rabbaynu Ovadia Sforno, *Commentary on Sefer Shemot*, 13:17.

shorter northern route because this route would quickly bring the people to the Land of Cana'an. The people were not spiritually prepared for the challenge of entering a land occupied by idolaters. Rather than conquering these nations, these liberated slaves would try to settle among the land's population. Quickly, they would assimilate and lose their identity. Before they could face the inhabitants of the Land of Cana'an, Bnai Yisael needed to develop and mature into a confident and thoughtful people. This required Revelation and the other experiences they encountered – including the destruction of their former masters.

However, Hashem did not reveal to Bnai Yisrael His full motives for not leading them directly into the land He had promised to them. He did not reveal to them the extent of their deficits and the extensive process of education and maturation that they must undertake. Instead, He only told the people that they were not prepared to face war.[95]

6. The search for freedom during life

Both of these approaches to explaining the *parasha's* opening passages share a common theme. Freedom is not achieved through removal or restraint. It is only achieved when the liberated individual develops the capacity to boldly and confidently make choices. Sforno explains that Bnai Yisrael were so fragile when they left Egypt, that they would have quickly abandoned their newly won freedom rather than face their masters. Netziv explains that without an extensive process of education, Bnai Yisrael would have squandered its freedom and quickly assimilated.

In many ways, our lives are an ongoing search for freedom. As teenagers, we seek freedom from our parents and the liberation of living away from home. As we enter the professional world, we strive to achieve financial freedom for ourselves and our families. As we become older, we contemplate retirement and freedom from the schedules and demands of our professional lives. We imagine, at each stage, the anticipated freedom that will change our lives and secure our happiness.

The story of our ancestors tells us that freedom is not easily achieved. Removing the restraints imposed by parents, financial responsibilities, or professional obligation does not result in personal freedom. Personal freedom is achieved when we understand ourselves, and when we seize the courage and confidence to pursue goals and objectives that are truly meaningful and transformative.

"And Hashem hardened the heart of Paroh the king of Egypt and he pursued Bnai Yisrael. And Bnai Yisrael left in triumph." (Shemot 14:8)

Pharoh's Choice

1. Pharoah possessed free will

The Egyptians are struck with the plague of the firstborn. Paroh agrees to allow the Jewish people to leave Egypt. Bnai Yisrael leaves Egypt and travels towards the wilderness. Hashem hardens Paroh's heart. He decides to pursue the Jewish people. This ultimately leads to the miracle of the splitting of the Reed Sea. The sea miraculously separates before Bnai Yisrael. The nation crosses the sea. The Egyptians follow and the sea closes upon them. Paroh and his

---

[95] Rav Naftali Tzvi Yehudah Berlin (Netziv), *Commentary Hamek Davar on Sefer Shemot* 13:17.

army are destroyed. Bnai Yisrael are redeemed. It is clear from our pasuk that the Almighty led Paroh and his nation to their destruction at the Reed Sea.

Paroh's heart was hardened by Hashem. This caused him to chase Bnai Yisrael into the sea. Rashi comments that Hashem carefully planned the route of Bnai Yisrael's escape.[96] His objective was to encourage Paroh's pursuit of Bnai Yisrael. After escaping from Egypt, Hashem told Moshe to lead the nation back in the direction of Egypt. He then commanded Moshe to instruct the people to camp near Baal Tzafon, an Egyptian deity. Rashi explains that these instructions were explicitly designed to mislead Paroh and his people. The backtracking implied that the nation was lost. The proximity of this confused wandering to Baal Tzafon implied that this deity was somehow acting against Bnai Yisrael. The deity was foiling the nation's attempt to escape.

Rashi's interpretation raises an immediate question. According to Rashi, the Almighty was enticing Paroh to pursue Bnai Yisrael. Why was this complicated plan needed? Hashem had hardened Paroh's heart. Paroh was forced to chase after the nation! Why was any inducement needed? It seems clear from Rashi's interpretation of the pesukim that Hashem hardened Paroh's heart through these inducements. Hashem did not just turn-off Paroh's ability to chose his course of action. Instead, Hashem maneuvered Paroh into a situation in which he would not be able to resist the urge to pursue Bnai Yisrael. The Almighty knows the inner workings of every person's heart. He knew that given the proper inducements, Paroh simply would not be able to resist the urge to chase after Bnai Yisrael.

2. We all can choose

This interpretation resolves an apparent contradiction in the writings of Maimonides. Maimonides explains in the fifth chapter of the Laws of Repentance that every person has the ability to choose the path of the good or the path of evil.[97] Hashem does not decree that any person should be evil or righteous. It seems that this is an unqualified statement. Every person has this ability to choose. Oddly, in the very next chapter, Maimonides explains that sometimes the Almighty withholds from an evil person the opportunity to repent from sin.[98] This is a punishment. This person performed willful evil. Hashem prevents the person from repenting. This assures that this evil individual will suffer for his or her wickedness. These comments seem to contradict Maimonides earlier assertion that every person has the freewill to choose between good and evil! How can these two statements be reconciled? Rashi's approach to explaining Paroh's experience provides a resolution.

Humans are created with the ability to choose between right and wrong. However, this does not mean that we can exercise this ability in every area of our lives. We are all subject to strong, overpowering feelings. Confronted with these powerful emotions, we may be helpless to choose freely between options. On balance, we have enough freedom to constantly choose to improve ourselves. We are responsible to make the proper choices in those areas in which we are empowered. If we make the proper choices, we become better individuals. We become more empowered. With time, we can even overcome desires that once were irresistible. In short, we have freewill. But this does not mean that we have volition in every area of our lives. It is

---

[96] Rabbaynu Shlomo ben Yitzchak (Rashi), Commentary on Sefer Shemot, 14:2.

[97] Rabbaynu Moshe ben Maimon (Rambam) Mishne Torah, Hilchot Teshuvah 5:1-2.

[98] Rabbaynu Moshe ben Maimon (Rambam) Mishne Torah, Hilchot Teshuvah 6:3.

completely consistent for Maimonides to state that every person has freewill. Yet, in a specific situation one may be bereft of the ability to choose. This is clearly illustrated by the experiences of Paroh. Hashem did not disable any faculty in Paroh. He did not suddenly hit a switch and turn-off Paroh's volition. Instead, he placed Paroh under the control of an irresistible urge. Paroh found himself outside of the area in which he could make choices. He had no option. He had to chase Bnai Yisrael.

And Paroh approached. Bnai Yisrael lifted its eyes and the Egyptians were traveling after them. They were very fearful and Bnai Yisrael cried out to Hashem. Bnai Yisrael said to Moshe: Are there not enough graves in Egypt – that you took us to die in the wilderness? What have you done to us in bringing us out of Egypt? (Shemot 14:10-11)

Perceptions and Reality

1. Bnai Yisrael's panic at the Reed Sea

Bnai Yisrael leaves Egypt. However, Hashem again strengthens Paroh's heart. Paroh amasses an army and pursues Bnai Yisrael into the wilderness. Bnai Yisrael see that Paroh and his army are approaching. They call out to Hashem. Then, they begin to sharply criticize Moshe. They confront and challenge him. They ask, "Why did you lead us out of Egypt if the sole outcome of our liberation will be our death in the wilderness?"

The commentaries note that the wording used by the nation in its criticism of Moshe is odd. They described their expected fate as "death in the wilderness". This seems to be a rather vague description of the fate that they feared. Paroh and his army were closing in pursuit. They should have described their expected fate as "death at the hands of Paroh and his army"!

Rabbaynu Ovadia Sforno offers an explanation for the people's phrasing of their fear. He suggests that the people were uncertain of Paroh's plan. They did not know whether he planned to attack or to merely block their path. They reasoned that Paroh did not need to enter into a battle with them in order to vanquish them. He could use his army to block their path and isolate them in the wilderness. Without a path of escape from the wilderness, Bnai Yisrael would not be able to secure water and provision and would die.[99]

Rashbam offers a simpler explanation for Bnai Yisrael's phrasing. He explains that Bnai Yisrael were protesting to Moshe that they were doomed regardless of the outcome of their confrontation with Paroh. Even if somehow they survived this impending conflict, they were destined to die in the wilderness from thirst and starvation.[100] According to Rashbam, the impending attack completely undermined any confidence that the people had achieved and it initiated an overwhelming panic. In their panic, the people foresaw inevitable doom. If Paroh and his army do not destroy them, then they will be annihilated by the harsh wilderness.

And Yisrael saw the great hand of Hashem at work in Egypt. And the nation feared Hashem. They believed in Hashem and Moshe His servant. (Shemot 14:31)

2. Bnai Yisrael regains it confidence

---

[99] Sforno 14:11.
[100] Rashbam 14.11.

Hashem rescues Bnai Yisrael. He separates the waters of the Reed Sea before them. They descend into the dry seabed, cross the sea, and ascend onto its shore. The Egyptians follow Bnai Yisrael into the sea. The waters come crashing down upon them and they are destroyed. Bnai Yisrael see their adversary's destruction. They are awed by the might of Hashem and they believe in Hashem and Moshe His servant.

Moshe then leads the nation in the Shirat HaYam – the Song of the Sea. In this song of praise, the nation acknowledges Hashem and gives thanks to Him for their salvation. They extol His praises. They express their confidence in the fulfillment of His promise that they will return to Cana'an and take possession of it.

Rashbam comments that with the destruction of the Egyptians, Bnai Yisrael not only recognized that they had been rescued from their adversary. Their confidence was also restored. Now, they were certain that they would survive their sojourn in the wilderness and enter the Land of Cana'an and take possession of it.[101] In other words, the intense panic that had overwhelmed the people subsided. In its place emerged a restored sense of confidence.

In summary, Rashbam's position is that within a few hours time the people experienced a series of intense and ever-changing feelings. The impending attack of Paroh and his army unleashed a sense of complete panic. The people lost all confidence and were certain of their impending death – either at the hands of their adversaries or through exposure to the harsh environment of the wilderness. With the destruction of the Egyptians, the nation embraced a renewed sense of confidence. They had been saved from their enemies. They would safely transverse the wilderness. They would conquer the mighty kings of Cana'an and take possession of the Promised Land.

This extreme swing in attitude and perception is not easily understood. In fact, it continues to characterize Bnai Yisrael's conduct throughout the balance of the parasha. At times, the nation again questions whether it can survive the wilderness experience. However, with the passing and resolution of each challenge, their confidence is restored – but only until the next threat or challenge arises.

Hashem is the strength and the song of Bnai Yisrael. He was my salvation. This is my G-d and I beautify Him. He is the G-d of my forefathers and I will exalt Him. (Shemot 15:2)

3. The encounter with Hashem at the Reed Sea

The above passage is from the Song of the Sea. It is translated according to Rashbam's understanding of its message. In his comments on the passage, Rashi quotes a famous teaching of the Sages. The people said, "This is my G-d!" Rashi comments that Hashem revealed Himself in His glory at the Reed Sea. The people pointed to Him with their finger and said, "This is our G-d." Rashi continues and explains that the most humble and simple person at the Reed Sea encountered Hashem at a level not achieved even by some of the greatest prophets.[102]

Rashi's comments are difficult on a number of levels. Hashem does not have a material form. He cannot be seen nor can one point at Him. Furthermore, the assertion that the most humble person at the Sea achieved some level of encounter with Hashem that exceeded the experiences of the greatest prophets seems remarkable. What is the basis for this contention?

---

[101] Rashbam 14:31.
[102] Rashi 15:2

Rashbam comments that the people did not actually see Hashem.[103] Apparently, Rashbam means that Hashem revealed Himself through His actions. He does not have a material form that can actually be observed. These comments reveal the meaning of the passage and Rashi's insight. It is human nature to accept the perception of the senses as being real. We have a saying: Seeing is believing. We are most convinced of that which we can see. Other information – facts or knowledge that is not observable – has less of an impact upon us.

Rashi's understanding of the passage is that the revelation of Hashem at the Reed Sea was so powerful that those present felt that they had seen Hashem. That is not to say that they believed they had observed a form or figure that they identified as Hashem. But the experience was equal in impact to a sensual encounter. The comparison of this encounter to the prophetic experience of the greatest prophets is intended to convey this understanding of the passage. This encounter with Hashem was similar in its intensity to the prophet's encounter with Hashem in the prophetic experience.

In this manner the righteous and the prophets appealed in their prayers to Hashem to help them in their pursuit of the truth. As David said, "Teach me Your way." He meant to say, "My sins should not prevent me from finding the path of truth. I wish to know Your way and (understand) the unity of Your name"…. (Maimonides, Mishne Torah, Laws of Repentance 6:4)

4. The forces that shape human perception

Based upon Rashi's comments, Rashbam's understanding of Bnai Yisrael's shifting attitudes and beliefs can be understood. However, it will be helpful to first consider an interesting comment by Maimonides. In the above quotation, Maimonides explains that the righteous and Hashem's prophets appealed to Hashem for His assistance in their search for truth. They believed that their shortcomings and sins could easily pervert their efforts and conceal the truth from them.

This is an amazing statement. However, it reflects a remarkable humility. Essentially, Maimonides asserts that the success or failure of our quest for truth is not merely a consequence of our intelligence and commitment to the pursuit. We can easily be mislead or led down the wrong path by our own shortcomings and sins. These cloud our mind, obscure the truth, and pervert our intellectual vision. Even the most wise and righteous realized that their inevitable shortcomings created an imposing barrier between them and the truth they sought. They prayed to Hashem for His help in overcoming this barrier.

The fundamental premise of Maimonides' comments is that our intellectual perceptions, our convictions, and our beliefs are as much a consequence of our moral and emotional state as our intellectual prowess. Our sins and wrongdoings influence and contribute to who we are. They help shape our personality and our moral state. These, in turn, strongly influence our intellectual perceptions and our conclusions regarding the truth.

Rashbam's comments illustrate Maimonides' contention. Bnai Yisrael were liberated from Egypt. They left with confidence and exultation. They did not flee bondage. They marched out of Egypt as free people. However, their confidence was a consequence of their understanding of their recent experiences and the emotionally liberating impact of observing their masters' humiliation. These factors combined to engender their sense of buoyancy and confidence. They

---

[103] Rashbam, Chorev edition, 15:2.

were not threatened by the prospect of crossing the wilderness and they were confident in their ability to conquer the Land of Cana'an.

Their mood changed when they saw their former masters in pursuit. Their confidence was shattered and their exaltation was replaced by fear and apprehension. Without their former confidence, their perceptions regarding their prospects changed radically. Now, they wondered how they had ever agreed to enter the wilderness. Why had they believed that they were freed of their oppressors or that they could cross the barren and hostile wilderness? Their understanding of reality changed – reshaped by fear and trepidation.

Then, they observed their adversary's destruction. Hashem was revealed to them! They experienced an intense encounter with Hashem. At that moment, doubt and hesitation became impossible. The people joined Moshe in the Song of the Sea. They declared their confidence in their conquest of the Promised Land. Doubt had been completely replaced by assurance in achievement of their destiny.

Of course, as the parasha continues, the impact of the encounter at the Reed Sea fades. With the weakening of its impact, old doubts reassert themselves. The balance of the parasha describes these recurring doubts and the people's internal battle to recapture the confidence they experienced as they marched forth from Egypt and encountered Hashem's revelation at the Reed Sea.

"And Moshe said to the nation: Do not be afraid. Stand firm and see the salvation of Hashem that He will do for you today. For although you will see the Egyptians today, you will not ever again see them." (Shemot 14:13)

The Generation Liberated from Egypt

Bnai Yisrael arrive at the Reed Sea pursued by the Egyptians. They fear that they will be destroyed. Moshe urges the nation to have courage. Hashem will save His people.

Bnai Yisrael had left Egypt armed. The nation included six-hundred thousand adult males. The Egyptians had been ravaged by ten debilitating plagues. Why didn't Bnai Yisrael confront their pursuers and fight?

Rabbaynu Avraham ibn Ezra explains that Bnai Yisrael could have fielded a formidable army against the Egyptians. However, two-hundred and ten years of slavery had undermined the confidence of the people. Newly gained freedom could not immediately erase the effects of their prolonged subjugation. The liberated slaves could not envision themselves opposing and overcoming their former masters.

Ibn Ezra explains that this same shortcoming prevented the generation that was liberated from slavery from entering the Land of Israel. It lacked the confidence to battle the fierce nations inhabiting Canaan. A new generation reared in the desert would be better prepared for this challenge. This new generation would not know slavery. It would be nurtured in an environment of freedom. Self-doubt would be replaced with self-assurance.[104]

Ibn Ezra does not intend to imply that the forty years of wandering in the desert were predetermined from the moment of the exodus. As the Chumash relates, spies were sent to

---

[104] Rabbaynu Avraham ibn Ezra, *Commentary on Sefer Shemot*, 14:13.

survey the land and plan its conquest. Instead, the spies emphasized the unassailable obstacles that awaited them. The nation accepted this report and the spies' conclusion that the conquest was unachievable. The people lost hope in regaining the homeland of the forefathers and questioned Moshe's leadership. It was in response to this failing of the people that Hashem decreed forty years of wandering in the desert.

Ibn Ezra is explaining the cause of this debacle. The crisis created by the report of the spies was a result of the nation's low level of self-confidence. The challenge posed by the conquest was more imagined than real. Hashem had assured the nation that He would defeat the nations of Canaan as He had destroyed mighty Egypt. But this generation of liberated spies that could not confront its former masters also lacked the self-assurance to wage a campaign against the inhabitants of Canaan. In short, heeding the counsel of the spies condemned Bnai Yisrael to wandering. But the self-doubt that underplayed this failing was exhibited first at the Reed Sea.

"And Moshe said to the nation: Do not be afraid. Stand firm and see the salvation of Hashem that He will do for you today. For although you will see the Egyptians today, you will not ever again see them." (Shemot 14:13)

"And the Egyptians will know that I am Hashem when I triumph over Paroh, his chariots and his calvary." (Shemot 14:18)

Convincing the Egyptians

Both of the above passages deal with the miracle of the parting of the Reed Sea. In the first pasuk, Moshe tells Bnai Yisrael that miracle Hashem will presently perform will complete the salvation of Bnai Yisrael and the destruction of the Egyptians.

Hashem tells Moshe to proceed into the sea. The water will be parted and the nation will transverse the uncovered dry seabed. Hashem tells Moshe that He has hardened Paroh's heart. He will cause Paroh to pursue Bnai Yisrael into the sea. Hashem will destroy the Egyptian army.

In the second pasuk, Hashem explains to Moshe that through the destruction of Paroh and his legions, the remnant of the Egyptian people will come to recognize the omnipotence of Hashem.

The two passages seem to communicate different messages regarding the parting of the sea and its collapsing upon the Egyptians. The first pasuk indicates that the objective of this miracle was the salvation of Bnai Yisrael. The destruction of the Egyptians was required to complete this salvation. The destruction of Paroh and his army will assure that the Egyptians will no longer pursue Bnai Yisrael. The second pasuk suggests that the destruction of Paroh and his army served another purpose. Hashem was concerned with the impressions of the Egyptians. He told Moshe that the destruction of Paroh and his army was designed to convince the surviving Egyptians of the greatness of Hashem.

Rabbaynu Ovadia Sforno confirms this interpretation of the second pasuk. He explains that the destruction of Paroh and his army would provide the remaining Egyptians with compelling evidence of Hashem's greatness. Hopefully, this demonstration will inspire them to repent. Sforno concludes by observing that Hashem does not seek the death of the wicked; rather, He seeks their repentance.[105]

Gershonides disagrees. He argues that the second pasuk does not intend to suggest that Hashem was concerned with the Egyptians' appreciation of His omnipotence. They had already been provided with the opportunity to discover Hashem. Why did Hashem wish to impress upon the Egyptians His omnipotence? Gershonides explains that this was not for the purpose of perfecting the Egyptians. Instead, Hashem wanted to deter the Egyptians from any other attempts to recapture Bnai Yisrael. Hashem presented the Egyptians with undeniable proof of His omnipotence. This convinced the survivors that they could not hope to overcome Hashem and recapture His nation. With this realization, they were discouraged from any further efforts to recapture Bnai Yisrael.[106]

And Hashem said to Moshe: Why do you cry-out to me? Speak to Bnai Yisrael and they should travel. (Shemot 14:15)

Too Much Prayer

1. Crisis at the Reed Sea

In the above passage, Hashem tells Moshe to stop praying to Him. It is odd that Hashem directs His prophet to not petition Him on behalf of His nation. To understand Hashem's objection, we must understand the context of the passage.

The Jewish people have left Egypt. They are traveling to Sinai and from there they will continue to the Land of Israel. Hashem tells Moshe that He will induce Paroh to reconsider his decision to release Bnai Yisrael. Paroh will amass an army and pursue Bnai Yisrael. Hashem will demonstrate His glory through the final destruction of Paroh and his mighty legions.

Bnai Yisrael arrive at the shore of the Reed Sea. They see Paroh and his army in pursuit. Their path forward is blocked by the sea. They turn to Hashem, petitioning Him for their rescue. Also, they challenge Moshe, "Why bring us into the wilderness to be slaughtered by the sword?"

Moshe responds to the people. He tells them that they should not be afraid. Hashem will wage war on their behalf. He will completely destroy the Egyptians. Moshe joins the people in prayer to Hashem.

This is the context of the passage. Hashem tells Moshe to not petition Him. He should simply lead the people forward. He then explains to Moshe that He will split the waters of sea. The Jewish people will pass between walls of water. Hashem will induce Paroh to lead his army into the parted waters and they will be destroyed.

2. Moshe should not pray

Why was Moshe told to stop praying? The nation faced a crisis. They were trapped between the sea and the Egyptians. Is it not appropriate to turn to Hashem when confronted with catastrophe? The commentators provide many responses. We will focus on two that are offered by Rashi.

"We learn [from the passage] that Moshe stood and prayed. The Holy One Blessed be He said to him, "This is not the time for protracted prayer. Israel is in distress!" Another opinion [states]

---

[105] Rabbaynu Ovadia Sforno, *Commentary on Sefer Shemot*, 14:18.

[106] Rabbaynu Levi ben Gershon (Ralbag / Gershonides), *Commentary on Sefer Shemot*, p 102.

"Why do you cry-out to Me? This matter depends upon Me, not upon you."" (Rashi, Shemot 14:15)

Both explanations present problems. Rashi's first explanation is that Hashem criticized Moshe for engaging in protracted prayer, while the people are in danger. Did not Moshe intercede on behalf of the nation for forty days and nights after the sin of the Golden Calf? As in this instance, they were in great danger. Moshe feared Hashem might destroy them for their sin. Why was the intercession at Sinai appropriate but lengthy prayer at the Reed Sea not fitting?

Rashi's second explanation is also troubling. Hashem told Moshe there is nothing for him to do. It is Hashem's place to take action. Moshe certainly realized that Bnai Yisrael required Hashem's intercession to be saved. He prayed for that intercession. Why did Hashem criticize him for such prayers?

3. The stakes at the Reed Sea

It is apparent that Moshe was not entirely confident that Bnai Yisrael would be rescued. He believed that their fate had not been completely determined. Hashem might allow them to be destroyed or harmed by the Egyptians. Hashem had assured him that He would destroy Paroh and his army. But Moshe had doubts. Since Hashem gave His assurance, the people had been overtaken by panic. They had accused him of bringing them into the wilderness to be destroyed. Moshe asked, "Were his people still worthy of the miracles Hashem had foretold?" Moshe prayed to Hashem to rescue His people and overlook their shortcomings.[107]

With this background, let us first consider Rashi's second answer. Hashem responded to Moshe that He will provide salvation. There is nothing for Moshe to do. He explained to Moshe that he was misinterpreting the situation. The people will be saved. Their rescue is not in doubt. Moshe does not need to pray on their behalf. Hashem's plan is materializing. Moshe must allow it to reveal itself. In other words, there is no real crisis. The plan is unfolding according to Hashem's design.

4. Types of prayer

Rashi's first answer is that Hashem criticized Moshe for engaging in protracted prayer while the nation is in distress. Why was this wrong? Should not Moshe pray for them until they are rescued? The hint or key to understanding Rashi's position is recognizing that Hashem did

---

[107] See comments of Sforno. Sforno attempts to resolve a difficult problem. Moshe seems to be in doubt of Bnai Yisrael's rescue. However, Moshe had assured Bnai Yisrael that Hashem would rescue them from Paroh and the Egyptians. The authenticity of a prophet is determined by the accuracy of his prophecies. If positive prophecies do not come true, then the claimant is deemed to be a false prophet (Rambam, Hilchot Yesodai HaTorah 10:1-2). How could Moshe be uncertain of Bnai Yisrael's rescue? He had shared with them his prophecy that Hashem would save them! Sforno responds that Moshe was confident they would be saved. However, he feared that they would not follow him into the parted waters of the sea. He turned to Hashem asking for His assistance in motivating the people to enter the sea. Hashem responded, "Why do you cry-out to me? You misunderstand the people. They will follow you." According to Rashi, it seems Moshe was not confident that the people would be saved. Rashi does not explain how he would resolve the difficulty addressed by Sforno.

not criticize Moshe for praying. He reproved him for engaging in lengthy prayer. Prayer was appropriate; extended prayer was not.

Rashi's position reflects an idea developed more fully by Rambam – Maimonides. Rambam explains that when the Jewish people are in distress they must turn to Hashem in prayer.

"This is part of the process of repentance. When an affliction occurs and they cry-out and sound the trumpets,[108] they all know that the misfortune came upon them because of their actions… This causes the affliction to be removed from them. But if they do not cry-out and sound the trumpets; rather, they say, "This is a natural event that has occurred to us. This affliction is happenstance", this is cruelty. It causes them to cleave to their wicked actions. It adds afflictions upon the affliction…" (Rambam, Mishne Torah, Hilchot Taaniyot 1:2-3)

Rambam explains that when confronted with a crisis, we respond with prayer. He explains that our prayers are part of the process of repentance. We are recognizing that our afflictions express Hashem's will and are a result of our faults and sins. This recognition hopefully leads to repentance.

Rav Yisroel Chait observed that it is interesting that Rambam does not say that the affliction is removed through repentance. He says we earn reprieve by recognition that our suffering is the consequence of our behaviors. Apparently, Rambam's position is that repentance is not required to cancel the punishment. Only the first step on the path of repentance is necessary. We must recognize that we have brought our suffering upon ourselves through our sins.[109]

Rambam is explaining that prayer is not only petitioning of Hashem. It is an acknowledgment of His role in our lives and our dependency upon Him. Typically, when suffering, we petition Hashem for His intervention. Rambam is asserting that the fundamental element of these prayers is not our fervent plea for rescue. It is our recognition that our suffering is a consequence of our sins. To summarize, prayer is not just petition. It is also an acknowledgment of Hashem's role in our lives.

5. The message of Moshe's prayer

According to Rashi, Hashem told Moshe, "You have prayed enough." He told Moshe that he does not need to plead for the rescue of the people. He needs only to ask Hashem – to demonstrate to the people that their approaching rescue is His response to their plight. Prayer is necessary. Without it the people may make the same error as the Egyptians. They may conclude that the winds parting the waters are an unusual but natural event. Moshe prayed before the people and then the water parted. The people recognized that they were being saved through Hashem's miracle.

6. Lessons from Rashi, #1

Bnai Yisrael believed they faced destruction. They were trapped between the sea and their enemies. Moshe was concerned. Hashem responded, "This is part of My plan. Yes, the

---

[108] These trumpets were sounded in the Tabernacle and in the Temple at times of affliction. They are an expression of prayer.
[109] Rav Yisroel Chait, author's personal notes.

Egyptians are directly behind you. But this will encourage them to follow you into the sea. They will be at your heels when the walls of the sea collapse upon them."

The lesson is familiar but important. Crisis does mean we are abandoned. We do not know Hashem's plan. Sometimes a crisis is the prelude to salvation. This does not mean that real tragedies do not occur. It means we should not lose hope when we experience a period of distress. Our distress may be the darkness before the dawning of a bright day.

7. Lessons from Rashi, #2

Rashi's second lesson is less obvious and more profound. Moshe was required to pray before the sea parted. His prayer was important because through it he demonstrated that Hashem parted the water. We are required to pray repeatedly. We may wonder why these persistent entreaties are required. Rashi's comments provide an important insight. In prayer, we petition Hashem. But this is not the only function of prayer. Rashi teaches us that prayer is also a statement. We acknowledge our dependence upon Hashem and that our blessings are bestowed by Him.

Our ancestors at the Reed Sea needed prayer to recognize that Hashem was parting the sea. We also need prayer to recognize that our blessings come from Hashem. We easily forget Hashem's role in our lives. We need to constantly remind ourselves of our dependence upon Hashem and that He grants us the blessings we enjoy. We need constant prayer.

"And Moshe extended his hand over the sea. And Hashem drove back the waters with a powerful east wind the entire night. And it made the seabed into dry land. And the waters were divided." (Shemot 14:27)

The Miracle of the Parting of the Reed Sea

1. Where the wind blows

Bnai Yisrael flee from Egypt. The people arrive at the shores of the Reed Sea. The sea stands before the nation. The Egyptians are directly behind them. Bnai Yisrael is trapped. Hashem performs one the greatest wonders recorded in the Torah. He parts the Reed Sea. Bnai Yisrael enter the sea. They travel across the sea over its dry seabed. The Egyptians enter the sea in pursuit of their escaped slaves. The sea closes upon the Egyptians and they are drowned.

The Torah provides some interesting details regarding this miracle. Generally, we imagine that Moshe extended his hand over the water and suddenly they separated and dry land was revealed. However, this is not the description of these events provided by the Torah.

According to our pasuk, the sea did not immediately split in response to Moshe's command. Moshe extended his hand over the water and a mighty wind arose. The wind blew the entire night. What was the function of this wind? Why did Hashem require this wind? Why did He not immediately part the waters?

2. Deception

Nachmanides explains that the wind was part of an elaborate deception. Hashem had brought the Egyptians to the Reed Sea. Here, they were to be destroyed. However, what was to induce the Egyptians to enter the sea? After all, if Hashem had parted the sea in order to save Bnai Yisrael, it was not likely He would allow the Egyptians to follow them! What would the point be of a miracle that failed to save Bnai Yisrael? Certainly, the Egyptians would realize that Hashem would not prolong His miracle for the benefit of his nation's adversaries!

Nachmanides suggests that the wind was part of a ruse. The Egyptians believed that the wind had split the sea. Bnai Yisrael were escaping into the sea as the result of remarkable good fortune. They just happened to reach the sea at the onset of a tremendous storm. The storm cleaved apart the waters. The Egyptians felt that they too could take advantage of this opportunity. The wind would continue to drive the waters apart. They could enter the sea and overtake Bnai Yisrael. The deception worked. The Egyptians were lured into the trap!

Of course, the Egyptians were mistaken in their interpretations of the phenomenon. They were not witnessing an unusual meteorological occurrence. They were seeing a miracle. They entered the sea and Hashem brought the waters crashing down upon them.[110]

3. The wind blew it

Rashbam adopts a completely opposite approach to explaining this wind. He contends that the wind actually parted the water. The Creator performed His miracle through the vehicle of natural forces. Rashbam adds some detail. He explains that the wind had two functions. First, it caused the water to back up. Once the water backed up, the seafloor was revealed. Second, it dried the seafloor and created a passable path across the seabed.[111] Ibn Ezra adds that the wind continued to blow as Bnai Yisrael crossed the sea. Only the power of the wind prevented the water from rushing in on Bnai Yisrael.[112]

In short, we are faced with two approaches for explaining this wind. Nachmanides maintains that the wind was not a factor in splitting the sea. The wind was merely part of a ruse designed to lure the Egyptians into the sea. Rashbam and others disagree. They insist that the miracle of the sea parting was brought about through this wind. Hashem used the wind to split the sea, dry the seabed, and hold the waters apart for Bnai Yisrael.

This raises an interesting question. We can understand the position of Nachmanides. Hashem is the Creator of the universe. He formed the seas and established the boundaries between the oceans and the continents. Obviously, He can alter these boundaries. If He wishes to create dry land in the midst of the sea, He can. He is omnipotent. He does not need any wind to assist Him. The position of Rashbam is more difficult to understand. It seems as if the Rashbam is limiting Hashem. He seems to deny his omnipotence. Why does Hashem need a strong wind to do His bidding?

The answer to this question is very important. It provides an insight into the Torah's understanding of the natural world. The answer also indicates the Torah's attitude toward scientific knowledge.

4. Nature

We all realize that we are required to observe the Torah. Observant Jews might dicker over the specifics of observance. However, we would agree that Hashem revealed the Torah with the intention that we observe its commandments. The reason for observance is obvious. The

---

[110] Rabbaynu Moshe ben Nachman (Ramban), *Commentary on Sefer Shemot* 14:21.

[111] Rabbaynu Shemuel ben Meir (Rashbam) *Commentary on Sefer Shemot* 14:21.

[112] Rabbaynu Avraham ibn Ezra, *Commentary on Sefer Shemot*, 14:21.

commandments are an expression of the will of Hashem. As His servants, we must submit to His will.

However, it must be noted that the mitzvot of the Torah are not the only laws that Hashem created. In addition to the mitzvot, He created the laws of nature. These are the laws that govern the movement of the galaxies and the behavior of the smallest subatomic particle. Just as the Torah's mitzvot are an expression of His will, so too the laws of nature are a manifestation of the Divine. It is reasonable for the Creator to expect that these natural laws should be observed.

Now, we can understand Rashbam's position. Rashbam does not deny Hashem's omnipotence. He is not positing that the Creator needs a wind to split the sea. He is asserting that a perfect Creator would not disregard His own laws. He would not capriciously suspend or violate the laws He had established.

Rashbam is also providing us with an important perspective on scientific knowledge. In order to understand this perspective, let us ask a question: What is religion's attitude towards science? The answer is that science and religion have often contended with one another. Many religions have resisted science. What is the reason for this conflict?

5. Science

There are many factors that have contributed to this contentious relationship. We will consider two of these. First, religion is often steeped in the mystical. For some, religion provides an explanation for the inexplicable. According to this perspective, religion begins where science ends and provides answers to the questions science cannot address. In such a relationship, the advancement of science must reduce the significance of religion. As science expands our knowledge of the universe, the realm of religion is reduced. Mysteries that were once explained through some mystical truth are interpreted by a set of scientific principles. The realm of the mystical is reduced, and the danger arises that religion will become trivial.

There is a second issue. In some religions, doctrine may seem to contradict science. Religious doctrine is regarded as a revealed or, at least, inspired truth. It is not subject to challenge. Therefore, any conflict with science must be eliminated.

When these conflicts arise, these religions must respond. There are a number of responses. At the extreme, the response can take the form of outright suppression of science. More commonly, these challenges lead to the disparagement of science and a marginalizing of its importance.

6. His infinite wisdom

It is noteworthy that many of our greatest Torah Sages possessed extensive knowledge of science. Apparently, these Sages did not perceive any conflict between their religious outlook and scientific knowledge. The attitude of these Sages suggests that science and Torah can peacefully coexist. What is the basis for this coexistence?

Rashbam's explanation of our pasuk provides a response. It is clear that Rashbam regarded the laws of the universe as a manifestation the Creator's will. They are an expression of His infinite wisdom. Even Hashem will not flippantly disregard these laws. This implies that these laws deserve our respect.

This attitude eliminates the conflict between science and religion. The discoveries of science are not viewed as a threat to religion. On the contrary, these insights are an inspiration to the Torah scholar. They provide awesome testimony to the infinite wisdom of the Creator. The expansion of scientific knowledge does not diminish the significance of the Torah. This newfound knowledge gives us a greater appreciation of Hashem. These insights are a source of inspiration in our service to Hashem through the performance of His mitzvot.

It is important to note that we are not suggesting that the study of science is a substitute for the study of Torah. This is a completely different issue. Even within a single science, there is a proper order for its study. For example, in mathematics, the study of algebra precedes that of calculus. In addition, some sciences are more easily understood and more suitable for general study. And of course, practical considerations can suggest that one science be given priority over another. All of these issues and others must be discussed in order to determine the relative merit of Torah study as compared to the study of science. Nonetheless, it is clear from the comments of Rashbam that scientific knowledge deserves our respect.

Thus Hashem saved Israel that day out of the hand of the Egyptians. And Israel saw the Egyptians dead upon the sea-shore. (Shemot 14:30)

Unity of Heart and Mind

1. The song of Bnai Yisrael

Parshat Beshalach continues the Torah's discussion of Bnai Yisrael's exodus from Egypt. The Torah relates that Paroh realized that Bnai Yisrael did not intend to return to Egypt. He regretted granting Bnai Yisrael permission to leave Egypt. He gathered his armies and set off in pursuit of his former slaves. Paroh overtook Bnai Yisrael as the nation was camped on the shores of the Reed Sea.

The Torah describes the reaction of Bnai Yisrael to the appearance of Paroh and his legions. They were trapped between the impassable sea and the Egyptian camp which was prepared to pounce upon them and destroy them. They initially responded to their perilous plight by praying to Hashem. Then, they began to criticize Moshe. They complained that they should have remained Paroh's servants in Egypt rather than die in the wilderness. Moshe responded that the people would soon witness their salvation and the utter destruction of their enemies. Hashem will fight for them.

Hashem then split the Reed Sea and Bnai Yisrael crossed upon the dry seabed. Paroh led his armies in pursuit. The sea closed upon them. The walls of the parted water came down upon them, crushing and drowning them within the depths of the sea. Bnai Yisrael observed the complete destruction of their enemies and, led by Moshe, they sang His praises.

Then Moshe and the children of Israel sang this song unto Hashem, and spoke, saying: I will sing unto Hashem, for He is highly exalted. The horse and his rider He has thrown into the sea.
(Shemot 15:1)

2. Song when salvation is complete

The above passage introduces the Shirat HaYam – the Song of the Sea. This is the praise that was composed by Moshe and recited by Bnai Yisrael in response to the destruction of their enemies. The passage begins by explaining that "then Moshe and Bnai Yisrael sang this song" of praise. The passage places emphasis on the moment selected for the recitation of the Shirat HaYam. It was recited when the nation observed the complete destruction of its enemies.

Rav Naftali Tzvi Yehudah Berlin – Netziv – explains that only at this moment was it appropriate for this praise to be recited. Only when their salvation was complete could this praise be sung to Hashem. Netziv's intention in this comment can be better understood in the context of earlier comments. Netziv notes that on two prior occasions Bnai Yisrael gave thanks to Hashem for their salvation. The first time was when Moshe initially came to them and told them that Hashem would redeem them from Egypt. The Torah states that the nation believed Moshe and responded by bowing to Hashem. Netziv explains that this act of bowing or prostration was an expression of thanks. Later, Moshe told Bnai Yisrael that the Egyptians would be smitten with the plague of the firstborn. Bnai Yisrael would be spared from the devastation of the plague through their participation in the Pesach offering. The nation responded by bowing to Hashem. Again, Netziv notes that the bowing or prostrating of the nation was an act of acknowledgment and a giving of thanks to Hashem.

In other words, the nation twice before expressed its confidence in Moshe's message that Hashem would redeem them from Egypt. On both occasions they responded with prostration and thanks to Hashem. However, on neither of these occasions did Moshe lead the people in song.

Apparently, Netziv is explaining why a song of praise was only recited after the destruction of Bnai Yisrael's enemies at the Reed Sea. He explains that such praise is only appropriate when the salvation is complete and not before that point. Although at these previous moments the nation responded to Moshe's message with appreciation and gratitude, these could only be expressed though bowing and could not find expression in a song of praise. Netziv does not provide a reason for this rule. Why can a song of praise – like the Shirat HaYam – only be recited when the salvation is complete?

Hashem is my strength and song, and He has become my salvation. This is my G-d, and I will glorify Him; my father's G-d, and I will exalt Him. (Shemot 15:2)

3. Awareness of Hashem

The above passage is from the Shirat HaYam. The people declare, "This is my G-d and I will glorify Him." The Sages are troubled by the use of the term "this". The term "this" is used to make reference to a specific object or person. In the passage it seems to be superfluous and misleading. The passage could have stated: Hashem is my G-d and I will glorify Him. What is added by the term "this"? Furthermore, the term indicates that there was some image or material presence to which the people referred. This is not possible! One of the Torah's fundamental principles is that Hashem is not material.

Rashi responds that Hashem revealed Himslef to the people at the Reed Sea and the people pointed to Him with their fingers and declared, "This is our G-d". He adds that even a former maidservant at the Reed Sea achieved a vision and experienced an encounter that was unsurpassed by the great prophets.

Rashi's comments are not only difficult to understand but also seem to contribute little to resolving the problems in the passage. He seems to suggest that the term "this" is used because there was an actual presence or image to which the people referred. This assertion only confirms the difficulties presented by the passage. How can Hashem be described as a material entity or presence to which the people referred?

Thus Hashem saved Israel that day out of the hand of the Egyptians. And Israel saw the Egyptians dead upon the sea-shore. And Israel saw the great work which Hashem did upon the

Egyptians, and the people feared Hashem; and they believed in Hashem, and in His servant Moshe. (Shemot 14:30-31)

4. Complete and compromised conviction

Rashi's comments can be better understood viewed in the context provided by the above passages. These passages are problematic. They explain that after Bnai Yisrael observed the destruction of their enemies at the Reed Sea they believed in Hashem and Moshe. These passages imply that prior to this point their conviction in Hashem and in Moshe was less than certain. Why were their convictions not complete until this point and how did their experience at the Reed Sea complete their convictions?

And when Paroh drew nigh, the children of Israel lifted up their eyes, and, behold, the Egyptians were marching after them. And they were sore afraid. And the children of Israel cried out unto Hashem. And they said unto Moshe: Because there were no graves in Egypt, have you taken us away to die in the wilderness? Why have you dealt thus with us, to bring us forth out of Egypt? Is not this the word that we spoke unto you in Egypt, saying: Let us alone, that we may serve the Egyptians? For it was better for us to serve the Egyptians, than that we should die in the wilderness. And Moshe said unto the people: Fear not, stand still, and see the salvation of Hashem, which He will work for you today; for whereas you have seen the Egyptians today, you shall never again see them. (Shemot 14:10-13)

5. Psychological perception and conflicting reality

In order to answer this question, it is important to consider a comment made by Rabbaynu Avraham ibn Ezra. Ibn Ezra poses a simple question on the above passages. The passages describe the response of Bnai Yisrael to the approach of Paroh and his armies. The passages communicate an image of panic and despair. Ibn Ezra notes that Bnai Yisrael included 600,000 able-bodied men. Their approaching adversaries had suffered through ten debilitating plagues. Certainly, both the health and numbers of Paroh's legions were severely depleted by these plagues. Why did Bnai Yisrael not face their adversaries and battle them?

Ibn Ezra responds that Bnai Yisrael were psychologically incapable of considering this option. They still viewed themselves as slaves and the Egyptians as their masters. They had witnessed the humiliation of the Egyptians through the plagues. Yet, as the Egyptians appeared on the horizon, Bnai Yisrael did not realize that their planned attack was the desperate final gasp of a dying kingdom. They saw them as the unvanquished and all-powerful masters to whom they were subservient. They could not imagine opposing or rising up against this invincible adversary.

Now, the passages introducing the Shirat HaYam are easily understood. Even before arriving at the Reed Sea, Bnai Yisrael had witnessed the plagues and seen the wonders performed by Hashem through Moshe. They intellectually understood that these wonders revealed the omnipotence of Hashem. They comprehended that Hashem had sent Moshe to rescue them from Egypt. However, their hearts and minds were not united. In their hearts, their awe of Hashem's omnipotence competed with their awe of their Egyptian masters. Their sense of freedom and deliverance from suffering could not be complete as long as they remained intimidated because of their subservience to Paroh and Egypt. Then, Bnai Yisrael witnessed the total destruction of Paroh at the Reed Sea. With ease and rapidity Hashem disposed of the invincible Paroh. Now, the people accepted Hashem in their minds and hearts. They could fully believe in Hashem and His servant Moshe.

Rashi's comments make the same point. Hashem revealed Himself to Bnai Yisrael at the Reed Sea. His existence, providence, and omnipotence emerged fully. With the total destruction of Paroh and his legions, the hearts and minds of the people became united in belief in Hashem. He became real; ambivalence was replaced by absolute certainty, and intellectual understanding was united with heartfelt wonder. Rashi is not suggesting that the people saw Hashem in the material sense. He is explaining that He became real and the people became certain in their conviction. The people expressed their new clarity of conviction by using the phrase "this is my G-d". They were giving expression to the overwhelming awareness of Hashem that they experienced at the Reed Sea.

6. Uncompromised convicton

A careful reading of the first passage of the Shirat HaYam reveals why it could only be recited at this time. The passage explains that the nation is singing Hashem's praises because of its awareness of His exalted greatness. He has thrown rider and chariot into the sea. Only after the victory at the Reed Sea did the people feel truly delivered from their oppressors. Only when they saw Paroh's complete destruction did they feel truly free. Now, their salvation was complete. Their hearts rejoiced in their deliverance.

Before, when they had expressed their thanks to Hashem for their deliverance, their sense of gratitude was compromised by their unresolved fear of their Egyptian masters. They could not recite Hashem's full praises because heart and mind were not united in their acceptance of Hashem as the only true ruler in their lives. Heart and mind were in conflict; ambiguity prevailed. At the Reed Sea, Hashem was revealed as the only G-d and as an absolute omnipotent ruler. Now, they were prepared and fit to sing Shirat HaYam.

Who is like unto You, Hashem, among the mighty? Who is like unto You, glorious in holiness, fearful in praises, doing wonders? (Shemot 15:11)

7. Seeking unity of heart and mind

We are obligated to serve Hashem with our entire being. We must draw close to Him through the effort of our intellect. However, intellect unaccompanied by heartfelt devotion does not produce true commitment and acceptance of Hashem. We must work to achieve unity of heart and mind. The work of the mind is not complete until the devotion of the heart is secured.

And Israel saw the mighty hand that Hashem had performed in Egypt. The nation feared Hashem. And they believed in Hashem and in Moshe, His servant. (Shemot 14:31)

Overcoming Doubts

1. Praise and thanksgiving

The first portion of Parshat BeShalach discusses the miracle of the Reed Sea. Bnai Yisrael emerged from Egypt. The nation began its journey to the Land of Israel. However, Paroh and the Egyptians reconsidered their decision to release the Jews from bondage. Paroh rallied his armies and they pursued Bnai Yisrael. The Jews were soon trapped on the shore of the Reed Sea. The waters of the sea were before them; Pharaoh and his armies were approaching. Bnai Yisrael entered the sea and Hashem parted its waters. They traveled along a path in the midst of the sea. The Egyptians entered the sea in pursuit of their prey. The waters of the sea collapsed upon them. Pharaoh and his mighty armies were instantly destroyed by the onrushing waters of the sea.

Moshe and Bnai Yisrael observed the destruction of their nemesis and recited a song of praise to Hashem. This song – *Az Yashir* – extolls Hashem's omnipotence and His destruction of Pharaoh and his mighty armies.

Only at this point did the Jews recite these praises acknowledging Hashem's omnipotence. They had observed His terrible plagues and the submission of Pharaoh and the Egyptians to the will of Hashem. They had departed from Egypt without opposition and left behind a defeated and completely vanquished nation. Why did they not extoll Hashem's greatness when they departed as a free people from Egypt?

The above passage introduces *Az Yashir*. It addresses this issue. The passage explains that only now – after observing the death of Pharaoh and his armies – did the people believe in Hashem and Moshe.

This explanation is difficult to understand. Apparently, until they observed the drowning of the Egyptians, the people were plagued by lingering doubts. They had doubts regarding Hashem and they were uncertain of Moshe's authenticity as His prophet. Now, these doubts were resolved and replaced by certainties. How did the miracle of the Reed Sea bring about this transformation? Why was this event able to resolve uncertainties that persisted even after they had observed all of the wonders that took place in Egypt?

There are a number of factors that contributed to the impact of the miracle of the Reed Sea. We will discuss one of these. This factor is identified and discussed by Rav Aharon Soloveitchik *Zt"l*.[113]

Therefore, say to Bnai Yisrael: I am Hashem. I will take you forth from under the burdens of Egypt. I will save (hatzalah) you from their servitude. I will redeem you with an outstretched arm and with great works. (Shemot 6:6)

And Hashem saved (yeshuah), on that day, Israel from the hand of the Egypt. And Israel saw Egypt die upon the shore of the sea. (Shemot 14:30)

My strength and my praise derive from G-d and He has been my salvation (yeshuah). (Shemot 15:2)

2. Two Hebrew terms describe salvation

Rav Soloveitchik suggests that the path to understanding this issue begins with an analysis of the terms used by the Torah to describe salvation. The Hebrew language includes a number of words for salvation or rescue. Two of those used in the narrative of the redemption from Egypt are *Hatzalah* and *yeshuah*. In the opening portion of Parshat VaEyrah, Hashem tells Moshe that He will soon redeem the Jewish people from Egypt. In the first passage above, Hashem describes various aspects of the redemption. In this description Hashem uses the term *hatzalah*. In our *parasha*, the Torah describes the rescue of the Jewish people at the Reed Sea. Here, the term *yeshuah* is used.

---

[113] Rav Soloveitchik discusses this issue in *The Warmth and the Light*, volume 1, pp. 127-131. His position is also discussed by his son Rav Chaim Soloveitchik in a recorded lecture. The following is based on both sources.

Rav Soloveitchik explains that the Torah's choice of terms is revealing. *Hatzalah* is used to describe the rescue of a passive individual. In speaking to Moshe, Hashem was describing the rescue of Bnai Yisrael from Egypt through the plagues. In this process, the Jewish people would be completely passive. They would not be required to participate in their redemption. In fact, the Torah describes Paroh and the Egyptians chasing Bnai Yisrael from Egypt.[114]

The term *yeshuah* is used to describe the rescuer acting in unison with the rescued to bring about the rescue. This is the term used in the second two passages above. These passages describe the rescue of the Jewish people at the Reed Sea. The use of this term indicates that Bnai Yisrael were not passive participants in the events at the Reed Sea. How did Bnai Yisrael participate in their own rescue?

And Bnai Yisrael came into the sea upon dry land. The water was for them a wall to their right and their left. (Shemot 14:23)

3. The Jewish people were required to act on their own initiative

The Tosefta describes the events immediately preceding the parting of the sea's waters. The Egyptians were to the back of Bnai Yisrael and the sea barred their path forward. Moshe told them to proceed into the waters. The tribes began to debate who should lead the nation into the sea. The tribe of Yehudah detached itself from this deliberation and proceeded into the waters.[115] The midrash adds that the sea parted only after the people waded into it and its waters had reached their noses.[116]

These comments suggest an obvious question. Where was Moshe? Why was Moshe not leading his people into the sea just as he led them out of Egypt? Apparently, the miracle of the Reed Sea were to occur in response to the initiative of the Jewish people. This miracle was intended to be a *yeshuah* and not a *hatzalah*. Moshe could not lead them into the sea. They were required to move forward on their own.[117]

---

[114] Sefer Shemot 12:33.

[115] Tosefta Berachot 4:16.

[116] Midrah Rabbah, Shemot 29:9.

[117] Meshech Chuchmah (Sefer Shemot 14:15) suggests that this expectation is explicitly expressed in the passages. When Bnai Yisrael set forth from Egypt, they followed a *malach* – an angel – of Hashem and a pillar of cloud. In Shemot 14:19, the Torah describes the *malach* and pillar moving from the front of the camp of Bnai Yisrael to its rear. The Torah explains that the *malach* and cloud took a new position separating and protecting the Jews from the approaching Egyptians. However, Meshech Chachmah explains that this repositioning of the *malach* and cloud had a second impact. The *malach* and cloud would not lead the people into the sea. The people would not be permitted to follow these leaders into the sea's midst. Instead, the people must lead themselves.

Meshech Chachmah further proposes that this *malach* was not a heavenly emissary. It was Moshe. This position is supported by the comments of Rashi on BeMidbar 20:16. In this passage, Moshe refers to a *malach* sent to rescue the Jewish people. Rashi explains that this *malach* is Moshe, himself. According to Meshech Chachmah's understanding of 14:19, Moshe was directed by Hashem to retreat from the front of the nation and to allow the people to act on their own initiative.

Let us now return to our initial question. Why only at this point did the people completely believe in Hashem and Moshe? Why did the plagues and miracles they observed in Egypt leave them with unresolved doubts?

4. Doubts derive from various sources

The answer is that doubt and ambivalence does not always derive from a deficiency in the evidence supporting a belief. In other words, even when the evidence of a truth is overwhelming, doubt can persist. In order to overcome this ambivalence, one must make the decision to embrace the truth proven by the evidence and to move forward on that basis.

Rav Aharon explains that this dynamic is demonstrated by this account. The plagues and wonders the nation observed in Egypt conclusively demonstrated Hashem's omnipotence and Moshe's authenticity as His prophet. The residual doubts were not the result of an insufficiency of evidence. The doubts reflected an internal conflict; a hesitancy to move forward and embrace the new truths that had been firmly established in Egypt. These doubts were not resolved by new overpowering evidence that emerged at the Reed Sea. Doubt was replaced by conviction because the people discovered within themselves the courage to embrace and act on these beliefs. Once they acted, doubt and uncertainly were brushed aside.

5. Developing conviction through action

Rav Aharon's insight has important practical implications. First, we must acknowledge that his perspective is novel. We assume that action proceeds from and follows belief and conviction. In other words, we assume that when we are completely convinced of a truth, we will act upon it. If we are struggling to move forward, we assume that our motivation is undermined by doubt. Rav Aharon is arguing that sometimes conviction proceeds from action. Our doubts are not the result of a deficiency in the evidence; they are based upon our resistance to embracing a challenging truth.

Let's consider an example. An acquaintance who became observant relatively late in life shared his story with me. He explained that many years ago, he and a friend sought out a rabbi in their community to study with them. They entered into their relationship with this rabbi only after establishing an understanding. The rabbi would study with them but not promote observance or any change in their lifestyles. The rabbi accepted the unusual arrangement. The rabbi and two friends studied together for many years. Occasionally, the rabbi would test whether there was any flexibility in the initial understanding. On each of these occasions, his study-partners assured him that they remained determined to not adopt observance or alter their lifestyles.

One day the rabbi asked his partners a question. "If you could observe a *mitzvah* without significantly altering your lifestyle, would you adopt that observance?" My acquaintance responded that he would consider it. The rabbi asked him whether he would consider shaving in the morning with an electric shaver. My acquaintance responded that he believed he could adopt that practice. He began to shave with an electric shaver. That little change was the first step in gradually implementing other changes.

No new evidence was provided to my acquaintance that finally won him over to the wisdom of the Torah. The barrier between him and observance was not authentic doubt reflecting a deficiency in the evidence of the Torah's wisdom. His internal resistances were undermining his advancement. Once he discovered – with the help of his rabbi/mentor – a path of action, his ambivalence was conquered.

We each should take a few moments to consider Rav Aharon's insight and this example. How often has this dynamic hindered us and prevented us from advancing and growing?

In short, once we have evaluated an issue and made a determination of the truth, we sometimes need to force ourselves to act on this determination. Only through moving forward will we overcome our resistances and the ambivalence they produce.

"Then Moshe and Bnai Yisrael sang this song to Hashem. And they said, "I will sing to Hashem for he is beyond all praise. The horse and its rider He threw into the sea." (Shemot 15:1)

6. Inadequate praise

Bnai Yisrael emerge from the Reed Sea. They have safely emerged and the Egyptians have drowned. Moshe leads Bnai Yisrael in a song of praise. Our pasuk is the opening passage of Shirat HaYam – the Song of the Sea. The translation above is based on the comments of Rashi.[118] According to this interpretation, Moshe begins with the pronouncement that Hashem is beyond all praise. This is a rather amazing introduction to his shira – his praise of Hashem. Essentially, Moshe is announcing that his praise is inadequate. But yet, this does not discourage Moshe from engaging in the praise!

"Then Moshe and Bnai Yisrael sang this song to Hashem. And they said: I sing to Hashem for He is the most exalted. The horse and its rider He threw into the sea." (Shemot 15:1)

The Angels Were Forbidden from Singing

1. Inappropriate

The Egyptians pursued Bnai Yisrael into the sea. The walls of water collapsed and the Egyptians were drowned. Moshe composed a song of praise to Hashem. This pasuk introduces Shirat HaYaam – the Song of the Sea. Moshe and Bnai Yisrael recited the song.

The Talmud comments, in Tractate Megilah, that the angels observed the destruction of the Egyptians and the salvation of Bnai Yisrael. The angels were moved to praise Hashem with song. Hashem protested. He explained that song was inappropriate. Bnai Yisrael had been saved – but only through the destruction of others. The Egyptians were creations of Hashem. The tragedy of their death was commingled with the salvation of Bnai Yisrael.[119]

This teaching gives rise to an obvious question. It was inappropriate for the angels to utter song to Hashem on this occasion. Why, then, was it fitting for Moshe and the Bnai Yisrael to compose and recite the Song of the Sea?

2. Objective and subjective

Rav Chaim Volozin Zt"l offers a brilliant answer to this question. He explains that a miracle can be evaluated in an objective and subjective manner. The angels do not personally benefit from the salvation of the righteous or the destruction of the wicked. Therefore, they are

---

[118] Rabbaynu Shlomo ben Yitzchak (Rashi), *Commentary on Sefer Shemot* 15:1.
[119] Mesechet Megilah 10b.

incapable of a subjective reaction. They can only analyze and react to the objective aspects of a miracle. The angels' reaction to the miracle of the Reed Sea must be understood from this perspective.

The angels were moved by the awesome significance of the moment. Hashem had revealed His mastery over nature. The wicked had been destroyed. The promise made to the Avot – the forefathers – was now closer to fulfillment. Indeed, the very purpose of creation was closer to being realized. Bnai Yisrael had been freed and were on the path to Sinai and Revelation. The angels reasoned that this objective analysis dictated that the moment be celebrated through song to Hashem.

Hashem responded that this objective analysis was incomplete. The Egyptians were also creations of Hashem. None of His creatures is created to be destroyed. Therefore, from an objective perspective, the miracle of the Reed Sea included an element of tragedy.

People, unlike angels, can benefit personally from miracles. We can evaluate a miracle on a subjective level. Bnai Yisrael had been saved. For the Bnai Yisrael, this was a great moment. The beneficiaries of Hashem's benevolence were obligated to recognize this kindness.

In an objective sense this miracle was not perfect. The angels could not offer praise. However, in a subjective sense, the event demanded recognition of Hashem. Therefore, Bnai Yisrael offered their praise to Hashem for their salvation.

"My strength and song is G-d. And this will be my deliverance. This is my G-d and I will glorify Him. He is the G-d of my father and I will exalt Him." (Shemot 15:2)

3. Blasphemy

Many of the passages in the shira – this song of praise – are difficult to translate. The exact meaning of numerous phrases is debated by the commentaries. The above translation of the latter part of the passage is based upon the commentary of Rashbam.[120] Gershonides expands on this translation. He explains that this passage is a continuation of Moshe's introduction. In the previous passage, Moshe acknowledges that Hashem is above all praise. In this passage Moshe is acknowledging that in his praises he will resort to material characterizations of Hashem.[121]

If the first passage of Moshe's introduction seems odd, this passage is amazing. One of the fundamental principles of the Torah is that Hashem is not material and that no material characteristics can be ascribed to Him.[122] Nonetheless, Moshe acknowledges that he will employ material imagery in his praise of Hashem. After this introduction Moshe uses various material images to describe Hashem. He refers to Hashem as a "man of war." He discusses the "right hand" of Hashem. In fact, virtually every praise that Moshe formulates ascribes some material characteristic to Hashem.

The combined message of these two first passages is completely confusing. Moshe first acknowledges that no praise of Hashem is accurate; it cannot begin to capture Hashem's greatness. In the second passage, Moshe excuses himself for ignoring one of our most fundamental convictions regarding Hashem – that He is not material. Instead of providing an

---

[120] Rabbaynu Shemuel ben Meir (Rashbam) *Commentary on Sefer Shemot* 15:2.
[121] R' Levi ben Gershon (Ralbag), *Com. on Shemot*, (Mosad HaRav Kook, 1994), pp. 111-112.
[122] R' Moshe ben Maimon (Rambam) *Commentary on the Mishne*, Mesechet Sanhedrin 10:1.

appropriate introduction to the shira, these two passages seem to argue that the entire endeavor is not only futile but is an act of blasphemy!

"I shall relate Your glory, though I do not see You. I shall allegorize You, I shall describe You though I do not know You. Through the hand of Your prophets, through the counsel of Your servants, You allegorized the splendorous glory of Your power. Your greatness and Your strength, they described the might of Your works. They allegorized You but not according to Your reality. And they portrayed You according to Your actions. They symbolized You in many visions. You are a unity in all of these allegories." (Shir HaKavod)

4. Dependancy

Our liturgy contains many profound insights. Unfortunately, sometimes, we do not carefully consider the meaning of the words. In many synagogues the Shir HaKavod – composed by Rav Yehuda HaChassid – is recited every Shabbat at the closing of services. The Shir HaKavod deals with the same issues that Moshe is discussing in his introduction to the Shirat HaYam. Let us carefully consider these lines.

We begin by acknowledging that we cannot see Hashem. In fact, we cannot truly know Hashem. Human understanding is limited. We cannot begin to conceptualize the nature of Hashem. This creates a paradox. How can we praise or even relate to Hashem? How can we relate to a G-d that is beyond the boundaries of human understanding? We respond that we will employ allegories.

But the use of allegories creates its own problems. If we do not know or understand Hashem's nature, then on what basis will we form these allegories? What allegory can we formulate for a G-d so completely beyond the ken of human understanding? We respond that we will rely on the allegories provided by the prophets. We do not trust ourselves to create our own allegories. Instead, we must employ the allegories that are provided to us by Moshe and the other prophets.

5. Limitations

Of course, this does not completely answer the question. Even Moshe was unable to achieve an understanding of the fundamental nature of Hashem. So, how can he help us? What allegory can Moshe provide for that which even he could not comprehend? The answer is that we never attempt to describe Hashem's nature. No allegory can be adequate. All of our allegories are designed to describe Hashem's actions and deeds. In other words, our allegories do not describe what Hashem is, only what He does.

Yet, at the same time that we employ the allegories of the prophets, we are required to acknowledge the limitation of these descriptions. We cannot – even for a moment – delude ourselves as to the accuracy of the terms we use when referring to Hashem. The allegorical terms are not in any way a description of Hashem's reality. This means these terms are not a true description of Hashem's real nature.

Finally, we acknowledge Hashem's unity. Hashem is a perfect unity. This means He has no parts or characteristics. The multitude of allegories that we employ cannot lead us to err on this issue of unity. All of the various allegories that we employ relate back to a G-d that in fact is one. He does not have various characteristics or any characteristics. He is the perfect unity. Even when we refer to Hashem as kind or omniscient, we must recognize the limitation of this reference. Hashem does not truly have the characteristic of being kind or the quality of omniscience. These are allegorical characterizations.

6. Accommodation

The Shir HaKavod provides a fundamental insight. It attempts to resolve an important paradox. We need to relate to Hashem. Yet, we cannot truly comprehend His exalted nature. How can we form a relationship with that which we cannot know? In response to our human need, the Torah allows us to employ allegorical terms in reference to Hashem. But we must recognize that this is an accommodation. We are permitted to use allegorical terms and phrases. We are not permitted to accept these allegories as being accurate depictions of Hashem's nature.

We can now understand Moshe's introduction to Shirat HaYam. At the Reed Sea, Bnai Yisrael experienced salvation. The people needed to respond. They needed to express their outpouring of thanks to Hashem. Moshe formulated Shirat HaYam in response to this need. But Moshe's shira – like all praise of Hashem – is a not an accurate portrayal of Hashem. Instead, it is an accommodation to the human need to relate to Hashem. We are permitted this accommodation. But there is a precondition. We must first recognize that it is an accommodation.

Our praise cannot capture the true greatness of Hashem – who is above all praise. And we must recognize that all of our praises rely on allegories, that are not true depictions of Hashem. This is Moshe's introduction. Before he led Bnai Yisrael in song, he explains the limitations of our praises. They are incomplete and are merely allegories, and not accurate descriptions of Hashem.

"And you should count, from the day following the holiday, from the day that you brought the omer wave offering, seven weeks. They should be complete." (VaYikra 23:15)

The Identity of the Days

1. Counting

This *pasuk* introduces the *mitzvah* of *sefirat ha'omer* – the counting of the *omer*. The Torah requires that we count seven weeks from the day on which the *omer* sacrifice was offered. The *omer* was a special grain offering brought on the second day of Pesach. Each of the forty-nine days of these seven weeks is individually counted. On the fiftieth day Shavuot is celebrated. The command is performed through verbally announcing the count each night.

The Talmud explains that this mitzvah must be performed by all males.[123] This law is derived from our pasuk. Ivrit differentiates between the second person singular and the plural. In this case the plural is used. This means that the counting is performed by many.

There is another instance in which we are required to count towards a date. This is the counting towards the Jubilee year – the *Yovel*. The *Yovel* occurred in the land of Israel every fifty years. This year was observed through a number of special laws. Jewish servants were set free. The land of Israel was redistributed to the descendants of those who had first occupied the land. The land was not worked during the *Yovel* year. Determination of the *Yovel* required counting. Forty-nine years are counted from a *Yovel* year. The fiftieth year is the next *Yovel*.

---

[123] Mesechet Menachot 65b.

Who was responsible to count the years between the *Yovel* years? This obligation was executed by the Great Court.[124] This raises an interesting question. The *mitzvah* of *sefirat ha'omer* is performed by individuals. The counting for *Yovel* is only performed by the Great Court. Why are these *mitzvot* assigned to different elements of the community?

A careful analysis of Maimonides' formulation of each *mitzvah* will help resolve this issue. In addition to counting the years leading to the *Yovel*, the Great Court is obligated to declare the *Yovel* year. These are two separate commandments. The court is obligated to count the years and declare the *Yovel*. Maimonides, understandably, relates these two commandments. The counting is requisite for the declaration of the *Yovel*. Both elements merge into a single objective.[125]

2. Causing Shavuot

The Great Court is responsible for the establishment of the Jewish calendar.[126] The court declared the beginning of each month and subsequently established our current calendar. The establishment of the *Yovel* year is also a calendar function. It is quite understandable that this *mitzvah* and the requisite counting should be responsibilities of the court.

Why is the counting of the *omer* an individual responsibility and not the duty of the court? We can only conclude that *sefirat ha'omer* does not determine the date of Shavuot. This occurs spontaneously with the advent of the second day of Pesach. The counting is not required to designate the date of Shavuot.

What then is the purpose of counting the *omer*? Through this counting we recognize the identity of these intervening days. We acknowledge the special nature of each day of the *omer*. As this is a personal act of acknowledgment, it must be performed by the individual. The court cannot perform this *mitzvah*.

"And you shall count for you from the morrow after the day of rest, from the day that you brought the sheaf of the waving seven weeks. They shall be complete." (VaYikra 23:15)

Make it Count

1. Incomplete redemption

We are currently involved in the mitzvah of sefirat ho'omer – the counting of the omer. We begin counting the omer on the second night of Pesach and continue the process up to Shavuot. This mitzvah requires that each night we verbally identify the new day's number within the fifty days of the omer. On the second night of Pesach we declare that we are in the first day of the omer. We declare the following night as the second day of the omer. We repeat this process nightly until we arrive at Shavuot. The first mention of this mitzvah in the Torah is found in our passage.

Sefer HaChinuch provides an explanation for this mitzvah. He explains that the fundamental purpose of this mitzvah is to link Pesach with Shavuot. Why is it important to make this connection? Pesach recalls and celebrates our redemption from Egypt. However, this

---

[124] Rabbaynu Moshe ben Maimon (Rambam) *Mishne Torah*, Hilchot Shemitah VeYovel 10:1.

[125] Rabbaynu Moshe ben Maimon (Rambam) *Mishne Torah*, Hilchot Shemitah VeYovel 10:1.

[126] Rabbaynu Moshe ben Maimon (Rambam) *Mishne Torah*, Hilchot Kiddush HaChodesh 1:5.

celebration is only completed with Shavuot. Shavuot recalls and celebrates the revelation of the Torah at Sinai. Our redemption from Egypt was designed to prepare us for receiving the Torah. This was the purpose and sole objective of our redemption from Egypt. Without the Torah, our redemption would have been meaningless. Therefore, we are required to acknowledge that the redemption that we celebrate on Pesach was – in itself – an incomplete event. It was a step in the progression towards revelation. We acknowledge this concept by linking – through our counting – the redemption of Pesach with the revelation of Shavuot.[127]

In our times, this remains an important message. Pesach is the most widely celebrated Jewish festival or annual event. It would seem that this popularity stems from its theme. The theme of an oppressed people achieving freedom from torment and bondage has broad appeal. This theme resonates with humanistic, enlightened values. However, it is unfortunate that this perceived theme of Pesach is not the actual message of the festival. We are not celebrating freedom in itself. Freedom is significant because of the opportunities that it provides. The virtue of freedom lies in the choices made by the free, unfettered individual or people. Freedom can be used wisely or destructively. We celebrate our freedom because of the opportunity that it provides us to serve Hashem. If this element is absent from the Pesach celebration, the festival has been fundamentally altered from the Torah's design.

This observation is not intended to suggest that we should not be gratified by the widespread celebration of Pesach. Instead, this observation should indicate to us that much work must still be done to communicate to the wider Jewish world the full meaning of Pesach.

2. Listening to another person count

The counting of the omer is an individual obligation. Each person fulfills this obligation through his individual verbal declaration of the number of the day. This raises an interesting question. The question requires a short introduction.

There are many Torah obligations that are fulfilled through verbal pronouncements. For example, each Shabbat night we are required to individually recite Kiddush. However, it is not the common practice for each member of the household to recite Kiddush. Instead, the head of the household recites Kiddush for the other members of the household and guests. How does the Kiddush recited by the head of the household fulfill the individual obligation of the others present?

The answer is that the others present fulfill their obligation through the legal principle of shomeah ka'oneh – one who listens is equated with the one who verbalizes. According to this principle, a person who listens to a verbal pronouncement is considered to have actually made the pronouncement. There are two important conditions that must be met for this principle to be applied. First, the person who wishes to fulfill his obligation with someone else's pronouncement must listen attentively. Second, both parties must share the intention to fulfill the listener's obligation through the other party's verbal pronouncement.

With this background, the question can be introduced. Can the principle of shomeah ka'oneh be applied to the counting of the omer? In other words, can a person fulfill his personal obligation to count the omer through listening to another person count?

---

[127] Rav Aharon HaLeyve, *Sefer HaChinuch, Mitzvah* 306.

One would expect that the principle does apply. After all, why should counting of the omer be different from reciting Kiddush? If a person can fulfill one's obligation to recite Kiddush through listening to someone else, it is reasonable to assume that one can fulfill the obligation to count the omer in the same manner. This is the position of Rav Yosef Karo.[128]

3. You count

Others disagree. Magen Avraham suggests that the principle of shomeah ka'oneh cannot be applied to the mitzvah of counting the omer. He offers an interesting explanation for his position. This explanation is based upon the Talmud's analysis of our passage. The passage instructs that "you shall count (the omer) for you." What is the meaning of the seemingly superfluous phrase "for you"? The Talmud explains that this phrase teaches us that each person must count.[129]

Tosefot comment that the Talmud distinguishes between the counting of the omer and the counting of the fifty years from one Jubilee to the next. The counting of the years between Jubilees is performed by the Sanhedrin – the high court. There is no obligation upon individuals to conduct this counting. In contrast, the mitzvah of counting the omer is not placed upon the Sanhedrin. In this instance, the individual is required to perform the counting.[130]

Magen Avraham explains that because the Talmud concludes that the obligation to count the omer is placed upon each individual, the principle of shomeah ka'oneh cannot be applied. Application of this principle would result in one person counting on behalf of many other individuals.[131]

Magen Avraham's comments are difficult to understand. It is unlikely that the message of the Talmud is that the Torah wishes to establish a proliferation of counters! The more reasonable interpretation of the Talmud's message is that the obligation of counting the omer should not be confused with the counting of the years between Jubilees. The counting of the omer is a personal obligation and not an obligation upon the Sanhedrin. Then, the counting of the omer can be equated with obligation to recite Kiddush. Both are personal obligations. Yet, the principle of shomeah ka'oneh does apply to Kiddush. Why should this principle not apply to the counting of the omer?

4. Understanding the word

Magen Avraham provides an important hint to his reasoning in his discussion of another issue. Can a person count the omer in a language that he does not understand? Magen Avraham discusses this issue in regards to the obligation to recite the Shema. He explains that the Shema can be recited in any language with the single provision that the person understands the language.[132] He adds that this ruling also applies to Kiddush, prayer, and the reciting of blessings. The implication of this ruling is that if a person recites the Shema in Hebrew, it is not necessary for the person to understand the language. Mishne Berurah confirms this interpretation.[133]

---

[128] RavYosef Karo, Bait Yosef Commentary on Tur, Orach Chayim 489.

[129] Mesechet Menachot 65b.

[130] Tosefot, Mesechet Menachot 65b.

[131] Rav Avraham Avlee, *Magen Avraham Commentary on Shulchan Aruch*, Orech Chayim 489:1

[132] Rav Avraham Avlee, *Magen Avraham Commentary on Shulchan Aruch*, Orech Chayim 62:2.

We would expect this ruling to apply to the counting of the omer. In other words, if a person counts the omer in Hebrew without understanding the language, one fulfills the obligation. However, this is not Magen Avraham's position. In the case of counting the omer, Magen Avraham rules that the person must understand the meaning of his statement. A person can only count in Hebrew if he understands the meaning of his words.[134] Why is the counting of the omer an exception to the general rule regarding Hebrew? Why in this instance is Hebrew only acceptable if the person counting understands the language?

5. Count, not pronounce

Let us begin with this last question. It seems that Magen Avraham is concerned with a basic issue regarding the mitzvah of counting the omer. Is this mitzvah fulfilled merely by pronouncing the appropriately formulated declaration on each night or must a person actually engage in a conscious act of counting? If we assume that the obligation is fulfilled through the pronouncement of the properly formulated declaration, then one should be permitted to count in Hebrew regardless of one's mastery of the language. After all, the appropriate formula has been pronounced.

The obligation is fulfilled. Magen Avraham rejects this interpretation of the mitzvah. His understanding of the mitzvah is that one must engage in a conscious act of counting. If one does not understand the meaning of the formula that he pronounces, then one has not fulfilled his obligation. In this respect, counting of the omer differs from the obligation to recite the Shema and other similar obligations. In these instances, one fulfills the minimal obligation through properly reciting the required statement. Of course, the mitzvah is performed on a more meaningful level when one understands the meaning of his statement. But on a minimal level, this is not required to fulfill the obligation.

We can not return to our original question. According to Magen Avraham, why does the principle of shomeah ka'oneh not apply to the counting of the omer? Magen Avraham is suggesting that this principle has a significant limitation. What is precisely accomplished though shomeah ka'oneh? This principle provides a means through which one person's pronouncement can be applied to another person's obligation to make this pronouncement. Again, let us consider the example of Kiddush. Through shomeah ka'oneh one person can recite Kiddush and this recitation can be related to and fulfill the obligation of all others who listen attentively.

However, according to Magen Avraham, the obligation of counting the omer is not fulfilled through producing a properly formulated pronouncement. Instead, each individual is required to engage in a conscious act of counting. The principle of shomeah ka'oneh cannot be applied to this obligation. One does not become a "counter" through shomeah ka'oneh.

A simple analogy will help illustrate this distinction. An organization sponsors a "walkathon". Supporters of the organization can participate in two ways. They can walk or they can sponsor a walker. The sponsor pledges a donation to the organization for every mile that the sponsored walker completes. On the day of the walkathon, the walkers and sponsors converge on the site of the event. The walkers embark on their walk and the sponsors stand on the sidelines. The sponsors are participating. They deeply identify with the walkers they have sponsored and feel very proud of their support for their walkers. At the end of the event, a medical team checks

---

[133] Rav Yisrael Meir Kagan, *Mishne Berurah*, 62:2.

[134] Rav Avraham Avlee, *Magen Avraham Commentary on Shulchan Aruch*, Orech Chayim 62:2.

the health of each walker. All of the walkers have elevated heart rates. They have enjoyed the cardiovascular benefits of the event. One of the sponsors asks a member of the medical team to check his heart rate. Should he expect to have enjoyed the same health benefits that the walkers have experienced? Of course not! He can take pride in his participation in the event. But he did not actually walk!

The principle of shomeah ka'oneh presents a similar phenomenon. The listener has participated. Through his participation, he fulfills his obligation. But he cannot be viewed as performing a conscious act of counting. Therefore, in the instance of counting the omer, shomeah ka'oneh cannot be applied.

Shavuot

And please, Hashem, our L-rd, make the words of Your Torah pleasant in our mouths and in the mouths of all Your people, the House of Israel. And may we and our offspring [and the offspring of our offspring] and the offspring of Your people, the House of Israel - all of us - be knowing of Your Name and studying Your Torah for its sake. Blessed are You, Hashem, Who teaches Torah to His people, Israel. (Morning Torah Blessings)

Seeking Truth

1. The blessings on the Torah

Each morning we recite the Berchot HaTorah – the blessings over the Torah. These blessings are composed of three components. They open with a reference to the commandment to study Torah. This is followed by petitioning Hashem to assist us in this study. The blessings conclude with an expression of gratitude to Hashem for selecting us from among the nations to be his Chosen People and to receive His Torah.

There are two interesting aspects of our petition. First, we ask that Hashem make the study of Torah pleasant for us. In other words, we ask not only for His assistance in securing success in our studies; we ask that the experience of study should be enjoyable.

Second, we ask that Hashem help us study for the proper purpose.[1] Why do we seek Hashem's help in guiding us to study for the proper purpose? Our discussion will focus upon this second issue.

Always, a person should engage in Torah and mitzvot even if not for their [true] purpose. For through [engaging in them] not for their [true] purpose, one comes to [engage in them] for their true purpose. (Mesechet Pesachim 50b)

[Regarding] any person who performs [the mitzvah] not for its [true] purpose, it would have been better for the person to have not been created. (Mesechet Berachot 7a)

2. Performing mitzvot for their true purpose

Before considering how our question might be answered, let us consider a related issue. The two statements above discuss the performance of commandments for personal gain. An example is performing mitzvot to conform to the standards of one's community. We can easily imagine a person who is not fully committed to observance but engages in Torah practices so that he or she will be accepted within the community. The first statement above encourages this behavior. The sage argues that through consistent engagement in Torah practice the person may advance in commitment. Eventually, the person will observe the commandments for their true purpose.

The second statement seems to contradict the first. This sage asserts that one who observes the commandments for some personal gain, is better to have not been created. How can these two statements be reconciled?

Rav Yitzchok Isaac Chaver suggests a simple and eloquent solution to this problem. He explains that the first statement encourages observance motivated by a personal agenda as a strategy for advancement. It addresses a person who would like to observe the Torah for its true

---

[1] Some versions of the blessings omit this reference to proper purpose.

purpose. However, he cannot move himself to observe the mitzvot for this exalted purpose. The sage encourages this person to think strategically. How can he motivate himself? He should identify and adopt a personal motivation as a step toward performing mitzvot for their true purpose. This person's ultimate goal is to perform the commandments for their true purpose. He is adopting a strategy to arrive at that goal. The second statement addresses a person who does not have a higher aspiration than his personal motivation. This person observes the commandments for a personal end and does not seek to advance himself or herself to a greater spiritual level. This person has perverted the mitzvot. He or she has made them a means for personal gain. It would have been better if this person had not been created.[2]

> Antignos of Socho received the tradition from Shimon the Righteous. He would say: Do not be as servants, who serve their master for the sake of reward. Rather, be as servants who serve their master not for the sake of reward. And the fear of Heaven should be upon you. (Mesechet Avot 1:3)

However, the science most needed for the [understanding of] the Torah is the most advanced science. It is the science of theology.[3] We are obligated to study it for the purpose of understanding and arriving at [the truth] of our Torah. But it is forbidden to study it for the purpose of gaining worldly benefits. (Rabbaynu Bachya ibn Paquda, Chovot HaLevavot, Introduction)

3. Mitzvot express love for and awe of Hashem

The above discussion distinguished between performing commandments for the proper reason and performing them for personal gain. What is the proper reason for observing mitzvot? The first statement above addresses this issue. The sage explains that we should aspire to serve Hashem and to observe His commandments as servants who serve their master naturally, without expectation of reward. Rambam – Maimonides – in his comments on this mishne, explains that we are to perform the commandments as an expression of our love of Hashem. He notes that this sage adds that we should also be motivated by our awe of Hashem. In other words, one who is deeply in love wishes to fulfill the wishes of the beloved. There is no consideration of personal gain. The needs and desires of the self are subdued by the drive to serve the beloved. Similarly, one who is in awe of a king performs his sovereign's wishes without thought of personal gain. It is a simple and natural response to recognition of their relative stations.

Rabbaynu Bachya discusses the study of theology – within which he includes the study of Torah. He explains that one's purpose must be to seek truth and understanding. It is forbidden to study Torah for personal gain.

Is Torah different from other mitzvot? Do we perform other mitzvot in service of Hashem but study Torah in service of truth? This is not Rabbaynu Bachya's contention. Torah study is a means of serving Hashem.[4] However, one must distinguish between the objective that is inherent in an action and its higher purpose.

---

[2] Rav Yitzchok Isaac Chaver, Ohr Torah, Commentary on Ma'a lot HaTorah.
[3] Rabbaynu Bachya describes this science as dealing with "knowing Hashem the Blessed One, knowing His Torah, and other spiritual matters, such as [the study of] the soul, the intellect, and the angels".
[4] See Rambam, Sefer HaMitzvot, Mitzvat Aseh 5.

4. Objective and purpose

An illustration will help clarify this distinction. Every organization – including commercial ones – should have a clearly defined mission. Is it correct for a commercial organization to describe its mission as enriching its owners? This is not the mission. The mission is the specific objective of its business. For a clothing retailer, the mission may be to provide customers with high quality evening-wear and excellent service. Through these means the retailer seeks to attire its customers in stylish and well-tailored outfits. This is the mission or the inherent objective of the business. Of course, if the business meets this objective but loses money each quarter, its owners will close it. This is because in addition to this mission, the business has an ultimate purpose. It must make a profit for its owners.

Rabbaynu Bachya is explaining that the inherent objective of Torah study must be the pursuit of truth. Of course, he agrees that this pursuit is a means of serving Hashem. When one studies Torah to gain recognition or for some other personal end, this person is not engaged in authentic Torah study. The perversion of the objective alters the very identity of the activity.

5. Torah study is unique

Let us now return to our original question. Why do we petition Hashem to assist us in studying Torah for its true purpose? From Rabbaynu Bachya's comments an important distinction arises between the study of Torah and the performance of other mitzvot. If one performs other mitzvot motivated by a personal objective, the performance remains valid. Consider a person who takes hold of and lifts the four species on Sukkot so everyone can admire his or her beautiful etrog – citron. As long as the person intends to fulfill the mitzvah, the performance is valid. The mitzvah is fulfilled. However, if one studies to earn the admiration of others and not in search of the truth, the fulfillment of the mitzvah of Torah study is impacted. By definition, study is a search for truth. When this objective is compromised, so is the fulfillment of the mitzvah. For this reason, we ask Hashem to help us tudy for the true objective – to discover the truth.

6. Torah study: searching for truth

This discussion has addressed two important issues regarding Torah study. Why study Torah? How do we overcome the natural resistance to increasing our commitment to Torah study? Torah study is a search for truth. We live in the information age. The enormous information market demonstrates that we want to be informed and we want to understand the world around us. Torah study provides us with a more profound and meaningful understanding of our world and our lives.

Our sages recognized that commitment to Torah study can be challenging and they invited us to be strategic. They suggested that we adopt, as an expedient, a personal motivator. With time, our commitment will strengthen and our artificial motivator will be replaced by the drive to seek truth.

Inconvenient Truths

1. The significance of the narrative portions of the Torah

Shavuot celebrates Matan Torah – receiving the Torah at Mount Sinai. Rambam – Maimonides – explains that, "Hashem selected Israel to be His portion. He crowned them with the commandments and He made known to them the manner of His service…"[5] At Sinai, we received the commandments and through these Hashem taught us how He is to be served. However, the Torah is composed of more than its commandments. It includes an account of creation and it describes important early events in the development of humanity. It includes the history of our nation. It describes the lives of our Patriarchs, the exile in Egypt, our redemption from bondage, Revelation, our travels in the wilderness, and the earliest stages of our conquest of the Land of Israel.

Much of the narrative material is important because it provides the foundation and context for the Torah's commandments. The account of Revelation, provides the foundation for observance of the commandments. The story of our exile in Egypt and our redemption from bondage provides the context for many mitzvot that recall aspects of our exile and redemption.

In short, some of the Torah's narrative portions are accounted for easily. Other narrative portions are not as readily explained. The Torah provides detailed accounts of episodes in the lives of the Patriarchs. What is the Torah teaching us through these portions?

One purpose of this material is explained by Rambam:

(And) all that is included in the Scripture (i.e. that) speaks ill of those who possess evil traits and deficient character traits, that denunciates their memory, and the praise of the righteous, and their eminence, the intent (of these condemnations and praises) is only as I have said to you. (It is) so that people will go in the way of these (the righteous) and distance themselves from the ways of these (the wicked).[6]

These comments suggest that some narrative portions of the Torah instruct us in proper values and behaviors that are not explicitly included within the commandments. The Torah teaches about the Patriarchs so that we can emulate them.

And there was a famine in the land. Avram descended to Egypt to sojourn there because the famine was intense in the land. (Beresheit 12:10)

2. Criticizing the Patriarchs

This understanding of the Torah's intent in its treatment of the lives of the Patriarchs impacts our approach to the study of its narratives. The above passage introduces an incident in the life of Avraham and Sarah. Hashem told Avraham that He would give his descendants the Land of Cana'an. Avraham travels through the land that will be the home of his descendants. A famine strikes the land and Avraham travels to Egypt to find relief. He is afraid the Egyptians will covet Sarah. They will kill him and take her. He asks Sarah to participate in a deception. She should identify herself as his sister. Avraham anticipates that suitors will appeal to him – Sarah's supposed brother – for her hand. He will make demands and place other obstacles before each suitor. In this way, he will delay the marriage and escape with Sarah.

Avraham does not foresee Paroh emerging as one of the suitors. Paroh does not need Avraham's permission to take his supposed sister as a wife. He assumes that Sarah's brother will welcome her marriage to the king.[7] He takes Sarah into his household without seeking Avraham's approval. Sarah and Avraham are saved only though Hashem's intervention.

---

[5] Rabbaynu Moshe ben Maimon (Rambam) Mishne Torah, Hilchot Avodah Zarah 1:3.

[6] R' Moshe ben Maimon (Rambam) Commentary on the Mishne, Intro. to Mes. Avot, chapter 5.

Ramban comments:

You should know that Avraham our Patriarch inadvertently committed a great sin in bringing his righteous wife into a situation of potential sin because of his fear that they would kill him. He should have trusted in Hashem that He would save him, his wife, and his possessions – for Hashem has the power to assist and to save. Also, in his going forth from the land (of Cana'an) – regarding which Hashem had commanded him from the outset – because of the famine he committed an iniquity. This is because Hashem would redeem him from death in famine.[8]

According to Ramban, Avraham committed two sins in his response to the famine. First, he abandoned the Land of Cana'an. Second, he represented Sarah as his sister. Ramban acknowledges that this second sin was inadvertent. It was a calculated strategy. However, it precipitated Paroh taking Sarah into his harem. Ramban's position is that Avraham should have relied upon Hashem to protect him from harm.

3. Objections to criticism of the Patriarchs

Rav Moshe Feinstein Zt"l's response to these comments was that they should be erased![9] Don Yitzchak Abravanel also rejects Ramban's position. His response is based upon two considerations. First, he cites the comments of Rabbaynu Nissim who explains that Avraham acted completely properly in his situation. Second, he objects to Ramban ascribing a sin to Avraham.[10] Rav Moshe based his criticism of Ramban's comments on this second objection.

And Hashem said to Moshe and to Aharon: Since you did not work to make them have faith in Me to sanctify Me in the eyes of Bnai Yisrael, therefore, you will not bring this assembly to the land that I gave to you. (BeMidbar 20:12)[11]

4. The Patriarchs are not above sin

This second objection is odd. It seems to attribute infallibility to Avraham. The Torah does not regard any human being as above sin. The Torah describes Moshe as that greatest of all prophets. "There did not arise another prophet in Israel like Moshe who Hashem knew face to face."[12] Yet, the Torah ascribes sin to Moshe. In the above passage, Hashem addresses Moshe and Aharon. He tells them that they will not bring the nation into the Land of Cana'an because they sinned and failed to sanctify Hashem before the people. If even Moshe is capable of sin, why can Ramban not criticize Avraham's behavior? In order to answer this question, we must more carefully consider Hashem's comments to Moshe and Aharon.

We will begin with a brief outline of the circumstances in which the sin was committed. The Jewish people were in the wilderness. They were camped at a location that did not have a water supply. They complained to Moshe and criticized him for bringing them to such a place.

---

[7] R' Nissim ben Reuven Gerondi (Ran), Commentary on Sefer Beresheit 12:11-13.

[8] Rabbaynu Moshe ben Nachman (Ramban), Commentary on Sefer Beresheit 12:10.

[9] Rav Yisroel Chait shared Rav Moshe's comments with me. I asked if he had heard his rebbe's remarks first-hand. He responded that he had and quoted Rav Moshe verbatim in the original Yiddish.

[10] Don Yitzchak Abravanel, Commentary on Sefer Beresheit, Parshat Lech Lecha.

[11] Translation based upon R' Sa'adia Gaon and Ralbag. Various other translations are abound.

[12] Sefer Devarim 34:10.

Hashem instructed Moshe to take his staff, to join with Aharon, and gather the people before an appointed rock. He should speak to the rock and it will give forth water. Moshe and Aharon gathered the people before the rock. Moshe then rebuked them. He described them as rebels. He challenged them rhetorically, "Will we bring water forth from this rock?" He then stuck the rock with his staff and water came forth.

5. Moshe's sin

The passages do not clearly identify the aspect of Moshe's behavior that was sinful. Because of this ambiguity the commentators present a number of opinions. Rambam explains that Moshe's sin was that he became angry with the people and described them as rebels. In Moshe, this behavior was a desecration of Hashem's name.

They learned from all his movements and words. Through them, they hoped to merit riches in this world and the next. How could he express anger, it is among the wicked behaviors!...

(And) he was not speaking with simple people and not with those who lack all virtue. Rather, (he spoke) with people whom the least among them was comparable to Yechezkiel the son of Buzi. All that he said or did they studied. When they saw that he was angry they said about him... he is not one who has deficient character traits. Were it not that he knew that Hashem had become angry with us for asking for water... he (Moshe) would not have been angry. But we do not find that Hashem, the Exalted One, in speaking to him (Moshe) was angry or outraged...[13]

According to Rambam, Moshe was a model for the people. He taught the people the Torah he received from Hashem. He also taught the people through demonstration. His actions and words provided instruction. The people understood Moshe's greatness and gave their attention to his actions and words. They studied them. Moshe's sin was that in his anger he communicated to the people a false message. His actions suggested that Hashem was angry with the nation.

6. Two principles of Biblical study

We can extract two very important principles from Rambam's comments:

- The actions and behaviors of the righteous should be studied. They provide lessons in proper conduct and insight into true values. Study should focus not only upon the actions of Moshe but upon those of other tzadikim – righteous individuals – in the Torah.
- When the righteous sin, as did Moshe, the Torah must be explicit in identifying the behavior as sinful. The Torah is completely frank about Moshe's sin and reiterates it multiple times. This is because the tzadikim in the Torah are intended to be studied as role models. If their sins are not openly acknowledged by the Torah, then in seeking to emulate their righteousness we will assimilate their flaws.

Now, Abravanel's criticism of Ramban is understood. He is not suggesting that Avraham is above sin. The Torah notes his errors and alludes to his failings. However, ultimately, we are expected to learn from Avraham's actions. We can assume that if Avraham had sinned in the Egypt episode, the Torah would have explicitly faulted him. Abravanel's criticism is that the Torah does not indicate that Avraham sinned in this incident. Therefore, Ramban does not have

---

[13] R' Moshe ben Maimon (Rambam) Commentary on the Mishne, Intro. to Mes. Avot, chp 4.

the authority to ascribe sin to him. Furthermore, in ascribing sin to Avraham, Ramban undermines the Torah's objective. Its objective is that we should study, understand, and emulate Avraham. If Ramban's position is adopted, rather than emulate Avraham's behavior we will disown it.[14]

And it was in the days of the judging of the judges that there was a famine in the land. A man from Bet Lechem, Yehudah, went to dwell in the fields of Moav – he, his wife, and his two sons.
(Megilat Ruth 1:1)

7. The marginalization of leaders

To this point we have discussed methodology in the study of Torah. Rav Moshe Feinstein and Abravanel criticized Ramban for apparently abandoning this method. We cannot know how Ramban would respond to this criticism. However, it is unlikely that he would dispute its basic premise. He would agree that, in general, we study the lives and actions of the tzadikim in the Torah and learn from them. Unfortunately, in our times, some "scholars" reject this premise. Let us consider this modern phenomenon.

The first passage of Megilat Ruth tells us that the events it describes took place during the period of the Shoftim – the Judges. The Shoftim led the nation after the death of Yehoshua. They continued to provide leadership until this role was assumed by Samuel, the Prophet – Shemuel HaNavi.

Commenting of the above passage the midrash declares, "Woe is upon the generation that judges its judges".[15] The message of the midrash is that the spiritual leadership of the Shoftim was compromised by the people's attitude toward them. They were very critical of the Shoftim and sought to find fault in these leaders. Through diminishing the spiritual stature of these leaders, the people weakened their spiritual authority.

8. Responding to inconvenient truths

This phenomenon needs to be understood. Why did the people denigrate and dismiss the moral authority of their leaders? This is a predictable response to confrontation with inconvenient truths. The responsibility of the judges was to lead; this included rebuking the people when appropriate. When rebuked we can respond by giving our attention to the issue and reassessing our actions. Alternatively, we can respond by discrediting our critic and thereby, dismissing his unsettling reproach.

The same dynamic can also influence our study of the Torah. The Torah's objective is not to teach us self-evident and universally appealing lessons. Hashem gave us the Torah because we are challenged in seeking and finding the truth. Therefore, it is inevitable that at times the views and values of the Torah will conflict with our own. How do we respond to these inconvenient truths?

Some will respond by finding fault in the messenger and the message. The behaviors of the Patriarchs and Matriarchs will be dismissed as expressions of cultural biases. The laws of the

---

[14] Rav Chait reported that Rav Moshe explained his own criticism of Ramban in this manner.
[15] Midrash Rabba, Megilat Ruth Introduction, 1. The comment of the midrash is based upon an ambiguity in the phrasing of the passage. The phrase "judging of the judges" can mean the judges were performing judgement or it can mean the judges were being judged.

Torah that conflict with our own values will be cast aside as residue from an archaic, less enlightened era.

This response is both self-serving and dishonest. It is self-serving because it is motivated by resistance to considering inconvenient truths. It is dishonest, because we should expect that a revealed Torah will conflict with our own human and more limited perceptions and positions. Those conflicts are not suggestive of obsolescence; they are consequences of the Torah's Divine origin.

A more honest approach is to recognize that inevitably some aspects of the Torah will be difficult for us to understand from our contemporary perspective. Nonetheless, these aspects should be honestly and objectively considered. Through this approach we can discover the wisdom of the Torah and refine our own views and values.

And Moshe went forth from the nation to greet the L-rd from the encampment. And they stood at the foot of the mountain. (Shemot 19:17)

The Mission of the Jewish People

The *pasuk* describes Bnai Yisrael as standing at the foot of Sinai. However, the Talmud comments that the nation stood under the mountain. Hashem uprooted Sinai and held it above Bnai Yisrael. He told the people that if they would not accept the Torah, they would be buried under the mountain.[16] If the comments of the Sages are intended to be understood literally, then it is strange that the Torah only makes reference to such a wonder through an allusion. Had this event actually occurred, the revelation at Sinai was very different from the description provided by the explicit meaning of the passages.

It seems that the Talmud is communicating to us two ideas. First, the development and existence of Bnai Yisrael is not a chance historical event. Bnai Yisrael was created and fashioned by Hashem. The nation was carefully nurtured in order to prepare it for revelation at Sinai and its acceptance of the Torah. This was Bnai Yisrael's destiny and its mission. Second, the exodus from Egypt and the awesome events of Sinai were essential elements of this process of preparation. These wonders were designed to provide overpowering evidence of the omnipotence of Hashem and revelation. They were designed to assure that Bnai Yisrael accept its mission. In short, Bnai Yisrael was created and formed for the moment of revelation; acceptance of the Torah was virtually predetermined or compelled. It was as if the mountain was raised over the heads of the people.

"And Hashem said to him, "Descend and then ascend – you and Ahron with you. And the Kohanim and the nation should not violate the boundary lest He send destruction among them." (Shemot 19:24)

Hashem's influence descends upon Sinai. Boundaries are set surrounding the mountain. The people are not permitted to approach the mountain beyond these boundaries. Hashem commands Moshe to remind the people that these boundaries cannot be violated. If this injunction is ignored, they will be severely punished.

---

[16] Mesechet Shabbat 88a.

Rashi explains that Moshe was permitted to ascend to the highest point on the mountain. Ahron could accompany him during most of his ascent. The *Kohanim* were allowed to ascend to a lower point. The rest of the nation was forbidden from approaching Sinai.[17]

What was the meaning of the boundaries? Why were these various individuals and groups permitted to ascend to different levels of the mountain?

Maimonides, explains that we cannot achieve complete understanding of the Almighty. Our material nature limits our ability. We can never completely overcome this limit. However, we can attain some understanding of Hashem. The level of comprehension we can acquire varies. This comprehension varies directly with one's spiritual level. Moshe reached the highest possible spiritual plane. He achieved a correspondingly profound level of understanding of the Divine nature.

Maimonides seems to suggest that this concept is represented by the various boundaries. Ascending the mountain represents attaining understanding of the Almighty. Moshe could climb to the highest point on the mountain. This symbolizes the unique understanding he achieved of the Almighty. Ahron was not as spiritually perfected as Moshe. He could not attain the same profound comprehension. This is represented by the prohibition against accompanying Moshe to his destination. The *Kohanim* and the nation were less spiritually developed. They were assigned boundaries corresponding with their levels. Their boundaries represent the levels of understanding attainable.

Hashem warns each group against trespassing beyond its assigned border. A person must recognize personal limitation. Passing beyond one's boundary represents striving for a level of understanding beyond one's ability. This will result in disaster. The individual who overreaches will not properly understand the Divine essence. Instead, this individual will develop a flawed conception. In order to avoid false conclusion regarding Hashem, each person must respect personal limitations.[18]

And the L-rd spoke all of these things saying: (Shemot 20:1)

The Challenge of Loving One's Neighbor

1. Serving Hashem through how we treat one another

The central element of the *parsha* is the Decalogue – the *Aseret HaDibrot*. The Decalogue is composed of ten statements which include a number of commandments. Why were these commandments selected by Hashem to be presented to the assembled nation and to be engraved on two tablets of stone? Rabbeinu Sa'adia and others suggest that all of the Torah's 613 commandments can be subsumed within the ten statements of the Decalogue.

The Decalogue reflects the diversity of the Torah's commandments and gives expression to one of the most remarkable aspects of our religious perspective. Our service and commitment to Hashem is inseparable from our responsibility to one another. The Decalogue commands us to serve Hashem exclusively and also admonishes us to not steal from one another or covet our neighbor's possessions. We can only serve Hashem if we honor and love one another.

---

[17] Rabbaynu Shlomo ben Yitzchak (Rashi), *Commentary on Sefer Shemot* 19:24.

[18] Rabbaynu Moshe ben Maimon (Rambam) *Moreh Nevuchim*, volume 1, chapter 5.

Do not covet you neighbor's wife, his servant, his maid-servant, his ox, his donkey, and anything that is your neighbor's. (Shemot 20:13)

2. How does one escape jealousy?

The Decalogue orders us to not covet our neighbor's spouse or possessions. Many of the commentators ask how the Torah can require that we regulate our feelings. How can we suppress the involuntary reaction of coveting? One of the interesting responses to this question is formulated by Rav Yoel Frumkin.[19] His comments deal with both coveting and other forms of jealousy. He explains that jealousy is a consequence of twisted thinking. He enumerates a number of perverse ideas that underlie jealousy. Among these notions is one that we would not naturally associate with jealousy. He points out that we are all brothers and sisters. We should rejoice in each other's success and exhilarate in each other's accomplishments. If instead our happiness is overwhelmed by our jealousy, then we demonstrate a complete lack of fraternal love.[20]

Let us consider this insight. The members of a family will inevitably have their rivalries. But in a healthy family these rivalries are tempered by the identification that the members have with one another. If one receives an honor or is appointed to a position of esteem the other siblings might feel an instinctual pang of jealousy but these siblings will recognize that they should rejoice in the success of their brother or sister. So, any jealousy would be tempered by their sense of fraternity. Bnai Yisrael is a family. We are a nation of brothers and sisters. Perhaps, a passing pang of jealousy is natural. But the harboring of this jealousy and its persistence indicates a sad lack of fraternal love.

And they said to one another: We are certainly guilty for our brother – that we saw the sorrow of his soul when he pleaded to us and we did not listen. Therefore, this affliction has come upon us. (Beresheit 42:21)

3. Compassion for those we must scorn

How far does the obligation to love one another extend? One of the most remarkable implications of our duty to love one another emerges from considering the sin of Yosef's brothers. The brothers considered killing Yosef. They reconsidered and instead, sold him into servitude. Eventually, the brothers recognized that they had sinned in their behavior toward Yosef. They articulated this realization. But the brothers' description of their sin is bewildering. We would expect them to confess that they had sinned in selling their brother into servitude. They do not focus on selling Yosef. Instead, the brothers declare that they sinned in disregarding Yosef's pleas. Why did the brothers focus on this aspect of their behavior?

Rabbeinu Ovadia Sforno explains that the brothers clearly remembered the deliberations that led to taking action against Yosef. To them, it was apparent that Yosef was self-absorbed and determined to dominate them. They understood that the sons of Yaakov had a destiny and they feared that Yosef would attempt to pervert that destiny for his own purposes. It was obvious to them that their father did not understand Yosef or the threat that he posed to their nascent nation. They felt that they were ethically compelled to remove Yosef from the family before he destroyed it.

---

[19] R' Yoel Frumkin, a student of R' Chaim Volozhin. Best known for his comm. on the mishnah.
[20] Rav Yoel Frumkin, Final testament. Included in *Asher Yitzaveh*, Ed. Anonymous, pp. 16-17.

The brothers did not condemn themselves for the action that they took against Yosef. They acted according to their understanding of the threat posed by Yosef and out of their commitment to the highest values. But, they did recognize that they had sinned in their callousness toward their brother. They declared, "How were we not moved by the cries of our brother? Why did we not recognize the tragedy of selling our own brother? Why were we not horrified by the prospect of cutting off our own flesh and blood?" They did not reproach themselves for the actions they took against Yosef; they condemned their cruelty, their insensitivity, their callousness.[21]

This is a profound message. When they sold Yosef the brothers believed that they had no other choice. They concluded that it was imperative to sever him from the family. They believed that their extreme measures were not only justified but demanded. Yet, they sinned in their callousness. They failed to recognize the tragedy in a brother acting against a brother.

How great is our obligation to love one another! Even when we must condemn or even eliminate from our community one its members, we must be aware of our brotherhood and mourn the tragedy of our loss.

If we must feel this fraternal bond even with one who deserves to be excised from our community, how great is our obligation to treat every Jew with love and compassion! Brothers and sisters do not always agree. Sometimes their differences are irreconcilable. Only the most extreme circumstances justify turning our backs toward another Jew. And if, G-d forbid, that circumstance should befall us, we should feel heart-broken as we turn away from one of our own.

"I am Hashem your G-d that took you out from the land of Egypt, from the house of bondage." (Shemot 20:2)

This passage is the first statement of the Decalogue. Maimonides understands this statement as a mitzvah. We are commanded to accept the existence of Hashem. Rav Elchanan Wasserman Ztl explains that this conviction is easily achieved. The complexity of the universe gives witness to the existence of a Creator. Nonetheless, many deny the existence of Hashem. Rav Elchanan explains it is not the inadequacy of the evidence that causes these denials. Instead, there is a basic human bias that interferes with recognizing Hashem. Once a person accepts that there is a Creator, one is longer one's own master. This Creator has the right to mandate action and demand obedience. Conversely, if one denies the existence of the Creator, one is free to act as one pleases. We do not need to answer to a higher authority. An interesting incident illustrates this point. There was a student of the Volozin Yeshiva that abandoned the Torah. Instead, he devoted himself to the study of philosophy and joined the Haskala movement. The student had occasion to visit his former yeshiva. There, he met with Rav Chaim Soloveitchik Ztl who was serving as Rosh HaYeshiva. Rav Chaim asked the young to explain his reasons for abandoning the life of Torah and pursuing worthless endeavors. The young man was shocked by Rav Chaim's confrontational tone. After recovering, the young man responded. He explained that he was troubled by various doubts and questions regarding the Torah. He could not find answers for his questions. So, he abandoned the Torah. Rav Chaim told the young man that he was willing to answer every one of his questions. However, the young man must first agree to answer a single

---

[21] Rabbaynu Ovadia Sforno, *Commentary on Sefer Beresheit*, 42:21. See also ibid. 37:25.

question. Rav Chaim's asked, "When did these various questions occur to you? Was it before you experienced the taste of sin of afterwards?" The young man was embarrassed. He responded that only after committing a serious sin had he begun to be bothered by questions. Rav Chaim responded, "If that is the case, these are not questions. Rather, they are answers you sought to excuse your evil actions." Rav Chaim continued, "I am sure that if you merit to achieve old age, your desires and yetzer harah will diminish. Then you will realize that you do not really have any questions. So, why not repent now?"

I am Hashem your G-d who brought you forth from the Land of Egypt. (Shemot 20:2)

Revelation: Parts I and II

1. The first statement of the Decalogue is a commandment

The above passage is the first of the statements of the Decalogue. The balance of the Decalogue is composed of commandments. This first statement seems to be an introduction of the rest of the Decalogue. The speaker and author of the Decalogue identifies Himself as the deity who redeemed the nation from Egypt.

This is not the view generally accepted among our Sages. Our Sages maintain that this statement is a commandment. The Talmud explains that 613 commandments are included in the text of the Torah that Moshe received at Sinai. The Talmud explains that although the number of commandments is not specifically stated in the text of the Torah, there is an allusion to the number in the text. Where is this allusion?

The Torah states, *"The Torah was commanded to us by Moshe. It is a legacy for the assembly of Yaakov."* (Devarim 33:4) Each letter of the Hebrew alphabet has a numerical value. The numerical values of the letters composing the word Torah is 611. The Talmud explains that this corresponds with the number of commandments the people received from Hashem, through the agency of Moshe. Hashem taught Moshe 611 of the Torah's commandments. Moshe taught them to the people. The Talmud adds that two other commandments were not received through Moshe. These the people heard directly from Hashem. They heard Hashem say, "I am Hashem your G-d, etc." They also heard Him say "You shall have on other gods before Me." The addition of these commandments to the 611 that were received through Moshe, provides a total of 613 *mitzvot*.

The discussion in the Talmud clearly treats the first statement of the Decalogue – "I am Hashem you G-d" as one of the 613 commandments. Based on this discussion, most of our Sages concluded that the Decalogue's opening statement is indeed a commandment.

What does this statement command? According to Maimonides, this statement commands that we know or accept that Hashem is the cause of all that exists and that all existence is sustained by His will.[22]

---

[22] This position engenders a number of problems. First, we assume that commandments are volitional. In other words, one who chooses to perform the commandment has it within his power to do so. Issues of conviction do not seem to meet this criterion. One cannot will oneself to believe in something of which he is not convinced. Second, specifically Maimonides' formulation of the commandment is confusing. In his Mishne Torah he states that one is obligated to know the existence of Hashem. In his Sefer HaMitzvot – as the text is typically translated – he states that one must believe in Hashem's existence. Both of these issues have

This first commandment of the Decalogue includes an interesting nuance of expression. The Hebrew language has two words for the first person singular pronoun – "I". One is *ani* and the other is *anochi*. The two words are near synonyms. However, they are not completely interchangeable.

> And Yaakov said to his father: I (anochi) am Esav your first born. I have done as you commanded me. Please arise and eat from my game so that you will bless me. (Beresheit 27:19)

> And Yaakov said to Shimon and Leyve: You have disturbed me by evoking hatred against me among the dwellers of the land – the Canaanites and that Prezites. I (ve'ani) am few in number. They will gather against me, strike me, and destroy me and my household. (Beresheit 34:30)

2. The difference between *ani* and *anochi*

Rav Yosef Dov Soloveitchik *Zt"l* suggests that the word *ani* is a simple first person singular pronoun. It does not, in itself, communicate anything beyond the identity of the speaker. *Anochi* is a more expressive term. It communicates the uniqueness of the speaker. *Anochi*'s the message is often "it is I and no other."[23]

The two passages above illustrate the contrast between *ani* and *anochi*. In the first passage Yaakov disguises himself as Esav in order to secure the blessings intended for his older brother. He approaches his father. Yitzchak's eyesight is failing and he asks his visitor to identify himself. Yaakov responds, "I am Esav your first born." Yaakov is responding to his father's uncertainty regarding the identity of his visitor. He responds: It is I, Esav, your first born. The term *anochi* is used because Yaakov is telling Yitzchak: It is I and no other.

In the second passage above Yaakov chastises his sons for destroying the city of Shechem. He tells them that they have incited the land's inhabitants against him. He says to them: I am a leader of a small group. He does not intend to emphasis the "I". Therefore, he employs the pronoun *ani*.[24]

Based on this analysis, can any message be derived from the use of the word *anochi* in the first statement of the Decalogue? Let us begin by considering another instance in which the word *anochi* is used.

> And Moshe said to G-d: Who am I (anochi) that I should go to Paroh and will I bring forth Bnai Yisrael from Egypt? And He said: For I will be with you. And this is the sign that I (anochi) have sent you – when you bring forth the nation from Egypt you will serve G-d upon this mountain. *(Shemot 3:11-12).*

3. Moshe's objection to his mission

In his first prophecy, Hashem spoke to Moshe and informed him that he had been selected to lead forth Bnai Yisrael from Egypt. Moshe questioned his suitability for this mission. He said to Hashem, "Who am I to challenge Paroh and demand that he release his slaves?" Moshe identifies himself with the word *anochi*. Based on the discussion above, this is to be

---

received extensive attention elsewhere.

[23] Rav Yosef Dov Soloveitchick, recorded lecture on aseret HaDibrot.

[24] The above examples support Rav Soloveitchik's interpretation of the words *ani* and *anochi*. However, it must be acknowledged that there are instances in which the use of these two words does not seem to conform to Rav Soloveitchik's view.

expected. Moshe seems to be asking Hashem why he has been selected. Why he and not someone more appropriate?

Hashem responds, "For I will be with you." Here too the word *anochi* is used. However, the reason for the use of this word and not the word *ani* is less obvious.

In order to understand Hashem's use of *anochi*, Moshe's objection must be reconsidered. Moshe could not understand how he could influence or coerce Paroh into releasing Bnai Yisrael. He protested that he had neither the eloquence to persuade nor the power to force Paroh. Hashem responded, "I will be with you." He was not contesting Moshe's analysis. He was not suggesting that Moshe could accomplish the task he was assigned. Hashem responded that He – Hashem – would be the agent of Bnai Yisrael's liberation. Moshe would not secure his people's freedom. Without revealing to Moshe the specific events that would soon occur, Hashem responded that He would be involved in the forthcoming events in an unprecedented manner.[25]

4. Hashem tells Moshe that He will be with him

Now, Hashem's use of the word *anochi* is explained. He responded to Moshe that He would be with Moshe. The emphasis was upon His uniqueness. Because He will be Moshe's companion on this mission and He is omnipotent, the otherwise unachievable is possible.

Hashem explained to Moshe that the Egypt redemption would be brought about through a manifest expression of divine intervention without precedent. Hashem had performed miracles for the *Avot* – the patriarchs – but these were subtle or minor compared to those that would be performed in Egypt. In Egypt, Hashem would reveal Himself as ruler over all creation. He would demonstrate His omnipotence to the Egyptians, Bnai Yisrael, and humanity.

From the passages in the Torah one cannot determine the level of detail that Hashem shared with Moshe at this point. However, it is clear that Hashem communicated to him that something unique and unprecedented was about to take place.

5. The sign offered to Moshe that Hashem will be his companion

Hashem then provided Moshe with a sign that confirmed His message. After emerging from their bondage, the nation would serve Hashem at Sinai. The commentators note that this is a difficult sign to understand. Hashem understood that Moshe required some assurance that He would be with him. He provided, as a sign, news of an event that will occur many months in the future. How would this sign reassure Moshe?

As explained above, Hashem had told Moshe that an unprecedented event was to take place in Egypt. Hashem would reveal and involve himself in the redemption of Bnai Yisrael to a degree that was never before experienced by humanity. He anticipated Moshe would receive this news with some degree of confusion. Moshe would not understand why Hashem would take such extraordinary measures on behalf of Bnai Yisrael.

Hashem responded that the explanation lay in the events that would take place at Sinai. At Sinai, the nation would serve Hashem. This Sinai experience would be a unique event in the experience of humanity. Hashem would reveal Himself to humanity and speak to Moshe and the

---

[25] Many commentators make this point. Some express themselves more clearly than others. See Rashi, Rabbaynu Yosef Bechor Shur, Emek Davar.

nation. The nation would experience Divine Revelation. Sinai would represent the initiation of a new stage in Hashem's relationship with humanity.

The *Avot* and other special individuals had sought out Hashem and discovered Him. They experienced their own personal revelations. However, Hashem had never before revealed Himself though manifestly interacting and demonstrating His presence to a nation. At Sinai, He would speak to Moshe and to Bnai Yisrael. Sinai would not be a private and personal revelation like those experienced by the *Avot*. It would be a public and manifest revelation. In other words, the Sinai Revelation would be the beginning of a new relationship between Hashem and humanity. No longer would Hashem be revealed only to those who relentlessly pursued Him. Now, each and every person would have manifest evidence of Hashem and His omnipotence.

This explained to Moshe Hashem's extraordinarily overt involvement in the Egypt redemption. The goal of the redemption was not only to liberate an oppressed people. The redemption was the opening act of a very pubic manifestation of Hashem's existence, His omnipotence, and His providence.

Hashem was not telling Moshe that the events of Sinai – once they occurred – would be a sign or provide evidence of His partnership with Moshe in Egypt. He told Moshe that the explanation for everything He had told him about Egypt lay in understanding the destined future of the nation – in appreciating the meaning of the Sinai experience.

6. The phases of Revelation

Now, let us return to the Decalogue. In its first statement Hashem says, "I am Hashem your G-d who brought you forth from the Land of Egypt." Hashem identifies Himself as *anochi*. Why does He use this form of the first person singular pronoun? Hashem is introducing Himself – He who now addresses the nation – as the G-d who revealed Himself in Egypt. He is explaining that the events of Egypt were the precursor to this wondrous moment. That omnipotent G-d who had triumphed over Paroh and over nature itself now spoke to the nation and gave His commandments to the people. In Egypt, He revealed Himself to the nation as the omnipotent creator and ruler of the universe. At Sinai, He introduced Himself as the G-d who was encountered in Egypt and who would now speak to the people as teacher and lawgiver.

He identifies Himself as *anochi*. He declares, "It is I – the G-d who redeemed you with wonders and miracles. I am the one who now speaks to you as teacher and lawgiver." In this introduction Hashem provided to the people a meaning for their experiences. Suddenly, they understood all that had occurred to them and its purpose. They had encountered the omnipotent creator in Egypt so that now they would understand and appreciate the G-d who addresses them.

I am Hashem your G-d Who took you out from the Land of Egypt, from the house of slaves. (Shemot 20:2)

Notes on the first statement of the Decalogue

1. The description of Hashem as Redeemer.

Parshat Yitro describes the communication of the *Aseret HaDibrot* – the Decalogue – to Bnai Yisrael. The first statement of Decalogue is contained in the above passage. In this statement, Hashem introduces Himself as the G-d Who redeemed the Bnai Yisrael from Egypt. Our Sages note that Hashem does not introduce Himself as Creator. Instead, He describes

Himself as the redeemer of Bnai Yisrael. Why does He choose to refer to Himself in this manner? Rashi quotes the Midrash as explaining that Hashem was communicating that the redemption of the nation from Egypt was in-itself an adequate event to bind the nation in service to Hashem.[26] In other words, the message of the Hashem's statement is that because He redeemed the nation from Egypt, the nation owes its service to Him.

Rav Yosef Dov Soloveitchik *Zt"l* explains that this first statement establishes the unique relationship between Hashem and Bnai Yisrael. This relationship was established or demonstrated through His rescue of the nation from oppression and the annihilation by the Egyptians. In this context – as a basis for the unique bond between Hashem and His nation – His role as Creator is not relevant. Acknowledgement and service to Hashem as Creator are responsibilities shared by all of humanity. He is the Creator of all humankind. Redemption from Egypt provides a basis for service to Hashem that is unique to Bnai Yisrael.

2. The purpose of the first statement of the Decalogue.

Rav Soloveitchik's interpretation of the Midrash's comments provides an important insight into the purpose and objective of this first statement of the Decalogue. The objective of this statement is not to educate the nation regarding Hashem's nature or His relationship with the universe and reality. If this were the intention of the statement, then it would have indeed been appropriate for Hashem to introduce Himself as the Creator and Sovereign of the universe. This description provides a more fundamental understanding to Hashem's relationship to all that exists than reference to His redemption of Bnai Yisrael. Instead, the objective of this introduction is to establish a basis or to serve as a preamble to the commandments that will follow. Bnai Yisrael are poised to enter into an exclusive relationship with Hashem. This introduction explains the foundation, rational, and the ethical imperative that underlie this relationship. We are compelled to serve the One who redeemed us from certain annihilation in Egypt.[27]

---

[26] Rabbaynu Shlomo ben Yitzchak (Rashi), *Commentary on Sefer Shemot* 20:2.

[27] Maimonides explains in his Sefer HaMitzvot that this passage is one of the 613 commandments of the Torah. He describes the commandment as recognition of Hashem as Cause of all existence. Others disagree and do not regard this statement as a commandment. Nachmanides, in his glosses to Sefer HaMitzvot, explains that those who dispute Maimonides' position, regard the statement as introductory to the commandments. Hashem introduces Himself to the nation. Once the nation accepts Him as Sovereign, then He will legislate the commandments. This dispute between Maimonides and his opponents can be readily understood based upon the above discussion. Maimonides opponents regard the statement as a rational or the basis for a moral imperative to serve Hashem. We must serve Him because He saved us. Maimonides disagrees. He regards the statement as an intellectual lesson. Hashem is providing the nation with the most profound understanding of the universe that humanity can achieve. Hashem is its Cause. He gives the universe its existence every moment. Maimonides regards the acknowledgement of Hashem's relationship with the universe and His centrality to its existence as a commandment. It is not a preamble to commandments or a rational for them. Instead, the statement is a profound and fundamental teaching that shapes the Jew's perceptions of the universe that surrounds him.

Of course, Maimonides' position seems suspect. Why did Hashem not describe Himself as Creator? Why did He refer to Himself as the Redeemer of the nation if His intent was to impart the profound understanding of Hashem and the universe that Maimonides attributes to this

3. Conflicting perceptions of Hashem.

Rashi continues his comments on the above passage. Again, drawing from the Midrash, he explains that there is an alternative explanation of the passage. The nation had observed Hashem at the Reed Sea as a young warrior vanquishing His enemies. Now, at Sinai, they see Him as a compassionate elder. These vastly different perceptions seem irreconcilable and suggest that the nation has witnessed the acts of two different deities – that the deity that had ruthlessly destroyed the Egyptians could not possibly be the same as the deity of Sinai. Hashem addressed this notion by responding, "I am Hashem your G-d that took you out to Egypt..." One deity destroyed Egypt and now, presents Himself at Sinai.

Rashi's comments from the Midrash present two challenges. First, it is clear from the Midrash that Bnai Yisrael believed that one god could not be responsible for both the destruction of Egypt and the Revelation at Sinai. Wherein lies the contradiction in these two perceptions of Hashem? Second, the Midrash seems to attribute a message to the statement that is not readily evident from the statement. What evidence does the Midrash find in the passage to support its interpretation?

Rav Soloveitchik explains that the Midrash is noting that the perception of Hashem's nature that emerged from the destruction of the Egyptians at the Reed Sea was that He is a G-d of vengeance. He destroyed the idolatrous Egyptians who had persecuted His nation. He showed no compassion for His enemies and granted them no mercy. The G-d revealed in the Decalogue was very different from this vengeful deity. He instructed His servant to treat each other with justice. He tought them to control their passions and not needlessly harm others. Hashem's servants must control their passions. They may not even covet another's possessions. These two perceptions seemed contradictory to Bnai Yisrael. It seemed that two different deities had revealed themselves – one a mighty god of wrath and vengeance, the other a god of love and compassion. At Sinai, Hashem responded: I am One. The G-d revealed at Sinai is the self-same G-d Who revealed Himself at the Reed Sea.

What evidence of this message did the Midrash find in the passage? Rav Soloveitchik explain that the Midrash is based upon the very first word of the passage. In the Hebrew language there are two words that can be used to communicate "I" – the first person. Most commonly the word *ani* is used. Occasionally, the word *anochi* is employed. What is the difference between these two words? Generally, the term *anochi* is used when the speaker wishes to emphasis himself as the subject. Often, he is identifying himself in distinction from others. *Anochi* means "I" in a specific sense and in distinction from anyone else. A few examples will illustrate one manner in which the Torah employs the word *anochi*:

---

statement? Nachamanides actually addresses this issue in his commentary on the Torah at the end of Parshat Bo. He explains that the redemption of Bnai Yisrael from Egypt through unprecedented miracles that contravened the laws of nature and the natural order demonstrated Hashem's omnipotence and sovereignty over the universe. This omnipotence can only be attributed to the Creator. In other words, it was impossible for the generation that stood at Sinai to have first-hand knowledge of creation – an event in antiquity. However, the miracles of Egypt provided first-hand proof – proof the generation witnessed – that Hashem was Creator. (Shemot 13:16).

- Hashem asked Kayin where his brother Hevel was. Kayin responded "Am I my brother's guardian?" Kayin was responding that Hevel's welfare was not his responsibility. He was saying, "Why ask me?" In this context the Torah uses the word *anochi*. Kayin was protesting his appointment as Hevel's guardian. He was protesting, "Why me more than someone else?"

- Sarah gave her servant Hagar to Avraham as a wife. Hagar conceived and began to act towards Sarah with condescension. Sarah protested to Avraham. She said, "I placed my servant at your chest. She saw that she had conceived and I became inconsequential in her eyes." Sarah was emphasizing the unjust irony of her situation. She was the one – no one else – who gave Hagar to Avraham and now, she was suffering from Hagar's attitude of superiority. Again, in this context the term *anochi* is appropriate.

- Yaakov appeared before his father Yitzcahak disguised as his brother Esav. Yitzchak asked him to identify himself. He responded "I am Esav your first born." His was telling his father that he is the real Esav. In other words he was saying, "I – and I alone – am Esav. Again, the appropriate term is employed – *anochi*.

In the first statement of the Decalogue, Hashem says, "I –*Anochi* – am Hashem your G-d Who brought you out of Egypt. The use of the word *anochi* indicates that Hashem is saying, "I Who speaks to you now at Sinai am the same G-d that appeared to you at the Reed Sea." Hashem is telling the nation that the G-d of Sinai is the self-same G-d that annihilated the Egyptians. Now, the Midrash's understanding of the passage is easily grasped. Hashem is telling the people that one G-d redeemed them from Egypt and now is delivering to them the gift of Torah. This statement must have been necessitated by the nation's confusion stemming from their varied perceptions of Hashem. Hashem responds that He is One even though He is perceived differently in different situations.[28]

I am, Hashem, your Lord that brought you out from the land of Egypt, the house of bondage. (Shemot 20:2)

Inclusion of Conviction in the Existence of Hashem within Taryag

This is the first statement of the *Aseret HaDibrot* – the Decalogue. It presents the most fundamental premise of the Torah. There is a G-d. Maimonides understands this statement to be a commandment; we are commanded to accept the existence of a G-d who is the source of all reality.[29]

The Halachot Gedolot differs with Maimonides. The author maintains that although acceptance of G-d's existence is fundamental to Judaism, it is not appropriate to classify this conviction as a commandment. Nachmanides explains the reasoning of the Halachot Gedolot. The six hundred thirteen commandments – the *Taryag Mitzvot* – can be compared to the decrees of a king. These decrees presuppose the acceptance of the king as sovereign. The act of acceptance is clearly not one of the decrees, but instead must precede them. Based on this reasoning, acceptance of the existence of Hashem logically precedes the *mitzvot* and cannot properly be viewed as one of these commandments.[30]

---

[28] Rav Yosef Dov Soloveitchik, Recorded Lecture on Aseret HaDibrot, part 1, 1969.
[29] Rabbaynu Moshe ben Maimon (Rambam) *Sefer HaMitzvot, Mitzvat Aseh* 1

Rabbaynu Chasdia Kreskas also differs with Maimonides. He presents a very powerful argument against defining acceptance of Hashem's existence as a *mitzvah*. He argues that every *mitzvah*, by definition, must engender some obligation or result. A command to accept G-d's existence could not meet this criterion. Why? To whom is the command directed? If it is directed to a person who is already convinced, then the command engenders no new outcome. This person is already convinced! The alternative is even more absurd. This would require that the command be directed to the non-believer. But the non-believer could not take such a command seriously! Through this argument, Rabbaynu Chasdai is illustrating the impossibility of legislating belief in G-d. Based on this argument, Rabbaynu Chasdia sides with the Halachot Gedolot. He concludes that conviction in the existence of Hashem precedes *mitzvot* and cannot be counted among *Taryag*.[31]

Another criticism of Maimonides' position questions the logic of a commandment that legislates any belief. A person can be commanded or compelled to act or behave in a specific manner. However, a person cannot be commanded to adopt a belief. I person either accepts or rejects a specific. Acceptance of a belief is not accomplished through an act of will.

How can Maimonides' position be explained? This issue provides a fundamental insight into Maimonides' understanding of *Taryag Mitzvot*. Apparently, Maimonides disagrees with a basic premise of the Halachot Gedolot. This premise is that the *mitzvot* can be equated to decrees. Maimonides seems to maintain that *Taryag* must be defined in a more inclusive manner. He includes among the *mitzvot*, commandments that legislate actions and behaviors and others that describe beliefs. Obviously, this second group of commandments cannot be regarded as legislative for the reason explained above. However, they are included because combined with the other commandments they describe a model or a representation of human excellence. Not all aspects of this model can be emulated through sheer willpower and determination. Convictions cannot be attained through an act of will. Nonetheless, these fundamental convictions are essential components to the Torah's model of human excellence. Without adoption to these beliefs, excellence has not been achieved.

In other words, according to Maimonides, *Taryag* can best be described as the basic blueprint for excellence in a person and nation. This blueprint includes the guide to achieving this excellence as well as the basic description of the behaviors and convictions of the individual who embodies this excellence. Based on this definition of *Taryag*, Maimonides' position can be appreciated. The most basic ingredient to human perfection is acceptance of Hashem who is the source of all other reality. No description of the *shalem* – the perfected individual – can be construed which does not include this fundamental conviction.

I am Hashem, your God, Who took you out of the land of Egypt, out of the house of bondage. (Shemot 20:2)

Conviction in the Existence of Hashem – the Creator

This week's *parasha* includes the Decalogue. The above passage is the first *pasuk* of the Decalogue. According to Sefer HaChinuch, this passage is the source of the commandment to

---

[30] R' Moshe ben Nachman (Ramban), *Critique on Maimonides' Sefer HaMitzvot, Mitzvat Aseh* 1.
[31] Rabbaynu Chasdai Kreskas, *Ohr Hashem*, Introduction (*HaTza'ah*).

accept that Hashem exists. He explains that this commandment requires that we respond to any inquiry regarding our convictions with the reply that we wholeheartedly accept the existence of Hashem. He adds that we are required to relinquish our lives for the sake of this conviction. In other words, we must affirm our conviction in the existence of Hashem and that there is no other is G-d. We are even required to sacrifice our lives in affirmation of this conviction.

Sefer HaChinuch adds that we should strive to establish clear proof of Hashem's existence. If we succeed in establishing such proof, then we have fulfilled the *mitzvah* at its highest level.[32] This is a troubling statement. It is understandable that complete fulfillment of the commandment requires basing our conviction on objective evidence. However, the implication of this statement is that even if we do not base our conviction on any evidence, the commandment has been fulfilled at least at to a minimal standard.

This implication presents two problems: First, Sefer HaChinuch acknowledges that one's conviction in the existence of G-d is the most fundamental element of Torah Judaism. All other elements of the Torah are based on this conviction.[33] If this conviction is not based upon evidence, then one's entire adherence to the Torah and observance of the commandments is based upon solely subjective belief. Among the Torah's commandments are various *mitzvot* that presume that the Torah is true and that other faiths are not valid. For example, the Torah includes many commandments directed against idolatry. These commandments include directives to execute idolaters. If our conviction in the Torah is based upon a completely subjective set of beliefs, then these beliefs are no more credible than those of the idolater. The Torah describes Hashem as a just G-d. How can a just G-d command us to execute those whose subjective beliefs – although different from our subjective beliefs – are every bit as credible?

Second, the implication that conviction in Hashem's existence based on subjective belief is adequate contradicts the position outlined by Sefer HaChinuch in his introduction to his work. There, the author explains that one of the unique elements of the Torah is the Sinai revelation described in this week's *parasha*. The Torah was revealed by Hashem to the entire nation. All of the people heard Hashem address the nation. The objective of mass revelation was to establish a firm basis for future generations' acceptance of the authenticity of the Torah as a G-d-given creed.

The details of Sefer HaChinuch's argument are beyond the scope of this discussion, but it is sufficient for our purposes to summarize his thinking. Mass revelation endows the giving of the Torah with the standing of an objective historical event. In other words, the Torah's account of revelation as a mass-witnessed event is so fantastic that the very acceptance of this claim indicates that it cannot be reasonably assumed to be a fabrication. No generation would have agreed to be the first to accept this fantastic claim were it not part of its established historical record.

According to Sefer HaChinuch, the objective of the Sinai revelation was to create a firm, objective basis for the authenticity of the Torah as a G-d-given truth. It is odd that, according to Sefer HaChinuch, Hashem gave the Torah through the Sinai revelation to provide an *objective* basis for our conviction in its authenticity – yet a *subjective* belief in Hashem's existence is acceptable!

---

[32] Rav Aharon HaLeyve, *Sefer HaChinuch*, Mitzvah 25.
[33] Rav Aharon HaLeyve, *Sefer HaChinuch*, Mitzvah 25.

Let us consider another issue. Conviction in the existence of G-d is, in itself, a meaningless requirement. Such a requirement lacks any description of the specifics of the required conviction. In other words, what is meant by "G-d"? Without a response to this question, the requirement is too vague to be meaningful. Sefer HaChinuch delineates three elements to the *mitzvah*: 1) We are required to accept the existence of a G-d Who is the source of all that exists; 2) This G-d is eternal; 3) This G-d redeemed us from Egypt and gave us the Torah.[34] These elements provide the specific details that give meaning to the requirement to accept the existence of Hashem.

Generally, Sefer HaChinuch adopts the position of Maimonides. However, there seems to be a disagreement between these authorities regarding the specifics of the *meaning* of acceptance of Hashem. In his Sefer HaMitzvot, Maimonides defines the commandment to accept the existence of G-d as a requirement to acknowledge there is a G-d Who is the cause of all that exists. [35] He does *not* include within the *mitzvah* a requirement to acknowledge Hashem as the G-d Who redeemed us from Egypt and gave us the Torah.[36]

Rabbaynu Yehudah HaLeyve also deals with the requirement to accept that Hashem exists. His position is very different from that of Maimonides. He explains that we are required to accept the existence of a G-d Who redeemed us from Egypt and gave us the Torah. He does *not* include within this basic requirement that we accept Hashem as the creator. He explains that while the Torah requires that we accept the existence of Hashem, this requirement does not include acknowledgement that He is the creator. There is a compelling reason for the requirement's exclusion of this element. Proof of a G-d Who is creator of the universe can only be attained through philosophical and scientific investigation and speculation. These investigations – and any proofs they provide of a creator – are subject to debate and criticism. According to Rabbaynu Yehudah HaLeyve, the Torah does not wish to base acceptance of Hashem upon speculations and investigations that can be debated and are not accessible to the average person. Instead, the Torah instructs us to base our acceptance of Hashem upon historically credible, public events such as the revelation at Sinai.[37]

It is important to note that Rabbaynu Yehudah HaLeyve does not intend to imply that acceptance of Hashem as creator is not a fundamental element of the Torah. This would be a rejection of the opening chapters of the Torah. The position of Rabbaynu Yehudah HaLeyve is explained by Rabbaynu Nissim Gerondi in his commentary on the Torah. He explains that acceptance of Hashem as the creator of the universe is an essential element of the Torah. However, this is a truth we know through revelation. The requirement to accept Hashem focuses on accepting Him as our redeemer from Egypt and the giver of the Torah. Once we accept the

---

[34] Rav Aharon HaLeyve, *Sefer HaChinuch*, Mitzvah 25.

[35] Rabbaynu Moshe ben Maimon (Rambam) *Sefer HaMitzvot, Mitzvat Aseh* 1

[36] Maimonides also does not include in this description of the *mitzvah* acceptance of Hashem as eternal. However, in the first chapter of his Mishne Torah, Maimonides elaborates on this *mitzvah*. There he explains that we are required to accept that Hashem is the cause of all that exists and that His existence is unique. His existence is more "absolute". This is apparently a reference to the eternity of His existence. In other words, it appears that according to Maimonides, this commandment requires us to accept that only Hashem's existence is "absolute" or necessary existence. All other things exist as a consequence of His existence and will.

[37] Rabbaynu Yehudah HaLeyve, Kuzari, part I, sections 11-25.

Torah as a revealed truth, it follows that we must accept the contents of this revealed truth. An essential element of this revealed doctrine is that Hashem is creator.[38]

Rabbaynu Yehudah HaLeyve seems to present a compelling argument for his position. Why does Maimonides insist that the essential element of the *mitzvah* to accept Hashem is the recognition that He is creator? In order to answer this question, we must address an astounding oddity in Maimonides' Mishne Torah. Maimonides' Mishne Torah is a codification of Torah law. However, the third and fourth chapters of this work can be described as a brief summary of physics and astrophysics. Why is this material included in this work of Torah law? Furthermore, as an introduction to each section of this work, Maimonides provides a list of the commandments that will be described and explained in the section. Presumably, the material in the section that follows is an elaboration of these listed commandments. The first section of the Mishne Torah is preceded by such an introduction explaining that the section will deal with ten *mitzvot*. The list of these *mitzvot* includes acceptance of His existence and His unity. None of the *mitzvot* in this list seem to provide an imperative for instruction in and knowledge of physics or astrophysics. Under which of these commandments does Maimonides subsume his discussion of physics and astrophysics?

Maimonides deals with this issue in the final passages of the fourth chapter. He explains that this discussion is relevant to those *mitzvot* that require we accept Hashem's existence and unity, and that we adore and hold Him in awe. How is Maimonides' discussion of scientific matters relevant to these *mitzvot*?

According to Maimonides, acceptance of the existence of Hashem, His unity, and our adoration and awe of Him must be predicated upon an understanding of our universe and His centrality to all existence. We must understand the universe and His role as the source of all existence. It is not adequate to merely accept this assertion as true. We are required to understand the nature of the relationship between Hashem and the universe.

An analogy will help us understand Maimonides' position. As I record these thoughts I am using my computer. I know that my computer is composed of a motherboard and various other circuitries. I have no idea how all these elements operate and work together. Yet, I know that these elements exist. I do not understand them nor do I have any appreciation of their operations. My acceptance of their existence is absolute; yet, my understanding of their nature and operation is negligible. Maimonides maintains that the requirement that we accept Hashem's existence cannot be fulfilled simply through acknowledging the fact He exists. This acceptance cannot be akin to my acceptance of the existence of a motherboard and circuitries in my computer. Instead, my acceptance of Hashem must be akin to the engineer's more fundamental comprehension of the computer. It must include an understanding and an appreciation of the nature of the universe and Hashem's role and relationship with reality.

This is the essential difference in the perspectives of Maimonides and Rabbaynu Yehudah HaLeyve. According to Rabbaynu Yehudah HaLeyve, we are required to accept as a revealed truth that Hashem is creator and that He sustains the universe. We are *not* required to understand or appreciate the full meaning of this assertion. Maimonides rejects this perspective. According to Maimonides, the *mitzvah* to accept Hashem requires our appreciation of His relationship to the universe and an understanding of His centrality to its existence. In other

---

[38] Rabbaynu Nissim ben Reuven Gerondi (Ran), *Commentary on Sefer Beresheit* 1:1.

words, this commandment addresses our overall understanding of reality. We are required to unmask the nature of the universe and the reality in which we exist.

We are now prepared to understand Sefer HaChinuch's position. Sefer HaChinuch adopts a position that is a compromise between these two perspectives. He agrees with Rabbaynu Yehudah HaLeyve that the *mitzvah* to accept Hashem requires that we accept Him as our redeemer from Egypt and the giver of the Torah. He adopts this position for the reasons that he outlines in the introduction to his work. The Torah must be based on objective evidence. It cannot be reduced to a set of subjective beliefs. Mass revelation and public miracles experienced by our ancestors provide us with the objective basis for our conviction in Hashem's existence. We do not need to resort of scientific proof and philosophical speculation in order to fulfill this most basic commandment.

However, Sefer HaChinuch is not willing to reject Maimonides' perspective. Our acceptance of Hashem is not complete without acknowledgement of His role as creator and sustainer of the universe. Our acceptance of Hashem must include this element to be meaningful. Nonetheless, Sefer HaChinuch does not completely agree with Maimonides' position. He asserts that although we should strive to achieve the level of understanding described by Maimonides, it is not essential to the minimal fulfillment of the *mitzvah*. However, an understanding of G-d in the manner explained by Maimonides is the highest fulfillment of the *mitzvah*.[39]

"I am Hashem your Lord that brought you out from the land of Egypt, the house of bondage." (Shemot 20:2)

This is the first statement of the *Aseret HaDibrot* – the Decalogue. It presents the most fundamental premise of the Torah. There is a G-d. Maimonides understands this statement to be a commandment. We are commanded to accept the existence of a G-d who is the source of all reality.[40]

In Maimonides' introduction to his *Mishne Torah*, he provides a list of the 613 commandments. In this list, Maimonides places the commandments in the same order that they appear in his *Sefer HaMitzvot*. The placement of the individual *mitzvot* on this list does not correspond with the placement of these commandments in the Torah. Instead, Maimonides constructed a hierarchical order. Maimonides' order reflects the relationship between the various commandments. The very first commandment in Maimonides' list is the *mitzvah* to accept the existence of Hashem. Apparently, Maimonides regards this *mitzvah* as fundamental to the system of *Taryag* – the 613 commandments.

In contrast to Maimonides, Rabbaynu Chasdia Kreskas argues that acceptance of Hashem cannot even be defined as a *mitzvah*. He presents a very powerful argument. He argues that every *mitzvah*, by definition, must engender some obligation or result. A command to accept G-d's

---

[39] It should be noted that none of these authorities ascribe to the position that acceptance of Hashem and the Torah can be founded upon blind faith. To my knowledge, this popular position has no basis or antecedents in the writings of the classical authorities. These authorities were unwilling to equate the Torah to other religions that are based upon personal belief and subjective conviction. Instead, the introduction of blind faith as a basis for acceptance of the Torah seems to be a relatively modern development. Perhaps, this more modern perspective is influenced by modern, conventional theology and existential philosophy.

[40] Rabbaynu Moshe ben Maimon (Rambam) *Sefer HaMitzvot, Mitzvat Aseh* 1

existence could not meet this criterion. Why? To whom is the command directed? If it is directed to a person who is already convinced, then the command engenders no new outcome. This person is already convinced! The alternative is even more absurd. This would require that the command be directed to the non-believer. But the non-believer could not take such a command seriously! Based on this argument, Rabbaynu Chasdia concludes that conviction in the existence of Hashem precedes *mitzvot* and cannot be counted among *Taryag*.[41]

How can Maimonides' position be explained? This issue provides a fundamental insight into Maimonides' understanding of *Taryag Mitzvot*. Apparently, Maimonides disagrees with the Rabbaynu Chasdia's basic premise. This premise is that the *mitzvot* can be equated to decrees. Maimonides seems to maintain *Taryag* must be defined in a more inclusive manner. He posits that the *mitzvot* are the basic blueprint for the complete person and nation. This blueprint includes the guide to achieving personal and national fulfillment as well as the basic description of the behaviors and convictions of the *shalem* – the complete individual.

Based on this definition of *Taryag*, Maimonides' position can be appreciated. The most basic ingredient to human perfection is acceptance of the Almighty, Who is the source of all other reality. No description of the *shalem* can be construed which does not include this fundamental conviction.

If we consider Maimonides' position carefully, an important premise emerges. The most basic and fundamental *mitzvah* of *Taryag* is not a command to perform any act. It is the description of a conviction that is fundamental to the perfection of the human being. In other words, the most fundamental element of human perfection is our conviction in the existence of Hashem.

Maimonides discusses this issue more thoroughly in his *Commentary on the Mishne*. He explains that in order to be regarded as adhering to the Torah, we must accept the basic convictions outlined by the Torah. Maimonides outlines thirteen principles – *ikkarim* – that are the fundamental convictions contained in the Torah. He explains that in order to be regarded as adhering to the Torah, one must accept all of these principles. If a person accepts these *ikkarim*, he is regarded as adhering to the Torah even if he is not perfect in his observance. In contrast, a person who is scrupulous in observance, but unconvinced of the truth of these thirteen principles, cannot be regarded as a Torah Jew. [42] It is clear from Maimonides' discussion of this issue that our convictions are essential to our identity as Torah Jews. Without these convictions our actions are hollow and loose their meaning and significance.

Maimonides' position differs markedly from the view that is popular today. Even many Jews who unequivocally identify themselves as Torah observant give little or none of their attention to clearly understanding these thirteen *ikkarim* of the Torah. Many Jews – observant and non-observant – do give some attention to the study of Torah *machshava* – philosophy. But this attention is generally directed to the study of *mussar* – ethical thought and philosophy. Maimonides' thirteen principles – which are remarkably devoid of any extensive discussion of ethical philosophy – are almost completely neglected. At most, the thirteen *ikkarim* are quickly recited at the close of morning prayers with little thought or understanding. The popular view is that actions are more fundamental than convictions. We can hold ourselves responsible for acting

---

[41] Rabbaynu Chasdai Kreskas, *Ohr Hashem*, Introduction (*HaTza'ah*).
[42] R' Moshe ben Maimon (Rambam) *Commentary on the Mishne*, Mesechet Sanhedrin 10:1.

properly but we cannot be expected to establish a clear system of convictions. Nonetheless, it behooves us to occasionally break from popular practice and give some serious thought to the thirteen *ikkarim* that Maimonides identifies as the underpinning of Judaism.

As explained above, Maimonides lists as the first *mitzvah* of the Torah acceptance of the existence of Hashem. Maimonides also lists this conviction as the first of the thirteen fundamental principles of the Torah. Of course, we need to define what we mean by Hashem. Maimonides explains that when we use the term Hashem or G-d we are required to understand that He is the cause of all that exists. In other words, all that exists is sustained by His will. In contrast, His existence is self-sustained and does not require any external cause.[43]

This principle is often confused with the Torah's assertion that Hashem created the universe. However, these two concepts are not interchangeable. Maimonides' first principle does not deal with the origins of the universe. It deals with the dependence of the universe upon Hashem's ongoing will. This is an important issue. The ancient philosophers – for example, Aristotle – were willing to acknowledge that the universe's existence is dependant upon G-d. However, they denied that He created the universe. They posited that the universe and

G-d share eternity. These philosophers maintained that although the existence of the universe is dependent on G-d, it is not created. Instead it is an emanation. It can be compared to the shadow of a wall. The existence of the wall causes the shadow. But the wall does not perform an act of creation in order to bring the shadow into existence. Instead, the shadow is a result of the existence of the wall. Similarly, these philosophers asserted that the universe is a result of G-d's existence but it not a creation of G-d.

It appears that Maimonides first principle does not contradict this perspective. It does not deal with the issue of creation. It merely asserts that the universe's ongoing existence is dependent upon Hashem.

"For in six days Hashem created the heavens, the earth, the seas and all that are contained in them. And He rested on the seventh day. Therefore, Hashem blessed the Shabbat and sanctified it." (Shemot 20:11)

Rav Yosef Albo criticizes Maimonides on this issue. He contends that Maimonides neglected to include within his thirteen principles the Torah principle that Hashem created the universe.[44]

We observe Shabbat every week. The above *pasuk* explains that Shabbat is designed to commemorate creation. It seems obvious that the attention the Torah gives to creation indicates that this is a fundamental element of the Torah. The Torah's emphasis on creation seems to support Rav Albo's criticism of Maimonides.

However, a careful study of Maimonides' thirteen principles indicates that they do include the assertion that Hashem created the universe. Maimonides' fourth principle is that Hashem is eternal and that no other existence is eternal. Maimonides elaborates on this principle and explicitly states that this principle includes a negation of the Aristotelian position. In other words, according to Maimonides' formulation of this principle, it includes the assertion that Hashem created the universe and it is not eternal.

---

[43]   R' Moshe ben Maimon (Rambam) *Commentary on the Mishne*, Mesechet Sanhedrin 10:1.
[44]   Rav Yosef Albo, *Sefer HaIkkarim*, volume 1, chapter 1.

It is amazing that Rav Albo criticizes Maimonides for neglecting to include within his thirteen *ikkarim* the Torah's assertion that Hashem created the universe. This is simply not accurate. As we have explained, Maimonides explicitly includes this assertion within his fourth principle! How can we explain Rav Albo's apparent error?

Appreciating Rav Albo's criticism requires a more thorough understanding of Maimonides' formulation of his thirteen principles. In order to reach this understanding, it is helpful to begin with a related question.

Maimonides' second principle is that Hashem is a unity. What is the meaning of the term "unity?" Maimonides explains that Hashem is not subject to division in any sense. This means that we can not view Hashem has having parts or even characteristics. We cannot view Hashem as possessing compassion or mercy. Such a view means that Hashem has attributes. The assignment of attributes to Hashem is inconsistent with the Torah's assertion that Hashem is one. It is true that the Torah does refer to Divine attributes. However, Maimonides explains that when the Torah refers to Hashem's mercy or other attributes it is resorting to an allegory and is not to be understood in a literal sense.[45]

Maimonides' third principle is that Hashem is not material and cannot be described as possessing any of the qualities or characteristics associated with material objects. It would seem that this third principle is superfluous. It is an obvious extension of the second principle. Hashem is a unity. This precludes conceiving of Him as material. All material objects have characteristics – for example dimension and size. It is quite impossible to conceive of a material object devoid of all characteristics. Similarly, Maimonides' fourth principle is that Hashem is eternal. This principle also seems to be an extension of the second principle. The reasoning behind this argument is somewhat abstract and is beyond the scope of this discussion. But the observation is nonetheless noteworthy. It indicates that the thirteen *ikkarim* are not independent of one another. They are interrelated and in some cases latter principles are easily derived from earlier principles.

This suggests a question. What are these principles? We would have assumed that they are similar to a postulate system. In a postulate system, each element is independent of the others. Postulates are basic building blocks. One cannot be derived from another. It is easy to understand the role of postulates in a postulate system. They are the fundamental principles. All other elements of the system are derived from the postulates but the postulates cannot be derived from one another. The postulates are the foundation. The remaining elements of the system are derived and built upon this foundation. But Maimonides' thirteen principles are not independent of one another. In fact, they are interrelated. If one principle can be derived from another, on what basis is a principle defined as fundamental?

The implication of this question is that Maimonides' thirteen *ikkarim* are not a system of postulates. Instead, they are Maimonides' outline of the basic theological framework of the Torah. They describe a structure of concepts. These concepts are interrelated. But in their totality they depict the basic outline of the Torah's theology. They are a basic sketch of the Torah's outlook. They are an abstract of the elements that compose the Torah's perspective. They can be compared to an architect's preliminary drawing of a structure. The architect begins with an outline that includes the basic elements of the structure. These elements give the structure its

---

[45] Rabbaynu Moshe ben Maimon (Rambam) *Mishne Torah*, Hilchot Yesodai HaTorah 1:9.

form and function. Later the architect adds additional detail to his drawing. But the basic form emerges from the preliminary drawing. It contains all of the elements that give the structure its basic form and function. Similarly, Maimonides' principles are such an outline. The basic form and structure of the Torah's outlook is contained in this outline. The Torah adds much more detail. But the fundamental structure is contained in these thirteen principles.

Now, Rav Albo's question can be appreciated. As Maimonides notes, the Torah's assertion that the universe is created can be derived from the fourth principle. But this does not mean that this assertion should not be treated as a separate principle. Rav Albo argues that certainly creation is a fundamental element of the Torah's outlook. It deserves to be treated as such and enumerated as a separate principle. It is not adequate to include creation within another principle!

What is the basis of this dispute between Maimonides and Rav Albo? This is a difficult question to answer. However, it is possible to present an approach or hypothesis. Rav Albo maintains that creation is a fundamental proposition of the Torah. According to Rav Albo, the Torah directs us to regard the word as a creation of Hashem and not as coexistent with Him. We must recognize that the universe that we know is not eternal and is a result of an act of creation. Our relationship with and understanding of the universe must be predicated on this acknowledgement.

In contrast, a survey of Maimonides' thirteen principles reveals that they deal primarily with our relationship with and understanding of Hashem. It seems that according to Maimonides, the essence of the Torah is the perspective it provides on Hashem and our relationship with Him. A fundamental element of this understanding and relationship is that we are required to appreciate Hashem's uniqueness. He is eternal. In His eternity, He is unique. Nothing else partakes of eternity.

Maimonides' understanding of the role of creation in Torah thought is predicated on his contention that our understanding of and relationship with Hashem is the most fundamental element of the Torah. The Torah's assertion that the universe is created is important because this assertion confirms Hashem's uniqueness. If we fail to accept creation, we do not appreciate the uniqueness of Hashem's existence and His central role in all other existence. Without creation, we cannot regard Hashem as the most fundamental reality and the most central element of all reality.

Based on this perspective, Maimonides does not enumerate creation as an independent principle. Instead, he includes it in his fourth principle. We are required to acknowledge that Hashem is eternal. Hashem's eternal existence is unique. Nothing else partakes of this eternity. Therefore, we must accept that the universe is created and not eternal.

"I am Hashem your G-d that brought you out from the land of Egypt, from the house of bondage." (Shemot 20:2)

This is the first statement of the Decalogue. Hashem identifies Himself as the G-d that redeemed Bnai Yisrael from Egypt. Most authorities regard this statement as a commandment. This presents a problem. A commandment engenders some obligation. It requires us to perform some action or accept some conviction. However, this statement is merely the presentation of a fact. What does this commandment require of us?

The Sefer Mitzvot Gadol offers an interesting interpretation of this *mitzvah*. His explanation is based upon a careful interpretation of the passage. The *pasuk* is the Almighty's introduction to the revelation of the Torah. He identifies Himself. He says that He is the G-d that redeemed the nation from Egypt. The Sefer Mitzvot Gadol concludes that the *mitzvah* requires that we acknowledge that the G-d that revealed the Torah is the same Deity that redeemed us from Egypt.[46]

Most other authorities maintain that this *mitzvah* obligates us to acknowledge the existence of G-d. This interpretation of the *mitzvah* presents an obvious problem. What is meant by the term "G-d"? This term has different meanings to different people. In itself, it is rather vague. The term needs some clarification. Precisely, in what must we believe?

Maimonides contends that the term "G-d" refers to a Deity that is the cause of all that exists. He explains that we are obligated to acknowledge that there exists a Deity that is the cause of all other existence. This means that all that exist is a consequence of His will. Without this will nothing would exist. However, if nothing else existed, He would still exist.[47]

Rabbaynu Yehuda HaLeyve, in his Kuzari, seems to object to this definition. In order to understand his objection, some initial clarification is needed. Rav Yehuda HaLeyve does not disagree with Maimonides' assertion that the Hashem is the cause of all existence. This is one of the lessons of the Torah. However, he points out that the commandment requires that we acknowledge the existence of G-d. His objection relates to defining the term "G-d" as the cause of all existence. What is the basis of this objection?

Rabbaynu Yehuda HaLeyve contends that the commandment does not obligate us in abstract philosophical speculation. In other words, the commandment cannot obligate us to prove through philosophical analysis the existence of G-d. Rabbaynu Yehuda HaLeyve assumes a skeptical attitude towards such speculations. The great philosophers have different understandings of G-d. Some acknowledge that He is the Creator. Others reject this conclusion. Even if the speculations were conclusive, they might exceed the ability of the common person. The "G-d" identified by the commandment must be a Deity that everyone can acknowledge, not just the great scholars.

On this basis, it seems that Rabbaynu Yehuda HaLeyve would reject Maimonides' description of the commandment. It is likely that he would argue that Maimonides defines the commandment in a manner that requires philosophical speculation. How would one prove that Hashem is the cause of all existence? This would require an analysis that may exceed the ability of the common person!

What is Rabbaynu Yehuda HaLeyve's understanding of the *mitzvah*? He explains that we are obligated to believe in the G-d of the forefathers that led Bnai Yisrael out of Egypt and gave the Torah. He contends that anyone can make such an affirmation. This is a G-d that was encountered through personal experience and is known to subsequent generations though an unassailable chain of tradition. In other words, this G-d is revealed in history. Anyone can accept an historical fact![48]

---

[46] Rabbaynu Moshe of Kotzi, *Sefer Mitzvot Gadol*, Mitzvat Aseh 1.
[47] R' Moshe ben Maimon (Rambam) *Mishne Torah*, Hilchot Yesodai HaTorah 1:1-3.
[48] Rabbaynu Yehuda HaLeyve, Kuzari, part I, sections 11-25.

In order to better understand the dispute between Maimonides and Rabbaynu Yehuda HaLeyve, it is helpful to consider a few scenarios. First, imagine a person that believes in G-d that delivered Bnai Yisrael from Egypt and gave the Torah. However, this person does not understand that this G-d is the cause of all existence. According to Rabbaynu Yehuda HaLeyve, this person's convictions do not conform to the Torah. However, it cannot be said that this person does not acknowledge the existence of G-d. Maimonides would clearly disagree. He would contend that this person does not fulfill the most basic of *mitzvot*. He does not acknowledge the existence of G-d.

Second, consider a person that accepts the existence of a Deity that is the cause of all existence. However, this person does not know that this G-d redeemed us from Egypt and gave us the Torah. Maimonides would contend that this person's belief system is not in conformity with the Torah. However, the primary command of acknowledging G-d has been fulfilled. Rabbaynu Yehuda HaLeyve seems to adopt the position that this person has not complied with the basic *mitzvah* of acknowledging G-d.

It is important to clearly understand the basis of the three positions we have described. Each position reflects a fundamentally different understanding of this commandment.

The position of the Sefer Mitzvot Gadol is the most astounding of the three positions. According to this interpretation, the commandment does not directly require an affirmation of the existence of G-d. Instead, the *mitzvah* requires that we acknowledge that the Deity that gave the Torah is the same G-d that redeemed us from Egypt. The commandment requires that we affirm the origins of the Torah. We must place the Torah in its proper context. We must appreciate that the Torah is a divinely revealed truth. Of course, this does imply acknowledgement of the existence of G-d. However, the commandment is formulated as an acknowledgement of the nature of the Torah. It is not inherently fashioned as an acknowledgement of G-d's existence.

Rabbaynu Yehuda HaLeyve and Maimonides disagree with this position. They argue that we are directly commanded to acknowledge the existence of G-d. However, they differ in the specifics of this obligation. Now, let us consider this dispute.

Rabbaynu Yehuda HaLeyve's position is more easily understood. We have already explained his reasons for rejecting Maimonides' approach to this *mitzvah*. However, it is important to appreciate the outcome of Rabbaynu Yehuda HaLeyve's formulation. Essentially, he contends that we are obligated to acknowledge G-d as He has overtly and manifestly revealed Himself. He made Himself known through the forefathers – the *Avot*, through the wonders He performs and through revelation at Sinai. We are obligated to acknowledge the G-d that is manifested through personal experience and known through tradition.

Maimonides requires that we acknowledge the existence of a Deity that is the cause of all that exists. What is Maimonides' reason for insisting on this somewhat abstract formulation of the *mitzvah*?

Maimonides provides an important insight into his position in his Moreh Nevuchim. He begins with the premise that the perfection of a person's soul is determined by the degree to which the person perceives actual reality. Therefore, various mistakes have differing degrees of impact on human perfection. A misconception regarding an insignificant issue does not have a substantial impact upon human perfection. However, an error regarding a basic reality has a serious impact upon the soul's perfection.

Let us consider a simple example. Assume a person thinks that Reuven is sitting. However, really Reuven is standing. How serious is this person's misconception of reality? It is not very serious. Consequently, this error has little impact on the person's soul. Let us contrast this with a person that believes that the earth is flat or a person that sees ghosts and demons around every corner. This person's perception of reality is seriously flawed. A more basic aspect of reality is denied. The impact of such a misconception is far more serious. As a result, these misconceptions have a significant impact on the person's perfection.[49]

Let us proceed one step further in this analysis. What is the most basic aspect of reality? The answer is that all that exists is a result of G-d. He is the most fundamental aspect of the universe and all that exists. Denial of the existence of a Deity that is the cause of all reality is the greatest possible misconception! No other single error can have the same degree of negative impact upon the soul.

We can now understand Maimonides interpretation of the *mitzvah* to acknowledge G-d. The Torah is a blueprint. It describes the convictions and behaviors of the perfected individual. Maimonides contends that this perfection requires more than mere acknowledgement of G-d. Human perfection is achieved through acknowledging the fundamental nature of reality. We must understand that the entire reality that surrounds us is based upon the existence of G-d. He is the basis and source of all reality.

For in six days Hashem made the heavens and the earth and all that is within them and He rested on the seventh. Therefore, Hashem blessed the Shabbat day and He sanctified it. (Shemot 20:10)

And you should recall that you were a slave in the Land of Egypt and Hashem, your L-rd, took you forth from there with a mighty hand and outstretched arm. Therefore, Hashem, your L-rd, commanded you to observe the Shabbat. (Devarim 5:14)

Mo' Money

Differences in the two texts of the Decalogue

The *Aseret HaDibrot* – the Decalogue – is presented twice in the Torah. It is presented first in our *parasha* and a second time in Parshat VaEtchanan. There are various differences in the texts of the Decalogue in these two presentations. Rabbaynu Avraham ibn Ezra dismisses many of these as inconsequential. He explains that in Parshat VaEtchanan, Moshe is reviewing the content of the Decalogue for the nation. His intention is to communicate its content, not to repeat it verbatim. Therefore, he chooses the words and phrases that he feels best communicate the material without regard to inconsequential deviations in the wording.[50]

However, some of the differences between the two presentation are not minor. Some are fundamental differences in content. One of these major differences is in the two presentations of Shabbat. The first quotation above is from our *parasha*. We are commanded to observe the Shabbat in order to reinforce a fundamental tenet of the Torah – the universe is the creation of Hashem.

---

[49]   Rabbaynu Moshe ben Maimon (Rambam) *Moreh Nevuchim*, volume 1, chapter 36.
[50]   Rabbeinu Avraham ibn Ezra, *Commentary of Sefer Shemot*, 20:1.

The second quotation above is from Parshat VaEtchanan. This is Moshe's presentation or review of the imperative to observe Shabbat. He explains that we observe Shabbat in order to recall our redemption from slavery in Egypt. Moshe makes no mention of Shabbat memorializing creation. In other words, each version presents its own explanation for the observance of Shabbat. This is not a minor discrepancy. How can it be reconciled?

Among the commentators there are a number of responses to this problem. We will focus upon the solution and insight suggested by Maimonides. This solution resolves the apparent contradiction between the texts, it addresses additional issues, and it suggests an important message regarding our values and priorities.

Moshe's objective was to motivate

Maimonides' solution is based upon an implicit premise. What was Moshe's objective in reviewing with the nation the *Aseret HaDibrot* before his death? Maimonides seems to assume that his objective was not limited to recapitulating the content. Moshe was also focused upon encouraging the people to observe the commandments. This objective impacted his presentation. It determined the elements of the Decalogue that he addressed and how he presented them. In other words, the original presentation of the Decalogue in our *parasha* is focused solely upon the fundamental content of the commandments. Moshe's review has a broader or different perspective. It is designed to encourage and even admonish the people to carefully observe the commandments.

Let's consider an analogy. It's Friday afternoon and a parent wants his son to straighten up his room before Shabbat. As soon as his son arrives home, the dad instructs his son of the expectation. These instructions are detailed. Of course, the son has other things to do before he gets to this task. Shabbat is approaching and the father realizes that if the room is to be straightened-up, the chore requires immediate attention. He speaks to his son again and reviews the expectation. This review of the expectation is different than the original presentation. There is no need for the father to review the details. He wants to make sure the chore is completed. In this presentation, the dad focuses upon the importance of preparing for Shabbat and explains that this is the son's opportunity to participate in honoring the Shabbat. In both presentations the father is discussing the same task. However, in the first the focus is upon the substance of the task. In the second, the substance of the task requires less attention. Now, the father focuses on motivating.

This illustration demonstrates how the same task will be presented differently as required by the situation. Maimonides employs this principle to explain the discrepancy between the presentations of Shabbat in the two iterations of the Decalogue.

The meaning of Shabbat

He explains that in the first presentation – found in our *parsha* – the Torah is presenting the basic concept of Shabbat. In this context, the Torah's focus is upon the innate meaning of Shabbat. It communicates the significance of the day. It is in this context that the Torah explains that Shabbat recalls the creation. Hashem created the universe. He fashioned it in six days and then rested on the seventh. The observance of Shabbat recalls and memorializes the universe's origin.

Shabbat was given to the Jewish people

Moshe's review focuses on *our* obligation to observe Shabbat. It explains Bnai Yisrael's selection for the role of observing this commandment.[51] We were selected because we were redeemed from Egypt. Our redemption endows this commandment – which is a day of rest – with a special significance. In other words, because of our redemption from slavery we are uniquely fit to observe this commandment. How does our experience of bondage and liberation endow us with this unique suitability?

Maimonides explains that in Egypt there was no day of rest. Our activities and our lives were controlled and fashioned by our masters. If on some occasion we did have a respite from our heavy burden, it was granted to us at the sole volition of a master. Such a hiatus in a slave's labor is not truly a respite; it is a reprieve that will soon be terminated at the whim of the master. Only a free person – one who is empowered to act upon is own volition – can experience authentic rest from labor and toil. According to Maimonides, our emergence from bondage into freedom uniquely prepared us to experience a day of rest. Any person can select a day of the week and decide to not labor on that day. But for us the designation of a day as a period for respite and contemplation has unique meaning.

Again, let's employ an analogy to understand this insight. A baseball team fields nine players. The coach must decide who will play shortstop. He considers his options and he selects a player who his very agile, has an accurate throwing arm, and is focused and alert. The position of shortstop has its own unique objectives. The shortstop covers the gap in the infield between second and third bases. He fields most of the infield grounders or one-hoppers hit in his direction and often has to handle line-drives. It is his job to throw out runners to first base and sometimes make a play to second, third or even home. This is the position. In selecting the player to play the position, the coach needs to consider the requisite skills, gifts, and talents. These are agility, accuracy in throwing, focus, and alertness. Returning to our discussion, Shabbat commemorates creation. Bnai Yisrael were selected to observe Shabbat because background and history rendered us uniquely suited for the role.

Let's summarize before continuing. The first iteration of the *Aseret HaDibrot* focuses upon the objective of Shabbat. Its objective is to recall that Hashem is the creator of the universe. The second iteration focuses upon the selection of the Jewish people for the role of observing Shabbat. In order to understand our selection, we must recognize how Shabbat communicates its

---

[51] Maimonides' interpretation of the message of the second Decalogue is not completely clear. One could argue that we were selected to receive the Torah; Shabbat is one of its *mitzvot*. No special explanation is required for our selection to receive a specific commandment. Abravanel, in his commentary on Maimonides' comments, suggests that we would expect Shabbat to be included in the laws given to the descendants of Noach. Its message that Hashem is creator is universal. It is relevant to Jew and non-Jew. Maimonides understands the second text of the Decalogue to address this issue.
Possibly, Maimonides' position can be understood in the context of his comments in Hilchot Melachim 10:9-10. There, he explains that generally, a non-Jew may adopt observance of any of the Torah's *mitzvot*. For example, a non-Jew may adopt observance of the *mitzvot* of *kashrut*. However, a non-Jew may not adopt observance of Shabbat. From these comments, it is clear that the relationship between the Jewish people and Shabbat is different than the relationship with most other *mitzvot*. We enjoy an exclusive relationship with Shabbat; a non-Jew may not join us in its observance.

message. The means is through observing a day of rest, every week. The character of the day as respite from labor and dedication to contemplation is most intensely experienced by a people who has emerged from slavery to freedom. Therefore, we were selected to receive the Shabbat.

Shabbat summarizes Hashem's love for us

Maimonides adds that these two presentations of Shabbat combine to create an integrated and comprehensive message. The observance of Shabbat recalls Hashem's creation. Our selection as the nation who observes Shabbat reminds us of our redemption from bondage. These two messages merge into a comprehensive expression of Hashem's lovingkindness toward the Jewish people. He has provided us with a spiritual legacy – a Torah that teaches us the most fundamental truths. He has provided us with the foundation for material advancement – our liberation from slavery.[52]

The Shabbat liturgy reflects the two version of the Decalogue

Maimonides' insight resolves a number of additional problems. The Friday night *Amidah* for Shabbat focuses upon Shabbat as commemorating creation. Its central blessing includes the passages from the creation narrative that discuss Shabbat. The *Amidah* of Shabbat morning does mention the meaning of Shabbat but its focus is overwhelmingly upon the selection of Jewish people to observe Shabbat. Based upon Maimonides' insight, we can easily understand these two treatments.

The central benediction of Shabbat *Amidah* of Friday night begins with the statement:

You sanctified the seventh day for Your name. It is the completion of the creation of heavens and earth. You blessed it from among all of the days and sanctified it from among all periods of time.

This introduction sets the tone for the benediction. It mirrors the first iteration of the Decalogue. Its focus is upon the meaning of Shabbat. Therefore, the blessing discusses Shabbat as the memorial of creation and does not make mention of our redemption.

The Shabbat morning *Amidah* is not focused upon the objective of Shabbat. Instead, its focus is almost entirely upon our selection to observe it. This focus is derived directly from the second iteration of the *Aseret HaDibrot*. The theme of this second iteration was adopted by the Sages in this *Amidah*. Therefore, rather than focusing upon the meaning of Shabbat, the central benediction discusses our selection for the role of observing Shabbat.

Wealth and its meaning and purpose

Finally, Maimonides' insight provides us with an important message regarding priorities. As he explains, Hashem's lovingkindness is expressed in the spiritual and material gifts that he bestowed upon us. Shabbat is one of these spiritual gifts. It focuses upon one of the great and fundamental truths of the Torah – Hashem's creation of the universe. It also reminds us of our rescue from Egypt. This is a material gift. Our freedom is the foundation of every material achievement that has followed and been built upon it. Shabbat is designed to remind us of both of these expressions of Hashem's lovingkindness. The integration of both messages within Shabbat suggests their intimate relationship with one another. Let us further explore and delineate this relationship.

---

[52] Rabbaynu Moshe ben Maimon (Rambam) *Moreh Nevuchim*, volume 2, chapter 31.

The experience of liberation gives the Jewish people the capacity to more fully appreciate a day of rest. In other words, material achievements create the foundation for a spiritual encounter. Also, the observance of Shabbat gives meaning and purpose to our liberation. The two acts of kindness complement one another. Liberation makes us more intensely appreciate Shabbat; observance of Shabbat endows freedom with meaning and purpose. This is an excellent model for the optimal interaction and relationship between our material and spiritual endeavors.

Our material achievements provide us with the opportunity to advance our spiritual development. Conversely, our spiritual endeavors provide meaning to our material achievements. Ultimately, Maimonides' message reminds us to devote ourselves to spiritual development. Focus on material achievement as an end in itself cannot really provide fulfillment and satisfaction. Once a person has provided for oneself and one's family, the pursuit quickly resolves into an exercise in greed or psychological insecurity. Greed can never be satisfied and deep insecurities do not yield to reason. Consequently, the single-minded pursuit of the accumulation of wealth does not end in fulfillment. However, the person who utilizes one's material wellbeing to support pursuit of spiritual development will endow these material accomplishments with real meaning. Furthermore, one who nurtures a strong spiritual life, will discover meaning and fulfillment.

Until the day following the seventh week, you should count fifty days. And you should present an offering of new grain to Hashem. (VaYikra 23:16)

The Sacrifices of Shavuot are Central to its Sanctity

1. The purpose of the listing of Festivals

The *parasha* reviews the various days on which *melachah* – work – cannot be performed and upon which special sacrifices are offered in the *Mikdash*. The Chumash begins this list with Shabbat. The Chumash continues and identifies each of the Festivals. In almost every case, the Torah explains that *melachah* is prohibited on the occasion and sacrifices are offered. The Chumash also mentions special *mitzvot* related to the *Chag* – the Festival. For example, we are commanded to eat *matzah* on Pesach. On Yom Kippur, the Torah requires us to fast.

The specific sacrifices that are required for each *Chag* are generally not enumerated or described. This seems slightly odd. After all, much of Sefer VaYikra is devoted to discussing sacrifices. The commentators offer a number of explanations. Nachmanides suggests that the Festival sacrifices were not offered in the wilderness but only once the nation entered the Land of Israel. Therefore, a description of the specific sacrifices was postponed until the people were poised to enter the Land. This detailed description of the sacrifices is included in Sefer BeMidbar.[53] Of course, this raises the question: What is the purpose of this list? Rabbaynu Ovadia Sforno responds that this list identifies the occasions upon which *melachah* is prohibited.[54] The requirement to offer sacrifices is mentioned without elaboration as the main purpose of the list is to identify occasions restricted in *melachah*. This explains an odd deviation within the list. The list begins with Shabbat. In listing Shabbat, the Torah describes it as an occasion restricted in *melachah*. However, no mention is made of the additional sacrifices offered on Shabbat. Only

---

[53] Rabbaynu Moshe ben Nachman (Ramban), *Commentary on Sefer VaYikra* 23:2.
[54] Rabbaynu Ovadia Sforno, *Commentary on Sefer VaYikra* 23:2.

much later in the chapter is any reference made to the Shabbat sacrifices (Sefer VaYikra 23:38). However, Sforno's comments explain this deviation. The list begins with Shabbat in order to identify the list's purpose and nature. Shabbat is the most fundamental and primary occasion of restriction from *melachah*. Any list of occasion restricted in *melachah* must begin with Shabbat. Because this list is an enumeration of such occasions, it first identifies Shabbat and then proceeds to the Festivals.

There are exceptions in the listing to the manner in which sacrifices are treated. The *Omer* sacrifice, offered on the second day of Pesach, is described. The special offerings of Shavuot are also outlined. The Torah describes the two loaves – the *Shetai HaLechem* and the accompanying offerings brought on this *Chag*. Why is a discussion of these sacrifices included in this section?

2. The definition of sanctity and the sanctity of the Land of Israel

Our section is introduced by an important *pasuk*. Hashem tells Moshe, "Speak to Bnai Yisrael and say to them, 'These are the special times of Hashem. You should declare them as sacred occasions. The following are my special times.'"[55] In other words, this section provides a list of sacred occasions. As explained above, the Torah then provides a list of occasions on which *melachah* is restricted. What does this reveal regarding the concept of sanctity – *kedushah*?

The term *kedushah* or sanctity has a specific meaning in *halachah*. *Kedushah* means that the object or entity is differentiated through *halachah*. Let us consider an example. The Land of Israel has *kedushah*. From the perspective of *halachah*, this means that the Land is different from all other lands. This distinction is created by the special *mitzvot* that apply only to the Land of Israel. In other words, the special *mitzvot* of the Land of Israel are not a result of its *kedushah*. They are the source and basis of its *kedushah*. It is these *mitzvot* that differentiate the Land from other lands, make it special, and endow it with sanctity.

3. The source of the sanctity of Shabbat and the festivals

Now, let us return to our section. The Torah is providing a list of days that have *kedushah*. These days are different from the other days of the year. What is the fundamental element that creates this *kedushah*? The characteristic that is the focus of the list is the prohibition against *melachah*. This restriction is this unique *mitzvah* that defines these days as sacred occasions.

However, the list also notes that special sacrifices are associated with each *Chag*. This suggests an interesting question. The sacrifices also distinguish these days from all others. Our section implies that these offerings do not, by themselves, create the sanctity of the day. However, do the offerings add an additional aspect of *kedushah*?

4. The role of the Shabbat and festival sacrifices

The answer seems to be provided by the liturgy accompanying these occasions. On each, a *Musaf Amidah* is recited. The *Musaf Amidah* makes reference to the special offerings of the occasion. The *Amidah* is a series of blessings. It is notable that the reference to the sacrifices is not formulated as a separate blessing. The reference is included in the blessing that discusses the *kedushah* of the occasion. The message of this formulation is clear. Although, the sacrifices do not create the *kedushah* of these days, they do add to this sanctity. In other words, the essential

---

55 Sefer VaYikra 23:2.

element differentiating these occasions from other days is the prohibition of *melachah*. The sacrifices create a secondary *kedushah* or distinction.

5. The unique sanctity of Shavuot

This analysis suggests that Shavuot is different from other holidays. As explained above, in discussing Shavuot, the Torah does delineate the special offerings for the *Chag*. However, there is another deviation in the manner in which the Torah discusses Shavuot. In enumerating the other Festivals, the Torah first states that *melachah* is restricted on the occasion and then notes the requirement to offer special sacrifices. In its description of Shavuot, only after describing the sacrifices is the prohibition of *melachah* mentioned. The implication is that the relationship between the sacrifices and the prohibition of *melachah* is reversed. These offerings are not a mere secondary source of *kedushah*. On Shavuot, these sacrifices create the *kedushah* of the *Chag*.

In summary, the section demonstrates that the fundamental element that endows Shabbat and Festivals with sanctity is the restriction from performing *melachah*. Sacrifices further contribute to the occasion's sanctity but are not an independent source of *kedushah*. In other words, the characteristic that distinguishes Sukkot from the days that precede it and follow it – that endow it with sanctity – is the restriction of *melachah*. Sukkot has many special sacrifices – more than any other Festival. However, these sacrifices are not the distinction that is most fundamental to the occasion's *kedushah*. The sacrifices only enhance and contribute to the sanctity. This role of the *melachah* restriction is the same for most other Festivals. It is the fundamental source of their sanctity. However, Shavuot is an exception. The sacrifices of Shavuot are its fundamental distinguishing characteristic. It is these sacrifices that give the occasion its identity and sanctity. In this instance, it is the *melachah* prohibition that is secondary. Rather than endowing the occasion with sanctity, the *melachah* restriction is a response to and enhances the Festival's sanctity.

You shall bring out of your dwellings two wave-loaves of two tenth parts of an ephah. They shall be of fine flour. They shall be baked with leaven, for first-fruits unto Hashem. (VaYikra 23:17)

And the Festival of the Harvest, the first-fruits of your labors, which you sow in the field; and the Festival of the Ingathering, at the end of the year, when you gather in your labors out of the field. (Shemot 23:16)

Shavuot's Dual Identity

1. Shavuot is described in the Torah as a harvest festival

According to tradition, the Torah was received by Bnai Yisrael on the sixth day of Sivan. Shavuot is observed on the anniversary of the Sinai Revelation. In the liturgy for Shavuot, it is described as "the time of the giving of the Torah". However, the Chumash never explicitly associates Shavuot with Revelation. Instead, the Torah consistently describes Shavuot as a harvest festival. The above passages provide two examples. The first passage is found in the Torah's most extensive discussion of Shavuot. In these passages, Shavuot is described as the festival upon which "a new grain offering" is brought. This is a reference to a unique sacrifice offered on Shavuot. It is comprised of two loaves of leavened bread baked from fine wheat flour. This flour was milled from the wheat of the new harvest. This meal offering and the *Omer* meal offering of Pesach together express our acknowledgement that the life-sustaining bounty of the new harvest is a manifestation of Hashem's *chesed* – kindness. The characterization of Shavuot as a harvest festival is even more explicit in the second set of passages. In these passages, Shavuot is referred to as the Festival of the Harvest.

The question raised by the Torah's descriptions of Shavuot is obvious. Why does the Torah not describe Shavuot as the celebration of Revelation?

And He said: Certainly I will be with you. And this shall be the token unto you that I have sent you. When you have brought forth the people out of Egypt, you shall serve G-d upon this mountain. (Shemot 3:12)

2. The strange order in which the narrative of Revelation is presented

Although the Torah provides a historical record of the development of Bnai Yisrael, its account does not follow a strict chronological order. Sometimes the Torah departs from a chronological presentation of events in order to preserve the continuity of its narrative. In other instances, strict chronology is abandoned in order to juxtapose events or themes and thereby, communicate a message. In other words, the coherence, the continuity of the presentation, and other considerations take precedence over strict adherence to chronology.

Based upon this principle, the content of the chapters of the Torah's narrative leading-up to the Sinai Revelation is surprising. Hashem explained to Moshe at their first encounter at the *seneh* – the burning bush – that Bnai Yisrael would be redeemed from Egypt in order to be brought to Sinai and there receive the Torah. Given that this was the stated objective of the nation's redemption, it follows that after the Torah's narrative of the exodus is completed, the narrative should proceed with a description of Revelation. However, the Torah concludes its account of Bnai Yisrael's escape from Egypt with its description of the destruction of Paroh and his legions at the Reed Sea and Bnai Yisrael's song of praise to Hashem. The narrative then describes a number of events that occurred during the interim between the nation's redemption and Revelation. The only apparent justification for the insertion at this point of these events into the narrative is the preservation of a proper chronology. However, as explained above, this is a poor justification.

And the people murmured against Moshe, saying: What shall we drink? (Shemot 15:24)

Then came Amalek, and fought with Israel in Rephidim. (Shemot 17:8)

And Yitro, the priest of Midyan, Moshe's father-in-law, heard of all that G-d had done for Moshe, and for Israel His people, how Hashem had brought Israel out of Egypt. (Shemot 18:1)

3. Bnai Yisrael's complaints, Amalek, and Yitro – their place within the Torah's narrative

The intervening material can be divided into three distinct sections. The first section records a number of occasions upon which the people complained about their lack of adequate provisions. This section culminates with a flock of quail descending upon the camp which provide the people with meat and the initiation of the falling of the *mun* – the manna. The *mun* continued to fall and to sustain the people throughout their travels in the wilderness.

The next section describes Amalek's unprovoked attack of Bnai Yisrael. This section concludes by describing the defeat of Amalek and Hashem's pledge to utterly destroy this wicked adversary.

The final section describes the arrival of Yitro – Moshe's father-in-law. Yitro has heard of the wonders that Bnai Yisrael has experienced. He wishes to hear more about these wonders from those who experienced and witnessed them. After hearing these accounts, Yitro recognizes and praises Hashem. This section concludes with an account of the introduction of nation's first judicial system. This system was designed by Yitro and implemented by Moshe. The placement of this final section in this point in the narrative is the most difficult to explain. Rashi suggests that this section is not even in its proper chronological place. He explains that a careful analysis of the text suggests that Yitro arrived after Revelation.[56] The placement of this section in this point of the narrative certainly requires explanation.

Rav Yosef Dov Soloveitchik *Zt"l* suggests an important explanation for the insertion at this point in the narrative of these final two sections. The following is based upon his explanation. However, it expands upon the insight of Rav Soloveitchik and is not intended as a precise record of his thoughts.

And Hashem said to Moshe: I come unto you in a thick cloud, that the people may hear when I speak with you, and may also believe you forever. And Moses told the words of the people unto Hashem. (Shemot 19:9)

4. The Revolution of Revelation

Rav Soloveitchik suggests that these two incidents are intended as an introduction to the Torah's account of Revelation. The ideas presented in the Torah were not only revolutionary in their content. They were also delivered in a novel manner. Prior to Revelation, one's choice of religion was completely subjective. Humanity's varied religions were the inventions of their worshipers. This led to the plethora of idols and deities. Of course, Avraham, his descendants, and followers had discovered truths that were not merely subjective products of the imagination. However, for most of humanity, these "truths" that Avraham and his followers promoted seemed to be no more established than competing religious notions.

In this historical context, Revelation was revolutionary. It was the climax of Hashem's revelation of Himself before the entire nation. This process began with the demonstrations of His omnipotence in Egypt. It continued with the rescue of Bnai Yisrael from their pursuers at the Reed Sea and the drowning of Paroh and his army. The events of Sinai were the final and most awe-inspiring expression of Hashem's revelation. Bnai Yisrael's conviction in Hashem's existence and the authenticity of Torah was based upon their first-hand experience.

However, this revelation that began in Egypt and achieved its climax at Sinai was not relevant to only Bnai Yisrael. For the first time, humanity had been presented with a revealed religious doctrine authenticated by the testimony of an entire nation present at its revelation. The evidence of an omnipotent Creator Who interacts with humanity and the authentication of the Torah as a revealed truth was directed and relevant to all of humanity. Every human being who heard of the wonders that Hashem preformed in Egypt and His revelation at Sinai was challenged to respond to these authenticated truths.

5. Two responses to Revelation

Rav Soloveitchik explains that the account of Amalek's attack upon Bnai Yisrael and Yitro's acceptance of Hashem are inserted at this point into the narrative in order to demonstrate

---

[56] Rabbaynu Shlomo ben Yitzchak (Rashi), *Commentary on Sefer Shemot* 18:13.

the two universal responses to the message of the Egypt redemption and Revelation. These responses are rejection and denial or acceptance and embrasure. Amalek exemplifies the first response. Rather than consider the message communicated by Bnai Yisrael's miraculous redemption from Egypt and the utter destruction of their oppressors, Amalek fled into denial. Amalek could not tolerate the message communicated by redemption. It responded by seeking out Bnai Yisrael and acting out its fantasy of denial. It attacked Bnai Yisrael – bent upon undermining the message of redemption through destroying the newly redeemed nation.

Yitro exemplifies the alternative response. Yitro understood the significance of redemption and Revelation. He understood the evidence these provided of an omnipotent Creator and a revealed Torah. With this realization, he came to the camp of Bnai Yisrael in order to learn more of a truth he now sought to embrace and make his own.[57]

6. Recalling Revelation – a doctrine or a commandment?

Rav Soloveitchik's comments provide insight into a dispute between two great Sages. Nachmanides maintains that we are required by a commandment of the Torah to not forget – even for a moment – the episode of Revelation. We are to remain continuously aware and cognizant of the events of Sinai.[58] Maimonides demurs. He agrees that our conviction in the authenticity of Revelation is a fundamental element of our religion.[59] Yet, he does agree that this doctrine is the material of a specific Torah commandment. Why does Maimonides reject Nachmanides' seemingly reasonable contention that a fundamental element of our religion should be the subject of one of the Torah's commandments?

Based upon Rav Soloveitchik's comments, Revelation emerges as not merely an important or even pivotal historical event. It is the distinguishing characteristic of the Torah. It is the foundation of the authenticity of the Torah and it differentiates Torah from other subjective religious doctrines. Perhaps, for this reason, Maimonides contends that conviction in the authenticity of Revelation cannot be the subject of a commandment. It is the foundation of every single commandment. Every commandment is performed as an expression of our conviction in the authenticity of Revelation. In other words, our conviction in the authenticity of Revelation is implicit in the performance of each and every commandment.

7. The relationship between Shavuot and Revelation

Aruch HaShulcan suggests that for this reason the Torah does not refer to Shavuot as the celebration of Revelation. With every commandment that we perform, we confirm Revelation. No day is needed to remind us of Revelation or to memorialize the event.[60] It is true that our liturgy refers to Shavuot as the time of Revelation. However, the intent is not to suggest that Shavuot memorializes or moves us to recall Revelation. Instead, we are merely declaring that the anniversary of Revelation is worthy of celebration as a day of thanksgiving.

An analogy will help communicate Aruch HaShulchan's perspective. A husband and wife should appreciate each other and love one another every day of the year. It would be ridiculous

---

[57] These comments are based upon a recorded lecture of Rav Soloveitchik *Zt"l*.

[58] Rabbaynu Moshe ben Nachman (Ramban), *Critique on Maimonides' Sefer HaMitzvot —* Negative Commands that Maimonides Neglected to Include.

[59] R' Moshe ben Maimon (Rambam) *Commentary on the Mishne*, Mesechet Sanherin 10:1.

[60] Rav Aharon HaLeyve Epstein, *Aruch HaShulchan*, Orech Chayim 494:2.

to have just a single day of the year devoted to appreciating one's wife or husband. This appreciation should be present and expressed every day. Nonetheless, the date of a married couple's anniversary should be special to the husband and wife. This day is the anniversary of one of the most important events in their lives. Even though the husband and wife appreciate and cherish one another every day, this day deserves special acknowledgment. Similarly, we express our conviction in Revelation with every *mitzvah* we perform. However, Shavuot – the anniversary of Revelation – deserves special acknowledgment as a day of awesome significance.

According to Aruch HaShulchan, the Torah does not explicitly refer to Shavuot as a celebration of Revelation. Such a characterization could be easily misunderstood to suggest that some commemorative celebration of Revelation is required rather than its commemoration through observance of the Torah's commandments. Only in the liturgy is Shavuot referred to as the time of Revelation. However, the intention in this reference is not to suggest that our commemoration of Revelation can be relegated to a calendar date. The intention is to proclaim the day that is the anniversary of Revelation as a day worthy of celebration and thanksgiving.

And you should declare on that very day (that) a sacred occasion it should be for you. You should not perform any work of labor. (This is) an eternal law, in all of your places of settlement, for all of your generations. (VaYikra 23:21)

The Torah's Mysterious Treatment of the Festival of Shavuot

1. The Torah does not reveal the purpose of Shavuot

The above is one of the pesukim in the Torah that instruct us to observe the festival of Shavuot. Shavuot corresponds with the date upon which we received the Torah at Sinai and commemorates that event. However, the connection between Shavuot and the Sinai Revelation is never explicitly stated in the Torah. Whereas the Torah teaches us that we are to observe Pesach in commemoration of our redemption from Egypt and that we are to celebrate Sukkot in order to recall our sojourn in the wilderness, the purpose and objective of Shavuot are not stated in the Torah. Instead, Shavuot's identity as a celebration of Revelation is only revealed in the Oral Law. Why is the Written Torah silent on the issue of Shavuot's objective and purpose?

And you should count for yourself from the day following the Shabbat, from the day of your bringing of the Omer wave-offering, seven weeks. They shall be for you full weeks. (VaYikra 23:15)

2. The Torah's strange treatment of Shavuot's date

Another oddity in the Torah's treatment of Shavuot is found in the above passage. The date of every other festival is identified by the Torah as a calendar date. Pesach's date is the 15th of the first month of the year. Rosh HaShanah's date is the first day of the seventh month of the year. Shavuot is the only exception to this pattern. It is not assigned a calendar date. Instead, we are instructed to count seven weeks or forty-nine days from the day after the first day of the festival of Pesach. On the fiftieth day Shavuot is to be observed.

The deviation from the typical dating standard – assigning each festival to a day of a month – can be explained. The apparent purpose of the Torah's dating scheme for Shavuot is to stress the relationship between Pesach and Shavuot. Shavuot completes the objective of Pesach. The redemption from Egypt was not intended to merely free us from bondage. We were freed in order to receive the Torah at Sinai. At Sinai, the objective of the redemption was realized. We became the people of the Torah and the nation of Hashem. This relationship is preserved in the manner in which the date for Shavuot is presented in the Torah. We count from the day commemorating our redemption to the date of Revelation. The counting joins the two festivals together and emphasizes the unity of their objective – redemption from Egypt for the purpose of Revelation at Sinai.

However, another aspect of the manner in which the date of Shavuot is indentified is not as easily explained and has been a source of consternation for the Jewish people. Rather than stating the counting to Shavuot begins with the second day of Pesach, the passage actually states that we begin counting on the "day following the Shabbat". The identification of the "Shabbat" in the passage as the first day of Pesach is provided by the Oral Law. As early as the Talmudic era, the Sadducees – who disputed the authenticity of the Oral Tradition – disputed the standard interpretation of the above passage. Therefore, they rejected the validity of the traditional date for celebrating Shavuot. Indeed, it is odd that the Torah describes the date for the initiating of the countdown to Shavuot as "the day following the Shabbat"! Why did the Torah not unequivocally identify the date as the day following the first day of Pesach? This would have avoided all of the subsequent debate and confusion generated by the ambiguity of the Torah's wording.

And it is customary to recite Shir HaShirim on the intermediate Shabbat (of Pesach)…

It is customary to recite Ruth on Shavuot … (Rav Moshe Isserles, Comments on Shulchan Aruch, Orech Chayim 490:9).

2. The custom of reading Megilat Ruth on Shavuot

The above source quotes the custom to read the Megilah of Ruth on Shavuot. There are various reasons suggested for this custom. Some identify only a very vague relationship between the contents of the Megilah and the celebration. However, perhaps some explanation can be found in the fundamental elements of the narrative of the Megilah.

The Megilah is an unusual work. The other works included in TaNaCh communicate a clear moral or theological message. In Megilat Ruth the message or messages are less clearly stated. The Megilah provides an account of the conversion of Ruth to Judaism. She travels to the Land of Israel with her mother-in-law Naomi. They live together in poverty, supporting themselves through collecting the annual agricultural charity-gifts provided at the time of harvest. Ruth impresses a wealthy and influential beneficiary Boaz. He is a relative of the family. Eventually, the relationship results in Boaz's rescue of the family from poverty and his marriage to Ruth. There are many important lessons included in this narrative. Yet, these lessons are not stated explicitly.

Perhaps, the lesson of Megilat Ruth is expressed in its final passages. In these passages, the Megilah traces King David back to the union between Boaz and Ruth. This ending suggests that the Megilah can be interpreted as an account of David's lineage. Such a conclusion is supported by the Talmud's position regarding the Megilah's authorship. According to the Talmud, the Megilah was composed by the prophet Shmuel.[61] Shmuel appointed David as king in place of Shaul. Apparently, Shmuel felt that it was important to create a historical record of David's ancestry. Why did he feel this was necessary?

And he took ten men from among the elders of the city and he said, "Sit here." And they sat. (Megilat Ruth 4:2)

---

[61] Mesechet Baba Batra 12b.

3. The controversy surrounding David's appointment as king

A possible explanation for Shmuel's concern with David's lineage is provided by the Talmud. The Talmud explains that David's eligibility to serve as king – indeed, his eligibility to be included within the community of the Jewish nation – was hotly debated. David descended from Ruth. Ruth was a convert from the nation of Moav. The Torah commands us to not accept into Bnai Yisrael converts from Moav.[62] Some authorities contemporary to David argued that this restriction disqualified him from membership within the community and certainly barred him from becoming king. Others argued that the restriction was limited to males from the nation of Moav and did not extend to women. These Sages contended that Ruth was a legitimate convert and David was fully qualified to be king. Eventually, this second group of Sages established their position as correct based upon the Oral Tradition.[63]

In composing the Megilah, Shmuel acknowledged David's ancestry and endorsed the ruling of these Sages. The Talmud actually asserts that Boaz also confirmed this ruling in marrying Ruth. In the above passage, the Megilah explains that Boaz gathered together ten elders before whom he announced his intention to marry Ruth.[64] The Talmud explains that he gathered these scholars together to publicly declare that the Torah restriction regarding Moav relates to the males and not females.[65] Boaz was an esteemed scholar and Torah authority. He was a master of the Oral Law and his ruling was accepted.

In short, the message of the Megilah is that although the Written Law might be interpreted to exclude males and females of Moav from inclusion in Bnai Yisrael, the Oral Law teaches us that the restriction is limited to males. Females may convert and join Bnai Yisrael. Therefore, David – a descendent of Ruth – was fully qualified to assume the mantle of leadership. This message is uniquely relevant to Shavuot.

The eighth foundation is that the Torah is from heaven. It requires that we accept that this entire Torah that is in our possession today is the same Torah that was given to Moshe and that it is entirely from Hashem... Similarly, its traditional explanation is from Hashem. (Maimonides, Commentary on the Mishne, Tractate Sanhedrin 10:1)

4. The Written and Oral Law are derived from Sinai

One of the Torah's fundamental principles is that it was communicated to Bnai Yisrael through Moshe at the Sinai Revelation. This import of this principle is so great the festival of Shavuot commemorates the event of Revelation. Maimonides explains that this principle does not apply only to the Written Torah. It also applies to the interpretation of the Written Torah. This interpretation is the Oral Law or Oral Tradition. In other words, the entire Written Torah and the basic components of the Oral Law were communicated at Sinai from Hashem.

Therefore, Shavuot commemorates not only our receipt of the Torah's written element but also its Oral interpretation. There is no better way to communicate that Shavuot celebrates the Sinai pedigree of both the written and oral components of the Law, than the method employed by the Torah. The Torah's written portion describes Shavuot in mysterious terms. It

---

[62] Sefer Devarim 23:4.
[63] Mesechet Yevamot 76b.
[64] Megilat Ruth 4:2.
[65] Mesechet Ketuvot 7b.

leaves its date vaguely and ambiguously stated. It provides no insight into the purpose and meaning of the festival's observance. These omissions and obfuscations compel the reader to acknowledge that the Law-Giver must have provided more. He must have provided an explanation in addition to the written material. Thus, the very command to observe Shavuot reinforces its identity as the festival that recalls the Sinai Revelation and communication of the entire Torah – its written and oral components.

Now, the connection between Megilat Ruth and Shavuot is quite clear. The Megilah provides an account of King David's origins and endorses his legitimacy. It accomplishes this by emphasizing the role of the Oral Tradition. David's kingship was predicated upon the legitimacy of the Oral Law as the true interpretation of the Written Torah. In reading the Megilah on Shavuot, we confirm our acceptance of the Oral Law as a fundamental element of the Sinai legacy.[66]

And you shall count seven sabbaths of years for yourself, seven times seven years. And there shall be to you the days of seven sabbaths of years – forty-nine years. Then you shall make a proclamation with the blast of the shofar horn on the tenth day of the seventh month. On the Day of Atonement you shall proclaim with the shofar horn throughout your land. And you shall sanctify the fiftieth year, and proclaim liberty throughout the land unto all its inhabitants. It shall be a Yovel unto you. And every man shall return to his possession. And every man shall return to his family. (VaYikra 25:8-10)

Yovel and Omer – Two Versions of Counting

1. The requirement to count the years of the Yovel cycle

Parshat BeHar discusses the laws of Shemitah – the Sabbatical Year – and Yovel – the Jubilee Year. The Sabbatical Year occurs in the Land of Israel every seven years. During the Shemitah year, the land may not be worked. The produce that grows spontaneously is shared by all inhabitants of the land. Every fiftieth year the Yovel year – the Jubilee year – is observed in the Land of Israel. The Yovel marks the culmination of seven Sabbatical year cycles. The Yovel shares many of the laws of the Sabbatical year. One of the shared laws is the restriction against farming the land.

Additional mitzvot apply to Yovel that are not in-common with Shemitah. In the Yovel year all Jewish indentured servants must be granted their liberty. This applies even to cases in which the servant wishes to continue his servitude. He is not permitted to extend his term of service beyond the Yovel year.

Another aspect of Yovel is land redistribution. After its conquests, the Land of Israel was distributed among the shevatim – the tribes. In turn, each shevet – tribe – divided its portion among its constituent families. The families divided their respective portions among their members. In each generation the land was further divided among the heirs of the land-holders. In general, a transfer of land was effective up to the Yovel year. With the arrival of the Yovel year all land was redistributed among the heirs of the owners to whom the land was distributed following its conquest.

---

[66] A similar presentation can be found in: Rav Yitzchak Mirsky, Higyonai Halacha (Jerusalem 1989), volume 1, pp. 134-140.

In the above passages, Bnai Yisrael is commanded to count the years of the Yovel cycle. Seven seven-year cycles are to be counted or a total of forty-nine years. The fiftieth year is to be declared the Yovel year.

And you shall count for you from the day following the day of rest, from the day that you brought the sheaf of the waving, seven weeks. They should be complete. Until the day after the seventh week you shall count fifty days. And you shall present a new meal-offering unto Hashem.
(VaYikra 23:15-16)

2. The requirement to count the days of the Omer

The Torah description of the counting of the years leading-up to the Yovel year is similar to the description in Parshat Emor of the counting of the days from the second day of Pesach to the festival of Shavuot. In both instances Bnai Yisrael is required to count seven cycles of seven or forty-nine time units and then sanctify the fiftieth unit. In the case of Yovel the time units that are counted are years – seven cycles of seven years or forty-nine years are counted and the fiftieth year is sanctified as the Yovel year. In the case of counting from Pesach to Shavuot, the units counted are days. Seven cycles of seven days or forty-nine days are counted and the fiftieth day is sanctified as Shavuot – the Festival of Weeks.

The days from the second day of Pesach until Shavuot are counted in the literal sense. Each evening we count by proclaiming the day's number. On the second night of Pesach we declare that the night initiates the first day of the Omer – the series of days between that night and Shavuot. Similarly, on the third night of Pesach we declare that we have arrived at the second day of the Omer. This process continues for forty-nine evenings. Because these proclamations fulfill the mitzvah described in the above passages, each evening the proclamation is proceeded by a blessing – as is typical before the performance of most positive commandments.

3. Are the years of the Yovel cycle formally counted?

The Talmud explains that every individual is required to count the days of the Omer. The Tosefot explain that in this requirement the mitzvah of counting the Omer differs from counting of the years the Yovel cycle. The responsibility of counting the years of the Yovel cycle rest upon the Rabbinic court. Individuals do not participate in counting the years of this cycle. The Tosefot then raise an interesting question. As explained above, the commandment to count the Omer is interpreted in a literal manner. Each night a formal counting is performed proceeded by a blessing by every individual. Does this same interpretation apply to the commandment to count the years of the Yovel cycle? Does the court, at the beginning of each year, recite a blessing and proclaim the number of that year in the Yovel cycle? The Tosefot raise this issue without coming to a resolution.[67] However, other authorities do take positions regarding the Tosefot's question. Rabbaynu Asher[68] and Maimonides[69] agree that the years of the Yovel cycle are counted by the court in the same manner in which the Omer is counted by individuals. Rabbaynu Nissim disagrees and argues that the years of the Yovel cycle are not formally counted. The court is required only to mark the years – in whatever manner – and declare each fiftieth year to be a Yovel year.[70]

---

[67] Tosefot Mesechet Menachot 65b.
[68] Rabbaynu Asher, Commentary on the Talmud, Mesechet Pesachim, Chapter 10, note 40.
[69] Rabbaynu Moshe ben Maimon (Rambam) Sefer HaMitzvot, Mitzvat Aseh 140.

At first glance it seems that the position of Maimonides and Rabbaynu Asher is more reasonable. The passages regarding the counting of the years of the Yovel cycle and those describing the counting of the Omer mirror one another. It is reasonable to assume that just as the counting of the Omer requires a formal proclamation each and every evening, so too, the counting of the years of the Yovel cycle is accomplished through a formal proclamation at the beginning of each year of the cycle. Why does Rabbaynu Nissim conclude that the court is merely required to keep the tally necessary to assure that the Yovel year is observed in its appropriate time but not actually formally proclaim each year?

4. An important difference in the Torah's descriptions of counting

A more careful review of the passages describing each counting is helpful. The two sets of passages are very similar. Each set describes an obligation to count forty-nine units which comprise seven cycles of seven units. However, there is a fundamental difference between the two sets of passages. The passages concerning the counting of the Omer describe the obligation as a process of counting from a starting point to an end point. We are instructed to count from the second day of Pesach to the fiftieth day – upon which Shavuot is observed. The element of counting from a beginning point to an end point is absent in the Torah's description of the counting of the years of the Yovel cycle.

What is the significance of the inclusion of this element in the Torah's directive to count the Omer? What conclusions may be drawn from the absence of this element in the instructions regarding the counting of the Yovel cycle?

5. The Shavuot anomaly and its explanation

Pesach, Shavuot, and Sukkot constitute the three Regalim – the pilgrimage festivals. During the era of its existence, we were required to appear at the Bait HaMikdash – the Sacred Temple – on these three festivals. It is interesting that Pesach and Sukkot are observed over a period of seven or eight days. Both begin and end with a day that is sanctified with a relatively comprehensive prohibition against performance of creative labor. During the intervening days the prohibition against performing creative labor is more lenient. In contrast, Shavuot is described by the Torah as a single day festival. How can this difference between Shavuot and the other Regalim be explained?

Nachmanides discusses this issue. He explains that Shavuot is actually an extension of Pesach. It is the culmination of an extended festival that begins with Pesach and extends through Shavuot. The intervening days between Pesach and Shavuot – although not subject to a prohibition against labor – are to be understood as akin to the intervening days between the initial and final sanctified days of Sukkot and Pesach proper.[71]

6. The fundamental difference between the two versions of counting

Based on Nachmanides' comments, the message communicated by the Torah's description of the counting of the Omer can be better understood. This Torah describes the counting of the days of the Omer as a process of counting from Pesach to Shavuot. This is because this counting is designed to express the relationship between Pesach and Shavuot.

---

[70] R' Nissim ben Reuven, (Ran) Notes to Commentary of R Yitzchak Alfasi, Mes. Pesachim 27b.
[71] Rabbaynu Moshe ben Nachman (Ramban), Commentary on Sefer VaYikra 23:36.

Through counting to Shavuot we demonstrate that it is connected to and the completion of the Pesach festival.

As explained above, the Torah's description of counting the years of the Yovel cycle differs from its description of counting the days of the Omer. The Omer counting is described as a process of counting from one date to another. In discussing the counting of the years of the Yovel cycle, this element is absent. The significance of this element is now evident. The process of counting the days of the Omer is designed to communicate the integral connection between Pesach and Shavuot. Merely counting-off forty-nine days on a calendar and marking the fiftieth day as Shavuot does not accomplish this task. It is through the process of counting that the connection between Pesach and Shavuot is communicated. In contrast, the counting of the Yovel cycle is not described in terms of counting from one date to another date that is fifty years in the future. The absence of this description suggests to Rabbaynu Nissim that the counting of the years of the Yovel cycle does not require a formal annual proclamation by the court. The objective of this counting is not to connect each Yovel year with the next Yovel year. The counting of the years of the Yovel cycle is instead a requirement upon the court to maintain a tally of the years and to declare each Yovel year in its proper time.

And you shall take from the first of all the fruits of the land that you shall bring forth from the land that Hashem your G-d gave to you. And you shall place it in a basket. And you shall go to the place that Hashem your G-d will choose to associate with His name. (Devarim 26:2)

The Species of Fruit Brought as Bikurim

This *pasuk* discusses the commandment of *Bikurim*. This *mitzvah* requires that the first fruits of each year be brought to the *Bait HaMikdash* – the Holy Temple. The *Bikurim* are brought only from the seven special species. These species are wheat, barley, grapes, figs, pomegranates, olives, and dates. These species are identified with the Land of Israel. The Land is considered blessed with these fruits and grains.

The Torah does not explicitly state that *Bikurim* are only brought from these fruits and grains. This law is derived from the *Torah SheBeAl Peh* – the Oral Law. Rashi explains that the source for this law is the word "land" used in the expression, "fruits of the land."[72] Rabbaynu Ovadia Sforno disputes this derivation. He explains that the law is derived from the word "first" in the phrase, "first fruits." He explains that the term "first" does not indicate that the *Bikurim* are brought from those fruits first to appear. Instead, the term refers to the significance of the fruits. *Bikurim* are brought from those species of the first or greatest significance. These are the special fruits and grains with which the Land is blessed – the seven species.[73]

This dispute provides an important insight into the *mitzvah* of *Bikurim*. The *mitzvah* of *Bikurim* is designed to demonstrate appreciation for the Land of Israel and its abundance. Rashi maintains that the seven species are central to the *mitzvah* because they are closely associated with the Land. Other fruits grow in the Land of Israel. However, they are not regarded as the species associated with the Land of Israel. In showing gratitude for the Land, it is appropriate to

---

[72] Rabbaynu Shlomo ben Yitzchak (Rashi), *Commentary on Sefer Devarim* 26:2.
[73] Rabbaynu Ovadia Sforno, *Commentary on Sefer Devarim* 26:2.

represent the Land through the fruits with which it is most closely associated. These are the fruits of the seven species.

Sforno maintains that the seven species are not chosen because of this association. The offering of *Bikurim* is an expression of gratitude. The quality of the offering is determined, in part, by the value of the object offered. Sforno maintains that since these are the best fruits that the Land produces, they are most appropriate for the offering.

In short, we are thanking Hashem for the Land. According to Rashi, the seven species are chosen because of their association with the Land. According to Sforno, they are chosen because their eminence makes them the ideal offering.

"And you shall take from the first of all the fruit produced by your land that Hashem your G-d is giving you. And you should place it in a basket and go to the place that Hashem your G-d will choose to associate with His name." (Devarim 26:2)

This *pasuk* introduces the *mitzvah* of *Bikkurim*. This *mitzvah* requires that the first fruit of the harvest be brought to Yerushalayim and presented to the *Kohen*. The *mitzvah* of *Bikkurim* does not come into effect until the land of Israel is conquered and settled.[74]

Our *pasuk* indicates that the *Bikkurim* are to be brought to the place that the Almighty will associate with His name. What place fulfills this requirement? Certainly, the *Bait HaMikdash* satisfies this criterion. However, the *Bait HaMikdash* was built by King Shlomo. How was the *mitzvah* of *Bikkurim* fulfilled prior to the construction of the *Bait HaMikdash*? The Midrash Sifrei discusses this issue. In order to understand Sifrei's response, some background information is required.

At Sinai Bnai Yisrael were commanded to build a *Mishcan* – the Tabernacle. This was a portable temple. During the travels in the wilderness, the *Mishcan* was the center for worship. All sacrifices were offered in the Tabernacle. When Bnai Yisrael entered the land of Israel, the *Mishcan* was not abandoned. It continued to function as the nation's holy Temple. It retained this status until the *Bait HaMikdash* was constructed. The *Mishcan* was initially erected in Shilo. It was then moved to Nov. Later it was transferred to Givon.

Sifrei explains that *Bikkurim* were brought to the *Mishcan* only when it was situated in Shilo. However, once the *Mishcan* was transferred the *mitzvah* of *Bikkurim* was suspended. Performance of the commandment did not resume until the *Bait HaMikdash* was completed. In other words, as long as it was located in Shilo the *Mishcan* fulfilled the requirements of the *mitzvah*. Once the Tabernacle was transferred from Shilo it no longer satisfied the criterion of the commandment.[75]

Why was the *Mishcan* only appropriate for the *mitzvah* of *Bikkurim* when it was at Shilo? Why did it lose its suitability when moved to Nov and then Givon?

Torah Temimah responds based upon a passage in the Navi. The Navi explains that the *Mishcan* was established in Shilo through the decision of Yehoshua, the elders and Bnai Yisrael.[76] Torah Temimah suggests that because of this consensus the *Mishcan* in Shilo was referred to as the *Bait Hashem* – the House of G-d.[77] The establishment of the *Mishcan* in Nov and Givon was

---

[74] Mesechet Kiddushin 37b.
[75] Sifrei Parshat Ki Tavo, chapter 2.
[76] Sefer Yehoshua 18:1.

not accompanied by this same level of consensus. The *Mishcan* was not referred to the *Bait Hashem* during its sojourns in these locations. Therefore, the *Bikkurim* could not be brought to the *Mishcan* while it was at these sites.[78]

Torah Temimah is providing a clear distinction between the status of the *Mishcan* in Shilo and its status when located in Nov and Givon. However, we must ask two questions. First, why can *Bikkurim* only be brought to the *Mishcan* when it has the status of *Bait Hashem*? Second, how did the consensus of Yehoshua the elders and the nation confer this status?

It seems that *Bikkuri* can only be brought to a *Mishcan* or *Mikdash* that is designated as the central location for worship. This designation is indicated that the title of *Bait Hashem*. In order for this designation to fully exist, it must emerge from the consensus of the leader of prophet, the elders and the nation. Only through the acquiescence of all these parties does the Tabernacle become the unique central location for worship – the *Bait Hashem*. In other words, the consensus endows the *Mishcan* with a higher designation and sanctity. This higher designation is essential to the *mitzvah* of *Bikkurim*.

Abrabanel suggests an alternative distinction between the *Mishcan* of Shilo and the *Mishcan* of Nov and Givon. He observes that the walls of the *Mishcan* in the wilderness were made of curtains. These curtains were supported by wooden boards. In Shilo these walls were replaced by a stone structure. Only the roof of *Mishcan* was still composed of curtains. In Nov and Givon the original system of curtain walls supported by boards was restored. Abrabanel contends that these walls endowed Shilo with the status of a House of Hashem. Because the Tabernacle of Nov and Givon lacked stone walls, the *Mishcan* could not be defined as a house while at these locations.[79]

It seems odd that the structure of the walls of the *Mishcan* would determine suitability for the *mitzvah* of *Bikkurim*! How did walls produce this effect?

It seems reasonable that the presence of stone walls indicated some level of permanence. Without these stone walls the *Mishcan* was essentially a portable structure. It had no relationship to its current location. Once the boards and curtains were replaced by stone walls, the *Mishcan* was transformed. It assumed a relationship with its location. It was a fixed feature of the land and location.

Abrabanel apparently maintains that the *mitzvah* of *Bikkurim* required more than a Temple. It demands a geographically unique location sanctified through the *Mishcan*. The *Bikkurim* cannot merely be brought to a holy structure. They must be must be brought to a location endowed with sanctity. A portable Tabernacle has not effect on the sanctity of its geographical location. There is no relationship between the *Mishcan* and the location. This changes once walls are erected. The *Mishcan* becomes a fixture of the land. Now the geographical location is sanctified.

Malbim suggests that the approach of Torah Temimah and Abrabanel are related. The *Mishcan* of Shilo was erected with stone walls as a result of the consensus. It seems the Malbim

---

[77] Sefer Shemuel I, 1:24.
[78] Rav Baruch HaLeyve Epstein, *Torah Temimah on Sefer Devarim* 26:2.
[79] Don Yitzchak Abravanel, *Commentary on Sefer Devarim*, p 245.

maintains that the *Mishcan* cannot be assigned a relationship with a geographical location without the consensus of the prophet, elders and nation.[80]

Malbim's approach explains another *halacha*. Maimonides explains the process for extending the boundaries of Yerushalayim and the courtyards of the *Mikdash*. He explains that this process requires the consensus of the king, prophet and Sages.[81] Why is this consensus needed? According to Malbim, we can understand this requirement. An addition to the city of Yerushalayim endows the geographical location with the sanctity of the city. Extending the courtyards of the Temple has the same effect. It bestows sanctity upon the location. The association of these sanctities with a geographical location requires the consensus of the nation. This only emerges though the participation of the king, prophet and Sages.

And you shall take from the first of all the fruit produced by your land that Hashem your G-d is giving you. And you should place it in a basket and go to the place that Hashem your G-d will choose to associate with His name. (Devarim 26:2)

The Status of the Mishcan at Its Various Locations

1. The Mishcan and its various locations

This pasuk introduces the mitzvah of Bikkurim. This mitzvah requires that the first fruit of the harvest be brought to Yerushalayim and presented to the Kohen. The mitzvah of Bikkurim does not come into effect until the land of Israel is conquered and settled.[82]

Our pasuk indicates that the Bikkurim are to be brought to the place that Hashem will associate with His name. What place fulfills this requirement? Certainly, the Bait HaMikdash – the Holy Temple – satisfies this criterion. However, the Bait HaMikdash was built by King Shlomo. How was the mitzvah of Bikkurim fulfilled prior to the construction of the Bait HaMikdash? The Midrash Sifrei discusses this issue. In order to understand Sifrei's response, some background information is required.

At Sinai, Bnai Yisrael were commanded to build a Mishcan – the Tabernacle. This was a portable temple. During the travels in the wilderness, the Mishcan was the center for worship. All sacrifices were offered in the Tabernacle. When Bnai Yisrael entered the Land of Israel, the Mishcan was not abandoned. It was erected at Gilgal and it continued to function as the nation's Temple. It retained this status until the Bait HaMikdash was constructed. The Mishcan was moved from Gilgal to Shilo. It was then moved to Nov. Later it was transferred to Givon.

2. Bikkurim were brought to the Mishcan only when it was at Shilo

Sifrei explains that Bikkurim were brought to the Mishcan only when it was situated in Shilo. However, prior to that point and once the Mishcan was transferred the mitzvah of Bikkurim was suspended. Performance of the commandment did not resume until the Bait HaMikdash was completed. In other words, as long as it was located in Shilo the Mishcan fulfilled the requirements of the mitzvah. Before its establishment in Shilo and once the Tabernacle was transferred from Shilo it no longer satisfied the criterion of the commandment.[83]

[80] Rabbaynu Meir Libush (Malbim), *Commentary on Sefer Devarim* 26:2.
[81] Rabbaynu Moshe ben Maimon, *Mishne Torah*, Hilchot Bait HaBichirah 6:11.
[82] Mesechet Kiddushin 37b.
[83] Sifrei Parshat Ki Tavo, chapter 2.

Why was the Mishcan only appropriate for the mitzvah of Bikkurim when it was at Shilo? Why was it not suitable for the mitzvah when it was at Gilgal, Nov, and Givon?

The finest first fruit of your land you should bring to the House of Hashem your G-d. Do not cook a kid in the milk of its mother. (Shemot 23:19)

And the entire assembly of Bnai Yisrael gathered at Shilo and they established there the Ohel Moed. And the land was conquered before them. (Sefer Yehoshua 18:1)

3. The Shilo Mishcan status as Bait Hashem

Torah Temimah responds based upon the two passages above and a third passage in Sefer Shmuel. The first pasuk discusses the mitzvah of Bikkurim. In this passage, the Torah stipulates that the Bikkurim must be brought to Bait Hashem – the House of Hashem. This is an interesting term. This term is not used to refer to the Mishcan when it accompanied Bnai Yisrael in the wilderness. The term is also not used by the prophets when referring to the Mishcan of Gilgal, Nov or Givon. The prophets only call the Mishcan the House of Hashem when referring the Shilo period.[84] Torah Temimah suggests that the Torah requires the Bikkurim to be brought to Bait Hashem. The Mishcan only achieved this status during its Shilo period. After, it was only the Tabernacle but not the House of Hashem. What was special about the Shilo period and how did the Mishcan attain its special status during this period?

The second of the passages above explains that the Mishcan was established in Shilo through the decision of the entire nation. Torah Temimah explains that the decision reflected the agreement of Yehoshua, the nation's elders and Bnai Yisrael.[85] Torah Temimah suggests that because of this consensus the special status of Bait Hashem was conferred upon the Mishcan in Shilo. The establishment of the Mishcan in Nov and Givon was not accompanied by this same level of consensus. The Mishcan was not referred to the Bait Hashem during its sojourns in these locations. Therefore, the Bikkurim could not be brought to the Mishcan while it was at these sites.[86,87]

Torah Temimah is providing a clear distinction between the status of the Mishcan in Shilo and its status when located in Nov and Givon. However, two questions must be asked. First, why are Bikkurim brought only to the Mishcan when it has the status of Bait Hashem? Second, how did the consensus of Yehoshua, the elders and the nation confer this status?

4. Transforming Mishcan into Bait Hashem

Perhaps, the explanation is provided by an interesting law related to the Shilo Mishcan. During the time that the Mishcan was in Gilgal it was permitted to offer certain sacrifices outside of the Mishcan. When the Mishcan was transferred to Shilo, these sacrifices became prohibited. This prohibition remained in place during the entire Shilo period. In other words, the Shilo

---

[84] Sefer Shemuel I, 1:24.

[85] Sefer Yehoshua 18:1.

[86] Rav Baruch HaLeyve Epstein, Torah Temimah on Sefer Devarim 26:2.

[87] Torah Temimah does not discuss status of the Mishcan during the Gigal period. The Mishcan was placed in Gilgal by Yehoshua and it seems reasonable that this decision should have the same status as his subsequent decision to move the Mishcan to Shilo. Perhaps, because Bnai Yisrael was still deeply involved in taking possession of the land, the mitzvah of Bikkurim was not yet in place during the Gilgal period.

Mishcan was the exclusive location for sacrificial service. The Mishcans of Nov and Givon did not have this exclusive status. During the Nov and Givon period and until the building of the Bait HaMikdash, it was again permitted to offer certain sacrifices outside of the Mishcan. This law suggests that the Mishcan of Shilo was designated as the central and exclusive place for sacrificial service and worship. For this reason, the prophets refer to the Shilo Mishcan and Bait Hashem. Bikkurim can only be brought to a Mishcan or Mikdash that is designated as the central and exclusive location for worship – as Bait Hashem.

This explains the significance of consensus. In order for this designation to fully exist, it must emerge from the consensus of the leader or prophet, the elders and the nation. Only through the acquiescence of all these parties does the Tabernacle become the unique central location for worship – the Bait Hashem. In other words, the consensus endows the Mishcan with a higher designation and sanctity. This higher designation is essential to the mitzvah of Bikkurim.

5. The relationship of the Mishcan to the Land of Israel

Don Yitzcahk Abrabanel suggests an alternative distinction between the Mishcan of Shilo and the Mishcan of Gilgal, Nov and Givon. He observes that the walls of the Mishcan in the wilderness were made of curtains. These curtains were supported by wooden boards. In Shilo these walls were replaced by a stone structure. Only the roof of Mishcan was still composed of curtains. In Nov and Givon the original system of curtain walls supported by boards was restored. Abrabanel contends that these walls endowed the Shilo Mishcan with the status of a House of Hashem. Because the Tabernacle of Nov and Givon lacked stone walls, the Mishcan could not be defined as a house while at these locations.[88]

It seems odd that the structure of the walls of the Mishcan would determine suitability for the mitzvah of Bikkurim! How did walls produce this effect?

It seems reasonable that the presence of stone walls indicated some level of permanence. Without these stone walls the Mishcan was essentially a portable structure. It had no relationship to its current location. Once the boards and curtains were replaced by stone walls, the Mishcan was transformed. It assumed a relationship with its location. It became a feature of the Land of Israel.

Abrabanel apparently maintains that the mitzvah of Bikkurim requires more than a Tabernacle. It demands a geographically unique location sanctified as the Land of Israel spiritual center. The Bikkurim cannot merely be brought to a holy structure. They must be brought to that special location in the Land that is endowed with sanctity. A portable Tabernacle has no relationship with the land on which it is situated. It has no effect on the sanctity of its geographical location or the land. It is on the land but not a feature of the land. This changes once walls are erected. The Mishcan becomes a feature of the land. Now the geographical location is sanctified and the Land of Israel has a spiritual capital.

6. Consensus endows Mishcan with its connection to the Land of Israel

Malbim suggests that the approach of Torah Temimah and Abrabanel are related. The Mishcan of Shilo was erected with stone walls as a result of the consensus. It seems that Malbim maintains that the Mishcan cannot be assigned a relationship with a geographical location

---

[88] Don Yitzchak Abravanel, Commentary on Sefer Devarim, p 245.

without the consensus of the prophet, elders and nation. Only when the walls are erected out of this consensus does the structure become a feature of the Land of Israel.[89]

Malbim's approach explains another halachah. Maimonides explains the process for extending the boundaries of Yerushalayim and the courtyards of the Mikdash.[90] He explains that this process requires the consensus of the king, prophet and Sages. Why is this consensus needed? According to Malbim, we can understand this requirement. An addition to the city of Yerushalayim endows the geographical location with the sanctity of the city. Extending the courtyards of the Temple has the same effect. It bestows sanctity upon the location. The association of these sanctities with a geographical location requires the consensus of the nation. This only emerges though the participation of the king, prophet and Sages.

"And it will be, when you come into the land which Hashem your G-d gives you for an inheritance, and possess it, and dwell therein. And you shall take of the first of all the fruit of the ground, which you will bring in from your land that Hashem your G-d gives you. And you shall put it in a basket and go to the place which Hashem your G-d will choose to cause His name to dwell there. And you shall come to the kohen that will be in those days, and say to him: I profess this day to Hashem your G-d, that I have come to the land which Hashem swore unto our fathers to give us. And the kohen shall take the basket out of your hand, and set it down before the altar of Hashem your G-d. And you shall speak and say before Hashem your G-d: A wandering Aramean was my father, and he went down into Egypt, and sojourned there, few in number; and he became there a nation, great, mighty, and populous. And the Egyptians dealt ill with us, and afflicted us, and laid upon us hard bondage. And we cried to Hashem, the G-d of our fathers, and Hashem heard our voice, and saw our affliction, and our toil, and our oppression. And Hashem brought us forth out of Egypt with a mighty hand, and with an outstretched arm, and with great terribleness, and with signs, and with wonders. And He brought us into this place, and has given us this land, a land flowing with milk and honey." (Devarim 26:1-8)

One of the mitzvot discussed in our parasha is the mikre bikkurim – the recitation accompanying the bringing of the first fruit. In order to discuss the mitzvah of mikre bikkurim, we must first review the mitzvah of bikkurim – the first fruit. This mitzvah only applies in the Land of Israel. We are required to bring the first fruit of each year's crop – the bikkurim – to the Bait HaMikdash. The bikkurim are then given to the kohanim. The mitzvah of bikkurim does not apply to all crops. We are only required to give bikkurim from the seven species that are associated with fertility the Land of Israel.

When the farmer brings the fruits, he is required to fulfill the mitzvah of mikre bikkurim. He recites a specific portion of the Torah that is included in this week's parasha. In this recitation he describes the tribulations experienced by our forefather Yaakov. He recounts his descent to Egypt. He describes the suffering and persecution our ancestors experienced in Egypt. Then, he briefly recounts our redemption by Hashem from bondage. He acknowledges that Hashem has given us the Land of Israel and that this produce is the product of that land. In short, the farmer

---

[89] Rabbaynu Meir Libush (Malbim), Commentary on Sefer Devarim 26:2.
[90] Rabbaynu Moshe ben Maimon, Mishne Torah, Hilchot Bait HaBichirah 6:11.

describes the fruit he is presenting as a manifestation of Hashem's redemption of Bnai Yisrael and an expression of His providential relationship with the Jewish people.

Why is this recitation required? Sefer HaChinuch responds that mitzvah is based upon an important principle that underlies many mitzvot in the Torah. The Torah requires that we accept specific truths. For example, we must recognize that Hashem is the creator. We must recognize that He exercises providence over Bnai Yisrael. However, it is not sufficient that we merely accept that these ideas are true. We must incorporate these ideas into our actual world-view and everyday thinking. We must live by these ideas.

In order to understand the significance of this principle, it is important to recognize that we do not always live by the ideas that we know to be true. A smoker knows that his habit endangers his health and wellbeing. He does not deny that this is true. However, his challenge is translating this knowledge into action. His trial is to live by his knowledge. This may seem like an extreme example. But we can all identify areas in our lives in which we experience this dichotomy between our knowledge and our actions. Life would be much easier if we could easily do all of the things we know are correct and reasonable. In our own individual ways, we all struggle with this challenge. According to Sefer HaChinuch, the Torah is not only interested in teaching us the truth. It is also concerned with assisting us in meeting the challenge of living by these truths.

This principle provides a solution to a well-known discrepancy in the writings of Maimonides. The first mitzvah of the Decalogue is conviction in the existence of Hashem. In his Mishne Torah, Maimonides defines the commandment as an obligation to know that there is a G-d who is the cause of all that exists.

Maimonides also discusses this commandment in his Sefer HaMitzvot. Maimonides wrote this work in Arabic. The standard translation of the Sefer HaMitzvot was composed by Moshe ibn Tibon. The first mitzvah in Sefer HaMitzvot is affirmation of Hashem. In Ibn Tibon's translation, the mitzvah obligates us to believe in the existence of a G-d that is the cause of all that exists. Why does Maimonides here describe the mitzvah as a requirement to believe in Hashem but in is Mishne Torah he tells us we are commanded to know He exists?

There are numerous approaches to understanding Maimonides' differing formulations of this mitzvah. However, one simple explanation is that the two formulations are simply dealing with different issues. In his Mishne Torah, Maimonides is explaining the substance of the required conviction. His objective is to precisely outline the truth that we are required to accept. In his Sefer HaMitzvot, Maimonides is describing the relationship we must have with this idea. It is not adequate to know that Hashem exists. We must achieve a stronger relationship with this truth. We must believe in this truth. Believing a truth is to wholly and unequivocally accept it. In other words, we do not fulfill this mitzvah by merely accepting Hashem's existence as an abstract truth. This truth must be the fundamental to our world-view. We fulfill the mitzvah through achieving complete conviction.[91]

---

[91] A similar interpretation is developed by Rav Yosef Dov Soloveitchik *Zt"l* (*Al HaTeshuvah* pp. 195-198). However, Rav Soloveitchik argues that Maimonides' formulation is his Mishne Torah reflects the requirement to achieve constant and uncompromised conviction whereas his formulation in his Sefer HaMitzvot is less rigorous.

Sefer HaChinuch explains that the mitzvah of mikre bikkurim is an example of one of the many mitzvot designed to translate ideas into meaningful convictions. How does the Torah assist us is meeting this challenge? Sefer HaChinuch explains that there is a reciprocal relationship between our thoughts and our actions. We all recognize that our thoughts and convictions influence our actions. Sefer HaChinuch points out that our actions influence our thoughts and convictions. If we wish to transform and idea into a meaningful and moving conviction, we must express the idea through actions. By acting on an idea we know to be a truth, we strengthen our conviction in this truth.

Sefer HaChinuch applies this principle to mikre bikkurim. Through the process of bringing the first fruit to Yerushalayim and reciting mikre bikkurim, we strengthen our conviction in Hashem's providence and benevolence. Through expressing these ideas in words and actions, we reinforce our conviction in the truth of these ideas.[92]

Don Yitzchak Abravanel offers a slightly different explanation of the mitzvah of mikre bikkurim. He suggests that mikre bikkurim is designed to address a basic human fault. When we are confronted with troubles, experience suffering, or pain, we recognize our inadequacies and frailty. In such situations we feel compelled to turn to a more powerful being for assistance. We call out to Hashem and beg for His deliverance. But when we are successful and we achieve wealth and comfort, we easily forget Hashem and attribute our successes to our own wisdom, ability and efforts. It is especially at such times that we must remind ourselves that all of our bounty is ultimately derived from Hashem's benevolence and that our efforts cannot succeed without His support.

Abravanel explains that the harvest time presents a challenge. As we gather our crops and admire the bounty that our efforts have produced, we may forget that this bounty is a result of the blessings that Hashem bestows upon the Land of Israel. The mitzvah of mikre bikkurim is designed to remind us of the true source of our success. We are required to acknowledge Hashem's role – His providence and benevolence.[93]

It is notable that Sefer HaChinuch and Abravanel agree that this mitzvah is designed to foster within us a proper and realistic attitude. Sefer HaChinuch suggests that many truths must be reinforced in order to become strong convictions. Mikre bikkurim is designed to provide such reinforcement. Abravanel agrees that the mitzvah is designed to strengthen our convictions, but he explains that the mitzvah addresses a basic human failing. We tend to take too much credit for our successes and to forget the role of Hashem.

Maimonides accepts this interpretation. However, he adds a subtle point. He explains that the mitzvah is also designed to foster proper character development. Personal humility is an important character trait. It is fundamental to human perfection. Our success can impair our sense of humility. Mikre bikkurim reminds us that our successful harvest is an expression of Hashem's blessings and benevolence. This helps us retain our sense of humility.[94]

---

[92] Rav Aharon HaLeyve, *Sefer HaChinuch, Mitzvah* 606.
[93] Don Yitzchak Abravanel, *Commentary on Sefer Devarim* 26.
[94] Rabbaynu Moshe ben Maimon, *Moreh Nevuchim*, volume 3, chapter 39.

"And now, behold, I have brought the first of the fruit of the ground which you, Hashem, have given to me." Then, you shall lay it before Hashem, your God, and prostrate yourself before Hashem, your God. (Devarim 26:10)

Many of us are familiar with the folk story of the ignorant shepherd boy that entered the synagogue eager to pray to Hashem, but did not know any of the prayers. The boy wished to reach out to Hashem but lacked the skills and knowledge to pray in the conventional manner. The kind rabbi of the congregation was moved by the earnestness of the young shepherd and advised him that despite his ignorance, he can effectively pray to Hashem. He need merely to recite the *alef bet* – the Hebrew alphabet. Hashem will form the proper words. In another version of the folk story, the rabbi tells the boy to whistle and Hashem will convert his whistles into beautiful prayers.

I am not sure of the true intent or meaning of this well-known story. However, it is often interpreted to mean that we need not be overly concerned with the details and nuances of the laws regarding *tefilah* – prayer. Much more important than our concern with this multitude of details, is our sincerity. If we are sincere, our prayers are appropriate. Some even assert that excessive attention to detail – to the extent that this attention distracts us from expressing our feelings – is counter-productive. This focus on the minutia of *halachah* may even undermine the effectiveness of our prayer and the meaningfulness of the *tefilah* experience.

S efer HaChinuch makes an interesting comment on this week's *parasha* that should cause us to reconsider this folk story and its popular interpretation. One of the *mitzvot* discussed in our *parasha* is the *Mikre Bikurim* – the recitation accompanying the bringing of the first fruit. In order to discuss the *mitzvah* of *Mikre Bikurim*, we must first review the *mitzvah* of *Bikurim* – the first fruit. This *mitzvah* only applies in the Land of Israel. We are required to bring the first fruit – the *Bikurim* – of each year's crop to the *Bait HaMikdash*. The *Bikurim* are then given to the *kohanim* for their consumption. The *mitzvah* of *Bikurim* does not apply to all crops. We are only required to give *Bikurim* from the seven species that are associated with the Land of Israel.

When the farmer brings the fruits, he is required to fulfill the *mitzvah* of *Mikre Bikurim*. He recites a specific portion of the Torah that is included in this week's *parasha*. In this recitation, he describes the tribulations experienced by our forefather Yaakov. He recounts his descent to Egypt. He describes the suffering and persecution our ancestors experienced in Egypt. Then, he briefly recounts our redemption by Hashem from bondage. He acknowledges that Hashem has given us the Land of Israel and that the produce that he is presenting is the product of that Land. In short, the farmer describes the fruit he is presenting as a manifestation of Hashem's redemption of Bnai Yisrael and an expression of His providential relationship with the Jewish people.

One of the interesting laws concerning *Mikre Bikurim* is that not every farmer who presents *Bikurim* is required or qualified to recite *Mikre Bikurim*. For example, *Mikre Bikurim* is only performed by males.[95] Why is the *mitzvah* limited to males? This limitation is based upon the above passage. The farmer states that the *Bikurim* are the product of the land that Hashem has given to me – to the farmer. The Torah provides instructions for the distribution of the Land of Israel among its inhabitants. When the Land of Israel was captured, it was divided among the male members of the nation. In subsequent generations, the Land was subdivided among the

---

95   Rabbaynu Moshe ben Maimon, *Mishne Torah*, Hilchot Bikkurim 4:2.

male descendants of these original land-holders. Land may be sold and purchased among these owners, or even to others who are not among these owners. However, with each Jubilee year – *Yovel*, the Land is redistributed to the male descendants of the original land-holders. In short, only the male descendants of the original land-holders can attain a permanent ownership right that is transmitted to their heirs.

How does this law regarding ownership impact the *mitzvah* of *Mikre Bikurim*? The passage above is taken from the text recited by the farmer. The farmer refers to the fruit as the product of the Land that Hashem has "given to me". This statement assumes that the farmer is a person qualified to receive the Land in a permanent manner. As explained above, only the male descendents of the original land-holders can attain permanent possession.[96]

Sefer HaChinuch makes an interesting comment regarding this law. He explains that this law provides evidence of the importance of the manner and precision with which we formulate our prayers.[97] How is this law indicative of the importance of precision in our prayers?

As we have explained, only males may recite *Mikre Bikurim*. This law is derived from the above passage. But let us more carefully consider how this law is derived from this passage. Many laws are derived from allusions and hints provided by the text of the Chumash. A nuance in the manner in which the Torah expresses itself – the choice of wording, a seemingly superfluous phrase, word, or even letter – can be the source of a law. A superficial consideration of the derivation of the limitation of *Mikre Bikurim* to males would indicate that this law is derived from such a nuance in our passage.

However, Sefer HaChinuch apparently maintains that the law is not derived from a nuance or superfluity in the passage. Instead, *Mikre Bikurim* can only be recited by a male, because the content of the recitation must be accurate. The person reciting *Mikre Bikurim* refers to the fruit as the product of the Land given to him by Hashem. If he is not a male, the statement is not true and accurate.

We can now understand Sefer HaChinuch's comment. *Mikre Bikurim* – and all prayers – must be accurate and precise. In the case of *Mikre Bikurim*, this requirement can only be realized when the recitation is given by a farmer who is male. Sefer HaChinuch admonishes us to require of ourselves the same precision in every prayer we recite. We must choose our text carefully and read or recite it precisely. Without this precision, a fundamental element of prayer is sacrificed.

What is this fundamental element that is only achieved through precision? In order to appreciate Sefer HaChinuch's response, another law regarding *Mikre bikurim* must be considered.

And you shall call out and say before Hahsem, your God: An Aramean [sought to] destroy my forefather, and he went down to Egypt and sojourned there with a small number of people, and there, he became a great, mighty, and numerous nation. (Devarim 26:5)

One of the requirements of *Mikre Bikurim* is that the passages must be recited in the *Bait HaMikdash*. This requirement is derived from the above passage. The *pasuk* tells us that the

---

96 Rabbaynu Moshe ben Maimon, *Mishne Torah*, Hilchot Bikkurim 4:2.
97 Rav Aharon HaLeyve, Sefer HaChinuch, Mitzvah 606.

passages must be recited before Hashem. Our Sages interpret this phrase to require that the recitation of the passages take place in the *Bait HaMikdash*.[98]

Minchat Chinuch notes that this interpretation of the phrase "before Hashem" does not seem completely reasonable. The Torah requires that we give a number of tithes from our crops. These tithes are not identical from year to year. However, they do have a fixed three-year cycle. At the end of each three-year cycle, one is required to declare that the tithes have been given properly. The Torah tells us that this declaration must be made "before Hashem." Indeed, it is preferable to make the declaration in the *Bait HaMikdash*. However, if one did not make the declaration in the *Bait HaMikdash*, it is nonetheless valid.[99]

Minchat Chinuch argues that it would seem reasonable that the phrase "before Hashem" used in reference to *Mikre Bikurim* should be interpreted in the same manner. It should indicate the preference for performance of the *mitzvah* in the *Bait HaMikdash*. But it should not suggest that recitation in the *Bait HaMikdash* is an absolute requirement.

Minchat Chinuch's question can be extended. The term "before Hashem" is used with some frequency by the Torah and our Sages. For example, when we recite the *Amidah* prayer, we are required to regard ourselves as standing before Hashem. When we confess our sins, we are required to regard ourselves as standing "before Hashem." In neither of these instances are we required to make a pilgrimage to the *Bait HaMikdash*. Clearly, in these instances the phrase "before Hashem" represents a state of mind. Why in the instance of *Mikre Bikurim* is the phrase interpreted more literally?

It seems that the term "before Hashem" can have two meanings. It can refer to a mental state – the person regards himself as standing before Hashem. The phrase can also represent a geographical or positional requirement – presence in the *Bait HaMikdash*. The *Bait HaMikdash* is a location in which Hashem's influence is uniquely represented and expressed. In instances in which the requirement is positional, it is fulfilled through standing in the *Bait HaMikdash*.

The proper interpretation of the phrase "before Hashem" is determined by the context. In the case of *Mikre Bikurim*, the recitation must accompany the offering of the *Bikurim*. The *Bikurim* must be presented in the *Bait HaMikdash*. Therefore, the phrase "before Hashem" is to be understood to include an absolute positional element. The recitation must take place in the *Bait HaMikdash*. In contrast, there is no particular relationship between the declaration regarding the tithes and the *Bait HaMikdash*. Therefore, the phrase is not interpreted to imply an absolute positional requirement. However, this answer suggests a new question. If the declaration concerning the tithes is unrelated to the *Bait HaMikdash*, why is it *preferable* for it to be recited at this location?

As explained, the phrase "before Hashem" sometimes implies an absolute positional element – as in the instance of *Mikre Bikurim*. In other instances, the phrase refers to a state of mind. In the instance of the declaration regarding the tithes, the requirement can be fulfilled anywhere. This indicates that "before Hashem" is essentially a mental state. However, the unique element of this declaration is that we are encouraged to reinforce the state of mind through a positional expression – through actually standing in the *Bait HaMikdash*. In other words, in

---

98   Rav Yosef Babad, *Minchat Chinuch,* Mitzvah 606, note 1.
99   Rabbaynu Moshe ben Maimon, *Mishne Torah*, Hilchot Ma'aser Sheyne 11:6.

making the declaration regarding the tithes, we are admonished to reinforce our state of mind through action – standing in the *Bait HaMikdash*.

Let us now return to our original question: Why is precision an essential element of prayer? Sefer HaChinuch explains that when we pray, we stand before Hashem. We address our thoughts and words to Him. We are expected to reinforce our sense of standing before Hashem through action. If we are to fully appreciate and recognize the significance of addressing Hashem, we must choose our words with extreme care and attention. This precision and attention to detail reflects and expresses an experience of awe. It communicates a cognizance of the significance – the gravity – of the experience. Through stating our prayers with precision and care, we reinforce the sense of standing before Hashem.

And you should rejoice in all the good that Hashem, your L-rd, has given you and your household – you and the Leyve, and the convert who is among you. (Devarim 26:11)

Be Happy!

1. Presenting the first-fruit

Parshat Ki Tavo discusses the Bikkurim – the first fruits. The Torah commands us to bring the first fruits of the harvest in the Land of Israel to the Bait HaMikdash – the Sacred Temple – and to present them to the Kohen. Although this mitzvah has been previously described in the Torah (Sefer Shemot 23:19), our parasha adds an element. When presenting the Bikkurim, the farmer recites a series of verses expressing thanksgiving. These verses retell the history of our people – our bondage in Egypt, our redemption, and our possession of the Land of Israel. The verses conclude describing the presentation of the Bikkurim as an act of recognition of Hashem's benevolence.

The above passage immediately follows the instructions for presenting the Bikkurim and for the recital of the verses. Moshe tells the people that they are to rejoice in recognition of the blessings that Hashem has bestowed upon us.

2. Rejoicing in bringing the first-fruit

How does the obligation to rejoice when bringing the Bikkurim express itself? Those bringing the Bikkurim are required to also offer a Shelamim sacrifice.[100] A Shelamim sacrifice is unique. A portion is placed on the altar, a portion is given to the Kohen, but most of the sacrifice remains the owner's. He shares the meat of the sacrifice with his family and others. This is one expression of rejoicing.

The presentation of the Bikkurim is accompanied by singing psalms of praise. This is another expression of rejoicing. When the procession of those bringing the Bikkurim reaches the courtyard of the Bait HaMikdash the Leviyim begin to sing psalms of praise.[101] However, even before reaching the courtyard, the Bikkurim are accompanied by rejoicing. They are brought into Yerushalayim in a celebratory procession. The residents of the city come into the streets to greet the pilgrims. When the procession reaches the gates of Yerushalayim, the pilgrims begin to recite

---

[100] Rabbaynu Moshe ben Maimon (Rambam) Mishne Torah, Hilchot Bikkurim 3:12.
[101] Rabbaynu Moshe ben Maimon (Rambam) Mishne Torah, Hilchot Bikkurim 3:13.

a psalm of praise. When they arrive at the Temple mount, they take-up a new psalm which they recite until arriving at the courtyard of the Bait HaMikdash.[102]

3. Bikkurim are unique

Bikkurim are presented in the Bait HaMikdash to the Kohen. Bikkurim is one of a number of gifts or tithes we are required to present to the Kohen. These include Terumah which is a portion of the harvest, and Challah which is a portion of every substantial bread dough. These other gifts are not accompanied by an obligation to rejoice. This obligation is unique to Bikkurim. Why does Bikkurim require rejoicing?

The requirement of rejoicing reflects a fundamental distinction between Bikkurim and the other gifts and tithes given to the Kohen. The tribe of Leyve, which is the tribe of the Kohanim – the priests – did not receive a portion of the Land of Israel. Instead, they were awarded cities in which to live. They were not given lands to cultivate and from which to support themselves. The nation is obligated to support the members of the tribe – including the Kohanim. This support is provided, in part, by Bikkurim and other gifts and tithes.

Bikkurim contributes to sustaining the Kohanim. However, it is also a thanksgiving offering. Thanksgiving requires rejoicing. The message of Bikkurim is that thanksgiving is incomplete if it is not accompanied by rejoicing. Why is this?

4. Acknowledgement brings rejoicing

The answer lies in the two different ways in which the rejoicing accompanying the Bikkurim is expressed. It is expressed through offering and consuming a Shelamim sacrifice. Consumption of the sacrifice provides direct gratification. This gratification is a form of rejoicing. Bikkurim are accompanied by psalms of praise. Reciting praise does not provide gratification. Instead, it nurtures or reinforces awareness of one's blessings and their source. This awareness evokes joy.

Why is joy an essential element of Bikkurim? The presentation of Bikkurim is an event. Its theme is thanksgiving. The psalms recited elaborate on the theme. Through presenting the Bikkurim we acknowledge the blessings that Hashem has bestowed upon us. Joy is the natural expression of this awareness. If joy is absent, then the awareness has not been fully achieved.

5. Blessings and happiness

This discussion explains an interesting comment of Rabbaynu Yosef Bechor Shur. He suggests that the above passage has a double meaning. We are obligated to rejoice with the presenting of the Bikkurim. However, the passage has another meaning:

"And you will rejoice – in the merit of this [mitzvah] the Omnipresent One will grant you joy."[103]

According to Rabbaynu Yosef Bechur Shur, the reward for bringing the Bikkurim and acknowledging Hashem's benevolence is that Hashem will grant us joy and happiness. This is a very odd interpretation. How can Hashem grant us happiness and joy? He can bestow His blessings upon us. But whether we will respond with appreciation, acknowledge our blessings, and achieve joy is in our hands. Happiness cannot be granted or coerced.

---

[102] Rabbaynu Moshe ben Maimon (Rambam) Mishne Torah, Hilchot Bikkurim 4:16-17.

[103] Rabbaynu Yosef Bechor Shur, Commentary on Sefer Devarim 26:11.

Apparently, Rabbaynu Yosef Bechur Shur is explaining that if we fully engage in the presentation of the Bikkurim, we sincerely acknowledge Hashem's blessings and His benevolence, then the blessings He will bestow upon us will bring us joy and happiness. Hashem does not grant us happiness. But if we properly prepare ourselves, His blessings will bring us happiness.

6. Opening one's heart to happiness

This is a subtle and astute point. Joy is not achieved simply because one has cause to be happy. One must open one's heart to joy. Two people with similar lives can have very different attitudes. One is grateful for his or her blessings and is happy. The other does not appreciate the blessings and instead, is troubled by the unfulfilled wishes and aspirations. How does one achieve joy?

One lesson of Bikkurim, according to Rabbaynu Yosef Bechur Shur, is that we achieve joy through developing our sense of appreciation. The more developed our capacity to appreciate our blessings, the more joy we experience in life. When we acknowledge and sincerely appreciate Hashem's blessings, they become a source of happiness and a cause for rejoicing.

And you should say before Hashem your G-d, I have removed the sacred from the house. And also I have given from it to the Leyve and the convert, to the orphan and to the widow, as required by your commandments that you have commanded me. I have not violated your commandments and I have not forgotten. (Devarim 26:13)

The Confessional Element of Veydoi Maasrot

At the end of a three-year cycle, a declaration is required regarding the giving of tithes. In this declaration, the person confirms that the annual tithes have been removed from the home and properly distributed. The tithe due to the Leyve has been given to him. The tithe required for the support of the poor has been distributed. This declaration is referred to as *Veydoi Maasrot*. This can be translated as "confession over the tithes." Why is this declaration described as a confession? A confession, in *halachah*, is made in order to repent from a sin. This person is declaring that the laws have been properly performed!

There are a number of answers offered to this question. Many involve providing an alternative translation for *Veydoi Maasrot* that does not include the element of confession. Rabbaynu Ovadia Sforno, however, offers a very simple explanation that preserves the straightforward translation.

Originally, the institution of the priesthood was awarded to the firstborn. Every tribe was to be represented in this honored group. At Sinai, the nation sinned through association with the *Egel HaZahav* – the Golden Calf. The only group that opposed the creation and worship of this idol was the tribe of Leyve. As a result, Hashem removed the priesthood from the nation's firstborn and awarded it to *Shevet Leyve* – the tribe of Leyve. This meant that the other tribes would not be represented within the priesthood through their firstborn.

Sforno explains that we are required to acknowledge our involvement in the sin of the *Egel*. This is done through the tithes. Through these tithes we acknowledge and support the selection of *Shevet Leyve* for the priesthood. Through this acknowledgement, we demonstrate that we accept our responsibility for the sin of the *Egel* and its consequences. *Veydoi Maasrot* is an affirmation of fulfilling our obligations of tithing. Therefore, it does have an element of confession. We are implicitly confessing the sin of the *Egel*.[104]

And you should say before Hashem your G-d, I have removed the sacred from the house. And also I have given from it to the Leyve and the convert, to the orphan and to the widow, as required by your commandments that You have commanded me. I have not violated Your commandments and I have not forgotten. (Devarim 26:13)

Paradigms of Confession

1. The tithes and their cycle

The Torah requires that we tithe our crops annually. Among the tithes that we are commanded to give are the first *ma'aser*, the second *ma'aser*, and the *ma'aser* for the poor. The first *ma'aser* is given to the Leveyim. The second *ma'aser* is taken to Yerushalayim and there the owner and his family consume the produce of the tithe. The *ma'aser* for the poor is distributed by the owner to those in need.

The first *ma'aser* is given to the Leveyim every year. The second *ma'aser* and the *ma'aser* for the poor are not given every year. Instead, they are given on the basis of a three year cycle. On the first, second, fourth, and fifth years following a sabbatical year the second *ma'aser* is given. On the third and sixth years following the sabbatical year the *ma'aser* for the poor is given.

Sabbatical year	Year 1	Year 2	Year 3	Year 4	Year 5	Year 6	Sabbatical year
No tithes	1st *Ma'aser*	1st *Ma'aser*	1st *Ma'aser*	1st *Ma'aser*	1st *Ma'aser*	1st *Ma'aser*	No tithes
	2nd *Ma'aser*	2nd *Ma'aser*	*Ma'aser* for poor	2nd *Ma'aser*	2nd *Ma'aser*	*Ma'aser* for poor	

2. The "confession over the tithes"

At the end of each three-year cycle, a declaration is required regarding the giving of tithes. A portion of the declaration is quoted above. In this declaration, the person confirms that the annual tithes have been removed from his home and properly distributed. The tithe due to the Leyve has been given to him. The tithe required for the support of the poor has been distributed.

This declaration is referred to by our Sages as *veydoi ma'asrot*. The term *veydoi* is used elsewhere in the Torah. In those instances the term means to confess.[105] If that translation of the term is applied to this context, then *veydoi ma'asrot* should be translated as "confession over the tithes." Why is this declaration described as a confession? A confession, in *halachah*, is made in order to repent from a sin. This person is declaring that the laws have been properly performed!

There are a number of answers offered to this question. Many involve providing an alternative translation for *veydoi ma'asrot* that does not include the element of confession.

---

[104] Rabbaynu Ovadia Sforno, *Commentary on Sefer Devarim* 26:13.
[105] See for example, Sefer BeMidbar 5:7.

Rabbaynu Ovadia Sforno, however, offers a very original explanation that preserves the straightforward translation.

3. Transfer of the priesthood from the firstborn to the tribe of Leyve

Originally, the institution of the priesthood was awarded to the firstborn. Every tribe was to be represented in this honored group. At Sinai, the nation sinned through association with the *Egel HaZahav* – the Golden Calf. The only group that opposed the creation and worship of this idol was the tribe of Leyve. As a result, Hashem removed the priesthood from the nation's firstborn and awarded it to Shevet Leyve – the tribe of Leyve. This meant that the other tribes would not be represented within the priesthood through their firstborn.

Sforno explains that we are required to acknowledge our involvement in the sin of the *Egel*. This is done through the tithes. Through these tithes we acknowledge and support the selection of Shevet Leyve for the priesthood. Through this acknowledgement, we demonstrate that we accept our responsibility for the sin of the *Egel* and its consequences. *Veydoi ma'asrot* is an affirmation of fulfilling our obligations of tithing. Therefore, it does have an element of confession. We are implicitly confessing the sin of the *Egel*.[106]

This is an imaginative yet reasonable explanation of the term *veydoi ma'asrot*. However, is there a more straightforward explanation for the term? Let us begin by revisiting one of Sefer Devarim's basic themes.

And you shall eat and be satisfied. And you will bless Hashem your L-rd upon the good land that He has given to you. Take care, lest you forget Hashem your L-rd and, thereby, not observe His commandments, His ordinances, and His statutes that I have commanded to you today. (Devarim 8:10-11)

4. Remembering that our blessings come from Hashem

The above passages are representative of the theme that Moshe repeatedly revisits in his final address to the nation. He explains that in the wilderness, the nation's awareness of the presence of Hashem was sustained by their complete, manifest dependence upon Him. They relied upon Hashem for their survival. He provided them with food, water, and responded to their other needs.

In the land that they will soon enter, conquer, and settle, His presence will not be as manifest. The nation will plant its annual crops. These will be watered by the rains falling from the heavens and harvested by the farmers. The people will consume the produce of their labors in safety and security. All of this will take place without the intervention of manifest miracles.

With the passage of time, the people will become accustomed to their comfort and wealth. They will come to regard the abundance that the land provides as a natural and normal outcome. They will take for granted their wellbeing. They will become complacent in their observance of the Torah. Complacency will develop into neglect. Neglect of the Torah will lead to abandonment of Hashem.

The people will no longer recognize that the blessings they enjoy are an expression of Hashem's benevolence. He provides for them in the land just as He provided in the wilderness. The falling rain, the healthy crops, the safety and security of the people are just a few of the

---

[106] Rabbaynu Ovadia Sforno, *Commentary on Sefer Devarim* 26:13.

many kindnesses that He bestows upon them. Every success and achievement that they attribute to their own efforts and initiative is realized only through Hashem's constant support and providence. He makes the rain fall. He protects the crops from disease and pestilence. He secures the borders of the land and dissuades other nations from contesting Bnai Yisrael's presence.

Finally, Moshe repeatedly warns the nation that if they abandon Hashem, then He will provide them will compelling evidence of His immense role in the wellbeing that they have enjoyed. He will not bring the rain down upon their crops. They will experience drought, disease, and pestilence. Their enemies will find the courage and the means to challenge Bnai Yisrael. The people will learn that Hashem's providence and benevolence are present even when not manifest. They will rediscover their helplessness. Let us now reconsider *veydoi ma'asrot*.

I did not eat any of it [second tithe] while in my mourning, nor did I consume any of it while unclean; neither did I use any of it for the dead. I obeyed the Lord, my God; I did according to all that You commanded me. Look down from Your holy dwelling, from the heavens, and bless Your people Israel, and the ground which You have given to us, as You swore to our forefathers – a land flowing with milk and honey. (Devarim 26:14-15)

5. Demanding from Hashem

The passages above complete the text of the *veydoi ma'asrot*. These passages contain two elements. The first element is a declaration that the *ma'asrot* have been treated properly and used for their appropriate purposes. The second element is a prayer. The person asks Hashem to bless Bnai Yisrael and the Land of Israel. How are these two elements related?

Rabbaynu Avraham ibn Ezra, explains that when one recites these passages, one is saying to Hashem, "I have observed the commandments with which You charged me. You have declared that You will respond to my observance by bestowing Your blessings upon me. I now ask that you respond to my perfect observance of these commandments. Bestow Your blessings upon me."[107]

This interpretation of the *veydoi* transforms it. It is not a typical petition in which the petitioner pleads with his benefactor for his kindness. It seems that the person reciting the *veydoi* is demanding that Hashem respond to his observance of the *mitzvot* with His blessings. Is this truly the intent of the *veydoi*?

*The L-rd then spoke to Moshe saying: Tell the children of Israel, "When a man or woman commits any of the sins against man to act treacherously against Hashem, and that person is [found] guilty, they shall confess the sin they committed, and make restitution for the principal amount of his guilt, add its fifth to it, and give it to the one against whom he was guilty."
(BeMidbar 5:5-7)*

6. The confession experience

These passages are one of the instances in the Torah in which the term *veydoi* is employed in its usual context. Here, it means to confess one's sin. What is the process that takes place in confession of sin? What is the experience? Confession is an acknowledgment. The person acknowledges that he has engaged in an activity that is wrong. However, acknowledgment is not synonymous with confession. Confession is a particular type of acknowledgement. It is an acknowledgement that emerges from a inner-struggle. The one who

---

[107] Rabbaynu Avraham ibn Ezra, *Commentary on Sefer Devarim*, 26:15.

confesses must triumph in an internal battle in order to pronounce his acknowledgment. He must overcome rationalization, and his self-serving perspective to acknowledge that his actions have – in fact – been wrong. In other words, confession requires acknowledging and embracing an unwelcome and uncomfortable truth.

Now, let us return to Ibn Ezra's comments. According to his view, when a person recites the *veydoi*, he describes his obedience to the commandments and he asks that Hashem respond to this obedience by bestowing His blessings upon him. In stating this request, there is an acknowledgement. The person reciting the *veydoi* acknowledges that he needs Hashem's blessings. His crops, his wealth, and his security are the product of these blessings. Without those blessings, his own efforts would not have been successful. He is also acknowledging that he cannot take for granted Hashem's blessings. Those blessings are a response to his observance of the commandments. He can only expect Hashem to bestow His blessings if he continues to be faithful to the Torah.

This acknowledgment has the characteristic essential to a confession – a *veydoi*. It is an acknowledgment that comes from overcoming the natural tendency that Moshe repeatedly identifies in Sefer Devraim – the tendency to take the credit for our accomplishments and to overlook or deny the role of Hashem in our lives and successes. The person who sincerely recites the *veydoi* overcomes this tendency and declares that his wellbeing is provided by Hashem and that his observance of the Torah's *mitzvot* is as fundamental to his success as his efforts as a farmer.

And it was in the days of the judging of the Judges, and there was a famine in the Land. And a man went from Bait Lechem of Yehudah to sojourn on the Plains of Moav – he and his wife and his two sons. (Megilat Ruth 1:1)

The Challenge of Accepting Less-than-perfect Leadership

1. The strange formulation of Megilat Ruth's first passage

The above passage introduced the Megilah of Ruth. The passage begins by describing the period during which the events of the narrative take place. These events in the Megilah occurred during the period of the Judges. The title Judge refers to those individuals who led the nation from the death of Yehoshua until the prophet Shemuel. This period began in approximately 1300 BCE and continued for almost 300 years. The passage continues and explains the context of the narrative. A famine struck Land of Israel and a man – who will later be identified as Elimelech – left the Land to seek relief from the famine in the Land of Moav. The Megilah will relate that in the Land of Moav, his sons took as wives two women from the nation of Moav. Elimelech and his sons died. They were survived by Elimelech's wife Na'ami and the wives of his sons. One of these wives returned to her own people. The other – Ruth – remained with Na'ami and returned with her to the Land of Israel. The narrative focuses on the relationship between Ruth and Na'ami and Ruth's experiences after joining the Jewish nation.

The commentators raise a number of questions regarding the message and the construction of the above passage. Among them are the following:

- The Megilah describes the events of the narrative as occurring during the era of the Judges. It seems that the intention of this statement is to identify the historical period of the events. However, the era of the Judges encompassed 300 years. If the Megilah's intention was to identify the historical period of the events, it should have identified the specific leader of the Jewish people at the time.

- The passage is oddly structured. In a single sentence, the term *va'yehi* – "and it was" or "and there was" is employed twice. The sentence should have been simplified: And it was in the days of the judging of the Judges, there was a famine in the Land.

- The passage describes the period as "the days of the judging of the Judges." Again, this is a rather tortured expression. The passage could have simply stated: And it was in the days of the Judges.

2. The Talmud's criticism of the Judges

This final question is discussed by the Talmud. The Talmud explains that the *pasuk* has an alternative translation. It can be translated as follows: And it was in the time that the Judges were judged. The passage is revealing that the events of the narrative occurred at a time in which there was a lack of confidence in the leadership. The people had judged or evaluated their Judges and found them to be deficient. The Talmud provides additional details. One of the responsibilities of the Judges was to provide the nation with moral guidance. This required that, at times, they critique and criticize the behaviors of the people. In order for the Judges' rebukes to be effective, their own moral character had to be untarnished. However, not all of the Judges succeeded in securing this high regard. When these less respected Judges criticized the nation, the people were unmoved by their rebuke. They responded to the Judges that they had no right to judge others when they themselves were flawed![108]

Rashi adds that the people were not merely imagining these flaws in their Judges' behaviors in order to excuse themselves from heeding their message. Some of the Judges were actually disappointing in their personal conduct and the people were responding to real defects in their leaders' characters.[109]

In short, the passage is constructed in its cumbersome style to communicate a dual message. It communicates the era in which the events of the Megilah unfolded and it tells the reader something about the era. It was an era in which sometimes the leadership did not have unquestionable moral authority. Because of their own shortcomings, the leaders were not respected moral guides.

3. The Midrash suggests that even a flawed leader may deserve our attention

The Midrash discusses this same difficulty in the passage as the Talmud but responds to it somewhat differently. It states: Woe unto the generation that judges its judges. Woe unto the generation whose Judges, themselves, require judgment. Like the Talmud, the Midrash is attempting to unravel the message of the difficult phrase, "And it was in the day of the judging of the Judges".[110] The Midrash accepts the basic approach of the Talmud. The passage has a dual meaning. It is intended to identify the era of the events and also comments on the nation's assessment of its leaders. The people judged their leaders and were disappointed. However, in the Midrash, another issue is added. It seems to criticize the people for their scrutiny of their

---

[108] Mesechet Baba Batra 15b.
[109] Rabbaynu Shlomo ben Yitzchak (Rashi), *Commentary on the Talmud,* Mes. Baba Batra 15b.
[110] Midrash Rabba, Megilat Ruth 1:1.

leader's behavior. This issue is difficult to understand. If the leaders were, in fact, deficient in their own behavior, then why should the people respect their moral guidance?

Clearly, according to the Midrash, the leaders' deficiencies were not so great as to justify the people's dismissive response to their criticisms. However, their flaws were adequate to provide the people with an excuse to ignore their leaders' rebukes. The message of the Midrash is that ideally a leader should possess moral and ethical excellence. The leaders own example will inspire others and encourage the people to seriously consider his messages. However, not every generation merits to be provided with leaders that match this ideal. In many generations, the leaders are less than perfect; they have real flaws. However, these flaws do not justify rejection of their message. Instead, the people of the nation must realize that their leaders are human – not super-human. They are less than perfect. Nonetheless, they have important messages and these messages should be considered.

In other words, it is true that some leaders so thoroughly compromise their own moral standing they do not have the right and authority to correct their followers. However, often the flaws that we identify in a leader are not of such great significance. These flaws are a reflection of the reality of the leader's humanity. Rejection of the leader's message in response to these lesser flaws is not justified. In such cases, the flaws are being seized upon as an excuse for not taking seriously the leader's message.

4. The message of the passage – rejection of the leadership led to famine

Based upon this analysis, Rav Moshe Alshich resolves the various difficulties in the passage. He explains that the passage is not intended to identify the specific era of the events. Instead, it is designed to identify their antecedents. The *pasuk* opens by describing the period as one in which the people rejected their leaders. They focused on their leaders' flaws and seized upon these flaws as an excuse to reject their messages. Without moral guidance, the nation degenerated. This was punished by a famine. In response to this famine, Elimelech took his family out of the Land of Israel and traveled to the Land of Moav.[111]

The message of this passage – as interpreted by the Midrash – is very applicable to our own times. Some of our supposed leaders are so corrupt as to deserve our disdain. However, in many instances, our criticism of our leaders focuses on flaws and deficiencies that merely reflect their humanity. We exaggerate the significance of these failings; we become virtually obsessed with each and every one of their flaws. When we do this, we are not only undermining their leadership. We are also seeking to excuse ourselves from listening to their messages.

"And it was in the times that the judges judged that there was a famine in the land and a man from Bait Lechem in Yehuda went to sojourn in the fields of Moav – he and his wife and his two sons." (Megilat Ruth 1:1)

One of the issues we encounter in teaching students TaNaCh is that the interpretations of our Sages often seem far removed from the literal translation and intent to the passages. It is important that the teacher relate these interpretations to the passage by explaining the basis for the insight within the wording of the passage.

---

[111] Rav Moshe Alshich, *Eynai Moshe – Commentary of Megilat Ruth*, 1:1.

The above passage introduces the Megilah of Ruth. The *pasuk* tells us the land of Israel was stricken with a famine. In response, Elimelech left the land of Israel with his family and relocated to the land of Moav. Malbim quotes the midrash that explains the there were actually two famines that afflicted the land of Israel. One was a famine involving a scarcity of foods. In addition, the land was also afflicted with a scarcity of Torah. The midrash does not elaborate on the specific form or nature of this scarcity of Torah. Neither does the midrash explain its basis for this interpretation of the passage. However, Malbim suggests that the nature of this scarcity of Torah is indicated by another teaching of the Sages. Based on his analysis, he also indicates the basis in the passage for our Sages' comments

Malbim begins by referring us to a comment of the Sages quoted by Rashi. According to our Sages, Elimelech was a wealthy person. As a result of the famine Elimelech was approached by many impoverished individuals needing his support. He fled the land of Israel in order to avoid his duty to support the poor. [112] At first glance, this seems to be another amazing comment that lacks any connection to the text. However, a careful analysis does provide significant support for these comments of our Sages.

Our passage describes Elimelech as "a man." Only in the next passage does the Megilah reveal his identity. Like the Chumash, NaCh does not waste words. Ideas are expressed in as precise a manner as possible. So, we would have expected the Megilah to reveal Elimelech's identity in the first passage instead of referring to him as "a man." The Sages often comment explain the term *eysh* – a man – usually refers to a person of importance. The Megilah is telling us that Elimelech was a person of significance.

Furthermore, the Megilah is referring to Elimelech as an *eysh* in describing his abandonment of the land of Israel. The implication is that his decision to leave was in some manner associated with his status as a person of significance. What is the connection to which the *pasuk* alludes?

In order to answer this question, we must ask one further question. In what sense was Elimelech an *eysh* – a person of significance? How was he special? The only remarkable characteristic of Elimelech that is mentioned in the Megilah is his wealth. It seems that the Sages concluded that this must be the distinction to which the Megilah refers in describing Elimelech as an *eysh*.

Now, we can better understand the message communicated in the passage in relating Elimelech's decision to leave the land of Israel to his status as an *eysh*. The apparent message of the passage is that Elimelech's wealth was the basis for his decision to leave the land of Israel.

So, how did Elimelech's status as a wealthy person influence his decision to leave the land of Israel? Our Sages conclude that his decision must have been motivated by a desire to preserve this wealth. They continue to explain that as a result of the famine Elimelech was accosted by the poor seeking relief. Elimelech was not willing to provide this support but neither was he comfortable turning the poor away. In order to evade his dilemma, he elected to leave the land of Israel and relocate to the land of Moav.

Based on the comments of the Sages quoted by Rashi, Malbim explains that nature of the famine for Torah. He explains that this famine was characterized by this attitude towards

---

[112] Rabbaynu Shlomo ben Yitzchak (Rashi), *Commentary on Megillat Rut* 1:1.

tzedakah – charity – expressed by Elimelech. In other words, the reluctance to provide support for the poor is described by the Sages as a famine for Torah.

In summary, although at first glance it would appear that the comments of the Sages are not reflected in the passage, a careful analysis of the passage does indicate that the Sages are responding to specific problems in the passage and resolving these problems based upon a thorough analysis of the text.

Let us now consider another issue. Malbim continues to explain that this is not the only instance in which the Sages use very harsh terms to describe a person who is remiss in performance of the *mitzvah* of supporting the poor. Malbim quotes two statements of the Sages. The Sages comment that anyone who hides his eyes from the poor is regarded as serving idolatry. In another instance, the Sages comment that anyone who does not involve oneself in acts of kindness is comparable to a person who has no G-d.

Malbim suggests that the Sages – like the TaNaCh – choose their words carefully. These two comments are not reiterations of the same idea. The subtle differences in the phrasing are significant. He quotes Rav Hai Gaon. Rav Hai explained that there is an important difference between hiding one's eyes from the poor and not involving oneself in acts of kindness. When one hides one's eyes, the person is attempting to not see something. In other words, there is a situation with which the person is confronted and the person turns away to avoid seeing and needing to respond to the situation. According to Rav Hai, this characterization describes the person that is confronted with a poor person – the poor person is knocking at his door – and he refuses to open the door or – like Elimelech – he flees from his responsibility. In contrast, in referring to a person who does not involve oneself in acts of kindness, the Sages are describing a different behavior. This person makes a decision to not get involved in acts of kindness. Perhaps, if a poor person came to the door, he would respond and provide assistance. But this person will not seek out the poor and those in need of help in order to provide for them.[113]

Although Malbim does not comment on the issue, it is interesting that the Sages refer to the person who hides his eyes as an idolater and the person who does not involve oneself in acts of kindness as not having a G-d. Can we explain the difference between these two characterizations and why each is used in reference to its respective behavior?

When a person turns away and avoids a needy person, a calculation is being made. The person is confronted with someone needing help and is aware of the obligation to respond. At the same time, that person is reluctant to give of his wealth. He balances his love for his wealth against his Torah obligation to support the poor and decides to ignore his obligation in favor of his attachment to his possessions. In this calculation, the person is giving precedence to his love for his wealth over his commitment to Hashem and His Torah. In deciding that the love of wealth comes first, the person has given his wealth a position in his outlook that is reserved for Hashem. He has placed love of wealth above love of Hashem. In assigning this position – reserved for Hashem – to his wealth – he has replaced Hashem with his wealth. In this sense, he is characterized as an idolater.

A person who does not involve oneself in acts of kindness is not making this calculation. In fact, through removing himself from involvement in acts of kindness – *chesed* – the person has avoided the necessity of any such calculation. However, this person is also making a clear

---

[113] Rav Meir Leibush ben Yechiel Michel (Malbim), *Geza Yeshai – Comm. on Megillat Rut*, 1:1.

statement regarding his relationship to Hashem. Who is this person? Our Sages accuse him of abandoning G-d because he does not perform *chesed*. The implication is that the Sages are referring to a person who is otherwise conscientious in his observance. But in the area of *chesed* he is remiss. He is establishing boundaries for his relationship with Hashem. He is establishing a realm or framework in which he must serve Hashem and defining a corresponding realm or framework in which duty to Hashem is irrelevant. This person is not denying that he must serve Hashem. Instead, he is establishing perimeters to this service. He relegates his service to the synagogue or the *bait hamidrash* – the study hall. But he banishes Hashem from important elements of his personal life. The message of our Sages now emerges more clearly. We cannot establish artificial boundaries designed to exclude Hashem from portions of our life. Devotion to Hashem – by definition – requires recognition of Hashem's mastery over all elements of a person's life.

An analogy will help convey this idea. Assume a king decrees that his subjects should pay a five-dollar tax every year. The subjects respond that although you are king, we do respect your right to demand taxes. You do not have authority over our possessions. Does this king truly have power over his subjects or does he rule only by virtue of the indulgence of his subjects? Cleary, he rules by virtue of their indulgence. They have the power to decide the areas over which he does and does not have authority.

Now, let us apply this analogy to our discussion. If we accept that Hashem has complete authority over us – that He is truly our G-d – then He does not need our indulgence in order to dictate behavioral expectations. We must acknowledge His authority in every aspect of our lives. However, if we insist that Hashem does not have the authority to prescribe behaviors in some areas, then we are implying that Hashem cannot dictate to us but instead rules through our indulgence. If Hashem requires our indulgence, then we do not really regard Him as our G-d.

So Naomi returned, and Ruth the Moabitess, her daughter-in- law, with her, who returned from the fields of Moab.And they came to Bethlehem at the beginning of the barley harvest. (Megilat Ruth 1:22)

The connection between Megilat Ruth and Shavuot

What is the connection between Megilat Ruth and Shavuot? Many responses have been suggested. Superficially, there is an obvious link. The events that compose the fundamental narrative occur during the harvest season in Israel. This season begins around Pesach with the barely harvest and continues through Shavuot which is the time of the wheat harvest.

Another obvious connection between Shavuot and the Megilah, is Ruth's conversion which is described in the first chapter. The "conversion" of the Jewish people took place at Sinai with their enactment of a covenant with Hashem. The basic elements of the conversion process are derived from the Torah's narrative of the Sinai covenant. Other elements of the process are derived from the description of Ruth's conversion.

A very interesting connection between Ruth and Shavuot is found in an aspect of the Megilah that is not explicit. The Torah prohibits us from marrying with members of the nation of Moav. Ruth was from Moav. Boaz persuaded the Sages that although the Written Torah may be interpreted to forbid marriage with any member of the nation of Moav, the Oral Law limits the prohibition to marrying with the males of Moav. Relying upon this ruling from the Oral Law,

Boaz married Ruth. In short, the marriage that is the climax of the Megilah is based upon the ruling of the Oral Law. Shavuot celebrates our receiving both the Written and Oral Laws. Reading Megilat Ruth is an appropriate aspect of the observance of Shavuot because it demonstrates the role of the Oral Law in our observance of the Torah's commandments.

All of these suggestions are credible. Moreover, it is very possible that for all of these reasons and for other reasons, as well, the Sages established the practice of reading Ruth on Shavuot. In the discussion that follows, we will develop another connection between Shavuot and the Megilah.

A basic challenge in understanding the Megilah

The Sacred Writings include five *megilot*. Two of these are narratives – Megilat Esther and Megilat Ruth. The remaining three do not contain narratives but are composed in a poetic style. Of the narrative megilot, Esther is the easier to understand. Its narrative recounts the saving of the Jewish people from Hamam's plot to destroy them. The Megilah contains a number of messages and lessons. These are clearly presented and developed. Megilat Ruth is more challenging. It presents the charming and moving account of the conversion of Ruth, her dedication to her mother-in-law Naomi, and Ruth's marriage to Boaz. However, the lessons that we are to take away from the account, are not explicitly stated and are not obvious from the text. However, important lessons are presented by the Megilah. We must search for themes in the Megilah in order to identify these lessons. Let us consider one of these themes and the lesson it communicates.

And Naomi said: Return, my daughters; why should you go with me? Have I yet sons in my womb, that they should be your husbands? (Megilat Ruth 1:11)

Ruth's decision to convert

The opening passages of Megilat Ruth provide an important introduction to the story that will follow. We are introduced to Elimelech. Elimelech decides to abandon the Land of Israel in response to a famine. He travels with his wife Naomi and his sons to the fields of Moav and settles there. Elimelech dies. His sons take wives from Moav. The sons die. Naomi finds herself alone with her two daughters-in-law. Naomi learns that the famine has ended in the Land of Israel and decides to return to her homeland. Her daughters-in-law, Ruth and Orpah wish to accompany her on this return journey. Naomi attempts to dissuade her daughters-in-law from joining her on her journey. She persuades Orpah to remain among the people of Moav. Ruth resists and refuses to abandon her mother-in-law.

Naomi offers a number of arguments in favor of her daughters-in-law remaining in their own homeland. One is that if they follow her, they will have little or no opportunity to remarry. They will be giving up the opportunity to have a partner and family. It is this argument that finally persuades Orpah to remain in Moav. Ruth is not moved by this argument and clings steadfastly to her mother-in-law. Ruth does not dispute Naomi's evaluation of her prospects. Instead, she responds that she is willing to endure the consequences of which Naomi warned.

It is important to understand the state in which Ruth arrived in the Land of Israel. She and Naomi were desperately poor. They had no food, housing, or prospects. They fully expected that their survival would depend upon the charity of those among whom they would live.

Ruth was confronted by another challenge. She was a stranger. Naomi had warned Ruth that she would not easily remarry and now was reliant upon the charity of a community that regarded her as a stranger.

Despite recognizing the challenges and disadvantages that would confront her, Ruth had decided to adopt Judaism and follow Naomi. From a practical or economic perspective, Ruth's decision seems foolish. She was motivated only by the righteousness and grace of her mother-in-law and her desire to emulate Naomi. In other words, she was completely sincere in her conversion.

And these are the generations of Perez: Perez begot Hezron. And Hezron begot Ram, and Ram begot Amminadab. And Amminadab begot Nahshon, and Nahshon begot Salmah. And Salmah begot Boaz, and Boaz begot Obed. And Obed begot Jesse, and Jesse begot David. (Megilat Ruth 4:18-22)

The destitute Ruth becomes the ancestor of King David

The desperate condition in which Ruth arrived in Bet Lechem leaves us completely unprepared for the closing passages of the Megilah. In these passages Ruth is married to Boaz. Boaz and Ruth have a son from whom, in three generations, King David emerges. In other words, the Megilah describes the unlikely series of events through which a destitute Moavite convert becomes the progenitor of the founder of the Davidic dynasty. How does this remarkable outcome evolve?

Ironically, Ruth's poverty played an enormous role in shaping her unlikely destiny. Upon arriving in Bet Lechem, Ruth suggests to Naomi that she support them by collecting the gleanings from the barley fields then being harvested. Ruth goes out into the fields and happens, by chance, upon the fields of Boaz. Also, by chance, Boaz comes to inspect the harvest while Ruth is collecting the gleanings. Boaz observes Ruth. He is impressed by her conduct and enters into conversation with her. The conversation confirms his impressions. He invites Ruth to collect gleanings from his fields throughout the harvest. Eventually, this relationship further develops and culminates in the marriage of Ruth and Boaz. In other words, poverty and chance came together to precipitate the encounter between Ruth and Boaz. Once the encounter occurred, Ruth's righteousness and Boaz's appreciation of that righteousness brought about their marriage.

And Ruth said: Do not entreat me to leave you, to return from following you, for wherever you go, I will go, and wherever you lodge, I will lodge; your people shall be my people and your G-d my G-d. (Megilat Ruth 1:16)

Making practical decisions

The theme that emerges is that our destiny can be very different from the one that seems most likely. When Ruth left Moav with Naomi her likely destiny was to die as an aged widow, destitute and obscure. The destiny that actually evolved was that she became the ancestor of King David.

Ruth eschewed the practical or utilitarian path. Instead, she chose to follow the beckoning of her spiritual soul. She elected to live a life of righteousness and poverty and was rewarded by becoming the ancestor of King David. In fact, her poverty and righteousness became the catalysts of her unforeseeable destiny. In other words, when Ruth decided to live according to the callings of her soul rather than to make the practical decisions, providence selected her for greatness. She became the ancestor of King David.

Choosing virtue over practical considerations

Ruth's experience provides us with an important life lesson. We are often confronted with situations in which our perception of self-interest comes into conflict with our ethics and morals. Sometime, we are aware of the conflict. We have to decide whether we will compromise our values in order to secure the outcome that we desire or need. This conflict can occur in our everyday life, in business, and in providing leadership to our community.

In some instances, we are not even aware of the compromise we are making. Our intense need or desire to secure the outcome we seek actually blinds us to the ethical compromise we are making. Without realizing that we are doing so, we rationalize our choice and dismiss the ethical compromise it requires.

Ruth's experience speaks to these situations. Her story reminds us that we are prone to overestimate our own power to shape our destinies. We suffer from an inflated sense of control over our fates. Because we believe that our fates will be determined solely by the measures we take to secure our destinies, we take every measure available to us – even those that compromise our ethics. In contrast, Ruth concerned herself only with acting properly. She accepted any destiny that might ensue. Because she was completely faithful to her values, she was selected for greatness by providence.

If you follow My statutes and observe My commandments and perform them, I will give your rains in their time, the Land will yield its produce, and the tree of the field will give forth its fruit. (VaYikra 26:3-4)

Two aspects of the Sinai covenant

Rabbaynu Avraham ibn Ezra explains that there are two aspects of the Sinai covenant. In Parshat Mishpatim the people declare that they will observe the commandments of the Torah. This commitment to observance is the first aspect of the covenant. In Parshat BeChukotai, Hashem describes the rewards He will bestow upon the people in response to their observance of the commandments and the consequences that they will experience if they abandon the Torah's commandments. According to Ibn Ezra, this is the second aspect of the Sinai covenant. Our destinies will be determined not solely or even primarily by our own endeavors but by our faithfulness to the Torah.

Earlier, we discussed some of the connections between Megilat Ruth and Shavuot. Among these were that Megilat Ruth opens with the conversion of Ruth and Shavuot celebrates the "conversion" of the Jewish people. Another connection is that the Megilah includes an instance in which the meaning of the Written Law is provided by the ruling of the Oral Law. Shavuot recalls Revelation, which is the source of the Written and Oral Laws. Both of these interpretations suggest that the Megilah is connected to the first aspect of the Sinai covenant. Conversion is essentially achieved through the acceptance of the commandments and the Written and Oral Laws are the source of these commandments.

The theme in Megilat Ruth developed above suggests that the Megilah is also closely connected to the second aspect of the Sinai covenant. The Megilah declares that our destinies are not in our own hands. Instead, our faithfulness to the values of the Torah and our commitment to the observance of its commandments can have a far greater influence on our destinies than our tireless efforts to secure our futures.

"Ribbi Elazar says about the Torah that the major portion of it is written and the minor portion is an oral tradition.. And Ribbi Yochanan says that the major portion of the Torah is an oral tradition and the minor portion is written." (Talmud, Tractate Gitten 60B)

The festival of Shavuot celebrates the revelation of the Torah at Sinai. The Torah received at Sinai is composed of two parts. It includes a written portion and an oral portion. The written portion is recorded in the five volumes of the Chumash. The Oral Torah was also received from Moshe at Sinai. This Oral Torah is an elaboration on the material in the Written Torah. It was not originally recorded. Instead, it was taught as an oral tradition and communicated through the generations by teacher to student. Eventually, a brief synopsis of this body was recorded as the Mishne. Later, a more detailed written account of the Oral Torah was created. This is the Gemarah. Over the centuries, an enormous body of writings has supplemented these early records of the Oral Torah. These works include all of the interpretations and elaboration on the basic material in the Written Torah. It is the product of the insights of Sages throughout the generations.

The text above recounts a dispute between two Sages. Ribbi Elazar asserts that the major portion of the Torah is contained in the Written Torah - in the Chumash. The Oral Torah is the smaller of the two components of the Torah. Ribbi Yochanan disagrees. He contends that the majority of the Torah is contained in the Oral Torah. The Written Torah is the smaller component of the Torah.

This is a perplexing dispute. One merely needs to look at any library of Torah works to understand the problem. The Written Torah is recorded in the five books of the Chumash. This work can be contained in a single volume. The Oral Torah fills endless volumes. It is true that the published material has grown over the centuries. During the time of Ribbi Elazar and Ribbi Yochanan, the published or written portion of the Oral Torah was quite limited. Nonetheless, the body of material encompassed in this Oral Torah surely was larger that the five books of the Chumash.

There is another problem with this dispute. Both Ribbi Elazar and Ribbi Yochanan were great Torah scholars. They certainly had disagreements. However, they studied the same Torah. They were both fully aware of the scope and detail of the Torah. Yet, the disparity between their positions is immense. How could they present such radically different accounts of the material they studied?

In order to answer these questions, we must ask one more important question. How does one measure the relative "sizes" of the Written and Oral Torah? The Written Torah has a size. It has a material form. We can measure the number of words or letters required to record it. But, how do we even measure the Oral Torah? We can count the number of words required to record it. However, this is not its true measurement. The Oral Torah existed before it was recorded in writing. It is a set of ideas. How does one assign a size to a set of ideas? How big is the theory of relativity? Is it larger or smaller than the Newtonian mechanics? These are absurd questions! Concepts do not have size.

It is apparent from this last question that Ribbi Elazar and Ribbi Yochanan are not disputing the relative material size of the Written Torah and the Oral Torah. This is not the basis for comparison. We have also shown above that, even if we make the questionable assumption that the Oral Torah can be assigned a size based on the words required to transcribe it, the dispute between the Sages remains enigmatic. They would both have to agree that the Oral Torah fills more volumes than the Written Torah. So, what are they disputing?

In order to understand the dispute between these two Sages, we must consider the relationship between the Written Torah and the Oral Torah. We will begin by outlining two fundamentally different possibilities.

The first possibility can be understood though imagining the following scenario. Consider an immense library. Some poor soul has been assigned the enormous task of preparing a single work that summarizes the knowledge contained in this entire library. How might he proceed in accomplishing this task? Let us propose the following. First, he should divide the library into sections. One section would be works on agriculture. Another section might contain all works on business and finance. Once the library has been so divided, these sections will be divided into smaller subsections. The business and finance section would include an accounting section and investment section. Once the sections and subsections are created, the real work can begin. A brief summary should be prepared of each volume in the library. Based on these summaries, a summary will be created of the works in each subsection. The subsection summaries will then be used to create a summary of each section. Finally, using the section summaries, a summary will be created that encompasses the entire library.

The Torah can be understood through applying a similar scheme. Each Tractate of the Talmud can be viewed as the summary of a large subsection of Torah concepts. The Mishne of the Tractate is a summary of the Tractate. The Written Torah is a brief summary of the summaries contained in the Mishne. In other words, the Written Torah can be viewed as the summary of an immense body of knowledge. This body encompasses all areas of the Torah - the entire Oral Torah.

There is an alternative way to characterize the relationship between the Written and Oral Torah. Again, let us consider an analogy. Shakespeare is probably the most thoroughly studied playwright or author. Let us consider just one of his works - Hamlet. Countless articles and books have been written analyzing and critiquing this work. These books and articles are commentary on Hamlet. They expand upon the issues and insights that the play reveals.

This description can also be used to characterize the relationship between the Written and Oral Torah. The Written Torah can be viewed as the more fundamental component, and the Oral Torah as a commentary and elaboration on the Written Torah. The Oral Torah explores the meaning and significance of each passage and nuance of the Written Torah. It reveals the Written Torah's full meaning.

These two relationships are very different. If the Written Torah is a summary of the entire Torah, it is - by its very definition - smaller than the Oral Torah. The summary is a condensation of the body it describes. However, if the Oral Torah is a commentary on the Written Torah, it is the less fundamental of the two works. Again, this is a result of its very definition. The commentary is an elaboration on the more fundamental work it explains.

We can now understand the dispute between Ribbi Elazar and Ribbi Yochanan. They do not dispute the relative sizes of the Written and Oral Torah. The issue they debate cannot be resolved through taking some measurement. They disagree over the relationship between these two elements. According to Ribbi Elazar, the major portion of the Torah is written. He maintains that the Oral Torah is a commentary and elaboration on the Written Torah. In this relationship, the Written Torah is the fundamental major component. The Oral Torah plays a secondary role. Ribbi Yochanan asserts that the major portion of the Torah is Oral Torah. He understands the Written Torah as a summary of the entire body of knowledge contained in the Oral Torah. In this relationship, the Oral Torah is the major element or partner in the relationship.

Tisha B'Av

'Comfort, comfort My people,' says your G-d. (Haftorah of Shabbat Nachamu, Yishayahu 40:1)

The fast of *Tisha BeAv* commemorates the destruction of the *Bait HaMikdash*. The *Haftorah* for the *Shabbat* before is related to the theme of *Tisha BeAv*. The *Haftorah* begins with our *pasuk*. In this passage, Hashem offers comfort to Bnai Yisrael. In the *Haftorah*, the Almighty assures His nation that their suffering in exile will end. The Almighty will reveal His kingship over all of humanity. The land of Israel, Yerushalayim and the Temple will be rebuilt.

This *Haftorah* offers an important insight into the observance of *Tisha BeAv*. In order to identify this insight, an introduction is needed.

Tisha BeAv is a date that is reserved for tragedy. Both Sacred Temples were destroyed on this date. Many other misfortunes befell Bnai Yisrael on this date. All of these catastrophes are historical events. None is part of our recent experience. Yet, despite the passing of time, we continue our annual observance of *Tisha BeAv*. This creates a problem. The tragedies commemorated by *Tisha BeAv* do not seem very relevant to us. These misfortunes are part of the distant past. Nonetheless, every year we repeat our commemoration of these events. It is difficult on a beautiful summer day to mourn a Temple we never saw. We are expected to feel genuine sadness over events that are not part of our experience. Other nations have also experienced tragedies. At first, they bemoan these misfortunes. However, with the passage of time, the memory of the trauma recedes. The nation moves on and focuses on the present and future. Why do we not place the past behind us?

Let us consider the problem from another perspective. Assume a person looses a parent. This is a terrible experience. The bereaved son or daughter is distraught. The child mourns the parent for a period of time. *Halacha* requires twelve months of mourning. Slowly, the son or daughter recovers from the loss. Mourning ends and life proceeds. Imagine the child could not overcome this loss. The son or daughter remained fixated upon the misfortune. We would conclude that this person is ill. We would suggest that the child seek help in overcoming this morbid depression. Are we not this child? Why do we not overcome our sorrow? Are we morbidly fixated on the tragedies of the past?

There are various answers to this question. We will consider one response. *Tisha BeAv* is a day of mourning. However, there is another element expressed in our observance of the day. This element is evident in an unusual *halacha* – law – of the day. On the eve of *Tisha BeAv*, the supplication *Tachanun* is not recited.[1] This supplication is also omitted on *Tisha BeAv* itself.[2] The reason for the omission of *Tachanun* is that *Tisha BeAv* is referred to in the Navi as a *Moed* – a festival. The prophet Zecharya prophesizes that in the Messianic era, the Temple will be restored and *Tisha BeAv* will be celebrated as a festival.[3] This element of festivity associated with *Tisha BeAv* is expressed in other laws as well.

It seems odd that in deference to Zecharya's assurance we add these elements of festivity to *Tisha BeAv*. We await the Messianic era. It has not yet occurred. Now we are in exile. The

---

[1] Rav Yosef Karo, *Shulchan Aruch, Orech Chayim* 653:12.
[2] Rav Yosef Karo, *Shulchan Aruch, Orech Chayim* 559:4.
[3] Sefer Zecharya 19:19.

Temple is destroyed. What is the relevance of Zecharya's prophecy to our current observance of *Tisha BeAv*?

The answer is that the destruction of the Temple is not merely a historical event. Its destruction and our exile represent an aberrant relationship with Hashem. This is the message of our *pasuk* and the *Haftorah*. We are the Almighty's nation. Our redemption and the restoration of the *Bait HaMikdash* are inevitable. The Messianic era is only delayed by our own failure to completely repent and return to the Almighty. With our wholehearted *teshuva* – repentance – the Messianic era will arrive.

This is the reason for the presence of a festive element in the observance of *Tisha BeAv*. This element reminds us that our fasting is in response to a current tragedy. We have not yet repented. Therefore, we remain in exile and the Temple remains destroyed. We can convert *Tisha BeAv* into a festival through changing our behaviors and attitudes!

Now we are prepared to understand the relevance of *Tisha BeAv* to our current generation. Other nations experience tragedies. They move forward. They forget the misfortunes of the past and enjoy the present and hope for an even better future. We too are not fixated on the past. We are not remembering an irrelevant past tragedy. We are commemorating a present misfortune. We are in exile and the *Bait HaMikdash* has not yet been rebuilt. We must repent in order to end our misfortune. In short, *Tisha BeAv* should not be regarded as a day that recalls a past misfortune. It should be observed as a day on which we mourn an ongoing tragedy. This tragedy is our own distance from the Almighty. It is a day that should inspire us to repent and restore our relationship with Hashem.

"There are other days on which all Israel fasts because of the tragedies that occurred on these dates. This is in order to move the hearts of the people and to open the road to repentance. And this is a memorial to our evil actions and the actions of our ancestors that were like our current behaviors to the point that these behaviors have brought these sorrows upon us and our ancestors. Through the recollection of these matters we will repent as it says: And they will confess their iniquities and the iniquities of their ancestors." (Maimonides, Mishne Torah, Laws of Fasts 5:1)

Recognizing the sins of our ancestors and our own iniquities on Tisha B'Av

Each year we observe four fast days that commemorate the destruction of the first and second Temples and the suffering associated with these events. The fast of Tisha B'Av is the culmination of these fasts and commemorates the actual destruction of both Temples. The above quotation introduces Maimonides' discussion of the laws governing these fast days.

In his concise manner Maimonides makes a number of important points:

- These fast days were created to commemorate the destruction of the two Temples and the associated suffering and to place us upon the path to repentance.

- The fast days should cause us to recall our own iniquities and failings and those of our ancestors.

- The destruction of the Temples and the related suffering are a direct result of our failings and the sins of our ancestors.

333

- Recognition of the relationship between sin and suffering should motivate our repentance.

- Repentance requires that we confess our own sins and those of our ancestors.

Maimonides' comments raise a number of questions. First, it is generally assumed that the observance of Tisha B'Av and the other three fasts commemorating the Temples' destruction and the related suffering are designed to recall these events and to recognize these events as national and spiritual tragedies. However, Maimonides does not support this position. Instead, he proposes that these fasts are observed in order to acknowledge our responsibility and that of our ancestors for these calamities. Maimonides' contention that we are responsible for these disasters is difficult to understand. The first Temple was destroyed in 586 BCE and the second was destroyed in 70 CE. However, Maimonides attributes these tragedies to the sins of our ancestors and to our own behaviors. How can we be held accountable for these disasters?

Second, Maimonides explains that these fasts are intended to lead us to the path of repentance through recalling these events. How does this occur? How does the recollection of these long-past calamities bring us to the path of repentance?

Maimonides' contention that subsequent generations bear responsibility for the destruction of the Temples is reflected in the statement of the Sages that any generation in which the Temple is not rebuilt is regarded as if the Temple was destroyed in its time.[4] On its simplest level, this statement means that the absence of the rebuilt third Temple is as great a tragedy as the destruction of the second Temple. However, on a deeper level the message of our Sages is that our behaviors and conduct determine when the Temple will be rebuilt. In other words, the Temples were destroyed as a result of the sins of previous generations. The Temple will be rebuilt through the repentance of their descendents. Every generation in which the Temple is not rebuilt endures its absence because of its failure to properly return to Hashem. Therefore, Maimonides' contention that the absence of the Temple is a consequence of the sins of our ancestors and our own iniquities accords with the position of the Sages. Our ancestors' behaviors led to the destruction of the Temples and our own failings are responsible for the delay in its rebuilding.

This explains Maimonides' assignment of responsibility for these events to generations living centuries after their occurrence. This interpretation of the Sages' comments also explains how recalling past calamities leads to repentance. In recalling these disasters, we are not merely remembering a misfortune in our ancient past. We are recognizing that the destruction of the Temples was the beginning of a calamity that continues into the present – our own time. We share responsibility with our ancestors for this disaster. Once we recognize that our behaviors are responsible for the continued delay in the Temple's rebuilding, we will be motivated to address and improve our behaviors.

We now better understand Maimonides' comments regarding these four fasts. However, in order to more fully understand Maimonides' position, it is helpful to consider his general perspective on the purpose of fasting.

---

[4] Talmud Yerushalmi, Mesechet Yoma 1:1.

"It is a positive commandment to cry out and to sound the trumpets in response to any affliction that comes upon the congregation .... This is characteristic of repentance. At the occasion of a tragedy, when the congregation cries out and sounds the trumpets, they all realize that the evil that has befallen them is a consequence of their actions.... And this will cause the removal of the affliction from upon them.... But if they do not cry out and do not sound the trumpets but say that these events are merely natural events and happenstance, this is the path of cold-heartedness and it will cause them to cling to their evil actions. And upon the affliction will be added more affliction ..." (Maimonides, Mishne Torah, Laws of Fasts 1:1-3)

Fast Days and their objective

In these opening sentences of his *Laws of Fasts*, Maimonides explains the purpose and objective of fasts. All fasts are a response to an affliction or suffering. The Sages may declare a fast in response to drought or famine. A fast may be declared in reaction to an impending attack by our enemies. The fundamental aspect of the observance is not cessation from eating and drinking or other self-imposed hardships endured during the fast. Instead, the most essential element is petition and supplication. More specifically – the essential element of the observance of a fast is recognition and acknowledgement that our suffering is not merely a consequence of simple misfortune or chance events but instead, it is a consequence of our actions. All blessings and suffering experienced by the Jewish nation are expressions of Hashem's will and His providence. In turn, He blesses or punishes us in response to our behaviors.

In the context of this perspective on the function and purpose of fast days it is possible to more fully appreciate Maimonides' understanding of Tisha B'Av and the other three associated fasts. According to Maimonides, all fasts days have three shared elements:

• They are a response to a present affliction.

• The ultimate objective of the observance is to relieve the affliction.

• This objective is achieved through accepting responsibility for the tragedy – through recognizing that our actions are the cause of the calamity.

Therefore, although Tisha B'Av and the other three related fasts are observed annually, they are fundamentally indistinguishable from a fast declared in response to an emerging, onrushing disaster. Both are responses to current afflictions. The delay in the rebuilding of the Temple is a current, present-day affliction and it is a consequence of our actions.

For the violence done to your brother Yaakov shame shall cover you, and you shall be cut off forever. On the day that you did stand aloof, on the day that strangers carried away his substance, and foreigners entered into his gates, and cast lots upon Jerusalem, even you were as one of them. But you should not have gazed on the day of your brother on the day of his disaster. Neither should you have rejoiced over the children of Judah on the day of their destruction. Neither should you have spoken proudly on the day of distress. (Ovadia 1:10-12)

Let Us Not Commit the Sin of Edom

1. **Ovadia's prophecy of the destruction of Edom**

The prophet Ovadia foretold the punishment that will be brought upon Edom for its iniquity. What was the sin of Edom? In the above passages, Ovadia explains that Edom was complicit in the destruction of Yerushalayim and the Bait HaMikdash – the Sacred Temple. Rabbaynu David Kimchi – Radak – explains that Ovadia, in his description of Edom's sin, is referring to events that will occur long after his own death. He foresees that the Roman general and future emperor Titus will lay siege upon Yerushalayim. He will ultimately breach the city's walls and destroy it and the Bait HaMikdash. Ovadia does not accuse Edom of directly participating in this tragedy. According to Radak, Edom's complicity will be expressed in its rejoicing in the destruction of Yerushalayim, the razing of the Bait HaMikdash, and the persecution and exile of Bnai Yisrael.

And command the people, saying: You are to pass by the border of your brethren the children of Esav, that dwell in Seir. They will be afraid of you. Take good heed unto yourselves therefore. Contend not with them for I will not give you of their land not so much as for the sole of the foot to tread on, because I have given Mount Seir to Esav for a possession. (Devarim 2:4-5)

2. The fraternal bond between Esav and Bnai Yisrael

Radak adds that Edom's behavior is especially egregious because of its relationship with Bnai Yisrael. The nation of Edom is comprised of the descendants of Esav, the brother of Yaakov. Edom and Bnai Yisrael share a fraternal bond. Esav's joy at the destruction of Bnai Yisrael was a repudiation of this fraternal relationship. Radak contrasts Esav's treatment of Bnai Yisreal and the attitude implicit in that behavior with the instructions that Hashem gave to Bnai Yisrael regarding its treatment of Edom.

In the above passages, Moshe reminds the nation of the instructions received from Hashem as Bnai Yisrael approached the Land of Edom. Edom's territory – the Land of Seir – was located to the southeast of the Land of Cana'an. The direct path into the Land of Cana'an lay through the territory of Edom. Hashem forewarned Bnai Yisrael that Esav's descendants were the sovereign rulers of this territory. Bnai Yisrael were forbidden from violating these borders or even threatening and intimidating Edom. Of course, these instructions were scrupulously obeyed. Bnai Yisrael extended its journey in order to travel around the territory of Edom.

Radak explains that Bnai Yisrael respected its fraternal relationship with Edom. It respected the sovereignty of Edom and acted toward this brother nation with deference. This behavior sharply contrasts with the behavior of Edom toward Bnai Yisrael. Bnai Yisrael treated Edom as a brother and with the respect and consideration due to a brother. Edom rejoiced in the destruction of Yerushalayim and the Bait HaMikdash. Edom observed with glee the agony of its brothers.[5]

3. Esav's implicit repudiation of its own rights

Rashbam, in his comments on the above passages from Parshat Devarim, provides the basis for an alternative interpretation of Edom's iniquity. He notes that Hashem explains to Moshe that Bnai Yisrael are to respect the sovereignty of Edom within the borders of its land because He has given this territory to Edom. In other words, just as Hashem granted Bnai Yisrael sovereignty over the Land of Israel, the Land of Seir was given to Edom as its homeland. He adds that Edom received this special treatment from Hashem because the nation is comprised of

---

[5] Rabbaynu David Kimchi (Radak), Commentary of Ovadia, 1:11.

the descendants of Esav and therefore, they are the descendants of Avraham. It is because of its relationship with our patriarch Avraham that Edom has been given as its legacy the Land of Seir.

Rashbam explains that the instructions that Hashem provided to Bnai Yisrael regarding Edom were also a timely reassurance that it will soon conquer the Land of Cana'an. The people may have been tempted to become despondent in response to the directive to delay their march into the promised Land of Cana'an. They may have been tempted to feel some element of doubt and despair. When would the long-postponed conquest occur? Hashem's instructions include a reassuring explanation of the detour. The sole reason for the detour is that Edom is comprised of Avraham's descendants. Hashem says to Bnai Yisrael that the legitimacy of Edom's rights to the Land of Seir is derived from the same source as Bnai Yisrael's right to the Land of Israel. The detour is actually an affirmation of the promise to Bnai Yisrael that it will receive the legacy promised to Avraham, Yitzchak, and Yaakov – the Land of Israel.[6]

Rashbam's comments suggest an alternative interpretation of Edom's sin. Edom rejoiced over the destruction of the Land of Israel and the exile of its people. In its rejoicing, Edom implicitly denounced its rights to its own ancestral homeland. Edom should have wailed and mourned the destruction of the Land of Israel and the exile of its people. If Bnai Yisrael could be separated from the Land of Israel, then what security did Edom have in its own homeland? Edom's sin was that rather than seeing the implications of the tragedy of the Jewish people and mourning this tragedy as the harbinger of its own potential exile and suffering, Edom rejoiced in the tragedy of Bnai Yisrael.

4. Not being like Edom

Both of these interpretations are relevant themes to contemplate with the approach of Tisha B'Av. Bnai Yisrael is a nation of brothers. We are dispersed to the corners of the earth but we form a single community. Regardless of the distances that separate us we must remember that we are brothers. We may be separated by miles, mountains, or oceans. We may be separated from one another by divergent perspectives, and outlooks. These distances and differences of opinion must not and cannot breach the fraternal bond that makes us one people.

We must also recognize that how we treat one another is an expression of how we expect to be treated by others. Edom failed to understand that in rejoicing over Bnai Yisrael's exile from its legacy it implicitly denounced its own right to the Land of Seir. When we treat another person with insensitivity or worse, we denounce our own right to be treated with sensitivity and dignity.

"Whoever mourns for Jerusalem will [merit to] see its rejoicing, and all who do not mourn for Jerusalem will not [merit to] see its rejoicing."[7]

The simplest understanding of this statement of the Sages is that Hashem operates *middah k'neged middah* (measure for measure). If a person acts according to God's wishes and is appropriately distressed over the destruction of the Beit HaMikdash, he will be rewarded with the opportunity to rejoice when it is rebuilt. If not, he won't deserve such a reward. In short: "If you show me you *really* want it, I'll give it to you, but if not, then I won't." This simple

---

[6] Rabbaynu Shemuel ben Meir (Rashbam) Commentary on Sefer Devarim 2:5.
[7] Masechet Ta'anit 30b

understanding might be true, but it is probably not what our Sages were getting at. There is a deeper meaning here.

In order to attain a deeper understanding of this statement of our Sages we must first examine the obligation of *aveilut* (mourning) on Tishah b'Av. Many people ask the question, "Why do we mourn for Jerusalem on Tishah b'Av?" This may be an important question, but it certainly is not a *strong* question. One could simply answer: "Because we are sad about the destruction of Jerusalem and the Beit haMikdash," and that would be the end of it. There is a stronger, more specific question we can ask: "Is our mourning on Tishah b'Av consistent with the structure of normative, halachic *aveilut*?" To understand this question and find an answer we must take a brief look at the halachic structure of *aveilut*.

Normative halachic *aveilut* takes place in three stages: the seven days of lamenting, the thirty days of weeping, and final twelve months, after which no more memorials may be held for the dead.[8] In each progressive stage, the severity of the strictures imposed upon the mourner is reduced. In each stage, the mourner is expected to grieve less intensely. After the end of the period of mourning, the mourner is expected to move on with his life. The main point: normative *aveilut* is time-bound.

Ostensibly, it seems as though the *aveilut* of Tishah b'Av is *not* normative. Normative *aveilut* shouldn't last past twelve months, and here we are, still crying over the destruction of Jerusalem after nearly two thousand years – a blatant breach of the clearly defined time boundaries of halachic *aveilut*! Not only that, but normative mourning *lessens* in intensity as time goes by, but with each Tishah b'Av that passes, our mourning *increases*! Furthermore, the Rambam says, "One should not indulge in excessive grief over one's dead, as it is said: "Do not weep for the dead, nor bemoan him,"[9] meaning, (do not weep for him) too much, for [death] is the 'way of the world,' and he who frets over the 'way of the world' is a fool."[10] It comes according to the Rambam that our *aveilut* on Tishah b'Av not only oversteps the bounds of normative *aveilut* but is also considered to be foolish! What is going on here?[11]

It turns out that we are not the only ones who mourn (or have mourned) excessively. We know that Ya'akov Avinu mourned for twenty-two years for (what he believed was) the loss of his son, Yosef[12]:

Then Ya'akov rent his garments and placed sackcloth on his loins; he mourned for his son many days. All his sons and all his daughters arose to comfort him, but he refused to be comforted.[13]

This is an outright contradiction to the halachic principles mentioned by the Rambam! How can it be that Ya'akov, one of the most righteous men to walk the earth, refused to be consoled, in stark opposition to the demands of halacha?

---

[8] Rabbeinu Moshe ben Maimon (Rambam), *Mishah Torah:* Hilchot Aveilut 13:10
[9] Sefer Yirmiyahu 22:10
[10] Rabbeinu Moshe ben Maimon (Rambam), *Mishah Torah:* Hilchot Aveilut 13:11
[11] At this point, Rabbi Fox made it clear that he was not in any way denegrating the *aveilut* on Tishah b'Av. He said that all of the mourning practices on Tishah b'Av make perfect sense, and that he is merely questioning the fact that the aveilut of Tishah b'Av deviates from normative halachic guidelines.
[12] Rabbeinu Shlomo ben Yitzchak, *Commentary on Sefer Bereisheet* 37:34
[13] Sefer Bereisheet 37:34-35

The answer lies in a distinction between normative *aveilut* and the *aveilut* of Ya'akov Avinu. This distinction is alluded to in the Midrash: "A person does not accept consolation over a living person whom he believes to be dead (*savur sh'meit*), for a [Divine] decree has been issued over one who has died that he be forgotten from the hearts [of the living], but this decree is not [issued] over one who is still alive."[14] The simple meaning[15] of this statement is as follows: one cannot be consoled over the death of a loved one until he has undergone *yei'ush* – until he has given up hope. The mourner must know and feel with absolute certainty that the person is dead and won't be coming back. When a person loses a loved one, he intellectually knows that that person is dead, but emotionally, his love still reaches out for that person. When he (emotionally) realizes that the person is no longer there, he becomes incredibly frustrated and distressed. The gap left behind by the deceased creates a gap between the mourner's mind and his heart, generating intense feelings of anxiety, confusion, and depression. Mourners tend to go through this intellectual/emotional battle for a period of time after the death, but eventually, their emotions catch up with their intellectual realization that the person is dead. Only then do they truly give up hope in both their minds and their hearts. Only then can they fully be consoled, and continue on with their lives.

Now we can see the distinction. Ya'akov's case was different. He could not be consoled. Why not? Because he had not given up hope. He only *believed* that Yosef was dead, but he didn't *know* with complete certainty. He lacked that absolute conviction necessary for the intellectual confirmation. If a mourner knows in his mind that his loved one is dead he may struggle emotionally, but his heart will eventually catch up with his mind. Emotional acceptance will eventually follow intellectual acceptance. But if a person lacks that intellectual conviction, consolation is impossible. As long as there remains room for doubt – even a remote possibility that the person is still alive – the mourner will invest his entire mind and heart into that possibility and refuse to let it go. The emotional acceptance will never come because the intellectual acceptance never took place. That is why Ya'akov's *aveilut* exceeded the normative boundaries of halacha. He was unable to be consoled because his mind had never fully accepted Yosef's death. To summarize, there are two objectives accomplished by mourning: 1) honor for the deceased, 2) closure for the living. The process of *aveilut* helps the living recognize and acknowledge the tragedy that has occured, and helps them get over it. So long as that second step remains unfulfilled, the process of *aveilut* can never end.

Back to Tishah b'Av. The Shulchan Aruch writes, "We do not say *tachanun* (Rema: or *selichot*) on Tishah b'Av and we do not fall on our face in supplication because Tishah b'Av is

---

[14] Cited by Rabbeinu Shlomo ben Yitzchak, *Commentary on Sefer Bereisheet* 37:34 from *Bereisheet Rabbah* 84:21; see also *Masechet Pesachim* 54b

[15] Rabbi Fox explained that although the term "decree" sometimes refers to miracles, that simply cannot be the case here. If this were a miraculous phenomenon, then Ya'akov should have known that Yosef wasn't dead from the fact that he was still sad after a year had passed. Furthermore, if this phenomenon were miraculous, we wouldn't have to worry about *agunot* (an *agunah* is a woman whose husband is believed to have died, but his death is not confirmed. She cannot remarry until it is established for a fact that her husband is dead). All you would have to do is ask the *agunah*, "Are you still sad?" and if she answered negatively, you could just say, "Yup! He's dead!" Obviously, if this phenomenon were miraculous, we wouldn't need the entire halachic process of establishing the death of the husband and we would never have to worry about *agunah* problems. Thus, the Midrash must be referring to a psychological phenomenon.

described as a *moed* (festival)."[16] This is a very strange phenomenon indeed. On Tishah b'Av we cry, mourn, afflict ourselves with fasting and the other four forms of affliction, refrain from studying Torah, refrain from donning festive clothing, and deprive ourselves of nearly every single pleasure – yet, we modify our observance of Tishah b'Av because we recognize it as a partial *moed*. Why should this be? It would be understandable if we made it a point to *omit* all *moed*-aspects until the arrival of Moshiach, when all fast-days will be nullified and celebrated as festivals[17]; that way, we would be drawing a full contrast between now (exile) and the future (redemption) . . . but that is not our practice. Instead, we take two *completely* antithetical themes – joyous *moed* and mournful fast – and bend over backwards to make sure both aspects are demonstrated and acknowledged. Why do we do this? Why try to uphold this paradox of including aspects of *moed* on a day of nation-wide mourning?

The Aruch haShulchan provides an insight into this conundrum. He explains that we refrain from reciting *tachanun* as a demonstration of our faith in the redemption.[18] Based on our understanding of Ya'akov's *aveilut*, we can understand the paradox. Our *aveilut*, like that of Ya'akov Avinu, oversteps the time-boundaries of normative halachic *aveilut*. Ya'akov continued to mourn because he could not be consoled. Why not? Because he had not yet given up hope over his situation. The same is true for *us.* The reason why we continue to mourn is because we have not given up hope over *our* situation. We fully trust in Hashem's promise that He will redeem us from our exile. We know that the exile is only temporary, and that the redemption can come at any moment. In fact, we are better off than Ya'akov. He was only *savur sh'meit* – he just *thought* that there might be hope. We *know* that there is hope, because Hashem has given us His promise!

Now our previous problem can be resolved. The clash of *moed* and *aveilut* on Tishah b'Av is no paradox. In fact, quite the opposite is true. By observing the *moed* characteristics of Tishah b'Av, we are demonstrating the *reason* why we continue to mourn and why we can't accept consolation: we *can't* be consoled precisely because we *haven't* given up hope! We have refused to be consoled for nearly two thousand years because we have not given up hope. We know that Hashem will redeem us.

Now we can fully appreciate the statement: "Whoever mourns for Jerusalem will merit to see its rejoicing, and all who do not mourn for Jerusalem will not see its rejoicing." Why does a person who mourns deserve to be redeemed? Because the fact that he *continues* to mourn is a demonstration of his conviction in the redemption! Conversely, one who does not mourn demonstrates the fact that he has "gotten over it;" by not mourning he is demonstrating that he has given up hope of redemption. Since he has demonstrated a lack of faith in the redemption and the rebuilding of Jerusalem, he does not merit to see its rejoicing.

He has drawn His bow like an enemy, standing [with] His right hand as an adversary, and He has slain all that were pleasant to the eye; in the tent of the daughter of Zion, He has poured out His fury, [which is] like fire. (Megilat Eichah 2:4)

---

[16] Rav Yosef Kairo, *Shulchan Aruch: Orach Chaim* 559:14
[17] Rabbeinu Moshe ben Maimon (Rambam), *Mishah Torah:* Hilchot Ta'aniot 5:19
[18] Rav Yechiel Michel Epstein, *Aruch haShulchan: Orach Chaim* 559

What He Wants

1. G-d becomes the enemy of Israel

Tisha B'Av – the fast of the ninth of Av approaches. We will mourn the destruction of our *Bait HaMikdash* – the Sacred Temple – and our exile. What are we mourning? We mourn the *Mikdash's* destruction. Its destruction represents Hashem's withdrawal from His nation. We mourn exile. In exile, we have been repeatedly persecuted and oppressed. However, there is another aspect of our mourning that we must identify and acknowledge.

In the above passage, the prophet Yermiyahu – Jeremiah – describes Hashem as the enemy of the Jewish people. Hashem draws His bow against us. He is our adversary. He pours forth his anger. He kills the best of our people. The characterization of Hashem as our enemy is the theme of the second chapter of Eichah. Is Hashem our enemy? What message is the prophet communicating? To answer this question let us begin by considering an interesting comment of the Talmud.

One who steals from his father and mother and says, "What is the iniquity?" is the companion of the man of destruction. (Sefer Mishlai 28:24)

2. Stealing from Hashem and Israel

In the above passage King Shlomo – Solomon – describes a child who steals from his father and mother. He rationalizes the behavior. The property of parents eventually is inherited by their children. This child reasons that he or she has not stolen. The child has taken an advanced payment on an eventual inheritance. Shlomo explains that this child is the companion of a villain or a sociopath. The child's rationalization provides the excuse to steal from his or her parents. Stealing will become routine. With time, the child will abandon the rationalization and steal from others. This child is on a path that will inevitably lead to degenerate behavior.

Shlomo emphasizes this inevitability by declaring that the moment the child embarks on this path, he or she is already the companion of the scoundrel.[19]

The Talmud offers another interpretation of this passage. We are required to make a blessing before we experience some of the benefits of this world. We make blessings before eating and before inhaling pleasant fragrances. The Talmud explains that King Shlomo refers to one who does not recite these blessings. This person reasons that Hashem placed us in this world and we have the right to enjoy it. There is no need to acknowledge Hashem each time we enjoy the benefits of our world.

Shlomo declares that this person steals from his father. This refers to Hashem. He steals from his mother. This is the community of Israel. He is the villain's companion. According to the Talmud, this is Yeravam – Jeroboam. Yeravam was the first king of the Kingdom of Israel. This kingdom was composed of ten tribes that rejected the leadership of King David's grandson, Rechavam – Rehoboam. He is notorious for formally introducing idolatry into his kingdom. He sinned and led his nation to sin.[20]

---

[19] Rabbaynu Levi ben Gershon (Ralbag / Gershonides), *Commentary on Sefer Mishlai* 28:24
[20] Mesechet Berachot 35b.

This interpretation raises several questions. How is one who does not recite a blessing stealing from Hashem? How does he steal from the community of Israel? Why is he compared to the villain Yeravam?

Rashi explains that this person steals from the nation because he engages in and promotes behavior that will lead to punishment. That punishment will be the destruction of the crops. He is the companion of Yeravam because, like Yeravam, his actions provoke a punishment that impacts the entire nation – the destruction of the crops.

How does this person steal from Hashem? Rashi comments, "He steals from the Sacred One, Blessed be He, His blessings".[21] What blessings is this person stealing from Hashem? It is generally assumed that Rashi is referring to the blessing the person should have recited before enjoying the benefit. Hashem was entitled to this blessing and the person did not recite it. He stole the blessing to which Hashem is entitled.[22]

Will a man cheat the L-rd? Yet you cheat Me, and you say, "With what have we cheated You?" With tithes and with the terumah-levy. You are cursed with a curse, but you cheat Me, the whole nation! Bring the whole of the tithes into the treasury so that there may be nourishment in My House, and test Me now with this, says the L-rd of Hosts, [to see] if I will not open for you the sluices of heaven and pour down for you blessing until there be no room to suffice for it. (Sefer Malachi 3:8-10)

3. Cheating Hashem

Rav Isser Zalman Meltzer[23] understood differently the Talmud and Rashi's comments. His interpretation is based upon the above passages. In these passages, the prophet describes the Jewish people cheating Hashem by not giving the required agricultural tithes. He declares that they are cursed and they cheat Hashem. Then, the prophet, speaking for Hashem, challenges the people to test his words. "Give the tithes and you will see that the curse that is upon you will be replaced by a blessing. The abundance of your harvest will be too great to store."

After the prophet describes the people cheating Hashem, he says that the people are cursed and they cheat Hashem. Why does he repeat they cheat Hashem? The prophet ends his message with challenges. Give tithes and you will be rewarded with enormous abundance. What is being tested? Apparently, the test will confirm that the curse upon the nation is Hashem's response to not giving tithes. However, if this is the purpose of the test, then the proof is not the abundance. It is the termination of the curse.

4. Hashem wishes to bless us

Rav Meltzer explains that the prophet is not rebuking the people for cheating Hashem out of His tithes. They are cheating Him out of the blessings He wishes to grant. The tithes they are withholding are how they cheat Him. By withholding them they prevent Him from bestowing His blessings upon the nation. Hashem would bless the nation of Israel. But instead, He must punish the nation for its wickedness.

---

[21] Rabbaynu Shlomo ben Yitzchak (Rashi), *Commentary on the Talmud,* Mesechet Berachot 35b.

[22] Rav Shmuel Eliezer Edels (Maharsha), *Commentary on the Talmud*, Mesechet Berachot 35a-b.

[23] Rav Isser Zalman Meltzer (1870-1953) studied in the yeshivot of Volozhin, Radin, and Slabodka. He was a Rosh Yeshiva and Rav in Europe and Israel. He immigrated to Israel in 1903.